D1338236

Bexley London Borough
LIBRARY SERVICE
This book is due for return on or before the date last
stamped otherwise a charge will be made. Books may
be renewed by post or telephone, quoting book
number and last date stamped below.

BLACKFEN 081-300 3010		CLOSED DAILY 1pm - 2.15pm	
1 5 JUN 1993			
13 Jul 93			
10 AUG 93			
2 0 AUG 1993			

499081

ITEM NO.

30109 0 11274142

One Hundred Days

Napoleon's Road to Waterloo

ALSO BY ALAN SCHOM

Trafalgar: Countdown to Battle 1803–1805

ALAN SCHOM

One Hundred Days
Napoleon's Road to Waterloo

MICHAEL JOSEPH

LONDON

11274142

MICHAEL JOSEPH LTD

Published by the Penguin Group
27 Wrights Lane, London W8 5TZ
Viking Penguin Inc., 375 Hudson Street, New York, New York 10014, USA
Penguin Books Australia Ltd, Ringwood, Victoria, Australia
Penguin Books Canada Ltd, 10 Alcorn Avenue, Toronto, Ontario, Canada M4V 3B2
Penguin Books (NZ) Ltd, 192–190 Wairau Road, Auckland 10, New Zealand

Penguin Books Ltd, Registered Offices: Harmondsworth, Middlesex, England

First published in Great Britain 1993

Copyright © Alan Schom, 1992

The map of the Battle of Waterloo at 7.30 PM, 18 June 1815, is
reproduced from *Waterloo: The Hundred Days*, by David Chandler,
© David Chandler 1980, 1987, 1990. Published by Osprey Publishing,
59 Grosvenor Street, London W1X 9DA. It is used by permission.

All rights reserved.
Without limiting the rights under copyright
reserved above, no part of this publication may be
reproduced, stored in or introduced into a retrieval system,
or transmitted, in any form or by any means (electronic, mechanical,
photocopying, recording or otherwise) without the prior
written permission of both the copyright owner and
the above publisher of this book.

Printed in England by Clays Ltd, St Ives plc

A CIP catalogue record for this book is available from the British Library.

ISBN 0 7181 3384 6

The moral right of the author has been asserted.

3.3.93

BEXLEY LIBRARY SERVICE

LOC	Cl. No.	944.05 Sch
BL		
PRICE	ACC	DATE	SKS
20-00	7-4-93	HD
COLL CODE		ANF
NF		
KEYER	LANG	CH	PR
A		MK	

In memory of my grandmother,
Fanny Schwab Stoler,
1890–1938

And my aunt,
Rose Stoler Ellison,
1912–1959

"Tis the time's plague when madmen lead the blind."

Gloucester in *Lear* (IV, 1)

"Humanity must perforce prey on itself
Like monsters of the deep."

Albany in *Lear* (IV, 2)

"I do not believe with the Rochefoucaults and Montaignes, that fourteen out of fifteen men are rogues. . . . But I have always found that rogues would be uppermost."

Thomas Jefferson

"The care of human life and happiness, and not their destruction, is the first and only legitimate object of good government."

Thomas Jefferson

CONTENTS

PROLOGUE xi

ACKNOWLEDGMENTS xv

I. "Ile du Repos" 1

II. The Sovereign of the Island of Elba 12

III. "The Disturber of the Peace of the World" 34

IV. The Brothers Bonaparte 57

V. A Deadly Enemy 85

VI. "The Most Wretched of All Professions" 107

VII. A Land in Turmoil 127

VIII. "Neither Peace Nor Truce" 160

IX. Mobilization 192

X. "Pour la Patrie" 221

XI. Eve of Battle 241

XII. Waterloo   262

XIII. End of the Napoléonade   295

EPILOGUE   320

APPENDICES   323

I. Chronology of Events   323

II. The Thirty-Two Military Divisions of Metropolitan France and Conquered Territories   325

III. Napoleon's Abdication Declaration, 22 June 1815   326

IV. Command Structure of French and Allied Armies at Waterloo   326

V. Napoleon's March on Paris, 1–20 March 1815   330

BIBLIOGRAPHY   331

NOTES   339

INDEX   385

PROLOGUE

"It seems to me an historian's foremost duty to ensure that merit is recorded, and to confront evil deeds and words with the fear of posterity's denunciations," Tacitus commented in his *Annals of Imperial Rome*. If Tacitus is correct, then Napoleon Bonaparte is surely one of the most fortunate of all historical figures, having managed to escape, as he has, such a confrontation with posterity. This is made all the more remarkable, in that most of his "evil deeds and words" are well documented, and recorded, and available for all to see and contemplate.

By February 1815 Napoleon had decided to escape from his island prison of Elba and attempt to overthrow the newly restored and internationally recognized Bourbon monarchy in France. The period of his return is generally known as "The Hundred Days," referring in fact to the period of Louis XVIII's absence from the French capital, from 20 March to 8 July, in reality a duration of 121 days.

A man apparently incapable of inner reflection, Napoleon could not believe, upon his arrival in Elba on 4 May 1814, that his career was over. Then when rumors of plots by the Allies either to kidnap or kill him, or to transfer him to a more distant island, were brought to his attention, combined with the very real fact of Louis XVIII's refusal to honor the Treaty of Fontainebleau and pay Napoleon and his family the stipulated six million francs due them, Napoleon felt fully justified in breaking his agreement with the Allies. And finally, when Fleury de Chaboulon and others reported to Napoleon that factions within France were rebelling under the Bourbon yoke, and demanding his return, any lingering doubts he may have had were dispelled.

Nevertheless, Napoleon did not invade France on 1 March in order to save that country, but, rather, himself. He felt, quite literally, at the end of his tether, that he had no future.

Apart from the military, however, and some of the urban proletariat, he did not find much real support from the people upon his return. Indeed, by the first week of June, more than half the country was rebelling against his rule in one form or another. Beleaguered by more than fourteen years of incessant Napoleonic warfare, with their economy utterly shattered, and an entire generation of their men systematically siphoned off and lost through conscription, the people had simply had enough. But now the Allies announced preparations for another invasion of France, and this for one reason only: to seize Napoleon Bonaparte and put him out of harm's way once and for all. There would be no war, no invasion of France a second time however if only Napoleon would abdicate. But, of course, he refused to do so.

By the beginning of June, hostility to Napoleon had increased so dramatically that he had to put numerous French cities in the south and west under martial law or the equivalent, leaving behind thousands of French troops to control, combat or crush them if necessary. Thus by June 1815, his popular support diminishing daily, Bonaparte knew he had no future in France. Clearly, his days were already numbered. The only way he could sustain his tottering throne and fill an empty treasury, he felt, was once again, as in 1805, to make war. Yet even before the battle of Waterloo, Bonaparte was finished.

Nevertheless, the extraordinary joint effort to rearm made by War Minister Louis Davout and Interior Minister Lazare Carnot was staggering. Their personal relations with the Emperor during this process proved equally fascinating, even as Police Minister Joseph Fouché did all in his power to betray him yet again. Throughout this book I have made an effort to bring historical events of the day into perspective by giving the personal background of the men making the decisions, and their evolving relations with one another and with Napoleon himself. A mere chronicle of historical facts and events, without providing the elementary human perspective responsible for shaping them, is in itself relatively meaningless, and, in my view, a distortion of history.

Given the extraordinary background of the times, the attitude of the French people, and the almost hostile attitude of the men whom Napoleon ultimately selected to lead his army into battle, it was astonishing that he nearly managed to defeat the combined Allied forces facing him in Belgium. In brief, he might well have shattered them, had he not made the disastrous choice of these three senior army commanders. Time and again Marshals Soult, Ney and Grouchy deliberately disobeyed or hindered Bonaparte's orders, thereby foiling his last chance to retain his position as head of the French nation.

Napoleon left Waterloo and returned to Paris a defeated and confused man. The very next day the joint Chambers of the Corps Législatif demanded and received his second and final abdication. And while he was permitted to escape trial and punishment, many of his loyal followers were hunted down and either killed by the people or executed by Louis XVIII, with the exception of some of the more politically slippery individuals, including Marshals Grouchy and Jean de Dieu Soult.

Nevertheless, several years after Napoleon's final departure from France and his demise, his reputation rebounded, reaching the reverential position it has retained ever since, in utter defiance of the facts, the woes, the hundreds of thousands of deaths and vast destruction he had everywhere brought to France and Europe forgotten, diminished or distorted by the treacherous and ever-elusive historical memory of man. Napoleon Bonaparte proved that he was indeed one of the few men in history ever to be able to escape legitimate judgment for all his heinous acts. Or, as a bewildered Chateaubriand put it, "When will Europe have put off mourning for his crimes?" This, then, is an account of Napoleon's final acts, which brought upon him the wrath of Europe and the ruin of France.

Alan Schom
Waterloo/Coursegoules
June 1991

ACKNOWLEDGMENTS

I should like to take this opportunity to thank the individuals and institutions who have aided me in the course of my research for this book, including the British Library, London; Bibliothèque de l'Ecole Supérieure de Guerre, Paris; Bibliothèque Nationale, Paris; Bibliothèque Cessole, of the Musée Masséna, Nice, and its Conservateur, Mr. Luc Thévenon; and the Musée Wellington, Waterloo. And finally, General Bruno Chaix, French Army (Retired); Colonel J-L Reynaud, Ecole Supérieure de Guerre; Lt-Col. L.S. Burr, OBE, RAOC; and David G. Chandler, Royal Military Academy, Sandhurst—for their most useful comments, suggestions and corrections of events at Waterloo. Mr. Bernard Chevallier, Conservateur en Chef, for plans and details of La Malmaison and its park and gardens; M. Philippe Martial, Directeur de la Bibliothèque et des Archives du Sénat, for a long personal tour and historical explanation of the parts of the Palais du Luxembourg associated with Marshal Ney's imprisonment, trial and execution; and finally His Excellency Walter J. P. Curley, United States Ambassador to France, for his help and that of his staff in facilitating my research.

Chapter I

"Ile du Repos"

"I felt . . . the utmost repugnance to anything like a treaty with him [Napoléon] after his déchéance had been pronounced."

> *Secretary of State Lord Castlereagh to*
> *Prime Minister Lord Liverpool, April 13, 1814*

"Let them kill me—I shall not stop them—but I do not want to be deported."

> *Napoleon to Sir Neil Campbell*

"Henceforth I want to live the life of an ordinary justice of the peace. . . . The Emperor is dead and I am no longer of importance to anyone . . . My only concern is for my little island; I require nothing more of the world . . . than my family, my little house, my cows and mules."

> *Napoleon to Sir Neil Campbell, at Elba,*
> *September 1814*

'Tis done—but yesterday a king!
   And armed with kings to strive—
And now thou art a nameless thing
   So abject—yet alive!

        Lord Byron
        "Ode to Bonaparte"

Armand de Caulaincourt, Duc de Vicence, Grand Equerry and Imperial French Foreign Minister, was appalled by what he saw as the agitated valet, Pelard, opened the door of Napoleon's dimly lit bedroom at three o'clock on the morning of Wednesday, the thirteenth of April 1814. Caulaincourt, who had served the Emperor so faithfully from the beginning as aide-de-camp, general, ambassador and statesman, and who had seen him create kings and address entire armies, hesitated as he stepped forward. Napoleon now lay in the small bed before him—his eyes sunken and haggard, his body racked by uncontrolled hiccoughing, his arms and legs stiffening, his abdomen and body arched up in excruciating pain, bathed in sweat and wrapped in a raging fever. Napoleon reached up for Caulaincourt's arm as he neared him. The tormented man had to vomit, but seemed to do all in his power to prevent it. It was now that Caulaincourt saw it, the small opened leather pouch with a black taffeta ribbon, on the bedside table, and next to it, the small empty vials that it had held. At once he understood what had happened. Two years earlier Dr. Yvan had prepared this poison at the Emperor's request, as he had no intention of falling into the enemy's hands during the Russian campaign. ("I am a man who can be killed, but not insulted," he had insisted.)[1] But now, no longer capable of bearing the pain and humiliation of seeing his self-made world and empire collapse about him, he had finally opened them.

As a veteran of the retreat from Moscow, Caulaincourt had often seen men die, even hideously, but never had he seen anything like this. The Emperor's servant had finally brought Dr. Yvan here—against Napoleon's protest and previous orders given when he was still *compos mentis*. There was little to be done now, however, for obviously he had taken the poison a few hours earlier. And yet that in itself was a good sign, the physician indicated, for clearly the poison had lost much of its original potency or Napoleon would have died immediately. If only he would vomit and cleanse his system, he had a chance of surviving, but the Emperor resisted that; he wanted to die.

Although Napoleon had once denounced the folly of suicide—there were always other options open, he had insisted—nevertheless it was shocking to see him, prostrate and helpless, this man above all others, the eternal optimist, with his amazing energy and endless plans.

The final draft of his acceptance of the new monarchy over the minuscular island of Elba lay on the desk of his study, this document which he had so long resisted, the final consequence of his unconditional abdication earlier on the sixth of April. And if that were not enough, there were certainly plenty of other reasons to explain this attempt at self-destruction: the collapse of his world, the defeat of his beloved Grande Armée, the mass desertion of friends, officials and high army officers—all of whom owed him everything for the positions they had achieved and the wealth they had accumulated. Even the servants of Fontainebleau, a few hundred of them, had fled, all but a mere handful remaining. Then, of course, the Emperor's family had evacuated Paris on 29 March, on Prince Joseph's decision, as the enemy approached the capital. The Russian Army under Czar Alexander, the Prussians under victorious Field Marshal Prince Blücher, and the Austrians led by Field Marshal von Schwarzenberg, were closing in on Paris from the north, the Rhine and Switzerland, while the Duke of Wellington's British force around Toulouse was securing the south, and by the end of March 1814, there was clearly no hope left for Napoleon Bonaparte.

At Frankfurt-am-Main on the first of December (1813) the Coalition had declared that they "were not making war against France, but against the loudly proclaimed preponderance which . . . the Emperor Napoleon has far too long exercised outside the limits of his Empire."[2] But still the French had resisted, if in vain, the massive invasion which had begun in January, gradually crushing them, and the British Foreign Secretary, Lord Castlereagh, for one, was growing most impatient. "The allies as well as the enemy must be considered as entitled to all the legitimate results of successful war," he insisted to Lord Liverpool,[3] and on 1 March 1814, the Allies signed a twenty-year alliance of military solidarity.

Nevertheless Napoleon alone continued to hold out, to the exasperation of his own commanders and diplomats, arrogantly hampering the negotiating process at Châtillon in February and March, despite Caulaincourt's warning—"If one negotiates at all, it is necessary to make it [peace], and to make it quickly."[4] But Napoleon refused to bend and the diplomats at Châtillon finally dispersed, empty-handed, and the fighting continued. But with his armies in disarray and even their marshals unpaid, Napoleon had been in no position to lay down terms since his great defeat at Leipzig in October 1813. Indeed, one or more of the Allies, continuously at war with the French Emperor since the days of the Consulate—apart from the one year of peace brought by the Treaty of Amiens, 1802–1803—they were now quickly losing what little patience remained, as were the French people themselves.

And thus on 29 March a cortège of green carriages bearing the imperial crest proceeding from the Champs Elysées with Napoleon's lovely young wife, Empress Marie-Louise; their son, the King of Rome; Napoleon's mother, Letizia; Jérôme's wife, the former Queen of Westphalia; and most of the imperial ministers, fled the capital for the safety of Rambouillet. Napoleon himself had finally abandoned the battlefield for Fontainebleau with Marshals Ney, Macdonald and Berthier, where they had arrived on 31 March, the very day Paris was officially surrendering. On the first of April the Senate appointed a provisional government headed by the indestructible Talleyrand, and even while Marshal Marmont was at Napoleon's side at Fontainebleau, they learned that his entire Sixth Army Corps, the last line of defense between Paris and Fontainebleau, had gone over to the Austrians and Russians. On the third the combined Corps Législatif officially deposed Napoleon, who in turn begrudgingly signed his abdiction on the sixth. That same April sixth, the French Senate and Deputies invited Louis XVIII to return and accept the very throne they had suppressed in 1793 after executing his brother.

Upon returning to Fontainebleau and passing the sentries and through the green-and-gold wrought-iron gates separating the sprawling sixteenth-century château from the town, Caulaincourt found all unusually still. There were no troops or horses in the courtyard. The château itself was empty, his steps echoing across the parquet floor of one empty reception room after another . . . all devoid of footmen, chamberlains, officials, soldiers and even of Napoleon's ubiquitous aides-de-camp. With the news of the abdication, Napoleon had been abandoned.

But apparently it was the startling announcement by Napoleon's old and dear friend, Marshal Alexandre Berthier, Prince de Neuchâtel et Valengin, his former chief-of-staff and War Minister, who was perhaps closer to him than anyone else, apart from the Imperial family, that proved the last straw. Although Berthier—unlike Marmont, who had joined his troops in fleeing to the Allies—remained at Napoleon's side, he announced that he would not be going into exile with him on Elba. The sixty-year-old warrior wished instead to hang up his sword forever and return to his estates with his twenty-nine-year-old German wife and their children, to enjoy a little peace in his remaining days. "That mark of attachment would have cost him nothing," Napoleon told Caulaincourt. "Who would have thought that he would have been one of the first to leave me?"[5] For an already shattered and superstitious Napoleon, this was perhaps the ultimate "betrayal," and to go on now without him seemed utterly unthinkable.

But the most humiliating part occurred on 11 April, when the three Allied Foreign Ministers, Hardenberg of Prussia, Nesselrode of Russia and Metternich of Austria, arrived to sign the Treaty of Fontainebleau, as it would be known, with Caulaincourt, Ney and Macdonald signing for and officially recognizing Napoleon's unconditional abdication of all rights to the throne of France.[6] And with the triumphant entry of King Louis's brother, Comte d'Artois, into the capital the following day, all indeed seemed over. Later that night of Tuesday the twelfth, Napoleon, who no longer saw an honorable way out and feared, as he said, deportation more than death, swallowed the vials of poison. But by dawn of the thirteenth, Dr. Yvan was able to inform an anxious Caulaincourt that the Emperor had survived the night and would live.

The Treaty of Paris, signed on 30 May, brought peace to the whole of Europe at long last. It was astonishingly lenient to France, thanks in no small part to the goodwill and offices of Czar Alexander. France was permitted to retain her frontiers of 1792, including parts of the Savoy border and areas taken previously from the Austrian Netherlands and the Holy Roman Empire. Basically it ended there, for as extraordinary as it now seems, the Allies demanded neither war indemnity nor foreign occupation of the country. Even the thousands of pieces of art stolen over the past couple of decades, looted from a dozen countries, were left in the Louvre (against the outraged protests of the Duke of Wellington). Literally millions of people had been killed, wounded and otherwise scarred in the course of the various wars waged by Napoleon;[7] hundreds of thousands of dwellings and buildings were destroyed, tens of thousands of women and girls raped, and untold agriculture and hundreds of thousands of farm animals destroyed. But what the Allies really wanted, above all else, was a lasting peace, and for that it seemed they were willing to pay a very high price indeed. They were in adamant unanimous agreement, however, that in order to ensure that peace one essential final measure had to be taken: the vanquishing of Napoleon Bonaparte.

"Général! I have sacrificed my rights in the interests of the nation, while reserving for myself the sovereignty and property of the Island of Elba, which has been consented to by all the Powers. Be so good as to have this new state of affairs made known to the inhabitants, and the choice I have made of their island—because of its climate and the gentleness of their ways—for my sojourn. Tell them they will be the constant object of my sincerest interests."[8]

Such was the proclamation Napoleon handed Brigadier General Jean-Baptiste Dalesme, the Governor of Elba, upon landing at the island's capital of Portoferraio on 4 May 1814, where he was greeted by a festive crowd, including most of the sovereign's 13,700 new subjects, shouting "Evviva il Imperatore!" as Mayor Traditi presented him with the keys to the city in a silver bowl.

Emperor Napoleon—the Treaty of Fontainebleau permitted him to retain his titles—quickly selected as his principal residence the rudimentary buildings known as "I Mulini," the windmills, which had earlier served as a court and garrison headquarters, some thousand feet above the port overlooking the Tyrrhenean Sea. Despite the humble setting—the "Palace" would have less than a dozen rooms, even after a second floor had been added as well as a large ballroom on the ground floor—the court, Emperor and his sixty-five servants were installed there, and in nearby buildings. Even as imperial court etiquette was rigorously reintroduced, the new officials were appointed, three men principally comprising the new cabinet, including his confidant and Grand Marshal General Henri Bertrand; Guillaume-Joseph, Baron Peyrusse, Treasurer and Minister of Finance; and General Antoine Drouot, as War Minister while also replacing Dalesme as the island's governor. A court of appeals was created, and General Cambronne given command of the capital's garrison of nearly a thousand men and the island's defenses, while Dr. Lapi was named Director of Domains and André Pons de l'Hérault, Director of Mines.[9] In addition to four chamberlains, the Emperor appointed seven Elbans to don the traditional green uniforms reserved for his ADCs.

Napoleon's initial reaction to his new kingdom was surprisingly positive; he referred to it as his *île du repos*, or island of repose, while one of Cambronne's troopers more facetiously called it simply "a great refuge for an old fox."[10] Napoleon's initial view held for some time, however, as he spent many hours in the saddle surveying all eighty-six square miles of his miniature realm, drawing up a list of more changes and improvements than the island had seen since the collapse of the Roman

Empire: customs and taxes were to be reorganized, a quarantine station was to be established near the port, a combination hospice-military hospital was to be developed, the island's fortifications improved and extended, proper barracks were to be provided for the increased garrison, a theater to be built, water supplies to be improved and streets paved, the two principal roads of the island were to be widened and improved to take carriages, and five new ones planned, not to mention the building of a tunnel to connect his residence with the port. Nor was the countryside ignored: vineyards were planted, studies were made for introducing the silkworm industry, distribution of the land was devised for the island's impoverished inhabitants, and the cultivation of virgin land was encouraged.

Napoleon never ceased, it seemed, appearing like a whirlwind to the drowsy island suddenly awakened from centuries of sleep. For the rather dim Colonel Sir Neil Campbell, the allied commissioner left there to keep an eye on things, all this activity was a bit much, complaining to London that he found Napoleon in a state of "perpetual motion" and frankly hard to keep up with.

Almost immediately the Emperor set about extending his realm by seizing the uninhabited adjacent island of Pianosa, where he planned to build fortifications and housing for thirty men. "Europe is going to accuse me of already having started on the road to conquest," he said humorously to Campbell while giving him a first-hand tour of his latest prize. [11]

Although his wheezing lungs were a continuing reminder of his suicide attempt and the past, Napoleon did his best not to dwell on either, preferring instead to keep as busy as possible, particularly with his new residences. As already seen, I Mulini was enlarged, including a spacious upstairs apartment for his sister Pauline Borghese, who joined him on 30 October. [12] His mother was given a house of her own in a nearby village. A small house serving as a summer retreat was also acquired at Portolongone, and Pauline later bought a grange for him at San Martino, which was also converted into a summer residence. He built another five-room house high up on Mt. Capanna with its stunning view of the sea, while a small hunting-estate acquired on the isthmus of Cap Stella completed his Elban domains.

Entertainment, naturally, was limited, but certainly not ignored. Every Sunday the traditional levée took place at the "palace," followed by mass and a turning out of courtiers in their Parisian finery, as if still at the Tuileries. Cards were always popular in the evening and of course the amateur theatre at I Mulini, which attracted the talents of the ladies of the court and wives of the officers in particular. And with the completion of the palace, in January and February 1815, Pauline launched a series of balls.

Napoleon Bonaparte's personal entourage on Elba was, to be sure, very small, Bertrand and his wife, Fanny, always in attendance as well as Drouot, Cambronne, Major Malet and Colonel Jerzmanowski. Sir Neil Campbell was, at Napoleon's personal request, a frequent visitor for the first few months in 1814. In addition a surprising number of foreigners also alighted on Elban shores—chiefly British and Italian—including Comte Litta and Lords Douglas, Ebrington and Bentinck,[13] not to mention Napoleon's two mistresses, Comtesse Walewska and Madame Palapra.[14] His family, however, was limited to Madame Mère, who had arrived on 2 August, and Pauline.

But even with all this activity, Napoleon had time to think and more and more frequently convened his inner council to discuss some nagging problems. One being the embarrassing situation regarding Marie-Louise and their son. Although the Fontainebleau treaty of 11 April did not forbid Napoleon's wife and son from rejoining him, what Napoleon did not know was that the Allies and the Austrian Emperor in particular had their own thoughts on the matter and were determined to prevent any such reunion. As has been seen, Marie-Louise and the King of Rome had fled Paris on 29 March, reappearing thereafter at her father's capital, Vienna, where Napoleon wrote to her time and again asking when she would be arriving at Elba. The few answers he received through his agents and physician were negative, however. Nor did Napoleon realize how determined his wife was never to return, as she indicated to Emperor Francis as early as 31 August 1814, and indeed was soon in the arms and bed of the Austrian Hussar general placed at her side to protect her, Graf Albrecht Adam von Neipperg. She had, she explained, just received "a letter [from Napoleon] in which he tells me he is passionately waiting for me to come at once . . . to the Island of Elba. Rest assured, dearest Papa, that today I have even less desire than ever to undertake such a journey and give my word of honor never to do so without first asking your permission."[15] She never changed her mind. And before the autumn was out a despondent Napoleon was confiding to Colonel Campbell—"My wife no longer writes to me. My son has been taken from me just as the children of the conquered were in former times, with which to proclaim and crown their victory."[16] And meanwhile Austrian Emperor Francis, fearing retribution by Napoleon and the rescue of his son, had him placed under heavy guard in the Schönbrunn Palace. The Allies were determined to keep father and son apart, for there must never again be another Napoleon on the throne of France . . . or anywhere else.

Of more immediate importance was the financial situation. Although Napoleon had left France with just over two million francs,[17] and was promised another two million annually by Article III of the Treaty of Fontainebleau, Louis XVIII thereafter not only refused to honor this commitment drawn up by the Allies—most of the money in fact to have come from Napoleon's sequestered investments left in France—but had publicly scoffed at the idea of ever doing so. This in turn caused considerable concern among the Allies meeting at the Congress of Vienna, including Castlereagh and Czar Alexander. What is more, back on 13 April the provisional government headed by Talleyrand had seized Napoleon's personal treasure of ten million francs from the imperial coffers at Orleans.[18] How then was he expected to pay his army, court and officials? What is more, King Louis was also withholding the annual sum of two and a half million francs stipulated by the Treaty of Fontainebleau for Napoleon's mother and his brothers and sisters, not to mention another two million set aside for gifts and payment to officers of his guard and court.[19] Thus, when he finally sat down with Finance Minister Peyrusse, Napoleon discovered that in reality the total annual income actually reaching him came to only 607,309 francs, and that from Elba alone—iron mine profits, salt sales, customs and taxes.[20]

As a result of the rumors reaching Elba of King Louis's boast to let him squirm and sink, Napoleon gradually became more restless, wary, withdrawn and despondent. Even the dull-witted Campbell—who privately claimed Napoleon was no more intelligent than some obscure deputy-prefect—gradually became more and more anxious about the implications and significance of this flagrant violation of the recently signed Treaty of Fontainebleau. If the Allies could break it without a qualm, why could not Napoleon himself rightfully do likewise? After all, he could not permit those dependent upon him to starve and his entire island to shrivel. Campbell felt that money was indeed the key to European peace, and as he informed London, "I persist in my opinion that if Napoleon receives the rent stipulated by the treaties, he will remain perfectly contented [at Elba], barring an extraordinary event in Italy or France."[21] It was little enough to pay to ensure European peace. But as Henri Houssaye pointed out "The Bourbon Government considered those clauses [of the Treaty of Fontainebleau] as completely null and void."[22] And by December 1814, Colonel Campbell noted that a hardened Napoleon was now deliberately avoiding him, except on public occasions.[23]

Even before this, stories of a possible escape by Bonaparte and his troops, with the intention of landing on the nearby Tuscan coast to join

Murat, or in France, were common enough.[24] In fact, they had perhaps been triggered off by even earlier rumors reaching Napoleon of plans by the Allies either to remove him to a more distant prison, or to kill him outright. Though some of the stories admittedly were farfetched, as such tend to be, others had a very sound basis. There was no secret, for instance, about the discussions by the two men who very much distrusted one another, Talleyrand and British Foreign Secretary Castlereagh, mooting the question of a more distant exile, such as Santa Lucia or Trinidad islands in the Caribbean or even far off Botany Bay in Australia.[25] As early as August and September (1814) Campbell had warned Lord Castlereagh of a plan by General Louis Bruslart, the commanding general of Corsica, to hire Corsairs to sail from Algiers to kidnap the Emperor.[26] "Napoleon frequently goes over to Pianosa," the French Consul General at Livorno, Mariotti, reported to Talleyrand on 28 September. "I have been assured that having no lodgings on that island, he always sleeps aboard one of his ships. It will be easy . . . to kidnap him and take him to Ile Sainte Margueritte,"[27] he argued. Other French officers simply wanted to assassinate him on Elba, and several plots were hatched, including one by a Colonel de C——— de B———, who proposed that Elban gendarmes in his pay could easily "do the job without much fuss." Indeed, it was even rumored that "some fanatical monks" at Rome wanted to avenge the Church with a dagger in his heart (or back).[28] If it came to a choice between an even more distant prison, and death, however, Napoleon had his own views on the matter, as he told Campbell. "Let them kill me—I shall not stop them—but I do not want to be deported."[29] But of course neither he nor Campbell was to have a say in that decision.

Despite the great engineering projects and bustling activity at Elba, the colorful masked balls, and the gracious receptions given to visiting English dignitaries, the island had nothing to offer him. How was he to meet his expenses six months hence, with King Louis openly refusing to pay the annual income for the maintenance of his court and family as stipulated by the Fontainebleau agreement? What is more, Louis XVIII had seized Napoleon's personal treasure at Orleans as well as his investments on the Bourse. Furthermore, the Allies at Vienna, while deploring the French King's actions and avowed intentions of seeing Bonaparte flailing in debt, nevertheless put no appreciable pressure on him to respect and execute the Fontainebleau arrangements that they themselves had negotiated on Napoleon's behalf. Indeed, having insisted on neither war reparations nor military occupation of French soil, they had no hold over Louis XVIII now. For the first time in his career Napoleon was all alone and only too well aware of this grim reality.

Nor did reports of allied plots to kidnap or assassinate him give Napoleon much faith in his position and future at Elba. No sooner was the ink dry on the treaties of 1814, than the Allies were violating the very spirit of them, plotting by one means or other to overthrow the sovereign of Elba. Clearly, Napoleon's days were numbered.

And finally there remained the stark fact that by December 1814, Napoleon Bonaparte was simply bored stiff. There were no armies to command, no battles to fight, no glory to win. This little man who had found the confines of French territorial frontiers too restrictive, this man who had marched his legions from the Adriatic to the Baltic, from the Rhine to the Moskowa, who had seized every major capital of the European continent, while even then contemplating wider operations in the Middle and Far East, felt *stifled* on Elba. What is more, on this minuscular Elba he was restricted to less than a dozen officers and officials of any personal interest to him with whom he would be compelled to spend the rest of his days, whereas in Paris he had been surrounded by hundreds of general officers, imperial officials, diplomats from the great courts of the world, not to mention the illustrious French savants and artists of the day. At Elba on the other hand, there was no one, nothing. And how long could the plans for a few kilometers of new roads, or the addition of a few new rooms to this travesty of a "palace" of a dozen rooms occupy this man accustomed to the splendor of the 1,800 rooms of Fontainebleau and who had ordered the construction of hundreds of new buildings and thousands of kilometers of roads just in France? Napoleon Bonaparte was slowly suffocating.

With the coming of the New Year in 1815, even if his coffers had been filled by Louis XVIII as promised, Napoleon knew that it was just a matter of time before he would have to escape from this gilded prison. Either he had to flee or die in the attempt, for there was no future on Elba, he felt. He had begun his political career in November 1799 with an act of brinksmanship, by a dangerous coup d'état that had nearly miscarried. And he would rather die gloriously now in another such attempt, rather than spend the rest of his days inertly contemplating the horizon and all that might have been if he had acted. It was simply a matter of time before the situation presented itself. But present itself it would, and of that he was sure.

Chapter II

The Sovereign of the Island of Elba

"I am the sovereign of the Island of Elba and have come with six hundred men to attack the King of France and his six hundred thousand soldiers. I shall conquer this kingdom. Are such things not permitted among sovereigns?"

Napoleon

"This man is nothing but an adventurer, which his final insane act now clearly proves."

Marshal Soult, March 12

"It is just as well that the man from Elba has attempted his crazy undertaking, for this will be the last act of his tragedy, the final curtain of the Napoléonade."

Marshal Ney, March 10

Former Imperial Deputy-Prefect Fleury de Chaboulon had arrived from France late on the twelfth of February, 1815, with reports from Marshal Davout and former Imperial Foreign Minister, the Duc de Bassano,

Hugues Maret.[1] Should Napoleon strike now? It must be his decision alone, his advisers agreed. Contrary to later reports by the Allies and the Bourbons, there was no carefully calculated plot by a special group of men to return the Emperor from Elba with the purpose of overthrowing Louis XVIII. To be sure, scattered former imperial officals and officers were sympathetic to the idea individually, and reports reached Elba of growing discontent among the masses and the French army under Bourbon rule, but there was nothing more mysterious involved now than that— there was no formal conspiracy afoot. Thus everything at this critical hour depended upon Napoleon himself. If he were to decide in favor of an attempted invasion, it would be with the knowledge that there would in fact be no concerted effort, no master plan, to help him once he was on French soil. Funds, troops and high-ranking commanders would not suddenly be at his disposal. It was an astonishingly desperate plan, but then Napoleon was an astonishingly desperate man. He had gambled many times in his career in the past. His coup d'état of 18 Brumaire (9–10 November 1799) had indeed been successful, but both his much vaunted plans to invade England (1803–1805) and his Russian Campaign had proven utter disasters. Yet to risk his last, final safe haven here on Elba—however, humble and tenuous it might be—could lead to utter catastrophe for himself and the house of Bonaparte. Within twenty-four hours of receiving Fleury's far from enthusiastic report, Napoleon nevertheless announced his decision: the invasion would go ahead! And even before Colonel Sir Neil Campbell left Portoferraio on 16 February for a rendezvous with his Italian mistress, Fleury had been dispatched to Italy and France with news of the momentous plans.[2]

Napoleon ordered the largest vessel of his rather motley, miniature "navy," the brig *L'Inconstant*, into drydock to have her two masts reinforced, her hull scraped and the entire vessel repainted to give it the appearance of a British warship. This then, along with two ninety-ton xebecs, *L'Etoile* and the *Saint-Joseph* (three-masted lateen sailers capable of holding more than three hundred men each), took on stores for their long journey. And while Colonel Jean-Paul Jerzmanowski's elite Polish lancers, ninety-four strong, began final intensive maneuvers, another large lateen-rigged vessel, the 194-ton "polacre," the *Saint-Esprit*, was seized and added to the fleet. It was designated now to transport most of the thirty-four horses, four caissons and their light cannon.[3] Finally, yet another lateen sailer, the *Caroline*, received last-minute repairs while the two remaining vessels of the "flotilla," the slender tartans *Abeille* and *Mouche*, were added, each capable of holding a maximum of thirty men. An expeditionary force of 1,026 men and officers (excluding the ships' officers and crews) made its final preparations. On Wednesday, 22 February, port authorities prevented all fishing boats from leaving Elban ports and the island sealed off as caissons, cannon, munitions, wagons, carriages and provisions were hurriedly loaded. On Friday the twenty-fourth, Napoleon formally convened the Elban officials, informing them of his forthcoming departure, without, however, disclosing his purpose or destination. And even as the mayor of the capital and president of the tribunal congratulated him, wishing him Godspeed, proclamations destined for both Elba and France were being secretly printed not far away.

By Sunday, 26 February, all was in readiness, a clear sunny sky, a welcoming sight after the recent winter storms, as the white Elban flag, with its diagonal red stripe and three bees, flew high above the port. All the officers had made their wills, said their good-byes to wives or mistresses, and had written their families, General Louis Alexandre Bertrand advising his own wife to seek refuge in England "if our efforts are not crowned by success."[4] Napoleon, dressed in his strikingly simple green uniform as Colonel of Grenadiers, attended mass at 9 A.M., an hour earlier than usual. By ten o'clock he was at the harbor with his four-man staff—Generals Bertrand, Cambronne and Drouot, and General Commissioner Pons—inspecting the troops, including the two principal units, the 551 grenadiers of the old Imperial Guard, commanded by Major Malet, and "the Corsican battalion" of four companies totaling 301 Corsican, Italian and Provençal troops.[5] Napoleon's traditional pre-battle speech before his Guard was brief and to the point, closing with a rousing—"Grenadiers, it has all been decided. We are going to France, we are going to Paris!" Hundreds of voices responded with the traditional "Vive la France! Vive l'Empereur!"[6] just as they always had done these past ten and a half years. At 5 P.M. the troops began embarking—though it was now found that there was not room enough for most of the horses after all—while Napoleon returned to the Palace for the last time to take leave of his mother and sister Pauline. By 8 P.M., everyone was on board, and at 9 P.M. Napoleon returned to the harbor amid a jubilant crowd, and joined his staff on board *L'Inconstant*, as Captain Cautard hoisted the signal for the flotilla to set sail. Portoferraio, filled to capacity with the population of the entire island, cheered, shouted, sang and danced, making such a racket that it was almost impossible to hear one think, as the island's newly appointed Governor, Dr. Lapi, informed the people that their "august sovereign" had been "recalled by Providence to continue his glorious career," though without divulging what he had been called upon to do.[7]

Meanwhile, just an hour earlier that same evening, Colonel Campbell, after receiving word that an expedition was being prepared by the exiled emperor, sailed on the frigate *Perdrix* from Livorno, the ships later passing each other unseen in the night.[8]

Apart from the sighting of a distant British warship, and a French naval brig, the *Zéphir*, off the Italian coast, which came within hailing distance—requiring all men in uniform to go below decks—Napoleon's vessels, all but the *Inconstant* lateen sailers typical of this area of the Mediterranean, apparently did not arouse suspicion, despite their unusual number. Nevertheless, the Comtesse de Boigne, with her father, Comte d'Osmond, the French minister to Turin, on a visit to Genoa on the twenty-eighth, claimed, while watching an artillery demonstration along the coast, to have seen "two small brigs" belonging to the flotilla.[9] In any event no French or allied men-of-war had been alerted or attempted to halt them, as they followed the coastline while remaining just over the horizon, continuing to France without incident and finally sighting the mountains of Cape Antibes at 10 A.M. on 1 March, when the Elban flag was replaced by the tricolor.

The seas were calm and azure blue, the sky clear and the sun warm, all seeming to bode well as the squadron sailed round the Cape, keeping the Ile Sainte-Margueritte well to the west as they entered the quiet waters of the Golfe Juan, where they anchored, unchallenged either by French royal navy vessels or coastal artillery. The chaloupes aboard *L'Inconstant* and the *Saint-Esprit* were quickly lowered over the side as sailors—some swimming, come rowing—guided General Cambronne and his initial landing party of fifty grenadiers to the sandy beach not far from Vallauris, halfway between Juan-les-Pins and the miniature peninsula of La Croisette, with Cannes just on the other side.[10] His men fanning out across the beach and meeting no resistance, indeed seeing no one, Cambronne signaled to the boats to continue with the landing and within an hour all 1,026 men were ashore—grenadiers, infantry and cavalry— they replacing their white Elban *cocardes* in their hats with tricolored ones.

Despite the inevitable noise, the proximity of a small outpost and the large garrison of Antibes and the Fort Carré, still no one seemed to take notice of their presence, and now that all was ready, Cambronne ordered the firing of two cannon to signal the arrival of the Emperor. A horse finally appeared on the beach coming from the direction of Vallauris and a Captain Carbonnel, a health inspector, accompanied by a few customs men, astonished by the sight of these men on a normally deserted beach, came up to the first French officer they saw and tried to arrest him, demanding to know who he and his men were, what they were doing there. But of course the French officials were helpless to do anything in the face of such a large force and finally withdrew some distance away.

With all the supplies, arms and artillery ashore, all the cannon aboard *L'Inconstant* suddenly exploded at 3 P.M., announcing the forthcoming landing of Napoleon, one gun from the brig firing every minute thereafter as he was rowed ashore. The local inhabitants, mainly potters and fishermen and their families living in huts along the "Royal Highway," (linking Antibes with Cannes) amid the thick maritime pines and olive tree plantations, gathered at a respectful distance. Apart from the disarming of two small local artillery batteries, the Battérie de la Courcade and the Battérie de la Gabette,[11] there was no other activity. The general staff congratulated themselves on such an easy landing as Napoleon stepped ashore, between two rows of sailors drawn up at attention, saluting him, shouting *"Vive l'Empereur!"*[12]

Meanwhile, the flotilla prepared to return to Elba later that night, except for *L'Inconstant*, which had orders to sail to Naples to inform King Joachim Murat of events, and the *Saint-Esprit*, which sailed to Marseilles to inform Marshal Masséna, who was now military commander of this district, representing Louis XVIII and the House of Bourbon.[13] While nothing appears to have been done by the health and customs officers to apprise the civil and military authority of Napoleon's arrival in France, the latter was giving instructions to consolidate his beachhead, for with the departure of his flotilla that evening, he would have no means of escape. He badly needed the support of Marshal Masséna (Prince d'Essling)—his former lieutenant, and a native Niçois—for Provence and the department of the Var had, with one or two exceptions, been traditionally hostile to Napoleon, and he thus had to act quickly to gather his few friends round him. In the event the *Saint-Esprit* did not reach Marseilles, however, Napoleon also dispatched his personal representative, Pons de l'Hérault, who was also to stop en route to see Admiral Ganteaume (who had commanded the fleet at Brest during the invasion preparations for Britain in 1803–1805). But because Napoleon wanted to gain as much local support as possible, and felt it essential to avoid a military clash, he instructed Pons to obtain a "passport" from the Mayor of Cannes, enabling him to cross the Var to Marseilles.[14]

Meanwhile, the important garrison at Antibes (where Napoleon had first met Marshal Berthier back in 1796)—the only large one in the vicinity between there and Toulon—had to be neutralized and General Bertrand sent an officer with a detachment of men to invite the garrison's commander to hand the fort over to them. This was not quite as mad as it might have appeared, however, as a Corsican officer, distantly related to Napoleon, Colonel Cunéo d'Ornano, was, in the absence of Colonel Poudret de Sevret, now temporarily in command of the garrison's regiment, while one of Bertrand's former young officers, Colonel Paulin, was second in command[15] and it was hoped that both men would look favorably on the situation.

What turned out to be the most significant and equally bewildering day of his life began at 3 P.M. on Wednesday, the first of March, 1815. The semiretired royal notary, and for some years now, Mayor of Cannes—a prosperous city of 12,000 souls—having just awoken from his siesta, was taking his usual stroll along the newly planted tree-lined promenade he had been so instrumental in creating. The daily routine of the sixty-seven-year-old François Poulle was interrupted suddenly moments later, however, when a clerk from the Hôtel de Ville came running up, stating that the Mayor was needed urgently back at his office.[16] A curious Mayor Poulle sauntered back to his office, where twenty minutes later his deputy, Antoine Vidal, informed him that a stranger in civilian clothes had arrived from Elba without a passport, but requesting one in order to continue on to Marseilles. The gentleman was of course Pons de l'Hérault. Poulle stated that regulations made it impossible for him to give a passport to someone not already holding one from the city where he resided. Shortly thereafter a gruff, unknown general appeared at the same office, and who, over the the next several hours was to give a variety of false names . . . Comber, Combier, Chambon and Camboin—also demanding a passport, this time for Toulon, but again unable to produce his old one. He therefore was likewise refused. The general—it was Cambronne, naturally—then brusquely left the office, only to return moments later, ordering the Mayor to the Golfe Juan where he was "to be given the commander's orders."[17] The Mayor, more than ever bewildered, declined to do so. Poulle was then informed that the city was surrounded by troops! In fact, Cambronne had already established detachments of troops blocking the three principal roads into the city: the one to Fréjus, just beyond the Chappelle Sainte-Pierre along the west coast, another at the northern route from Grasse, and along the Royal Highway connecting Cannes with Antibes and Nice. In short, the city was completely sealed off, and the Hôtel de Ville surrounded.

By now it was 4:30 P.M. and Poulle dictated the first notice of the landing of foreign troops to his assistant for the Prefect of the Department of the Var, Comte de Bouthillier de Chavigny,[18] which would be slipped past the troops and sent on to the sub-prefect's office at Grasse, who would then forward it to Draguinan. He informed the Prefect that "sixty grenadiers" and their general, from the former imperial guard at Elba, had landed at the Golfe Juan and were now in Cannes, where they had begun requisitioning transport for themselves. "They are acting very mysteriously about the whole thing. They are taking horses from travelers, making them get down and paying them on the spot for their animals." He added that the general had "some dispatches for General Masséna."

By five o'clock other messages had been dispatched secretly to Fréjus and the gendarmerie post in the Esterel. At about the same time the Duc de Valentinois (the future Prince Honoré V of Monaco) was arrested as his coach approached Cannes along the Grasse road, his carriage and horses seized, and he himself locked in a room at the nearby Auberge Pinchinat, with a soldier left on guard.[19] Meanwhile, Cambronne, who had already purchased twenty-one horses and some wagons, now returned to Poulle's office at 6 P.M. to requisition twelve carriages and another forty-eight horses, for which he paid with a chit. He then left abruptly, returning an hour and a half later with another order for the Mayor—to provide three thousand rations of bread and meat, to be ready at "midnight sharp."[20] The figure startled the already much perplexed notary. Three thousand! Not sixty? "I summoned all the butchers and bakers," he later noted, "and explained the [general's] order that had to be filled."[21] Three head of cattle were then slaughtered, and the bakers too set to work, with the first large orders ready for distribution by 11 P.M., the remainder by 1 A.M. Cambronne could of course demand whatever he wished for, and there was very little Mayor Poulle could do about it. There was no garrison to protect the city, and just a few gendarmes. Nor was there even an armory from which citizens could have drawn weapons. And as Valentinois later put it, even if the worthy burghers had been so foolhardy as to attack professional soldiers, no doubt they would have seen the city sacked and burned.[22]

But the real identity and purpose of these men were only revealed to the mayor and the municipal councillors—who were by now crowding his office—when, at 8:30 P.M., an officer arrived with a batch of proclamations for distribution, proclamations signed by Napoleon and General Bertrand.[23] Dated March 1, 1815, Golfe Juan, and in large print, "NAPOLEON, by the grace of God, Emperor of the French," and addressed "TO THE ARMY," Napoleon appealing to the army to return to him and join his force. "We have not been conquered. . . . I heard you calling me in my exile, and I crossed every obstacle and peril [to return to you] . . . Take up those colors that the nation has prescribed, those colors around which we rallied for twenty-five years, fending off the enemies of France. Wear the tricolor *cocarde* that you also wore during our finest days! . . . We have been ordered to forget that we have been the masters of other countries, but at least we do not have to suffer the interference of others in our national affairs. Who would dare claim to be our masters? Who would be powerful enough to do so? Take up the eagles again that preceded you at Ulm, Austerlitz, Jena, Eylau, Friedland. . . . Soldiers! Come and rally round the banners of your Leader!"

Meanwhile, the detachment Cambronne had sent to Antibes had met with an unexpected check, for upon presenting itself and inviting the garrison there to join Napoleon's ranks, found itself arrested by Dauger Cunéo d'Orano and locked up in the Saint-Esprit Church, as the town's gates were closed and the drawbridge raised. Cunéo sent the officer leading that detachment back with an unopened letter, which Napoleon had addressed to him. At the same time in the commercial district of Antibes, the chief administrator, Dr. Arnoux, and Mayor Tourre sounded the tocsin, calling the citizens to arms,[24] while a second detachment sent by Cambronne proved equally unsuccessful.[25] But at least Cunéo was not ordering an attack on the Elban troops still on the beach, and since time was of the essence, Napoleon simply gave orders to bypass Antibes altogether. If he were to succeed now, he had to reach Paris quickly. He certainly had no plans to cross the River Var, where the Niçois were later to be warned by the Duc de Valentinois of the Bonapartist expedition.[26] In fact, Napoleon probably would have encountered stiff resistance in Nice, where Lieutenant-General Louis Cacherano d'Osasco, Governor of the Comté de Nice, summoned the 600-man-strong Queen's Regiment, along with two companies of Chasseurs de Savoie, and the city's National Guard, as well as dispatching a detachment of forty men with two cannon to the left bank of the Var to secure the narrow stone bridge, the Pont Saint-Laurent, even as the French Consul at Nice, the Marquis de Candolle, apprised Paris of the situation.

"Toward two A.M. someone came to announce the arrival of Bonaparte, who was setting up a bivouac in the sand dunes just outside the city, near Notre-Dame [du Bon Voyage]," Mayor Poulle informed the Prefect, "where he had a large fire lit, surrounded by his troops and many townspeople as well."[27] "Stay calm," he assured his anxious municipal councillors and the citizens maintaining the vigil with him at the Hôtel de Ville that night. "Neither strength nor courage is needed now, just a little caution. Rely on me and we will come out of this all right."[28] Moments later Napoleon summoned the Duc de Valentinois, and although spending quite a bit of time with him, the duke later acknowledged that he was only asked "a few trivial questions," and was then returned under guard to his inn.[29] But the duke, much miffed by the high-handed treatment he had received at the hands of Napoleon, later complained to War Minister Soult—"If you had only had some troops at Cannes, the landing would never have succeeded. . . ."[30]

Between four and five o'clock on Thursday morning, the second of March, Napoleon's "army" broke camp hastily—so hastily that they left behind over 1,700 rations of meat and bread. Equipped now with a couple of dozen carriages and a variety of carts for faster travel, they followed the winding road, which would eventually take them to Grasse, from where their journey—if unimpeded by resistance at that city—would begin in earnest. Napoleon passed through what he called "my beautiful countryside" enjoining his troops "not to fire a shot, for I want to return to my throne without a drop of blood having been spilled by us."[31] The men moved quickly now, with vehicles and horses pulling artillery and carrying the dozens of cavalry saddles, boxes of ammunition and supplies. Cambronne, with an advance contingent of one hundred grenadiers, was the first to reach Grasse that morning, issuing orders for the royalist Mayor of the city—Jean-Paul Lombard, Marquis de Gourdon—to provide more provisions and horses.[32] Upon descending from his sheer clifftop castle overlooking Grasse, Gourdon found Napoleon's main force already arriving, bypassing the city proper along the Chemin de Saint-Hilaire, mounting the hill and bivouacking on the heights immediately above the city itself. Cambronne found the mayor, municipal officials and people here even more outspokenly anti-Bonapartist than those of Cannes. But when the Marquis ordered General Gazan to summon the city's National Guard, only thirty men appeared armed with rifles, and it was at once evident that any resistance would be foolhardy.[33] The twisting narrow streets of this ancient town, which over the centuries had witnessed Greek, Roman and Arab invaders, now simply closed its doors on yet another intruder, shops and houses remaining firmly shuttered, not a single welcoming gesture to the man from Elba with his ragtag force and collection of dusty eagles. Provisions therefore had to be taken by force. But still nothing had been seen of King Louis's troops from Draguinan, Toulon and Marseilles, nor had word been received from Marshal Masséna.

Napoleon decided to press on, despite the exhaustion of his troops, and at 11 A.M. the bugle was sounded again to break camp, heading toward Paris via the only route where he knew there would be no major garrisons or large hostile crowds—the lower Alps via Digne, Gap and Grenoble. If once Napoleon reached the safety of the mountains rising sharply before him, his small force would have at least a meager chance to succeed, and thus he had urged on "his old groaners,"[34] his faithful troops, up the narrow twisting road—more often than not, a mere path— more frequented by shepherds than by carts or travelers—to the northwest towards Castellane. But the going was hard on both men and and animals. Carriages and even cannon were abandoned along the first fifty kilometers as they marched past Saint-Valliers, Escragnolle and Seranon. The weary men heaved the heavy saddles to their shoulders as they trudged through snow. When the carriage wheels could no longer advance they stopped for their first real sleep since landing in the Golfe Juan.[35]

In fact, Napoleon's decision to push on quickly was a wise one, for the authorities had been apprised early of his actions. Draguinan's church clocks had not yet struck three o'clock on the cold morning of Thursday, 2 March, when the recently appointed royal Prefect of the Var, Comte de Bouthillier-Chavigny, was rudely awakened by his valet to inform him that a messenger had just arrived from Cannes via Grasse. If when dressed for an official reception the plump, gray, frizzy-haired little Prefect with his languid smile, managed to look reasonably civilized, in his dressing gown and nightcap at his ungodly hour, he looked as truly ugly as he really was. He was handed the first note dictated by Mayor Poulle the previous afternoon, notifying him of the arrival of an Elban general and sixty men at Cannes. Hardly the sort of thing worth waking up a Prefect for! But this was followed in short order by two more reports, one from Raymond de Lacépèdes, Mayor of Fréjus, and another from a sergeant at the Esterel gendarmerie, confirming this news while increasing the troop estimates.[36] Bouthillier now notified the garrison commander, General Baron de Morangiès, who gave orders to have fifty men of the 87th Regiment mounted and ready to leave in short order.[37] At the same time the Prefect contacted Major de Lanautte, commanding the gendarmerie of Draguinan, to prepare a company of men also to accompany him. Meanwhile, Morangiès' superiors, Lieutenant General Baron Abbé, commanding the royal troops in the departments of the Basses Alpes and the Var, and Marshal Masséna, commanding officer of the 8th Military District (comprising the Basses-Alpes, Var, Bouches-du-Rhône and the Vaucluse) were also notified before dawn broke that Thursday morning.

Finally, before setting out, the Prefect also hurriedly apprised the Director General of Police in Paris that "a landing of grenadiers formerly of the imperial guard and coming from the Island of Elba" were somewhere in the vicinity of Cannes.[38]

As there was still no indication where the troops were heading, General Morangiès had to assume it was westward—the usual route to Marseilles, Aix or Paris—and left at 6 A.M. with his troops and the company of gendarmes, accompanying a perplexed Comte Bouthillier to the road cutting across the Esterel plain at Le Muy. His force was quite sufficient to deal with sixty soldiers. In a notice he had prepared to be circulated throughout the Var, the Prefect had stated "that announcements of these troops, however real or exaggerated they may prove to be, require our presence there to advise what measures are to be taken to ensure the safety and defense of the region. . . ."[39] And as they advanced across the Var the Prefect called out the few existing National Guard units of the sparsely populated plain.

It was not until he had reached Fréjus, however, that Mayor de Lacépèdes—himself a former naval officer—informed him that there were "about two hundred men," not sixty, and that they were not heading for Le Muy as he had first thought, but for Grasse and "they go so far as to claim that Bonaparte is leading them."[40] In addition to rallying the departmental defenses, Bouthillier continued along the coast to gather information, and later arms at Antibes, before returning to Draguignan via Grasse. On the second, rumors reached the Prefect that perhaps up to 1,000 men had landed. That same Thursday a by now much agitated Bouthillier dispatched a messenger to Masséna "to inform you that troops, HEADED by Bonaparte would be at Digne today."[41] By noon all the proper authorities, whether at Marseilles or at Paris, were being informed of what was happening. By 7 P.M. on the second, Bouthillier had prepared another report for Interior Minister Montesquiou in Paris that Bonaparte's troops "are heading for Digne and then Grenoble," with a force of between "1,600 to 1,800 men. . . .[42] I am taking all the necessary measures in my power to ensure the safety of the State and the King's interests. But, on the one hand, there are not enough troops here, and on the other, I make no attempt at deceiving Your Excellency, that a National Guard as badly armed [as they had there] is of very little real help. . . ."[43] In other words, by Thursday evening Bouthillier no longer had the slightest hope of trying to capture such a large force. But at least he took the basic steps expected of him, while the Mayor of Cannes in turn assured the royal Prefect of his personal dedication to King Louis, "of his love for his august person, and strongly condemned the man whom the sea had vomited up on the shores of Provence."[44] It was after this meeting with Mayor Poulle that Bouthillier revised his estimates of Napoleon's force yet again, ordering his deputy in Draguinan "to organize a detachment under the orders of Colonel Ferru as quickly as possible. . . . Send them to Castellane and Barrême. Bonaparte definitely has no more than 6 to 800 men with him. . . . *Vive le Roi!*"[45]

By Friday, 3 March, despite the dense pine forests extending between Seranon and La Garde, and the difficult ice and snow up the Col de Luens (well over three thousand feet high), the straggling column bereft of cannon, carriages and most of their horses, reached Castellane. After requisitioning 5,000 provisions for the troops, along with forty carts and 200 mules,[46] Napoleon then dispatched Dr. Emery to Grenoble to alert Colonel de La Bédoyère and former Foreign Minister Maret of his imminent arrival, while trying for a second time to send Pons de l'Hérault to Marshal Masséna at Marseilles. But fearful of the very real threat of pursuit by the large garrison at nearby Draguinan, he then gave the order to proceed to Digne.

And it was just as well that he did so—despite the primitive roads and trails that lay ahead of them as they advanced with difficulty through the rugged mountain wilderness separating Digne and Castellane—with troops already on their way from Draguinan. But Bouthillier for one, was now more confident that the ex-Emperor, the "adventurer," would soon be stopped. "It is quite impossible for those troops to advance for long in a country entirely devoted to H. M. [Louis XVIII] before receiving their just deserts for their rash act," the Prefect assured Paris and the Interior Minister on 3 March. He reiterated that he was taking "all precautions necessary . . . to ensure that this aggressor would be repulsed."[47] While in Marseilles, the actions of Marshal Masséna, as Military Governor of this region, were more questionable, however. But as usual the crafty Masséna covered his tracks reasonably well, afterward claiming he had first received word of Napoleon's landing in France at 2 A.M. on 3 March, when he received a gendarme's report from the Esterel "that fifty men from the Guard of the ex-Emperor Napoleon, coming from the Island of Elba, landed in the Golfe Juan yesterday."[48] According to Masséna, Napoleon was not even reported to be present. Was Masséna—who owed his spectacular promotions, honors and wealth solely to Napoleon—in fact apprised of the landing *prior* to the event, perhaps by Fleury? Did he receive the Emperor's personal message via the *Saint-Esprit* (which was never again mentioned by anyone)? Although it seems extremely likely that the old fox knew precisely what was going on, he continued to claim complete ignorance of an important political event—the first and only time in his life he ever did so—and in any case was certainly playing all cards close to his chest. He was not about to lose his wealth and accepted position, which he had been fortunate enough to retain under Louis XVIII (who was still dubious about Masséna's loyalty), to jeopardize all for Napoleon on his risky gamble, one which Ney himself was to call "simply crazy." If Napoleon succeeded, well, then he would see, but until success was ensured, he for one would simply procrastinate, hamstringing local administrators and military commanders. That, however, was the extent of his cooperation with Napoleon. He had, he insisted, no other information about the force of "fifty men" at this time early on the third, "neither about their present whereabouts, nor their objectives."[49] The same day, however, Prefect Bouthillier had written from Fréjus stating for the first time that 1,000—not fifty—troops had landed, troops definitely headed by Napoleon personally and moving in the direction of Digne. Whatever the reason for the unusually slow response to the threat posed by Napoleon's reappearance, even three days later no serious action had been undertaken by Masséna to cut off and capture that force. He merely dispatched two or three agents in different directions to gather more precise information,[50] only later sending General Millis and the 83rd Regiment to Sisteron to pursue the invader.[51] He assured the fervently anti-Bonapartist people of Marseilles—who had seen their thriving maritime economy shattered during the Empire (and their sea-going merchant marine fleet of three hundred thirty ships reduced to less than a dozen)—"You can count on my zeal and devotion. I swore my fidelity to the legitimate King. I shall never deviate from the path of honour. I am ready to spill my own blood in order to support his throne."[52]

Meanwhile, General Morangiès, in addition to calling out the 87th Infantry Regiment and arming more gendarmes, also summoned the National Guard units of Le Muy, Puget-sur-Argens, Roquebrune, Bandols, Fayence and Seillans (the latter of course merely to defend their own communities).[53] As for Bouthillier, he only set out for Saint Vallier on 4 March, where, after learning of Napoleon's good head start, complacently returned to Grasse the following day.[54] He had made his token defense of the kingdom.

Such was the resistance Napoleon met during his first four days in France, the splendid Bouthillier commenting afterward to Paris that "if the neighboring departments had been organized as well as mine,

Buonaparte would not have passed through the Lower and Upper Alps with impunity."[55]

Without the carts and mules, the Emperor could never have moved so quickly over the difficult terrain of the *arrière-pays* that lay before him on the third. But thanks to his loyal followers and his own desperate determination to succeed, Napoleon was able to push on with startling speed, given the conditions in this geographically difficult part of France. By the fourth he was in Digne, and Gap on the fifth, and on the morning of 7 March, at La Mure, only thirty-eight kilometers from Grenoble.

Two major obstacles barred the way between Napoleon and Paris: Grenoble and Lyons. Both cities had turbulent pasts, as well as large garrisons of several thousand men each and arsenals well stocked with artillery and ammunition. Thus it was at Grenoble, as Napoleon well knew, that his fate would first be decided. The garrison there would either crush or join and support him. Without fresh troops to bolster the nucleus of his "army," he would never reach Paris. The commanding officer at Grenoble, General Jean-Gabriel Marchand, the holder of the Grand Aigle of the Legion of Honour and a considerable private fortune— both of which he had acquired under Napoleon—had been one of the first imperial officers to betray the Emperor in 1814, allying himself with the House of Bourbon, for which King Louis had duly rewarded him with this post. Learning of Napoleon's approach, General Marchand now ordered Major de Lessart to leave immediately with a battalion of the 5th Infantry Regiment, a company of sappers, cavalry and artillery (perhaps 700 to 800 men in all) with which to halt the invaders at La Mure. He did so with the full support of the Prefect of Isère, Fourrier, who, ironically had been first named to his present position by Napoleon (before also abandoning the Imperial cause with Marchand the year before).

Upon reaching General Cambronne's advance contingent at noon on 7 March, at a position about a league from Laffrey, de Lessart sent a message making his position perfectly clear to the general: "I am determined to do my duty. If you do not retire, I shall arrest you."[56] Napoleon, who was a mile or so away, at the rear of the column, upon being informed of this check, leapt on a horse and rode forward quickly past the hundreds of blue capotes and the tall bearskin busbies of his Old Guard and the tense ranks of his Polish lancers—all with weapons at the ready. He pulled up abruptly ahead of Generals Cambronne, Bertrand and Drouot, while de Lessart, recognizing the little man with the big hat and famous gray campaign coat, stood speechless before the living legend of France. De Lessart, as well as his own officers, were astonished when Napoleon ordered them to have their troops shoulder their arms, thereby hoping to defuse this critical situation. There was then a period of utter silence while the battalion from Grenoble continued nevertheless to train their weapons on Napoleon's troops. Suddenly, Captain Randon, one of Marchand's ADCs accompanying the battalion, ordered the men to open fire. Nothing happened. Napoleon proving again what an extraordinary man he was, stepped forward. Bringing his right hand to his hat, he saluted Captain Randon with the bayonets pointing at him. "Soldiers of the 5th Infantry Regiment, I am your Emperor," he shouted out in an unusually loud parade-ground voice, as he opened his coat, revealing the Grand Cordon of the Legion of Honor across his bared chest. "If there is any soldier among you who wishes to kill his Emperor, here I am," he continued defiantly, holding his coat wide open. There was a stunned silence, then the spontaneous deafening shouts of *"Vive l'Empereur!"* as the troops from Grenoble broke ranks behind their officers, running up to Napoleon, kneeling down before him, kissing his sword and even the hem of his coat, while others threw away their white cocardes or hoisted their shakos on their bayonets. A bewildered Captain Randon fled the field in utter dismay even as Major de Lessart stepped forward handing Napoleon his sword, the Emperor embracing the major warmly in return.[57]

Shortly thereafter Colonel Charles de La Bédoyère, commanding officer of the 7th Infantry Regiment of Grenoble—who had been corresponding secretly with Napoleon at Elba—advanced with his entire regiment, all of them joining Napoleon's ranks. Lighting torches in the wintry darkness, they led the way back to Grenoble, and by nine o'clock that evening were passing through the Bonne Gate of the city.

Napoleon now discovered, however, that both General Marchand and Prefect Fourrier had fled, but at least La Bédoyère had prepared the way for him earlier. His enthusiasm when addressing his regiment spread to the others. "Take up your eagles again," La Bédoyère harangued them, "and all of you run to join us. Emperor Napoleon marches at our head!"[58] And as a result, Napoleon now met with no further resistance from the numerous garrisons there, including three regiments of engineers, the 4th Artillery Regiment, the 5th Infantry and the 4th Hussards (the troops that had left with Marchand earlier but then revolting would soon return as well).[59]

The following day Napoleon reviewed the eight thousand or so troops now at his disposal in the Place Grenette where Mayor Renauldon in his tricolor sash proclaimed that "the inhabitants of Grenoble [were] proud to have the conqueror of Europe within their walls. . . . Order us, sire! Your children are ready to obey!"[60] This was followed by the appearance of the Municipal Council, the magistracy, the clergy and teachers of the academy, all coming to pay homage to him. It was the first time since arriving in France that a large city and its burghers had freely welcomed him.[61] The white Bourbon cocarde was everywhere being replaced by the troops and national guardsmen with the revolutionary tricolor, which Napoleon now ordered to be hung from the city halls and belfries of the entire nation.[62]

At 4 P.M. on Thursday the ninth of March, Napoleon, cheered on by the populace of the city singing the "Marseillaise,"[63] preceded by the company of Polish lancers and his coach flanked by his imperial guard, set out from Grenoble. The most important immediate question facing him now, was what sort of reception Louis XVIII was planning for him, in particular at Lyons. For he knew it was simply a matter of days before the King's forces would be sent to stop him.

In fact, on the ninth of March, the King's brother, Charles Philippe de France (or the Comte d'Artois, as he was better known), was addressing General Brayer's thousands of troops gathered in the Place Bellecour in Lyons, attended by Comte Damas and Marshal Macdonald. Charles Philippe was chiding the soldiers that Bonaparte had landed with just "a handful of men" and that "with such feeble means he now claimed the right to be able to again impose his yoke on a great nation," the very nation he had left in ruins just months before. Enough of this, soldiers of France, he declared, "put an end to these criminal projects. We are all going to advance together on the enemy!"[64] But when Artois then ordered them to join him in shouting "Long live the King!", the smartly assembled battalions remained ominously silent. Visibly shaken by this untoward event, and after hurriedly convening a war council, including the Duc de Tarente and General Brayer, the garrison commander fled Lyons on the road to Paris early the next morning.[65] A few hours later a gloomy Macdonald, after learning that even Brayer had boldly declared his support for Napoleon, followed in Artois's tracks.

At 10 P.M. that same Friday the tenth, the triumphant Emperor, at the head of thousands of troops, drove through the open gates of Lyons as others captured the carriage of a fleeing General Mouton Duvernet, still bravely sporting his white cocarde. Pulling up in the Place Bellecour where the Comte d'Artois had stood just hours before, Napoleon was greeted warmly, throngs shouting *"Vive l'Empereur! A bas les prêtres! A bas les nobles! A l'echafaud les Bourbons! Vive la liberté!"*[66] ("Down with the priests! Down with the aristocrats! Hang the Bourbons! Long live freedom!") He made his temporary headquarters in the nearby Archbishop's Palace (that had formerly been the residence of his uncle, Cardinal Fesche), while sporadic pockets of resistance by "republicans" and aristocrats fought it out in the suburbs that night.

At 10 A.M. the following morning, with all resistance broken, the Mayor of Lyons, the thirty-six-year-old Comte de Fargues, welcomed Napoleon officially in the Place Bellecour, praising his virtues. This was followed by a review of the garrison by Napoleon and the local commander, General Brayer—the same garrison that the day before had declined Artois's appeal to defend the city against this very man.[67] While at Lyons Napoleon finally took the step he had long dreaded, but knew was inevitable if he were to succeed: He issued proclamations making a token compromise with the country's reburgeoning republicanism. "I am coming back," he assured the people, "to protect and defend the interests that our revolution has given us. I want to give you an inviolable constitution, one prepared by the people and me together," he declared, as he announced the abolition of the old aristocracy and any feudal obligations reintroduced by the Bourbons. At the same time he ordered the replacement of the Bourbon flag with that of the revolutionary tricolor throughout the land, while assuring the nation that the laws of the Constituent Assembly and Chambers would be vigorously supported by him. As for "the individuals who have obtained their national honors from Us, as a form of national recognition for their services to the country," all those Imperial titles would remain valid.[68]

With that unpleasant task out of the way, he removed 600,000 francs from the local office of the Banque de France (with which to fill the empty coffers of the "Imperial Treasury"), and then wrote to Marie-Louise to announce his forthcoming arrival in Paris on March 20 (the birthday of their son). Bidding his "Adieux and thanks to the Lyonnais,"[69] he left the city on Monday, 13 March with several thousand additional troops, including the 30th and 23rd Infantry Regiments and the 13th Dragoons, setting out on the road to Macon, Auxerre and Paris.[70] Little did he realize, of course, that Marshal Ney, of all persons, was now at the head of the country's eastern army corps (including the troops of Franche-Comté and Burgundy) forming on the path before him at Lons-le-Saunier, while General Comte Dupont, commanding officer of all royal troops in central France at Tours, was ordered to march eastward in a pincer movement toward Montargis. Also, a reserve army (theoretically 60,000 strong, with 150 pieces of artillery) was to form just outside Paris at Melun, the crossroads where the highways to Auxerre and Montargis met. All three forces were ordered by an anxious King Louis to stop Napoleon's advance once and for all.[71]

"The time has come to provide a fine example," the King proclaimed. "We expect all the energy a free and valiant nation can put forth. It will find Us ready to lead her in this enterprise upon which the safety of France depends. Measures have been taken to stop the enemy between Lyons and Paris."[72]

The cortège of five carriages headed northwestward, including Napoleon's calèche drawn by a fresh relay of six horses, flanked by the faithful Polish lancers in their red-and-gold uniforms. They were preceded by General Brayer (who had replaced the irritable and poorly organized Cambronne as commander of the advance guard), with perhaps 14,000 well armed troops and thirty pieces of field artillery.[73] Reaching the banks of the Yonne, Napoleon passed through the Faubourg Saint-Gervais and into Auxerre at 4 P.M. on 17 March. Throughout France uprisings that had begun with the news of Napoleon's landing on the first of March had since spread throughout much of the north, the north central and eastern regions of the country. Tricolor *cocardes* replaced the white. By the time Napoleon reached Auxerre he was met with a formal welcome by city officials, attended by a much warmer one by near-hysterical townspeople.

Just six days before this, however, on March 11, Prefect Gamot had informed the Interior Minister that Auxerre and his entire department were completely loyal to Louis XVIII: "I believe I can assure you that the Department of the Yonne is as a whole in a good frame of mind . . ." and that "His Majesty's subjects cannot find enough means of expressing their deep veneration, confidence, love and admiration for him."[74] Nevertheless, "the strictest surveillance" was being maintained along all the principal roads and the guard doubled everywhere. "I believe I can indeed assure Your Excellency that we have nothing to worry about . . . in this department where the greatest calm now reigns. . . ."[75] When Napoleon's envoy, General Ameil, arrived at Auxerre on the morning of the sixteenth, ordering General Boudin to surrender, Boudin simply had Ameil thrown into jail.[76] But over the next few hours as disastrous reports reached General Boudin of the magnitude of Napoleon's advancing forces (which he could not even begin to match here), the first tricolor cocardes began to appear on open display. The previous morning, Wednesday, the fifteenth, Prefect Gamot had "appealed to every man of good will, in the name of the safety of the country and the defense of the [Bourbon] Throne" to step forward to form reserve battalions for the protection of the department. But by that same evening the situation changed dramatically. Grave reports of mass desertions from Louis XVIII's forces everywhere were added to the débâcles of Grenoble and Lyons. Also, Gamot's brother-in-law, Michel Ney, had sent a message declaring his own intentions. The result was that Gamot himself now stepped forward appealing to the people of Auxerre and the Yonne *to abandon the Bourbon cause* and support the invader. "Inhabitants of the Yonne, throughout his life Napoleon has produced one prodigious achievement after another. . . . Let us unite around this hero whom national glory has recalled to us. Honor is the sole sentiment guiding our armies. Let every Frenchman follow their example. Let all our passions be reduced to a single one, for the love of our Country and our Sovereign [Napoleon]."[77]

When Boudin read this extraordinary document, written by a hitherto loyal supporter of King Louis, he knew all was indeed lost, even as more reports reached him of the swelling strength of Napoleon's quickly approaching columns. Thus at 3 P.M. on 16 March, General Boudin, commander of all the troops of the Yonne, fled alone in his carriage. In his inordinate haste, he left behind his papers, baggage, wife and children to their fate.[78] Two hours later Prefect Gamot descended the same steps into another carriage, and rode out of the city—in *his* case, to the south, in the direction of Lyons, to greet the conquering hero.

Given the small amount of time left between his "conversion" to the Bonapartist cause, and the arrival of Napoleon, Prefect Gamot had accomplished a great deal. By the time the five carriages bringing the Emperor's entourage appeared at 4 P.M. on Friday the seventeenth, the citizens had decorated the city lavishly with large tricolor flags and festive bunting. An old red revolutionary cap was found and placed on the clocktower of the Abbaye Saint-Germain, and an immense tricolor was suspended from the Tour de l'Horloge.

Napoleon was greeted there by Mayor Robinet de Malleville, who assured the "worthy inheriter of Charlemagne's throne" of "the devotion of the people of Auxerre" to him and his cause.[79] But of course the day before the same mayor and city council had been equally "devoted" to the Royalist cause, and Napoleon had no illusions about this abrupt transformation and switching of allegiance. Cries of *"Vive l'Empereur!"* rang through the stone streets, drums rolled and instruments played as the carriage now approached the Place du Département, moving into the courtyard of the Prefectural Palace. Prefect Gamot, who had joined the procession of carriages hours earlier, now showed Napoleon into the former archbishop's palace where King Louis's bust had just been discreetly removed and replaced with those of Napoleon, Marie-Louise and the King of Rome. The ambitious Gamot—from whom Napoleon could scarcely conceal his scorn—had even dug up a copy of Gérard's enormous wall-length coronation portrait of Napoleon.[80] After climbing the elegant staircase, Napoleon's staff, including the ever-faithful Bertrand, and his two principal secretaries, Rathery and Fleury de Chaboulon (who had just rejoined Napoleon at Lyons), set to work writing and copying letters and posting instructions; wherever Napoleon appeared, there was always an almost unceasing flurry of activity, as dictation followed dictation in rapid fire, then dispatched to high army and civilian officials. Although he had taken no real rest all day, at six o'clock he went out in a fresh downpour to review the 14th Infantry Regiment in the Place Saint-Etienne. There was simply no stopping this man whose mind appeared to be a perpetual dynamo. Nor was there any denying the sincere loyalty many felt throughout the country, exemplified now when the officers escorting him suddenly formed a triumphant arch with their drawn swords under which the wet but exhilarated Emperor passed.

Meanwhile the King and War Minister Soult were now counting heavily on Marshal Michel Ney and his reserve forces at Lons-le-Saunier. Ney, though Napoleon's age, was a tough, muscular man, with an equally tough reputation, if a limited set of values. Like most of the generals of the early empire, he had risen rapidly in his career thanks to Napoleon, and after distinguishing himself in every theater of war was elevated to the peerage with the title Duc d'Elchingen and Prince de la Moskowa. Although scarcely literate when he had been first commissioned in the revolutionary army, he had educated himself to a minimal level. "The brave of the brave," as he was affectionately known throughout the French army, never made much of a pretense at being able to express himself in a very civil manner, or even of possessing the thinnest veneer of culture. He was no Berthier. Now at Lons-le-Saunier, before dawn on 14 March, in the presence of the Prefect and Sous-Prefect of the Ain, he described Napoleon—the man who had crowned his career and given him wealth, as "a mad dog upon whom one must fling oneself in order to avoid his savage bite. If I have the good fortune to arrest him, I hope to bring him back to Paris alive in an iron cage!"[81]

Ney, like Macdonald, Masséna, Marmont and so many of Naopleon's former senior commanders, had no sense of loyalty to anyone. In fact, he had already heard of Napoleon's amazing successes at both Grenoble and Lyons, of course, and knew he was facing a force of at least 14,000 men at this stage; that is, one twice the size of his own. Furthermore, Ney was furious with Paris, which since his arrival on the eleventh had failed to communicate with him, to give him further instructions or even indicate what regiments he was to expect or draw upon for his force in the Franche-Comté (which the Duc de Berry had been originally assigned), most of his present force consisting simply of the troops he could find in the immediate vicinity.

Now, without warning, Ney suddenly announced he was throwing in his hand *with Napoleon*, and sent an officer to him with a personal letter to this effect.[82] When an astonished Prefect Baron Capelle (of the Ain) protested vigorously at this betrayal of their king, Michel Ney calmly replied: "Do not worry about a thing. Napoleon is returning with the finest intentions in the world. He wants to forget the past and instead reconcile all parts of society and save France."[83] Within a matter of twelve hours Napoleon, for Ney, had changed from a vicious "mad dog" to the "savior" of the country. Ney immediately drew up a proclamation to his newly formed army corps, declaring that "the Bourbon cause is lost forever! The legitimate Dynasty which the French Nation has adopted is going to return to the throne. It is to Emperor NAPOLEON, your sovereign, alone who has the right to rule over our splendid country. . . . Officers, Noncommissioned Officers and Soldiers! I have often led you to victory. Follow me now and I will lead you and this immortal Phalange, which is marching with Napoleon on Paris. . . . Long live the Emperor!"[84]

But his senior staff officers—Generals Bourmont, Lecourbe and Mermet—whose support was critical to him, were as dedicated to King Louis as the exasperated Baron Capelle. In order to win them over now and rally their men, Ney did as he had so frequently done in the past, resorted to an outrageous lie—"Gentlemen, the matter is settled. The King has already had to leave Paris,"[85] and with that the ineffable Ney dispatched his message to Napoleon.

Early evening on Wednesday, 15 March, Napoleon was just beginning to dine with a few of his staff at the Hôtel de la Poste, in Autun, when an officer arrived with Ney's letter. Opening it then and there, he beamed an unaccustomed if cynical smile, as he announced the good news—Ney and some six thousand troops were on their way to join them.[86] If Lyons had marked a significant military coup in Napoleon's advance on the nation's capital, assuring him as it did of sufficient loyal forces with which to meet a royalist challenge, he still had no major national military figure, not a single one of his celebrated marshals, on his side. But now Ney, whose name carried great weight among the rank and file of the regular army, was linking his name with the Bonapartist cause. Napoleon ordered the hotelier to bring forth his finest reserve. If it was a cynical celebration—for Napoleon utterly detested this man who had betrayed him in his hour of trial—he needed him, and like all the marshals he had created, Napoleon himself was a tough, practical man, siding with the devil himself when necessary.

Arriving late on Friday the seventeenth, Marshal Ney did not meet Napoleon till 8 A.M. the next morning, when the Emperor embraced him and invited him to join him for breakfast. Napoleon, for one, saw no reason to dwell on the past now, while all the embarrassed Ney could manage was to mutter the insistence of his unswerving patriotism to France. With that tense moment out of the way, they got down to breakfast and business, Napoleon questioning him about the units under his command and the situation in Paris. After explaining his current position and immediate objectives, he ordered Ney to take his troops to Dijon, where he was to assume command of all units there, and march on Paris, where he would meet him [on 23 March, as it turned out].[87] Napoleon now had one excellent commander in the field, and if he could prove trustworthy, there was plenty of work for him. His intention was to arrive in Paris on 20 March, and he had much to do before then, as he organized the twelve regiments and a few odd units at his disposal.[88] There was no Berthier to help him now, and logistics for some 20,000 troops and thousands of horses and wagons had to be drafted. What force they would encounter before Paris, probably at Melun and Essonnes, where the Duc de Berry was purportedly assembling a large army, no one knew. Napoleon had confidence in his own numbers now, however, if they could all be trusted. Paris was an unknown factor, to be sure, and he did not want to have to fight his way in, which would prove disastrous for his cause. He hoped that by giving the King enough time, the main opposition would melt away and the King himself would flee.

If there appeared to be chaos all about Napoleon's Auxerre headquarters now, it was the organized chaos typical of a new, hurriedly assembled fighting force, while the same could not be said of Paris, where outwardly there appeared to be no confusion—the King in residence, the Chambers meeting, newspapers appearing regularly and café and theatre life flourishing. But in fact, the Tuileries and the King were in a state of near panic, as Louis continued to listen primarily to only one man, and he not even a member of the government, the Comte de Blacas.

Chapter III

"The Disturber of the
Peace of the World"

*"What utter madness could have seized the Emperor? But he will soon be
its first victim. Who will support him? Not a soul."*

Aglaé-Louise Ney [Marshal Ney's wife]

*"A band of five or six thousand fugitives flatter themselves that they can
conquer France and impose their laws on a nation of twenty-five million
people."*

Journal des Débats, March 18, 1815

*"I am convinced that Bonaparte's undertaking will come to nought and
that it will not be necessary to call upon the foreign powers to intervene
once again. Nevertheless it is always wise to take the necessary
precautions."*

Talleyrand to Jaucourt, Vienna, March 12, 1815

The news of Napoleon's landing in the Golfe Juan reached Paris—via
messenger as far as Lyons, and then by military "telegraph" (or signal
flags) to the capital—just after noon on Sunday the fifth of March. As is

often the case with someone upon receiving a startling piece of news, the King, in this instance, at first seemed neither shocked nor unduly disturbed.[1] Surely such a desperate undertaking—with just a few hundred men and no organized support within the country—could not advance very far inland before being stopped by royal army units. Indeed, what could a small landing party do against a standing army of over 200,000 men! What is more, Napoleon had landed in one of the traditionally most hostile parts of the realm, the Midi, a region that had always been staunchly pro-royalist and anti-Bonapartist throughout the Empire years.

In fact, Napoleon's whole enterprise now was more one of blind faith buttressed by an equally blinded egotism, in blatant defiance of all the known realities, which had become agonizingly clear, even by the end of 1813, at a time when the Emperor was still in control of the Tuileries. In December of that year an alarmingly large number of secret prefectoral reports from departments and cities throughout France—from the Nord, Pas de Calais, Picardie, Normandie, the Vendée, Britanny, the Auvergne, the Ardèche, Le Gard, Lyons, Marseilles, Toulouse and Bordeaux—attested unequivocally that imperial decrees were not only being ignored, but that public opinion was now flauntingly critical of Napoleon, declaring the last years of his rule to be calamitous for the nation. The wartime economy, for so long bolstered by staggering trains of war booty, a continual flow of war indemnities from conquered nations, and lucrative army contracts, not to mention the subsequent wealth gained from those regions as commercial outlets, had long since dried up, once artificially expanded frontiers had begun to shrink drastically in the wake of the fiasco of the retreat from Russia in 1812. With dwindling treasury resources to meet the expenses of a country continually at war, taxes—many of those very taxes earlier suppressed by the Revolution—had been reintroduced as early as 1804, including the "collective duties" on drinks (at various levels of production and distribution), salt and tobacco.[2] In addition, when farmers were not hit by bad harvests, they were now increasingly, systematically, struck down by enforced military requisitions—for horses, cattle, fodder, grain and wine. Entire regions of France proper were left without sufficient work animals for the plowing and harvesting of fields. But War Minister Soult, a singularly insensitive man, and responsible for ordering this nationwide policy of rapine of a country which was still four-fifths agricultural, merely replied to pleas of protest with his habitual—"You must assist us . . . even if it means providing the army with the last kernel of corn, and the last forkful of fodder."[3] Career officers, of course, were rarely known to show any sympathy for farmers. But the army was not the only reason for the by now endemic draining of financial resources and a dwindling of treasury reserves. The Continental System, closing off British goods and markets from the entire European mainland—and, of course at the same time, French goods from British markets—as well as as the extraordinary costs of maintaining a growing number of "nonproductive" imperial court officials and officers— were also contributing to undermine the economy. Napoleon, intent upon creating another Versailles mentality in the guise of his own "aristoc- racy," one loyal to and dependent upon him alone, had created a new peerage, with hundreds of counts and dozens of dukes (without duchies for the most part) and princes, and with each title went large sums of gold from the civil list. Each of the twenty-six "marshals" he had created over the years was granted an ever-increasing fortune, including estates, thereby gradually rendering them so rich—Berthier, for one, had become one of the wealthiest men in France—powerful and independent, that by 1813 most of them could afford to ignore their Emperor's orders and complaints with impunity.[4] Unlike Louis XIV, Napoleon had quickly lost control of his "Versailles," the monster he had created, and which had shown little gratitude in return. The Bourbons had had centuries in which to create and mold their aristocracy. Napoleon had lost control of his own less than ten years after creating it. But Napoleon steadfastly continued to believe in the efficacy of his system, insisting that the distribution of this astonishing largesse and plethora of new titles was all to the nation's— and of course his own—good. Naturally, ministers and friends, too, greatly increased their personal acquisitions, Talleyrand achieving the foremost position with his vast estates and by now immeasurable wealth, and even the self-proclaimed "puritanical" former Police Minister, Joseph Fouché, having salted away millions before being fired in 1810.

With this growing financial drain and accompanying inability of a nation to pay its bills, the few new burgeoning industrial centers of the country began to collapse after 1812. The subsequent closing of more and more of Europe to them resulted in a shortage of cash, materials and, of course, markets for their products, leading in turn to chronically crippling unemployment (as witnessed at Lyons for instance).[5] In the year 1813 alone, 5 percent Consols—securities in which so many of the wealthy had invested their money—dropped from 80 to 50 on the Bourse, while the gilt-edge shares of the Banque de France plummeted from 1,480 to 690 francs. The critical wine industry was likewise hard hit as prices fell continually year after year, a *tonneau* of red wine (906 liters) dropping from 2,850 to a mere 850 francs by 1813, despite growing inflation.[6]

Another cause of national decline—all related to the constant state of war insisted upon by Napoleon—was the now-desperate government quarterly conscription of recruits for the army, which stripped hundreds of farming areas of most of their male labor force, as more and more fields fell fallow and production slumped drastically. Indeed, by 1813, it is estimated that Napoleon had conscripted over 1,800,000 men[7]— even before the Russian débâcle—sending back in return a steady stream of tens of thousands of permanently crippled veterans and amputees.

Nevertheless, these heady facts had not deterred the Emperor from descending upon France in 1815, attempting to rouse the people yet again, nor even from his personally complaining of King Louis's oppressive reign during his first year on the throne. "Let's forget the past, the royalists say. In that case, Frenchmen would be forced to forget all the wives who have been raped [sic], *their properties that had been devastated [sic], and France, her very glory destroyed, her name dishonored—all by the Bourbons. Are the people then to forget that the wolves have replaced the shepherds?"*[8] he harangued the populace, having apparently forgotten that all the above calamities, which he now laid to the Bourbons, were in fact the results of his own rule, and that over the past fourteen years he had *willfully* destroyed the country's economy as well.

By the end of 1813, the complaints reaching the Tuileries could be summed up in one word—peace. Everyone, from every sector of society was clamoring for, *pleading for, peace,* even close confidants and loyal Bonapartist supporters. And National Guard units often declined to muster when summoned, rejecting outright the very idea of any sense of fealty and further blind obedience to the ruthless policies of Napoleon. Indeed, even the one minister who had remained at his task faithfully since the days of the Consulate declared his open hostility to this continuing state of warfare and to Napoleon's obduracy in rejecting one peace initiative after another. "Do you really want me to tell you the unvarnished truth?" Naval Minister Admiral Decrès asked Marshal Marmont bluntly. "The Emperor is crazy [*fou*], completely crazy, and is going to throw us over, landing us in an incredible catastrophe."[9] "Peace is the country's only desire and the need of mankind. . . . Sire, by one final effort worthy of you, obtain peace for yourself and the French people," Napoleon's hand-picked Senate officially implored him in December 1813.[10] The Deputies of the Corps Législatif were even more outspoken in their criticism of him. "Commerce has been annihilated . . . industry is on its last legs. . . . What has been the cause of these unutterable woes? A vexatious government, overtaxation, the deplorable means applied for the collection of taxes, and even more cruel, the excesses of the system used for army recruitment . . . Conscription has become an odious plague for the entire country. . . . For the past two years, the men of the nation have been harvested [*on moissonne*] three times a year. *A barbarous and pointless war** has been periodically fed by our youth, torn from their education, agriculture, commerce and the arts," the angry deputy from Bordeaux, Joachim Laîné, now stated forcefully in support of a motion before the Corps Législatif calling for peace. As a result of this "senseless" [*sans but*] continuation of warfare, "All the country's frontiers are now threatened, and we are going to suffer an end unparalleled in our history. . . ."[11]

France was being systematically destroyed *from within*, losing everything it had gained since the Revolution. The nation wanted peace now, immediately, before being overtaken by total disaster. If Napoleon could claim that this was just the sort of isolated rhetorical complaint one might expect from the traditionally royalist city of Bordeaux, he could not so easily explain away the following vote on Deputy Laîné's motion to initiate peace talks: *223 for, 51 against.* Nor by the same token could Napoleon so readily dismiss the pleas of those loyal to him and his cause. "We want only one thing, peace. It is the general cry from everyone and from every corner of the land," Senator Lapparent pleaded.[12] But still a stubborn Bonaparte—unwilling to admit years of colossal error and of course his own rapacity—held out, blinded by his insuperable arrogance and egotism, refusing to acknowledge publicly that the very core of his imperial policy since the renewal of war following the scuttling of the Peace of Amiens, in May 1803, had been an unmitigated disaster for France and all of Europe.

With the Emperor still in the field on 4 March 1814, ex-King of Naples and Spain, Joseph Bonaparte, in his brother's absence as head of the Regency Council, had written to the Emperor about this very problem. With France now surrounded, and 100,000 Allied troops closing in on Paris itself, peace, he said, was inevitable. "The forthcoming peace, whatever else it may be, will be indispensable; but good or bad, we must have peace. When the day comes that people believe that Your Majesty has preferred the continuation of war to peace, even a disadvantageous one, no doubt they will react harshly. I cannot deceive myself on this point, like everyone else, seeing it as clearly as I do. We are on the verge of *total disintegration*,* for which there is only one possible answer—peace."[13]

It was a nation utterly exhausted and bewildered that subsequently

*Author's italics.

saw the Duke of Wellington leading thousands of occupying troops into Paris in the spring of 1814, as King Louis XVIII (brother of the executed Louis XVI) replaced Napoleon in the Tuileries. So thoroughly had Napoleon removed—in one fashion or another—all organized opposition during the last nearly ten years of his tyrannical Empire, that not a single competent leader—of any political persuasion—capable of capturing national support for a new government could be found with whom to replace Bonaparte. The Allies had thus been faced with a dilemma. They neither liked, admired nor wanted the return of the Bourbons, but in the end had not much choice. Either they could have retained Napoleon to administer the country—albeit under severe safeguards and constitutional restrictions—or perhaps a regency could have been formed in favor of his wife or son. Or Louis XVIII could be brought to France, and the latter decision was of course finally taken, after Talleyrand and Fouché did everything in their power to turn the Allies against the idea of a regency, which they were seriously considering.

The newly occupied France, however, remained effectively leaderless under its new king and, not surprisingly, in numbed postwar shock. Few Frenchmen could remember the rule of France under the Bourbons prior to 1789. Few knew anything about King Louis or even what he looked like, nor even the names of the royal family. Over a period of twenty-five years—nearly a full generation—the Revolution and Napoleon Bonaparte had effectively *erased the historical memory of the nation*. Thus support had to be carefully cultivated and this was undertaken in the southwest, and in such cities as Bordeaux, Toulouse, Nîmes and Marseilles, artificially nurtured by a group of men, members of a fanatical secret religious society known as the "Chevaliers de la Foix" (Knights of the Faith)—including among their numbers some of the most prominent names of the Faubourg Saint-Germain: Alexis de Noailles, Armand and Jules de Polignac, and the brothers Eugène and Mathieu de Montmorency.[14] Nor would even their support alone suffice to have installed "the immense corpulence of the King" (now so obese he could only be moved by a large, specially reinforced chair on wheels) in the Tuileries Palace in 1814. Nevertheless, after weeks of debate, wangling and intrigue, the Allies accepted the Bourbons as the only practical solution for the moment. *Someone* had to rally the nation and restore order. It was as simple as that.

It was hardly surprising then that the reign of the new Bourbon King had done nothing to increase his popularity throughout the remainder of the year 1814. If he had acquiesced in the matter of the new Constitutional Charter, foisted upon him by the Allies (but which was ultimately modified by the King himself to meet his own needs), it had done little to allay a dictatorial mentality still living in pre-revolutionary France of the eighteenth century, when the current king had fled the country. Louis XVIII was not familiar with the people he now ruled and the changes wrought over the past decades; nor did he wish to be so, all of which was aggravated by his natural secretiveness and tendency to listen to only one adviser, the Comte de Blacas d'Aulps.

When the seventy-four articles comprising the "Constitutional Charter" were signed on 4 June 1814, they ensured a system—with the blessings of the Allies—placing all the executive powers in the hands of the King. He alone could name and dismiss ministers, and he alone was able to initiate legislation. In general he had the same powers as Napoleon before him in controlling the armed forces, the judiciary and the administration, and he alone could declare war, or name the life members of the Senate to the Chamber of Peers (with no restrictions on number). The one sop granted the Deputies in the lower Chamber was that of approving all legislation creating direct taxation, though even the Deputies were controlled by the King through voting and office-holding restrictions. To be able to vote in France one had to meet stiff property qualifications devised by King Louis, requiring the minimum payment of 300 francs a year in direct taxes, which at once limited national suffrage to perhaps 90,000 persons out of a population of 25 million. But then in order to be eligible to hold office as a Deputy—and they were only elected indirectly by electoral colleges—one had to pay at least 1,000 francs a year in taxes, which left a mere 10,000 persons in the country qualified, a number further reduced when the minimal age requirement (of forty years) was subsequently applied.[15] Although all religions were in theory tolerated by the new Charter, the Roman Catholic Church became the official State religion and indirectly, through the strong reintroduction of long forgotten religious customs and ceremonies, Protestants and Jews were made to feel more and more the outsiders of a society from which they were deliberately excluded, a society rigidly directed by a small nucleus of the old aristocratic families.

Although a new freedom of the press was introduced and greatly welcomed—after Napoleon had surgically reduced the number of daily national papers in Paris to a mere three—the heavy hand of press censorship was soon reintroduced, much dampening the initial enthusiasm of publishers and politicians. A further source of discontent was the reduction of the standing army from over 500,000 to just over 200,000 which included immediate mandatory retirement of a corps of some 12,000 disgruntled officers.[16] Three hundred thousand demobilized soldiers sud-

denly thrust upon a country where commerce had long been in a state
of stagnation and unemployment rife, did not bode well for the new King's
popularity. Within the remaining army the King's authority and influence
were further undermined by the fact that he lacked among his supporters,
a sufficient number of qualified military officers to assume command of
large military units. The King was thus forced to retain most of Napoleon's
marshals and senior generals. For example, his 6,000-man "Household
Guard" itself was commanded by two of Napoleon's principal officers,
Marshals Berthier and Marmont. And even in the civilian realm, the King's
aristocratic supporters were so few in number that he could hardly begin to
fill the Senate properly. The same applied to the important vacant positions
of prefect and sous-prefect, for which he likewise lacked a sufficient number
of properly qualified aristocratic gentlemen, and he was determined above
all to reintroduce the old aristocracy and have it supplant Bonaparte's home-
spun variety of half-literate army officers inherited from the Revolution. King
Louis symbolically capped the introduction of his Bourbon restoration on
January 21, 1815 with the transfer of the remains of Louis XVI and Marie-
Antoinette to the traditional royal crypt at Saint-Denis.[17]

Unfortunately for the King, a not terribly astute or competent national
leader, he chose to surround himself by men who were, by and large, as
incompetent or inadequately prepared for leadership as himself. His principal adviser and confidant since 1800, during his exile at Hartwell in
England was the Comte de Blacas, who bore no political title and held
only the honorary position as "Maître de la Garde-Robe."[18]

Such was the situation in France at noon on Sunday the fifth of March,
1815, when King Louis received word of the landing of Napoleon and
his troops.[19] After consulting Blacas, and then War Minister Soult (who
had replaced General Dupont in that position just before the new year),
it was decided to take some necessary precautions, although it seemed
hardly likely that Napoleon would ever reach the Alps (whereas in fact,
by March 5 he was of course already at Gap). The King's nephew, the
Duc d'Angoulême (son of Louis's younger brother, the Comte d'Artois)
and his wife were on a State visit to Bordeaux at this time when the King
dispatched a messenger to inform them of the possible crisis, ordering
him to proceed to Nîmes, where he was to form an army of at least ten
thousand men and pursue Napoleon wherever he might be by then. Back
in Paris the Comte d'Artois's other son, the Duc de Berry, was summoned
directly to the Tuileries and then sent to eastern France in the Franche-

Comté where he was to assemble all the military units of the region to form another army, while the Comte d'Artois and Marshal Macdonald were dispatched to Lyons where War Minister Soult was in theory mobilizing another army corps, 30,000 strong.[20] Soult's intention then was to launch that force southward in the event Napoleon reached the Rhône. But of course, as already noted, that plan came to nought with the unforeseen departure from Lyons of Artois and Macdonald.

One of the main elements in all these military preparations was naturally, Marshal Soult, who now proved—what Napoleon had long ago discovered at Boulogne during the invasion preparations for Britain over ten years earlier—that he was as incompetent as he was vain, as the King was about to learn for himself. To be sure, two premature military uprisings between Paris and the Belgian frontier led by Generals Drouet d'Erlon and Lefebvre-Desnouëttes, were put down in very short order, and fortunately for King Louis, France—despite Napoleon's absurd and fictitious claims about the King's actions and alleged brutality—though scarcely enthusiastic, was at least not openly vexed with or hostile to the King. On the other hand King Louis was still very much an unknown quantity to the nation and the result was that, through apathy, jaded and wary regular royal army and national guard units almost everywhere failed to rally in sufficient numbers to form effective military resistance for the defense of the country. They had heard that patriotic plea to defend throne and nation far too often in the past. If the people were as a rule not anti-Louis, they certainly remained largely too unsympathetic to any fresh appeal to arms to wish to lay down their own lives. They had had enough troop mobilizations and battles under Napoleon and were not about to support such a a national effort for an unknown King who had been absent for the past twenty-five years, a King so hideously obese that he could not even stand up unattended to review his own Household Guard!

Masséna, of course, had deliberately dragged his feet before making even a token move in pursuit of the invader back on 3 March,[21] and Artois had witnessed for himself how apathetic the royal troops at Lyons were, while to the east, the King's nephew never even reached the Franche-Comté. It was humiliating, it was shocking, it was disastrous. Indeed, King Louis grew so anxious about unsettling reports of fresh antiroyalist feeling among garrisons stationed within Paris to protect the royal family and the capital that he ordered them all out of the city (except for his own 6,000-man Household Guard), mostly to Villejuif and Melun, where the Duc de Berry was now reassigned as commander in chief with Macdonald as his second-in-command. Meanwhile, Soult, who as a former Bonapartist army commander, had many enemies in the Tuileries following the débâcle of Lyons—for which he alone was held responsible—was denounced as a traitor by Blacas, charged (albeit without any proof in hand) of plotting with Napoleon to overthrow the Bourbons. The "rebellion" at Lyons, Blacas claimed, had occurred in fact on Soult's orders. Army units in the Franche-Comté and the Midi had failed to assemble because Soult had managed it that way. Little did Blacas realize that much, if not all of this, was now taking place due to Soult's mismanagement and incompetence. In any event, Marshal Soult now resigned in a huff and was replaced at the War Ministry by the Duc de Feltre, General Clarke, a man who if anything, was even less fit for that particular post.

One former imperial army officer after another was letting the King down. But the King was still sanguine, for there remained one last hope, one of Napoleon's former officers who was known not only as an outspoken critic of the former Emperor—that sadomasochistic Napoleon, who had humiliated him time after time, as he had done to just about everyone round him—the Bonaparte he had betrayed the year before (when he, Caulaincourt and Macdonald had abandoned him to his fate at Fontainebleau), the one man still universally respected throughout the army as a tough soldier's soldier, the ill-tempered hero of numerous imperial battles, Marshal Michel Ney. A desperate King Louis had ordered Ney to Lons-le-Saunier, to assemble the army that Berry had so singularly failed to do, and then to prepare to advance on Napoleon. Ney, with a shallow ego admitting of no inadequacies, promptly accepted the task, arriving at Lons on the eleventh, informing Suchet that he hoped they would "soon see the end of this insane venture."

This was the situation as the King understood it at three o'clock on Thursday, 16 March, as he set out from the Tuileries in a downpour to address the hurriedly reconvened Chambers in the Palais du Corps Législatif (as the Bourbon Palace was now called). The cortège included the recently returned, if crestfallen, Comte d'Artois, the ever-hopeful Duc de Berry, the devious Duc d'Orléans (the future Louis-Philippe), as well as all the principal State and Palace officials, and a large retinue of admirals and generals. They in turn were preceded and followed by cavalry units of the Paris National Guard as well as by the King's colorful musketeers in their red-and-black uniforms—as the State carriages crossed the Place du Carrousel, Place Louis XV (Place de la Concorde— where the King's brother had been executed) and over the Pont Royal to the Palace.[22] A couple of hours earlier, his brother, the Comte d'Artois, had returned from a review in the Place Vendôme of General Dessolles's

13th Legion of the National Guard, where Artois, as Prince Colonel-General, had received a warm welcome, the troops cheering him and the King. But by now the King needed both assurances and moral support, especially after the gloomy ministerial meeting held at the Tuileries earlier that morning when Blacas and Secretary of State Baron de Vitrolles had discussed the disagreeable possibility of a French civil war in the event Bonaparte were not checked immediately.[23] As the carriage made its way, the King to his chagrin, heard very, very few shouts of *"Vive le Roi!"* that Artois had reported from the Place Vendôme, and the continuing rain did little to lighten already well-dampened spirits.

Nor did the delayed arrival of the King do anything to ease the tension at the Palace, as Comte de LaMothe-Langon, an eye-witness, noted. "There were moments of crisis when confusion spread everywhere. The continuing booming of the cannon at the Invalides, the noisy crowd gathered just outside the Corps Législatif, the roll of drums, the loud music from the military band, created an atmosphere of almost electric excitement as the King's cortège approached the Palace. Although the scene outside struck me as rather disturbing," LaMothe acknowledged, "inside I found something altogether different . . . [where] a great crowd gathered in this hour of national jeopardy, distinguished by the magnificence of their clothes, the richness of their appearance, and even more noticeable, by an almost universal feeling of love, concern and anxiety, all giving a very special atmosphere to this solemn occasion."

With the announcement of the King's arrival at 4 P.M.—*"Le Roi Messieurs, le Roi"*—Louis's entourage began descending from the long queue of carriages, as ushers, Deputies, State messengers, officers of the King's Chamber, his heralds at arms, pages, equerries, gentlemen-in-waiting all proceeded, then the Prince de Condé, the Duc d'Orléans, H.R.H. Monseigneur le Duc de Berry, His Highness Monsieur (Artois) and finally the King himself, literally supported by the Duc de Duras and the ubiquitous Comte de Blacas. "The Monarch made his way slowly, the real anguish of the effort reflected in his drawn features, though his eyes were calm and his forehead exuding that usual aura of majesty. The shouts, the formal greeting accompanying such an occasion, followed him to his throne. Trumpeters' fanfares filled the air, the ladies waved cloth of lillies and white handkerchiefs . . . it was like a snow storm . . ."[24] And in the background standing together, the Montmorency brothers, Eugène and Mathieu, Alexis de Noailles, and finally, of course, Armand and Jules de Polignac.

As the King settled on the throne and his brother and the royal dukes took their places to the right and left of him, Louis in turn signaled the

Chancelier de France, the Chevalier d'Ambray, to invite first the Peers, then the Deputies to be seated before him. All the pomp and tradition of yesteryear were reintroduced today as if they had never been interrupted by the past historical chasm. To the troubled and uncertain, it was reassuring to see the old pageantry and customs played out again, as they had been for centuries, whenever the monarch of the realm had appeared among his subjects. After all the changes, disruptions, violence and social turbulence wrought by the Revolution, it was indeed reassuring again to see the King back on his throne, ensuring badly needed national stability in the lives of the French people and their institutions. It was worth forgoing some liberties—even a parliamentary monarchy such as Britain enjoyed, for example—in order to have regained this cohesion and national calm.

But outside, from a cold, overcast sky, the rain continued to pour, from the Channel to the Jura Mountains, enveloping the nation portentously, while just a few hundred miles to the east an even more forbidding storm threatening Paris and the Government was steadily advancing, prepared at any cost to overthrow this newly and dearly wrought peace and stability, not yet quite a year old. Thus, despite the appearances of reassurance reflected in this distinguished assemblage now in the Palace, glittering in the light cast by a thousand brilliant candles and dozens of exquisite chandeliers, the hour was a grave one for France. Indeed, nothing less could have persuaded this habitually indecisive King to convoke an emergency session of the Chambers today for such a purpose. Rumors, always rife in Paris, had begun to assume a more ominous tone the past few days when first the news of the fall of Grenoble to this "Corsican Ogre" (as the London *Times* referred to him) followed by that of Lyons, accompanied by the utterly unthinkable revelation that most of that city's ten-thousand-strong garrison had gone over to Napoleon. To be sure, the *Moniteur* and *Journal des Débats*—on direct orders from Vitrolles and the Tuileries—had contradicted this direful news, blatantly informing the few thousand literate Frenchmen and women that Napoleon had been repulsed.[25] "Marshal Ney," said the *Journal des Débats*, "is leading a corps some ten thousand strong . . . all in excellent spirits."[26] Paris was certainly safe, it assured the people, ringed as it was by "an army of 35,000 men. . . ."[27] A band of five or six thousand fugitives flatter themselves that they can conquer France and impose their laws on a nation of twenty-five million people. . . ."[28] "Louis XVIII," the *Débats* continued, "has given us peace, the Constitution and freedom. What is Bonaparte bringing us? . . . Frenchmen! Be true Frenchmen! Let us at least die as Frenchmen if that is what is required of us. . . ."[29] And yet

Artois and Macdonald, sent to Lyons to lead that great counteroffensive against "a handful of rebels covered in the blood of their brothers"[30] were in Paris here today, a grim reminder of present realities, indeed, in this very hall where they should not have been at all had Napoleon really been forced to fall back to the Mediterranean. It was in fact quite embarrassing. And, indeed, if all had truly been going well, why the melancholy countenances of the ministers, generals and members of the royal house, to a man, and a pall of gloom hanging over this entire ceremony? Indeed, why this ceremony at all and the presence of the King at this untoward moment? The fact was that France was menaced once again—not by the Allied armies of 1814—but by a French force, French troops facing French troops, threatening to overwhelm the nation in bloodshed and political chaos.

No moment could have been more fraught with suspense now as the King prepared to speak, when everyone present hoped they would soon learn precisely what was indeed happening. "The King, having lost none of his noble serenity, or love and confidence of the people," LaMothe blandly continued, "greeted the assembly, then, in a strong sonorous voice" addressed his subjects.

"Gentlemen, in this moment of crisis, which—having taken root in one part of the kingdom—threatens the freedom of all the rest, I come in the midst of you to draw close those ties uniting you to me, and which are the very strength of the State. . . .

"I have seen my fatherland again, and I have reconciled it with all the foreign powers, which will remain—have no fears about it—faithful to those treaties which have brought us peace.

"I have labored for the happiness of my people, and I have received and indeed daily receive, marks of their love for me. And now at the age of sixty, could I end my career in a finer manner, than by dying in the defense of my country? . . . I fear nothing as regards myself, but I do fear for France. Those who come among you lighting the torches of civil war bring also the plague of foreign war.

"He who does that comes in order to put our nation under his own iron yoke.

"He comes to destroy this Constitutional Charter . . . this Charter that every French citizen cherishes, and which I have sworn to uphold. . . .

"Then let us rally, Gentlemen, let us rally round it [the Charter], let it be our sacred standard. The descendant of Henri IV will be the first to do so, followed in turn by every Frenchman.

Finally, then, Gentlemen, let the two Chambers give it the force of authority it requires and this war will then truly prove to be a national war, showing what can be done by a great people united together by their love for their King and by their fundamental love of the State."[31]

Two days earlier Interior Minister Montesquiou had assured the King that "Marshal Ney . . . is advancing on Lyons," and in fact, Ney was certainly the King's last hope of checking the force even at this late hour. But now, upon returning to the Tuileries, following his address before the Chambers, King Louis was informed of Ney's treachery . . . of his having gone over to Napoleon, when that marshal had himself best summed up the King's situation: "The Bourbon cause is lost."[32]

The news of Ney's betrayal had cast aside the last shadow of doubt, and the candles of the King's apartments in the Tuileries burned very late into the night of 16 March and the early morning of the seventeenth, as advisers, ministers and generals came and went. Further confirmation of Ney's heinous act received over the next few hours finally jolted the King into action. General Nicolas Joseph Maison, Governor of the 1st Military Division, around Paris, was summoned, even as the Duc de Berry was riding out to assume command of the ten thousand or so troops (not the 35,000 claimed earlier by Soult) ordered to Melun, where the young duke intended to make a last stand against Napoleon and his "handful of men."[33] As Berry was shortly to discover, however, even these greatly reduced numbers of troops now refused to move past Villejuif, and Melun remained all but an open crossroads.

Meanwhile, at the Tuileries, Generals Maison and Dessolles reassured a much-shaken King of their profound loyalty to the Bourbon cause and of their determination and willingness to head fresh armies against Napoleon . . . in exchange for an immediate payment that very afternoon of 200,000 francs each![34] The King, who apparently did not seem shocked at this outrageous blackmail, agreed there and then and Maison returned to his headquarters, where he finally issued orders for the troops of his military district "to consider themselves on active duty." . . . "Look at your King, so full of confidence in your loyalty and fidelity. . . . Soldiers, get ready to march!"[35] and thus more troops set out for Melun, even as the equally loyal General Dessolles rallied the Paris National Guard. Meanwhile, the Comte de Blacas, inspired no doubt by the King's resolution and speech the day before, and taking literally his willingness to head his troops, even if it meant "dying for the fatherland"—and in this act of heroism seeing the immobile monarch somehow transformed into a younger, more lithe Henri IV—now personally urged the King to go and do just that. He must proceed to Melun and in the best feudal manner, lead his troops into battle against Napoleon. Vitrolles, who was present at this meeting, at first aghast at this proposed piece of folly, then caustically interposed—"Monsieur le Comte, you have quite forgotten to have your procession preceded by the Holy Sacrament, borne forth by the Archbishop of Paris himself!"[36] With alarming reports reaching them of the growing number of troops abandoning the Bourbon flag, joining Napoleon on his seemingly relentless and thus far unimpeded march on the capital, the smug Blacas asked Vitrolles in turn—whom he loathed, a sentiment fully reciprocated by the latter—to state his own solution for the defense of the country. "Have all the royalist volunteers assembled at Orléans, Tours, Blois, Saumer and Sanger, there to hold a solid line along the Loire," Vitrolles immediately snapped back. "Let us organize a strong resistance on the spot as we march through the western provinces: in Anjou, Poitou, the Vendée, Britanny, and a large part of Normandy."[37] With "fifty or sixty million francs in the Royal Treasury" and these troops, they could also hold the principal ports in their hands: Brest, Rochefort, Toulon, supported by an entirely loyal navy. But Blacas and Montesquiou vetoed the idea then and there.

Later that night (17 March), the ruthless and power-hungry Duc de Raguse, Marshal Marmont, at his own insistence, held a secret meeting with a hesitant, if still despairing, Vitrolles, when he presented his own answer to the immediate crisis—a modified palace coup. Blacas, as the King's principal adviser, was the cause of all the present woes, and thus must be disposed of. He should be seized and sent to America, well out of harm's way. Vitrolles should then lead a new government as Prime Minister and, of course, appoint Marmont commander in chief—not simply of the nation's army, but of the navy as well. "Monsieur le Maréchal, the enemy is at our very door," Vitrolles calmly pointed out. "You have chosen this precise moment in which to form a new government and an absolute monarchy—this in spite of the King's wishes, in spite of the princes, in spite of the Chambers, in spite of public sentiment to the contrary—all of whom would unite against you? Under those circumstances the troops would not obey you for even twenty-four hours," and with that dismissed Marmont's mad scheme with a sigh.[38] Soldiers never did understand politics.

✦　✦　✦

"I shall enter Paris just as easily as I did Grenoble and Lyons. The garrison and commanders are all behind me," Napoleon confidently told his secretary, Fleury de Chaboulon.[39] Everywhere villagers and communal mayors came out to greet the Emperor's calèche, protected as usual by his Polish lancers in their red-and-gold uniforms and shining metal helmets, albeit now dripping in the continuous rain as nearly twenty thousand men continued on their way to the nation's capital without meeting the least resistance. Miraculously, not a shot had been fired, nor had anyone been killed. It was a remarkable feat. But crowds could be fickle or simply pro-Bourbon, and Napoleon's views of the French working class and the lower bourgeoisie are well known: "In them I only see the rabble of the country,"[40] he said over and over again, even when that "rabble" consisted of drunken civilians and soldiers storming through towns and cheering his own cause. Rampaging crowds could just as easily be turned against him, as he knew only too well. But the crowds followed him everywhere. "Light-hearted demonstations verged on the delirious," Fleury noted en route from Auxerre. "The people are rushing and shoving to get close to him [Napoleon], to meet him, to speak to him. His lodgings [that night] were quickly surrounded and laid siege to by such a large and determined crowd that it was quite impossible for us either to enter or leave without having to pass through the entire population of the place."[41]

Napoleon needed more popular support, but at the same time he personally feared and distrusted the all-too-frequently veering violence of hysterical, unreasoning mobs, and had few illusions about their real or lasting loyalty, significance or influence. And thus, whenever possible, Napoleon continued to enter large cities in particular at night, to avoid such demonstrations, even when they were—as they now invariably were—friendly. Before proceeding, Napoleon therefore took whatever measures he could to ensure that the crowds he would encounter—which always appeared to be composed of the same faces he had seen among Parisian mobs he had fired into in the 1790s—would not be hostile, and that the army garrisons ahead were indeed safely committed to his cause. The troops in Paris "are in my camp," he boasted, but could not really believe it till he saw it for himself. His "brave soldiers" and their commanders had turned against him in 1814, and had barred the way at Antibes upon his return to France. Garrisons from Draguinan and Marseille had pursued him, ordered to "run him down"[42] as he advanced through the Alps, and had almost checked him completely at Grenoble. No one could ever be counted on, and Napoleon, who had also been abandoned by his wife, Marie-Louise (who had thus far refused to return his son to him as well), had few illusions about human attachments, even when it concerned the highest military leaders. "Ney," he pointed out, "was firmly committed to attack me, but when he saw that his troops would not allow it, he was forced to go along with popular feeling, at the same time seeking a way to profit from a situation which he could not prevent. Rest assured, that was indeed the case. . . ."[43] With equal frankness—after all, his entire future now depended on clear vision—he acknowledged that his real support throughout the country came from two elements "the people"—i.e., the working classes, and "the army," and it was not for them that he had written the *Code Napoléon*, or Civil Code, but for the solid people of property and education. And yet he admitted that these very solid bourgeois "fear me and therefore I simply cannot rely on them"[44] and that rightly disturbed him very much. Four-fifths of French society was still largely composed of the peasantry, mostly unorganized and illiterate, who in turn were traditionally controlled by the remaining one-fifth, the one-fifth he now badly needed to win over.

Before leaving Auxerre on Sunday, March 19, Napoleon addressed a final letter to Marie-Louise:

> "My good Louise,
>
> The people are running to me in droves. Entire regiments are quitting and joining me. . . . I shall be in Paris by the time you receive this letter. . . . Come and rejoin me with my son. I hope to embrace you before the month is out. . . ."[45]

Dispatching this now, little did Napoleon realize that one week earlier, his wife—who had taken General Neipperg as her lover several months earlier—had just written a public letter to the Austrian Emperor formally renouncing her husband and the French crown, refusing to return their son to his father.[46]

A sense of impending doom, matched by grim wintry skies, pervaded the French capital by Saturday the eighteenth. Nevertheless a few public officials did remain optimistic, including the brash new War Minister, General Clarke, who went so far as to smugly assure the troops: "Now you can put on your boots again . . . all the damage has been repaired [now that he had replaced Soult and was in charge]. The general staff, which were not even organized [eight days earlier under Soult] are now working perfectly. Officers are rejoining their regiments."[47] While the

Journal des Débats, as a government organ, went even further: "After having retaken Grenoble [from Napoleon], General Marchand [the Bourbon commander there] has executed a junction with Marshal Masséna, Prince d'Essling, and his army. It is reported that they have retaken Lyons."[48] In this same edition the now pro-Bourbon liberal, Benjamin Constant, referred to Napoleon as "this Attila, this Genghis Khan . . . this man stained with our blood. . . ."[49] It was a tissue of lies from beginning to end, of course: Grenoble and Lyons were now firmly in Bonaparte's hands, even Marchand joining him. As for the wily Masséna, he had not even considered leaving Marseilles. But even before the print was dry on the Saturday edition of the *Débats*, the Duc de Berry had found that the troops at Villejuif were refusing to follow orders, indeed, failing to salute the King's name or to proceed in any numbers to Melun, where in fact gathering staff officers almost outnumbered their troops. Nor had his brother, the Duc d'Angoulème, sent much good news. After having set out from Bordeaux late on the ninth, he had intended to rally the nucleus of at least ten thousand men from the royalist southwestern region of the country, at Nîmes, and to pursue Napoleon up the Rhône.[50] And although royalist sentiment was certainly stronger there than elsewhere, and the royal duke had been duly greeted on his arrival at Nîmes on 15 March by loud acclamations of *"Vive le Roi! Vive la famille royale!"* he ultimately found a mere 5,500 men ready to march under his banner. After losing several more valuable days arming and organizing his force, he was only to reach Valence on April 3, by which time Napoleon was already in Paris.[51]

Given this sad state of affairs, the official "propaganda" could in no way alter the truth. The upper bourgeoisie and aristocracy hurried to the Hôtel des Postes to apply for their passports, their elegant carriages soon heavily laden with cumbersome trunks as they fled Paris in a mass exodus via Saint-Denis heading for the northwest, led in their panic by the wives of the most prominent government officials, including the Duchesse d'Orléans, the Comtesse de Blacas and the Princesse de Talleyrand. Even as the *Journal de Paris* appeared on the street trying to allay fears, imploring the people "not to believe a word of what those traitors are saying, they who—with their hypocritical and perfidious private interests at stake—are deliberately exaggerating the dangers of the situation."[52] Even as a now desperate General Dessolles, keen on earning his enormous bribe, was hurriedly calling up the law and lycée students of the capital to don uniforms and patrol the streets, while King Louis was issuing one last equally desperate proclamation appealing to his subjects, his "children" . . . "To win or die for her [*la patrie*], let that be our war cry." As for the tens of thousands of troops—that is to say, his "children" who had gone over en masse to Bonaparte—they were not really bad, he insisted, just led astray [*égarés*] in the heat of the moment. "Therefore renounce your error and come and throw yourselves into your father's arms. . . ."[53] If armies could not hold back "Attila," nor could such patriotic words and fatherly sentiment, even as Treasury Minister Louis was making arrangements to transfer the 25 million francs in silver, in Paris, to the north (most of which, in fact, never left the capital).[54] And then, as if Saturday, 18 March were not already a fiasco and total disaster, Marshal Macdonald suddenly appeared at the Pavillon de Flore insisting upon an immediate audience with the King. At this meeting he tendered his resignation because his superior, the young Duc de Berry, had made such a hash of the defenses, first of the Franche-Comté, then of Paris. Refusing to accept the loss of one of his few remaining competent commanders (who, in fact, did not even demand a bribe), the King fired Berry, replacing him with the angry Scots marshal. That same Saturday, another of Napoleon's former generals, Augier, rose before the Chambre des Députés, proposing a motion for the declaration of war against the invader, a measure tabled for further consideration.

By Sunday the nineteenth, some 20 million francs had been withdrawn from the private accounts of French banks, or otherwise transferred abroad by Bourbon supporters fleeing the country.[55] The King, who had till this point been unflappable, was now more than a little shaken. As Vitrolles acknowledged, "The knell of our agony was ringing across the land. Even now, at the last critical moment, they [the King and his advisers] remained as indecisive and as inert as before." The King had by habit refused to take the necessary steps and give the urgently needed orders, and "none of his ministers was prepared to assume the responsibility and authority required, indeed none was capable of doing so . . . M. de Blacas even less so than the others. As a result, a sort of paralysis set in," Vitrolles noted.[56] In fact, the King had resolved on one thing: to flee. But fearing another Varennes, another humiliating capture of the royal family by angry mobs barring his route to freedom across the Belgian frontier, the King now informed only the most essential personnel and court officials of his decision, not even trusting to apprise his own ministers. The most influential and dedicated aristocrats of the land—Chateaubriand, Montesquiou, Montmorency, Noailles, Richelieu and the faithful Vitrolles among them—remained ignorant of his plans. The King further concealed his intentions by scheduling a royal review of the Household Guard at the Champs de Mars at noon that day (19 March). It was all the more ironic, then, that the only two senior military commanders he did choose to confide in at this most critical hour were former Bonaparte cronies—Marshals Macdonald and Berthier—though not his own War Minister, General Clarke.[57]

Due to increasingly unfriendly crowds along the scheduled route for the military review, the King put off his departure for a few hours, leaving the Tuileries just before 4 P.M. But his fears, rather than being allayed by this delay, had only been reinforced by the hostile greetings the King now encountered as he set out. In fact, they had proceeded no more than a few hundred yards—as far as the Champs Elysées—when he decided to go no further. Stopping then and there "to review" some detachments of the Guard stationed at that point, he immediately turned back to the palace. He did not even have the courtesy to send word of his change of plans to the rain-soaked Marshal Marmont, who remained sitting on his horse before the Ecole Militaire, awaiting the King. And yet it was Marmont who was to command these same Household Guard during the King's flight. It was not until later that night that the Comte de Blacas finally informed the ministers of the plans for the King's departure. They hurriedly agreed to follow him . . . after being offered an inducement of 100,000 francs cash each (readily accepted to a man).[58] Summoning Baron de Vitrolles to his apartments at 11:30 P.M. that evening, the King at last informed him personally of his intention to leave *in half an hour* and ordered Vitrolles in turn to leave at once for the Midi, to help the Duc d'Angoulême rally troops for this force round Nîmes and to instruct the Duchesse d'Angoulême ("The only man in the King's army," Napoleon said of her) "to hold Bordeaux as long as possible. Following these words, the King held out his hand, which I kissed . . . I certainly being more moved [by the tragedy of this moment] than the King himself."[59]

At midnight the doors of the Salle des Maréchaux were thrown open as the King bade farewell to the faithful who had remained with him to the very end only to learn now that they were being abandoned, though the King assured them he would be seeing them again "soon." Then entering his carriage with the aid of his two traveling companions, Marshal Berthier (of all people!) and Comte de Blacas, another Bourbon King fled north in the night to the safety of the frontier and the protection of foreign armies.[60]

Napoleon intended to arrive in Paris in two days' time, advancing from the southeast via Fontainebleau, and if he were to keep to that schedule, he had to make the final dispositions for his troops. At this moment he badly needed and sorely missed the one man above all others responsible for organizing his armies ever since 1796, Marshal Alexandre Berthier, his former war minister and chief of staff, and closest friend (as much as anyone could have claimed that distinction). Berthier had a genuis for organizing, but without him at his side—and it seemed an ill omen to the superstitious Napoleon that he had chosen to remain with King Louis—Napoleon was at a severe disadvantage, having now to work as his own chief of staff, though Bertrand, who still bore that title, no doubt did his best. It was too important to leave to men of lesser abilities, however. Feeding and housing some 20,000 men[61] was a major logistical problem here in a region unaccustomed to large army garrisons, and the sooner they left Auxerre and were dispatched to Paris, the better—hence the decision to divide his forces as they approached the capital. A few thousand troops would accompany the Emperor, but perhaps up to 9,000 or 10,000 would be sent ahead, on barges and boats down the River Yonne, while most of the cavalry would also set out in advance on the road to Melun, to clear the way for Napoleon. Despite the jubilation along the muddy banks of the Yonne, where the last traces of snow were fast melting, as company after company of troops—cheering, and singing the "Marseillaise," "Ça Ira" and the "Carmagnole"—embarked on the makeshift transport flotilla, a wary Napoleon nevertheless knew that not only angry soldiers could start shooting innocent people, firing indiscriminately, but festive, delirious troops could as well, and so he decided to keep the men moving.

From the very beginning at Cannes, he had enjoined meticulous control of his troops in order to avoid alienating the people he was just beginning to win back. He knew he would greatly increase his following in his role as harbinger of future peace, set on a peaceful rule as opposed to the traditional view of him as the belligerent conquering soldier. But with Paris practically in sight, the situation was never more delicate, with thousands of troops, often drunk, in and around Auxerre. And thus on 19 March Napoleon again reminded the generals commanding these various units of the necessity of maintaining strict discipline. "I am told that your troops . . . are bent on reprisals against the royalist forces they encounter," he informed General Girard. "But, General, the only people you are going to meet are Frenchmen. Therefore call your soldiers. Tell them I have no intention of entering my capital with troops covered with French blood."[62]

The jubilant troops thus duly pulled out of Auxerre during the night, Napoleon's closed calèche in their midst, setting out on the 104-kilometer stretch of road to Fontainebleau, where they arrived just after 4 A.M., on Sunday the twentieth, the hoofs of thousands of horses clattering against the cobbles of the streets of the sleeping provincial town. Passing through the imposing green-and-gold wrought-iron gates, bringing them suddenly before the enormous château, they entered the Cour du Cheval Blanc, filled with hussars, staff officers, infantry, engineers and limbers with dozens of pieces of artillery. But Napoleon, for one, was too exhausted to take in this scene of his triumph now—here where just a year before he had nearly died, followed by his public humiliation and deportation.[63]

Despite his fatigue, after taking less than three hours' sleep, the Emperor again convened his inner staff—Bertrand, Drouot, Brayer and his treasurer, Peyrusse—to outline the final stage of this journey and what was to take place in Paris. Messengers arrived constantly with fresh reports of the continuing disintegration and withdrawal of Macdonald's few forces making a last stand at nearby Melun and Essonnes, most of whom were already indicating their intention of changing sides and joining Napoleon. The important news he had been so longing for, however, only arrived at noon, from Napoleon's former director of the postal communications in Paris, the Comte de LaVallette, who had seized the Hôtel des Postes just two hours earlier that very morning. "Hasten, Sire. The King has left. The Tuileries is yours."[64] The courier brought other items as well, from two former Police Ministers, Savary and Fouché, Hugues Maret, and his step-daughter, Queen Hortense—describing the King's flight and the welcome Napoleon would receive at the Tuileries, which had been reoccupied by Excelmans's cavalry and the National Guard. Shortly thereafter, Napoleon boarded the same vehicle he had been using since Lyons (having declined the use of the more magnificent state carriages brought from the stables at Fontainebleau) and set out on the last eighty or so kilometers and the final leg of this Odyssey, which had begun at Elba less than a month before.

Arriving in the suburbs after dark, Napoleon's long cortège of carriages and large cavalry units passed through Essonnes, reaching the heart of the capital, then crossing over the Seine on the Pont Louis XV, where tricolor flags could be seen in the lamp light, approaching the usual entrance of the Tuileries, passing under the arches at the Pavillon de Flore, where a battalion of National Guardsmen smartly presented arms as a large crowd of officers and civilians rushed up to the mud-splattered carriage.[65] The main entrance of the palace "was filled with such a solid mass of generals, officers, guardsmen and a large quantity of distinguished persons, however, that the carriage could not proceed to the stairs at the main entrance," Saint-Denis reported. "Seeing that he could advance no further, the Emperor descended in the midst of the immense crowd, which quickly engulfed him."[66] But before Napoleon could utter a word, he was snatched away from Bertrand, Drouot and Caulaincourt (who had joined him hours earlier at Essonnes) and hoisted upon the shoulders of several young officers and carried up the Grand Escalier. Practically crushed in the onslaught of enthusiastic supporters inside converging at the entrance with those outside, it was only with extreme difficulty that Napoleon, already weakened by the journey, gladly escaped immediately into his apartments. It was a far cry indeed from Cannes! But exhausted or not, he was greatly moved and excited by this astonishing welcome—perhaps even more so than at his own coronation—as General Bertrand recalled. "I never saw him so exhilarated, and so terribly proud." And he kept repeating to Bertrand—"It is really those who had nothing to gain who brought me back to Paris, it was the second-lieutenants and privates who did it all—it is to the people, the army, that I owe everything." Around him old friends and a few members of his family now gathered, Hortense in black (the sad reminder of Josephine's recent death) and Queen Juli (Joseph's wife), but not his own wife, Marie-Louise and their son, the King of Rome, whose fourth birthday Napoleon had been determined to celebrate in Paris this day.

Chapter IV

The Brothers Bonaparte

"Just be satisfied with being a prince and stop worrying about the consequences of that title."

Napoleon to Joseph Bonaparte, November 1804

"My mistress is Power. I have gone through a great deal to make that conquest, to permit her to suffer or be ravished by anyone else coveting her."

Napoleon

All eyes were now on the brothers Bonaparte, indeed on the entire Bonaparte clan. It was hardly surprising that following Napoleon's forced abdication on 11 April 1814, the Allies had insisted upon the isolation of every member of the clan from one another, including the suppression of all communication. The brothers were deliberately cut off from one another—which in fact they much preferred to permanent internment on Elba with Napoleon—while at the same time finding themselves spied upon and openly harried by local officials and police. The Bonapartes had controlled and dictated European destiny throughout nearly ten years of the Empire: waging wars, interrupting international trade, undermining national economies, not to mention shattering the homes and lives of millions of people. It had taken years of turmoil, instability and destruction resulting from Napoleonic rule before France and all of Europe had been in a position to put an end to the havoc wrought by this one man's egotism and unsated appetite for wealth and power.

Thus with the return of Napoleon in March 1815, this remarkable if unpredictable family once again became the major concern of the chancelleries of Europe. One of the first preoccupations of statesmen everywhere naturally was to consider what sort of vengeance Napoleon and his family would wreak, in light of the humiliations they had suffered following their calamitous defeat. But how different France had been some two decades earlier when that Corsican clan had first inflicted itself upon this ancient land.

The brothers Bonaparte were to prove the key to the events which followed. If in Napoleon's four brothers—Lucien, Joseph, Louis and Jérôme—instability of character in varying degrees including inordinate egotism, a general sense of irresponsibility, ruthlessness and sheer perversity were to be found, in Lucien alone did they form the character of a political bounder par excellence.

Born in 1775 and thus six years younger than Napoleon, Lucien was sent to join him briefly at his school at Brienne, from which he was withdrawn two years later following his father's death, and transferred as a full scholarship student to Uncle Joseph Fesch's seminary at Aix. Although Fesch was to emerge shortly thereafter as an ordained priest of the Church, the unruly Lucien soon left without any qualifications whatsoever. With very little formal education behind him, and unlike Joseph, neither interested nor talented in business matters—and at one time so impoverished he was forced to take work as a warehouse watchman—Lucien did early indicate a strong interest in Jacobin left-wing revolutionary politics.

But politics in 1795 could also be very lethal. After displaying strong leadership qualities, it was hardly surprising that the outspoken young man found himself in a crowded Aix prison that July, following a crackdown by counterrevolutionaries on both former Jacobin followers of Robespierre and on their more moderate branch, the Thermidorians, who were everywhere attacked, murdered or imprisoned. As a revolutionary firebrand and the brother of General Napoleon Bonaparte (a friend, in turn, of the notorious Robespierre's brother, Augustin), Lucien found himself in an unpleasantly prominent position despite his mere twenty years.[1]

Thanks to Napoleon Lucien was finally released unharmed. A month later (October 1795) Napoleon showed his gratitude to the newly installed Directory by training forty cannon on riotous pro-royalist crowds in Paris, which he quickly reduced in a frightening massacre. It was Napoleon who now obtained for young Lucien his position as "commissaire politique," or political officer, with the French army, which brought with it a good salary and the lucrative possibilities of many unsavory forms of income. With Napoleon's reward now as commander of the Army of Italy, the Bonaparte family was finally on its way to establishing itself.

Prisons apparently did not deter Lucien, however, for by 1798 he was running for public office as a member of the Council of Five Hundred (of the new national assembly in Paris). That he was only twenty-three years old, and thus did not qualify for this position—twenty-five being the minimal age stated by the constitution—did not appear to perturb the young man, who shared his fellow Corsican countrymen's traditional scorn for such legalities. Upon presentation of fraudulent birth records, he was duly elected a Deputy for Liamone and whisked off to Paris. And in the same year, 1798, as Napoleon was preparing to embark a large army with which to invade Egypt (the idea of invading England having been dropped), Lucien was joining Joseph, Uncle Fesch and Letizia in a little private venture of their own: purchasing and arming a coastal vessel called the *Patriote*. On their orders the captain captured on the high seas a Turkish (or Moroccan?) ship with a rich cargo, which they then had openly sold at Ajaccio, bringing them 180,000 francs profit. It took some legal maneuvering, however, and no doubt a considerable portion of their newly acquired loot, with which to bribe the authorities and keep them out of prison for piracy.[2] Letizia, who could not understand why her family was so put upon, indeed persecuted, for something which had been done continually by Corsicans for centuries, roundly condemned the French and Corsican magistrates. Hence it was that with the threat of yet a second prison sentence now safely behind him and cast from his mind, Lucien proceeded to Paris to assume his new duties as a member of the Council of Five Hundred.[3]

The following year, 1799, was to prove of singular importance for the entire Bonaparte clan. Lucien was proving to be a rather spectacular deputy, distinguishing himself with remarkable rapidity as a result of his dramatic and effective impromptu speeches, while collecting the traditional bribes and followers in rather impressive numbers, culminating in his surprise election as President of the Council of Five Hundred the same year (at the age of twenty-four). Meanwhile, newly accrued riches permitted him and his young wife, Christine, and their child to move into the luxurious country estate of Plessis-Chamant[4] north of Paris, just outside Senlis (and not far from Chantilly and Joseph's country place, Mortefontaine).

In October, General Bonaparte returned hurriedly to France (after abandoning his army in Egypt) and on 18–19 Brumaire* (9 and 10 November) arrived with troops at Saint-Cloud, where the Council of Five Hundred was meeting, and promptly overthrew the French Government. In fact, this coup d'état nearly failed on 10 November, and was only saved thanks to the direct and vigorous intervention of President Lucien Bonaparte. The Directory was immediately dissolved, the Consulate—with Napoleon Bonaparte at its head—created, and the foundation laid for the new Bonaparte Empire, which would soon encompass not only France but much of Western Europe.

In December 1799, First Consul Bonaparte rewarded young Lucien—who had had no administrative training whatsoever, and just a few months' experience in national politics—with perhaps the most difficult and exacting of administrative portfolios in the new government: Minister of the Interior,[5] which thereby placed him in charge of the entire internal political structure of the country.[6] And it was hardly an accident that First Consul Bonaparte now decided on "legalizing" his illegally established government, by ratifying the new Consulate in a new Constitution (the Constitution of the Year VIII, as it was referred to), which he submitted to the people in the form of a national referendum. Lucien Bonaparte, as Interior Minister, set about arranging this plebiscite and the machinery with which to tally the election figures. With Lucien's deft hand guiding this operation, the results were hardly in doubt. Of the little more than 3 million votes recorded, according to the Interior Ministry, 3,011,007 supported Napoleon's new role as Consul and the new Constitution, a mere 1,562 of the nation's 9 million eligible voters rejecting it. In fact, the greatest vote-rigging fraud in the history of France had been executed, reversing and suppressing the true pulse of the nation. In reality a maximum of only one and a half million electors voted "yes"[7] for the new government, a majority deciding against them.[8] Thus Lucien Bonaparte, an old hand at doctoring documents, was responsible for the acceptable election result, at once assuring Napoleon (and of course the whole clan) of a happy and prosperous New Year in January 1800.

Lucien had now saved Napoleon and his career for a second time in just a few weeks, and thus was ultimately responsible for the introduction

*The Revolutionary calendar was currently in use and would be until the creation of the Empire in 1804.

of the following fourteen years of Napoleonic domination of France. The requisites for both blatant piracy and unabashed political manipulation, it would appear, were not so different after all.

But over the next several months Lucien followed up his two major coups with one mistake after another, again in the same overtly offensive manner. He proved an ineffective, egotistical administrator, and published a pamphlet critical of the Consulate (*Parallèle entre César, Cromwell, Monk et Bonaparte*) suggesting drastic changes in the structure of government—to which were added confounding reports of serious irregularities in the administration of Interior Ministry funds (at a time when Lucien Bonaparte was making major purchases for Plessis-Chamant). The outcome was not difficult to anticipate. In the first week of November 1800, the young Interior Minister was summoned to the Tuileries in the presence of his hated foe, Police Minister Joseph Fouché, when Fouché formally charged Lucien with leading a scandalous private life (especially his egregious affairs with well known demimondaines, including the leading actress of the Théâtre Français, Mlle. Mézeray, for whom Lucien had already purchased expensive jewelry and a posh Parisian mansion[9] during his wife's third pregnancy, mortal illness and subsequent interment). Fouché further accused Lucien of making large-scale speculations on the Stock Exchange and of illegally conceding national monopolies (in exchange for substantial sums), not to mention engaging in illegal or at best equivocal maritime transactions—once a pirate, always. . . . All of this was rendered all the more dramatic as Lucien was now living in such shockingly new luxury—at a time when the French economy was in a shambles and poverty rife—as to compromise the new First Consul and his regime. On the other hand, Fouché heroically managed to avoid the rather delicate matter of ballot-rigging during the recent plebiscite (of which he himself was a conspirator). Napoleon, who had never made any pretense at liking Fouché, listened painfully as the police officer coldly concluded his long and detailed report.

It was now the First Consul's turn to launch into his younger brother, who had so humiliated him, resulting in an unpleasant altercation between the two brothers, no doubt to the amusement of the Police Minister. Finally, Napoleon announced Lucien's "resignation" as Interior Minister, which resulted in a further outburst. Over the next couple of days Lucien fulminated to friends against his ungrateful brother, and on 9 November 1800—one year to the day following the coup d'état—Lucien was abruptly dispatched to Madrid as the new French Ambassador.[10] Indeed, so quickly was the matter decided by Napoleon to rid himself of this fraternal affliction that he did not even give Foreign Minister Talleyrand time in which to submit Lucien's credentials to the Spanish King for his approval, contrary to established international procedure.

Despite some initial blunders at his new post, Lucien's natural charm and affability won over a reluctant King Carlos IV. As part of his role in Spain, Lucien, albeit on his own authority, decided to negotiate a peace treaty—the Peace of Badajoz as it was to be known—between France, Spain and Portugal, the initial draft of which was duly signed on 5 June 1801. This resulted in the evacuation of Portugal by all foreign armies (although Napoleon wanted to maintain Franco-Spanish troops in at least three provinces of that country, to oppose the British), while gaining a little territory for Spain and small war indemnities for France.[11] When submitted to Paris, however, the treaty was rejected out of hand, which meant that Lucien and the other negotiators, who had by tradition accepted substantial bribes from Spain and Portugal, were required to return them. The Spanish King in particular had broken all records, presenting Lucien with *five million francs' worth of diamonds*, not to mention twenty paintings by old masters.[12] But there was an equally old Bonaparte tradition of never returning "remuneration," whatever the source or form, and Lucien for one was very much a Bonaparte, and thus, without even waiting to request the return of his credentials or take leave of the generous Carlos IV, escaped from Madrid with his immense new fortune intact.[13] The ex-President of the Council of Five Hundred, ex-Interior Minister and now ex-Ambassador to Spain, reached Paris in a record five days on 14 November 1801,[14] much to the astonishment of First Consul Bonaparte. At the age of twenty-six, Lucien was certainly one of the richest political bounders in a French capital already boasting its fair number of that curious fraternity.

Initially, Napoleon had placed high hopes in the intelligent, if erratic, Lucien. But recent events had cast considerable doubt as to his future reliability and usefulness. General Bonaparte had to do something with him, to be sure, and for the time being had him reelected to the Tribunate.[15] And yet that was hardly sufficient to occupy the restless young man. Like all the Bonapartes—male and female—Lucien was ambitious, and, in the words of historian Louis Madelin, through his "complete lack of any moral sense, pushed ambition to the point of utter frenzy and the thirst for riches to sheer robbery," so that even Napoleon began to realize that his younger brother had to be considered "really dangerous."[16] In fact, Lucien already had an eye on the position of First Consul for himself, especially after mid-1802 when Napoleon made it clear that he intended to modify the Constitution of the Year VIII in order to allow himself to become First Consul "for his lifetime." At the same time he indicated a preference to name another younger brother, Louis, and his children as his political heirs.

Needless to say, a jealous and angry Lucien, driven to "frenzy," could in his position as member of the Tribunate do a great deal to undermine the First Consul's position. In the summer of 1802 Napoleon decided to remove the troublesome Lucien from the limelight of national politics by forcing him to accept the higher, more prestigious and lucrative—if less politically significant—honor as Senator.[17] Greatly stymied by this act, Lucien now revealed a "complete lack of stability" as he tried seriously to undermine Napoleon's position. To a family friend, Miot de Melito, he loudly condemned the First Consul's "caprices," as he called them, boasting—"I intend to obtain real political freedom and suppress *all despotism*."[18] But even by this early date Napoleon was too well entrenched and too powerful to have to worry about Lucien's sniping. Even Germaine de Staël found herself expelled from the French capital to seek the refuge of her estate of Coppet, in Switzerland, where she criticized Napoleon for replacing the liberal members of the Tribunate (including her favorite, Benjamin Constant), with a fresh batch of his own lackeys.

The inevitable break between Lucien and Napoleon came in the early spring of 1804, as Napoleon prepared to exchange his position as First Consul for that of "Emperor of the French," bypassing Lucien altogether in the legal succession to the imperial purple, in the event of his early demise. The immediate reason for the break resulting in Lucien's decision to quit France permanently for Italy, however, was ostensibly over Lucien's choice of Alexandrine Jouberthon (née de Bleschamp) as his second wife. Younger than Lucien, very tall, with "the figure of a goddess" and "admirably beautiful" as Elisabeth de Vigée-Lebrun described her,[19] a cultivated woman of the world, perhaps of the demimonde. The daughter of an impoverished provincial lawyer, she was the alleged widow (though no one could ever prove it) of one Hippolyte Jouberthon, who had earlier fled to the West Indies after being involved in some banking irregularities. Left with a baby girl, Alexandrine Jouberthon received society *chez elle*, but also frequented artists' studios, while becoming the mistress of a rich young man, Comte Alexandre de la Borde.

Lucien met her in 1802 when he returned to Paris. He installed her as his mistress at Plessis-Chamant, where in May 1803 their bastard son, Jules-Laurent-Lucien, was born, followed by a hurried, secret civil wedding. It was the news of this marriage that proved to be the proverbial final straw for Napoleon—whose wife, Josephine, had also been a merry widow and a well-known mistress of several leading politicians. He found

Lucien's choice of a wife simply deplorable, indeed shocking and degrading, and ordered an annulment, but in vain. One could never *order* Lucien to do anything. "Betrayal! Betrayal! It's sheer betrayal!" Napoleon stormed before Josephine.[20] And thus it was that Lucien Bonaparte and family went into exile on 4 April 1804.[21]

Little did the arrogant Lucien realize as he set out on the long journey to Rome, that now, at the age of twenty-eight, he was effectively ending his political career in France, and would not be returning for the next eleven years. If in theory Lucien refused an annulment or divorce of his second marriage, to Alexandrine, who was eventually to provide ten children for him (the only woman he was genuinely happy with, despite his other affairs and liaisons) one cannot help but wonder how the opportunistic young man would have acted had circumstances between himself and Napoleon been different, on a sounder footing. The fact is that Letizia Bonaparte had suckled a band of brigands and bounders on her venomous milk, pitting every child against the other, inculcating little if any sense of public or private morality, or even family responsibility.

The relatively untrained and undisciplined maverick Lucien, thus now settled in Rome in the spring of 1804, where, through sheer charm, he won over a simple if powerful gentleman who had no reason for liking the Bonapartes. Pope Pius VII made the mistake of helping the wily Lucien, even naming him a Roman Prince, and acting as godfather to one of his children, a distinction reserved for only the most influential of aristocratic families. Never would he return to France and bend the expected knee to Emperor Napoleon, though Lucien let it be known that he would accept, among other possibilities, either the Italian or Spanish crown—if he could keep his wife. The Emperor of course continued to insist upon the dissolution of Lucien's marriage, as he shortly did for his own marriage when exigencies of State required it.[22]

With the French seizure of the Papal States in 1808, and following the Pope's bull excommunicating him on 11 June 1809, an angered Napoleon arrested the defiant Pius VII one month later.[23] Meanwhile, Lucien suddenly found his numerous estates and palaces in occupied French territory and himself required to apply to the French authorities for written permission whenever he wished to leave one property to travel to another. By 1810 an unrepentant and still much exasperated Lucien had had enough and decided to sell many of his possessions and art treasures with the secret intention of moving to America. On 5 August of that year he, his wife and their family of seven children bade their adieux to friends and family and set sail on an American ship, the *Hercules*.[24] But when inadvertently forced by a violent storm to put into port at Sardinia, he was arrested by British officials there and transferred with his entire family to Malta and then to Britain.

Placed under "house arrest," he was confined to the vicinity around the comfortable estate of "Thorngrove" in Worcestershire, where he quickly purchased countless paintings and statues and entertained the social elite, and in this manner managed to idle away the next four years of his life, while studying astronomy and writing a seemingly unending attack on Napoleon in the form of an epic poem entitled *Charlemagne*.[25] With the news of Napoleon's defeats and abdication in the spring of 1814, Lucien and family were released and given permission to return to Rome.[26]

Although Lucien later claimed to have been in communication with Fouché, Carnot and Murat upon his return to Italy—with the purpose of restoring Napoleon to his imperial throne—there is no written record to support this, other than Lucien's own dubious *Secret Memoirs*.[27] If, as seems likely, the Roman banker friend of Lucien, Torlonia, made a loan of up to 50 million francs available to Napoleon when still on Elba, whatever happened to that money is not known and Napoleon, for one, barely had funds enough to underwrite the expedition from Elba to Paris.[28] In fact, of course, apart from possible desultory correspondence among the alleged Bonaparte supporters, there was no concerted plot to return Napoleon, and as already seen, he ultimately reached Paris without the assistance of Fouché, Carnot, Murat, or Lucien. What is more, while living at his estate in Canino, Lucien, although well informed regarding the escape from Elba in February 1815 (thanks to the Princess of Wales, Caroline of Brunswick, and his mother),[29] made no attempt to rush to Paris for the first month, venturing no further than Rome. Indeed, a somewhat more cautious Lucien, chastened and wisened by the instructive intervening events he had witnessed over the past eleven years, waited until he had received word of Napoleon's successful return to Paris before deciding on 24 March to join him.[30]

But even then it was not quite as simple as that. With all of Europe quickly rallying to encircle and isolate France, the Bonapartes, naturally, were everywhere persona non grata. Hence the difficulty in obtaining the necessary "passports" required for crossing frontiers. Although Lucien finally reached French territory, at Bellevue, on Lake Geneva, a reconciliation between Napoleon and Lucien had yet to be achieved. The family mediator, Joseph Bonaparte, *"le Roi Joseph,"* once again stepped into the breach and set to healing old wounds. The result was that on 9 May 1815, the forty-year-old Lucien was finally warmly embraced by Napoleon in the Tuileries and at a public ceremony awarded the Grand Cordon of the Legion of Honor, proclaimed a *"prince français,"* and given the Palais Royal as his principal residence.[31] Napoleon, already in a desperate situation, needed every family hand he could muster.

If four of the five Bonaparte brothers were rapacious, egotistical, grasping, vain and unstable, the eldest, Joseph (born in 1768), was the best example at the other extreme, indeed, the only brother who could be described as possessing a modicum of public and fraternal responsibility. Like Napoleon and Lucien, Joseph was educated in France. Unlike Napoleon, he learned to speak French without an accent and to write it perfectly, while maintaining a fluent knowledge of Italian as well (again, unlike Napoleon). After completing five years' work at the Collège d'Autun, he went on to the ancient university town of Pisa, where he was awarded a law diploma, without, however, being formally enrolled as a student there.[32] Of all the brothers Joseph had the most complete cultural background, as well as genuine cultural interests later in life.

The financial beginnings of the indigent Bonapartes were difficult for the three older brothers, Joseph beginning his career as a minor magistrate in Corsica. He then became a "commissaire militaire" attached to the French army, thanks to Napoleon's intervention, bringing him the first solid financial returns of his life. But it was his early marriage to the wealthy Julie Clary on 1 August 1794[33] that changed his life completely. She was very small, with a thick nose, a large shapeless mouth, and otherwise graceless features. In addition, she was painfully thin and frequently ailing, but loyal, stable, tender and entirely devoted to her family. Julie, the daughter of a wealthy merchant established in Marseilles, and one of a closely knit brood of a dozen siblings, was also religious and very honest, stubborn and intelligent, and hence at once the very antithesis of Bonaparte values in general.

Therefore, at the age of twenty-six, Joseph became the first of the Bonaparte brothers to marry and find a substantial financial base, ensuring his position as head of the family since his father's premature death eight years earlier. Napoleon in turn, recently promoted to Brigadier General, began courting Julie Clary's younger, beautiful sister, Désirée, equally an heiress in her own right. And despite the uncertainty of the times—Robespierre had been overthrown violently at the end of July 1794—Joseph, who prized his position as head of the family, was perhaps never again happier than at this moment before Napoleon began his meteoric rise in his military career. Joseph was also responsible for family finances as well, including most of the investments for Napoleon and their brothers, and was soon returning substantial dividends.

It was Joseph's acceptance by the Clary family and his obvious fondness of Julie that naturally explains why the rest of the Bonapartes were later accepted without too much close scrutiny, those Bonapartes who were ultimately to bring such upheaval and tragedy to the Clarys.

For the next couple of years all seemed to bode well for the future, and the relationships between Joseph and Napoleon seemed unshakable. Thus, for example, we find Napoleon writing to Joseph in tones that, in light of the events of the following years, seemed almost surreal: "Whatever circumstances fate reserves for you, you certainly know, my friend, you can have no better friend than I, who hold you most dear and who desire most sincerely your happiness. Life is a wisp of thought that disappears before our eyes. . . . If you leave, and feel it will be for a considerable time, send me your portrait; we have lived together for so many years, and have been so closely united, that our hearts are one and you know better than anyone, how fond I am of you. I find in writing these words an emotion I have rarely felt in my life. . . ."[34] It was an extraordinary glimpse into the thinking and values of Napoleon in his mid-twenties, one which would rarely be repeated or revealed again as his military career began to soar to astonishing heights. The growing complexity of his life hereafter would leave less and less room either for family or sentiment, transforming him over the next five years into one of the most ruthless men in Europe. And when in October 1795 the Committee of Public Safety named him Commander in Chief of the Army of the Interior,[35] these close fraternal relations and concerns ended abruptly.

Henceforth Joseph's own career would evolve more clearly, emphasizing a growing greed, jealousy and weakness of character, as he gradually fell more and more under Napoleon's sway and domination. Through expanding contact with national politicians in Paris—including the influential Paul Barras—Napoleon also introduced Joseph to the highest political circles, coaxing him to leave his easy, assured existence in the Midi and come to Paris, where real fortunes could be made. To further entice the cautious Joseph, Napoleon arranged at Joseph's request lucrative *lettres de marque* to be issued, permitting him to fit out and arm two more corsaires (legally this time), with which to prey upon unsuspecting merchantmen in the waters between Corsica and France.[36]

The first serious challenge to the fraternal allegiance of these two brothers came on 9 March 1796 with the announcement of Napoleon's secret marriage to Josephine (Marie-Josèphe-Rose Tascher de la Pagerie), widow of Vicomte de Beauharnais. Until this point the Clarys and Joseph considered the marriage of Napoleon and Désirée as good as settled, and this betrayal caused an immediate and permanent chill in relations between the two families thereafter.[37] And yet there was more to it than just that. The Bonapartes themselves deeply resented the intrusion of Josephine into their clan, bringing down upon her the full wrath of Letizia in particular.[38] The rift between them and Josephine was never to be healed. Nor did Josephine's children, Hortense and Eugène, accept the news of this marriage cheerfully, considering it an embarrassing social blunder and humiliation.

Meanwhile, life went on, Joseph finding his hitherto humdrum existence now invaded and unsettled forever by the swirl of events involving the French political scene of 1797, first in his role as a newly elected Deputy of the Council of Five Hundred, followed swiftly by his appointment as French Consul at Parma. But even before he could officially assume either of those positions, Joseph received a warm letter on 6 May 1797 from the Directory's Foreign Minister, Charles Delacroix. "Citizen, the Executive Directory has felt that you would be more useful to the Republic in a more eminent post than that to which you have first been assigned," it began, informing him that instead he had been named Minister Plenipotentiary to Rome, where one of his first tasks was to make "every effort to introduce representative democracy" and supervise the "establishment of this [new] Government."[39]

With a generous installment of his new salary (60,000 francs per year) in his pocket—in addition to an already substantial private income—"Ambassador Bonaparte" duly arrived on 31 August 1797 set on fulfilling his mission of subversion, if not greatly liking it. On 2 September he was received in audience by Pius VII and his credentials accepted.[40] The pope took an immediate liking to the amiable French Ambassador and even went to the unusual trouble of giving him two splendid horses for his carriage, not realizing of course that the Ambassador had been sent to bring the French Revolution to the Papal States. Balls and receptions were quickly arranged in Joseph's honor, reciprocated by the staff of the new embassy at the spacious Palais Corsini.

But while Joseph was dancing with elegant aristocratic ladies, his military counselors, and General Duphot in particular, were hard at work stirring up antipapal revolutionary circles, including a group of "patriots," or revolutionary leaders, recently released from papal prisons.

On 28 December a small group of these well-rehearsed men appeared in the courtyard of the Palais Corsini, calling for French intervention and protection in Rome. Joseph immediately ordered them to leave. But before they could do so a contingent of papal troops arrived on the premises and tried to arrest the would-be revolutionaries (who then fled deeper into the embassy's grounds). At that moment General Duphot arrived with three other high-ranking officers drawing their swords and ordering the papal troops to leave, which they finally did. The whole incident should have ended there, but Duphot and his colleagues, who apparently had orders to cause just such an "incident" that would justify French military intervention and the occupation of Rome, drew pistols, pursuing the departing troops down the street and around the corner. Moments later shots were fired and the French officers returned to the embassy carrying Duphot's bloody corpse! Joseph, for one, panicked, ordered the servants to pack their trunks and close the embassy, as he sent a messenger over to the Vatican to request their passports. At 6 A.M. the following morning, 29 December 1797, Joseph, his wife and embassy staff were in carriages heading for the French frontier. Thus ended his first diplomatic post, after just four months.[41] The French Foreign Minister and Directory were simply delighted with the results, as they ordered French military contingents into the area. General Berthier arrived from Mantua with his troops on 15 February 1798, to proclaim the new Roman Republic.[42] Joseph's embassy had achieved its objective.

Like all the Bonapartes, Joseph was an avid collector—first of money, then real estate, works of art and an equally dazzling array of mistresses (despite his alleged affection for his wife). Like Jérôme and Lucien, Joseph was especially fond of large country estates, and if Lucien's favorite property was Canino, Joseph's—situated just north of Paris near Senlis and Chantilly—was Mortefontaine, acquired in October 1798. Alas, its last owner, a banker by the name of de Ruey, had met an historical, if uncomfortable, death by guillotine five years earlier. Joseph put down the full 258,000 francs required for the initial purchase, and though a large sum for this relatively modest estate, it was nothing as compared to the many hundreds of thousands of francs he was to pour into that property over the next eight years, transforming the gardens, adding new buildings and extending the château itself, while he continued to acquire many hundreds of additional acres of fields, woods and dozens of smaller houses and outbuildings, finally giving him an aggregate of thousands of acres of prime real estate.

Nevertheless such rustic pastimes did not prevent Joseph from dipping pen into ink to do a little creative writing—apparently a family genetic necessity, later repeated by Lucien, Louis and even Jérôme. And if Joseph's efforts produced neither a masterpiece nor a work of any length, his friends—to whom he humbly read it—found his novella *Moïna* harmless and amusing (which is more than Napoleon could say later of Lucien's extraordinary poem, *Charlemagne*).[43] Another distraction, in fact more of a duty, was Joseph's assumed task of finding a suitable husband for Julie's lovely but jilted sister, Désirée. He finally settled upon—and Désirée agreed to—one of the French generals most critical of nearly every political step Napoleon had taken—Jean [Baptiste-Jules] Bernadotte.[44] Antipathy to Napoleon by the unforgiving Désirée gave the couple a mutual bond of understanding. Little did they realize, of course, that one day they would be wearing the crowns of Sweden and Norway, while Napoleon remained a British prisoner on an island they had never heard of.

Like Lucien, Joseph was an active participant in behind-the-scenes maneuvering in preparation for Napoleon's famous coup d'état of 18 Brumaire. It was from Joseph's Paris mansion in the rue de la Victoire, with Joseph at his side, that Napoleon set out for Saint-Cloud that fateful morning.[45] If Joseph was not rewarded with a post in Napoleon's newly formed government [he was nevertheless named a Conseiller d'Etat] the growing problem of his receding importance in the family as its titular head, was already apparent to all.

The problem of naming a successor—a position which Joseph clearly sought—proved at once irritating and pleasurable to Napoleon, whose sadism was becoming increasingly evident. His brothers had the irritating habit of reminding him that as an active soldier it was indeed possible that he could be killed early in life, and that it was imperative to name a successor. Lucien, of course, was probably the most insensitive and ruthless of the Bonaparte brothers, and he soon let it known that *he* hoped to replace the First Consul by means of a national election, while insisting that he also be made Napoleon's official successor. Joseph for his part also began to reveal an increasing greed for power, privileges, riches and honorary posts in the government. "Clearly you do not understand me at all, if you think I lack initiative to defend my interests where my personal honor is concerned," Joseph said angrily. ". . . I have to remind you of my position and of the decisions I shall be forced to take, that you might not misjudge my apparent moderation concerning the ultimate choice you make. I hardly have to say more on this point," Joseph admonished First Consul Bonaparte.[46] Napoleon knew he could invariably manipulate Joseph, regardless of his threats or protests. Nevertheless, from now on Napoleon witnessed a hitherto unknown level of anger and jealousy from all his brothers, all of whom were to plague and undermine his administration of the country from 1800 onward. But given his natural indolence, Joseph's insistence on fresh honors was probably the result of a growing, embittered jealousy of Napoleon, who was, he felt, usurping his own seniority and position in the family. Unlike Lucien, whose opposition to Napoleon often took the form of bitter quarrels with him, Joseph attacked him a little more subtly. He would befriend and invite Napoleon's respectable republican opponents to his estate of Mortefontaine (e.g., Mme. de Staël and Benjamin Constant), going even so far as to personally have Constant named to the Tribunate.[47] These were perhaps mere pinpricks, but they angered Napoleon nonetheless.

Within the clan proper, Joseph's principal role was that of treasurer. He was responsible for investing their funds—including Napoleon's—while also paying out family allowances and income, even to Josephine. At the same time Napoleon did call upon Joseph for his help, especially in diplomatic matters; his signature occurred on the Treaty of Mortefontaine over the sale of Louisiana to the Americans, and on the Concordat with Rome—both signed in 1802 (though they had been almost entirely negotiated by Foreign Minister Hugues Maret, and merely brought to Joseph at the end). In the case of the Peace Treaty of Amiens, also concluded in 1802, Joseph did indeed participate actively, successfully resulting in a most favorable if temporary peace for France with Britain. That same year Napoleon offered Joseph the Presidency of the Cisalpine Republic, in northern Italy, but as a result of Joseph's adamant insistence on major policy changes in that Republic (including the withdrawal of all French troops), it fell through, Joseph refusing to compromise.

For a while Joseph continued to remain aloof, rejecting most state honors as well as high appointments, arguing that he was happy enough living the life of a country gentleman. "Why then do you want me to change such an existence without good and substantial reasons?" he asked.[48] If Joseph now refused the largely honorary title of Colonel General of all Swiss troops serving in France, not so the chair as Senator (representing Bruxelles). But when in addition Napoleon offered him the well-paying post as Chancellor of the Senate, Joseph declined at this stage, declaring such duties to be "detrimental to my existence and character, for whatever usefulness I might contribute would not merit the personal sacrifice it would require of me . . . [therefore] . . . I ask of your friendship . . . that you not insist upon placing a charge on me which would in fact prove a great burden. . . ."[49] Translated into reality, however, this was simply Joseph's way of indicating that he would now accept only the highest of honors and posts.

By 1803 Joseph was so jealous of Napoleon's own astonishing political success that he complained about him whenever his back was turned,

lamenting to Lucien "the filching of my rights as eldest of the family."
He repeated to friends and family, "He will never again deceive me! I
am sick of his tyranny and vain promises . . ." And then he admitted
frankly, "I want everything or nothing at all. He must either treat me as
a simple private citizen or he must offer a post which assures me a
position after him! . . . But if he refuses that, then he can expect nothing
from me in return. . . ." If Napoleon continued to ignore Joseph's wishes,
he said, he would work to overthrow him and "his caprices." In an
astonishing outburst he claimed that he would "work with Sièyes, or
Moreau if needs be, and with any other Frenchmen who are true patriots
and friends of liberty, in order to oppose his tyranny."[50]

Napoleon's answer to such threats and unpleasantness, however, remained inevitably the same—money. In November 1803 Joseph received
"a gift" of 200,000 francs in cash from the First Consul, followed by an
additional 300,000 francs a few months later.[51] This may have kept
Joseph silent for a while and provided money for extra acreage and
baubles for his actresses, but it did not address the festering problem of
naming Joseph as Napoleon's successor. Then one day at a semiformal
family dinner at Mortefontaine, Joseph placed his mother as guest of
honor to his right, instead of "the first lady," Josephine, resulting in a
furious outburst by Napoleon before the entire assembly. On another
occasion Joseph picked up a pistol and shot at the First Consul's
portrait hanging in his library.[52] Clearly something had to be done.
Napoleon desperately sought an appropriately lofty post with which to
assuage the irate head of the family, while at the same time hopefully
putting some distance between the two brothers, but that would take
some time.

With the creation of the First Empire in May 1804 and the announcement of a new law on the family succession, the situation vis-à-vis
Napoleon and his brothers—Lucien had just left France permanently with
his family—became even more acute. The descendance would be "from
male to male," but a special clause permitted Napoleon to bypass direct
descendants by adopting the children or grandchildren of his brothers
once they had reached their majority at the age of eighteen. Thus Joseph,
for one, while not excluded from inheriting the crown, was informed that
in the event Napoleon had no children of his own—which seemed
likely—Napoleon's first preference was for Louis's, then Jérôme's, children.[53] The Emperor had to soften the blow to Joseph, which he did by
raising him to the dignity of a "French prince" and Grand Elector. While
these titles carried no great powers with them, they did provide Joseph
with additional annual income of 1,333,333 francs, not to mention out-

right gifts totaling another 350,000 francs, with the Luxembourg Palace thrown in for good measure as his new official residence.[54]

Nevertheless, in due course Joseph resumed his grumblings among his liberal friends and brothers, demanding his rights and more power as the eldest male of the family. When this got back to Napoleon, he snapped: "My mistress is Power. I have gone through a great deal to make that conquest, to permit her to suffer or be ravished by anyone else coveting her. . . ."[55] You forget, therefore, that my brothers are nothing without me, that they are only great today because I made them so. . . . But let's get down to facts: Joseph is not destined to reign; he is older than I am . . . and, moreover he was not born of a distinguished rank in his own right. I was born in misery and want . . . I raised myself by my own actions, while he remained at the same level at which he was born. To rule in France, one must either be born to a high position . . . or else be a man capable of distinguishing himself above all others."[56]

This of course in turn then got back to Joseph, who announced his refusal to attend the imperial coronation in Notre Dame Cathedral on December 2, 1804. "Place yourself in a hereditary monarchy and be my first subject," Napoleon replied. "That is quite a handsome role to play, being the second man of France and perhaps of all Europe. . . . Therefore be a prince and stop worrying about the consequences of this title." But, "if you refuse to come to the coronation and fulfill your functions there attributed to you in your quality as Grand Elector and Prince . . . as of that moment you are my enemy . . . and I shall destroy you. . . ."[57] Joseph duly attended the coronation.

In 1805 Prince Joseph grudgingly accepted the command of a regiment of the Grand Army then poised near Boulogne for its invasion of Britain. But he felt that the rank of colonel was humiliating—his younger brother, Louis (a career officer), was already a general and in command of the entire Paris garrison. When Napoleon was then forced to rebuke him for giving orders to the Army's commander in chief, Marshal Soult, Joseph promptly deserted his post, retiring to Mortefontaine.[58] Napoleon's plans for an imperial dynasty across the face of Europe now seemed the appropriate solution and convenient way of dealing with a recalcitrant Joseph, who instead by all rights should have been brought up before a general court-martial. And thus it was that the Emperor first offered Joseph the crown of the Kingdom of Lombardy (or Northern Italy), which he declined (when informed it would result in his forfeiting all rights to the throne of France as well).[59] He accepted, however, Napoleon's second offer in 1806 of the crown of Naples and Sicily. To be sure, Naples was just one part of Napoleon's master plan for the Grand Empire, which would see members of his family directly ruling all of Italy, Holland, Westphalia and Spain.[60]

Adhering to Napoleon's schedule for implementing this plan, the newly promoted "General" Joseph Bonaparte entered Naples in February 1807.[61] Indeed, for the first time in years he now seemed surprisingly content here in Naples, where he found ideal scope for himself and his ideas as a liberal, enlightened monarch. Despite his inherent laziness of character, Joseph had other qualities which now emerged, putting him in good stead with the Neapolitans, who appreciated having an affable new king with good intentions for his people. Liberal, gallant and generous, Joseph found the appalling living conditions of the people simply shocking and set out to ameliorate them. War and harsh Bourbon rule had led to this state of affairs and it must now be changed drastically, he decided. War must end, replaced by prosperity and well-being.[62] And when Napoleon immediately insisted upon Joseph's raising millions of francs annually to pay for the large French army of occupation in Naples, Joseph protested vigorously in a vain attempt to protect the impoverished people from his ruthless brother. At the same time Joseph began to confide less and less in friends, even in his closest advisers.

Meanwhile, Napoleon went ahead with his plans to Bonapartize as much of Europe as possible, placing Louis on the Batavian, or Dutch, throne, and Jérôme on that of the Kingdom of Westphalia, while he, the Emperor, also assumed the crown of Italy (disregarding his earlier promises to reserve it for Eugène). However, as Lucien remained obdurate and aloof, refusing to accede to the Emperor's dictatorial commands— including that of divorcing his wife—Napoleon had to look elsewhere when seeking a family member for the Spanish throne in 1808. After having successfully forced King Carlos IV to abdicate on 5 May 1808, and his son, Fernando, to abandon his claims to that throne five days later,[63] Napoleon's egoism and ill-concealed lust for power led to his decision to invade, occupy and incorporate Spain into his Empire. Naturally, such an important new acquisition must have a Bonaparte on the throne, and after considerable negotiations, a most reluctant Joseph (who had by now become deeply attached to the Neapolitan crown and people) accepted this new burden. On 7 June 1808, the "Junta de Estado" and the Council of Castille duly invited Joseph to assume the crown of Spain and the Indies. Meanwhile, his brother-in-law, Marshal Joachim Murat (and sister, Caroline) replaced him and Queen Julie in Naples.[64]

Spain, however, quickly proved to be a mass of political, financial and military quicksand—by the end of 1809 Napoleon had 191,905 crack

French troops there[65]—and Joseph once again became his old, jealous, grumbling, bitter self. In fact, he soon discovered that not only was he given no real authority over French army commanders there, but that Napoleon was intervening directly in Spanish politics while demanding staggering financial exactions. Angry, frustrated and disillusioned, Joseph replied to Napoleon with an ultimatum. "I am only King of Spain as a result of the presence of your troops. I should like to become that, however, through the love of the Spanish people for me in my own right. But to achieve that I have to be able to govern as I see fit. . . . I shall be King in a manner befitting the brother of Your Majesty, or I shall return to Mortefontaine, where I shall ask for nothing better than the simple happiness of being able to live without being humiliated, permitting me to do so with peace of mind."[66]

If the French and Joseph continued to remain in Spain year after year, it was with the knowledge that they were in fact losing the battle for the control of that harsh but proud country. Then, with the advent of the débâcle of the Russian campaign later in 1812, and Wellington's successes in the Iberian Peninsula, even a Napoleon had to recognize the failure of French arms and policy in Spain, which Joseph was permitted to abandon (if not the crown itself), returning home "to defend the frontiers of France" in 1812.[67]

Despite the grave situation facing France in 1813, Joseph refused to return to the capital itself and support Napoleon, unless the Emperor continued to recognize him as "King Joseph." At the same time Louis was insanely insisting on Napoleon's returning his crown of Holland (and evacuating French troops and advisers there), and Jérôme was evacuating Westphalia in the wake of French military disasters there. Napoleon, his back to the wall in 1813 (when Pauline was even selling her jewelry to help her Emperor brother in the emergency),[68] gave in to Joseph (but not to Louis), naming the eldest Bonaparte his "Regent" during his absence.[69] Napoleon's last memories of Joseph as Regent in early March 1814 were of him arguing on behalf of France—"Sire, you are now all alone. Your Family, all your ministers, your army, want the peace which you refuse to accept."[70] Despite Napoleon's obstinacy, that same month Joseph authorized negotiations with the Allies[71] as an incredulous Napoleon finally abdicated.

Jérôme, the youngest of the Bonaparte brothers, was only fifteen years old when Napoleon overthrew the French government and established the

Consulate in 1799. Due to the instability of all public institutions in the country during the preceding ten years of revolution, Jérôme had received very little formal education as late as January 1796, when an anxious Napoleon summoned him (then in Marseille) to Paris, where the general immediately enrolled him as a boarder in a college to study Latin, mathematics and music.[72] And in December 1797, he entered the prestigious and recently reopened Collège de Juilly, where several members of the Beauharnais family had been educated, including Eugène. For the next two years Jérôme was all but forgotten by his mother (who preferred her real favorite, Lucien). He languished unvisited by his brothers till the autumn of 1799,[73] when he was finally withdrawn, although he had received considerably less education than any of his brothers. A warm, charming and delightful young man—especially before women—Jérôme quickly became outrageously spoiled by all the family and seemingly could do no wrong. Nor did Napoleon help matters by overlooking nearly every infraction, constantly indulging the boy's growing sense of irresponsibility,[74] for which Napoleon was later to pay most dearly.

Without actually enrolling him in the military, Napoleon did have him privately instructed now as a cadet officer with some Hussards volunteers. As any officer worth his salt had to have had at least one good duel to his name, Jérôme decided to pick a quarrel with a young comrade by the name of Davout. Meeting him in the Bois de Vincennes, they stepped off twenty-five paces, and then sat down with a box of cartridges, continuing to fire their pistols at each other until the jolly Jérôme received a bullet squarely in his chest, lodged in his sternum. There were, however, no long-lasting effects—despite the inability of surgeons to remove the lead safely—and he was soon on his feet,[75] the miniature ball remaining in his bone the rest of his life.

Upon his return from Egypt, Napoleon decided on a naval career for Jérôme and on 22 November 1800 the young midshipman was handed over to Admiral Ganteaume at Brest. "General, I am sending you Citizen Jérôme Bonaparte," General Savary informed the squadron commander, "to prepare him for his naval apprenticeship. As you know, he must be subjected to the strictest discipline in order to make up for lost time. See to it that he fulfills all his functions punctiliously."[76] Entrusting Jérôme to the plump, pink-cheeked, indecisive, pleasure-loving Honoré Ganteaume was a mistake that greatly shaped the rest of Jérôme's life. Enthusiastic, energetic, fairly intelligent, but rather wild and lacking any sense of discipline, motivation and sense of purpose, he was at a stage when a good, firm admiral could have still shaped his character, preparing him for a useful career. Alas, Ganteaume was not that admiral, as he now completely ignored the consular instructions for the sixteen-year-old boy, who refused even to share the midshipman's mess, and instead dined daily with the admiral, from whom he had the cheek to borrow large sums of money. Jérôme far preferred good society to the annoying necessity of clambering up and down rigging and learning the seemingly infinite list of names of the parts of a ship. Ganteaume further aggravated the situation by praising the boy outrageously to Napoleon, who privately counseled the midshipman, "Not to permit anyone to do your work for you." Naturally Jérôme ignored this advice in the best of spirits.[77] Indeed, he quickly got completely out of control, going so far as to address his commanding officer jauntily as *"mon cher admiral,"* taking the most outrageous liberties that even a senior captain would never have ventured to do, Jérôme knowing that brother Napoleon was there to protect him.

Following a first year's cruise, Ensign Bonaparte returned to Paris a swaggering, conceited and arrogant young man, lecturing the highest officials of the government on naval matters, even criticizing flag-rank naval officers. After one such evening at Ganteaume's, where talk turned to recent naval campaigns, Jérôme reported back to the Tuileries: "They look at everything like army officers, and after a lot of nonsense spoken, I took my hat and said to them: 'I am going away, for you think like a lot of fools and fireside tacticians.' "[78] Having the First Consul's seventeen-year-old brother under one's command was not altogether that agreeable, and thus when Jérôme was transferred to Admiral LaTouche-Tréville's expedition destined for Santo Domingo and the retaking of Port-au-Prince in 1802, Ganteaume no doubt sighed with relief.[79] Following that campaign, he sailed to the Antilles again, now in the newly launched corvette *l'Epervier*, sporting the uniform of a *"capitaine des Hussards de Berichiny,"* while his new if complacent commanding officer promoted Jérôme to the rank of lieutenant and handed over command of the vessel. At this time Napoleon was paying Jérôme an allowance of 30,000 francs a year (i.e., the equivalent of a cardinal's salary), in addition to which Jérôme took the liberty of cashing bills of exchange, trebling or quadrupling his annual salary.[80]

From Martinique, Lieutenant Bonaparte sailed to America—against the orders of his commander in chief—where he dropped anchor off Maryland for a good many months and found a bride in "La Belle de Baltimore," Elizabeth Patterson, the eighteen-year-old daughter of a very wealthy businessman.[81] Jérôme and the beautiful, svelte and accomplished brunette were married by special license on 24 December 1803, in a religious service performed by the Bishop of Baltimore,[82] but without having asked the permission of First Consul Bonaparte, which proved to be a great error. Despite a reiteration of orders from both Napoleon and Naval Minister Admiral Denis Decrès, instructing him to put to sea forthwith, the young bridegroom declined to do so with remarkable insouciance, refusing to leave the allures and charm of the young country and his pretty wife.

Upon receipt of the news of Jérôme's wedding, Napoleon informed him that he refused to recognize it, forbidding any French ship from transporting Elizabeth Bonaparte to France. "I shall receive Jérôme," Napoleon informed Decrès, "if, on leaving America, the young person in question returns to me and associates himself fully with my regime. If, however, he brings her with him, she is not to be allowed to set foot on French · territory."[83] "If he comes alone, under these conditions," Napoleon informed his mother, "I'll overlook his momentary transgression and consider it merely a youthful indiscretion."[84] The entire Bonaparte clan fully supported Napoleon's stand on the issue, including Letizia, who cast the most outrageous aspersions on the young bride, refusing to countenance this "foreign marriage ceremony."

With the declaration of the Empire in 1804, Napoleon retaliated by having the recalcitrant Jérôme's name struck from the roster of hereditary succession, while ordering an official government newspaper to describe Elizabeth Bonaparte alternatively as "his mistress" and as "his so-called wife."[85] The sadistic Napoleon pretended that the marriage by this Roman Catholic bishop had never taken place. Just as he continued to distort and manipulate war and international news in the *Moniteur* and the *Journal des Débats*, he now also did so in the case of his family.

Regardless of such threats, on 25 October (1804) Jérôme and Elizabeth Bonaparte finally set sail on the privately leased American brig the *Philadelphia*, which foundered in a fierce storm just out of port. The young couple lost most of their money and belongings, and barely escaped with their lives. Another attempt two months later was foiled by blockading British warships. And while Jérôme's mother continued to denounce "any marriage illegally contracted by my son, Jérôme Bonaparte, in a foreign country and without my consent,"[86] Napoleon seconded this by cutting off all French funds. The Emperor gave a variety of reasons for his refusal to recognize this marriage, including that of religion. "It is important for France herself that there be no Protestant girl associated with my rule," he insisted,[87] although another "Protestant girl" was soon to be accepted in her place. Jérôme responded to these obstacles now by refusing to leave the United States altogether.

Thus it was that Jérôme and Elizabeth Bonaparte were in America on 2 December 1804, when Napoleon's imperial coronation was taking place in Paris. Angered by this defiance, Napoleon retaliated in turn through an official imperial act of 11 March 1805, declaring their "marriage and marriage ceremony null and void, and the illegitimacy forever of any children resulting from the said marriage."[88] The Emperor of France of course had no authority to annul an act legally and duly performed and recognized in America, any more than he could annul a Roman Catholic marriage ceremony.

Unaware of this latest imperial challenge, however, Jérôme and Elizabeth set out for France for a third time, now in the American brig the *Erin*, owned by the bride's father. Upon reaching Lisbon on 8 April 1805, however, the French chargé d'affaires refused to issue a visa permitting "Mademoiselle Patterson" to enter France.[89] And while the *Erin* was continuing on its way, sailing to Amsterdam for a second landing attempt, Napoleon was writing to his mother scornfully of his troublesome brother, "this prodigal child," while threatening to disown him entirely if "he continues his liaison. . . . That is my final word on the matter. . . ."[90] His wife again forbidden to land, a stymied Jérôme finally broke at the end of April, agreeing to abandon her "temporarily" and return alone to Paris.

Napoleon's response on 6 May was generous as usual. *"Mon frère,* there is no fault in my eyes that cannot be erased by your repentance. Your union with Mademoiselle Patterson is void in the eyes of religion [sic], just as it is from a legal viewpoint [sic]. Your marriage now declared invalid at your own request [sic] I thus offer you my friendship. . . ."[91] A bewildered, rejected and defeated Elizabeth Bonaparte sailed for England and out of Jérôme's life forever, and on 7 July gave birth to their son, Jérôme-Napoléon Bonaparte, a bastard, according to the new imperial law, but in fact Jérôme's only legal offspring during his entire life. Indeed, what Jérôme never discovered was that when in May 1805 Napoleon—despite all his blustering—wrote to Pius VII, insisting upon an immediate annulment of the marriage of Jérôme and Elizabeth performed in America "by a Spanish priest" [the Bishop of Baltimore], the Pope's secretary replied that "it has been impossible for him to declare the said marriage null and void."[92]

Thus ended the first, but not the last, of Jérôme's several bitter clashes with the Emperor. It had been a most humiliating experience for Napoleon as well, this boy's outrageous, recalcitrant behavior before French ministers and officials—and then dragged out for so many months. But now that Napoleon had the young man back in France, he was determined to keep him there, whatever the price. Upon his return to Paris, Jérôme was informed that most of his debts in America—amounting to a few hundred thousand francs—were paid, and that this twenty-one-year-old junior lieutenant was to be given command of a division of three frigates and two brigs (which, in fact, required someone with at least twenty years' experience and holding the rank of rear-admiral). Then on June 2 he was promoted to the rank of frigate captain. But this did not suffice for the young man, who, unilaterally—without the knowledge or authorization of his commanding officer, the Naval Minister or the Emperor—illegally *promoted himself* to the rank of a senior captain, donning that prestigious uniform. Then compounding this folly, he promoted (illegally) several of his officers, who were just as promptly demoted by an irate Naval Minister shortly thereafter.[93]

Despite Jérôme's flagrant acts, Napoleon continued to pamper him while ordering the nefarious Police Minister, Joseph Fouché, to keep him "informed of the actions of a young man whose lively passions continue to lead him astray."[94] Meanwhile, the maddening Jérôme continued to sport a captain's epaulets, regardless of the growing outrage of career officers and a by-now-seething Decrès. Perhaps even more irritating to the irascible Decrès was Napoleon's persistence in *praising* the troublesome lad! "Monsieur Jérôme has character, is intelligent and decisive, and has a sound-enough general knowledge of his profession to need his own staff now," Napoleon informed an astonished Naval Minister.[95] Thus he needed a higher command and greater responsibility, although of course Jérôme had sedulously avoided learning his profession thoroughly, only managing to squeak through by depending upon better-trained fellow officers willing to cover for him. Admiral Decrès attempted to argue with Napoleon, but was hardly prepared to risk a good land berth as Naval Minister for a mere Jérôme Bonaparte. As for the self-promoted Captain Bonaparte, he managed to find time—when not entertaining a bevy of actresses—to write Madame Jérôme Bonaparte in England and reassure her of his own misery. "Life is nothing to me without you and my son. . . . [But] not to worry, your husband shall never abandon you."[96] (He, however, sent no money to her, although Napoleon settled 60,000 francs a year on her and the child, which Jérôme tried to get away from her.)

Nor was Jérôme doing much to endear himself to Napoleon, apart from heading an expedition of five vessels to Algiers to free 231 European "slaves" (mostly Italians) by paying a ransom of 450,000 francs.[97] Indeed, he otherwise refused to put to sea in 1805, preferring the feminine delights offered him in the ports of Genoa, Toulon and Brest, while continuing to spend much more money—none of it on his wife and son—than he possessed or ever expected to see. And yet Napoleon's generosity had certainly been princely, having given his younger brother, in 1805 alone, in addition to his salary as prince, of 150,000 francs, 191,000 francs in cash—not to mention another gift of 100,000 francs received from Joseph.[98] Regardless, the debts continued to accrue, causing Napoleon to snap: "I definitely intend to let him be imprisoned for debt if he cannot live on his salary. . . . It is quite inconceivable what these problems with that young man cost me, and after all that, he still contributes absolutely nothing to my régime."[99]

In the following year, after deserting Rear-Admiral Willaumez's squadron in the West Indies—giving no prior indication to that stunned commander of his intentions—Jérôme returned to France, in August 1806, where he was received with open arms by Napoleon (for having captured some valuable, if undefended, merchantmen—in the best family spirit). Indeed, for his valiant efforts, Jérôme was raised to the rank of Imperial Prince and decorated with the Grand Aigle of the Legion of Honor. At the same time, his forthcoming marriage to the daughter of the Protestant King of Württemberg, Her Royal Highness, Princess Fredericka Catherine Sophia Dorothy,[100] was officially announced.

As he felt that his own imperial decree invalidating the American marriage ceremony of Jérôme and Elizabeth would not suffice in the eyes of the world, and in light of the Vatican's negative reply to annul that marriage, Napoleon set out desperately to find someone willing to oblige him. He finally came up with a priest and honorary canon in the diocese of Paris—Father Pierre Boileu (Doctor in Canon Law)—who was willing *to override the Pope's decision* and on October 6, 1806, solemnly "declared that there had not been a marriage contracted between the minor Jérôme Bonaparte and Elizabeth Patterson."[101] That this decision, no doubt munificently rewarded by an anxious Emperor, was neither authorized nor accepted by the Vatican and hence remained illegal and invalid, did not appear to disturb the Tuileries unduly. Nor did the bride's obliging father question the situation and wedding plans went ahead with great jubilation, as Jérôme strutted about in the new uniform of a rear-admiral (that is, when not wearing the alternate uniform as a French *général de division*).[102]

The civil and religious marriage ceremonies took place in Paris on August 22 and 23, 1807, and in November of that year the happy, if bigamous, Jérôme set out with Catherine for their new kingdom in Westphalia, Jérôme leaving in his wake another *3 million francs* worth of unpaid bills incurred just over the past two months.[103] As the marriage ceremonies remained illegal, however, and the young royal couple never went through a proper ceremony after Elizabeth Bonaparte finally obtained a legal divorce in Maryland in 1813, Jérôme's and Catherine's children remained bastards—a fact that French historians generally decline to acknowledge.[104]

Giving a kingdom to the utterly irresponsible Jérôme was an utterly irresponsible act in itself (for which Napoleon would later pay most dearly), and what he could have been thinking of when he did so is not clear. Upon reaching his new capital at Kassel, Jérôme's follies resumed anew, but now on a royal scale, and continued in magnitude over the next few years, commensurate with his more exalted whims and rank. If, under King Jérôme, the Kingdom of Westphalia achieved prominence in little else, at least it did so as the merriest capital of the new French Empire. Balls and extravagant parties were given weekly, in addition to the usual theatrical presentations, and, of course, the presence of the omnivorous gaming tables attracted every bounder and rake in Europe. Money flowed as freely as champagne at the new court as Westphalian jewelers, gown and boot makers were inundated with orders. Jérôme, who had early appreciated colorful costumes, had splendid new uniforms designed for his court and army, decorated with new ceremonial orders of chivalry, attended by new titles galore, in turn matched by lavish outlays of latifundia in gold coin and munificent estates. Jérôme had indeed found his magical world of fantasy, in a fairytale kingdom, which included the creation of his very own army, while he continued to command the French troops of occupation (the upkeep of which cost Westphalians tens of millions of francs annually). The result of this unmatched prodigality was debt, ever-increasing debt. And when the millions paid out by Napoleon and the various State treasuries proved insufficient—as they invariably did—Jérôme had recourse to impressive lending from private bankers.[105] His personal debts of a hundred thousand francs as a naval captain now burgeoned into a more princely tens of millions.

Nor did it end there. French officials and officers whom Napoleon had placed with Jérôme were replaced by the young king, even at the ministerial level, with men sometimes wanted for fraud or other legal infractions in France. Napoleon finally grew so exasperated with this monster whom he had so encouraged, shaped and indeed created that he halted almost all direct communication with Kassel. The good-natured, if feckless, Jérôme, amazed to find himself beyond the pale, totally ignored and treated like a truant schoolboy, cut off by an impenetrable wall of silence, pleaded like the child he was. "I have not been writing, because I have nothing to say to you," Napoleon finally replied coldly, after a silence of several weeks, then launched into a sharp attack. "I have met very few persons whom I could rank as low as I do you. You know nothing, not even what is happening around you. You do not make a decision by thinking out a problem carefully, but rather according to the mood of the moment. . . . Nothing you have done meets with my approval nor holds with the truths I have learned through hard experience. As far as I am concerned, if you continue in this manner you will never amount to much!" It was very straight talk, and should have shaken the young man, but was weakened immediately by the last line, which belied all the harsh words, for no matter what he did, Jérôme was, and remained, Napoleon's favorite younger brother. "*Mon ami*, I love you, but you are furiously young!"[106] Hence, over the months and years ahead, Jérôme's appalling conduct continued unabated, indeed with astonishing stupidity even by his standards, involving women and court scandals of all sorts, enlivened by more balls and hunts, financed of course by irresponsible public and private borrowing, resulting in an indebtedness that undermined the stability of the country itself. As for Jérôme, he continued to shirk most of his real work, while declining to provide Napoleon with the troops he required in his incessant wars. But the Emperor continued to put up with it all, despite occasional harmless outbursts of anger, until one day, that is, when even Jérôme finally overreached himself.

The King of Westphalia's many whims included supporting British goods, products and trade, in defiance of Napoleon's Continental System, contrived especially to put an end to just such commerce in Europe. Indeed, Jérôme went so far as to authorize large shipments of goods into Westphalia—all very profitably—then selling them in other French imperial territories, including his western neighbors, the Grand Duchy of Berg and the Batavian Republic. Once again Jérôme had perversely flaunted Napoleon's orders, undermining his authority and making a mockery of him at the same time. Needless to say, the French Emperor did not particularly appreciate this latest princely prank and without warning set up armed customs stations ringing and isolating Westphalia, giving strict orders to halt the flow of this illicit trade once and for all. Jérôme countered this, ordering Marshal Berthier to have the French customs agents disarmed "while awaiting the Emperor's orders to have them punished." Then, without waiting for a reply, he ordered a convoy of three hundred wagons—escorted by mounted Westphalian gendarmes—out of his realm and past the helpless French customs agents, into the rest of the Empire.[107] Germany's new Corsican Till Eulenspiegel had acted even more quickly and brazenly than the mighty Napoleon himself. But there was a price to pay as a result, and the existing bad relations between Kassel and Paris quickly deteriorated, never again to improve. Unfortunately for Napoleon, Jérôme was just one of four cantankerous brothers causing havoc with his grand imperial design and from now on till the end of 1813, he was forced to spend nearly as much time on them and their unruly kingdoms, past and present, as on all those created by his European enemies combined.

Even after having been forced to evacuate Westphalia, Jérôme remained selfish, myopic, spoiled, irresponsible and ungovernable to the end, despite the obvious disintegration of the Empire about him, as foreign troops closed in. Even in these last desperate hours, although now back in France, Jérôme refused to cooperate with his brothers and help save the crumbling imperial edifice. Still Napoleon failed to accept Jérôme for what he really was, and since Jérôme, of all the brothers, had shown some recent military spirit and talent in the defense of the Westphalian monarchy, the Emperor now confided on him the command of the last large army corps—garrisoned at Lyons—while at the same time ordering him to disband the remnants of his Westphalian court, which had followed him to France. A much peeved Jérôme adamantly refused to lose his courtiers, however, and what is more, resented receiving his new military orders from a mere War Minister, instead of from Napoleon himself. In 1812 Jérôme had deserted Napoleon's armies during the Russian campaign, and now in 1814 petulantly refused to oblige him in one last stand. If Napoleon would not permit him to have his lackeys, then he would not proffer his military services. That foreign troops were closing in on Paris was irrelevant, that is, if he could not be treated with the proper respect due the King of Westphalia.[108] And thus, in March 1814, Paris fell as Jérôme looked on.

Of the remaining male clan members, the mentally ill Louis Bonaparte was not to make an appearance during these hundred or so days, nor Napoleon's capable but alienated stepson, Eugène de Beauharnais. Thus, for better or worse, it was to be Napoleon, Joseph, Lucien and Jérôme versus France and Fate.

Chapter V

A Deadly Enemy

"M. de Talleyrand had taken possession of his ministry like Fouché that of the police; each had created his own role for which there could be no understudies."

Victorine de Chastenay

"Political regimes may come and go, but France always remains. Occasionally one may betray all his country's interests by serving one particular regime too fervently, and yet in so doing, at least one is sure of only betraying her intermittently."

Talleyrand

"Once again this morning I have been reproached for changing my mind. But can anything better establish my sense of loyalty, than by remaining faithful to my own inconstancy?"

Talleyrand

"He [Talleyrand] had the means at his disposal to do great harm. He used them."

Queen Hortense

Even as Proconsul Fouché was reporting to the Convention, in September 1794, that the uprising in Lyons had been satisfactorily subdued, an old-fashioned carriage emerged from the forest of ancient elms and maples a few miles west of Albany, New York, along the Troy-Schenectady road running parallel to the Mohawk River. The farmer's wife, dressed in a long blue skirt and brief dark jacket, looked up at the rare sight of a vehicle here in the midst of the great American wilderness, as it turned into the lane leading up the hill to the wood and brick farmhouse.[1] A most elegant forty-year-old gentleman, attired in the rich silks of a Parisian style hitherto unseen this far north, stepped awkwardly down from the carriage. His right crippled foot with a heavy steel brace made progress an ordeal as he slowly approached the young woman, Henriette-Lucy, the Marquise de La Tour du Pin de Gouvernet and her two-year-old daughter. She, the niece of the Bishop of Narbonne, warmly welcomed the former Bishop of Autun and fellow émigré, Charles-Maurice de Talleyrand-Périgord, after sending one of the slave girls back to the house to prepare tea for their unexpected guests. In Philadelphia, New York City and even up here in the harsh New York hinterland near Albany could be found hundreds and hundreds of émigrés forced from their homes and country by the Robespierres and Fouchés of France, indeed fleeing for their very lives to escape the vengeful truths and awful freedoms bestowed by the French Revolution.

With the little money they were able to salvage, in part thanks to this same Monsieur de Talleyrand, the Marquis and Marquise de La Tour du Pin were able to buy this primitive farmhouse and the surrounding acreage. Sitting down in the still autumn air, Monsieur de Talleyrand brought the latest news of their stricken homeland, of the outer world and of their own finances with which he was occupying himself. He also offered his condolences to her and her husband, Frédéric (who was then away on business), for the name of yet another victim to the guillotine in the Place de la Révolution in Paris—her husband's father. Talleyrand, a cold, unemotional man, greatly liked and respected this very feminine but determined young lady, who had been brought up in the luxury of the Court, and whom he had known since her childhood. And although he had not seen her for many years, indeed since her marriage, he was an old friend of her soldier-diplomat husband of better days. Both of these formerly great landowners were now stranded in America and surviving. One had no choice, but the lovely woman was doing so more cheerfully than most, and even seemed to enjoy the challenge of her new existence, despite the great restraining difficulties of her position.

The Marquise, for her part, found Talleyrand "kind as he has always been to me, with that delightful conversation so unique to him."[2] Although unlike most French women who knew Talleyrand, she was bound closely to her family and husband (by whom she ultimately bore six children), nevertheless she was fully aware of the reputation of this excommunicated ex-bishop. But if her husband's distinguished family proudly traced its roots to the fourteenth century, Talleyrand's had been prominent in the tenth, and in any event he was not the sort of person one could ignore. To be sure "one personally regretted having so many reasons for not being able to respect him," she acknowledged, "but after an hour's conversation, all was forgotten."[3] Nevertheless, the contradictions of his character were puzzling, given his *"indulgence pour les vices,"* as Queen Hortense later put it.[4] Indeed, one could have applied to him what Montesquieu had said of Caesar, Madame de La Tour du Pin observed: " 'This man had no faults, although a good many vices.' "[5] Curiously enough, "disregarding his own foibles, he nevertheless felt a real repugnance in those he found in others. To hear him speak, without knowing who he was, one would have thought him a virtuous man."[6] That even the good Marquise could be fascinated by this man was hardly surprising. "While maintaining his noble bearing and elegant manners, he was both charming and amusing, and his conversation always in good taste. One found in him the *grand seigneur*, a feminine streak, a catlike nature and a bit of the priest, the priest and the *grand seigneur* predominating,"[7] commented a perceptive Comte de Molé. "And when he wished it, perhaps no one could quite fascinate you as did M. de Talleyrand."[8] "Really, in spite of everything, I must confess that I found in him a charm that I never discovered in any other man," the Marquise de La Tour du Pin confessed.[9] "The day he condescends to speak to you, he is already too kind, you feel, and you are fully ready to adore him if he so much as asks after your health," admitted Queen Hortense years later.[10] "One could be armed with every bit of information one had about his immorality, his conduct, his personal life, about everything he was reproached with, and yet he always won you over to him, like a bird hypnotized by the serpent."[11] Even an unhypnotized Napoleon found him "the King of conversation."[12]

Talleyrand marked his memorable sojourn in the wilds of the Mohawk River valley by planting a mulberry tree, the farm known thereafter as Mulberry Hill, while presenting Madame de La Tour du Pin with a splendid saddle and bridle. And later, when she was very ill with pulmonary problems, he sent her expensive medicines hundreds of miles across primitive roads from New York City and Philadelphia.

Although to old friends like the La Tour du Pin, Talleyrand could appear pleasant, yet there was one essential quality he lacked: warmth. Consequently, "one never really feels at ease with him."[13] To most, including the aristocratic ladies of the Faubourg Saint-Germain, in Paris, with whom he surrounded himself, he was charming, seductive, and in the words of Victorine de Chastenay, "most witty . . . and remarkably able to an unusual degree."[14] If in public he was generally a man of few words, when however he did have something to say, it was invariably to the point. Later, even Czar Alexander I found himself stopping in midsentence to listen to him. And "when he spoke," Madame de Chastenay remarked, "Talleyrand made it abundantly clear that he would brook no interruption by *anyone*."[15] Or "he could chat and tease with inimitable charm" while his "persiflage was simply ingenious, and his jesting at once light and biting." "But," said his colleague Molé, "when he was angered, the conversation of this phlegmatic statesman could take a strong, bitter turn, becoming harsh and coarse."[16] And the legendary haughtiness and self-confidence attendant on such occasions was dramatically enhanced by his physical appearance—his "supercilious expression" set off by his "dead eyes"—as Molé referred to his dull blue expressionless eyes—and "his mouth reflecting at once debauchery, satiety and utter disdain."[17] This encompassed in a feminine face and an elaborate coiffeur worthy of a princess of the reign of Louis XIV, and a fair complexion reduced "to pale, dead, sagging skin," made the sixty-year-old Talleyrand of 1815 look like the ghost of another century and at least seventy-five years old. And because of his slow, awkward, slithering gait when he approached, "one could almost see in him one of those fabled monsters of yore, half man, half serpent."[18]

Yet despite his unique appearance, the embonpoint resulting from six decades of sheer physical idleness and overindulgence, not to mention a certain notoriety as rake and reprobate, women continued to flock round him, and his social life certainly appeared to be undiminished. Indeed, the magnificent Louis XV salons of his four-story mansion at the corner of the rue de Rivoli and Saint Florentin, overlooking the Tuileries gardens, were filled every week with a select bevy of friends, chiefly female. Madame de Chastenay nevertheless remained more of a pessimist about him and his celebrated soirées, than of her friend Fouché. Talleyrand, she noted perceptively, kept his friends, "I am almost tempted to say, as one does one's dogs, to lead about and for amusement, without really taking any notice of them."[19]

This same Prince de Bénévent was quite incapable of living by himself. To be sure, Napoleon had forced him to marry his mistress Cathérine-Noël Grand, back in 1803, after the wives of the diplomatic corps had refused to meet him in his official capacity as Foreign Minister in the presence of la belle Grand, who by the age of forty had had more lovers than Talleyrand mistresses. Since then, however, she had been banished permanently to the provinces by her husband, an imposing list of other ladies taking her place thereafter at the rue Saint Florentin, including the Duchesse de Courlande, and her incomparable daughter, Dorothée.

Talleyrand rarely appeared in public before 11 A.M. The doors of his salon opened at 11 P.M.: generally he would join his guests before midnight, when a light supper was served, followed by a game of whist—which he preferred to play with three ladies. And more often than not this would be followed by gambling with his male friends, when he frequently lost large sums, sometimes hundreds of thousands of francs, without batting an eye. He could always make up for it easily enough on the morrow, by demanding fresh bribes from foreign diplomats wishing to curry favor with him.

With the outbreak of the Revolution Talleyrand's career had shifted from the Church to politics. He personally proposed the seizure of all Church property in the land—with Fouché's full support—and instituted a Constitutional Clergy, that is to say, one swearing allegiance to the French Republic and no longer to Rome. Leaving France in 1792, he spent the next few years in exile, in Britain and America, until 1796 when his name was finally removed from the list of proscribed émigrés. But his real career lay before him and in 1797, at the age of forty-three, when the Directory named him Foreign Minister, a post in which he excelled, and continued in until 1807.

If Talleyrand proved a most effective Foreign Minister under Napoleon Bonaparte, it was not always because the two men were in agreement with one another. Like Police Minister Fouché, he was no soldier and found no attraction in war, and generally advised governments against it throughout his career. To his mind, the continuing forays of French armies beyond their frontiers into northern, central and southern Europe simply ensured an unprofitable state of affairs for Europe, resulting in political and economic instability, strife and war. Like Fouché, he envisaged a Europe at peace, which meant peace with Great Britain, Russia, Prussia, Austria and Spain.

On the other hand, Napoleon, as a soldier, was set on his primitive quest of unsettling world affairs, threatening and invading neighboring States in order to achieve his objective: the conquest of the world. For indeed it was not merely Europe that was involved in his plans, but the Middle East and even India, and this, of course, was clearly at odds with his Foreign Minister's entire policy. That the relationship of the two men proved stormy, was inevitable. Talleyrand carried out his meetings with Napoleon—two or three times weekly—in a calm, polite, even gracious, manner. Not so Napoleon, however, who while admiring Talleyrand's gifts, found these occasions and Talleyrand's aristocratic haughtiness maddening, resulting in the frustrated Emperor losing his temper. Thus such occasions would frequently turn into bitter encounters.

While in some respects Talleyrand greatly admired Napoleon, particularly certain of his achievements, it did not prevent him from opposing Napoleon, or even working to overthrow him when he felt that the Emperor was no longer acting in the best interests of France. For his part, Talleyrand wished to see a strong, respected France, an influential member of the international community, yet one safely back within her traditional borders.

Unlike his colleague Joseph Fouché, Talleyrand was not the first to arrive each morning at his ministry, in the Hotel Gallifet in the rue du Bac, nor the last to leave; indeed, quite the contrary—he arrived late and stayed only for a very brief spell. Talleyrand's administrative philosophy was again quite in keeping with the ancien régime: all work that could be delegated to lesser officials should be so disposed of. The fact is, Charles-Maurice de Talleyrand-Périgord was a very lazy gentleman. It was not his task to read every report and dictate every reply to Napoleon, foreign governments or French diplomatic staff abroad. After all, the appropriate departmental officials of the Foreign Ministry were there precisely to deal with such matters. If, for example, a report had to be prepared for the French Emperor, Talleyrand would explain to the pertinent head of a department what in general was required, then order him to prepare a draft for him to study. If upon reading it Talleyrand did not feel it was satisfactory, he would simply reply, "No, that is not it," while declining to explain *why*. The bewildered subordinate would leave to prepare a more acceptable version, hopefully reading the Minister's mind as to what was required. It was a frustrating "system" and not very intelligent, but that is the way the slothfully perverse Talleyrand did things. Once the document was found to be satisfactory, Talleyrand would simply remark, "Yes, that is it."[20] In the event the document was particularly important and intended for Napoleon himself, Talleyrand would copy it in his own hand and sign it, though he found that rather tedious. "I have always made others work to avoid doing it myself," the Foreign Minister admitted. "One should not permit oneself to be buried under a lot of papers . . . [which thereby] gives the day more than twenty-four hours."[21] And yet the aloof, arrogant Talleyrand, or Prince de Bénévent as he was known after 1806, was generally liked by the Ministry personnel and greatly admired by his subordinates Jaucourt and Caulaincourt.

To his senior officials Foreign Minister Talleyrand defined what he perceived to be the basic characteristics and philosophy required of a good diplomat. "Circumspection," "discretion," "a disinterested dedication, open to no outside influence," "a certain elevation of feelings which makes the individual feel that it is grand and noble to be able to represent one's country . . ." At the same time one also needed "skill in the art of dealing with matters . . . the requisite facility to permit one to seize upon and expedite the objective in hand" as well as "a good general overview of the situation" all supported by "a penchant for the study of political relations. . . ."[22] (All this at a time when an ambassador's salary was only 10,000 francs a year, compared, say, with a marshal's 100,000 francs.) Talleyrand's motto at the rue du Bac was *festina lente*," make haste slowly and proceed with a good degree of caution. "One must always have time to reflect," he insisted, "and it is better to put off for tomorrow what one cannot do readily and well today, than to act precipitously, leading everyone to believe that this is being done because one has too much other pressing work to do."[23] And to Ambassador General Andréossy, for instance, he added; "Given the present state of Europe, no delay in acting will put our political transactions in imminent danger." Quite to the contrary "a negotiator or minister . . . can, by giving an immediate, definitive answer without adequate consideration, do, in a thoughtless moment, such harm to his cause and country that often cannot be undone afterward even by several years' good service."[24] Hence when negotiating directly with a foreign government, always stall when an answer is demanded—"the lack of instructions and the necessity of consulting one's government are always legitimate excuses . . . in order to obtain delays in political affairs. . . ."[25] Therefore, "never give an immediate reply to any proposition made to you, nor to any complaint or unexpected offer."[26] And to foreign ministry officials Talleyrand added for good measure: "After you have spent some time dealing with European interests with the Emperor, you will see how important it is not to rush and carry out his orders,"[27] for this Napoleon could frequently change his mind three times in as many days, as all the other ministers could attest with a vengeance.

Despite Talleyrand's shortcomings, Napoleon felt that he, like Fouché, was an essential man to have in his government. "His own self-interest," said the Emperor, "guarantees for me his loyalty, much more than his character does,"[28] to which were added other attributes: his ancien régime sense of dignity, as well as a knowledge of the international scene unequaled among foreign ministers anywhere in Europe, not to mention a sense of "legitimacy," which his presence gave to Napoleon, a legitimacy his regime otherwise lacked.

And yet Talleyrand's arrogance and independence of thought—not to mention his astonishing private life—also resulted in getting the Emperor's hackles up, to the point of his denigrating the Foreign Minister and his accomplishments before Comte de Molé.[29] "Part of his reputation is due to luck more than his own merit, thus resulting in his negotiating and signing several peace treaties. I could not honestly tell you that we gained much from his presence then, nor did he create and provide the expedients or any profound skill. I do not even think . . . that he is very intelligent, certainly not extraordinarily intelligent—in fact, all you have to do is look at his private life to see that. He was by birth and class one of the first personages of the nobility and clergy, and yet he did all in his power to bring them down. Upon his return from America and following the close of the Terror, he publicly defiled and demeaned himself by attaching himself to an old, unintelligent hag [Mme de Talleyrand]. Since the signing of the Concordat [with Rome], I had been hoping that he might extricate himself, in spite of himself, from the filthy situation he was in by asking the Pope for a cardinal's hat for him, and I was prepared to get it. But, oh no, he would not hear of it, and in spite of me, he married his disgraceful mistress—to the scandal of all Europe*—a woman who could not even hope to give him children. As we all know, he has stolen more than anyone else in the world, and yet he does not have a sou to his name, and therefore I am obliged to support him out of my private funds, as well as pay off his latest debts."[30]

As usual in the case when Napoleon wished to humiliate someone—in this instance, Talleyrand—he uttered a lot of gibberish (mixed with some half-truths), which court officials were only too well familiar with, and thus generally ignored.

Nevertheless, there was a very dark side to Talleyrand, revealing

---

*In fact, Napoleon had given him an ultimatum: either to throw her over, or marry her.

something sadistic and sinister. This was best seen regarding the Duc d'Enghien, whose kidnapping and execution Talleyrand "suggested" to Napoleon, and which was to bring down upon the Emperor the wrath of Europe, and for which he would never be forgiven. Talleyrand managed to convince Napoleon that Enghien, who was living in exile on the German side of the Rhine, was directing royalist plots in conjunction with the Chouan leader, Georges Cadoudal, to overthrow Napoleon, and thus had to be made an example of.[31] Napoleon put a plan into effect and on 15 March 1804 the Duc d'Enghien was arrested. At 3 A.M. on the twentieth, he was summarily executed, without counsel or trial, in the dry moat outside the dungeon of Vincennes.[32] That Napoleon had no right to kidnap people, in France or in foreign countries, was not only self-evident, but irrelevant. He held the power and could do anything he wished to do. Thunderstruck, Josephine hounded Napoleon thereafter, as Alexander's court in Saint Petersburg went into mourning for the lamented Duke. But the very next day Talleyrand, who was delighted with his sadistic success, while marshaling more enemies in his fight against Napoleon, casually mentioned to his lady friends over a hand of cards: "By the way, the last of the Condé family has ceased to exist."[33] And when later reproached at the Foreign Office by the Comte d'Hauterive, Talleyrand replied quizzically: "But what is so extraordinary about that?"[34] The successful execution of the plot he had hatched to kidnap and murder another human being, a fellow aristocrat, named and targeted by him, left the effete Talleyrand totally unmoved.

From a documentary point of view, the French Foreign Minister as usual had covered his tracks reasonably well. Admittedly he had suggested this plan to assassinate the last member of France's most ancient family, the Condés, at a cabinet meeting on 10 March before witnesses (a mistake he would not repeat in the future): Fouché, Cambacérès and Murat—to which two of them, Fouché and Murat, gave their full support. But of course the orders to execute every detail of this brutal plan were issued by Napoleon, who afterward admitted his role: "I had the Duc d'Enghien arrested and judged, because the safety, interests and honor of the French people required it. . . ."[35] But later, with the unexpected storm of protest blasting the newly launched French Empire that spring, Napoleon publicly rebuked and blamed Talleyrand, pointing out the whole thing as his brainchild.

Although Talleyrand had the sheer effrontery to insist upon the importance of maintaining "a disinterested dedication open to no outside influence" in his instructions to ministerial and diplomatic officials, that by no means proved an obstacle to his personal financial interests and pursuits when advancing his own "diplomatic career." Indeed, there was no secret about the astonishing bribes demanded and received by this self-same Foreign Minister Talleyrand. To be sure, negotiators of international treaties invariably received "gifts" from all sides—usually in the form of jewel-encrusted snuff boxes or a handful of precious gems, the more lucrative ones coming from the winner of the particular issue of the moment. Or when foreign governments anticipated special favors from France, for instance, a bribe of some sort was mandatory, as everyone knew—except, apparently, the diplomats of the young American republic, who rejected outright such propositions. But as Talleyrand distinguished himself in international diplomacy as the finest statesman and negotiator of the age, so too did he achieve inordinate financial success as well. Indeed, over the years he set European records for the types and amounts he received in "gifts" from grateful parties, which included one-time installments of 800,000 francs from General Murat, 1 million francs from the Margrave of Baden, 3,700,000 francs from King Ferdinand IV of Naples—all of whom wanted to ensure their titles to the lands they claimed or hoped to obtain. The King of Saxony offered him 6 million francs in exchange for a Berlin prison,[36] while receiving some 7 million francs from all parties for his having successfully concluded the Treaty of Lunéville.[37] And although less successful in obtaining the presidency of the Batavian Republic for Prince van Weilbourg, he was none the less contented with the 5 million franc fee he received for that attempted intervention. It is equally true that Talleyrand received at least 10 million from several German princes vying for claims to and recognition of the newly revised Rhineland states. One exasperated German diplomat, Baron von Gagern, outraged by this blatant extortion, complained publicly that Talleyrand "considered his high diplomatic situation a gold mine," even demanding payment in "hard cash."[38] And yet the French Foreign Minister kept his sense of humor throughout the process, and after receiving an acceptable offering from one minor German ruler, Prince von Reuss, he scribbled in the margin of the treaty concerning him: *"La République française est charmée de faire connaissance avec le prince von Reuss."*[39] Say what his detractors might about the inimitable French Foreign Minister, no one could fault the man's style. How much did Talleyrand ultimately extort from foreign governments and office seekers over the years? One cannot even begin to guess.

Despite the uncertainty of the year 1805 for France and the imperial regime—the treasury was empty, the much vaunted invasion armada at Boulogne, 167,000 strong, had not budged an inch in the last two years, and the disastrous naval battle at Trafalgar had literally destroyed the entire combined Franco-Spanish Fleet in October—relations between Emperor Napoleon and Foreign Minister Talleyrand were never better. And although later denied by both men, a special relationship did, in fact, now exist. When for instance Napoleon left Talleyrand at Strasbourg in October 1805, to lead his armies against those of Franz II of Austria, the usually phlegmatic Talleyrand acknowledged he "felt an emotion that is impossible to describe,"[40] while in a private letter to Josephine, Napoleon likewise admitted that he found it "most painful to leave the two persons [Josephine and Talleyrand] I most love."[41] It was an astonishing admission and brings forth new questions about their relationship. As for Talleyrand, this period certainly marks the apogee of his career, for following Napoleon's double victories at Ulm (in October) and Austerlitz (in December 1805) and the subsequent Peace Treaty of Pressburg ratified in January 1806—which reputedly brought Talleyrand another five million francs[42]—a jubilant French Emperor personally rewarded everyone in sight, and in the case of Talleyrand, with nothing less than a principality, that of Bénévent[43] (which admittedly cost him nothing, he simply having confiscated it from the Papal States).

Although Talleyrand publicly paraded his altruistic pacifism, indeed, boasting how he had managed to tone down the harshness of the anti-Austrian provisions of the Peace of Pressburg, all the while he secretly acted as Napoleon's architect in dismembering the Habsburg's thousand-year-old Holy Roman Empire. Thus, for instance, from its remnants he created the two new kingdoms of Bavaria and Württemberg as a part of the newly emerging Confederation of the Rhine in July 1806. This total upheaval all along this mighty river now was hardly the best means of ensuring peace, though it was soon to be further undermined by Napoleon's secret plans for the introduction of a Continental Blockade, intended to deny access of all British goods to the European Continent.[44] If any single measure were to assure the British Government's determination to crush the French and their leader, it was this. And when the Prince of Peace, Manuel de Godoy, later informed Napoleon at Berlin that Spain would certainly not adhere to such a blockade, Napoleon determined to crush the Spanish Bourbons and invade their kingdom. Talleyrand, for his part, seeing the utter madness of both the creation of the new Confederation and the Continental Blockade, remained a silent participant in the process while biding his time until the downfall of the house of Bonaparte, which, as of the summer of 1807, he knew to be inevitable.

During this period (though probably beginning as early as 1804 or so), while Talleyrand was receiving the rich fruits of his cultivated relationship with the French Emperor—e.g. including the 19,000-hectare estate of Valençay, which the Emperor had just bought for him at a cost of 1.6 million francs (bringing an annual net income of 180,000 francs)[45]—the French Foreign Minister was secretly plotting with the Grand Duke Dalberg of Frankfurt—"a puny but quick little man of extraordinary malice"[46]—and his nephew to overthrow Napoleon. Indeed, Dalberg's nephew, who headed the Russian espionage network acting out of the Russian Embassy in Paris, even passed on its vital information and reports to St. Petersburg via French Imperial diplomatic pouch and couriers, thanks to Talleyrand! Some of this information (e.g., on French Channel naval orders and fleet dispositions) was also passed on to Great Britain.[47] If Napoleon, as a native Corsican thought he knew a thing or two about duplicity, he was but an innocent compared with the French master par excellence, Charles-Maurice de Talleyrand. The Emperor, remarked Jean Orieux pithily, had been "blinded by incense."[48]

Talleyrand's overriding interest in a general peace was real enough, however, at least most of the time, and after the bloody near-defeat at the Battle of Eylau in February 1807, he was determined more than ever to do whatever was necessary to achieve a lasting settlement. The great French victory of Friedland in June (1807), he felt, afforded the perfect opportunity for this, Talleyrand telling Napoleon frankly that he hoped this battle would be "the last one he would have to win."[49] But after Napoleon's meeting with Czar Alexander at Tilsit (July 1807) Talleyrand definitely felt that all was lost, for the French Emperor made it clear that he had no intention of putting an end to his incessant wars and conquests. "This conquest would kill any chance of peace . . . this long, calamitous aberration of history . . . this military dictatorship" would inevitably lead to *"la catastrophe"* for France, Talleyrand lamented.[50] He left Tilsit depressed and disillusioned. And when Napoleon decided not to create an independent Polish state after all, despite his previous declaration to do so,* Talleyrand lost all hope for the future.[51] "The first priority for Europe, its greatest need," he submitted, "was therefore to banish the doctrines of [Bonaparte] usurpation and to revive the principle of legitimacy, which is the sole remedy for all the woes afflicting it."[52] There could be no peace in Europe so long as there was a Napoleon, he felt, and upon returning to Paris in August (1807), Talleyrand resigned as Foreign Minister, never again to resume that post under the empire.[53]

Napoleon, taken aback by this act of "treason," said he would never

---

*Talleyrand had received 4 million francs in bribes for Polish patriots for the creation of the new state.

forgive this haughty, ungrateful Prince de Bénévent, though he was later to offer him that same portfolio on more than one occasion. "Why did he want to leave the ministry?" a perplexed Napoleon asked Caulaincourt six years later. "He could have still been there now, if he had so wished. . . . He was one of those who helped establish my dynasty."[54] Napoleon simply could not understand something as basic as the need for law, order and peace in the world . . . at least not in *his* world, and as Talleyrand himself so succinctly put it, "I do not want to be the Empire's executioner."[55] But in fact there were also personal reasons, grievances for Talleyrand's abandonment of Napoleon. At Tilsit he had been humiliated before everyone to find that though present, he had not been invited to participate in the negotiations and thus had no hand in drawing up the final agreement between Napoleon and the Czar. Also the Prince de Bénévent felt that since the creation of the Empire he had not been sufficiently rewarded, either in titles and honors, or financially, for after all he was only receiving a total annual income of some five hundred thousand francs (exclusive of his negotiating perks).[56]

In the final analysis, however, it was the discarding of his own plans for Europe, and France's role in it, that discouraged the French Foreign Minister. "My humble brain has much trouble in convincing itself that what we are doing beyond the Rhine will outlive the great man who is creating it.[57] . . . Ambition, pride, anger and some imbeciles he listens to, often blind his vision. He suspects and ceases to believe me the moment I urge moderation, and you will see how he will finally compromise himself in the future, by his *imprudentes sottises*."[58]

And yet Talleyrand was not quite so innocent or prescient as he later made out. To be sure, he had been plotting against Napoleon for years, in one form or another, quoting Corneille's famous lines as justification— *"La perfidie est noble envers la tyrannie"**—and at Erfurt, in 1808, secretly informed Czar Alexander that he, Prince de Bénévent, and others supported him, advising him that Russia and Austria should work actively against Napoleon, who was overreaching himself.[59] "The only time I ever plotted in my life," Talleyrand later protested, "was when I had most Frenchmen as my accomplices, and when the well-being of the country required it."[60] Some took a different view of his acts, however, as Chateaubriand quipped: *"Quand M de Talleyrand ne conspire pas, il trafique."*[61]

Despite his calls for peace, this same year Talleyrand supported Napoleon's plans to intercede in Spain, including a second kidnapping,

*"Treachery is a noble thing when enacted against tyranny."

of the Spanish royal family at Bayonne, even permitting them to be kept prisoner *under his own roof* afterward, at his estate of Valençay.[62] "The Crown of Spain has belonged to the French royal family since the reign of Louis XIV," he pointed out to Chancellor Pasquier by way of explanation for his act, "and the Emperor must collect the entire inheritance; indeed, he has no right to abandon any part of it."[63] Years later, of course, Talleyrand denied any participation in the scheme to depose the Spanish ruling family in favor of French military intervention, just as he later denied his role in the kidnapping and execution of the Duc d'Enghien. (Interestingly enough, the imperial files on both incidents— documenting Talleyrand's active involvement—disappeared from the archives during Napoleon's reign.)

That December 1808, while at his Spanish military headquarters at Vallodolid, Napoleon received news that not only the French people were turning against him—some 300,000 army conscripts having recently revolted or fled the authorities—but that Talleyrand and Fouché were plotting with Murat and others to overthrow his regime.[64] Following the events at Erfurt, this was too much for the French Emperor, who rushed back to Paris where on January 28, 1809, he summoned Talleyrand and Fouché before Cambacérès, Lebrun and Decrès. To the bewilderment and embarrassment of these witnesses, Napoleon singled out Talleyrand, calling him a "thief . . . a coward, a faithless wretch . . . All your life you have failed to fulfill your duties, you have deceived and betrayed everyone . . . nothing is sacred for you! You would not think twice about selling out your own father! I could break you like a glass. I have the power to do that. I really don't know why I haven't had you hanged from the gates of the Carrousel!" He even went so far as to accuse his former Foreign Minister of permitting his wife to become the mistress of one of the Spanish princes at Valençay.[65] The tough Admiral Decrès—hardly a squeamish chap—found this scene a bit unpleasant. Talleyrand was no doubt deeply upset by this humiliating harangue, but of course remained perfectly true to his austere reputation, and as his carriage passed the very green-and-gold wrought-iron railing from which Napoleon had just threatened to hang him, he turned to Fouché and commented—"A pity, don't you think, that such a great man was so badly brought up."[66]

The following day Talleyrand was informed that he had been removed from his last official post as Imperial Chamberlain, and that was the end of it, at least for him. Napoleon had no written proof with which to convict him, but he would no longer be in the Emperor's trust, or appear at court. "I want no more of that Talleyrand!" exclaimed an angry Napoleon afterward. "It is not that I fail to recognize his talents, for he is superior to everyone else, *mais c'est l'or à côté de la merde.*[67] As for Talleyrand, he considered himself most fortunate, for after all, Enghien had been murdered for much less, indeed, for nothing at all. The following year (June 1810) Fouché was likewise dismissed from office as Police Minister for corresponding with the British and Ouvrard, helping to break Napoleon's precious Continental Blockade.[68] Fouché was then exiled far from France for years to come. Talleyrand, however, managed to remain. Even in disgrace Napoleon appreciated the difference between a commoner and *"un grand seigneur."*

To be sure, thereafter Talleyrand distanced himself from the Tuileries, which did not prevent Napoleon from asking him again in 1813 to resume his old place in the rue du Bac . . . though in vain. As he had said earlier, "the doctrines of usurpation" now had to be replaced with "the principle of legitimacy," and he was not about to aid the "usurper" at this late hour.[69] "I believe that he [Napoleon] is finished, for the only thing he is doing now is personally destroying everything good he has built and accomplished."[70] "I forgive Talleyrand, I have mistreated him," a repentant Napoleon confessed in the spring of 1815. "The Bourbons will do well to employ him. To be sure, he likes money and intrigue, but he is a most capable man. My affairs went well all the time that Talleyrand was in charge of them . . . and in the final analysis, he is the one man who best knows and understands France and Europe."[71]

With the allied entry into Paris, in March 1814, Czar Alexander, the King of Prussia, Ambassador Prinz von Schwarzenberg of Austria and Lord Castlereagh met in Talleyrand's mansion in the rue Saint Florentin to resolve the many problems facing France.[72] On 2 April Talleyrand was elected President of the Provisional Government and the same day voted to overthrow Napoleon. "It is legitimate vengeance," Napoleon said upon receiving the news. "I was wrong to have left him the time to avenge himself."[73] But he added sadly, "I appear to be destined always to find myself betrayed by the ingratitude of the men upon whom I have heaped the greatest benefits."[74]

And just as the Emperor had predicted, Talleyrand was indeed accepted by the Bourbons upon their return in the spring.[75] But all was not clear sailing in France, even with Napoleon finally out of the way . . . or was he? Talleyrand, for one, was by no means so sure. Is it true, then, that he ordered his secretary, Roux-Laborie, to meet the Comte de Guerry-Maubreuil on that same April second, with the purpose of hiring him to kill Napoleon and perhaps even his brothers? Talleyrand admitted to knowing Maubreuil, as well as about his meeting with Laborie on that date, though scoffing at the idea that he had offered the Count a great deal of money to assassinate Napoleon. (Nor did he ever acknowledge being behind the kidnapping and murder of the Duc d'Enghien.) And yet police records reveal that Maubreuil then set out and attacked King Jérôme's carriage, only to find it occupied instead by the Queen of Westphalia, whom he merely robbed. In fact, it sounds very much like the sort of thing Talleyrand would do—with someone else's financial support—when he knew all the Allies were whispering similar thoughts themselves.[76] "Beware of that man," Napoleon had warned his brother Joseph on 2 February 1814; "he is most certainly the greatest enemy of our house."[77]

Napoleon abdicated on 6 April, followed by the signing of the Treaty of Fontainebleau on the eleventh, and on the nineteenth, Talleyrand himself signed the armistice on behalf of France with the Allies.[78] Czar Alexander's formerly friendly relations with Talleyrand had, since Erfurt, declined rapidly, which the meetings held at the rue Saint Florentin apparently did nothing to improve.

Talleyrand, who was now formally switching allegiance from the House of Bonaparte to that of Bourbon, finally met the sixty-year-old Louis XVIII on 29 April. "I cannot begin to describe to you my disappointment when I met him for the first time," he later acknowledged to a friend, portraying his king as "selfish, insensitive, epicurean, ungrateful and the greatest liar I have ever seen"[79]—which is almost precisely how one society lady had earlier referred to Talleyrand himself. Nor were the King's impressions of Talleyrand any more encouraging for the future. Reporting to his own sovereign, Metternich explained that "Talleyrand is feared at Court, more than he is liked. I believe the King is hardly inclined to bestow his unlimited confidence on this minister."[80]

And yet Talleyrand had achieved a great deal, for, as already noted, his Treaty of Paris signed by all parties on 30 May 1814 proved surprisingly generous, sparing France both war indemnity and occupation by foreign troops.

It was at the Congress convening at Vienna, beginning in September 1814 and continuing well into the following year, however, that the sixty-year-old Talleyrand succeeded in enjoying perhaps his finest hour by bringing off two more astonishing coups. The purpose of the Congress was to resolve many of the outstanding issues caused by the years of Napoleonic upheaval, including the adjustment of several national frontiers and territorial claims. At the same time, this had an essential aim of ultimately "containing" France in the event of any future militaristic sallies beyond her reduced frontiers.

To the north, Prince William, shortly to become King William of the Low Countries (in February 1815) was jockeying for his own recognition and for the addition of Belgium and Luxembourg to Holland and his proposed realm, while King Frederick William II of Prussia was reaching out in every direction for territorial aggrandizement, as rewards for his part in the destruction of Napoleon's army, including claims to the whole of Saxony, Swedish Pomerania and some Rhineland states. Austria wanted the return of her lands in northern Italy, and Czar Alexander demanded no less than the throne of the whole of Poland. Others sought a change in Naples, notably the removal of King Joachim (Murat), Wellington arguing that "if he [Murat] were gone, Bonaparte in Elba would not be an object of great dread."[81] As in all such ventures, there were to be found strongly conflicting interests, and in this case the confusion wrought by the devil's advocate, France, in the guise of Talleyrand, only added to the problems.

According to the Secret Additional Article I of the Treaty of Paris (30 May 1814), the French Government was not entitled to participate in any form at the Congress of Vienna. Nevertheless, the wily Talleyrand insinuated his way to the bargaining table, and when at the opening a declaration was read, beginning with the term "Allied Powers,"—clearly intended to exclude France—Talleyrand interrupted: "Allied?" he queried. "Against whom? It cannot be against Napoleon, for he is defeated and on Elba; nor can it be against France, as peace has been achieved. Surely it cannot be against the King of France, for he is the very guarantee of that peace."[82] And continuing in that vein, Talleyrand managed to have his credentials accepted as a fully fledged negotiator, thanks in large part to the British Foreign Secretary, Lord Castlereagh. That very acceptance was Talleyrand's first great achievement. His second one was the disruption of the Congress by creating a major division of interests between the members.

Although Counts von Nesselrode and von Hardenberg, and Prince Klemens von Metternich were also principal negotiators at Vienna, it was Talleyrand and Castlereagh who dominated the proceedings. Viscount Castlereagh, as Robert Stewart was known after 1796, was at once Talleyrand's staunchest ally and most powerful enemy. Although both men were intelligent, well informed and most determined on achieving their ends, such ends, however, were very different indeed, which the forty-six-year-old Castlereagh discovered from the outset when he found Talleyrand forcefully opposing his own effort to have the international commerce of slaves outlawed. For Castlereagh, who had espoused Catholic emancipation for Ireland, it was only natural to support this cause, though soundly defeated in the attempt at Vienna.

Of much more immediate importance for all parties negotiating the fate and the redrafting of the map of Europe were the decisions to be taken regarding Prussia's Saxon, and Russia's Polish, claims. To be sure, all of Europe—Austria and England in particular—were wary of the growing Russian giant, which had already swallowed up Bessarabia and Finland within her remarkably expansive borders. And yet Castlereagh, more than anything else, wanted to work on the larger issues facing Europe, and therefore felt that Russia should be won over amiably, if at all possible, to working in conjunction with the Allies. The long-term peace and prosperity of the continent were his objectives. Talleyrand, on the other hand, was constantly dragging his feet, deliberately sidetracking the diplomats to minor issues, with no deep-seated interest in seeing a happy, reasonably unified Europe, regardless of his professions to the contrary. Indeed, his principal objective now was to foil any attempt made by Castlereagh. "He spoils, he plots, he manipulates in a hundred different ways daily," Ambassador Pozzo di Borgo attested.[83] And although not so explicit, Castlereagh fully concurred. Surveying the results of those tactics at the highest level, the British statesman complained privately to the Duke of Wellington on 25 October (1814): "You will perceive from my several dispatches that the difference in principle between Talleyrand and me is chiefly that I wish to direct my main efforts to secure an equilibrium in Europe" while Talleyrand plotted and quibbled about minor or irrelevant issues that would serve to neutralize that equilibrium.[84] Wellington replied that he had urged King Louis's government "in the strongest manner to have instructions sent to Monsieur de Talleyrand to lay aside all considerations upon small points, and to unite cordially with you [Castlereagh] in a great effort to produce the union of all the Powers in Europe against the projected aggrandizement of Russia."[85]

As a part of this overall strategy, Castlereagh also hoped to make Prussia "a useful ally"[86] and saw a couple of alternatives for maintaining this equilibrium. He thought "a union of the two great German powers [Austria and Prussia], supported by Great Britain, and thus combining the minor States of Germany, together with Holland" serving as "an intermediary system" to separate the two great warlike powers in Europe, France and Russia, would prove ideal. Less agreeable to Castlereagh might be a "union of Austria, France and the southern States against the northern Powers, with Russia and Prussia in close alliance. . . . Necessity," he told Wellington, "might dictate such a system, but not choice."[87] It was not that he liked the idea of pitting one bloc against another, however, as he admitted. "It would have been to be wished that the arrangements upon a peace could have been effected in Europe without giving rise to any combination whatever of this nature, and that at the end of so long a struggle, the several Powers might have enjoyed some repose, without forming calculations that always augment the risks of war, but the tone and conduct of Russia have disappointed this hope, and forced upon us fresh considerations."[88] With France now at bay, Castlereagh found Talleyrand "very averse to Russia and impatient of the notion of any union between Austria and Prussia,"[89] though Castlereagh personally felt there was "no reason to fear that the union between Austria and Prussia will be such as to endanger the liberties of other States."[90]

Although the British Foreign Secretary did everything in his power to woo Frederick William and Prussia into his camp, he failed, as the question of Saxony and Poland, aided by the spoiling hand of Talleyrand, irrevocably divided the Congress of Vienna. Prussia, continuing to insist on seizing the crown of Saxony, was encouraged and abetted by Russia, in return for Prussian support of the Czar's claims to Poland. If Prussia and Russia succeeded in seizing their mutual quarry, however, France threatened to "withdraw their Ministers from the Congress," Wellington informed Castlereagh, "declaring they would not acknowledge these arrangements, and that Europe would remain in a feverish state, which, sooner or later, must end in war."[91] With this threat in mind, Castlereagh, anxious, as he said, about Russian "encroachment and dictation,"[92] was thus in part manipulated, by Talleyrand as well, into forming a secret defense pact with France and Austria. This was duly signed by Castlereagh, Talleyrand and Metternich on 3 January 1815, each signatory promising to field 150,000 men and to come to the aid of one another in the event they were attacked by Russia or Prussia.[93] Talleyrand had indeed succeeded in formally dividing the seemingly mighty Allies, who had just conquered his country. "The coalition is dissolved, and dissolved for ever," Talleyrand wryly informed Louis XVIII.[94]

With the issue of alliances and divisions finally settled, the English Government, bent on resolving the outstanding territorial disputes once and for all, concentrated their energies on attacking Frederick William's Saxon claims. "I confess little kindness for the King of Saxony personally," Lord Liverpool informed Lord Castlereagh, "but I do not wish to see the system of totally annihilating ancient States extended beyond what is necessary,"[95] while admitting nevertheless that he would be happy to remove Murat from Naples "if it is just and practicable."[96] After further intense negotiations with Hardenberg and Nesselrode, the issues were finally resolved. Although Prussia withdrew her claim to all but a small portion of Saxony—in exchange for significant territorial compensation elsewhere—Russia proved more intractable, insisting on retaining her military occupation of Poland. Indeed, only two Polish concessions were wrenched from the Czar's unrelenting grip: Krakow was declared to be a free city (under Austrian supervision), and Thorn was ceded outright to Prussia.[97]

Naturally, the other most common topic of conversation at Vienna—apart from the charms of the ladies—was Napoleon, his past depredations, and his current situation on Elba. Nobody, it seemed, was at ease with his close proximity. Working from the Kaunitz Palace in Vienna, Talleyrand, in particular, did all in his power to keep the world's attention focused on his former chief. While admitting to Madame de Staël for instance that he "detested . . . Bonaparte's [past] successes . . . it was his principles that were shocking, and which must be expelled from Europe once and for all. . . ."[98] To ensure the very extinction of those militaristic principles, Talleyrand once again conspired against the dethroned Emperor. "Yes, we have removed him from the battlefields, *mais il est au bout de notre lorgnette*," he warned Schwarzenberg. "It is all because of Alexander that Napoleon is so close, on the Island of Elba," Castlereagh added. "If they had listened to us, Talleyrand and me, he would have been deported 16,000 leagues from here."[99] Indeed, as Talleyrand had emphasized back in February 1814, during the congress held at Châtillon-sur-Seine—"The Powers cannot take enough precautions in the treaty they will be preparing, if they do not wish to be put to fresh [military] expense next year. *Les mauvais restent toujours mauvais.*"*[100] With a man like Napoleon, one could never be wary enough. To be sure, while meeting in the rue Saint Florentin earlier in 1814, the Allies had discussed the possibility of sending him to the Azores, or even to Saint Helena, but Czar Alexander's moderation had won out.

Once this was established at Vienna, however, there was growing concern among the Allies that Bonaparte might yet make an unscheduled and most undesired reappearance. As seen earlier, there was talk of sending Algerian Corsairs, or even a special mission of elite troops from Corsica, for instance, to kidnap him, though in the final analysis, appar-

*"The bad ones never change their ways."

ently, it was a less rigid plan by Talleyrand and Castlereagh that was adopted. They would entice Napoleon from Elba—he thereby breaking his treaty obligations with the Allies—permitting them to seize him and take him to Saint Helena. To this end Talleyrand and Castlereagh allegedly dispatched an Austrian commissioner to Elba to urge the Emperor to escape and try to recapture France, convincing him that the French people were awaiting him with open hands.[101] It was the sort of thing that would have appealed to Napoleon's ego, as they well knew. How effective this was is not clear, but a few independent reports by Bonapartists in France, capped by those brought by Fleury de Chaboulon in February, did finally resolve Napoleon to act. Nor did he know how well informed Talleyrand and Castlereagh were of the secret military preparations under way at Elba. "I personally helped in the loading of 60 cases of cartridges on board the *Inconstant*," read one such report dated 21 February 1815. Nevertheless, this information either arrived too late or was not coordinated with French and British naval vessels in the Mediterranean, whom Napoleon's flotilla managed to elude with remarkable ease.[102]

The basic settlements had already been made when news of Napoleon's escape reached Vienna, as Lord Clancarty explained to Castlereagh on 11 March 1815. "We were at Court the night of the arrival of Burghersh's dispatch, containing the news of Buonaparte's flight; and though there was every attempt to conceal apprehension under the masque of unconcern, it was not difficult to perceive that fear was predominant in all—[including] the Imperial and Royal personages there assembled.[103] The overwhelming circumstance . . . hourly occurring in France," Clancarty admitted a few days later, left nothing but "black and bloody prospects" for the immediate future.[104]

Fortunately, with Allies still at the conference table, swift action was possible. On March 13 the seven Powers and France signed a declaration announcing that by fleeing Elba and breaking the Treaty of Fontainebleau, thereby "destroying the sole legal title to which his existence is attached . . . he has deprived himself of the protection of the laws, and had manifested in the face of the universe that they can have neither peace nor truce with him." They concluded by declaring him, therefore, "outside civil and social relations, and that as an enemy and disturber of the peace of the world, he has delivered himself over to public prosecution."[105] Twelve days later, Great Britain, Austria, Russia and Prussia signed another treaty at Vienna, binding themselves to mobilize their armies and prosecute a fresh war against Napoleon until he was "put absolutely outside the possibility of exciting troubles."[106] They had declared war on him; there would be no turning back.

With the announcement by Napoleon's new Foreign Minister, Armand de Caulaincourt, of the discovery of the secret treaty back on January 3, 1815, against Prussia and Russia, the single question Castlereagh was worrying about was whether the four major Powers would indeed be willing to reform their coalition after all, and work under a united standard to destroy Napoleon once and for all. Mastering their anger with and distaste for Britain, France and Austria, however, King Frederick William and Czar Alexander nevertheless immediately proclaimed the greater necessity of prosecuting the war, and ordered the mobilization of their forces. "If we are to undertake the job, we must leave nothing to chance," Castlereagh advised Wellington after signing the new treaty. "It must be done upon the largest scale . . . you must inundate France with force in all directions. If Bonaparte could turn the tide, there is no calculating upon his plan."[107] Finally, on April 3, Castlereagh was able to assure Wellington "that there is no hesitation on the part of the Prince Regent's Government . . . in prosecuting the war against Napoleon . . . and will embark heartily in the contest . . . for the salvation of Europe."[108] And Nesselrode quickly assured Castlereagh of Russian solidarity. *"C'est pour nous tous, le cas du* last shilling,* [of the] last drop of blood."[109]

"I have the honour to acquaint you," Lord Clancarty informed Stratford Canning, "that his Grace the Duke of Wellington set out this morning from Vienna, to take command of the army in the Low Countries."[110] The war was on, and fortunately for Europe, Talleyrand's machinations had failed after all.

*"We will spend every penny we have and fight to the last man, if needs be."

Chapter VI

"The Most Wretched of All Professions"

"Louis XVIII has partially formed a new government at Ghent, including Beugnot [Naval Ministry], Louis [Finance], Clarke [War] and Chateaubriand [Interior]. But who heads his police ministry?" asked one of Napoleon's officials. "Monsieur Fouché, no doubt," Napoleon smiled.

Bourrienne, April 1815

"I shall be appointed one of his [Napoleon's] ministers, and in three months' time, either he or I will no longer be there."

Fouché to Madame de Chastenay,
Mid-March 1815

"It is certainly the most wretched of all professions, that of Minister of the Police."

Talleyrand

If Napoleon found his reception at the Tuileries on the twentieth of March exhilarating, and crowded anterooms bustling with familiar faces, this was hardly the moment for festivities, and well before midnight he closeted himself with his advisers to take up the urgent task of appointing a new government. In the past, of course, the grandees and aspirants of Imperial Paris had fallen over one another, vying for the privilege of holding a ministerial post under Napoleon. But despite the outward excitement of the moment now, all was different. Not only were most of the principal politicians and generals not present—some in foreign countries, others secluded at their estates, the rest attached to Louis XVIII's court at Ghent (e.g., Berthier, Beugnot, Clarke, Jaucourt and Talleyrand)—but those "available" were either wary of associating themselves too closely with this new regime already denounced and threatened by the Allies at Vienna, or simply declined outright, bluntly, the offer of any official position. Nevertheless, there were still some familiar faces at the Tuileries now and decisions had to be made. To be sure, naming the Duc de Bassano, Hugues Maret, as Secretary of State, was easy enough, as was the appointment of the faithful Admiral Denis Decrès to his old post at the Naval Ministry. But if Martin-Michel-Charles Gaudin, Duc de Gaëte, took over the Ministry of Finance, François-Nicolas Mollien hesitated, however, before reluctantly accepting the Treasury. Pleading poor health, Mathieu-Louis Molé, for his part, declined the sensitive post of Justice Minister (preferring the nonpolitical and less lucrative office as Director of Ponts-et-Chaussées), the ever-obliging Jean-Jacques de Cambacérès stepping in temporarily to hold that fort. Marshal Davout likewise initially refused the War Ministry, though finally giving in under strong pressure from Napoleon. Whether he served the Emperor now in the field or as a member of the government, he had burned his bridges vis-à-vis the Bourbons and the Allies, and would never find employment again should the Empire fall a second time. The Duc de Vicence, General Armand de Caulaincourt, resisted the senior portfolio for Foreign Affairs, preferring to lead troops in the inevitable battles that lay before them. Although finally acquiescing to Napoleon's badgering twenty-four hours later, his pessimism remained unchanged. "This undertaking of the Emperor's is simply mad," he confessed privately to his old friend Pasquier after less than a week in office. "You and everyone else are by now familiar with the Allied Declaration against him promulgated at Vienna on the 13th. . . . Therefore he is going to be up against the whole of Europe. . . ,"[1] he sighed with resignation. And yet he had accepted this critical post, for which there was no one else better qualified, apart from Talleyrand—who of course was with King Louis—and perhaps Maret, who was already Secretary of State. No one else had such an intimate knowledge of foreign affairs and diplomatic channels, combined with a first-hand acquaintance with most of the leading international statesmen of the day. Clearly this was no office for a neophyte, and of course his own long-established contacts and standing with them would be of inestimable value. The choice of Antoine Chamans de LaValette naturally was an easy one for the Postal Ministry—his former post—after he had first declined the difficult Interior Ministry, recommending instead to Napoleon "a man well known during the Revolution."[2] To be sure, France was in turmoil; there were strong signs of a resurgence of former revolutionary slogans, views and threats. Thus, following his advice, Napoleon's choice fell upon none other than Lazare Carnot, who, when summoned to the Tuileries on the evening of 21 March, hesitated, and then accepted the Interior Ministry. "At a time like this, one could refuse him nothing," he admitted afterward.[3] Lastly came the controversial position of Police Minister, which after having been declined by the Duc de Rovigo, or René Savary, was offered surprisingly to the oft-proven disloyal Joseph Fouché himself. "Thus," summed up ex-Chancellor Pasquier, "the government was completed, but not without very considerable difficulty."[4]

Descendants of a long line of merchant ship captains from Nantes, the Fouchés were financially comfortable and Joseph Fouché received an excellent education at the Oratory of Jesus seminary of Nantes, later teaching physics and science there, at Arras and Juilly. But with the outbreak of the Revolution in 1789, other interests and values now emerged in the thirty-year-old schoolmaster, as he turned to the world of politics. Having been brought up in strict religious circles, he now openly and permanently turned against the Church, and most priests and Churchmen, apart from those affiliated with the Oratory. "It is they who have gradually been enslaving us more and more over the past 1,300 years," he proclaimed. And in so doing "this handful of liars"[5]—the priests—had led the people astray, away from all logic and reason, while causing irreparable damage to their political development. Surrounded by priests all his life, he felt stifled by them, their teachings, their restrictions and manipulations, and their haughty domineering unchallengeable authority. Religious orders should be disbanded, Church wealth and property seized for the use of the State and the people, urged the newly converted revolutionary and *Montagnard*,* Joseph Fouché.

*Political faction during the early Revolution; ruthless men supporting extreme actions and repression.

Henceforth, his carefully controlled, but long pent-up, anger against authority figures—the Church, the monarchy and his father—now burst the constraints of his past, and, indeed, even with the blessing of the authorities of the day. A deep-seated thirst for intrigue and power, abetted by a vein of subconscious cruelty and sadism, was revealed on 17 January 1793, as he voted for the execution of one authority figure, the King, while upholding the mass use of the guillotine and the political use of terror and destruction by which, in theory, to avenge the poor and the downtrodden. The aristocracy, the well-to-do, manufacturers, business-men, tax-farmers (or tax collectors), men like his father were in his eyes a plague on the nation. They had to be destroyed, or at least brought to their knees and humiliated in public. His reaction to aristocracy was typical of his almost schizophrenic view of things. He had been born a bourgeois, not a nobleman, and very much resented this inferior social position, though he was later raised to a peerage, and accepted by the aristocracy, the old aristocracy, almost as an equal, even as a friend.[6]

From the outset many were puzzled by this self-proclaimed atheist Fouché, who disliked loud political meetings, and neither drank to excess nor strayed from the hearth of his young wife and family. And yet his atheism and hatred of Christianity and the Catholic Church were profound and well known. In the autumn of 1793 French revolutionary forces captured a recalcitrant Lyons, the country's second largest city, which under a combi-nation of aristocratic and bourgeois leadership had rejected the Revolution. The Convention's notorious Committee of Public Safety ordered the extirpa-tion of religious and counter-revolutionary leaders and values, and Collot d'Herbois and Joseph Fouché—who had voted for the confiscation of all Church property throughout the realm—were called in to "de-Christianize" this city and restore order along with true revolutionary values. They were to do so with the cold, calm vengeance worthy of madmen.

"The City of Lyons is to be destroyed," read the orders of 17 October 1793, which Fouché received from the Committee of Public Safety, "Every building inhabited by the rich is to be demolished . . . A column will be raised on the ruins of the city, which shall commemorate for posterity the royalists' crimes and punishment," bearing the inscription— "Lyons waged war on freedom, now Lyons no longer stands."[7] But was it true, did the Revolutionary Government really expect this mass destruc-tion of a city and the execution of its two hundred thousand inhabitants? The previous Proconsul, Couthon, had in fact just been recalled because of his leniency, he having only executed a handful of aristocrats, while the unsentimental Fouché, for one, apparently had no qualms about car-rying out such instructions.

Fouché personally set about attacking the clergy, many hundreds strong, desecrating churches and convents, humiliating priests and nuns alike. Crucifixes, missals, statuary, religious relics and objects were thrown out by mobs, burned and smashed. Bishop Lamourette's residence was invaded and that gentleman ejected unceremoniously. His chasuble was attached to an ass, his miter strapped to the unfortunate animal's head, and a Bible and crucifix tied to its tail as it was led through the city to the howling approval of the city's population and that of a smiling onlooking Fouché,[8] pleased to find his orders executed so enthusiastically. But it was more than rank and privilege, it was wealth, greed and jealousy that were really at the heart of this government-approved scene of mayhem. It was the wealthy and educated in particular who were terrorized, literally night and day, as Fouché and his colleague in destruction, Collot, gave orders for continual sporadic searches for riches and incriminating documents[9] regarding plots against the government, or containing attacks against Jacobin ideals.

A malicious desire to wield power, especially over the formerly powerful, ruled the day. Fresh orders were given for thousands of house searches and the sequestration of their contents, extending to hats, jackets, trousers, shirts and shoes, after which the judges, professors, aristocrats, bankers and wealthy merchants were forced to parade in rags and sabots before the mobs. The have-nots were having their day; the French Revolution was a success. But the reign of terror was only just beginning as the orders were given to demolish the houses of this entire class of city leaders and some 15,000 men, women and children gleefully looted 1,600 of the city's most beautiful eighteenth-century residences,[10] which were attacked with picks, shovels, explosives and fire. Then came the Convention's orders for victims, for the traditional rites of purification worthy of the ancient Aztecs, demanded by "the people." "We are causing much impure blood to flow, but it is our duty to do so, it is for humanity's sake,"[11] Fouché and Collot assured Paris. They were good at following orders, any orders, all orders. *Kristallnacht*-type nightly roundups heightened fears and brought forth fresh batches of prisoners and executions. But when irate inhabitants in the rue Lafont complained that the gushing blood of guillotined victims was overflowing the gutters, causing a terrible stench and seeping into some houses, the execution ground was moved out of the city to Brotteaux field, along the Rhône (where Montgolfier's celebrated creation, the first hot-air balloon, had risen during a happier, more civilized hour). Firing squads and even mobs were loosed upon bound prisoners, as the blood-bath begun in late 1793 continued unabated into the new year and the early spring of 1794. At its most efficient, the guillotine killed only one person every two minutes, hence the reversion to firing squads and letting the good people of Lyons set upon prisoners with household weapons. (The meat cleaver, tested on the neck of a twenty-six-year-old nun[12] who persisted in her religious obstinacy to praise God, was a favorite.) "We must be fierce in order not to fear becoming weak and cruel. . . . Let us strike like lightning and let the very ashes of our enemies disappear with the approach of freedom,"[13] Citizen Fouché preached to the fanatic Pierre Chaumette in Paris. And his orders continued to be followed as sixty-four young men of good family were next experimented on with a more dramatic form of murder. Bound in a long, straggling row in Brotteaux field, cannon were brought up before them a few yards away and the victims were "shot." Those who were not dismembered and killed outright were attacked with sabres, bayonets, and, of course, the meat cleaver. All told, 1,905 men and women were thus "executed" on Government orders.[14] The Revolution was clearly making great strides forward, bringing democracy and civilization to the land. "Terror, salutary terror," Fouché proudly informed Paris, "is now the order of the day here."[15]

By 1815 the thinning reddish blond hair of the fifty-six-year-old Duc d'Otrante, Joseph Fouché, had started to turn gray, setting off his fair "bloodless" complexion and small, pale, watery-gray Breton eyes, in an angular face matched by an equally thin, angular, if tall and stooped, body. Although never physically strong, and prone to pulmonary weakness, like Napoleon he had never had much need of sleep and found little patience in having to sit through long dinners, however sumptuous. Nor, apparently, did any of the lovely women about him succeed with their charms and wile. On the other hand, an indefatigable worker, constitutionally incapable of remaining inactive, he was always the first to arrive at the dreaded Police Ministry in the Quai Voltaire overlooking the Seine, and the last to leave.

Surprisingly, Joseph Fouché was a sociable individual, albeit after his own languid, emotionless and haughty manner[16]—which nevertheless attracted and misled women—belying the real nature of this man who was ceaselessly ferreting out the secrets of all those about him. Although an interesting conversationalist and well-read (aided by a superb memory), in public he remained insensitive to nearly every emotion, a flicker of his eyelids perhaps occasionally betraying a fleeting reaction, only his constantly agitating hands revealing an impatient, tense inner self. Many tried but most failed in interpreting his expression at any given moment, his sphinx-like façade only occasionally permitting one to discern perhaps the faintest of caustic smiles. Victorine de Chastenay, who as a family friend, and like many women, thought she understood Fouché better than the others, felt that in addition to his "true talents" there was also something of "the charlatan"[17] about the man. To the more intimate of his friends, including Madame de Chastenay, he revealed an annoying sense of "superiority over all men, all social ranks, over every opinion and passion, giving one the impression that he alone was in full control and that everything was happening according to his calculations. . . ."[18] And what "a true Breton he was, invariably meddling in everything that was happening, even when it did not concern him."[19] But he always acted with "much dignity," she stressed sarcastically, irritated that "upon leaving his office one always felt that one had been given some confidential, top state secrets,"[20] only to discover subsequently that he had disclosed nothing significant. Nevertheless, she attributed to him "a certain nobility of character" and "an independent and real goodness,"[21] which, of course, the history of his own shameful past explicitly refuted, and which she apparently preferred to ignore. Nor could a stranger have realized in this quiet man attired in dark, simple clothes (in contrast to the heavily bemedalled imperial officials all round him) that he had before him the second-most-powerful official of the realm—a regicide, a mass killer, a relentless policeman and manipulator who had sent thousands to prison and torture cells, and, indeed, who invariably had everyone present under surveillance and their correspondence read, his notorious ministry casting a long menacing shadow across the Seine to the Tuileries itself.

If women tended to find him disarmingly quiet and attractive, men, as a rule, saw in him someone ugly and sinister. And yet this selfsame Fouché was extolled by friends and enemies, men and women alike, as the model husband and doting father. Unlike both Napoleon and Talleyrand, Fouché remained faithful to his wife, who was in her turn as "passionately in love and as jealous of him as if she were only twenty."[22] Following her death, he remained equally devoted to his second wife, Gabrielle de Castellane, his family always coming first. "You may perhaps have been told that they [his children] are spoilt, but they are so pleasant, the real delight of my life," he admitted to Madame de Custine.[23] Indeed, much to the amusement of visitors, "the children would run round the room wildly, and when someone chided them on their unruly behavior, Fouché would roar with laughter,"[24] like the humblest bourgeois; for the Duc d'Otrante, his hearth was the center of his universe. "Follow my example," he counseled his close friend, Gaillard; "dictate correspondence to your wife. It is so enjoyable being able to kiss your secretary," he beamed with a rare smile. "My only wish," he conceded "is to make life pleasant for my wife and children."[25] And to his sister, Alexandrine Broband, he gave the same advice regarding her daughters as he followed regarding his own: "Recommend that they deport themselves properly in public. Let them know that a woman's empire in society is established by the firmness of her principles, spirit and moral values, and that this empire is destroyed forever the day she forgets her duties."[26] (All very touching from the man who had ordered the execution of dozens of young women their age in Lyons many years before.) Given his general contempt for mankind, and the intensity of his feelings for the sacredness of his family, it was hardly surprising that few court officials were ever invited to share the intimacy of his hearth and a family dinner, or to watch him spoil his four children, including his favorite, his daughter Josephine (named after Napoleon's first wife, of whom he was a confidant), although the Archbishop of Paris, Cardinal du Belloy was one of those rare, privileged official guests.[27] What is more, the Duc d'Otrante rarely permitted his wife to appear at court receptions or public functions, nor did she wish to do so. Of course, men were almost always most vulnerable through their wives, and Fouché, as a policeman, was only too well aware of imperial mores and peccadillos and of their far-ranging consequences.

Napoleon for his part admired his Police Minister as a model paterfamilias, someone almost as unique in promiscuous Parisian society as an iceberg in the Seine. Nor, unlike Talleyrand, Decrès and just about everybody else, could Fouché be easily bribed. Not even at Lyons, as he was signing death warrants by the hundred, could he be deterred by his orders from the capital. And yet he did discreetly accept some huge sums and chatted easily with the mistresses of his colleagues and even arranged for a few of them to visit Napoleon himself from time to time. The contradictory aspects of his character continued to bewilder those about him. "One finds a mixture of everything [in Fouché], religion along with an impious character, virtue with vice, the royalist with the revolutionary . . . I have never found such a bewildering combination in anyone," Chateaubriand, for one, readily acknowledged.[28] And yet Fouché was not unaware of his own reputation and did everything he could to encourage it. And as Madelin put it, the Duc d'Otrante had "a strange and continuous need to mystify," veiled and confounded in the black turbulence of his "continuous duplicity."[29]

On the other hand, should anyone dare thwart Fouché's plans or professional work, he found himself in for a rude awakening, as many could attest, including Robespierre, Barras, Sieyès, Savary, Carnot, LaFayette, and even Talleyrand and Napoleon. And because of Fouché's total lack of emotion and "supreme unflappability," he could look upon events in his own life, even in adversity, with a remarkable calm. "I am by nature sanguine even when in official disgrace and during the most trying of times," he calmly agreed.[30] When Napoleon would on occasion challenge him to his face or fling back at him what others would only dare whisper behind his back, Fouché remained as unmoved as ever. "You voted for the death of Louis XVI, Monsieur le duc d'Otrante?" Napoleon now reminded him. "To be sure, Sire," he replied. "That was the first service I was able to render Your Majesty."[31] And Napoleon was simply delighted, for Fouché was—like Talleyrand—one of the very few men in the Empire who would never cringe before him. On another occasion the Emperor, who enjoyed taunting and baiting his courtiers, once mischievously asked Fouché: "What would you do if I were killed in battle or in an accident?" "Sire, I should assume as much power as I possibly could in order to avoid being overtaken by events," the Police Minister coolly replied,[32] and again Napoleon beamed with pleasure at this answer worthy of a fellow Corsican. Who else would have been so forthright? That Fouché also, like himself, openly despised a free press and parliamentary government only added to Napoleon's sense of assurance that he knew his man very well indeed, whereas in reality he had not a clue. Fouché once said to some disgruntled aristocratic friends— seemingly in jest—"When you have something bad to say about the Emperor and government, wait for my arrival. The spies will disappear when they see me there."[33] The story would get back to the Tuileries, Napoleon would smile all knowingly—ah, that Fouché—but in reality not understanding at all. "Duc d'Otrante, I ought to have you beheaded," Napoleon said to him shortly after discovering a fresh plot following his return in 1815. "I am not of the same opinion, Sire!" the phlegmatic Fouché parried, as Napoleon burst into laughter, but still not understanding his man.[34]

As the statesman and historian François Guizot later pointed out, "Fouché had maintained a certain bold independence ever since his days as proconsul [in Lyons] in 1793–1794"[35] and once decided on a policy "he sometimes revealed a stupefyingly bold and furious force of energy in executing it."[36] "I must be the complete master when I am placed in charge," said Fouché,[37] in order to achieve a program, then undertaking whatever that entailed. "Resorting to extremes is always unpleasant, to be sure, though a wise necessity in some instances all the same," he temporized.[38] He carried out his functions at the Quai Voltaire, working in the greatest detail, reading every line of every report sent to him by his agents and *"mouchards,"* or spies, while never losing sight of his overall objective. And for Police Minister Fouché, there was no such thing as "indecency or impossibility" in executing a policy or plan. "An unrivaled genius for intrigue,"[39] he was a frighteningly insensitive man when it came to human beings, which when combined with a most calculating methodology and singleness of purpose resulted in a police expertise feared and renowned throughout all of Europe.

One of the reasons why both friends and enemies could rarely fathom the man was because he was, like Napoleon himself, a supreme gambler and juggler, constantly weighing and juxtaposing opportunities and possibilities. "Under the government of the day, he was always the man of tomorrow," as Madelin so aptly put it,[40] already anticipating his role in the new government that would require his symbiotic presence. "One must have one's hand in many pies," Fouché frankly told Chancellor Pasquier,[41] and thus had to be ready to take advantage of every situation, whether it concerned fanatical Jacobins, a despotic Napoleon or a Bourbon monarch. In short, "this man's entire life was one long unbroken calculation, applied with an intensity of purpose which he never relaxed even for a moment."[42]

In order to facilitate his policy of maintaining himself in office by clinging to the leader of the moment, he made friends with various influential groups, most of them in sharp political conflict with one another, he alone among them enough of an actor to transcend all social and ideological barriers. Thus he could be found in the republican salon of Germaine de Staël, chatting with Benjamin Constant and Gilbert de LaFayette, or elsewhere with Grégoire, Sieyès, Carnot, Tallien and Méhée, or among old Jacobins such as Thibaudeau, Boulay and Réal. He would mix with friends of the Oratorian fraternity, including Daunou, Gaillard, Perrier, Malout, Jay, Chênedollé and Pardessus, or be found socializing in the aristocratic bastions of Bourbon legitimacy in the Faubourg Saint-German, including those of Princesse de Vaudémont, Marquise de Custine, René de Chateaubriand, the Comtesse de Narbonne, the Duchess de Duras, Charles de Calonne, Mathieu de Montmorency, Alexis de Noailles, and the Duc de Guignes, and of course he could be seen most mornings riding in the Bois de Boulogne with none other than Adrien de Montmorency.[43] The Duc d'Otrante was the only member of Napoleon's regime in 1815 to be able to bridge all these social circles, enough of a political chameleon to enable him to be accepted as a member of each. Even Napoleon marveled at this astonishing coup, Fouché's "chef d'oeuvre," Madelin called it. In fact, the Fouché who had ordered the execution of dozens of aristocrats at Lyons, including that of a harmless seventy-five-year-old lady, the Comtesse Albanette de Cessieux, was at heart a snob—his second wife was an aristocrat—who felt more at ease in the Faubourg Saint-Germain than in the circles of imperial glitter. And Napoleon continued to accept the Police Minister's explanation that by mixing with everyone, he was winning over new friends while gaining access to opinions and information which might otherwise not be readily available to the Tuileries.

On the other hand, unlike Napoleon, who though possessing a great many faults, did at least have very specific ideas and programs for France (educational changes, financial, legal, administrative), Fouché to the contrary had little in mind and certainly no master plan to replace everything else proposed. Basically a destroyer, a policeman, a superspy . . . not a creator, he was only good at executing the policies handed down to him, at least when he felt inclined to do so, as for instance earlier when he had executed the Convention's de-Christianization policy at Lyons by harassing church officials, stripping priests of their authority and work, and desecrating the city's churches. Guizot was struck by the strange qualities of the man, by his "hardy, ironic and cynical indifference, indeed phlegmatic attitude, applied in his unsated quest for embroilment, his obstinacy in doing everything possible to succeed—not for any particular goal—but rather according to the fleeting opportunity of the moment."[44] Here the perspicacious Guizot alone, of all Fouché's critics over the decades, finally captured and understood the spirit and essence of the man: Fouché had to plot and plan, but could not create, and thus by temperament he could never have led a government successfully. If he was in part imbued with an understanding of some of the requirements for effective government, he just as often undermined those very elements. He had no conception of "fidelity" to any one political leader, party, government or principle, but rather was "prepared to serve all governments, and then to betray them,"[45] as indeed he did in the case of the Convention, the Directory, the Consulate, the Empire and finally the restored Bourbon monarchy.

Apart from the well-being of his family, and his constitutional necessity of remaining in office and of manipulating people, the only other real objective the Duc d'Otrante adhered to with extraordinary pertinacity was wealth. "Let us scorn vile gold and silver, and leave these monarchical gods in the filth where they belong,"[46] Proconsul Fouché had proclaimed repeatedly at Nevers, Moulins and Lyons some twenty years earlier as he ordered private wealth confiscated and magnificent houses and mansions looted and destroyed. And yet, this very Revolutionary and self-righteous patriot Fouché later expended enormous effort in building up his own wealth—his picture galleries, stunning collections of objets d'art and gems, the best silver plate, the finest carriages and resplendent mansions. If acclaim and public honors made little impact on him, the gold and silver that he had found so "vile" a few years earlier now became his gods, indeed the primary ones in his pantheon.

And he succeeded admirably, with a total income of 223,000 francs from all official sources at the height of his career (when a marshal earned 100,000 a year) as Police Minister, exclusive of income from bribes, enormous "gifts" by Napoleon, from his private investments on the stock exchange (often based on "insider's" information, such as prior knowledge of French victories at Austerlitz and Wagram, before the results were known to the public), not to mention the income from his vast estates. A good friend of millionaire financiers Ouvrard, Hingerlot and Perrégaux, Fouché invested wisely and reaped fortune after fortune. He has also been called "the greatest property owner" in France,[47] for, in addition to his two mansions in Paris (one of which was an official residence), he owned two prestigious ones beyond the capital—Pont Carré and Ferrières, two entire provincial parishes, as well as dozens of farms and houses in the south, not to mention large German and Italian estates. To these had to be added family sugar and indigo plantations in Santo Domingo.[48] Joseph Fouché owed at least ninety-five percent of this vast wealth—which was ultimately estimated conservatively at 15,000,000 francs in value—directly or indirectly to Napoleon Bonaparte and his service as police minister.[49]

"Bonaparte does not like me," Fouché admitted to Victorine de Chastenay, "and he knows that I do not like him . . ."[50] and this mutual antipathy extended to both Lucien and Joseph Bonaparte as well. Nevertheless Fouché and Napoleon apparently felt the other to be necessary in the scheme of things, at least for the moment. Fouché certainly proved to be the best police administrator in French history, whose vast network of spies—in the Tuileries (even Napoleon's letters were intercepted), in all the ministries, all the major salons, in every prefecture and in the major European capitals as well—proved stupendous and deadly. But Fouché always considered himself much more than a policeman: he was a national statesman, or at least wanted to be. He advised Napoleon—

sometimes uninvited—on all major national and many international undertakings. He enjoined Napoleon time and again to make peace in Europe and with England in particular, warning him equally against the Spanish invasion and that of Russia.

Thus as a policeman and counselor, in certain respects Joseph Fouché was an efficient and effective official, but all this was negated in Napoleon's eyes by the Police Minister's two great disabling qualities. He was a devious, dishonest minister and "a magnificent plotter," and therefore, not being in a position to trust him, Napoleon found that he had to keep the country's first policeman under subtle surveillance. Each thought he was more clever, talented and powerful than the other, which led to a continued clash of wills. And Fouché, for his part, never groveled before the great man, an attitude he also had in common with Talleyrand. But Fouché was also a potential threat because of his intimate knowledge of too many scandalous family secrets. In fact, over the years he had personally witnessed a few dozen calamitous confrontations between Napoleon and his brothers and sisters—e.g., regarding Jérôme's astonishing spending sprees and Lucien's corruption and plotting—and was also in possession of complete files on the rest of the Bonapartes, including the embarrassingly exact and long list of Pauline's lovers, although Napoleon's occasional searches for them proved fruitless. As long as the Emperor kept Fouché employed, and provided him with a munificent annual income—for nothing less would suffice—he had some control over the man, or so he hoped. The Bonaparte family indiscretions would remain carefully concealed, but if Fouché were dismissed outright, what havoc, what utter embarrassment, the man could wreak. Napoleon, for one, knew only too well just how much dirty linen had been swept out of sight, enough to make him the laughingstock of Europe, and if there was one thing he feared above all, it was public humiliation!

Despite the threat posed by the presence (or absence) of Fouché, Napoleon apparently continued to feel that he alone was master of the men and the situation, and able to cope with whatever happened. But when word of Fouché's various intrigues reached him, he fumed with rage, calling the Police Minister on the carpet. But these very intrigues were mystifying. To be sure, in some instances a rational explanation could be found, as when Fouché "negotiated" secretly with the Austrians, Russians or British, sending out peace feelers in an attempt to bring the state of seemingly incessant warfare to a close. But at other times he was plotting, it would seem, with the primary purpose of overthrowing Napoleon, though without having anyone with whom to replace him, or even with a suitable program of his own. And if later Fouché decided to accept a Louis XVIII in lieu of a Napoleon I, he was in turn soon plotting to overthrow that monarch for "someone else." In effect, he was constantly putting both career and life in jeopardy, simply for the pleasure of displaying the power he could wield and plots he could weave. Constitutionally, something in him had constantly to challenge authority and the powers that be, to fly in the face of great dangers, to defy the world and show one and all that *he*, Joseph Fouché, was powerful enough to threaten, to undermine, to bring down any individual in the realm . . . *any*! Biographer Stefan Zweig rightly likened Fouché unto a blind mole, a little animal constantly burrowing out of sight, beneath the surface, undermining everything around him.

And twice Napoleon acted against him, unmasking his duplicity and intrigues, in 1802 and 1810. Fouché had done everything in his power to prevent Napoleon from being named Consul for life, successfully plotting with key senators, and even Josephine (who now feared divorce once Napoleon—without heirs—achieved this office), the Senate ultimately rejecting Napoleon's demand, however, offering him instead a consulship for a mere six years. Overruling the Senate and successfully launching a national plebescite to approve his Consulship for life, Napoleon decided to dismiss the meddlesome Fouché, which he then did by suppressing the Police Ministry itself.[51] And although Fouché was reinstated with the creation of the Empire in 1804, his pro-Jacobin past was not forgotten, nor allegations that he had aided royalist Georges Cadoudal and Generals Moreau and Pichegru in their conspiracy to assassinate Napoleon in 1803. Cadoudal and Pichegru were condemned to death, of course, while Moreau, the great victor of the battle of Hohenlinden against the Austrians (which in turn resulted in the favorable Treaty of Lunéville) was exiled. Fouché, as usual, had carefully covered his own tracks in the affair.[52] By 1810 an embittered Napoleon had once again accumulated fresh evidence of Police Minister Fouché's contrary views and actions, purporting to undermine Napoleon and bring down the Empire. When, for instance, Talleyrand was dismissed as Foreign Minister in 1807, he had begun plotting with Police Minister Fouché to find a successor to rule the country. Matters dragged on interminably, however, and it was only in 1810 that the Emperor discovered that for the past year Fouché had been negotiating secretly with the British government to achieve this dénouement. Napoleon dismissed him for a second, final time while taking the precaution, however, of exiling him far from France, by appointing him to a variety of lesser diplomatic posts, concluding as Governor-General of Illyria at Trieste. As for Fouché, he was willing to bide his time.

With the downfall of the Empire in April 1814, the Duc d'Otrante, now back in France, endeavored to find a snug royalist berth in the new Bourbon government. But although he had remarkably powerful supporters in official circles, the King, his family—except his brother, Comte d'Artois—and most of their counselors at this time, advised strongly and successfully against the ex-regicide, ex-Jacobin, ex-Police Minister, and for keeping him at arm's length. Fouché thus began burrowing again, unseen, indirectly, but always toward his objective, now mainly by insinuating himself into the good graces of highly placed aristocratic ladies, who proved more vulnerable to his charms, it would seem, and, in turn, ultimately winning over their husbands, brothers and friends, as in the case of Madame de Vaudémont and the Montmorencys. "The entire faubourg swears by no one but M. Fouché," a bemusedly flummoxed Talleyrand related to Etienne Pasquier. "Every letter and person reaching the King and the Princes for the past fortnight have spoken only of him and of the great services he has rendered to the royal cause."[53] "After all, in the final analysis, who are the real enemies of the royal family?" Bailli de Crussot asked Jacques Beugnot. "The Jacobins, and frankly, he [Fouché] holds them in the palm of his hand. Once he is on the King's side, we shall all finally be able to sleep at night. We of the Faubourg Saint-Germain are getting old, my dear Beugnot, we have all been through a great deal. We need some rest."[54] Clearly Fouché was the man to ensure such rest.

And with such support behind him, the Duc d'Otrante already envisaged himself a royalist minister, perhaps even foreign minister. Thus he wrote to Czar Alexander, he wrote to British officials and to Louis XVIII and his adviser, the Comte de Blacas, explaining to each what had to be done in order to consolidate the Bourbons on the throne in a country where the King was still utterly unknown by the masses. Between June and September 1814, Fouché met with Blacas, Montesquiou and the King's brother, Comte d'Artois, counseling the introduction of greater democracy in France—though Fouché personally had no liking for this concept—and "opening the arena of parliamentary legislative debates,"[55] as a sop to public opinion, for the days of sheer despotic rule were over. Ironically, the infamous proconsul of Lyons, who had ordered the confiscation of the wealth of the ruling class, now advised the King to request that "the Chamber of Peers and Chamber of Deputies establish a national tax with which to indemnify the unfortunate and the indigent people [who had suffered losses of property and wealth during the Revolution], so worthy of being assisted by an heroic nation." He specially referred to the "multitude of Frenchmen devoted to the Bourbons throughout all their misfortunates," viz. those very royalist and upper-middle classes whom Fouché had personally terrorized, despoiled and forced to flee the country twenty years earlier. All this by the same Fouché, who at Nantes in 1794 had demanded harsh measures against émigrés, echoed later in 1799, following Napoleon's successful coup.[56] To the royalists he pleaded the royalist cause, to the Republicans, he complained of royalist abuse, and to both sides he denounced Napoleonic despotism. Fouché was as unprincipled and supple as Machiavelli himself.

It is ironic that throughout this period, in 1814, it was Fouché's old foe, Talleyrand, who appeared everywhere with him now, arm in arm, supporting his cause, abetted by Mesdames de Custine and de Vaudémont.[57] To anyone who would listen, Fouché advocated the return of Belgium to Austria, while maintaining Murat on his Neapolitan throne, where he could be of use. But if Louis XVIII's government proved unsuccessful, Fouché guardedly mooted the possibility of *its* replacement. He opposed the candidature of both Napoleon and the Duc d'Orléans, he said, but accepted the idea of a Bonaparte regency for Napoleon's baby son, Napoleon II. "If Napoleon were mounted on an ass, and led by a peasant, he would be accepted by everyone," he nevertheless acknowledged caustically.[58] Precautions therefore had to be taken. But at this stage Fouché still had the King's ear, however indirectly, warning the monarch that "if within a few months our coasts are still left so unguarded, spring will bring Bonaparte along with the swallows and violets."[59]

But despite everything he did, Fouché's offer to join the government was rejected, that is until the last minute, in March 1815, following news of Napoleon's return to France. The King, by then in desperate straits, had sent the Comte d'Artois to negotiate with the former police official at the residence of Chancellor Dambray,[60] though the practical Fouché instead now chose to bide his time in order to open negotiations for a place with Napoleon, as he caustically commented to the Marchioness de Custine on 9 March (1815)—"I admire the patience of the monarch, who has resigned himself to closing his eyes to the reality of the situation."[61] Finally on 14 March, with Napoleon now closing in quickly on the capital, Chancellor Dambray had suggested another urgent meeting, this time at Fouché's residence in the rue Cerutti, when he asked him to form his own government as Prime Minister.[62] And again Fouché rejected the impossible, while boasting to Victorine de Chastenay that Napoleon would soon be sending for him, when "I shall be appointed one of his ministers," and then adding with frightening accuracy, "and within three months' time, either he or I will no longer be there."[63]

The next day, 15 March, Fouché was summoned to yet another meeting, this time at 10 P.M. at the mansion of Princesse de Vaudémont, where the Comte d'Artois personally pleaded with him on behalf of the King to assume the office of Prime Minister, Fouché declining with the parting words: "My Lord, you must save the King. I shall save the monarchy."[64] In reality, of course, Fouché had no intention of "saving" the Bourbons, and in fact was already in secret communication with several prominent Bonapartists, to prepare a place for himself with the new government in the event Napoleon did indeed succeed in wresting the crown from the King.

With news of d'Artois's failure that night, the King summoned Director of Police André, who in turn summoned his new Prefect of Police, Napoleon's former secretary and ambassador—previously dismissed from his imperial post for financial irregularities—Louis Bourrienne. Fouché refused to support the King, then he must be conspiring against him, and hence must be arrested, along with Davout, Savary, LaValette, Maret and other former high imperial officers.[65] The following morning the police came to the rue Cerutti to execute the Prefect's orders. But through a ruse, the former Police Minister managed to escape by the skin of his teeth through a door in the rear garden leading into the property of his friend and neighbor, Queen Hortense.[66] He remained in hiding until Napoleon's arrival on the twentieth, as the last of Louis XVIII's court and police fled the city.

"Fouché! Let Monsieur Fouché pass!" was the exclamation of astonishment passing from anteroom to anteroom of the Tuileries[67] just before midnight on 20 March, as the Duc d'Otrante made his way to the reception room where he had been informed by one of his minions that Napoleon was now waiting for him. In fact, Napoleon had been most indignant after his arrival in Paris, to hear everyone round him *praising* Fouché, declaring the immediate necessity of his presence in any new government. It was quite extraordinary: Barère, Benjamin Constant, Chancellor Pasquier, the Duc de Bassano, Réal, Marshal Davout, Regnault—almost every known enemy of the police official was, in this dramatic hour of trial, urging Napoleon to reconsider, to put aside his numerous past grievances against this slippery, disloyal Fouché, and to give him back his old portfolio, where his talents could be put to good use. Indeed, it almost seemed stage-managed, a melodrama, Fouché the fugitive, dodging the King's police, only safely reappearing thanks to Napoleon's timely arrival. For the first time in his life, Joseph Fouché emerged publicly smiling, nodding, the hero of the hour! Fortunately for him at this moment Napoleon was most unhappy with his last Police Minister, Savary (Duc de Rovigo) even more than he was with Fouché.

And Fouché had the advantage now of excellent contacts with Talleyrand in Ghent and Metternich in Vienna, and indeed with all the important leaders of French society—former Jacobins, revolutionaries, liberals, even royalist circles—whose immediate support Napoleon needed if he were to maintain order and ensure national and international acceptance and peace. Fouché alone could accomplish this. Nor was there another candidate capable of reorganizing, restoring the old system of administration, anyone who had the loyalty of the key police and prefectorial officials, most of them already in place. And although Napoleon could not overlook the past treachery of Fouché, by the same token he could not overlook the sound advice this same Fouché had given him in the past.* There were few others around the Emperor who could boast an equal record. That all Napoleon's supporters now rallied around the hated Fouché was probably instrumental in finally swaying the Emperor, who offered him his old post at the Police Ministry in the Quai Voltaire—just as Fouché had predicted earlier—although he would have preferred the Foreign Ministry.[68] But Napoleon's initial reactions to Fouché were correct and this was to prove a catastrophic decision.

In addition to forming a new Police Ministry forthwith,[69] Napoleon instructed Fouché to establish immediate contacts with London, via Mr. Marshall, the senior British representative in Paris, to see whether or not he could begin negotiations for a settlement to defuse the tense international situation caused by his coup d'état. "The Emperor," Fouché instructed Marshall on the twenty-first, "has arrived in Paris to the acclamation of the entire population . . . convinced that the Bourbons did not suit the new France and that the Emperor alone could represent and unite all the various interests of the nation while guaranteeing the rights and situations born of the Revolution . . . The Emperor," he concluded, "was prepared to receive any proposition from the English government honorable to both countries, which would ensure a solid and lasting peace,"[70] while quietly confiding to ex-Chancellor Pasquier that, "that man has not altered one bit and has returned as despotic, as set on conquest . . . in fact, as crazy as ever," and as a result, "all of Europe is going to hurl itself at him . . . and within four months' time, he will be finished."[71] In any event, the allies—Great Britain included—who had already declared Napoleon a "disturber of the peace" and "outlaw," were not taken in by such a ruse now by a man whose word in the past

---

*Especially in international affairs: to make peace with England, not to marry an Austrian, not to break with Czar Alexander and certainly not to invade Russia or overcommit himself in Spain.

had proven utterly worthless. Accordingly, on 25 March they signed a new treaty of alliance, forming a seventh military coalition, with the intention of crushing Napoleon and the French people once and for all, though they still had no one with whom to replace him and certainly were, if anything, most disinclined to restore the uncooperative and feeble Bourbons yet again.

Meanwhile in the seven new police districts into which the country was divided, now administered by two Inspecteurs Généreaux de la Police, Pasques et Foudras,* an older and somewhat altered Fouché presented yet another face to history, in the knowledge that all his actions were now under the closest scrutiny by Louis XVIII and the Allies, as he introduced an enlightened policy for the guidance of the national police—one, moreover, intended purely for public consumption. "Police surveillance is . . not to exceed the requirements of public or personal safety," he informed the country's police on 31 March, "nor to carry out detailed surveillance of individuals just for the sake of collecting data (i.e., without a specific object or complaint in mind), nor to hinder the actions and deny the civil rights of individuals through a system of harsh police intervention and practices otherwise unauthorized by law."[72] In brief, in theory the new liberal empire was to "abandon the former unrelenting police policies of taking direct action against individuals, without sufficient and proper reason or suspicion, and avoiding the usual excitement and turbulence resulting from threats, torments and harassment— and instead guarantee and respect citizens' rights." Hereafter, the nation's prefects and police were "to adhere to the restrictions and limits of a new liberal and positive police policy" that would be operational "everywhere under all circumstances, protecting and looking after the happiness of the people, ensuring their right to work and repose."[73] It was crass showcase balderdash intended to allay fears and to whitewash Fouché's role in Napoleon's government (in the eyes of the Allies) and to drive home the point, the Police Minister had this new policy published in the *Moniteur* on 4 April (1815), while nevertheless secretly placing a group of royalist "friends" under *"la surveillance de la haute police."*

In addition, Napoleon also ended State censorship of newspapers, though Fouché instead managed to assign one agent or, rather, editor to each paper to carry out "autocensorship" from within each periodical.[74] Indeed, by careful manipulation of the new censorship laws, Fouché was able to arrange for newspapers to publish *pro-royalist propaganda*, by quoting from Chateaubriand's official Bourbon newssheet at Ghent, the

*Foudras was the inspector who had attempted to arrest Fouché on March 16.

new *Gazette Universelle*, such as fresh decrees by Louis XVIII ordering the people of France to oppose Napoleon in every way possible, e.g., by refusing to pay taxes and serve in the army, while another decree officially disbanded the existing French army immediately.[75] Napoleon objected to the appearance of these articles, but apparently lacked the will and confidence of the days of yore, now for the first time permitting himself instead to be manipulated by the Police Minister. Times had indeed changed.

Nevertheless, the energetic Fouché had in practice not changed *his* ways much or let up, as his new *"police libérale"* quietly intercepted all correspondence once again, private and official, to and from every member of the Bonaparte family, including Napoleon, as well as that of his ministers and high officials. To the last, Fouché remained Stefan Zweig's mole, bent on intrigue and undermining all his opponents. He went so far as to inform the nation's eighty-six prefects—in correspondence *not* published in the *Moniteur*—that they were quietly to forget several of Napoleon's recent decrees and orders, in particular those relating to the arrest of several royalist supporters and officials and the sequestration of their property—including Ferrand, Dambray, André, Séguier, Jaucourt, Montesquiou, Vitrolles and Clarke to mention a few. And for the most part it was Fouché, not Napoleon, who was obeyed, only Vitrolles finally being arrested and imprisoned. But some of Fouché's other surreptitious activities were soon to come to light with an éclat reminiscent of 1810 all over again.

Chapter VII

A Land in Turmoil

"*I have just created the constitutional monarchy. Men are powerless to arrange the destinies of nations; only institutions can guarantee that.*"

Napoleon

"*I do not want to be King of a jacquerie. Revolution is one of the worst afflictions of mankind.*"

Napoleon

"*France wonders what has become of the Emperor's firm hand, that hand which she needs in order to control Europe.*"

Napoleon

"*Every day has its problems, every situation its law, to each his own nature. As for me, clearly I am no angel.*"

Napoleon

"*Napoleon had said: the Empire, it's the Revolution. He had also said: the Empire, it's peace. He refused to reintroduce the Revolution and was incapable of maintaining the peace.*"

Henri Houssaye, 1815

"There is no word so prostituted as 'patriotism.' It is part of the base coinage of controversy. . . . It urges to heroism, to self-sacrifice, to assassination, and to incendiarism. It rebuilt Jerusalem and burned Moscow; it stabbed Marat, and put his bones in the Pantheon. It was the watchword of the Reign of Terror, and the motto of the guillotine. It raises statues to the people whom it lodges in dungeons. It patronises almost every crime and every virtue in history."

Lord Rosebery (1882)

"Fouché . . . if he wanted to, and more importantly, if he could, destroy Bonaparte now, no doubt would do so without hesitation, because he would then find himself the most powerful man in France."

Pozzo di Borgo to Foreign Minister Nesselrode, 11–23 May 1815

With the Allied Powers' joint declaration of 13 March 1815, deploring the return, and outlawing, of Napoleon Bonaparte, followed on 25 March by their formation of the seventh coalition to bring down the freshly reconstituted French Empire,[1] any real hope that Napoleon or his Foreign Minister, Armand de Caulaincourt, may have had about negotiating a peaceful solution for their coup d'état was destroyed. But in any event, whether it was to be war or peace, Napoleon's first objective was to reorganize the country and consolidate his hold, before either the revolutionary Jacobin Left could act, repeating the bloodshed and political convulsions of the early 1790s, or the royalist Right initiated a full-scale civil war to regain the Bourbon throne.

"I wish to be less the sovereign of France and more the first of her citizens," Napoleon had declared at Lyons. "I am a product of the Revolution . . . [and] have come to free the French people from the enslavement in which the priests and nobles wanted to entrap them . . . I shall hang the lot of them!"[2] If in fact the Church proved no very serious threat to his return, and like any good politician, Napoleon was simply manipulating the current powerful anticlerical sentiment throughout the country, he did intend to act immediately against the still influential royalist element. On 22 March he ordered all royalists to leave the French capital and remain at least ninety miles from it, while issuing warrants for the arrest of thirteen pro-Bourbon royalists including, Talleyrand, Marmont, Montesquiou, La Rochefoucauld, Lynch, Bourrienne, Bellart, Beurnonville, Jaucourt and Dalberg,[3] and the general sequestration of royalist properties. "They want the men whom I have covered with wealth and benefits to be used to conspire against me," Napoleon protested. "That cannot be, that will not be!"[4] On the other hand, despite his fire-breathing revolutionary-like proclamations before reaching Paris, he had no intention of introducing another reign of terror, of unleashing the populace "to lynch them."

Indeed, what Napoleon deeply feared instead—apart from any military attack by the Allies—was the threat of the French masses thirsting for blood. That he had two former revolutionaries with the best credentials now on his side—Fouché and Carnot—was hardly an accident. He needed every influential person available to keep this potential threat in check. The Left had acted immediately against Napoleon's proclamation calling for a new Liberal Empire; indeed, most Jacobins complained only of his leniency with aristocrats.[5] "Abandon your unsettling moderation. How can you claim to maintain peace and calm when you protect the enemies from within! They must be extirpated from our breast like a cankerous wound!"[6] "The insolent nobles are calling out to the foreign armies to come and put us in chains, and cut our throats. . . ." Banish them "and let's seize their property . . . Lynch the aristocrats!"[7] "If we are not careful," warned one anxious prefect, "we shall see the same bloody scenes of [17]92 all over again."[5] "I am fearful of the upheaval threatening us, ready as it is to vomit forth terror and proscription over France yet again,"[8] an uneasy Comte de Molé confided to Napoleon, "I find the hatred of priests and nobles as widespread and as violent today as it was at the outset of the Revolution. It is whipped up to a fury!"[9] Others, however, felt Napoleon could ill afford to alienate himself from the revolutionary Left. "The use of violence was his best bet," Benjamin Constant believed, in securing the Empire. "It is by rejecting these powerful and frightening auxiliaries that the imperial government was creating dangers for itself," he insisted.[10] Napoleon needed every bit of support he could gain. On the other hand, Madame de Staël felt that the very appearance of "this burly bear," of Napoleon himself, aroused terror in the people, inviting their brutal reaction. And therefore "it was sheer folly . . . the moment we accepted Bonaparte, a return to dictatorship was inevitable. . . ."[11] But of course in reality Napoleon feared the people's fury as much as did the fair Germaine de Staël herself. Revolution—or the use of revolutionary threats and methods—was the last thing the Emperor wanted, as he afterward recalled. "The Empire had become legitimate. A regular government cannot employ the same ferocity or odious acts as a mob. I had no intention of becoming a King of the jacquerie. A revolution," said this one-time supporter of Robespierre, "is one of the worst afflictions on mankind."[12]

But of course times had changed and Napoleon could no longer rule as he had done in the past, as an unchallenged or unchallengeable military dictator, like Madame de Staël's "burly bear." Therefore, upon overthrowing King Louis's legitimate government in March 1815, he attempted to tread a very narrow path, accepting some popular concessions to a nominally more democratic form of society, while retaining the real essentials of power in his own hands. At the same time he had no intention of giving up a monarchical-style society and aristocratic titles—old or new. Distinctions and privileges would remain firmly in place, despite the protests of Lazare Carnot, who was shortly to find himself raised to a peerage! Slavery—earlier abolished by the Revolution but reintroduced by Napoleon and upheld steadfastly by Louis XVIII—was now abolished again, as a sop to the Allies, and to Great Britain in particular.[13] Press censorship, too, was abolished,[14] at least in theory, and new newspapers—including those in opposition—appeared or were permitted to reappear, e.g.: the *Gazette de France, Le Journal Général, Feuille du Jour, Journal de Paris*, the *Nain Jaune*, the *Journal des Débats*. Although Police Minister Fouché did maintain some control over these newspapers, his hand was light and subtle. Thus, for instance, King Louis's decrees issued at Ghent were published in them, and some direct criticism of Napoleon himself allowed as well, which admittedly did not sit well with devoted Bonapartists, and exasperated General Hugo for one—the father of the poet and novelist—"Is it possible to so horribly outrage the great man!"[15] he protested to War Minister Davout about one particularly offensive article. And yet when the *Censeur des Censeurs* of Auguste Comte publicly denied Napoleon's newly assumed imperial rights, declaring his regime to be merely provisional, it was seized and closed down—just a fortnight after the announcement of the ending of such government interference.[16] Meanwhile, however, one or two clandestine royalist papers, including the *Journal de Lys*, continued untouched, calling Napoleon "the monster" and his followers, "the rabble." Other, more blatant attacks appeared in the guise of hundreds of anonymous pamphlets, referring to "the great man" as "the thief who stole Louis XVIII's throne," as "a common criminal" and as "that wretched juggler."[17] On the other hand, those on the left accused Napoleon of "having forgotten the Revolution," while a minority supported him. "We do not just love the Emperor, we adore him,"[18] read one excessive piece. The vast majority, however, were neither pro-royalist nor Bonapartist, but rather for a more liberal, parliamentary democracy.

Greatly to his regret now, much earlier Napoleon had promised that electoral colleges would be convened in Paris in May "in order to modify our constitutions according to the interests and will of the nation."[19] At first he thought it would make a colorful, if harmless entertainment— "Just imagine, thirty thousand people gathered in the Champs de Mars. What a spectacle!" he had beamed to Comte de Molé at the thought of those delegates from all over France gathering to rewrite the nation's constitution.[20] It would capture the imagination of the whole country as well. Such an open-air gathering of legislators had never before been seen, certainly not on such a grand scale. It was precisely the sort of pageantry that appealed to Napoleon, who liked larger-than-life events, worthy of an artist's largest canvas—he fully appreciating its magnetic attraction for and impact on the French people. No one now could deny his earnestness in promulgating his new "Liberal Empire," he thought. The harsh decrees of the military dictator of yore, were, he insisted, a thing of the past, replaced by his recognition of the will of the French people and of their rights to a reasonable portion of happiness. Even some of his most outspoken opponents who had denounced Napoleon just days before his arrival in Paris, now praised the idea. On 19 March, for example, Benjamin Constant had firmly declared in the *Journal de Paris*: "I have seen that freedom was possible under the monarchy and I have seen the King rally the nation." Therefore he, Constant, could never give his allegiance to the Napoleon who was at that hour threatening the Bourbon capital. "I shall not change and become a wretched turncoat, going about with hat in hand, from one regime to another, covering such infamy by sophisms, babbling profane words simply in order to provide a secure, if shameful, existence for myself."[21] And following this bold and magnificent declaration in a major Parisian daily, Constant told Juliette Récamier privately: "Along with Marmont, Chateaubriand and Laîné, I am now certainly one of the four most compromised men in the whole of France. If we [the Bourbon party] don't win, in another week I shall most certainly be outlawed [by Napoleon] or else a fugitive." He then concluded, "I would rather perish than fall into his [Napoleon's] hands."[22]

But upon the arrival of Joseph Bonaparte at the capital a few days later, one of the first tasks assigned him by Napoleon was to win over the outspoken, if whimsical, liberal royalist, Constant, which resulted in an invitation—accepted by Constant—to the Tuileries.[23]

After his first reluctant meeting with the Emperor on 4 April, the outspoken Constant changed his tune, much to the astonishment and consternation of Juliette Récamier: "What an amazing man he is," Constant exclaimed. "Tomorrow I am to bring him an outline for a new constitution!"[24] It was one of the most startling political conversions in French history, and apparently Constant was willing to offer his "sophisms" and "profane words" to the entire world by way of explanation of his extraordinary behavior, and to accept "a shameful existence" and the sobriquet of "turncoat." When news of Constant's inconstancy and apostasy reached Ghent, his old friend Chateaubriand commented: "These weaknesses of a superior man are the same black traits that in antiquity were sacrificed to the gods of the netherworld, and yet they still persist among us."[25]

On 19 April Constant returned to the Tuileries with his "Benjamine" in hand, as Montlosier facetiously referred to it—the new "Additional Act," which Napoleon now invited him to read. In it Constant echoed Napoleon's initial call for the abolition of all press censorship (reintroduced by King Louis's June 1814 Charter) while demanding that any legal action against the press now be heard before a jury, not by a judge alone. Civilians were no longer to be tried by military tribunals. There was to be complete freedom of religion and no State religious affiliation. Ministers were no longer permitted to interpret laws as best suited them. The proceedings of the Chamber of Peers were to be published; both Chambers were to have the right to amend laws, as well as to propose laws on specific subjects. Hereafter, all conscription had to be authorized annually by the Chambers. Henceforth, cabinet ministers were to be given greater authority and the legislative branch was to have the right to supervise the executive branch. And yet the Emperor retained the right to appoint the Chamber of Peers (who were to be hereditary), and the nation's judges, and could unilaterally prorogue and dissolve the Chambers. He could accept or reject the newly elected President of the Chamber of Representatives (elected by that Chamber), and could propose new legislation. Napoleon also retained the right to issue an imperial pardon to anyone for any crime or misconduct in office.[26] Upon completing the reading of the sixty-seven articles an anxious Constant looked up for the Emperor's reaction, this Emperor whose powers he had just proposed curtailing. To his surprise Napoleon was smiling and indicated a willingness to accept the whole thing, with only a few modifications.[27] Times had indeed changed, or had they? In any event, the "Benjamine" was then to go on to the Constitution Committee for more detailed study.

Behind his welcoming acceptance of the new Additional Act of 19 April, Napoleon was in fact furious at the idea of anyone limiting his powers, including now the right to conscript troops whenever he felt it necessary.

"They are pushing me in a direction I do not like," he complained after Constant's departure. "They are weakening me, tying my hands. France is putting me in the background and can no longer see me. . . . They ask what has become of the Emperor's famous firm hand, which France needs now in order to master Europe. They can talk to me all they want to about their concepts of 'goodness,' 'abstract justice' and 'the natural laws!' But the first real law is 'necessity' while the most essential form of 'justice' is national safety."[28] "That man has learned nothing and has returned as much of a despot, as keen on conquest, as insane as ever," Fouché told Pasquier after returning from one such tirade at the Tuileries.[29] Nevertheless, Napoleon was not too upset to overlook a reward for Benjamin Constant's unique contribution, and the following day named him a State Counsellor along with a handsome salary.[30]

Napoleon clearly saw the Additional Act as a necessary evil, if as an insult, a "constitutional yoke," as Constant well realized. When his own Imperial cabinet asked him to submit it, article by article, for discussion prior to submitting it to a final public vote, Napoleon simply rebuffed them in feverish haste, insisting that the Constitution Committee accept it then and there, as a unit. He was not quite ready for the role as democratic benefactor. Indeed, he then forced their hand on the twenty-third by announcing in the *Moniteur* his acceptance of the Additional Act. At the same time, he called for a national plebescite to approve it, promising to announce the results at a magnificent state assemblage at the *"Champ de mai"* ceremony in Paris on 26 May (later postponed till the first of June).[31] The Emperor's firm hand had not lost all its cunning and determination. It was in fact high-handed and typical of the old Empire, all rushed through in twenty-four hours before the bureaucratic wheels could even begin to roll, before anyone could protest.

But if many Bonapartists were most disappointed with the new constitutional act, which they felt too greatly weakened the power and prestige of the Emperor, others were not. "It is quite impossible that he does not realize that his position now is quite different from what he had originally hoped for. Everything has changed in France since his departure [in 1814], and the people's expectations have developed far beyond those of the past,"[32] Caulaincourt pointed out. LaValette saw things differently, however—"Do not rely on this liberal constitution [the Additional Act], which he appears willing enough to give us today. Once at the head of a victorious army again, he will have soon forgotten it."[33] And as a skeptical A. N. de Salvandy so pithily remarked upon reading the new Additional Act: "He has learned nothing, he has forgotten nothing."[34]

As for Benjamin Constant, he not only remained proud of his grand *oeuvre* and claim to fame, but as optimistic as ever—despite much criticism from royalist and liberal friends for his betrayal. The fact is that Constant never quite understood the reality of the times, including Napoleon's character, and when the Emperor himself expressed some doubts about enacting the new Additional Act, Constant replied—"When the people see that they are now free, that there is representative government, that you are putting dictatorship aside, they will certainly realize that the Act is not making fun of them."[35] Napoleon, of course, was hardly worrying about that, or indeed of what "the people" thought. Quite the contrary, his misgivings about his "Benjamine" stemmed from the feeling that he had given away *too much power*, which in turn would result in reduced public respect for him (i.e., for having given in to public pressure). Ironically, the feeble Constant, of all persons, instead now tried to convince Napoleon that by having consented to the Additional Act he had shown courage and determination. "In the final analysis, there is indeed an advantage in it: showing me acting decisively," commented Napoleon. "They will think I am my old vigorous, determined self. But we shall see what happens."[36]

Accordingly, on the first of May, the Emperor drew up a decree concerning the convening of the electoral colleges to elect the new Deputies to the Chamber of Representatives, which would then be called into session following the official proclamation of acceptance of the Additional Act. Meanwhile, Joseph Bonaparte, who had been working behind the scenes to gain the cooperation and trust of the liberal majority, was invited by Napoleon to prepare a list of 120 candidates for the proposed new Chamber of Peers, from among whose numbers Napoleon would select the requisite eighty members.[37] Between 26 and 30 April (1815) the national plebescite was then launched, giving the French people an opportunity to accept or reject the Additional Act.[38] Would they endorse it, however? Or had he gone too far by offering this extension of democratic liberties, Napoleon wondered? On the other hand, perhaps other steps could be taken—as in the past under Lucien—to ensure a guarantee of fortuitous election results. In fact, if the Additional Act, as a supplement to the existing French Imperial constitutions* *were rejected*, would that mean the end of Napoleon and his regime? Indeed, given Napoleon's precarious situation, could he risk jeopardizing his entire future, based on the results of this election? In fact, unknown to him, a malaise of uncertainty, extending far beyond

*The "Imperial constitution," in fact, took the form not of a single document, but, rather, of dozens of Senatus-Consulte.

this single issue, was already pervading every sector of the people and of the new Imperial regime.

Only someone with Napoleon's charismatic personality could have possibly gathered any of his former élite round him now in his illegally established government, and even the most faithful among them had some misgivings, if not grave doubts, about the new regime's future— Caulaincourt, Davout, LaValette, Mollien—all felt ill at ease. "The Emperor is not in an enviable position," Regnault confided to Pasquier, "It will take a great deal of work before he is solidly established."[39] And Foreign Minister Armand de Caulaincourt's reactions typified them all. He felt the entire restoration of the imperial enterprise to be "insane" (*fou*) and complained that "He [Napoleon] simply refused to listen to any sound criticism or warning,"[40] which meant that war with the Allied armies was inevitable. "He will of course be defeated, but in the meantime what will become of France? She will be ravaged and perhaps even partitioned,"[41] he predicted. "As for the Emperor, it is quite inconceivable that he is not aware that his situation is very different indeed from what he had originally expected. Everything in France has changed since his departure [for Elba], for the expectations of the people have risen sharply since then." It was particularly ironic that the introduction of the ideas of new freedoms offered by King Louis—as opposed to Napoleon's former dictatorial ways—"renders the old-style imperial government quite intolerable to Frenchmen today." And yet, "he simply dare not grant the sweeping freedoms everyone wants. He has promised them, to be sure, but only as a temporary measure, until he is on his feet and his old ways and values take root again. . . . What direction is he heading in now? He does not even know himself. For instance he is appealing for the support of the men of the Revolution, and yet fears them above all others. . . . He is heading in the wrong direction, his step is uncertain and illogical. He is entirely out of his depth. And why is he so blind to the fact that the only real feeling he inspires in the people is fear itself?" (I.e., of war, disaster, chaos and revolution.) "What then will be the result of this inevitably terrible war he is imposing on us? The most determined generals are themselves afraid. The nation cannot but be afraid as it approaches and it will revolt and then blame him for all the suffering they have had to endure."[42] "I solemnly pledge that despite the assurances [of maintaining peace] that he [Napoleon] has given us, the whole of Europe will soon be throwing itself against us," Fouché declared adamantly to Pasquier, "and there is nothing one can do to resist and stem the inevitable tide, for in any event the whole thing will be settled within four months' time."[43]

"I am the last person to wish to deny praise to the First Consul: had Bonaparte produced nothing other than the Civil Code, his name would deserve to be passed on to posterity. And yet . . . if a citizen has once restored political freedom . . . would it then be right to reward him by offering to suppress that very freedom?"

Carnot on Monarchy

"Everything that has been said up to this point on absolute power simply goes to prove the occasional necessity of a temporary dictatorship in times of national crisis, but certainly not on a permanent basis."

Carnot on Monarchy

"It is less difficult to form a republic without anarchy than a monarchy without despotism."

Carnot on Monarchy

"War is nothing other than anarchy in uniform and despotism in fancy dress."

Carnot

"Without a sufficiently strong political power capable of rewarding every individual effort and that of every faction in society, one is left only with anarchy; the natural law of the strongest then immediately establishes itself.

"Since a strong political power is necessary [to govern a State] it is a question of knowing upon whom to confer it.

"If this power is the appanage of a hereditary family, it becomes despotic.

"If it is conferred by elections, there will be a dispute over the choice of persons selected to run.

"If it is given to a Senate, there will be divisions among its members.
"If it is given to those elected by the people, they will become ambitious and oligarchical."

Carnot

That these were extraordinary times, no one could deny, but such times also demand extraordinary leadership. Louis XVIII had been forced out in the power struggle because he lacked Napoleon's drive, energy, determination and awesome talents. France in 1815 was in a most perilous position, with the Allied armies preparing to pounce on her from without, while the forces from within, including the liberals, demanded sweeping political reforms. "No more arbitrary actions," they declared. "We must have personal safety and freedom of expression."[44] Maintaining some sort of balance was no easy feat, as both Caulaincourt and Fouché had averred. Napoleon for his part wanted to win over both the Allies and the French people, and the liberals in particular, if he could, demonstrating to everyone that he wished to comply with their wishes and acting with restraint. At the same time the shrill cries of the spokesmen for the uneducated masses were calling for blood and destruction. "Oust the aristocrats once and for all . . . Lynch them!" they cried from every corner of the land. "The people must make their strength felt,"[45] they insisted loudly enough to frighten Napoleon in the process. And although he ordered the army to take strong measures to maintain law and order, nevertheless outrages occurred, some aristocrats were seized by mobs and a few châteaux were looted and burned, notably in the Isère and Seine-et-Oise. The situation was more than tense, it was explosive.

In fact, Napoleon found at least four important political forces clashing with one another for control of opinion and the government at this time: Bonapartists, independent liberals, conservative royalists, and the discontented masses of a Jacobin tendency. No one man, however, not even a Napoleon, could maintain a government, even in the best of times, without the firm assistance of talented, reliable lieutenants. And now it was that the validity of Napoleon's choice of ministers would be put to the test, to heal the wounds and misunderstandings, to restore faith in government and order in this much troubled land. And to no individual did a heavier burden fall than to Interior Minister Lazare Carnot, with his chiseled face and equally strongly chiseled determination, and upon whom so very much now depended if chaos were to be averted and the disparate conflicting elements in this volatile society to be brought under control.

The son of a prosperous Burgundian notary of Nolay, Lazare-Nicolas-Marguerite Carnot, after receiving a good education, had decided on a military career, ultimately graduating from the Army Engineering School of Mézières as a lieutenant at the age of twenty in 1773. But although a most intelligent and industrious young man, by 1791 he had only reached the rank of captain, thanks to the artificial constraints of a royal law requiring that for further promotion, one had to establish that all four quarters—that is, all four grandparents—were of aristocratic birth, and, of course, Carnot was a bourgeois through and through.

Like Joseph Fouché, Carnot, too, was enticed forth by the sirens of the Revolution, though in Carnot's case, reinforced by his personal dissatisfaction with an unjust system curtailing an otherwise promising career. Thus it was, in October 1791, he found himself sitting as a Deputy, first in the Legislative Assembly, and later in the National Convention. Along with Fouché he voted for the death of King Louis in January 1793, and later fully supported the necessity and principles of the Reign of Terror, even joining the Committee of Public Safety that same year when it replaced Danton's Committee for General Defense.[46] He was also appointed "Commissaire," attached to the Armée du Nord, these special envoys provided with sweeping emergency powers, including the right to create revolutionary tribunals to summarily try and execute enemies, to search houses and seize food and property. Carnot also personally agreed to the necessity of "the extermination of brigands" and the use of "torch in hand and a bayonet on every rifle."[47] In his capacity as a member of the all-powerful Committee of Public Safety in August 1793, he decreed the *levée en masse*, calling for nationwide conscription, insisting on vigorous defense of the homeland while remaining opposed to an offensive war plunging beyond French frontiers and leading to foreign conquests. But as a member of this heinous Committee, he also fully supported its harsh suppression of revolts at Lyons, Marseilles, Toulon, Nîmes and Bordeaux, condoning mass arrests and executions of thousands of French men and women, including those ordered by Fouché.[48] Times of inordinate national danger, Carnot felt, required very bold measures. "Everything said thus far about the use of absolute power, merely goes to prove the necessity of a temporary dictatorship in times of national crisis," he insisted, though he did call for its removal once the danger had passed.[49] Upon leaving the Committee of Public Safety in March 1794, he continued to play an active political role in the country and was soon elected President of the Convention,[50] reflecting his growing prestige.

As a member of the new Legislative Corps, in November 1795, Carnot was elected one of the five members of the Directory,[51] the new ruling oligarchy. He held this post until August 1797, when he clashed with Barras over Bonaparte's wish to continue an aggressive, foreign war. When national elections were annulled by the Directory in September (1797), Carnot and fifty-five other recalcitrant deputies were then summarily ordered to be deported to a tropical prison in French Guiana. Carnot, however, took matters into his own hands and fled to Germany, though his private property was subsequently confiscated.[52]

It was only after Napoleon's coup d'état late in 1799 that Carnot was permitted to return to France, when he was first named *Inspecteur Général aux Revues*, and then on 2 April 1800, the First Consul's War Minister.[53] In fact, Napoleon desperately needed a vigorous hand to reintroduce stiff discipline into the army and to stop its pillaging, and Carnot was just the man for that.

Ever the idealist and patriot, Lazare Carnot remained dedicated to the early principles of the Revolution, that revolution he described as the beneficent "storm that cleanses the air and brings a calmer sky."[54] He had been the only member of the Directory, for instance, ever to refuse to accept a bribe or even a favor, and Napoleon certainly respected him for that unique feat at a time when almost every member of government was quickly enriching himself as a result of open bribes. At the same time Carnot had little sense of humor, and despite his social standing and background, lacked not only the social graces, but enforced his rough manners in a most uncomfortable bluntness, as First Consul Bonaparte discovered in 1800 when discussing his plans for life-consulship with his ministers. "I shall vote against the reestablishment of monarchy in *any form*," he told the embarrassed First Consul to his face.[55] The Revolution had been "a struggle between the salons and the great mass of people,"[56] as he put it, and reestablishment of monarchy under any guise now would be betraying that Revolution, which had fought to rid the country of lifetime and hereditary officials, and thus in October 1800 Carnot retired in a huff, first to Saint-Omer, then to his farm at Presles, in Burgundy. And although he continued to serve as a member of the Tribunate, from 1802 until it was disbanded in 1807, he never again served Napoleon in a high capacity.

Life at Presles (near La Ferté-Alais) was hardly a trial for Carnot, where as a happily married man the former War Minister found a warm, if unpretentious, hearth, a loyal wife and two bright sons, Sadi and Hippolyte (whose son, François-Sadi Carnot, later became President of the Republic). As an adherent of revolutionary ideals, Carnot, despite the high office he had held, lived simply—two servants sufficing for a sprawling house, with a single horse and cabriolet—in addition to several hands to work the land. His wife, Sophie (du Pont), the daughter of a successful munitions manufacturer,[57] played the piano and harp, or worked on her tapestry. But most of the time Carnot spent behind closed doors in his paneled study, where he concentrated on his two obsessions: military fortifications and theoretical mathematics, over the years producing a series of learned papers and pamphlets on both subjects, including studies on "balance and movement," the "correlation of geometric figures," trigonometry, and his most important mathematical work, *Réflexions sur la métaphysique du Calcul infinitésimal** (a work admired by Auguste Comte, and still in use today), not to mention his textbook on military engineering, *La Défense des places fortes*. He also participated in the proceedings of learned societies, including the Institute's Academy of Sciences, where he reviewed and analyzed papers on combustion engines, hydraulic machinery and submarines.[58] The man's energy never flagged, nor did the numerous projects on his desk ever seem to diminish, and he was to hand down this scientific enthusiasm to his son Sadi, who became a distinguished physicist in his own right and the creator of the first law of thermodynamics.

It was not until the last critical days of December 1813, however, that Carnot finally again offered his services to defend the country, and on 25 January, as a divisional general, he was named Governor General of Anvers, to protect the northern approaches to France from the gathering allied armies. Although leading a successful defense, following Napoleon's abdication, General Carnot retired once again from the scene.

There was nothing delicate about Lazare Carnot, including his appearance at the age of sixty-one, as he took office as Interior Minister in March 1815. The rough features of a pockmarked face, lined by the grief he had experienced at the untimely death of his wife, Sophie, two years earlier, dominated by a large nose and powerful chin, were hardly sympathetic. On the other hand his small blue eyes set off in stark contrast

Reflections on the Metaphysics of Infinite Calculus.

against his pale complexion and blond hair turning gray gave nothing of the air of a man bent by age or intimidated by the humiliating surrender of his country the year before. Though his stocky body stood perfectly erect—he was slightly above average height—there was certainly nothing distinguished-looking about him, indeed quite the contrary, his enemies going so far as to describe him as looking "false and cruel."

"He [Carnot] is most irascible and vindictive," said one critic and "teasing and opinionated" claimed Réveillière Lépeaux.[59] But regardless of the opinions of his character and personality, no one could deny that he was as active and as vigorous now as at the age of sixty, and ever impatient to see his ideas and concepts put into effect. "He is very intelligent and a first-rate administrator," the corrupt Paul Barras observed and to which Napoleon could well attest.[60] Some of his colleagues wrongly interpreted his strong belief in his own ideas and panaceas for the country as "sheer vanity," and "pride." "He is devoured by ambition," a friend noted, "but with the ambition to take charge and do everything in his own manner." Like most Frenchmen in a position of power, he was too sure of himself, and felt that he alone could solve the problems at hand. "He is a hard man to do business with," one ministry official complained, "and makes himself hated by his subalterns,"[61] for individuals were, in fact, of little import to this tough dynamo of a man, who was more preoccupied with mankind as a theory than in its daily reality. And although on occasion he could be "fascinating and gay" in conversation, it was when occupied with ideas, not concerning people, the latter tending to find him instead "always cold and caustic," but "never warm and affectionate."[62] Indeed, at such times he was more like some intellectual in his ivory tower, an enthusiastic scientist warmly expounding some new theory before his colleagues or students. He was a dedicated worker, of course, and loyal to his cause, and never even considered going over to the Czar and Wellington, unlike so many of Napoleon's army commanders and politicians. Thus, in February 1814, Carnot—despite his hopeless military position at Anvers—had rejected von Bülow's offer to join the Allies and turn against Napoleon. It would have probably paved the way for future employment with the Bourbons, but to Lazare Carnot, loyalty and honor came first . . . very rare commodities in Imperial France. Quite unlike the treacherous Fouché, Carnot was unwilling to plot against Napoleon or France to save his own skin. He loved his country too much to use it as a pawn with which to improve his personal political ambitions, and thus, he had finally surrendered his garrison to the Bourbons.[63] They had fought to the end with all their might and lost, but the wounds of war now had to be healed.

"Monsieur Carnot, I really got to know you far too late," Napoleon later lamented at Saint Helena.[64] Carnot was "a sincere and hardworking man," Napoleon had earlier told Metternich, and he had "nothing to complain about concerning him."[65] Las Cases later confirmed that Napoleon found him "loyal, honest, industrious and always upright,"[66] in stark contrast to just about everyone else surrounding him. "The good, excellent Carnot," Michelet exuberantly described him.[67]

And yet there was a decidedly ugly side to Carnot's character, seen clearly during his earlier role as a member of the Committee of Public Safety, which the brutal, corrupt and ruthless Louis Bourrienne, for one, attempted to whitewash. Carnot, he insisted, "was the representative of the Reign of Terror from outside," only indirectly involved, "whereas his colleagues were the representatives from within."[68] He was only responsible for the technical, military aspects of the Committee's infamous deeds as "the organizer of victory," he insisted, not for its human repression and degradation. But that of course was utter rot. Carnot had openly admitted his role in authorizing arrests and executions throughout France over a period of several months. There was indeed something monstrous, "hard and cruel" about the man. The genes controlling human sympathy, understanding and compassion were simply missing. Carnot for his part saw the whole situation in a different light. "We felt we had grasped the illusion of national happiness," he later reflected. "We believed it was possible to achieve a republic without undergoing anarchy, and to achieve freedom for us without political factionalism. Experience proved how utterly deceived we were."[69] And one of the powerful "factions" that had so disappointed him was that calling for French military aggression and expansion. (The mass murders had not disturbed him unduly.) On this point, however, Carnot was much more in agreement with Robespierre. "It is not by rhetoric nor by warlike acts that we will subjugate Europe, but by the wisdom of our ideas, by the majesty of our political deliberations, and by the grandeur of the French national character."[70] Carnot could not have said it better himself.

The Interior Ministry that Lazare Carnot accepted in March 1815 had been unsuccessfully offered to Molé, LaValette and Maret, and Carnot himself diffidently protested that he knew nothing about its administration.[71] But once accepting this daunting task, as usual he threw everything into the effort, which included supervising the great technical services of the nation: public works, mines, agriculture, public welfare and health, the beaux arts, public education, conscription and the National Guard, of the publishing industry and the general administration of the political structure of the country.

Carnot's immediate task was of course to restore the effective functioning of the State machinery as well as order in the nation's provinces. To do that, he adopted the same method used during the Revolution; he dispatched special *"commissaires"* throughout the land to assess the situation, who were to expedite reports of their results to Paris. Within less than a fortnight their initial findings warned Carnot that most of the country's prefects were either unenthusiastic about Napoleon's return, or downright hostile, and the report on the Prefect of Isère, for instance, was typical. He openly criticized the Emperor and "Bonaparte's crooks."[72] Although King Louis had kept at least half of Napoleon's prefects and deputy-prefects, Carnot found that few could be trusted. Confusion, distrust and discontent had reached and undermined nearly every corner and *département* (province) of the land. "Gangrene has set in in the civil administration everywhere," one official advised the Interior Minister early in April, "and nothing will be done until the Prefect, Deputy Prefect, Secretary-General . . . indeed, just about everyone, is replaced."[73] "Reports from numerous *départements* are in full agreement in pointing out that the mayors (for the most part, former *seigneurs*) are one of the principal obstacles preventing a restoration of law and order. . . . They terrify the good citizens, dampening the enthusiasm of the French people, predicting fresh disasters and spreading unsettling rumors," Police Minister Fouché confirmed. "The Prefects are bad, the mayors worse."[74] And War Minister Davout complained to Carnot of the adverse effect of their actions on his department, stating that if immediate action were not taken to remove obstructive officials, "one can expect all government operations concerning the military to be hindered or paralyzed."[75]

The administrative structure was far more severely corroded than Napoleon had realized. With good, reliable prefects and mayors (the latter in France having far-reaching powers and influence), anything could be undertaken by the head of State. With this cadre unresponsive or hostile to the orders from Paris, however, there was no future, and Napoleon, who as a good army officer knew and understood the importance of a solid reliable chain of command, was just as anxious as Carnot.

But as Napoleon's intimates were now discovering, their Emperor was a changed man from the one they had known in the old days. In public he often seemed ill at ease and pale, and ever since his attempted suicide the year before, a handkerchief was constantly ready to control the flow of saliva seeping from the corner of his mouth. His breathing was hard and irregular, and his speech often interrupted by a cough. Even his own person seemed somewhat unkempt, his underwear frequently visible, as his clothes stretched, opening around his greatly protruding paunch. Before leaving Elba he had known there was no future for him, that he was lost, and could never succeed again in France, but there was no other choice for him, as he saw it. There was neither a present nor a future in Elba—he had to act now, or at least die in the attempt, and the distinct decline in his health made his forty-six years seem like sixty. But the reports reaching him now from two hardened realists—Carnot and Fouché—simply could not be ignored. Somehow new, reliable prefects had to be found and *immediately*, and all important officials down to and including mayors, replaced.

If Carnot did not act at once, Napoleon was lost, but if he did act precipitously, without sufficient time to sift the files to find the very best men, all was equally lost. He could not win, for time was of the essence. To be sure, Napoleon had taken some immediate action upon returning to Paris, to win over public support. First the capital must be squarely behind him, for he had no intention of becoming another Louis XVI, a prisoner of "the people" in the Tuileries. He announced the creation of large-scale public works projects to reduce the swelling number of unemployed: three thousand men were to be hired by the imperial government to build a new market in Saint-Germain, to work on the immense fountain and elephant erected on the site of the former Bastille, and to repair the Louvre. Another two thousand men—including gunsmiths, carpenters, tailors and coppersmiths—were taken on by the War Ministry, repairing rifles, ironwork, a variety of military equipment and clothing, while another four thousand were to rebuild walls and fortifications at Montmartre, Belleville and Mont-Louis. To the people of Paris, Napoleon was a hero—overnight nine thousand families suddenly had work, food and hope.[76]

Paris was immediately festive and the people made triumphant promenades to the Tuileries and Palais-Royal, where workers laid violets and wreaths of flowers around imperial war monuments, at the column of the Grand Army, and at busts of Napoleon. Refrains of the "Marseillaise" rang through ancient streets and public gardens, attended by fireworks, while Napoleon's 7,300-man Imperial Guard gave a banquet round the Ecole Militaire for some 15,000 troops from Lyons and Grenoble garrisons who had brought Napoleon back to Paris, when one of the thousand officers feasting in the courtyard suddenly shouted, *"A la colonne!"* Grabbing a bust of Napoleon from the Ecole and hailing some drummers, the entire group of officers was soon marching to the Place Vendôme, shouting *"Vive l'Empereur! Vive la liberté!"* magnified a thousand-fold, while at the Opéra, the Théâtre Français and at the Feydeau, enthusiastic Parisians were singing patriotic songs between performances of plays and shows.[77] Indeed, so boisterous did this pro-Bonaparte reception become over the ensuing days and weeks that Napoleon was finally forced to flee the luxurious but noisy Tuileries for the more secluded residence of the military governor of Paris at the Elysée Palace, the governor in turn forced to seek shelter elsewhere.

But cheers in Paris in no way diminished the reality reported by Carnot's special emissaries. In fact, if the country was not on the verge of immediate military rebellion . . . then at least it was in the act of subverting the entire imperial political machinery, while the only obvious indicator of this in Paris was apparently the continuing gradual decline of government securities on the Stock Exchange.

Carnot, staggered by the enormity and implications of the reports reaching him from the provinces, took the bull by the horns and by the end of the first week of April dismissed 61 of the nation's 87 prefects.* And although the situation was as potentially dangerous as it was dramatic, he discovered that the post of prefect, usually so desperately sought after, frequently including the exchange of substantial sums, was not only difficult to fill, but as equally difficult to keep occupied. Over the next several weeks he had to name an additional 109 prefects or deputy-prefects, reflecting just how shaky Napoleon's newly restored Empire really was. Then, to complete the measure, on 20 April Carnot fired every mayor of every town or commune with a population of less than 5,000 persons.[78] Fouché, on the other hand, remonstrated with his colleague that "such violent measures, far from breaking resistance [to the new regime], to the contrary will only result in aggravating and increasing it."[79]

Sure enough, so powerful and universal was the sense of outrage to this measure that ten days later Carnot was forced to issue a fresh decree, rescinding the mayoral decision of the twentieth, thereby restoring the old mayors who would instead have to face mayoralty elections. Alas, when the election results duly reached Paris, Carnot was chagrined to find *two-thirds of the former mayors reelected*, reflecting serious lack of Bonapartist grass-roots influence and confidence throughout the provinces. As for the prefects named by the Interior Ministry, a great many proved either apathetic, lazy, or fearful and uncertain of the present and future, and thus directly or indirectly uncooperative with a much dis-

---

*Eighty-seven including the prefect for Corsica.

mayed Carnot. And yet he had given his "commissaires" and provincial officials stern and precise instructions: "The magistrates [appointed or elected] had to be selected with the best interests of the people in mind. . . . All public officials [must be] men enjoying the people's confidence and animated by the finest public sentiments."[80] And unlike Fouché, who as Police Minister had his new "liberal police" policies published for all to see (and praise), while personally neither believing in nor respecting any of them, Carnot's decrees, so firmly representing his sincere aims and values, did not as a rule appear in the Parisian press. Carnot was therefore doubly disappointed both by the commissaires' reports on the prefectorial replacements and communal election results.

Everywhere the authority of the government was challenged or greatly flaunted, leading the few conscientious prefects to despair, and as Regnault acknowledged to Pasquier, the situation was "neither as fine nor as sure as most people think. . . . The Emperor is certainly not in a secure position and is going to have to work very hard indeed to establish himself solidly."[81] Indeed, Deputies and public officials were permitted to act outrageously, and with complete impunity, the influential Joseph Laîné, for instance, currently serving as President of the Chamber of Deputies, openly calling upon his constituents in Bordeaux to neither heed Paris nor pay the imperial tax collectors.[82] And this brought home the point all the more that in the final analysis everything really depended on the goodwill of the mayors who were responsible for implementing the mechanisms of national government at the grass-roots level: charged with collecting taxes, dispatching recruits to the army, calling up the National Guard when required, supervising all elections—local and national—finding billets for troops stationed in the region, and, of course, enforcing government orders and posting fresh decrees.[83]

With mayors and deputies publicly defying Paris, acts of rebellion and worse quickly increased in number. Following Laîné's harangue, at Bordeaux, two hundred rioting army recruits were only brought under control by the force of arms, resulting in a brutal skirmish and the death of one man. Elsewhere in the country army officers were insulted or even attacked in public, and in one case, a group of National Guardsmen actually opened fire on some regular army officers. At Avignon other officers were insulted in the streets, while Marshal Brune, governor of the VIII Military District in the Var, received crude death threats, warning him what would happen in the event France were again threatened with an Allied invasion. (He was subsequently murdered.[84]) At Marseille rocks were thrown at some officers sitting at a café, demonstrators shouting "Death to the Bonapartists!"; at Lisieux a regimental colonel was horsewhipped in public.[85] Everywhere mayors, in particular, abetted such acts and when these seemingly untouchable officials now frequently refused outright to cooperate with Paris, the machinery of the nation literally ground to a halt, leading either to a stuporous state, chaos or open rebellion. Reports from prefects in all regions now reached Paris and Carnot's desk with greater frequency and unanimity: "The Government's action here is entirely null and void," read a typical such report from the south. "Everything is collapsing and dissolving in a state of anarchy."[86] At Boulogne the white Bourbon flag was flagrantly hung from the cliffs overlooking the sea; at Sète, the imperial arms were torn down by a mob in the main square; at Poitiers rebellious citizens smashed Napoleon's bust in broad daylight; at Aix-en-Provence royalists demonstrated before the hôtel de ville; at Bayonne, Marseille, Versailles and Amiens government posters bearing proclamations and decrees were torn down and often replaced by those of King Louis. In a dozen other cities wild crowds gathered shouting "Down with the Eagles! Napoleon to the gallows! Up the royalists! Death to the Bonapartists!" This repeated at Alençon, Le Mans, Beauvais, Abbeville, Armentières, Dunkerque, Calais, Saint-Omer, Bordeaux, Montpellier, Avignon, and Marseille.[87] In some cases these acts and demonstrations were carried out by *fédérés* workers; in others, by pro-royalist groups; while everywhere they left confusion and a feeling of unrest. Carnot had to admit to Napoleon that his choice of Prefects had been too rushed and that those of Lyons, Marseille and Bordeaux, for instance, lacked "energy and firmness," while local ringleaders, particularly the mayors, continued to go unchecked. "All the reports received express the same apathy and ill will on the part of the mayors," a dejected War Minister Davout confirmed.[88]

Nor was the situation very different in other sectors. In the traditionally conservative bastions of the judiciary, resistance to Napoleon was only too apparent, where judges at all levels declined to take the new oath of allegiance to the Emperor, and there were not sufficient numbers of qualified jurists to replace them. In the lycées created by Napoleon years before, headmasters frequently were unable to rouse a *"Vive l'Empereur"* from the assemblies of angry boys who knew only too well that they were shortly to be conscripted to form another army. The Church of course remained opposed to the new Empire as it had to the old. "The clergy are animated by the greatest ill will. They are doing a great deal of harm," read one prefectorial report typical of dozens of others. The Church was perhaps much more effective in its resistance than other branches of society, having as it did the right to deliver sermons every

Sunday, openly encouraging revolt and dissension. Prefects and commissaires found that large numbers of priests refused to chant the *Domine Salvum* for Napoleon, while the bishops of Agens, Soissons and Vannes preached open disobedience to the new French government.[89]

If the old anti-Bonapartist antagonism of 1813 and 1814 now revived, unchanged, from every direction, nowhere did it find a more unanimous and more vehement rallying point and protest than around the issue of conscription and rearmament. As both War Minister Davout and Interior Minister Carnot quickly discovered, if there was one thing the entire country was agreed upon, it was the determination not to support fresh wars. It has been estimated that *at least* 900,000 French men between the ages of 23 and 45 alone were killed directly or indirectly during Napoleon's long series of wars,[90] while some scholars would double that, and the French people clearly were in no mood now to provide fresh cannon fodder for Napoleon Bonaparte or anyone else. Everywhere initial enthusiasm for Napoleon had quickly waned by mid-April 1815. Napoleon needed troops, he said, in face of the new Allied threat. There would have to be fresh conscription yet again and the National Guard would also have to be called out. Carnot dispatched commissaires including Roederer, Thibaudeau and Dumolar to Lyons, Dijon, Besançon, Moulins and Grenoble to oversee the call-up of National Guard units. Other special commissaires were attached to each of the country's military divisions, again as in the days of the Revolution, to clean up the military command and organization, bringing some semblance of order and efficiency, while reinfusing patriotic motivation.[91] But in general the reports sent to Paris were discouraging. Everyone was complaining, everywhere resistance was evident and mounting. War again, all because one man, Napoleon Bonaparte, had returned to France—it was simply too much for an emotionally and physically exhausted French nation, and even in Paris, along the rue de Rivoli, the invasion of posters gradually encroached upon the Tuileries: "Two million francs reward for anyone finding the peace lost on 20 March," read one found on the palace walls.[92]

The reports reaching Carnot were almost invariably negative. There was, in addition to everything else, powerful anti-imperial resistance from the commercial world, from the manufacturing cities and the ports—fishermen, shipbuilders, cotton weavers—Paris, Lyons, Dunkerque, Nantes and Marseilles—all reported resistance in one form or other.[93] But not one to give in easily, Carnot initiated several new measures to gain support of the masses.

Communicating the government's ideas and programs to the peasantry was naturally considered the most difficult task, but the peasants composed the majority of the population and Carnot felt the effort had to be made. He hit upon the idea of creating and publishing a national village newspaper, the *Feuille Villageoise*, as he called it, a brief newssheet written in simple language, explaining the government's agricultural aims and policies. As most of the peasants were completely illiterate, this required someone reading the sheet to their leaders in every village of the land, a cumbersome and largely ineffective system at best. And if, for instance, as was too often the case, the local mayor opposed the government, the newspaper and its news would not be distributed. Furthermore, Fouché for his part did his utmost to prevent its publication by opposing the editors selected by Carnot, and as a result, its first issues only appeared early in June 1815, too late to have any effect on subsequent events.[94]

Nor could Carnot act quickly in the fields of commerce and industry. Nevertheless, he did launch the mechanism by which to reach the pertinent representatives, by creating the Conseil d'Industrie Nationale (National Industrial Council), through which he called upon leaders of commerce, industry and agriculture to introduce improved methods of production and distribution. Carnot encouraged the use and development of modern machinery—including steam engines and hydraulic machinery—in industry and agriculture, offering a 50,000-franc annual award for the best new piece of machinery invented.[95] At the same time Carnot felt that it was foolhardy for France—a predominantly agricultural land— to try to challenge British industry. To be sure, industry could improve greatly, but he believed it could never equal or replace British industrial output. But to win over agricultural, commercial and industrial leaders, Carnot drafted a project for the election of national deputies in the legislative body in blocs, according to their economic constituency; e.g., so many deputies to represent commerce, so many to represent industry, and then agriculture, but the brevity of the reimposed Empire did not permit it to develop properly. Finally, Carnot also drew up plans for national workshops where the large numbers of unemployed could be trained for new skills. A shattered economy, however, was not the only cause for concern threatening national stability, as anxiety about rebellion and even civil war gradually attracted more and more attention.

"Fears of civil war in the West have now completely disappeared," the Préfecture at Angers reported to Paris early in April. "I was able to travel across the entire Vendée with just three gendarmes. Everywhere the people are happy," read another report covering not only the Vendée but Maine-et-Loire and Deux-Sèvres. Throughout the West Country, between 31 March and 7 April, official reports seemed reassuring:[96] the royalist forces, until recently led by the Duc de Bourbon, had been captured or disbanded. So confident of the return to normalcy was Marshal Davout initially, for example, that he ordered all large army units withdrawn from that entire region, leaving only a skeleton force of supply depots, garrisons and gendarmeries. To be sure, this western region and parts of Brittany had not always been easy to understand. The *chouans*, or pro-royalist groups of armed bands, had traditionally rallied to the French royal house, whereas equally large portions of the peasantry and working classes were often opposed, even brutally so, to anyone with title or wealth. That the gentry and peasantry occasionally joined forces in times of national emergency merely confused the matter more.

With the Allies rallying again to prepare another campaign, however, the decision by Napoleon's officials to ignore this traditionally cantankerous western region was certainly premature, for if King Louis were to rally forces from within France, he would begin here and in the Midi. The calm of early April was indeed deceptive, for all the while a dozen or so royalist leaders were meeting in as many secret rendezvous and châteaux to prepare for a major spring uprising against Napoleon. Though many vied for the leadership, most finally accepted Louis, the Marquis de La Rochejacquelein, and his younger brother, Auguste, as their commanders, and the various regional leaders could be seen occasionally thereafter quietly entering the medieval Rochejacquelein castle at Saint-Aubin de Baugine. King Louis's proclamations and the Allies' March declarations were read before, and heatedly discussed by, these conspirators: d'Autichamp, Sapinaud, Saint-Hubert, de Suzannet, Robert, the Charette nephews, La Salmonière, d'Andigné, d'Ambrugeac, Picquet du Boisgny, and others. If at first the calm seemed real enough, Napoleon's orders now to call up troops who had already completed their military service or who had retired, as well as the civilian National Guards throughout the region, gradually invited fresh discontent and grumbling. This in turn led to new recruits for the royalist movement, by men willing to do anything to get rid of Napoleon and his militaristic policies once and for all.

And with the western region of the country already stripped of most large regular army units, the time seemed ripe to act. Beginning on 10 April the peace was broken as the first series of coordinated royalist attacks were unleashed against gendarmerie headquarters and garrisons and even against some opposing civilians, at Ancenis, Bressuire, Chollet,

Fougères, Gallais, les Herbiers, Machecoul, Rennes, Saint-Brieuc, Savenay, and Vannes.[97]

Fouché, Carnot and Davout suddenly found themselves inundated with a rash of hysterical reports pleading that no more government troops be withdrawn, and that fresh assistance be sent. As early as 16 April, a seasoned veteran, General de Caffarelli, personally appealed to Paris for more troops. "The revolt here will explode out of control if the remaining troops are withdrawn," he told War Minister Davout. "Then we will need an entire army in Brittany."[98] But Napoleon, for one, did not take a series of ill-armed minor uprisings that seriously. If he had had forces to spare, of course, things might have been different, but with the growing menace of Allied invasion to the north, his thoughts and concerns were centered there, and not in the West country. "All the troops are needed at the frontier now, for a victory in the north will do more to calm the interior than a few regiments left in the West," the Emperor argued.[99]

Meanwhile the royalists in the West were escalating their attacks, Auguste de La Rochejacquelein, d'Autichamp and Suzannet holding another war council at Chapelle-Basse-Mer on 11 May to assess the situation.[100] Though they would continue with smaller operations, they decided to hold off their large-scale confrontation to coincide with that of King Louis and the Allies' offensive in the north planned for June. Rochejacquelein's elder brother, the Marquis de La Rochejacquelein, had already concluded a satisfactory meeting with the King in Ghent to coordinate their efforts, whence he had gone on to London to obtain fresh military aid, and the British frigate *Astrée* was now due off the coast momentarily to land badly needed rifles, ammunition and supplies.

By the time the Marquis de La Rochejacquelein himself finally disembarked from the *Astrée* at Saint-Gille on 15 May with some 2,000 rifles—they had been promised 14,000—the royalist movement had swollen to impressive numbers in Brittany, Morbihan, Maine-et-Loire, Deux-Sèvres and the Vendée, with forces estimated from between 15,000 to 31,000 men.[101] Most of them were badly armed, however, two-thirds of them, perhaps, having ancient hunting rifles or old-fashioned muskets, while the remaining third had only pikes, clubs or pitchforks. But they were angry and they were determined, and facing only a total regular army force—moreover scattered in small garrisons—of about 4,000 men. Thus they felt most confident in the outcome and without awaiting King Louis's offensive in the north, Rochejacquelein's bands now impetuously attacked Ancenis, Boispréau, Bressuire, Chemille, Cholet, Sables and Soullans.[102]

"It's civil war just like [17]93 all over again!" wrote an anxious

General Charpentier. "The entire Department of Morbihan is in rebellion. . . ."[103] "Rennes is being threatened," wrote General Bigarré. "I am surrounded by ten thousand insurgents!"[104] And although many reports were inevitably exaggerated—including the number of "insurgents" and the quantities of their arms, estimated to include some 30,000 modern rifles and four million cartridges—clearly the situation was deteriorating, General Travot alone asking for "reinforcements of 10,000 men."[105] "The country is in danger," Carnot echoed, "discontent is general and continuing to spread in the provinces as in Paris. Civil war is about to break out in several parts of the country."[106]

Finally, late in May, Napoleon acquiesced, ordering the few remaining troops to stay where they were, while placing General Lamarque at the head of a new army to be sent there to relieve the threatened region, the new force to include 2,800 gendarmes, two regiments of the "Young Guard" (from the Imperial Guard), twenty-five battalions of infantry, eight squadrons of cavalry, and three batteries of artillery, for a total of more than 20,000 men.[107]

But to Napoleon and Fouché there seemed a more intelligent, far more expeditious, if seemingly incredible, means of defusing the situation, as the Police Minister arranged a meeting in Paris with an outlawed, former-royalist senior army officer, the Comte de Malartic.[108] Malartic, who had considerable influence over the great nobles of the West, was asked to intercede, to prevail upon them to halt their rebellion, at least for the moment. Had the idea come from anyone less than the tough, practical Fouché, one would have laughed at the very idea. But Fouché, who, back on 27 April, had predicted to Marshal Davout the very inevitability of this uprising in the first place, now on 23 May predicted he could quash it *without* the use of great armies. Fouché had been called many things by his enemies, but never a dreamer.

"This premature insurrection is in fact harmful to the very cause it hopes to serve," the Police Minister pointed out to Malartic, "for it is going to permit Bonaparte to take violent countermeasures. The West will be ravaged, the rabble will be armed, and the Emperor will be given new armies with which—after reducing the Vendée—he will then in turn use to prolong his resistance against the Allied forces. Therefore, understand fully well that the reestablishment of the [Bourbon] monarchy in no way depends upon a war in the West. It is in the North that the fate of France will be decided." And to calm a by-now bewildered Malartic's anxiety in considering such action now, Fouché added uncannily—"Hostilities will not begin until mid-June. But in any event, by that time it will be too late, for your uprising will have been already crushed. Help me in stopping this useless spilling of French blood."[109] Fouché of all people, concerned about the spilling of French blood! It took some doing, but General de Malartic was finally convinced, and agreed to accept the infamous Police Minister's "peace mission." "It is the only way left," Fouché insisted.[110]

Accordingly, Malartic along with two other influential aristocrats from that region, Messieurs de Flavigny and de La Béraudière, set out from Paris on 26 May with safe-conduct passes, reaching one of the royalist commanders, the Comte d'Autichamp, in the Vendée at Mortagne-sur-Sèvre three days later. In fact, Malartic's mission was a desperate one, for if he failed, there were strong rumors of the uprising spreading south-ward to Bordeaux—already a powder keg—then eastward to the Languedoc and up to Provence. But d'Autichamp, who had already seen some heavy fighting during the past few weeks, fell in with Malartic's proposal. Continuing on their way, they next won over Suzannet, who in turn wrote to their commander-in-chief, La Rochejacquelein, of their decision, who had just seen his 8,000-man force defeated at Aizenary by General Travot's mere 1,000 men.[111]

A bitter La Rochejacquelein was furious at the very idea of standing down, however. It was sheer treason! "As commanding officer of the Grande Armée de la Vendée, I order you to appear before me to receive your instructions. You will be punished as a traitor and rebel should you persist in your defection!"[112] And although the Marquis de La Rochejacquelein now also ordered the mayors of every town and village of the Vendée to conscript all men between the ages of twenty and fifty for the royalist struggle, on 31 May three of the Marquis's principal commanders—d'Autichamp, Suzannet and Sapinaud, by now desperately short of arms and ammunition—met at Falleron and drew up a formal statement renouncing any further fighting at this time. In it they called upon "M. le Marquis de La Rochejacquelein to return to his estate to await the official outbreak of hostilities along the northern frontiers, before deploying all the forces of the Vendée." "All the officers will simply have to accept this arrangement," Suzannet added in a personal plea to his chief, "Adieu, mon cher Louis."[113]

Bereft of his principal field commanders and their forces, Louis de La Rochejacquelein found himself in a hopeless position. The royalist uprising of the West was doomed. But after his enormous personal effort, and intensive negotiating, including traveling earlier to Ghent to gain the King's support, thence to London to plead his cause before Lord Liverpool's ministers, and with further British arms deliveries imminent— not to mention a promised British troop landing—he was in no mood to accept the Declaration of Falleron. Replying immediately, he castigated Sapinaud, Suzannet and d'Autichamp . . . "for having added to the infamy of disobedience, that of the blacker one of treason, and of a willingness to accept an arrangement with the Devastator-Tyrant [*tyran dévastateur*] of France."[114] Louis de La Rochejacquelein, his name, word and honor at stake, would continue the struggle, regardless of the betrayals and impossible odds, and on 3 June he was killed in a skirmish near Saint-Jean-de-Monts, in an attack by the forces of Brigadier General Estème, thus effectively reducing the major part of the uprising in the West.[115] Fouché's fantastic proposal and estimation of the situation had proven correct after all, and Napoleon, for one, was most impressed.

But unknown to the Emperor, at this very moment his Police Minister was quietly predicting to ex-Chancellor Etienne-Denis Pasquier (himself then harried by the Paris fédérés at Napoleon's instigation) that Napoleon was doomed! He would soon be fighting the Allies, he pointed out—"He will be forced to leave for the northern army. . . . Once he is out of the way, we shall remain masters of the situation. Let him win one or two battles, he will finally lose the big one and that is when our role will begin in earnest. . . . [116] I ask for nothing better than the return of the Bourbons.[117] . . . Believe me, all will turn out well in the end." He smiled with his usual calm. "This man has returned from the Island of Elba crazier than when he left. His fate is as good as settled," and he would soon be defeated once and for all.[118]

Russia's astute ambassador to France, Pozzo di Borgo, for one, however, was not taken in by Fouché's machinations. "I beg of you, do not count too much on Fouché's intrigues," he warned Foreign Minister Nesselrode. "That man is planning on working with us when we return to Paris, that is to say, when we will no longer need him. He intends to use us to remain master of the day, in spite of us." Indeed, Pozzo warned, "if he wanted to, and more importantly, if he could, destroy Bonaparte now, no doubt he would do so without hesitation, because he would then find himself the most powerful man in France."[119]

In the meantime Fouché continued to play his double game, now having thousands of anti-Bourbon posters circulated throughout Paris, caricaturing a fat King Louis in a chair hoisted high in the air by struggling porters, carrying sacks of gold looted from the Banque de France, his hands filled with diamonds torn from his crown, as he commanded an army of invalids. What *was* Fouché's game? No wonder even Napoleon could not understand him. And yet, as Pasquier points out—"What is even more astonishing is that the Emperor could have been completely unaware of his activities. Yet he has left him with his portfolio, which has kept him in a position where he [Fouché] had the means at his disposal to do a great deal of harm! Did he feel that he would be more of a problem outside the cabinet, than within? Or else was M. Fouché protected by his well-known custom of deceiving everyone? Be that as it may, what is certain is that Napoleon has been duped by him, and yet this very error seems all the more bizarre in light of the fact that the men most devoted to him—M. de Bassano, M. de LaValette and a good many others—have never stopped warning him about Fouché!"[120]

Neither for Napoleon nor King Louis, the sinister Fouché was in fact attempting to destroy both—just as Pozzo had surmised—while negotiating tentatively with Vienna for the Duc d'Orléans as a possible substitute for the French throne.[121] In fact as early as the end of April and beginning of May 1815 the French Emperor had conclusive proof of Fouché's treasonous contacts with the Allies, and Prince von Metternich in particular, after one of the latter's agents had been intercepted with messages for Fouché. Unknown to the Police Minister, however, Napoleon had replaced his (Fouché's) agent with his own—none other than Fleury de Chaboulon—dispatching him to a secret rendezvous on 3 May at Basel, Switzerland, with the Viennese Baron Ottenfels—or Henri Werner, as he now called himself incognito—where the primary topic of Napoleon's possible successor (following the downfall of the Empire) was discussed at length, including the name of the Duc d'Orléans.[122]

Thus, well before Fouché's famous attempt to stave off a royalist uprising in the Vendée, Napoleon had summoned the Police Minister, confronting him with the irrefutable proof of his latest conspiracy to remove him. "You are a traitor, Fouché. I ought to have you hanged!"[123] he bellowed furiously before witnesses. And yet, incredibly enough, *Napoleon then did nothing*, somehow convincing himself that the obvious betrayal was not that at all, just Fouché's lamentable penchant for enjoying the feel of power and being in personal contact with all the famous names of the day. "It simply is not in Fouché's best interests to betray me," he afterward said to Fleury, in an attempt to convince him (and perhaps himself). "He is simply a born intriguer, and no one can prevent him from doing it."[124] (Curiously enough, there was something to that explanation.) Thus he was little more than a naughty child and must be humored! If Napoleon was not quite the dupe Pasquier made him out to be, nevertheless he was no longer the old Napoleon who had once acted so vigorously against unfaithful lieutenants. And keeping Fouché in his sensitive and powerful position at the Police Ministry now, reflected the sharp decline in Napoleon's facilities and willpower. In some respects he was a broken man, clearly, and through his apathy, acting against his own best interests. All was lost, the play was ending, but he refused to be denied all the main, familiar actors who had to remain with him till the curtain came down. "What direction is he heading in?" Caulaincourt asked, as bewildered as anyone else by Napoleon's incongruous acts since his return. "He does not even seem to know himself," he sighed.[125]

Meanwhile Fouché was also secretly negotiating in another direction, contacting the Duke of Wellington to arrange a place of exile for himself and his family in Great Britain should the Napoleonic axe finally fall on him.[126]

Be that as it may, the royalist uprising in the West, in bringing havoc to the country, would certainly have caused severe problems for Napoleon by leaving him so weakened with *two military fronts*, and a divided military force, that victory would have been rendered impossible. One moment Fouché was acting to overthrow him, the next to help him, all in a defyingly irrational pattern. Indeed, the question of Fouché's mental stability must certainly be raised.

To complicate matters further, another de-stabilizing element also emerged at this time, the *fédérés*, or federated forces—founded originally at Rennes by property owners and students there, then spreading to other western cities, as a reaction against royalist-chouan threats of violence spawned by La Rochejacquelein (but not in order to defend Napoleon's new government). And thus the fédérés, which soon expanded to include what Fouché referred to as *"la canaille,"* the rabble, the working classes, of which he had warned the Comte de Malartic, were to prove equally vexatious for Napoleon as the royalists. The federated movement quickly spread throughout the entire western region, then elsewhere in the country, almost overnight posing as a possible third force (i.e., in addition to the regular standing Imperial Army units, and Rochejacquelein's royalist forces) and keeping it under control was to prove no easy matter for Napoleon.

Finally forced to face the possible threat posed by the fédérés (not to be confused with the National Guard), he decided to act, taking the initiative *by personally sponsoring them*, to maintain them on his side, and to serve as a counterforce against royalist unrest.[127] But it was a very dangerous game—and more often manipulated unseen by Fouché's agents, than Napoleon's—and was in fact a reflection of the dangerous escalation of intense French national discontent and instability. And what is more, a politically active and militarily armed fédéré movement would obviously overlap and conflict with the National Guard and their role, two organized units of armed citizens in every city and commune vying with each other. Napoleon for his part had enough trouble in trying to rally and maintain the loyalty of the bourgeoisie represented in the traditional National Guard units, many of which also soon proved so much of a threat—either by their actions or failure to obey orders—that some of them had to be disbanded and disarmed.[128] Meanwhile the petit-bourgeois, working-class-dominated fédérés attempted to replace the National Guards, declaring that they were organizing "to defend freedom" and "to put down the counterrevolution."[129]

In fact, their organization quickly became large and dangerous, fédéré units springing up in Brittany, Picardy, the Moselle, Alsace, Lyons, in Bordeaux and Les Landes, Toulouse, Angoulême, Le Puy, Bouches-du-Rhône and the Var.[130] By mid-May the situation was becoming ominous, despite fédéré professions of loyalty to the Empire. Then when thousands of their members marched as infantry units through the Paris working-class suburbs of Saint-Marceau and Saint-Antoine, no one could be in doubt as to the potential crescendoing threat posed by these neo-revolutionaries so reminiscent of those who had supported the outrages perpetrated by the National Convention and Committee of Public Safety. The same faces and mentality had rendered the reign of terror a reality and a permanent blot on human decency and French history.

When on Sunday, 14 May, some 15,000 of these fédérés suddenly emerged unannounced from the slums of Paris, converging on the Tuileries unbidden and unwanted, then and there demanding the right to protect the Empire and country, a cold chill went up many a spine, especially of those court officers and officials who had witnessed these same crowds bursting forth from the slums before these very gates at the Tuileries over two decades earlier, prior to their rampaging through this palace, capturing and then executing Louix XVI and Queen Marie Antoinette. It was indeed a delicate situation for Napoleon as these revolutionary ghosts exhorted the little man from Elba, their hero and savior, proclaiming their grievances: "We don't like kings imposed on us by the enemy. We have welcomed you back enthusiastically because you are the man of the nation, the defender of the fatherland and because you protect the rights of the people. . . . The country must give arms to those who have shed their blood for her. Sire, give us arms in her name. We swear we will . . . only fight for her sake and yours. Long live freedom! Long live the nation! *Vive l'Empereur!*"

Unlike Louis XVI, however, who had cowered behind well-protected closed doors, Napoleon, completely unguarded, came out smiling to address this mob, and a terrible silence fell upon them as shuffling, pushing and shouts died down.[131]

"Federated soldiers, I have come here alone because I was counting on the people and the army. You have now justified my confidence, and I accept your offer! I shall give you arms! Federated soldiers, if there are some men born in the upper classes of society who may have dishonored the French nation, the love of the fatherland and the feeling of national honor nevertheless have been maintained fully intact by the people and the army. . . . I have faith in you! *Vive la nation!*"[132]

The effect was electric as thousands of men roared their instant approval, cheering their Emperor, and in later weeks they marched again, this time down the rue de Grennelle and Saint-Honoré singing old revolutionary favorites, "Ça Ira" and the "Marseillaise," while burning the white Bourbon flag.[133]

A few days later Napoleon decreed the formation of twenty-four battalions of *"tirailleurs fédérés,"* or infantrymen, for a total of 17,280 men,[134] but who were to be officered and trained by regular army personnel. Nevertheless, Napoleon—who had enough worries with too many unreliable armed National Guard regiments—had no intention of keeping his word about arming these people. After all, if they wanted to fight, the army was crying out for recruits. Six weeks later a mere 3,500 unarmed muskets had been distributed for drilling purposes only. And although both War Minister Davout and Interior Minister Carnot argued with Napoleon to arm these men and use them, the Emperor, with Fouché's full support, stoutly refused to do so. He would never lose his fear of the masses bursting forth from the tenements of the Faubourg Saint-Antoine, those very people against whom, as a young general, he had fired his deadly cannon over twenty years earlier in this very city. But despite his blatant refusal to keep his word and arm the fédérés, tens of thousands of them throughout the country remained loyal to the Empire, thereby neutralizing for the moment another possible threat to the war effort on the home front.[135]

If Napoleon could not count on the fédérés, he did need to call up troops to defend the country against the "hateful injustice of the Allies" and the military threat they posed.[136] While it fell to Davout to supervise the regular army, Lazare Carnot would have to bolster that effort, reinforcing it with the National Guard, though admittedly it was not clear to what extent he could depend upon the latter. Accordingly, on 27 March, Napoleon duly instructed the Interior Minister to take the necessary dispositions.

It was just like old times as General Mathieu Dumas and Carnot conferred hurriedly to draft the necessary measures to help put the country on a war footing once again. And on the fifth and tenth of April, Carnot shocked the French nation by sounding the familiar war tocsin as he promulgated two important decrees, one organizing some 2,200,000 men (between the ages of twenty and sixty) into National Guard units, vastly expanding the old organization; the second decree, immediately activating two hundred four battalions, or some 144,000 men.[137] At the same time, he continued to encourage a vigorous program for the manufacture of arms and war matériel, though he only met with some real success in the northern and eastern regions of the country, notably between Paris and the Rhine.[138] But without a convinced patriotic republican of Carnot's stature and unimpeachable reputation and standing, it is doubtful whether Napoleon could have successfully gathered any significant defense force. Clearly, even a more lethargic Napoleon—and he was certainly no longer his old dynamic self—appeared to realize this, as he now rewarded Lazare Carnot, first by promoting him to the rank of Grand Officer of the Legion of Honor and then by raising him to the peerage, as Count of the Empire.[139]

There was of course one other man necessary for launching French armies once again for an all-out war effort. War Minister Marshal Davout was certainly the third man in the equation, the one who could now make or break Napoleon's bold venture.

Chapter VIII

"Neither Peace nor Truce"

"After having been the greatest of conquerors, now prove yourself the most peaceful of sovereigns: your glory requires it, and our well being demands it of you."

> Electoral College of Seine-et-Oise
> to Napoleon, 14 May 1815

"We all want peace, but at the same time are well prepared for war."

> Napoleon to the Electoral College of
> Seine-et-Oise, 14 May 1815

"In the event of war, everything indicates a successful outcome."

> Napoleon

"There can be neither peace nor truce. There can be no reconciliation with this man [Napoleon], and all of Europe feels the same way."

> Czar Alexander to Queen Hortense

Napoleon's choice of Marshal Davout as War Minister reflected the strain of circumstances. If to all the world this nominee seemed natural enough, to those familiar with court life and the complex mesh and clash of relationships so haphazardly thrown together by Fate, History and Napoleon to form the curious assortment of individuals comprising the upper echelons of French Imperial society, the selection of Marshal Davout (Duc d'Auerstaedt and Prince d'Eckmühl) was little better than the selection of Fouché or Carnot.

To be sure, Louis Davout had at first declined the appointment, which many another might have coveted. In fact the forty-five-year-old Davout had doubted his ability to work with Napoleon, a former "in-law" of sorts, and had only accepted after an unexpectedly disarming plea for help.

"Very well then, I am going to speak to you most frankly," Napoleon had begun. "I have let it be understood that I was acting in concert with my father-in-law, the Emperor of Austria, and that the Empress with [my son] the King of Rome were on their way here. . . . The truth of the matter is, there is nothing to any of that, that in fact I stand here alone, alone against all of Europe. That is my situation! Are you, too, going to abandon me?"[1]

Napoleon knew Davout well, of course, and had chosen this surprisingly blunt, emotional argument for the notoriously unemotional Davout with great care. By implying that he, Davout, was even considering "to abandon" him, had clinched his support, for if there was one man in the entire country who took the word "loyalty" seriously, it was Louis Davout, regardless of how unsatisfactory their personal relationship had been for the past several years. Indeed, it was insulting even to suggest disloyalty in Davout of all persons, who had grimly held on in Hamburg in 1814 as the Allies encircled and closed in on him, at a time when most of Napoleon's other commanders were already wavering, fleeing or surrendering.

Somehow or other these two men, so close in age (Davout being just a year younger) and in professional outlook, had always narrowly missed getting to know and accept one another, and their almost sharing the same military school at the same moment seemed representative of this missed connection, which continued in the following years. Back on 27 September 1785, "gentleman-cadet" Louis Davout had just entered the Ecole Royale Militaire of Paris, where he met several of the men who were to become famous in the future and whom he was to encounter throughout his brief, meteoric career—MacMahon, de Noailles, de Suzannet and de Narbonne, among others[2]—but not Napoleon Bonaparte, who had been commissioned a second lieutenant in the French army leaving these very portals on 21 September for his first military appointment. They had missed meeting each other by just six days; it might as well have been six years.

Unlike Napoleon, Davout was the scion of the ancient, if minor, French aristocracy from Burgundy, where they had been established since 1279, the family taking their name from their principal estate, the château d'Avot, near Dijon. Like his father and many an ancestor over the centuries, the Chevalier Louis-Nicolas Davout was destined for a military career, first attending the Ecole Royale Militaire at Auxerre, before completing his studies in Paris. His father having been killed in a hunting accident when Louis was only nine years old, leaving the family bereft of father and fortune,[3] life thereafter had been one continuous struggle for Davout's determined mother and his three brothers and sisters. But determined they were, for failure meant total ruin for this proud family already hovering on the brink of collapse as a result of this untimely demise of a husband and father who had had little respect for money, making no provision for the future—alas, a trait his son Louis was to inherit.

Unlike most of his fellow aristocrats at the Ecole Militaire, to Davout, who had been appointed a second lieutenant in his father's former royal cavalry regiment in February 1788, the outbreak of the French Revolution the following year seemed just what the nation needed. And although like any normal young man eager for promotion, Louis Davout also firmly believed in the revolutionary gospel of freedom and fraternity, and above all, in the honor and glory of his country. He was a patriot to his very marrow, despite two spells served in revolutionary prisons solely because of his noble birth, incidents which might easily have deterred others less firm in the convictions of their revolutionary beliefs.

Regardless of the prejudice of various superior officers concerning his ancestry, Davout rose rapidly in his military career. By the time General Louis Desaix summoned him to Paris in March 1798 to meet the much talked about General Bonaparte, Davout was already a Brigadier General. This curious meeting was to change Davout's life, for Napoleon, impressed by what he had heard, and now saw for himself, immediately liked this fair, snub-nosed, prematurely balding young man with the enormous domelike head. Seconded to Citizen Bonaparte's Egyptian Expedition, Davout found himself in the company of fellow general officers who were soon to bring fame and glory to French arms: Berthier, Desaix,

Dumas, Kléber, Reynier, Verdier, Leclerc, Lannes, Murat and Damas.[4] It was a very special fraternity indeed, whose members were never to be forgotten by a grateful Napoleon after seizing power and the French government in November 1799.

In Egypt Davout personally distinguished himself time and again as a cavalry commander; his astonishing courage, audacity and ingenuity, embellishing his brilliant battlefield tactics, were accentuated by his remarkable self-possession even in the heat and turmoil of battle. For as Napoleon pointed out when describing what he considered to be the basic traits essential to a good military leader, "The first one," said he, "is to be able to maintain a cool head, permitting one to see things clearly and objectively."[5] In the confusion of battle a commander naturally received all sorts of feverish, often contradictory, reports, and one had to be able to evaluate them and the situation of the moment calmly, accurately and yet quickly. Davout stood out as one of the very few commanders capable of doing that. Furthermore, Napoleon continued, Davout possessed "character and intelligence," though adding wryly that he felt it to be "much more important for an officer to have more character than brains."[6] And even if some of his numerous enemies might later question Davout's character, everyone had to acknowledge that, despite his youth, he had always planned and executed his military operations carefully, had supreme self-confidence in his own decisions, handled great responsibility with considerable ease and was not afraid to alter orders and campaign plans when unexpected midbattle events necessitated it. And yet he always followed Napoleon's plans down to the last detail when at all feasible. This naturally impressed General Bonaparte enormously, who in turn praised Davout in his reports to Paris.

And yet as time passed, Napoleon found he did not particularly enjoy having him around, for General Davout was certainly no courtier. He did not have the tact and patience to cultivate important high-ranking officers and politicians and, indeed, had no patience for that particular sociopolitical process, which he found to be just so much nonsense carried out by second-rate minds. Like Carnot and Napoleon, he had discovered very early that life was a very tough proposition and had to be tackled with all one's might and ability. Under the circumstances, then, it was hardly surprising that Davout had little patience for drawing-room conversation or society, his presence in the chic salons of Paris as rare as a smile on his lips. In short, he was a singularly stern, intense, single-minded young man—forever fault-finding and stubborn—and, like Napoleon, had no qualms about freely expending the lives of his troops when the occasion warranted it.[7] On the other hand—unlike most of his fellow general officers—Davout was considered to be most honest and scrupulous in all things, even winning the praise of his enemy, Bourbon Prefect of Police Anglès, who succinctly attested that he was "irreproachable when it comes to money matters," highly praising "this very rare incorruptibility."[8]

Scrupulous in money matters and objective in evaluating situations, Napoleon knew that he could trust him explicitly. But Davout was also a tough commanding officer, with a well-deserved reputation for his "harshness and critical attitude," which his subordinates frequently found nearly unbearable. Davout demanded intelligence and boldness in his ADCs and staff officers, and needless to say, his hard-driven qualities did not make him a popular man in the army. On the other hand, his staff always had the greatest confidence in him on the battlefield, something rare enough then as now, where indecision and incompetence were the norm. Napoleon himself praised Davout's "distinguished bravery and decisive character" in his "5th Bulletin at the Grande Armée."[9] Indeed, in later years, in a "Cours de Stratégie et de Tactique Générale" at the Ecole de Guerre, one celebrated officer, in discussing Napoleon's finest commanders, described Davout as "the one man of war who could understand, and who was permitted to discuss, his [Napoleon's] major operations with him" and therefore "capable of fully appreciating the true Napoleonic genius."[10] But at the same time Davout for his part had even less of a sense of humor than Napoleon, and if anything, was even more serious, spending most of his time and energy on his career. He was a stickler for detail, and like Napoleon, was ever impatient to see his orders executed forthwith, haranguing his subordinates until that was done.

Under the circumstances, then, it was hardly surprising that if Davout's military career proved an early success, such was not the case with his private life. His first marriage, at the age of twenty-one, to the daughter of the distinguished and wealthy de Seuguenot family had proven a disaster, his wife's infidelities leading to divorce after just two years.[11] His second marriage, ten years later, on 7 November 1801, seemed better fated. An alliance with Aimée, the younger sister of General Victor Emmanuel Leclerc (the husband of Pauline Bonaparte), seemed to portend well. Not only was Aimée Leclerc attractive, cultivated, in good health and relatively wealthy (the daughter of a substantial grain merchant from Pontoise), but of course was the sister of a famous general linked directly to Bonaparte himself, who, along with his wife Josephine, spurred on the initial courtship and later witnessed the signing of the marriage contract.[12] And although the thirty-one-year-old Davout had very little money of his own, his prospects seemed brilliant even then, for upon the establishment of the Consulate, Napoleon quickly rewarded everyone who had been on the Egyptian expedition with him. Davout, who on 3 July 1800 was promoted to the rank of Général de Division, or Major General, was soon dispatched with the Army of Italy on its successful campaign there, in company with six other celebrated soldiers: Berthier, Masséna, Suchet, Moncey, Dupont and Macdonald.[13] And in Italy his abilities were again confirmed by brilliance and audacity in the field. As a result, on 19 May 1804, Napoleon promoted the much-decorated Davout (by now an established member of the Bonaparte clan) as one of the first nine Marshals of the newly created first Empire.

As the riches now suddenly poured in, Davout spent them with a natural aplomb worthy of his spendthrift father. His purchases included a Paris mansion, the former "Hôtel de Monaco" in the rue Saint-Dominique (not far from the War Ministry) for 425,000 francs (including repairs and a complete refurbishing),[14] as well as a splendid country estate at Savigny-sur-Orge, just south of Paris near Essonnes, for a mere 760,000 francs.[15] But the round of activities for the young married couple was quickly reduced to a fairly regular exchange between the Tuileries and Josephine's Malmaison in the western suburb of Rueil, for neither Louis nor the lovely Aimée were socially inclined, both in fact being rather taciturn by nature and unemotional. Gradually the young couple showed a distinct preference for the calmer delights of the countryside at Savigny to the glitter of the fabulous *hôtels particuliers* acquired by Napoleon's nouveau riche and sometimes rather bumptious imperial society. But Davout's idea of hearth and home was soon dashed. His young wife (thirteen years younger than himself) became cold and reclusive, and after the deaths of a few infants, the couple drifted apart. Davout turned to other women for the warmth and comfort his wife declined to provide. He became gloomier than ever and more and more preoccupied with military affairs.

In the campaigns of 1805–1806, including the battles of Austerlitz (2 December 1805) and Auerstaedt (14 October 1806), Davout proved his real military brilliance by single-handedly inflicting a stunning victory over a major Prussian army twice the size of his own. Napoleon showed his appreciation two years later by granting him the title of Duc d'Auerstaedt.[16] This only tended to increase the jealousy and antipathy toward Davout by so many of his fellow general officers who felt that Davout's well-documented abilities and achievements on the battlefield were clearly overrated by Napoleon—for family reasons. Nor was this helped by Davout's unflinching loyalty to the Emperor and his own extraordinary zeal and perseverance in his career. Though often rich and successful themselves, his colleagues continued to snipe at the marshal, who proved an easy target, with his perpetually solemn nature and total lack of geniality and charm. Bernadotte, Berthier, Caulaincourt, Ney and Murat, for instance, detested Louis Davout with an often vigorous rancor, which he fully reciprocated. At the battle of Jena-Auerstaedt (in October 1806) for instance, Davout, facing a Prussian army of more than 50,000 men, appealed to Bernadotte to throw his still uncommitted corps into the battle and come to his aid. Bernadotte was in fact ordered to do so by Marshal Berthier, but he steadfastly refused, forcing Davout to fight it out alone. Although finally winning a superb victory, he did so at the price of 26 percent French casualties.[17] Upon meeting one of Bernadotte's officers immediately after that battle, an angry Davout—then in the process of going over his appalling casualty list—snapped at him: "When I meet him [Bernadotte] I'll horsewhip him!"[18] Alexandre Berthier—no field commander, but a superb chief of staff—was apparently jealous of the younger Davout's quickness and achievement in the field—a jealousy exacerbated by Davout's occasionally ignoring Berthier's orders[19] and then succeeding in spite of them. On an another occasion, during one of the German campaigns when Murat, as King of Naples, insisted on Davout addressing him with the respect due a king, Davout sharply reminded him that on the battlefield he was simply a general like the rest of his colleagues and that he, Davout, would address him accordingly. Some of these quarrels among marshals and generals took place before Napoleon, who simply loathed such undignified scenes, seeing his highest commanders belittling themselves in public and before court officials like so many children, with their bickering and jealous squabbles.

After 1806, with Davout's marriage already in disarray and his reputation for solitude and arrogance by then well established, and his own dissatisfaction in knowing that unlike Murat (married to Caroline Bonaparte) he was not destined for a kingdom or even a principality of his own, his relations with Napoleon began to chill. This was aggravated by occasional outspoken language by Davout to Napoleon.[20] In any event, Napoleon decided to keep Davout as far away from Paris as possible, naming him Governor General of the Grand Duchy of Warsaw, where Davout, amid courtly ceremony and opulence, "ruled" with an iron hand. During the Russian Campaign of 1812, Davout, at the head of the first corps of the Grande Armée, displayed astonishing tactical battle feats. But with the destruction of the French Army, thanks to his own incompetence, Napoleon—as bitter as ever toward Davout—had Murat, Duroc, Berthier and Caulaincourt accompany him on the premature return journey to Paris, leaving behind Prince Eugène, Davout and Ney to salvage what they could of the once-powerful legions.[21] Following the Russian Campaign, Davout was next posted as Governor of Hamburg and the Hanseatic coast, where his ruthless administration won him few German admirers.

During the final campaign in 1813 and 1814, at the head of the Thirteenth Corps around Hamburg, Davout fought with unparalleled tenacity against the Russian onslaught, only surrendering on 23 May, long after Napoleon himself had capitulated. And as Louis Chardigny has aptly said of Davout, "His soul was better than his character, and if he had very few friends, at least he was faithful to them."[22] But most of all, regardless of his differences with Napoleon, Louis Davout remained loyal to him.

If the War Ministry in the rue Saint-Dominique had not changed since Marshal Davout's last visit there years before, there was one great difference now: on the morning of 21 March (1815) Davout stepped from his carriage into the quiet courtyard and entered the semidarkened building as the newly appointed War Minister; now he was responsible to only one man in the entire Empire—Napoleon Bonaparte. To be sure, the name of Marshal Louis Davout would be no more welcome here as War Minister than that of Vice-Admiral Duc Decrès was across the Seine at the Naval Ministry. Both men were renowned for their humorless, hard-driven character and as dedicated, no-nonsense career officers. However, Decrès had the great advantage of fully knowing his job and all that it comprised, having held it throughout the full span of the Empire, whereas Davout had never held any ministerial post. He had much to learn: the political channels of command, bureaucratic procedures, even how to apply for funds allocated by the budget. Clearly this was no time for a neophyte in this critical post and he knew it as well as any man, which is one of the reasons why he had argued so vehemently with Napoleon earlier, trying to dissuade him from this very appointment. Commanding a few thousand men in the field was not the same as commanding all the armies of the land, providing food, housing and arms for more than two hundred thousand men! To arrange for the maintenance of tens of thousands of horses and transport vehicles, of every piece of ordnance, of hundreds of buildings, barracks and forts, while creating sufficient supply depots, was going to be a nightmare. To complicate this situation was one final damning factor: Davout's poor working relationship with Napoleon, with whom he had barely been on civil terms these past ten years. And yet Davout was one of the very few competent, loyal, scrupulous, persevering and dynamic soldiers of his eminence available now for this post. No one less could have been considered—and certainly no political appointee—and yet was he the right man? It would not be easy in such a post under Napoleon. But, in an age where all seemed to be controlled by self-interest, money and lust for power, loyalty and competence were extraordinarily rare commodities. Then, too, honesty and dedication to hard work had to be considered and Davout was one of those rare men who combined all these qualities at a time when most marshals and senior generals had grown rich, fat and slothful. And yet Davout was no desk officer, no administrator. Nonetheless Napoleon knew that, though Davout might make some initial errors, especially when he thought his own views should prevail over those coming from the Tuileries, he could still be relied upon with his bulldog tenacity to stick to the task until it was achieved. What is more, he was utterly devoted to the empire and could be depended upon, unlike just about all the others. Marshals Augereau, Gouvion Saint-Cyr, Kellermann, Marmont, Masséna, Ney, Oudinot, Perignon, Soult, Victor, even the faithful Berthier, had "betrayed" Napoleon's sinking ship.[23] If, however, Napoleon were to reject all who had betrayed him, he would now have no one to lead his armies and hold government posts, and the Emperor's reputation for excusing past misdemeanors and transgressions by former colleagues was as legion as the number itself.

But there were few secrets in an army, even when that reborn army was just a few hours old, and while the wartime capital slept, wrapped in the cold, late wintry March darkness, carriages and horses were already beginning to arrive in the rue Saint-Dominique, bringing the first seekers of posts and commands, loudly insisting that they be admitted to the War Minister at once, though usually not getting past the new Minister's anteroom. Davout would need every capable hand soon enough. The situation was reminiscent of the exciting and bustling Paris of November and December 1799, following the creation of the Consulate. Nevertheless, it would be many hours before Davout would be in a position to see most of the couple of dozen generals and colonels already pacing the corridors and anteroom. Davout, who had been among the first of the ultimately twenty-six to be raised to the rank of Marshal of the Empire, knew nearly every brigadier, divisional (or major) general and full general in the army, and a good many other officers as well.

First things first, however; he had to organize his office and ministry. Who of the permanent War Ministry officials and staff would remain with him? He needed secretaries, department heads, a full complement of ADCs—all superior officers, trustworthy men. Lists had to be drawn up and analyzed, secretaries and clerks dispatched to find files. There were many questions that needed answers. Which of the army commanders were to remain at their posts, and how many of them could be depended upon? *Where* were the French armies now? What was their strength? How many troops were following Louis XVIII to Belgium, and who were their officers? How many of those that remained would be loyal to the returning Napoleon, who had so shocked the nation just the year before by proving he was not invincible after all, that even *he* could be subdued, broken and dismissed. France today was a country in chaos, her illusions shattered. Faith had to be restored, along with order.

Davout, with a mind nearly as quick as Napoleon's himself, wanted everything done at once. Situation reports were ordered, the whereabouts of former army colleagues had to be established, as a growing staff of younger officers hurriedly entered and left the Minister's office and polished tabletops soon disappeared beneath oversized maps and stacks of files, reports and documents. Davout had only been in his office a few hours and already it seemed like the good old days, the mad bustle of the military machine that he and Napoleon had always found so enthralling, indeed intoxicating. Davout now barked out orders, frowned, sifted hurriedly through sheaves of papers, mumbled that all was sheer chaos, and like Napoleon going through a similar scene at the Tuileries, loved it, imbibed of it, as essentially as he did the air he breathed, for it was his very existence, his raison d'être. Those two men, Napoleon and Davout, may not have liked one another any better today than they had ten years earlier, but *they understood one another perfectly as soldiers*, and shared the same values and ultimate aims—viz., to gird the nation for war yet again. Although Davout's notorious short temper and bleak moods were well known to every career officer in the army—causing even brave officers to flinch at the thought of having him as head of the Army—yet even they all knew that Davout's reputation of utter dependability and devotion to the army were solid and very real indeed. Digging his razor-sharp spurs into the flanks of the nation, a determined Davout would drive it on to fulfillment regardless of the pain it caused or blood that flowed, for if he could not get something done, no one short of a Napoleon could. And now the clank of swords, the tread of heavy glistening boots and the growing din of voices gathered in intensity throughout the War Ministry. The "street of the marshals," the rue Saint-Dominique and the courtyard filled with horses, carriages, orderlies and officers, overflowing in the direction of the Invalides and the Ecole Militaire, past the nearby mansions of five celebrated imperial marshals, those of Kellermann, Masséna, Soult, Suchet, and, of course, that of Davout himself.[24] Clearly, Napoleon had returned, and things were back to normal.

The bald, forty-five-year-old War Minister's torrential energy continued unabated as dawn broke unobserved over the French capital, but this had to be if he were to regain contact with the tens of thousands of troops scattered throughout the nation's twenty-three military districts,* and come to grips with the current situation, in order to be able to provide Napoleon with the information he impatiently awaited and desperately needed. From now on until the second week of June, three, four, five and sometimes six officers from the rue Saint-Dominique would be daily passing their counterparts for the Tuileries wearing the Emperor's personal livery, their horses clattering past pedestrians lunging for safety as they crossed the river to relay the feverish messages of their lords.

King Louis was fleeing to the northwest, though it still was not clear whether it would be to the Channel and England, or the Belgian frontier. And if Napoleon deliberately now ordered that he be permitted to leave the country unhindered and unharmed, he did want the State treasury funds he was thought to be carrying, along with his troops' arms and horses. Meanwhile Davout was already dispatching ADCs to the North to establish the loyalty and strength of the armies, and the state of fortifications and supply depots, in the unlikely event of an imminent attack by the Allies.

Mobilizing the nation's defenses would require vast amounts of money of course, and as the War Department's 1815 budget under Louis XVIII no longer applied, there was nothing Davout could do about estimating expenses until Napoleon presented him with the new one, including monthly breakdowns, or with the assurances of a full treasury with money on hand. Nevertheless, the country had to be organized and armed. How this was to be financed was Napoleon's problem, or to be more precise, that of Finance Minister Gaudin and Treasury Minister Mollien. But the rest of the country, the west, south and southeast in general, too, had to be secured, solid pockets of royalist resistance crushed, and every trace of the white Bourbon fleur de lys scourged from the land and replaced by the tricolored cocarde. The Vendée, Bordeaux, Toulouse, Montpellier, Nîmes, Marseille—all were powerful traditional royalist or republican strongholds even in the best of times and unsympathetic to the Empire, and now, of course, were agitated by the Bourbon army gathering under the direction of the Duc d'Angoulême.

*See Appendix II.

Yes, Louis Davout had his work cut out for him. In his anxiety to succeed he, as usual, tried to outthink Napoleon, all the while expediting the Emperor's orders, drafting reports, submitting urgent projects, and preparing the nominations of new commanding officers. No minister in the new government would be communicating more frequently with the Emperor than Davout, but given the domineering nature of these two men, could this tenuous relationship work, or would the choice of Davout for the War Office prove not only a grave error on Napoleon's part, but perhaps a fatal one for France?

If the number of officers milling about the War Ministry seeking commands was large, what Napoleon faced at the Tuileries was a veritable inundation. Suddenly, many who had smartly disappeared over the past year had reappeared demanding favors of various kinds—offices, commands, honors, titles, pensions, rewards—but rarely asking what they could do for France. It came as no surprise to Napoleon, of course, as he now sealed himself off from most court life, closeting himself with his staff, imperial officials, ministers and senior army officers.

In addition to affairs of state, Napoleon was also concerned about the fate of his beautiful young wife, Empress Marie-Louise, and their only child, the King of Rome, whose fourth birthday he had celebrated so dramatically on 20 March by overthrowing the French government. Publicly he confidently announced his wife's forthcoming return along with his son—even having her suite and the nursery completely refurbished and the official court *accoucheur* and governess reinstated—and Foreign Minister Caulaincourt had special couriers dispatched to her to arrange for her return, though it appears that all were intercepted by the Allies before reaching their destination. One earlier letter from Elba had, indeed, reached the French Empress, though she had solemnly handed it over to her father, Austrian Emperor Francis I, at the same time formally renouncing any intention of ever returning to France and Napoleon. Meanwhile, much to the amusement of the diplomats attending the Congress of Vienna, as well as the light-hearted Austrians, Marie-Louise had taken General Adam von Neipperg as her lover, the idea of the dainty Empress cuckolding the mighty Napoleon appealing to everyone's sense of humor. As for Napoleon's only legitimate son, Prince Francis Charles Joseph, King of Rome, he was removed for safekeeping to the Schönbrunn Palace, where, isolated and heavily guarded, he would be better protected against any kidnapping attempt expected now by his disconsolate father.

Nor was this threat taken lightly, for this Emperor, after having success-fully kidnapped the Duc d'Enghien along with several British diplomats from foreign soil in the spring of 1804, had proven himself a skilled practitioner in that treacherous Corsican art. After nearly a year's absence Napoleon was understandably in a desperate enough state of mind to do anything to regain his son and heir.

As for women, feminine attachments had never meant very much to Napoleon since his divorce from Josephine, and the occasional need for such company was easily enough met by willing young, and some not so young, courtesans longing to claim the privilege of his bed. But this was hardly the time for such escapades, when the Empire and his throne were threatened both from without and within.

Despite Emperor Napoleon's stern, derisory, self-confident appear-ance, his occasionally brisk, determined stride and sharp, usually deci-sive orders, despite the presence of old forms, customs and uniforms, surrounded by familiar faces and a bevy of secretaries and ADCs in smart attire—he was in fact fighting desperately to hold on and entrench his position. The old pre-1814 confidence had been all but obliterated by the desertion of his general officers and imperial officials, by his own failed suicide attempt, by his forced abdication and, finally, by his wife's desertion.

Time, however, was now short. He calculated that he had until July or August, at the latest, before the Allies, with their large dispersed armies, would be in position again along France's northern borders for an attack, this time massive enough to shatter him completely. Therefore, he had to do something before some possibly 600,000 Allied troops would be threatening him. To be sure, he went through the diplomatic rituals, writing to kings, princelings and prime ministers of his good faith and peaceful intentions. He duly instructed Foreign Minister Caulaincourt to send secret agents not only to the capitals of the great European powers, but to The Hague, Denmark, Sweden, Bavaria, Württemberg, Baden, Hesse-Darmstadt, Nassau, Saxony, Naples, Tuscany, Rome, Spain and Portugal, to assure them "of my intentions and friendly dispositions re-garding them."[25] His sole wish now was to live in amity and brotherhood with the world, he professed, and his appeal to the King of England was typical.

"*Monsieur mon frère*, the reestablishment of the imperial throne was necessary for the happiness of the French people" and he, Napoleon, had been "carried to the heart of my capital by their love. My cherished wish is to repay such affection by maintaining an honorable calm [*une honourable tranquillité*] . . . and the confirmation of the peace of Europe [*le repos de l'Europe*]. Many changes have taken place and let us now put the years of battle behind us, replacing that military rivalry with one striving instead for the advantages of peace, for the holy struggle and happiness of the people. . . . France is most sincerely pleased to proclaim this noble goal . . . [and to assure] that her steadfast policy henceforth will be to respect absolutely the independence of other nations. If, as I am confident, such are also the personal feelings of Your Majesty, the general calm is assured for a long time, and justice, lodged within every individual country, alone will suffice for the protection of international frontiers."[26]

There would be no more French Armies in Amsterdam, Bruxelles, Hamburg, Berlin, Dresden, Vienna, Warsaw, Moscow, Milan, Naples or Zürich, and clearly no further attempt on London would be made. The leopard had changed its spots, Napoleon had returned from Elba, not as the knight and warrior of old, but as the wisened bearer of peace—peace for France, peace for all of Europe. But England, which had heard this same appeal in 1803, indeed almost word for word, did not bother to reply.

Such professions were, to be sure, for public consumption only. Even the previously moderate Czar Alexander, seeing through them, now declared the utter impossibility of ever again working with, or trusting, Napoleon, whose word and signature on the abdication papers signed at Fontainebleau on 11 April 1815 had proven as worthless as Napoleon's Treaty of Amiens a dozen years earlier.

If Napoleon was publicly renouncing war, there was only one realistic policy at home, however, "defense" of the homeland, he called it. "All Frenchmen must rally now to prevent a civil war and repulse the foreigners,"[27] War Minister Davout echoed, admonishing the highest military officers of the land, ordering them to return to Paris forthwith. The results, however, were shocking: refusals, excuses, or more often than not, no reply at all, as was the case with the elusive, noncommittal Marshals Gouvion Saint-Cyr and Oudinot. Davout threatened to have them "arrested and declared traitors of their country." He also threatened to confiscate their wealth and estates, and to have them report not to the rue Saint-Dominique, but to the dungeons of Vincennes.[28] André Masséna, Prince d'Essling, also remained aloof, hedging his bets in silence at his 8th Military District headquarters in Marseille,* and Napoleon frankly had no idea what to expect from that brilliant commander whose services he so badly needed. Accordingly, Davout softened

---

*Masséna resided in Marseille, though technically the H.Q. were in Toulon.

the message sent to him, explaining that "the Emperor realizes you are in a difficult position in the midst of a rebellious population."[29] In any event, nothing could be done regarding Masséna without a good long interview with him, to clarify the situation.[30] In the meantime, Napoleon proclaimed his policy loud and clear to the War Minister: "Forget the past, but take harsh measures against traitors and agitators."[31] And yet was he in a position to enforce it?

Meanwhile within France's frontiers, order and confidence had to be restored, and without order there could be no confidence, not even within those now much reduced imperial borders. When on 27 March General Pajol informed the War Minister that there was some unrest in the Vendée, some sort of Chouan uprising, Davout dismissed it out of hand: "I do not think that can be of any serious consequence," he replied. "A few days of vigorous action by you will put everything to rights and peace will be quickly restored." And although confidentially assuring Marshal Suchet that "the Bourbons have been completely broken," he nevertheless closed with a firm: "But there must be no civil war, a curse upon those who wish to stir one up."[32] In the meantime, to ensure the crushing of the last signs of rebellion, Davout ordered General Clausel to march on and suppress the city of Bordeaux, and Marshal Suchet and General Grouchy to the east, to secure Lyons and pursue the Duc d'Angoulême to the south.[33] As early as 26 March Napoleon ordered the reorganization of the nation's armies,[34] issued decrees calling up retired former soldiers[35] and for the bolstering of the Imperial Guard, followed shortly thereafter by the mobilization of the National Guard.[36]

Henceforth, from the day of his return on 20 March, the keynote of Napoleon's activities would be not merely defensive military measures, but active war preparations. On 3 April he might indeed instruct Caulaincourt to dispatch secret diplomatic agents behind the scenes to reassure European statesmen of his alleged peaceful intentions, while simultaneously secretly ordering the creation of the single largest cavalry force of any individual country in Europe, one larger than Wellington's and Blücher's combined force.[37] And while frontier fortresses, batteries and redoubts were arguably essential for the defense of the land, cavalry regiments, particularly the large numbers of light cavalry Napoleon was now envisaging, were deployed primarily for quick offensive purposes, for attack, and always entailed very heavy extraordinary expenses for the Army and the State. If anything gave the early lie to Napoleon's "*bonnes intentions*" vis-à-vis the Allies for the maintenance of peaceful coexistence, it was this phenomenally large cavalry force—up to 46,000 strong—which would permit the Emperor to carry out lightning strikes beyond French frontiers before the Allies could even act. (The usually observant Wellington was later to pay a very high price for failing to take note of this act.) The second factor giving the lie to Napoleon's true intentions was seen in his orders, letters and decrees issued between 21 March and the second week of June, 95 percent of which were addressed to his various ministers and officials about only one subject, war preparations: to Davout and the Army, to Carnot for the National Guard, to Gaudin and Mollien regarding funds for the war chest (while perhaps more than 70 percent of those were addressed directly to Davout). The remaining 5 percent, though dealing with nonmilitary matters, were often indirectly related, such as the appointment of more loyal and efficacious prefects, mayors and public officials, tax collections, the sale of national forests and property, the cutting of national timber for war revenue purposes, or the rebuilding of houses in northeastern France destroyed by the fighting in 1813 and 1814 (whose inhabitants Napoleon would need on his side in the event of war now) and finally the convening of electoral colleges (to gain official public support for mobilization).

In brief, Napoleon had returned to France bent on war and reestablishing himself firmly as a military leader of the French, to which these hundreds of official documents flowing from the Tuileries so dramatically attest. Not a single long-term project was mentioned or drafted for the improvement of the life of the French people. Nor had the Emperor returned from Elba with sincere projects for improving relations with the other European powers, whom, until his own downfall, he had been attacking and overrunning for the past decade. There were no plans to change the military-oriented curricula at schools, to correct national histories explaining the true nature of French depredations in Europe, to expand education or improve commercial facilities and transport. As Fouché had said to Pasquier, "that man has learned nothing, and has returned as despotic as ever."[38] Despite the usual Tuileries rhetoric that he had come to rule France for and with the people, under fresh constitutional constraints, the facts speak for themselves. He had made this one last extraordinary attempt, or gesture, to regain power for *himself* and his family. It had nothing to do with the needs of France or of the French people who would, to their detriment, be dragged into yet another war because of his obstinacy and personal objectives. After all, what was an Emperor without an Empire? If perhaps he was reconciled—albeit half-heartedly—to accept the old, restricted French national frontiers, recognizing that further aggression in Europe could not be considered again (for the moment, that is), at least he could restore his own regime.

But what became strikingly evident within the first weeks of his return was that even if the European powers convening at Vienna agreed to peace (of which there was not the slightest indication), the French people were not reconciled to Napoleon Bonaparte. As War Minister Davout, Interior Minister Carnot and Police Minister Fouché were beginning to corroborate, the number of reports reflecting strong resentment against Napoleon was growing daily, extending to the Channel ports, sweeping southward across Brittany, Deux-Sèvres, Morbihan, the Vendée, to Bordeaux, Toulouse and the whole of the Languedoc, Marseille and the Var. The depth and vigor of this royalist, anti-Bonapartist feeling and agitation was simply astonishing.

The only way he could possibly counter it and reunite the country behind him was by going to war and roundly defeating the powerful seventh coalition now gathering to the north, thereby hoping to mollify his critics, as he had always done in the past, beginning with Austerlitz in 1805. Then, too, he probably would have lost his crown, with the treasury empty, commerce in dire straits and the massive two-year invasion preparations for England an utter fiasco, had he not returned—not just with a victory—but a stunning one.

In fact the intensity and grass-roots origins of the fresh anti-Bonapartist feeling across the land now in 1815 were much stronger and better developed than in 1805. What is more, it no longer seemed certain that even the greatest victory in history over the Allies could ensure him a secure future in France, for the French people were weary beyond measure of armies, of seeing a repetition of the massive French casualty reports—21,000 at Aspern-Essling, 25,000 at Eylau, 32,000 at Wagram, 73,000 at Leipzig, 50,000 *annually* in Spain and over four-fifths of the entire Grande Armée during the 1812 Russian Campaign, including perhaps a quarter of a million Frenchmen (of the original 300,000 or so who had set out on the death march to Moscow).[39] Nearly an entire generation of youth had been swept away or shattered, and the national economy diverted for the sole purpose of building armies. And although Napoleon—through his monopoly and manipulation of the nation's press—had suppressed the full extent of these horrific facts and statistics, by 1815 the French people could see for themselves, unaided, and had little patience or loyalty left for him and his blood-stained imperial glory. If they did not particularly like the Bourbons or Louis XVIII, one enormous compensating factor remained in their favor, in spite of the King's harebrained religious fanaticism and medieval ideas of restoring feudal privilege and government. For all his impressive failings, at least Louis XVIII was no soldier, and had not the slightest interest in war and armies. Napoleon, on the other hand, had no ploy with which to counter

Emperor Napoleon

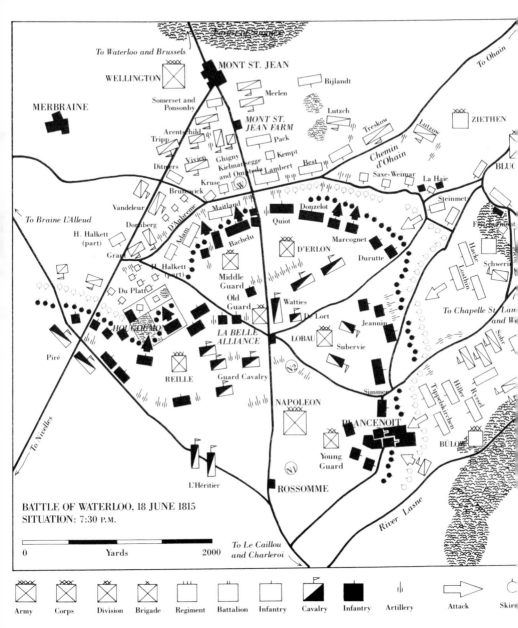

BATTLE OF WATERLOO, 18 JUNE 1815
SITUATION: 7:30 P.M.

| 0 | Yards | 2000 |

To Le Caillou
and Charleroi

Symbols Used on Military Map

| Army | Corps | Division | Brigade | Regiment | Battalion | Infantry | Cavalry | Infantry | Artillery | Attack | Skir |

KEY W Wellington's main position
     N1 Napoleon's first position
     N2 Napoleon's secondary position

that stark fact, unless of course he had decided to retreat to Elba, leaving France in the peaceful state in which he had found it and which King Louis's presence had ensured. From his viewpoint, however, it was now too late even for that. He had burned his proverbial bridges, and the Allies were adamant about putting an end to the threat he posed once and for all. Some wanted his execution, others were satisfied with a sturdy prison, but this time one very, very far from Europe. As Napoleon saw it, he could either go forward into battle or . . .

The time factor also seemed against the Emperor from the start, this for several reasons. Unlike the situations in the past, he now had to reorganize the entire armed forces, call up and train the 1815 conscripts and the National Guard, name new loyal commanding officers at all levels, prepare arms, equipment and provisions in massive quantities, and raise the necessary funds for this effort. This at a time when the Allies—already formed into a powerful coalition with armies in the field, or on the way—had, rare even for coalitions, clearly demonstrated the strength of their consensus by their singular determination to destroy Napoleon and crush the untrustworthy French people whose signature on peace treaties appeared to mean nothing, to give them one final lesson they would never forget. For twenty-five years their armies had been causing upheaval throughout Europe; they must be stopped permanently. As for the present situation, it was all due to their (the Allies') leniency the previous year, the leniency so warmly espoused by Czar Alexander. What is more, for the first time in many a year, the Allies no longer had to fear lightning attacks from Napoleon's crack legions with a united country behind him, that is, from legions which no longer existed and a country torn by strife and dissension.

Nor, of course, would there by any legions without money, and the French Emperor had urgently summoned the Finance Minister, Duc de Gaëte (Martin-Charles Gaudin), and Treasury Minister Comte Mollien to the Tuileries, instructing them to come up with a lot of answers and quickly: What were King Louis's 1815 budget estimates for the expected annual national revenue remaining to be collected over the next several months, and the amount actually in the treasury? How much could be allocated now? But if the Emperor could bully army commanders into moving troops quickly, experience had taught him long ago that Treasury and Finance Ministers were independent men sure of themselves and their own value, who at the same time made heads of state realize it took time to gather the data and estimates in order to make the calculations required of them.

Hence it was not until 14 April that Messrs. Gaudin and Mollien finally returned to the Tuileries, now attended by a bevy of secretaries armed with reports, analyses and projections. King Louis's budget for this year had been 298 million francs, not nearly enough to meet the costs for national mobilization, and Napoleon ordered Finance Minister Gaudin to revise it sharply upward, initially to four hundred million.[40] And yet even this would hardly suffice, for in theory it cost forty million francs to mobilize each entirely new army corps, and he was initially calling for at least eight of them, at a cost of three hundred twenty million francs (and he anticipated creating perhaps two additional corps later). To be sure, increasing national taxes by a full third above the existing levels would make onerous demands on the people of France, whose economy had been practically destroyed as a result of ten years of Napoleon's nearly incessant warfare. It could only be done at bayonet point, whereas the Emperor could not afford to alienate further a people who would now have to yield up their sons and husbands, as well as their last penny, yet again.

Nevertheless, what a contrast from earlier days in the Empire, when Napoleon never had less than five hundred millions. The first imperial budget, for 1804—at 588,066,203 francs—had risen to 744,392,027 francs by 1810 and then to 876,266,180 francs in 1812.[41] Direct taxes and property registration fees certainly accounted for the two largest basic sources of annual revenue, aided by customs receipts, the *droits réunis*, the national lottery, and the post office. But what was hidden from the French public was the amount "contributed" by what they euphemistically referred to as "the countries which have gradually been joined to France since the beginning of the Revolution," that is, all the lands conquered and subjugated by French armies. In the case of the above 1812 revenue figures, for instance, the Benelux countries alone provided 153,805,239 francs, and obviously not on a voluntary basis. (The Dutch, of course, had seen their Treasury and Navy seized and their houses occupied by French troops, and thus were hardly enthusiastic about paying these large sums to fill French coffers, part of which in turn paid the very troops that held bayonets at their throats, forcing them to continue paying.) Meanwhile the funds poured into the French treasury from Parma, Turin, Genoa, Florence, Sienna, Rome, Livorno, Spoleto, Hamburg, Bremen, Aachen, Osnabrück, Mainz, Münster, The Hague, Amsterdam, Anvers, Bruges, Bruxelles, Luxembourg, Geneva and Nice, totaling 226,389,345 francs just in 1812.[42] (Naturally, this excluded the vast sums extorted from Spain.)

But French bayonets could no longer provide these annual contributions, and additional funds had to be found elsewhere, as the War Ministry alone would need close to 70 million francs a month over the next several months,[43] and thus, if that figure were applied beginning in May, the entire national budget would not suffice just for Davout's needs. On a more optimistic note, Mollien reported that taxes had been coming in fairly regularly under Louis XVIII, who in his inordinate haste to flee in March, left 50 million francs in cash in the Treasury. Another 150 million could be raised by an emergency national loan, he felt,[44] and when consulted later, the wizard of French finance, Gabriel-Julien Ouvrard promised another 40 million. Gaudin said Napoleon could probably count on an additional 240 million francs over the next several months.[45] But promises were one thing, translating them into a flow of hard cash would be another, and the final bill for war expenses was always far greater than originally presented to the Chambers voting the funds. For instance, to keep the proposed Armée du Nord in the field in peacetime, clothed and armed, would cost 5 million francs a month, or 40 million francs by the end of the year, and that was just one army. Another 24 million would be needed initially just to clothe and equip the national guards[46] (an amount not even included in the War Ministry's budget), although the Chambers were not to be informed of these problems until mid-June, by which time much of that money had already been spent.

Moreover, by squeezing hard and the use of legerdemain, over the remaining months of the year the Treasury Minister promised Napoleon 440 million francs in "extraordinary revenue"—above and beyond that allocated by the annual civilian budget requirements: 80 million francs from the sale of State and communal properties, 300 million from the sale of State forests and cut timber, and 60 million from the "*centimes de guerre*," special war taxes and contributions.[47] And yet, how realistic was this? When rushed sales of seized land and property had been attempted years earlier during the French Revolution, it had proven a disaster, the market glutted with property, forcing down prices, and, of course, when too much was offered to the people, they suddenly became wary. What is more, during the Revolution, as now, large amounts of property—frequently with no proper title, or at best of a dubious nature—were offered to the public without proof and assurances that claims to such title would not be overturned or rejected by the next government, the next political regime, and if nothing else was sure and predictable in history, it was that at least there would always be a "next government." As a result of the acquisition of such property, new proprietors—even if their titles were recognized and upheld by subsequent courts—sometimes found themselves obliged to pay a second time to ensure their title. But anticipating that all 80-million-francs' worth of State and communal property (excluding State forests) could be sold profitably and the money collected within just a few months, was wishful thinking, and even Napoleon knew that.

Nevertheless, from his viewpoint, the worst of it was that this sum of 440 million francs was earmarked—not for the armed forces and the waging of war—but for repayment to all the ministries for *previous* wartime expenses, notably army equipment and provisions. If this were not done, however, and faith not quickly restored in government contracts and promises, Napoleon certainly could not expect the nation to offer services and products again now, to meet the new, looming national threat. These funds were also to be used to repay cities and individuals for requisitions and destruction incurred due to previous enemy attacks, confiscation and occupation. Arrears in salaries to government officials were also included, "for I wish . . . to repay all that I owe various departments of the country and thus put an end to this whole business," an impatient Napoleon informed the Treasury Minister.[48] Old, unpaid bills, like any other old, nagging problems did not simply vanish of themselves.

But when even the entire national budget could not begin to cope with Napoleon's present financial demands for the army budget, compounded by Mollien's latest report that less than 700,000 francs remained in the treasury of the original 50 million found there on 20 March, the Emperor threw up his hands in despair.[49] He was now reaping the inevitable whirlwind he had sewn years before, leading to the commercial isolation and collapse of France and, indeed, to the destruction of the French national economy.

When even the projected 1815 naval budget of 70 million francs—i.e., for the entire year—could not be met, Napoleon informed Admiral Decrès on 22 April that it would have to be cut to 50 million francs (i.e., by a reduction of 28 percent),[50] in other words, well under a single month's Army budget. The officers and crews of all but five of the Navy's ships of the line were to be reassigned to shore duty, along with hundreds of pieces of naval artillery, to man coastal and even interior defenses.[51] The few remaining smaller vessels were to be left to protect the principal Channel ports and harbors. As Napoleon now informed a much flummoxed Naval Minister, he was virtually putting the French Navy in mothballs: "Given the present situation, we cannot do anything for the Navy before the month of September at the earliest . . . [and therefore] I should like to see these 50 million francs *spent on the army and national defense.*

So long as this crisis lasts, *it really does not much matter whether or not we have a navy*,"[52] and then even ordered the last five armed battleships to be stripped and drydocked.[53] Decrès was simply staggered. Never since his original appointment to this post in 1801, never in the bleakest days of the Empire, had he seen *the entire French Navy put into mothballs*! It was a very bitter pill indeed for the admiral to have to swallow. What a comedown from the summer of 1805, when the French Navy boasted some forty superb ships of the line just in European waters. But after the débâcle of Trafalgar (21 October 1805), Napoleon had never again taken the French Imperial Navy seriously, and now, with the country threatened on all sides, he announced the final humiliation, the beaching of the last of the great warships. No wonder the Naval Minister had gained in girth and turned more and more to heavy drinking. As for Britain's Royal Navy, little did they realize that France was theirs for the taking!

But Emperor Napoleon was interested only in Emperor Napoleon. He was and remained essentially a soldier at heart, with a soldier's aims, interests and values, not a civilian, with projects for rebuilding France. Apart from ordering the Duc de Bassano to select an historian to sift through the tons of imperial records, to draft a massive history of his great *chef d'oeuvre*, from its inception in 1804, Napoleon's eyes were turned only on the army preparations and the timetable for war. He would show the Allies that he was not yet finished, that as he repeatedly put it now, his "hand had not lost its cunning." The Allies would very much regret the humiliation of Elba, or at least, he, Napoleon, would die gloriously in the attempt. And even if Gaudin and Mollien could only come up with excuses for an empty treasury, that would not prevent him—the greatest military juggler in European history—from launching his legions in another great war . . . even if it were to be his last. As for those hundreds of millions of francs needed to pay for that great event, payment could be put off and delayed over the next few months and by then, with another great military victory in hand, the money— foreign money, of course—would fill the State coffers once again. And if he lost . . . well, then it really would not matter, would it?

Meanwhile, dissident regions of the country had to be rallied and won over to his cause, uprisings put down, patriotism stimulated, and what better way to raise additional sums than by repeating his astonishing triumph of 1803–1804 when he had called upon every French citizen and organization to make *"offrandes patriotiques"* for the building of the nation's defenses. To be sure, in those far-off days, he had been able to squeeze money out of the conquered Belgians, Dutch, Swiss and Italians, and that could no longer be done today, but at least he could appeal to the generous French people. By 1804, for instance, he had raised a total of 24 million francs for similar "patriotic offerings,"[54] which had helped pay for part of his impressive invasion fleet, and if he realized that the amount raised today would be less, given the state of the French economy, at least he would produce a respectable amount, while more importantly reviving the spirit of patriotism and pride, resulting in new unity in the land.

And thus the word went out from the Tuileries, or to be more precise, orders to the various ministers, especially Carnot and Davout, to inform prefects, school directors, public officials and army commanders to stimulate this great patriotic gesture, "to encourage" contributions from the people, however humble, and gradually the funds trickled in. "I am enclosing the 100 francs I received for the sale of my jewelry," wrote one Cornélie, a working-class Parisienne, to a much-moved Carnot.[55] The lycée students of Grenoble were ordered to send 400 francs, those of Nancy, 500.[56] Not to be outdone by the youngsters, the Collège de France produced 1,500 and the more patriotic Ecole Polytechnique (with its future engineering and artillery officers) 4,000 francs. The commanding officer of the Rheims National Guard offered to pay out of his own pocket an annual 250 francs pension to each of the four most outstanding recruits. One Mabillion, a veteran of Napoleonic triumphs and disasters in the Egyptian campaign of 1798–1799, offered his emperor his entire meager pension of 1,081 francs for the next four years. The Comédie-Française sent the Treasury half of one night's receipts, 1,500 francs. Considerable pressure was put on reluctant state employees, even those in badly paid positions, Carnot's Interior officials coming up with 5,777 francs, those of the Foreign Office with 5,000, Davout's War Ministry producing 14,000 francs, LaValette's Postal Department 20,000 and Mollien's hard-pressed Treasury 27,839 francs. Nor were prefects, judges and even court clerks exempt from this artificial, if limp, patriotic revival, the Paris Prefect of Police producing 20,000 francs, the courts of Paris proffering 6,000 francs, and those of Douai and Poitiers, for instance— 2,000 and 3,000 francs respectively—while the revenue agents of Colmar contributed another 5,300. In addition, each regimental commander "encouraged" his officers and men to forgo one, or even two, days' pay, the 7th Régiment de Tirailleurs redefining the word "patriotism" by offering five days' pay. As a rule, officers were persuaded to contribute individually 100, 500, 1,000 or even 4,000 francs each according to their rank and personal wealth. A group of merchants from royalist Bordeaux surprisingly offered to clothe and equip two National Guard companies, some grain merchants in Les Halles offering 3,700 francs, one Parisian sending 10,000 francs directly to the Treasury, matched by a similar sum from one Frédéric, a Mulhouse manufacturer. Davout received an offer of 2,000 francs "for the first soldier to capture an enemy flag," a distiller from Jonzac presented forty casks of eau-de-vie, an arms manufacturer donated 100 muskets, a saddler from Boulogne presented several cavalry saddles. Small anonymous contributions reached the desks of Davout, Carnot, Gaudin, Mollien and Napoleon, while a patriotic Parisian by the name of Delorbe offered 60,000 francs a year "as long as the war lasted." And on 14 May, during Napoleon's review of the Paris fédérés, one woman approached Interior Minister Carnot and suddenly shoved a thick petition into his hands, then just as quickly disappeared anonymously into the crowd: upon opening it, Carnot discovered twenty-five 1,000-franc bank notes, tied together by a red Legion of Honor ribbon.[57] But the vast sums offered by the cities and eighty-seven departments in the past—frequently amounting to hundreds of thousands of francs each— simply did not materialize and the national appeal turned out to be a colossal flop, bringing perhaps less than one tenth of the amount offered for the appeal in 1804, a true barometer of Napoleon's declining popularity and fortunes. Even a Napoleon, it would seem, could not force history to repeat itself in this instance.

Regardless of the obvious resistance he was meeting, the Emperor was not to be denied his special moment now for the only program he had prepared during his long frustrating months on Elba . . . war. An army of course was only as good as the men who led it, and for what Napoleon envisaged, this meant having commanders who both knew him and what he expected of field officers, and who at the same time had already proven themselves capable of handling whole divisions and corps, and that meant marshals or senior generals. But the problem was, how many of them could he consider loyal and trustworthy, and of those few, how many were now in France and willing to serve under him?

Of the twenty-five marshals he had created thus far during the Empire, only one had neither abandoned him at Fontainebleau in March and April 1814, nor had gone over to serve Louis XVIII since then— Marshal Davout. Not only had the prickly Davout remained fully trustworthy, but he (along with Masséna) was probably his most capable field commander, as he had proven time and time again. In any event the Emperor needed "big names" in his cabinet to attract other big names, and at this stage, Davout was the the one well-known person he could rely upon one hundred percent. The Duc d'Albuféra, Marshal Louis-Gabriel Suchet, was also available, but hardly of the same caliber as Davout. Ney, of course, had changed sides once again, having now rejoined Napoleon—a fairly good commander, no doubt, but no more than that, and about as loyal and trustworthy as a polecat. Marshals Brune, Gouvion Saint-Cyr, Jourdan, Kellermann, Lefebvre, Macdonald, Masséna, Moncey, Mortier, Oudinot, Pérignon, Sérurier, Soult and Victor, to be sure, were in or near France, but until March, heading Bourbon armies or retired, and now refusing to offer their services. Napoleon, however, was desperate enough to consider them for important commands if they would betray Louis XVIII publicly and return to the fold.

Fortunately, the list of loyal generals capable of commanding a corps or division was longer, including Clausel, Drouet d'Erlon, Drouot, Exelmans, Foy, Gérard, Grouchy, F. E. Kellermann (the Marshal's son), Lamarque, Lecourbe, Mathieu, Milhaud, Morand, Pajol, Piré, Rapp, Reille and Vandamme—and perhaps a few more out of a list of several dozen, though some of these very far from the best. At the same time, Napoleon also drew up a shorter list of known disloyal general officers, including Briche, Clarke, Curto, D'Aultanne, Dessoles, Dupont, Leclerc, Loverdo, Maison, Monnier and Souham, whose names he had struck from the army rosters.

As for the highest commanders, his marshals, he had only seven—including the newly promoted and twenty-sixth but hardly first-rate Grouchy—Brune, the self-serving Soult, Suchet, Mortier, Ney and, of course, Davout. But Davout, it was felt, could not be spared for a field command and Grouchy would have to replace the Masséna of yore, probably at the head of the cavalry. As for Mortier, Ney and Soult, Napoleon was not yet ready to commit himself. In brief, of the twenty-two living imperial marshals, only four—Mortier, Ney, Grouchy and Suchet—were available to head an army corps into action. If Napoleon could not pull rabbits quickly out of his famous round hat, he would be going to war with only four marshals in his entire army as field commanders (two of whom of uncertain loyalty), as compared with ten in the Russian campaign of 1812. Moreover, from these few dozen superior officers now willing to rejoin Napoleon, commanders had to be selected for the country's twenty-three military districts. He simply needed more senior officers, for the situation was nearly out of hand. Then to compound the problem, the armies were lacking hundreds of good junior officers as well.

As for the problem of loyalty, Soult proved a typical example. What to do about him? He was first named Imperial Marshal in 1804, when he headed the immense army of 167,000 men gathering at Boulogne for the invasion of England, which was then converted into the Grande Armée that was launched against the Austrians and Russians at Austerlitz in December 1805. This same Soult, of course, abandoned Napoleon in 1814, not merely going over to King Louis, but becoming his War Minister. Could he really be trusted now? Davout summoned him—"*par amitié pour vous*"—back to Paris to take the "loyalty oath" to Napoleon and Empire, though many weeks were to pass before the slippery Soult finally committed himself, throwing in his hand with Napoleon.[58] But if most other marshals did not return now to the Tuileries on bended knee to renew their allegiance to Napoleon, officially renouncing the Bourbon throne, it was hardly surprising. Indeed, given the circumstances, it would have been foolhardy for anyone to want to return to Napoleon now, when his situation was demonstrably as dubious as it had been in the fateful early months of 1814. Napoleon was stymied by the reluctance or outright refusal of those who turned their back on him, or of those who did return but refused to take the loyalty oath he insisted upon. In the past, no official, no officer, held a commission or post without first swearing before the imperial eagles. "A large number of individuals refuse to swear their allegiance to me" a perplexed Emperor informed Acting Justice Minister Cambacérès, "What should be done about them?"[59] He really did not know, nor did Cambacérès.

Nevertheless, as it turned out, loyalty oaths were the least of his problems now, for Napoleon had to take whomever he could find. If Ney (and later Soult and Mortier) did associate themselves with the Empire, they were not given immediate commands of troops, Soult instead finding himself temporarily restricted as Inspector General of the northern defenses, while Ney was kept far from Paris and the sensitive northwest, where large armies were now gathering—that is, until the very last minute. As for Oudinot, Mortier, Victor, Gouvion, Pérignon and Kellermann, they were permitted to return to their residences in Paris or the provinces, but under loose house arrest, Mortier alone finally offering his services.[60]

Although determined to reorganize the entire military establishment and transform it into an effective war machine as quickly as possible, Napoleon initially found his hands tied because of his own earlier proclamations enunciating his own peaceful intentions. The allied declaration against France on 25 March[61] had immediately changed all that, however, and the next day he announced the creation of eight *Corps d'Observation* along the French frontiers, a month later converting four of them into fully operational "armies" (indicating their new "offensive" as opposed to nominal "defensive" roles). The Armée du Nord was to be the principal one, joined by the Armée de la Moselle, the Armée du Rhin and the Armée des Alpes,[62] supported by the Observation Corps of the Jura, of the Pyrénées and of the Var (mobilization authorization of this latter corps postponed for the time being, however). In addition, four reserve corps were to be created at Bordeaux, Toulouse, Lyons and Paris (under the command of Comte Lobau), while a "temporary army," that of the Loire, was of course also created later in May and placed under the command of General Lamarque with orders to quell the civil war in the West.

The regular army corps were to be reinforced by the calling up of a large portion of the National Guard's total of four hundred battalions,[63] to be drawn from up to ten percent of each department's population, under the direction of Interior Minister Lazare Carnot. But once activated, National Guard command was transferred to the War Minister and the Army, and one lieutenant-general named to command each Guard unit in each of the twenty-three military districts. To meet the current emergency, the Guards were divided into two classes: the élite, or mobile, National Guard and the "sedentary" units. While the sedentary Guards—usually older or less fit male citizens up to the age of sixty—were assigned to defend their own particular city or region, the younger élite Guard were created to man the northern frontier forts, defenses, garrisons and depots, extending from the English Channel right across the country to the Rhine and the Alps. At a stroke they would thereby release tens of thousands of trained regular army troops for badly needed front-line duty, leaving behind only experienced artillery units with the National Guards. Initially, Napoleon ordered the élite Guardsmen to be in place along the northern frontier by 10 May, though this deadline was to come and pass, and be delayed more than once thereafter. In most cases Guards units were not actually called up, equipped and dispatched to the north until early June, and then in inadequate numbers. Although hundreds of regular army officers were seconded to the National Guard, and 14 million francs released by the Interior Minister with which to clothe and equip them, the process proved longer and more arduous than anticipated. The nation's defenses were to be manned "*au son du tocsin*" ("at the sound of the tocsin") by a general *levée en masse*, drawing on every possible source, the National Guard naturally remaining the basic reserve force.

In May, notwithstanding mounting military costs and insufficient funds, Davout finally convinced Napoleon of the necessity of creating the Corps d'Observation du Var, comprising the large, troublesome 8th Military District with a strength of three divisions to be commanded by

Marshal Brune.[64] That same day Napoleon promoted Emmanuel de Grouchy to the rank of Marshal (the twenty-sixth, and as it turned out, the last, to be so nominated) who was to exchange the command of the Armée des Alpes at Lyons for that of the French Army's entire cavalry force.[65] Unlike in previous military campaigns, on this occasion Napoleon was aided in the drafting of his campaign plans and strategy by Marshal Davout and General Andréossy's "Section de Guerre" of the Conseil d'Etat (including the Comité de Défense, whose work involved assessing technical and intelligence reports—e.g., regarding the efficacy of northern fortifications and defenses, and numerous engineering problems, recommending the appropriate corrective measures as required).[66]

Troops for the defense of France ultimately were to fall into several categories: recruits, "former soldiers" (an euphemism including some 85,000 deserters from 1814),[67] retired soldiers who had already completed their military service, men on temporary leave, national guardsmen, the gendarmeries, forest wardens, customs officials, fédérés and "volunteers." For a variety of reasons mobilization of this manpower was proving much more difficult than anticipated, for which Napoleon reprimanded Davout.

Although prefects, mayors and municipal councils throughout the country were literally ordered by Napoleon "to show the flag," the people had heard that patriotic appeal too often in the past. Mayors in many regions now declined to encourage recruits to appear either for the Army or the National Guard, and in some dramatic instances, those National Guard regiments that did assemble—particularly in the Midi—because of disloyalty had to be replaced in part or entirety, including numerous officers.[68]

If recruiting troops and organizing armies were to prove much more agonizing than Davout had expected, the problem of supplying uniforms, arms and munitions, and food for up to an additional 340,000 men[69] proved an unmitigating nightmare from the very beginning, as he designated the three principal supply depots for the northern armies at Soissons, Laon and Avesnes, with smaller depots at Meaux, Guise, Vitry, Langres, Metz and Strasbourg.[70] Although originally intended to hold enough provisions to sustain 100,000 men and 20,000 horses,[71] on 3 May Napoleon revised that sharply upward, requiring enough stores—including wheat, rice, eau-de-vie and vegetables—for some 250,000 men, and fodder for 40,000 horses, for a period of up to six months, which in effect meant *23 million rations* for the troops and *4 million* for the horses! "Then the Army will not have to resort to requisitions," Napoleon explained, apparently seeing no particular significance in these phenomenal figures, which excluded the purchase of over 7,600 head of cattle.[72] In the past the commandeering of food supplies by local army commanders had always been a source of friction between Napoleon and the French people. Frequently, entire communities found not only food but horses and wagons suddenly removed, sequestered without appeal, an officer simply handing them a chit in receipt with a promise of reimbursement later. Just how onerous this had become was borne home on Napoleon on 29 April 1815, when he was handed a bill for 118 million francs demanded as compensation for communities that had suffered from Napoleon's ruthless requisitioning in 1813–1814, that is to say, a sum over twice Admiral Decrès's naval budget for the entire year, and even then excluding the vast cost of rebuilding entire villages and houses destroyed in the fighting.[73]

Hence the Emperor's growing concern for adequate supply depots to avoid this problem in the future, though the Army's Munitionnaire Général was allocated a basic monthly budget of only 1 million francs for this purpose (exclusive of a series of contracts with various private firms). Thus, for instance, during the previous regime, Louis XVIII's government had signed a major victualing agreement with a contractor by the name of Doumerc, who had, since Napoleon's March coup d'état, suspended operations. Upon investigation it turned out that Doumerc was merely a front man acting on behalf of none other than Gabriel-Julien Ouvrard. With northern army warehouses still largely empty and a hungry army to feed, an exasperated War Minister Davout took matters into his own hands, ordering numerous prefects to intervene personally and conclude subcontracts with local suppliers, regardless of the price, and to charge the whole thing to Doumerc's government account (Doumerc, of course, being in no position to lodge a complaint). If these were at best stopgap measures, they did have a more salutory effect, forcing Doumerc's—i. e., Ouvrard's—hand, to sign a fresh contract with Davout on 24 May 1815, requiring the merchant to provide four million francs' worth of food supplies for the northern armies over the next four weeks.[74] The result was that by mid-June all the northern armies and depots had four months' provisions, if not the full 23 million rations ordered.[75]

If the victualing problem was thus largely resolved for the moment, others remained as Napoleon was vividly reminded by a barrage of daily complaints reaching him from Daru (Intendant General in charge of manufacturing and otherwise procuring army uniforms), Carnot, and especially from the unrelenting Davout, regarding the lack of uniforms, boots, arms and munitions, the Emperor in turn then assailing Gaudin: "None of the army's victualing and supplies' services is working," he pointed out bitterly,[76] because of that minister and an empty treasury. This, he continued, was hamstringing every aspect of the mobilization effort for the defense of the country. Old bills had not yet been paid, and contractors balked at filling new orders. Nor did the Emperor spare one of the principal contractors, one Montessuy, when he failed to meet his commitments to the Army's "Victualing Services," further criticizing that businessman's demands for "excessive prices" and "most onerous terms of payment."[77] Thus, even if Napoleon were able to double or triple the number of regiments, nevertheless the plain fact remained that, despite all his efforts, he could neither feed nor clothe them on time.

Even after Napoleon had ordered the creation and government supervision of national workshops for the manufacture of muskets and uniforms, current production failed to meet the quotas he set, inevitably resulting in reprimands for both Gaudin and Davout. Thus, for instance, on 13 April the Emperor complained to the War Minister that "the Prefect of Police has informed me that a large number of workers who have gone to the workshops for employment have been turned away."[78] Why? Because of inadequate space and material. Therefore a crash program had to be inaugurated for increasing these craftsmen, even if they had to work at home on such items as gunstocks and small metal parts, which he felt was perfectly feasible.[79] He also demanded immediate expansion of new rifle production, for they were still nowhere near meeting the additional 240,000 muskets he required for his armies.[80] "The manufacture of weapons is the best means of safeguarding the country," the Emperor instilled time and again upon the harried War Minister.[81]

Davout too frequently now found himself swamped and behind his own rigorous schedule, despite his demanding twenty-hour workday—which included the selection of hundreds of commanding officers at all levels, as well as devising large-scale troop movements and transfers from one military district to another—when it came to the civilian side of his job, coordinating efforts, as in the case of musket production, directing the entire operation (for the army was placed in direct charge of their manufacture), he was a neophyte and well beyond his depth (where Carnot would have been better employed) and Napoleon was quick to remind him of it: *"Mon cousin, voilà* two weeks lost already. The new arms workshops are still not in operation," he wrote impatiently on 15 April.[82] "Do not wait for word from the Tuileries to appoint officers and create these gunshops. You know perfectly well that you hardly need my authorization to assign 20 or 30 officers for that."[83] Paris was filled with unemployed artisans, he was to use them to manufacture musket parts, ramrods, bayonets. "Appoint a colonel, eight majors, eight captains, sixteen lieutenants to organize this today and do not write to me anymore about this, just take all the steps necessary to execute it. . . . If lack of large factories proves a problem, take over army barracks, slaughter houses, my churches, even the music halls, but . . . let's see some action!"[84] "And why not extend musket production to the provinces—little Maubeuge, for instance, could no doubt produce four hundred muskets per month, and Charleville four thousand nine hundred—and then multiply this by dozens of such towns and cities,"[85] he said. "It is distressing that all this was not dealt with three weeks ago . . . if we had a million muskets ready, I could use them today. We must have one hundred thousand muskets ready in fifty days' time"—or 200 per day—he ordered,[86] later changing that to "300 to 400 per day . . . in the shortest possible time," he now estimating a current shortage of 300,000 muskets.[87] Nor was there any reason why new muskets could not be purchased through third parties from England and Switzerland.[88] Why did he, Napoleon, always have to point out the obvious? . . . He added caustically—"I presume that at least our regular army is completely armed?"[89]

In fact, there were large numbers of muskets available simply requiring minimal repairs and replacement of parts, which could be brought into service quickly. Then again pulling statistics out of his hat—accurately this time—Napoleon mentioned forgotten caches of broken muskets in dozens of places, the existence of which Davout knew nothing about. There were 350 muskets to be repaired at Montreuil he told Davout, 1,100 at Dunkerque, 5,791 at Douai, 11,686 at Lille and so on, in every depot and fortress of the country,[90] altogether totaling some 74,000 muskets.[91] With all these arms available, why had not Davout thought of this, why had he not set the wheels in motion? "War could break out at any moment and yet . . . nothing has been done," he exclaimed.[92] Davout had done nothing.

It was absurd, of course, for no War Minister had ever worked harder and Napoleon knew it, but he was always a most unreasonable man when he wanted something done. If that meant producing 100,000 muskets overnight, then he wanted 100,000 ready at that garrison today, if not the following day, at least within a week.[93] But there was also a personal acrimonious element in this relationship, for he was riding Davout very hard, sending him ten times the number of critical, indeed harassing, letters and orders than he was doing to all the other ministers combined.

Likewise the serious lack of uniforms was beginning to make itself felt. Even as early as April, fresh troops assembling at army depots found the quartermaster's clothing supplies nonexistent. The objective was to see each army regiment in roughly the same uniform, hopefully in the same shade of blue or gray, in an attempt, at least, of maintaining regimental uniformity. And in addition to a musket, each man was also to have two extra pairs of boots in his knapsack (though in reality even one additional pair was rare, and at one time twenty regiments lacked any boots at all),[94] and without an extra dry pair on hand, soldiers would rightly earn the sobriquet given long ago by Napoleon to his troops, the *grognards*, the groaners.

The ominous tone, the multiplicity of negative reports received from armies and supply depots at the War Office by mid-April, soon reached epidemic proportions, leading Marshal Davout to complain again in turn to the head of the uniform procurement program, Comte Daru.[95] Soldiers could not be inducted into the army, or trained, while soldiers without uniforms lowered all aspects of army morale. A smart uniform gave a soldier a sense of dignity, of belonging, and pride in the army itself. Naturally, Davout in turn passed on these anxieties to Napoleon, who in this case directed his wrath against Comte Mollien and the Treasury. "Large numbers of recruits arriving at every corps in the country still cannot be clothed,"[96] an impatient Napoleon snapped. Why even bother to call up men when we have nothing ready for them? "I have 100,000 men at the induction centers whom I cannot even use, because of the lack of funds with which to provide clothing and equipment for them. The fate of France boils down to that," and ordered Mollien "to work day and night" and to have that money available "within a week's time."[97] For, as he put it, "Provided they [the recruits] have a musket, a greatcoat and some sort of military uniform, that suffices. Our primary objective is to increase the number and strength of our battalions."[98] The result? Fourteen million francs credit were found before the week was out, permitting the manufacture of 1,250 uniforms per day in dozens and dozens of workshops in Paris and some northern cities,[99] later extended to Lyons, Toulouse and Bordeaux.[100]

With a steady supply of muskets, munitions—the Vincennes cartridge production figure was now up to 6 million per month—and immediate victualing and clothing problems reasonably under control at long last, Napoleon was free to focus all his attention on the army, prodding and bullying the reluctant French people into preparing for a crash mobilization program.[101]

Chapter IX

Mobilization

"What will be the outcome of this terrible war into which he is leading us? The most valiant generals themselves are clearly anxious, and upon seeing the approach of hostilities the nation will take fright and turn against him [Napoleon]."

Caulaincourt to Pasquier

"Napoleon, by the grace of the devil and the constitutions of hell, Emperor of the French, have and do hereby decree the following: Art. I. I shall be supplied with 300,000 victims per year. Art. II. According to the circumstances, I shall increase this number up to three million. . . ."

Royalist Broadsheet, 1815

"The word 'impossible' is but the hobgoblin of the timid and the excuse of poltroons."

Napoleon to Molé

"If a nation wants happiness, it must obey orders and remain silent."

Napoleon to Cambacérès

Within twenty-four hours of the Allied declaration of 25 March, Napoleon had ordered the creation of eight army corps. Mobilization for this was a cumbersome task that literally required restructuring most of the French Army. In addition to his role as War Minister, Davout unofficially, temporarily and not very successfully, acted as Supreme Chief of Staff, with the task of coordinating all the army's efforts. But, of course, Marshal Alexandre Berthier, who had held this post most of the time since the beginning of Napoleon's meteoric rise, beginning with his Italian campaigns back in the 1790s under the Directory, and who had so deftly managed everything, making Napoleon's astonishing subsequent chain of victories possible, was no longer there. However, Marshal Davout, for all his loyalty, intelligence, good intentions and extraordinary energy, was floundering in his attempt to assume both jobs now, for he lacked Berthier's unique, detailed knowledge of all aspects of army organization—for instance: how much under strength were the third and fourth battalions of the 7th, 11th or 19th Infantry regiments? How many transportation wagons, carts and carriages were available at Lille, Avesnes, Laon, Nancy or Belfort? How many cavalry horses were still needed at Lyons or nearby Versailles? What was the state of defenses of Dunkerque, Soissons, Charleville, or Givy? How many cannon, mortars and howitzers did they have on hand, how many thousands of kilos of gunpowder, how many rounds of ammunition for muskets, how many cannon balls, especially for the 6- and 12-pounders? What supplies of rice, cereals, eau-de-vie, vegetables and meat were in each and every supply depot of the land? How many saddles and bridles was the cavalry short; how many months' supply of fodder did they currently have at Meaux—and if any of those elements was missing, say at Soissons, who was responsible for obtaining and executing that? How was each contract to be negotiated and deficiences made up and by whom, and when would they be completed? How long would it take for these supplies—whether bridles, oats, eau-de-vie, bread, greatcoats, gunpowder, or extra ramrods for muskets—to reach, say, the garrison at Le Havre or Calais or Amiens, Belfort or Chambéry? These were typical of the hundreds of such questions facing the War Minister.

Also on a more subtle level Berthier had invariably, intuitively understood Napoleon's way of thinking regarding new plans, any plans, however sketchily they were presented to him, thereby permitting Berthier—without further orders or explanations—to interpret and anticipate what the

Emperor really desired, effortlessly engaging and expediting the appropriate bureaucratic mechanism. Davout, for all his diligence and dynamism, could not even begin to provide this particular, unstated but essential requisite.

Thus, although it was Berthier, who, as Chief of Staff, had resolved most of the strategic planning problems in the past, it was hardly surprising that Napoleon relieved Davout of much of that task now, assuming it for himself, for the time being, while looking for the full-time chief of staff he would need at his side in the field, in the event of war. Meanwhile other roles had been assigned to the Conseil d'Etat's Section de Guerre under the guidance of General Andréossy, who directed the Comité des Finances to provide important military financial analyses, while appointing three generals with a large staff to head the studies carried out by the Conseil des Défense (e.g., how many horses did the cavalry need in the event Napoleon attacked the northern frontier by the first of June, or did army engineers have enough pontoon sections and transport on the Sambre, the Moselle or the Meuse; how long would it take to move three cavalry regiments from Versailles to their new positions near the frontier?). In brief, Napoleon drew up the final orders and Davout then executed them, and on 30 April the Emperor announced his momentous decision. . . .

Ready or not, on that day he ordered the transformation of seven Corps d'Observation into four powerful armies, capable of launching a massive offensive operation against the Allies in Belgium.[1] The Armée du Nord, comprising the 2nd and 16th Military Districts, and destined to spearhead this attack, was to be the largest one, comprising the 1st, 2nd, 3rd and 6th Corps, as well as three divisions of cavalry; the Armée de la Moselle—encompassing the 3rd and 4th Military Districts—was composed of the 4th Corps; the Armée du Rhin, the 5th Corps; and the Armée des Alpes (in the 7th and 19th Military Districts) consisted of the 7th Army Corps. The remaining three corps were to include the Corps d'Observation du Jura between Belfort and the mountains up to the frontier at Geneva in the 6th Military District, and that of the Pyrénées, the 9th, 10th and 11th Military Districts covering the entire southern region of the country down to the Spanish border.[2] A final corps d'observation, on the drawing boards, but in this case still a mere theoretical possibility, that of the Var, would be dealt with shortly.

By June Napoleon envisaged having a regular army force of some 300,000 men (compared to King Louis's force of 200,000 in March).[3] In addition the combined front line and reserve army forces were to be beefed up immediately by some 112,000 "former soldiers" (drawn from roughly 32,000 retired soldiers or men on extended stay,[4] and 85,000 deserters from his army in the spring of 1814), and by 120,000 recruits from the anticipated 1815 conscription lists.[5] Most of these additional 232,000 men were to be absorbed into the four Armées de Réserve planned for Paris, Lyons, Toulouse and Bordeaux, though much to Davout's consternation, Napoleon only belatedly authorized the drafting of this project on 3 May.[6]

In most instances the initial drive to attract volunteers, former soldiers and recruits proved slow and disappointing, so that by 12 May, a mere month before operations were scheduled to begin, a desperate Napoleon personally ordered the creation of special press gangs, similar to those used traditionally by the navies of France and England, albeit larger and better armed, including tough "mobile columns," 125-men strong each, "to make the former soldiers rejoin," as the Emperor put it.[7] Next came orders to call up the 1815 recruits, though by May Napoleon was no longer counting on the 120,000 young men so designated, but closer to 85,000,[8] whose effective numbers were already eroded daily now by interference or plain lack of support by mayors and departmental officials everywhere, reducing considerably the number of recruits eventually reaching registration centers and army depots, particularly in the west, southern and southeastern third of the country. Indeed, even the 85,000 figure was to prove overly optimistic.

Time and again Napoleon, Davout and Carnot attempted to stir up a sense of patriotism and duty in recruits and former soldiers alike, as when the Emperor addressed the Army on 9 April, reminding the men why he and France needed them now: "Soldiers! We do not want to interfere in the affairs of other countries, and woe to those who would do so in ours, daring to treat us like another Genoa or Geneva, imposing laws on us unacceptable to the nation! Soldiers! The French people and I are counting on you. And you can count on the people and me!"[9]

The Army's final corps, that of the Var, sometimes also called the Corps d'Observation de Provence, whose main forces were to be stationed between Antibes and the Italian frontier was authorized on 12 May,[10] then only after a terrible scene between Davout and Napoleon. Although Napoleon himself approved the new chain-of-command of this new corps on 12 May,[11] instructing Marshal Brune to activate its two divisions, the next day when the War Office duly submitted the request for the funds required to launch this new corps, Napoleon, apparently pushed beyond limits by the continued strain under which he had been working incessantly since 20 March, lost all control, and lashed out at a bewildered, equally exhausted Davout. "I never thought you might involve me in an expense of some 40 millions without my first having considered, then confirmed it by a decree. I had approved the idea in principle only, but you have then executed it in such a manner as to create sheer chaos. . . ."[12] It would take extreme boldness on the part of anyone to do such a thing given the perilous state of our finances,"[13] though, of course, Napoleon had given written orders regarding the implementation of the new corps, even ordering Davout to have the new corps commander, Marshal Brune, to be at his new headquarters "by 8th June at the latest."[14] In fact, this was simply one of a few dozen serious, aggravating criticisms unleashed against Davout, beginning in April, and now reaching the War Ministry with alarming regularity by the end of May. "It would appear that the offices of the War Department have forgotten the standard operating procedure so long in practice," he chided his minister. If these incredible actions by Davout were to continue, Napoleon stated menacingly for the first time, "then it would necessarily mean a parting of the ways,"[15] and he would have Davout replaced.

But this really was almost the last straw for the hard-pressed War Minister, who had had just about all the abuse from this thankless Emperor he was going to take. And yet attack Marshal Davout as he may, if in fact there was one man in all of France whom Napoleon simply could not afford to alienate or lose at this precise moment, it was this haggard, impatient Louis Davout, whom no understudy was even vaguely equipped to replace.

After snatching a few hours' sleep on the camp bed hastily erected in the corner of his office, Davout could think clearly enough to realize that if he resigned now, Napoleon would find himself "thrown into a state of chaos" far greater than he had ever conceived, probably resulting in the collapse of the Empire itself. For nothing less was at stake at this critical hour, and like it or not, at this stage at least, all very much depended on Davout, if mobilization preparations were to continue apace. And Davout for his part tried to accommodate a Napoleon who, although definitely no longer his old self, nevertheless was still surprisingly dynamic and certainly just as impatient to see everything executed forthwith. The Emperor lashed out at Mollien, Daru, Decrès and especially at Davout. His political and marital frustrations, his recent knowledge of fresh attempts at deception and betrayal by Fouché, aggravated his anger, which was released in a bewildering barrage of criticism, any subject now serving as pretext for a series of withering attacks on the competence of the War Minister.

Ironically Davout's own impatience was growing as a result of Napoleon's frequent wavering and indecision. Occasionally, if not actually creating his own orders and decisions in place of Napoleon's, Davout would at least bypass one phase of their implementation by neglecting to obtain the written consent the Emperor always insisted upon, prior to action being taken, as in the case of the creation of an Army for the Var. But as Napoleon refused to delegate authority, someone had to act, even without that authority. Thus, for instance, when armies, divisions and brigades cried out for good officers and he and Napoleon had discussed specific commanders orally, Napoleon, indicating his approval of such and such an appointment, would then forget or delay sending off the written authorization he had promised. In a few instances Davout expedited matters by ordering the appropriate generals to their new commands, pending the receipt of this written imperial confirmation, only to get his knuckles rapped in the process: "It is standard procedure that generals cannot be appointed to commands without my approval," Napoleon reminded him. But as Davout had indeed done this, "I therefore find myself obliged to reorganize the entire divisions mentioned where you have placed generals whom I find unacceptable."[16] In the same breath Napoleon then reprimanded him for still *not having named* the commanding generals for the Vendée, Deux-Sèvres and the Loire Inférieure![17]

Meanwhile the pressure on everyone continued to crescendo alarmingly throughout the hectic month of April, becoming nearly intolerable by the third week of May. Musket production was behind schedule at Maubeuge and Charleville, for example, because "the workers have not been paid for nearly six weeks,"[18] while everywhere in general production was grossly inadequate. "You have done nothing," Napoleon complained.[19] The cavalry was short thousands of saddles and bridles, and Napoleon even had to explain to him the names of a dozen different depots where they could be found—something a good war minister should have known, he insisted.[20] The system for transferring mounts from the gendarmeries to the army was cumbersome and inefficient, resulting in unnecessary delivery delays averaging a good fortnight.[21] Consequently, there were only 2,800 horses at Versailles instead of the 8,000 ordered. "Cavalry preparations are not going at all well,"[22] Napoleon lamented. Army contractors were delaying supplying food, despite signed contracts, while their prices were exorbitant and terms of payment unreasonable, if not unpatriotic.[23] Troops continued to be armed and clothed far too slowly— "I have received complaints from everyone! Entire regiments have no funds, so that many troops reaching their corps cannot be clothed,"[24] he repeated ad nauseam. National Guard units were excruciatingly slow in replacing garrison troops all along the northern frontier, why? "Our aim is to increase the strength of our battalions as quickly as possible!" But how could this be achieved with such insuperable obstacles?[25] When Davout submitted his fortification plan for the defense of Lyons, Napoleon rejected it;[26] likewise he found the War Minister's report on the state of readiness of the army engineers' pontoon bridge companies at Strasbourg, Metz, Douai and Laon "rather vague . . . resubmit a more complete study."[27] One of Napoleon's ADCs, General Dejean, returning from an inspection tour along the northern frontier, informed him that "the Provisions and Catering Services are very poor" and that "our situation is simply shameful. Send me a report on this immediately," explaining why this was happening there and how it was to be corrected. Davout had given Douai and Lille too many artillery batteries, while leaving Montreuil and Charlemont undefended. "Correct this," the Emperor ordered.[28] The War Minister had permitted the state of rebellion in the Var to get completely out of hand and he must therefore "establish strict police enforcement there" and arrest the ringleaders.[29] Napoleon found Davout's proposed budget for 1815 "to be inadequately explained,"[30] and what is more, "you are placing orders for equipment for which no funds have been allocated. . . . You must therefore rectify this [for] if you order equipment beyond your budgeting means, you create chaos. . . . It seems that the War Office have forgotten the well-established practices and procedures in such cases. Your administrative philosophy seems to be that money is unimportant," reminding him finally that "the Treasury is the basis for everything. . . ."[31] He then chided Davout for handing over his private imperial correspondence to the press—"I have just found one of my letters to you published in a newspaper. I have never seen anything like it before! Your predecessor kept my letters under lock and key in his office."[32] It turned out, however, that in this instance Davout had done nothing of the kind, whereas, of course, the Minister's predecessor, General Clarke, though having never let his papers leave his office, did, nevertheless, remove his own person, going over to the enemy, joining Louis XVIII as his own War Minister. When Davout protested, the Emperor retaliated promptly by returning two of Davout's latest orders, marked "NOT APPROVED" (one regarding the formation of an infantry company in the Mâcon,[33] the other appointing a minor officer of the 31st Light Infantry Regiment at Chambéry).[34] But for an angry Napoleon, that did not suffice, now venting his spleen on those around him, or better yet, those who stubbornly refused to return to the fold, including the hapless former Imperial Chancellor, Etienne-Denis Pasquier, whom Napoleon now had harried with the threat of being drafted as a private in a fédéré company.[35]

Meanwhile, a fortnight later, after personally instructing Davout "to use all the force necessary to round up the 'former soldiers' " (that is, deserters and retired soldiers who had failed to come forth), he reprimanded the War Minister about "complaints [he had received] that you are using force" to execute those very orders, "for what we are concerned with here is public support, and if they [the public] are unhappy with us, they will not serve [their country]."[36] Following a review at the Tuileries on 28 May of five artillery batteries, Napoleon whipped off another negative report to the War Minister, noting that "several of the caissons lacked the little grease boxes required by the maintenance manual."[37] Little grease boxes!

Clearly, Napoleon was carrying out a senseless, vindictive policy of harassment, riding Davout remorselessly. As a result, for the next few days, the infuriated War Minister adamantly refused to answer a single order or note sent by the Tuileries—literally cutting off all communications with the Emperor—bullying his own subordinates as they and his ADCs sought refuge as best they could from the storm in the rue Saint-Dominique. But for Davout it was an insult—he was not a Fortfait, a Schimmelpenninck, a Murat or Francis I, to be treated in this manner. Working flat out, he scarcely stopped to eat, only grabbing occasional snatches of sleep for weeks on end—rarely even leaving to see his pregnant wife (who had already lost a few children over the past ten years)—all this, and why, to have to put up with Napoleon Bonaparte, who in turn repaid this by humiliating him. That he took out his frustrations on his own officers was hardly surprising, and when, in May, Marshal Soult—now reinstated by Napoleon—not only disobeyed one of Davout's direct orders, but issued his own instead, Davout warned him that he would be dismissed forthwith if he did not shape up.[38] Next he snapped at Daru regarding the backlog of undelivered uniforms, while criticizing Carnot's prefects and officials for hindering the war effort through their low morale, and poor public support and cooperation.[39]

The army, already reduced in numbers by circumstances described earlier, was further limited by the Emperor's insistence that only seasoned veterans were to be used for the principal corps and divisions whenever possible, an injunction that he applied even more stringently to the cavalry. And apart from the defense of cities, all artillery batteries along the frontier and coast were to be manned by career officers and crews, though supplemented by naval artillery units and personnel.

Given the great number of troops deployed in the provinces to maintain public order and quell political opposition—e.g., Lamarque's Armée de la Loire, Clausel's Corps d'Observation des Pyrénées and Brune's

Corps in the Var—the National Guard's role in the defense of the country became critical. Eight divisions of élite National Guardsmen were to be mobilized to create "the second line of defense" by manning forts and protecting cities, thereby releasing tens of thousands of regular army troops in the process. One National Guard division each was to be seconded to the Armies of the North, the Moselle and the Rhine, two to the Jura Observation Corps, and the remaining three to the Armée des Alpes.[40] The lieutenant-general commanding each National Guard division was also charged with encouraging "the formation of partisan units" to protect forests, river crossings, canyons, and mountain passes, thereby preventing enemy light cavalry, army convoys, foragers and couriers from passing into France. The National Guard divisions were to be stationed all along the northern and eastern frontiers in the Ardennes, the Argonne Forest, along the Rhine, in the Vosges, the Jura, in Franche-Comté and the Alps.[41] In addition each city was to have its own National Guard force with which to prepare a last-ditch defensive effort in the event enemy armies broke through again, as in 1814. The commander-in-chief of each regular army (e.g., of the North, Moselle, Rhine and the Alps) commanded all troops—including guardsmen—within his military region.

Napoleon's initial orders to have all National Guard units in place, manning northern forts and garrisons by the second week of May,[42] proved overly optimistic, most of those units not arriving for another month, and even then in disappointing numbers.[43] If as a rule Davout proved himself a skeptical realist when assessing the Army's potential capabilities and current strength, not so Lazare Carnot vis-à-vis his national guards. Two and a half million men (nearly 10 percent of the country's population) could be called up in a *levée en masse*, the Interior Minister asserted. In fact, however, of the initial 234,000 national guardsmen ordered to arms by mid-June, a mere 90,000 or so materialized,[44] over 50,000 of whom were assigned to the northern frontier, the rest to the defense of cities and depots.[45] Carnot's mobilization of the National Guard proved a disaster. But that was just the beginning, for other shocks lay in store. Of the 211,800 former soldiers, deserters and men on leave receiving their call-up orders, a mere 52,446 actually appeared in June, and many of them only at bayonet point.[46] Of the 445,800 men promised and counted on by his ministers responsible for national mobilization, only 142,446, or 32 percent, had materialized by June, a desperate Davout then activating 14,000 gendarmes, 12,000 customs officials and 6,000 volunteers (in special regiments) to help make up for those embarrassing shortages.

As for the regular army, it seemed in better shape. When the Imperial

Guard, which had comprised a force of 7,390 men on 20 March, was increased by another eight regiments for a total of 20,755 men, as well as 46,419 recruits, Napoleon mustered a total force of 178,929 men available for the front lines. The remainder of the grand total of 284,090 men were dispersed among the garrisons and depots of the country,[47] or were claimed by the great upheaval along the Channel, in the west, in the south and southeast.

In fact, opposition to Napoleon was not only growing quickly, but was nearly out of control. Although War Minister Davout had proclaimed to Napoleon on 10 April that "the Bourbon yoke has been broken,"[48] he had quickly discovered that this assessment was shockingly wrong. Even the reasonably solid Lyon proved to be no bastion of Bonapartism and imperial loyalty where Emmanuel de Grouchy requested the immediate replacement of both its mayor and prefect.[49] Davout remarked similar antipathy in Dunkerque, Abbeville, Cherbourg, Rouen, Agen and Marseille,[50] whose officials openly hindered tax collection and the induction of the 1815 army conscripts, thereby greatly undermining Napoleon's efforts to consolidate his new, still tenuous position in France and ability to launch his war preparations.[51] "Execute a harsh policy toward all agitators," he riposted.[52] Not only were new conscripts and troops slow in coming forth, but as already seen, the new resistance, especially along the Channel ports, in the west including the Vendée, as well as around Marseille, finally required the sending of additional regular army units to maintain order.[53] And it was not simply "the sparks of civil war" as Davout referred to the situation in the west and south where the royalist uprising discussed in the previous chapter was just beginning,[54] but a gradually pervasive spreading of rebellion and obstruction throughout most of the country. And despite Napoleon's euphoric announcement to Marshal Davout on 16 April that "the tricolor flag is flying over Marseille," ordering the firing of one hundred cannon at the Invalides to commemorate the conclusion of national resistance to his government, this proved as premature as Davout's earlier declaration.[55]

And thus, just a fortnight after the celebratory barrage at the Invalides, on the first of May, Interior Minister Carnot belatedly prepared the draft decrees for Napoleon dispatching "commissaires extraordinaires" to all military districts where "they will remove from office then and there all those opposing us, and whose replacement is required for the good of the State," which included mayors, and public officials, and even

National Guard officers throughout the country.[56] "You must appeal to the honor and patriotism of the people everywhere," Napoleon reminded the superpatriot Lazare Carnot, who, at that moment, was in the process of removing the obstructionist prefects of the Somme, Pas-de-Calais, Calvados and Chartres.[57] Napoleon's policy of alienating the commercial community by delaying payment for bona fide government contracts, while attempting to take away the fathers and sons of a couple of hundred thousand families once again for an unwanted and equally unnecessary war, were resulting in a lethal anti-Bonaparte contagion sweeping across the land.[58]

Nevertheless, the French people, still wary of Napoleon's great power and legend, did not speak up with a single national voice against him, thereby sending the Emperor mixed signals. "We all want peace, but we are fully prepared for war," Napoleon stormed before the Electoral College of Seine-et-Oise on 14 May. Therefore, "I expect much patriotism and understanding from the Chambers."[59] It sounded very much like the threat it was, rather than an appeal for support. "After having been the greatest of conquerors, now be the most peaceful of sovereigns: your glory requires it of you, and our happiness demands it of you,"[60] they boldly replied for once, only to give in once again to the dictator, assuring him of their support in this national crisis. Napoleon, for his part—and to his ultimate regret—chose to ignore their momentary, if wise, appeal for peace.

Elsewhere in the country, however, the people themselves were gradually proving less timid in expressing their discontent with both Napoleon and their representatives. At Dijon the aristocratic officers of the National Guard refused to obey orders to activate their battalions;[61] at the national workshops, musket and clothing production were still weeks behind government orders, while recruitment of troops lagged, even for the new "Young Guard" regiments of the prestigious Imperial Guard, as officers and recruiting sergeants returned from Amiens, Rouen, Orléans and Burgundy with quotas unfilled. "Parade the flag," Napoleon impatiently instructed Comte Drouot, the Imperial Guard's commanding officer. "Do what has to be done . . . music and drums . . . arouse the enthusiasm of the young people!"[62] But neither smart marching columns nor immense, waving tricolor flags seemed to avail as the morale of the artificially revived Empire fluttered weakly and then plummeted.

A stymied Napoleon finally ordered Police Minister Fouché to carry out more mass arrests of known royalist agitators at Boulogne, in the Seine-Inférieure, at Clermont-Ferrand, Toulouse, Montauban, Montpellier, Perpignan and Bordeaux, including for good measure "anyone seriously suspected of being on their side," even if hard proof were lacking.[63] It was with this situation in mind that the Emperor appointed Carnot to edit and direct the *Journal Général de France* in order to intensify the propaganda effort. "It is my intention that you give a patriotic impetus to this paper to counter the furor of the attacks by the government's enemies."[64] If armies were needed to defeat Allied armies abroad, newspapers served as effectively as regiments at home.

As for the "rebellion" in the West, in Brittany, Deux-Sèvres, the Loire, Morbihan and the Vendée, Napoleon only finally acknowledged its significance to his Council of Ministers on 21 May. "We can no longer delude ourselves. Civil war is really breaking out in the Vendée. We can no longer afford to put off the measures required in organizing an army with which to fight that rebellion."[65] And as already noted in Chapter VII, he then personally announced the formation of the Armée de la Loire, 20,000 strong, under the command of General Lamarque, ordering him "to act vigorously" to crush, arrest or deport its ringleaders, and in the case of La Rochejacquelein, "to burn down his house."[66] Much of this was now happening, Napoleon said, because of England, which was "encouraging this uprising and thereby committing serious hostilities against us."[67] And he really believed it, temporarily deluding himself that he alone might not possibly be the real reason for this rebellion, though of course there was little or no "English influence" in all the major cities of the south and southeast where other significant clashes against imperial authority were also taking place.

But if the situation in the southern cities was critical, by 22 May, that in Marseille was out of control, as Napoleon ordered the removal of most of that city's powerful arsenal—100,000 kilograms of gunpowder and 500,000 cartridges from its principal fortress, Fort Saint-Nicolas—transferring it to Toulon and Lyons, thereby leaving only Fort Saint-Jean fully defended. "It is essential that such a large supply of munitions not be left in such a hostile city as Marseille,"[68] Napoleon told Davout as he ordered the immediate disarming and disbanding of its entire national guard—four thousand strong—to be replaced by another, much smaller force, "but this time," he insisted, "one composed of patriots and of the people."[69] It was in part because of the desperate situation in Marseille that Napoleon now consented to the creation of an extra corps, after all, that of the Var, ordering Marshal Brune to head these two new divisions with strict orders "to crack down" on Marseille.[70] And yet even these tough and extraordinary measures did not suffice. On 3 June the Tuileries ordered the War Minister to organize and arm strong units of fédérés throughout the South.[71] Desperate times require desperate measures, and

Marseille, Toulon, Arles, Tarascon, Perpignan, Toulouse, Montauban, Bordeaux, Le Havre, Nantes, Poitiers and Cherbourg, among other prominent cities and ports were put on a special danger list of "hostile cities" whose officers and National Guard units were to be disbanded as Napoleon acquiesced, agreeing to Davout's pleas for even more drastic action by placing them either under direct martial law, or the near equivalent, as if they were occupied enemy territory.[72] It was a damning indictment of Napoleon the dictator and all he stood for. France was now on the threshold of another war and contingents of foreign troops were already reported moving in along northern and eastern frontiers. And the question no doubt arose among those who knew how grave the internal situation really was, whether or not France might not even collapse *before* the Emperor ever advanced to the Belgian border to meet Wellington's forces.

Nevertheless, after an extraordinary effort by the extraordinary Napoleon, the groaning, cumbersome prehistoric beast of war was at long last awakening, so painfully and reluctantly that echoes of this astonishing exertion were heard in every corner of the land. National Guards, conscripts, retired soldiers, deserters, gendarmes, customs officials, students, even the much-despised fédérés were moving forward, albeit in reduced numbers and hardly in an enthusiastic state of mind. Cannon fodder was cannon fodder, however, and Napoleon was not choosy, whether it was a question of a seventeen-year-old lycée student or sixty-year-old shopkeeper.[73] After dramatic exhortations by the Tuileries, repeated with harsh insistence by the War Ministry, some 40,000 cavalrymen were being assembled by the newly promoted Marshal Grouchy at the principal staging centers of Versailles, Beauvais and Troy,[74] as thousands of wagons and primitive carts on enormous rumbling wooden wheels brought provisions and munitions to the great depots at Laon, Soissons and Avesnes.[75] The transportation park at Sampigny grew daily in girth. The nation's 13,947 artillery pieces were distributed along the coasts and among the armies, cities, the two large burgeoning parks at Vincennes and the Invalides.[76] The Navy rushed nearly seven thousand artillerymen and officers to Paris and Lyons, adding the remainder of their men to the impressive Channel defense network of over 60,000, which included army units and volunteers and was supported by sixty-six batteries and some six hundred cannon.[77] And thus with an army 284,000 strong, the giant beast, still weary and reluctant from the great effort the year before, once again heaved itself onto its feet for yet one more "final effort." At last, with the appointment of Marshal Davout as the acting commander in chief of the capital during his anticipated absence, Napoleon cast his attention to the preparation of the defenses of Lyons and Paris.

Next to Paris, Lyons, as the second largest city of France, naturally occupied Napoleon's thoughts more and more, and with the clearing of the snow and ice, the Alps would soon be vulnerable to any Allied attack sweeping down from the Swiss mountain passes. Unhappy with the overly elaborate defense plans submitted by the War Minister, the Emperor modified them, eliminating all but the most essential works. Then on 12 May he authorized an emergency budget of 400,000 francs and the use of some 4,000 laborers to prepare Lyons,[78] including repairs of the city's ramparts and walls and the creation of thirty artillery batteries (comprising 150 cannon)—to be brought up from Toulon and manned and commanded by the Imperial Navy—supported in turn by one army division and nine thousand National Guardsmen.[79] But when by the beginning of June he found the basic defenses barely begun and the magazines still desperately short of powder and munitions, a furious Napoleon immediately fired the previous commander and military governor (General Brayer), replacing him with the more dynamic General Dulauloy, at the same time releasing additional funds with which to spur on the effort.[80] The river approaches being critical to that city's defenses, the Emperor discussed the work required for each and every bridgehead (which he named and described in remarkable detail), as well as the creation of drawbridges, redoubts and battery sites for all approaches to the city, including those controlling the heights above the Rhône and Saône.[81]

But, naturally, it was Paris that was especially to occupy the French Emperor as the last days of April quickly slipped by, giving way to a prematurely warm May. Allocating a budget of 500,000 francs (independent of the army budget) on 2 May, Napoleon instructed his aide-de-camp Comte Dejean, Inspector General of Army Engineers, to prepare works tackling these diverse defense problems. Some 5,000 laborers were assigned to build the redoubts and batteries on the heights of Montmartre, Ménilmontant, and at Belleville and Saint-Denis.[82]

"Do everything in your power to organize and hasten the defensive measures now in progress," Napoleon urged in one of four messages sent to the War Ministry that same second of May. He advised the use of 6- and 12-pounders and a single caliber of howitzer for the city's wall of artillery in order to simplify the supplying of ammunition for the batteries and thereby anticipating and eliminating possible later confusion.[83] Initially, more than three hundred such guns were to be assigned to the new batteries, exclusive of a forty-five mile defensive perimeter erected well beyond the city including Meaux, Melun, Trilport, Château-Thierry, Nogent, Montereau and Arcis-sur-Aube—most of which was to be manned by volunteers.[84] Within Paris proper and its immediate suburbs, Admiral Decrès was made responsible for bringing another seventeen flying artillery batteries of 136 guns up the Seine, part of the hundreds of guns being transferred from the dismantled fleet at Brest and Cherbourg.[85] The suburb of Saint-Denis was to have twenty siege guns and two mobile batteries (of sixteen guns) while another four more flying batteries (of thirty-two guns) were assigned to protect the critical Saint-Denis Canal— the Navy being responsible for those batteries as well—all of which were exclusive of the fixed artillery sites in the redoubts and at the bridge-heads, and ordered to be operational by 6 June.[86] Eight more naval batteries, comprising sixty-four guns, were assigned to other suburbs, including Belleville, Charenton and Montreuil.[87]

Within the heart of Paris, some thirty siege cannon and eight smaller guns were being laboriously hauled up the steep incline for the four impressive new redoubts atop Montmartre. Other batteries were hurriedly traced along the right bank of the Seine, and braces of guns with a sweeping field of fire were placed in the main boulevards of the capital. The largest concentration and the main artillery park within Paris itself, which included more than a couple of hundred artillery pieces, all but obliterated the large green expanse before the Invalides extending down to its own quayside on the Seine, where barges were constantly unloading immense stacks of supplies and munitions twenty-four hours a day.[88] Not content with these measures, Napoleon ordered an additional one hundred naval artillery pieces from Toulon for Lyons, as well as three hundred more (along with one hundred caissons) from Le Havre for Paris, with half of the latter shipment intended to reinforce positions at Soissons, Reims, Vitry, Laon, Langres and Château-Thierry.[89] Despite the chaos and bustle of hundreds of naval officers directing 6,000 artillerymen, not to mention thousands of workers feverishly building redoubts and fortifications, and dozens of army and national guard regiments erecting strong barricades and additional guns in the principal street intersections of the capital, and the impromptu inspection tours of Napoleon himself to spur on these preparations, even a month later, in the first week of June, much of the essential work was still not completed. Two hundred badly needed naval guns were still on barges coming up the Seine somewhere between Rouen and Paris.[90]

Generals Hulin, Durosnel and Darricau, commanding the army regiments, National Guardsmen and tirailleurs,[91] meanwhile found themselves with insufficient forces for the defense of the capital. A mere 36,000 men were assigned to defend the sprawling outer perimeter and another 24,000 to man the walls of the city, while a total of 90,000 troops were dispersed throughout Paris, including 30,000 National Guardsmen, 20,000 men recruited from a last-minute levée en masse of untrained citizens, 20,000 marines brought in from the Channel by Admiral Decrès and another 20,000 citizens guarding the various depots of munitions, supplies and provisions.[92] But even with the nearly seven thousand naval artillerymen and officers, crews were lacking for many batteries, a shortage that Napoleon now overcame by drafting students from the Ecole Polytechnique and the new Saint-Cyr Military Academy, who were given crash courses in gunnery practice at the Invalides, where their constant salvoes shattered the usual calm of the *quartier* Saint-Germain, setting neighbors' nerves on edge and intensifying war jitters.[93]

Paris had been stunned on 23 April to read the new *"Acte Additionnel,"* promulgated and imposed upon them without warning or consultation. While "the people" had felt it imperative to introduce new constitutional liberties and safeguards to avoid the despotic rule of the past, it was likewise expected that they should be consulted in that process, when deputies could suggest modifications, deletions or additions. Instead they had been deliberately, even arrogantly, ignored. Sixty-seven new articles were foisted upon them as a final, integral text. They were, of course, left to vote on them, as a fait accompli, but only as a single, unalterable text. A plebiscite, a national referendum, would determine the acceptance or rejection of this text, just as similar plebiscites had determined the acceptance of Napoleon's Life Consulship in 1802, and then the creation of the new Empire in 1804. To be sure the voting had been rather crudely rigged in both instances, resulting in 3,011,007 and 3,572,329 consecutive affirmative—if fraudulent—votes declared, without anyone at that time daring to challenge these results, despite the palpable absurdity of a mere 2,579 negative votes being cast in the case of the Empire, for example. Less than one dissatisfied person in every village, town and city of the realm? It was sheer nonsense. And thus now for Cambácères, at least, the pending plebiscitory results were hardly in doubt when he recalled a comment made years earlier by Napoleon after dinner one night at Malmaison: "Louis Sixteenth's only mistake was his love of legality; all is lost for a sovereign when he permits his people to question his power and rights." Then, reinforcing his scorn for any form of parliamentary government, or even a plebiscite, Napoleon angrily asserted: "If a nation wants happiness, it must obey orders and keep quiet. Grandees, magistrates, priests, citizens, everyone must be reduced to the same level of obedience, that is the secret for maintaining public tranquillity and the stability of the throne."[94]

Despite national public silence, the people were shocked by Napoleon's high-handed measures. Regarding the plebiscite of the "Acte Additionnel," pro-Bonapartist Fleury de Chaboulon acknowledged "The promulgation [of 22 April 1815] paralyzed and put an end to the previous goodwill [vis-à-vis Napoleon] that I had seen until this point. That same day I met various men known for their sincere attachment to the Emperor, but even they complained bitterly about this event."[95] Indeed, Carnot himself, as trustworthy a minister as he could hope to find, pleaded with Napoleon to reconsider. "Sire, I implore you, do not fight public opinion Your 'Acte Additionnel' has upset the nation. Promise the people you will modify it to meet their wishes. . . . I am not deceiving you when I tell you that your well-being and ours, depends upon your heeding the wishes of the country."[96]

But, of course, he did not listen; he never did. When on the first of June Napoleon duly announced the usual favorable plebiscite results (1,532,357 versus 4,802),[97] bitterness quickly hardened and spread, pervading the country, further undermining his already most precarious position. In fact, even the few details Napoleon deigned to release about these official, if fraudulent, statistics were alarming: 4,802 negative votes—this in a country of 26 million people—99.9 percent voting in favor? It was preposterous, of course, as even a totally illiterate peasant could have attested who chanced to see the thousands of irate French men and women, in Marseille alone, throwing stones at French troops and tearing down new imperial decrees and orders. Only 4,802 votes opposing Napoleon and his new Constitution? It was a farce. Clearly Police and Interior Ministry officials, aided by troops, had intimidated perhaps up to 2 million persons or simply had disposed of their votes, while brazenly increasing the number of affirmative ones. To this was added the double insult of the trumped up, nicely rounded military figures (at a time when perhaps 95 percent of all soldiers and sailors were illiterate, most being incapable even of writing their own names). Nevertheless, according to Napoleon Bonaparte, "222,000" soldiers (that was the precise official figure) for the Acte, and 320 rejecting it. Another remarkable coincidence occurred with naval registers, where precisely 22,000 affirmative votes were recorded and only 275 negative ones. The Army and Navy were now manned by thousands of men "recruited" often at bayonet point by press-gangs, and yet the combined armed forces voting a mere 595 opposing votes? (And one can scarcely forget that 85,000 French soldiers had felt strongly enough opposed to him the year before to desert his armies in wartime.) And who decided on the use of all the "twos" and "zeros" in the final count? Compounding this, Napoleon rejected *all votes* from the eleven southern and western *départements* currently in revolt against Paris. The Ministry of Interior's excuse for this was that they arrived "too late" to be counted.[98] And then, for good measure, all votes from fourteen entire army regiments were also rejected, allegedly on the basis that they also had arrived too late to be counted.

But war and politics did not preoccupy the Emperor all the time. While he had finally given up hope of seeing the Empress and his son at this time, at least part of his own family now rejoined him: Joseph, Julie and Hortense, as well as Madame Mère, Jérôme, and Cardinal Fesch, who had safely reached France from Italy aboard a French warship on 26th May.[99] However, the remaining two passengers accompanying them now, King Joachim (Murat) of Naples, and his wife, Caroline Bonaparte, were certainly less welcome. But once again the family met almost nightly for dinner—Joseph, for one, always present—where music, wine and conversation flowed as of yore.

It was at his public lunches where Napoleon particularly shone, however, as he entertained the scientific, literary, artistic and theatrical celebrities of the day, including his favorite actor, Talma, famous for his historical roles, whom he taunted, if in a jocular manner. "Now tell me, Talma, what is this I heard at Elba, that you were boasting of having taught me how to sit properly on my throne?" "Sire," a smiling Talma replied, "clearly you sit on the throne most admirably. Indeed, I have come here today for the very purpose of observing just how it is done." Occasionally in the evenings Napoleon would seek other company, including visits from either of his two favorite mistresses, Emilie de Pellapra and Marie Walewska.[100] But in general the celebrated balls and glittering festivities were a thing of the past; the tempo of life, much more subdued in the capital, readjusted to the tread of marching troops. Nor did the return of the King and Queen of Naples lighten any hearts.

Murat and Caroline had, of course, publicly denounced Napoleon in 1813 and 1814, signing alliances with the Allies in exchange for recognition of their throne. But when the Allies turned on Murat, he foolishly proclaimed Italian independence at Rimini, on 30 March 1815, and attacked Austrian armies in northern Italy. The Allies understandably, but incorrectly, believed he had done so at Napoleon's behest. After having been completely routed by them beginning at Occhiobello in April and concluding with Tolentino in May, Murat withdrew to Naples only to flee his capital under the threat of British guns on 19 May, landing at Cannes on 26 May.[101] Napoleon reluctantly permitted the royal couple to remain in France, but on condition that they did so at a secluded estate in eastern France between Lyons and the Alps. However, Murat never got beyond the warm limpid waters of the Riviera throughout the one hundred days. Although Lucien—making his way independently from Switzerland—did successfully reach Paris, it hardly seemed to bode well that Napoleon's favorite sister, Pauline, was detained in Italy by illness. Jérôme, although back in Paris, had not yet made his official appearance because of Napoleon's refusal to receive him as King of Westphalia, and also because of Napoleon's offer of the command of a mere division instead of an army or corps. Jérôme left Napoleon in a huff and the feud between them continued unabated, although Jérôme did promise to make an appearance for the Champ de Mai ceremony.

In the last week of May, the long drawn-out meeting and reconciliation between Lucien and Napoleon had been successfully negotiated by Joseph Bonaparte, when after many weeks of wrangling, it finally took place just after Napoleon had moved into the Elysée-Bourbon Palace.[102] Napoleon, while not warmly embracing his tiresome brother in private, at least did so in public. His valet, Marchand, approached Lucien with a gold salver bearing the brilliant red Grand Cordon of the Legion of Honor, which Napoleon placed around his taller brother's handsome head, then paraded through the white-and-gold anterooms to announce their reconciliation to the world. Now having Lucien reinstated as both senator and "French prince," Napoleon installed him just across the rue de Rivoli in the sprawling galleries of the Palais Royal, where, unlike in the past, he lived a quiet, even secluded, existence. And thus with most of the family back in the capital, the much-vaunted but greatly delayed Champ de Mai festivities could finally take place on Thursday, 1 June. To the superstitious, however, it seemed yet another ill omen that a traditional May ceremony and military parade dating from the Merovingian past should take place in June. Napoleon, who had already changed history, was now changing the French calendar.

A couple of hundred thousand Parisians and out-of-town visitors crowded the vast green acres reaching down from the Ecole Militaire and overlooking the Seine. The river itself was filled with hundreds of boats and barges, their passengers and crews attempting to catch a glimpse of the ceremonies. Troops lining the streets approaching the Ecole Militaire tried to keep traffic open both to the nearby Invalides and the War Ministry just beyond, as well as to the Pont d'Iéna leading back to the Tuileries.[103]

Imperial Architect Pierre Fontaine had created the high ceremonial stands for the event held today at the south end of the Champ de Mars, consisting of an enormous pentagonal hemicycle, its wings facing the gaunt gray stone—columned façade of the Ecole Militaire, now largely obstructed by the wooden structure erected before it, including two long tribunes with seating for several hundred people on either side of the raised pavilion in the center upon which the Emperor's throne was placed.[104] This in turn was covered by a triangular roof of Nordic design, crowned by two tricolor flags, and from which immense folds of red drape serving as backdrop, and hung along the sides, the only relief to an otherwise stark edifice.

The overcast early-morning sky soon gave way to a sunny, indeed, sizzling day. Thousands of invited guests, including the five hundred electoral college delegates and representatives, arrived at the hemicycle at nine o'clock, on either side of an elevated altar built in the middle of the large open space. Forty-five thousand officers and troops representing every regiment of the Army and Imperial Guard filled the raised stands on either side of the hemicycle. An hour later the highest officers of the Legion of Honor, along with members of the Conseil d'Etat, the Cour de Cassation, the Imperial Court, the Cour des Comptes, the Paris Municipal Council and luminaries of the university in their array of gorgeous gowns and gold- and silver-encrusted uniforms filed into the tribunes on either side of the throne facing the vast bustling audience.

Suddenly, at 11 A.M., an ear-shattering blast rang through the wooden structure, momentarily startling, shaking and silencing the spectators: One hundred cannon along the quai of the Tuileries thundered over the Seine, simultaneously matched by another five hundred mighty guns before the Ecole Militaire, the Invalides, the Pont d'Iéna, Montmartre and Vincennes, announcing the departure of the imperial procession from the Carrousel of the Tuileries and the awesome might of the man responsible for the day's events.

But it was not until after noon that the Imperial Guard's legendary Red Lancers Cavalry Regiment leading the procession clattered across the Pont d'Iéna and made the long approach to the Ecole Militaire. Another salvo of six hundred cannon again reverberated through the capital, numbing ears and panicking horses. Hundreds of solemn drums began to roll as thousands of bayonets glittering in the sweltering sunlight lining the route along the River Seine snapped to attention. The Imperial Guard was then followed by the Governor of Paris, the Comte de Lobau on a magnificent mount, heading his general staff and cavalry units, and a mounted platoon of heralds at arms bearing violet coats of arms, embroidered with golden eagles, preceding nineteen elegant State carriages, each drawn by six immaculately groomed horses, preparing the way for Napoleon's golden State carriage—first seen at his coronation over a decade earlier—with its mirrored panels bearing the gold-encrusted imperial arms—drawn by eight magnificent steeds caparisoned with large white plumes worthy of a sultan. Along either side of this carriage astride handsome horses, in the most resplendent military uniforms of the Empire, the navy blue velours embroidered heavily in gold from their wrist to the tip of the high stiff collar, came Marshals Grouchy, Jourdan, Ney and Soult, accompanied in turn by aides de camp, ordnance officers, écuyers and pages in their red, green and golden imperial uniforms, as the Duc de Rovigo (A.J.M. R. Savary) at the head of grenadier and dragoon cavalry units brought up the rear.

It was impressive, it was stunning. It no doubt sent shivers of excitement up the spines of the Parisian populace witnessing this atavistic splendor so reminiscent of the great ceremonies of the past that had inaugurated Napoleon's imperial regime, and seen by many present today at an earlier, happier hour in the Empire when all the joys and disillusionment yet lay before them. But the thoughtful and reflective among them were no doubt also reminded of another, more solemn military review by the triumphant Allied armies here on the Champ de Mars by the Duc d'Angoulême and the Duke of Wellington just the year before.

Despite the imperial tergiversations, deaths and alienation within court society since then, many familiar faces were now recognized here by alert Parisians priding themselves on such knowledge, including the much-dreaded, but smiling, Fouché, who, regardless of the silver braid of his blue court uniform, appeared as cunning and deadly as ever. Then, of course, in his ancien régime elegance, the Comte de Montesquiou, the Prince Cambacérès, the Duc de Vicence (Caulaincourt), the Duc de Gaëte (Gaudin), Duc Decrès, Comte Mollien, Comte Carnot, and the four distinguished Ministres d'Etat—Comte Défermon, Comte Regnault de Saint-Jean d'Angély, Comte Boulay de la Meurthe and Comte Merlin, not to mention the Comte de Ségur (who as Grand Maître des Cérémonies, had organized this day's entire events). Nor could one mistake the scowling, humorless, haggard-looking Prince d'Eckmühl, Marshal Davout himself, upon whom so much now depended, accompanied by lesser known celebrities including the two most recently elevated peers of the realm,

General Comte Brayer and the newly promoted General de La Bédoyère,[105] as well as rows of anonymous officials, officers, magistrates and dignitaries, uniformed and gowned, bemedaled and beribboned, in a mass blending of reds, blues, white, grays and greens. Yet striking among almost all of them was the singular lack of joy, celebration or even evidence of mild optimism, in stark contrast to the years of the Consulate and the early Empire.

A low murmur rose from the spectators as Napoleon finally appeared, attended by his brothers Joseph, Lucien and Jérôme. Dressed in white velvet, they mounted the steps to the high platform, set off by the red of the drapes, while all but secluded by them in the lodge, sat the two former Queens, Julie of Naples and latterly of Spain, and Hortense of Holland—with her two young sons—now reduced to the rank of mere imperial princesses.[106] Marshals Moncey, Kellermann, Sérurier, Lefebvre, Oudinot and Masséna, persuaded at the last minute to make an appearance today for old time's and solidarity's sake, stood on the steps below the throne, segregated by Ségur's pen[107] like the outcasts they had become.

A sudden hush now fell upon the tens of thousands of spectators, as Napoleon stepped into full view before the throne. It was unbelievable, it was absurd, indeed grotesque. In this ceremony allegedly called to proclaim the expansion of liberty and the new Constitution, Napoleon had just pulled one of the greatest gaffes of his career—appearing now in white coronation robes, complete with black velvet toque surmounted by white heron feathers. Taken out of camphor-filled trunks lost in the labyrinthine attics of the Louvre, this was the very costume he had worn by the side of the now-deceased Josephine back on 2 December 1804. Napoleon was pathetically attempting to relive, if not revive, artificially, the specter of the past. But a lifeless specter it was, despite, and because of, this horrible mummery—all rendered almost obscene by the tight-fitting jacket and shirt made originally for a younger, much more slender Emperor, whose greatly developed paunch and chest threatened now to burst seams and buttons. And as Henri Houssaye put it, "Napoleon, who at this solemn moment might have rightly appeared before the people and army in the simple grenadiers uniform he had worn at Austerlitz, preferred instead the stage costume of a Talma in *Les Templiers.* . . ."[108]

Yet what was just as striking now was the obvious absence of those who had been present at the Coronation ceremonies a decade earlier, those no longer present as a result of intervening historical events: ex-Chancellor Pasquier, for instance, and Talleyrand, as well as ambassadors of all the greater and lesser European powers, including Prussia,

Russia, Great Britain, Austria and Spain, not to mention a bevy of German Rhineland princelings. But it was neither the nefarious Talleyrand nor the distinguished diplomats whom Napoleon personally missed today, as he reflected on the significance of the event. "What I most want to see here is Berthier" he had earlier lamented unconsciously before his valet, Marchand.[109] To Napoleon's mind it was the "betrayal" and absence of this soldier in particular that was most painful for him. It was the faithful Berthier who had served beside the Emperor in all his major battles, as well as at the coronation ceremony in Notre-Dame Cathedral, whose absence today emphasized the great chasm separating Napoleon from the past. Little did he realize, of course, that on this very day, at nearly this very hour, his grief-stricken Berthier—after having gone over to King Louis in 1814, only to abandon him in despair in March 1815—was leaping from a high tower window of a castle in Bamberg to a dreadful death.[110] But even without this knowledge, everything about this ceremony before the Ecole Militaire, where he had received his army commission thirty years before, now seemed lugubrious, despairing, a travesty of the very Empire he had created. The event poignantly dramatized to everyone just how much had really transpired, failed and altered over the years—all reflected starkly in the sullen, somber faces weakly attempting to emit an occasional *"Vive l'Empereur."*

But despite martial music, forced patriotic cheers and acclamations filling the air and the officers of crack regiments bellowing out their orders before the towering throne, another portent, if not ill omen, was evident: the presence of a mere handful of the twenty-two remaining Imperial Marshals whom Napoleon had created during an earlier, more youthful Empire. Nothing could have been more strikingly symbolic to those with an intimate knowledge of Court affairs than the fact that even these few marshals had agreed to appear today only on condition that following the ceremony they would be permitted to retire quickly to the seclusion of their estates, and hence distance themselves as far as possible from Napoleon Bonaparte and his mad schemes.

These ceremonies—originally convened as a mass meeting of "30,000 electoral-college delegates" from all across the nation wherein they were to discuss and vote on a new constitution—had since been altered unilaterally by Napoleon. Thirty thousand delegates were reduced to a mere five hundred while the debate was eliminated altogether, transforming today's ceremony into a great patriotic rally to whip up and unify public support for the war he was about to drag the nation into. This was to be capped by a great display of loyalty, as all the officials and troops of the land traipsed before him swearing their allegiance to throne and Empire.

Standing in the strong June sun before the altar amid the vast audience, with his arms upraised, Fallot de Beaumont, Archbishop of Bourges—attended by Cardinals Cambacérès and de Bayanne and the bishops of Nancy, Meaux, Versailles, Parma and Liège[111]—next called upon the Supreme Being for his blessing. Following this the deputation of five hundred electoral delegates stepped forward, en masse, to the foot of the imperial throne[112] as their spokesman, Dubois d'Angers, prepared to address the Emperor:

"A new contract has been formed between the nation and Your Majesty," he declared, and they, the delegates had "gathered together now from every part of the Empire to acknowledge the tables of the law . . . just sanctioned by the people." Then turning to the current situation facing France, he noted that times were grave, with the enemies of the nation threatening them again with hostilities. "But what do all these Allied kings want with us—arrayed before us with their armies, drawn up for a war which so astounds Europe and afflicts humanity? By what act of ours, by what violation have we provoked their vengeance and aggression?" asked this indignant official. "Even with the artificially reduced frontiers we now find foisted upon us, we find ourselves threatened by invasion." Why? Because Napoleon had returned. "Because France wants to be France [and choose her own leader], does she deserve to be degraded, torn apart, dismembered, reserved for the same fate as Poland?" France, however, a proud nation, would not be dictated to, he asserted. "If they force us to fight, then let one great cry resound in every heart. Let us march on the enemy! . . . Sire, nothing is impossible, no effort will be spared to ensure our honor and independence . . . everything will be done to reject the ignominious yoke they wish to force upon us. . . . Every Frenchman is a soldier," he concluded. "Victory will follow our eagles, and our enemies who have counted on divisions within our ranks will soon regret having provoked us."[113]

Of course, what all but a handful of those present knew, however, was that this was not the delegates' original speech. Having insisted upon its being submitted well in advance for his prior approval, Napoleon had been dismayed by what he had found, and ordered his henchmen, Acting Justice Minister Cambacérès and Jean-Antoine Chaptal, to rewrite much of the text, eliminating its numerous critical and distasteful declarations, including the forcefully painful judgment: "We have rallied to you because we hope that you have brought to us from your retirement the full repentance one might expect from a great man,"[114] a statement whose chiding arrogance had simply infuriated the Emperor. Fortunately, being Emperor, he still had the power to delete disrespectful criticisms and utterances, at least from speeches, if not quite so successfully from people's hearts, and had substituted instead stock phrases from so many of his own repertoire of previous speeches ("Nothing is impossible," "What have we done?" "Every Frenchman is a soldier." "Victory will follow our eagles," etc.). Indeed, it was most embarrassing for Napoleon's ministers and court officials to listen to this pathetic travesty of what was self-evident to all in the know. Napoleon rigged ballots, Napoleon rigged the chambers and Senate, Napoleon manipulated the press, and now he rewrote the speeches of the elected delegates of the people. Far from indicating a willingness to accept new constitutional reforms to help France rebuild its moral and political base, Napoleon had now shown his utter contempt for the French people, their wishes, institutions and aspirations. It really was the supreme insult, this doctored speech. That it was greeted by the polite, lukewarm applause of the electoral delegates, offset by the obscenely robust cheers of the tens of thousands of troops and officers standing behind them, merely intensified the entire farce. This in turn was followed by the official announcement of the results of the national plebiscite: 1,532,357 approving the new Acte Additionnel, opposed to 4,802 negative returns—it was national unanimity itself, though of course a total fabrication by the Emperor, who now addressed the nation:[115]

"Messieurs les électeurs des collèges de départements et d'arrondissements; Messieurs les députés des armées de terre et de mer au Champ de Mai.

"As Emperor, Consul, Soldier, I owe everything to the people. In prosperity, adversity, on the battlefield, before the council, on the throne, in exile, France has been the sole and constant object of my thoughts and actions.

"Like the Athenian king of yore, I sacrificed myself for my people [in 1814] in the hope of seeing fulfilled the Allied promise to maintain intact France's natural frontiers, her honor and her laws.

"Instead, our indignation on seeing these sacred rights—acquired as a result of twenty-five years of victories—discarded and lost forever, the outcry resulting upon finding our national honor sullied, and the wishes of the people denied, led me to return to this throne . . ." In so doing "I had counted on a long era of peace" but that has now proven impossible, and instead "it has been necessary to prepare for war. However, before personally running the risks involved in fighting, my first concern was to instruct and advise the nation [in the preparation of a new enlightened Constitution] and the people have now accepted this Constitution which I submitted to them." Nonetheless the very independence of France was now at stake. "Frenchmen, you are about to return to your departments. Tell the citizens how serious the situation is!!! but that with unity, hard work and perseverance we will emerge victorious from this struggle of a great people against its oppressors. . . . Tell them that all the foreign kings whom I have raised to their thrones, or who have been able to maintain their crowns due to my help (all who in prosperous times allied themselves with me and accepted the protection of the French people) today direct their attacks against my person. If I did not realize that it was in fact this country that they really want, and not just me, I would gladly give myself up to them." But so long as "the French people continue to manifest the many examples of their love for me, the rage of our enemies will be rendered harmless. Frenchmen, my wish is that of the people. My rights are theirs, my honor, my glory, my happiness are in fact the honor, glory and happiness of France itself."

Napoleon's first official address to the nation in person since his return to Paris was "very warmly received," said a biased eyewitness, Comte Fleury de Chaboulon, as cries of *"Vive l'Empereur!"* filled the Champ de Mars, notably, however, from the troops under his orders, whereas only a dull applause could be discerned from the two hundred thousand spectators ringing this last great imperial spectacle. Parisians above all knew the price one paid later for the applause and glory of the present.

An irritable Napoleon himself seemed deadly aware of just how badly his speech had been received. The Archbishop of Bourges next approached the throne and on bended knee held out the New Testament to the Emperor, upon which to take his oath, raising his right hand as he pronounced loudly: "I swear to observe the constitutions of the Empire and have them enforced,"[116] which was repeated in turn by all the court officials and entire assembly echoing their loyalty and adherence—*"Nous le jurons!"* followed by the *Te Deum* and the parading of the imperial and regimental flags as Interior Minister Carnot, Naval Minister Decrès and War Minister Davout, surely three of the gloomiest faces in the hemicycle, stood mutely bearing immense imperial flags on behalf of the National Guard, Navy and Army. It was hardly a scene to rouse warmth or fervor. A seemingly distracted Emperor prepared to distribute over a hundred eagles to the presidents of the provincial electoral colleges and officers of every regiment. But after awarding just three medals he departed, without warning, from the schedule of ceremonies now already over an hour behind time and abruptly turned away without explanation and rapidly descended the steps. Ministers, marshals and officials quickly moved aside to make way for the Emperor, who then marched at a fast clip straight across the hemicycle—to the utter astonishment of all—followed by dozens and dozens of scuttling flag bearers and ADCs. Then, continuing, he left the ceremonial structure and passed beyond into the open air of the Champ de Mars, where he mounted a fifteen foot pyramid-like platform and was immediately encircled by the flag bearers who had by now caught up with him. Thousands of troops, primarily Paris National Guards and some twenty thousand Imperial Guards, formed in a deep square around their fiery, unpredictable Emperor, as he distributed hundreds of eagles to the troops, stopping briefly only to invoke their dual allegiance.

> I hereby confide the eagle to the national colors. Do you swear to perish if needs be in the defense of the nation? . . . Do you swear never again to permit foreigners to defile the capital of our great nation . . . and to die rather than allow them to come and dictate their laws to us!

Each phrase uttered now was interrupted by jubilant, deafening outbursts—"We swear it!" over and over again, like peals of thunder echoing across the sky, as swords and bayonets danced in the sunlight above their heads, accompanied by triumphant *"Vive l'Empereur!"* over and over again.[117] It was simply electrifying, and if the previous part of the ceremony had been limp, lukewarm and contrived, the present scene with the Emperor surrounded by a sea of soldiers was one of untamed ecstasy. "It is impossible to describe its magnitude," one English witness, John Hobhouse, later wrote.[118]

But in retrospect this great spectacle was one with which the French people were by now only too familiar. Once again bands had played stirringly, drums had rolled dramatically, whereas, apart from the troops, there had been little warmth or response demonstrated by a people bled white as a result of having answered such appeals too faithfully in the past. The ghosts of hundreds of thousands of slain French soldiers completely diminished and all but neutralized the Emperor's charisma and pleas today. Perhaps for the first time, he appeared to the people to be the very small, if dangerous, man he was, ready to jeopardize and destroy everything and everyone, in order to achieve his ends—ends that clearly were against the best interests of France. Indeed, even Napoleon's faithful lieutenant, Fleury de Chaboulon, reluctantly acknowledged "the dissatisfaction of a certain number of his supporters who openly complained about the current situation."[119] The official electors who had come today for the great national congress, expecting to find themselves and a new constitution the center of attention, had found instead just another patriotic war rally, with the usual distribution of ribbons of the Legion of Honor, eagles for the flags and the trooping of the colors. Old revolutionaries, hoping to see Napoleon rid himself of the Empire altogether, replacing it with a republic, were equally disappointed. Still others closer to the Tuileries, including Caulaincourt and LaValette,[120] were even more concerned that Napoleon had not taken advantage of this ideal occasion—at a time when so much personal hostility to him was manifest throughout most regions of the country—to step down, perhaps declaring a regency in favor of his son, Napoleon II, thereby preventing this patently absurd and unnecessary war.[121]

And thus somber citizens, magistrates, public officials and regiments left dreams behind in the trampled grass and empty stands, as the imperial coronation carriage—already an historical museum piece like Napoleon himself—bearing the brothers Bonaparte in deadly silence, led the cortège back to the Tuileries for the receptions, sumptuous dinner, elegant ball and *feu d'artifice* that were awaiting their return on this most festive day.

Napoleon's last full day in Paris, Sunday, 11 June, was unrelenting. Having reinstated Marshal Soult in May, then appointing him his new chief of staff and sending him north to prepare the Army for his arrival, the Emperor now received the delegations of the combined Chambers at the Tuileries. They were completely behind him, the handpicked Chambre des Pairs assured him; even "military reverses shall not weaken the inseparable link"[122] between the nation and him. These sentiments were strongly reinforced by the delegation from the Chambres des Représentants, which fully supported the necessity and right to defend themselves against "the most unjust aggression," declaring the forthcoming hostilities to be "a legitimate war," the success of which was assured by "the union of the people and throne," whose only intention was "to seek in victory a means of reaching a lasting peace."[123] As for the earlier dissenting voices, exemplified by the anti-imperialist General Gilbert de LaFayette, dubbing these two chambers "the Napoleon Club," they were today forgotten, the Emperor himself informing them of what they had come to hear: "I shall be leaving tonight to join and lead my armies. The movement of the various enemy corps makes my presence there indispensable. . . . In all my undertakings my step will be firm and straight. Help me now save the country."[124] The Emperor was clearly tired and tense, and the less than eloquent farewell address reflected that.

In the last hours of the day Napoleon gave the inevitable final orders, checking all arrangements, adding a few last-minute surprises, including summoning Marshal Masséna—"if he wishes to appear"—to take command of the 3rd and 4th Military Districts[125] while also informing Marshal Ney of his departure, inviting him to be at imperial headquarters at Avesnes on the fourteenth—"if he wishes to be present at the opening battles."[126] It was the first and last time he would "invite" principal army commanders to fight, if they "wished to do so."

Napoleon next convened the Council of Ministers in the throne room for the last time.[127] He informed them that in his absence they would be meeting under the presidency of "*notre frère le prince Joseph,*" seconded by Prince Lucien, and that in addition to the usual eight ministers (Cambacérès, Davout, Caulaincourt, Gaudin, Mollien, Decrès, Fouché and Carnot) would be added the four Ministres d'Etat (Défermon, Regnault, Boulay and Merlin). All important matters were to be decided in his absence by majority vote.[128]

Upon returning to his state chambers later that evening, Joseph handed him 800,000 francs worth of diamonds, which in addition to the necklace worth 300,000 francs given him at Elba by Pauline, were to be stashed away in his carriage, to see the Emperor through unforeseen circumstances. Then, after ordering Marchand to deliver two large caches of arms to Mesdames Pellapra and Walewska, Napoleon sent for his secretary and awarded the payment of a 2,000-franc pension to the widow of a former superior officer long forgotten back in the Revolution.[129]

At three o'clock in the morning of Monday, 12 June, Napoleon Bonaparte, once again attired in his green grenadier's uniform, entered his carriage in the courtyard of the Tuileries, accompanied by his ADCs, ordnance officers, two pages, and Messrs. Gaudin and Cambacérès. Escorted by four hundred Imperial Guardsmen, including his faithful Red Lancers, he gave the order to take the road to Soissons . . . and to another war.

Chapter X

"*Pour la Patrie*"

"*Glorious news! Nosey has got command! Won't we give them a drubbing now!*"

> Sergeant Wheeler, 51st Regiment

"*I have got an infamous army, very weak and ill equipped, and a very inexperienced Staff. In my opinion they are doing nothing in England. They have not raised a man.*"

> Wellington to Lord Stewart
> 8 May 1815

"*For every stout-hearted Frenchman, the time has come to conquer or perish.*"

> Napoleon, "Ordre du Jour," 14 June 1815

If the Wesleys continued to propagate and young Arthur Wesley—as the future Duke of Wellington was baptized following his birth on 1 May 1769—was one of five siblings, it was because the human condition and English tradition required it. That there might not be enough money to go round—the Wesleys had already lost most of their wealth and property—and children were considered more of a hindrance than a delight, nevertheless they appeared with ceaseless regularity over the centuries. But perhaps the most remarkable thing about the Wesley family was that after having spent centuries in Ireland as members of the Anglo-Protestant ruling elite, they had achieved absolutely nothing remarkable. Indeed, the reasons why the future Duke's unimpressive father was raised to a peerage—if only an Irish peerage—"are not obvious," as the Duke's biographer, Elizabeth Longford, put it.[1] In any event, less than ten years before the boy's birth, his father had become Earl of Mornington, and Professor of Music at Trinity College, Dublin, where he led the orchestra and composed musical pieces, mostly madrigals and glees, including a Dublin favorite, "When for the world's repose my Chloï sleeps." And though a violin was foisted upon the reluctant Arthur Wesley at an early age, he later managed to burn it without any particular traumatic effect upon his subsequent development. (Wellington with a fiddle, it is hard to imagine!)

Because his parents were "frivolous and careless personages"—as their eldest son, Richard, later described them—and their mother a shallow, insensitive woman only too pleased to be rid of the lot of them, young Arthur was conveniently dispatched to Eton. There he remained, singularly undistinguished in any subject or endeavor, even sports, as he segregated himself successfully from all group activities, fleeing the playing fields of Eton, even avoiding the arduous pastimes of boating and cricket, with set purpose of mind. Lord Mornington having left his family in straitened circumstances—brother Richard had to leave Oxford before taking his degree—Arthur's mother put off time and again the decision regarding a career for Arthur. As a result, by the age of eighteen, he was still wandering aimlessly, his mother loudly lamenting—"I vow to God I don't know what to do with my awkward son Arthur," though the family for the most part did not take her remiss attitude too much to heart. And then one day shortly thereafter upon entering the Haymarket Theatre in London and looking about, Lady Mornington suddenly exclaimed to her companion: "I do believe there is my ugly boy Arthur." Concluding from this incident that he was good "food for powder" and nothing more,[2] she arranged for a commission and whisked him off to the army, safely out of sight and mind once and for all, as his 76th Regiment embarked for Ireland.

Despite his Irish roots, young Wesley did not enjoy his years in what he called "that country of scoundrels," and although serving briefly in Flanders under the Duke of York, he much preferred his next significant assignment, in British India. Although he had very little money of his own, a fairly frugal existence, along with his family's help, permitted him to purchase promotion, and this added to the sums received from the sharing of booty won in battle saw him reach the rank of colonel by the age of twenty-seven, in 1796. Curiously enough, the life of a soldier fully agreed with this former musician. Although he shared a natural interest in horses with his fellow officers and had attended the famous gentlemen's Equestrian School at Angers, France, for nearly a year before joining the army, and was an excellent horseman—the other traditional amusements of his army brethren rarely attracted him. The polo field, the raucous, heavy drinking of the regimental mess, if anything, repelled him. Instead, while others were gambling heavily or carousing in local bordellos, Wesley preferred the quiet company of a few friends, or could be found reading the dozens of books he had brought with him from London, to make up for what he now acknowledged to be a rather sketchy education at best. Needless to say, a young officer preferring John Locke's *Essay Concerning Human Understanding*, or *Treatise on Government*, to the jovial fraternity of the mess, was deemed unusual, if not downright ungentlemanly, but then again the Wesleys—unlike most officers—were Tories, not Whigs.

It was not altogether surprising, therefore, that Arthur Wesley's entire Indian philosophy was extraordinarily mature and almost unique for his day. For one, he worried about maintaining good health in a country whose climate was notorious for breaking the hardiest of souls. To survive here, year after year, he reckoned one had "to live moderately, to drink little or no wine, to use exercize, to keep the mind employed, and, if possible, to keep in good humour with the world,"[3] a philosophy echoed by an American statesman thousands of miles away in Virginia, Thomas Jefferson.

And Wesley's career continued to develop, thanks in part to his own common sense, though more through the appointment of his eldest brother, Richard, Earl of Mornington, first as Governor of Madras and then as Governor General of India.[4] But despite his parents' neglect, the young colonel maintained his own standards of integrity, which puzzled many of his peers, but gradually earned him the respect of his junior officers. He loathed "greediness" and "dishonesty" in British officials and officers, deploring the prevalent "system of dubashery [corruption] and rapacity"[5] he found everywhere. And at one point feeling so disheartened by it all he even considered resigning his commission, so embarrassed was he for the Raj. Officers too frequently abused their power, even to the detriment of the troops under their own command, as for instance when one Lieutenant Colonel Saxon was found stealing large amounts of army saltpetre, stores and guns, and selling them privately.[6] The sense of honor in Colonel Wesley was simply outraged. Time and again he did all in his power to have such officers courtmartialed and cashiered from the Army, though usually in vain, as soldiers covered up well to protect their own.

Colonel Wellesley (his family had changed its name from Wesley in 1798) had a good reputation as a commanding officer, despite his youth, quaint philosophy and singular uprightness of character. He was a good commander, thorough in everything he did, thoughtful and liked by the ranks, but because of the position of his brother, Lord Mornington, he encountered considerable jealousy among his fellow officers. There was another reason for such puerile animosity, however: his outstanding ability on the field of battle, which he displayed on at least two well-known occasions.

At the end of the eighteenth, and beginning of the nineteenth, century, India was in a state of rapid change, as the East India Company and the British Indian Army (close to a couple of hundred thousand strong, including sepoys), were extending their influence and control, everywhere entrenching themselves deeper and deeper. Some areas proved particularly worrisome, however, and none more so, perhaps, than the 29,500 square miles comprising the tumultuous Hindu state of Mysore, which ranked fourth in size and importance after Jammu and Kashmir, Hyderabad, Kalat and Jodhpur (Marwar) of the more than 120 "Salute States."

Mysore, located in the southern tip of the Indian subcontinent and wedged between Madras to the east and Goa to the northwest on the Arabian Sea, had been in flux, indeed in a state of war, for years, thanks to the rapacious rule of Tipu. Heading the 33rd Regiment, many thousands of Indian troops and over 10,000 bullocks hauling ammunition, artillery, food, supplies and baggage, Wellesley successfully fought off hundreds of Indian cavalry elephants, traversing steaming jungles and immense irrigation canals, to take Tipu's mighty fortress of Seringapatam on 4 May 1799. Killing Tipu in the fighting and seizing his fabulous treasure—then conservatively estimated worth over £1,100,000 just in gold and jewels[7]—Colonel Wellesley celebrated his thirtieth birthday as Seringapatam's new Governor, with a personal windfall of £4,000 for his troubles. It had been an arduous but most successful campaign,[8] and shortly thereafter Wellesley, despite his relatively low rank, was promoted as Governor of the entire state of Mysore (an area three times larger than modern Lebanon).

The other battle that greatly enhanced Wellesley's reputation took place in September 1803 when the Governor General called upon his brother, Major General Wellesley (promoted in April 1802) to put down fresh disturbances to the northeast of Bombay and to the north of the Nizam's threatened state of Hyderabad, in the Deccan Plateau, when in November 1802 the rampaging Holkar of Indore attacked and defeated two fellow Mahratta chiefs, the Peshwah of Poona and Sindhia of Gwalior. In December 1802 the Governor General, taking advantage of the Peshwah's critical situation, forced the Treaty of Bassein on that ruler—hitherto the independent head of the Mahratta Confederacy—thereby reducing him to British protection and his state, like that of Hyderabad, Mysore and Oudh, thus becoming yet another British puppet. It was good politics for the British, and Wellesley, a staunch imperialist, headed an expedition from Mysore, far to the south, to put down the militant Holkar once and for all.[9] With the appearance of Wellesley, however, the Peshwah was safely returned to his throne, as Holkar fled into Hindustan. But by the summer of 1803 more trouble developed as Sindhia and the Bhoonslah, themselves fearing British control, now threatened the Nizam's neighboring southern frontier.

The entire affair came to a climax in September 1803 as Major General Wellesley, with a total force of 7,000 men single-handedly attacked Sindhia's army of some 40,000 in the steaming summer heat. Approaching Assaye between the Juah and Kaitna rivers, Wellesley found his greatly inferior force and twenty-two field guns facing the Mahratta's French-trained army and more than one hundred cannon. It defied everything any attacking officer had been taught, going on the offensive with numerically inferior infantry, cavalry and artillery, against a formidable army in a well-entrenched position. But after reconnoitering the area, Arthur Wellesley, always known for his prudence and accurate assessment of a situation, threw away the military textbooks. Attacking on 23 September, he decisively defeated the Sindhia's troops, inflicting some 6,000 casualties in a most bloody encounter, and costing the British force some 2,200 men. Wellesley himself, as usual, had been in the midst of the heaviest fighting, and twice had horses killed under him, though, also as usual, escaping unscathed.[10] He had won an astonishing victory against intimidating odds, thanks to his superior maneuvering and boldness of plan and action. In many of the future battles, however, restricted manpower and resources were to allow for little display of his skill in such maneuvers.

At this battle of Assaye, he carried out certain actions that were always to be typical of him as a commander regardless of the campaign, whether in the Iberian Peninsula or Indian Subcontinent, although in some ways detrimental to good command. For example, though rightly complaining now and throughout his career of the poor quality of officers under his command, Wellesley rarely confided in even his more trusted ones. There were few stimulating *conseils de guerres*, few or no prebattle consultations. And once hostilities had commenced, Wellesley was loath to delegate authority, resulting from a combination of his basic distrust in the ability or loyalty of others and a wish to capture all the praise for himself. And yet, ironically, Wellesley was no grand egotist like Napoleon, Masséna or Soult, but rather, no doubt, was simply reacting to a childhood bereft of even a minimal amount of love or attention by his parents. "The real reason why I succeeded in my campaigns," he later acknowledged to his old friend, Philip Henry, Earl Stanhope, "is because I was always on the spot—I saw to everything and did everything myself. If I had not been there to . . . restore the battle, we should have lost the day."[11] He was not boasting, but simply stating the fact. And yet it was a damning fact regarding his own principles of command. To intervene personally occasionally in order to save a situation from disaster was one thing—as in the case of stopping the mass desertion of troops— but to do so continually was poor leadership, reflecting lack of judgment. And yet he was to do it time and again in every battle he fought. "The general was in the thick of the action the whole time . . . I never saw a man so cool and collected as he was," attested one young officer at Assaye.[12] He was always there because he felt all would go wrong without him. That two horses were killed under him, that bullets and cannon balls flew past, killing and wounding those all about him, apparently did not worry him. He never seemed to have much awareness of his own personal safety and could not have cared less. "When one is strongly intent on an object, common sense will usually direct one to the right means," he once said. But common sense required a good commanding officer to stand back at a distance to be able to appraise the overall campaign, to give advice, help and orders accordingly, and not entering the fray like a company commander, thereby neglecting his real task and even jeopardizing the overall operations. Napoleon, too, was a brave man, never overly concerned with the personal risks of a battlefield, but he remained aloof and directed the general situation, not local tactics. Wellington lacked that quality and ability. And yet his very intervention rightly earned for Wellington the admiration, confidence and pride of the men in the ranks, as well as the officers under his command, who knew they could always count on him. He always gave his best.

Although other battles ensued, and further territories consolidated— resulting in Wellesley's being awarded the prestigious Order of the Bath in

September 1804—by then the British Government had greater, more pressing concerns than Mahratta chieftains. Britain was again at war with France, and Napoleon Bonaparte, who had just been proclaimed Emperor in May, and was once again actively pitting his forces against them and most of Europe. And it was in this political climate that a now victorious and fairly wealthy General Wellesley embarked in March 1805 for Great Britain, after more than eight years' service in India. Having arrived an unknown and unproven colonel, he returned almost a national figure, intent on marrying the girl of his dreams.

Like many a successful soldier and public leader, Wellesley was not destined to find success in his private life. His offer of marriage to Catherine "Kitty" Pakenham, the daughter of Earl Longford, having been rejected in 1793, Wellesley had long since put all thoughts of the fashionable and wealthy girl out of his mind, that is, until recently. Then mutual friends took matters into their own hands and artificially revived a long-dead romance, resulting in General Wellesley's renewed proposal by correspondence to Kitty Pakenham now being accepted.

But the passage of time, he found to his dismay, had brought about great mental and physical changes in the once-blooming young woman he had left behind. The shock of no longer finding a twenty-two-year-old beauty, but a retiring, fast-fading thirty-four-year-old struck him most forcefully, making him immediately regret his second offer of marriage sight unseen. "She has grown ugly, by jove," he muttered to his younger, clergyman brother upon first laying eyes on her again after a hiatus of twelve years.[13] But for better or worse Wellesley was always a man of his word, even when he found he had made a less than satisfactory bargain. He and Earl Longford's* sister, Kitty, were duly united, in Dublin on 10 April 1806: "I married her because they asked me to do it & I did not know myself what I was getting into . . . in short, I was a fool," he admitted to a lady friend sixteen years later.[14] Instead of finding a cheerful, outgoing, sociable creature, the thirty-seven-year-old general found a prematurely retiring, indeed reclusive, woman, aging beyond her years, unsure of herself, frequently ailing for weeks at a time, to the point of later failing to attend most important public affairs and receptions, even those given in honor of her husband. Nor could she give either the love or the warmth a husband might expect, though at least she was close to the two sons she provided in short order, and to whom she clung, almost in desperation. The young general found that he could

---

*Her brother, Thomas, had succeeded to the title years earlier and had been responsible for declining Wellesley's initial proposal of marriage.

neither confide in nor respect this hysterical woman, and as a result, soon sought the company of other society ladies as well as a foreign command that would put much distance between him and his wife.

But their long separation in the future, rather than putting things in perspective and eliminating differences between them, increased them. Communications gradually became rarer and more perfunctory, leading almost to estrangement when Wellesley discovered that Kitty had secretly diverted many hundreds of pounds of her housekeeping money to her brother, Henry, to pay his gambling debts. Had she been forthright in the first place and simply asked for his financial help, Wellesley no doubt would have paid the debt himself—as he had done on more than one occasion for his junior officers in India. But pure deceit on the part of his wife, of all persons, was more than he could stomach. Nor did this improve Wellesley's relations with his two sons, Arthur and Charles, in whom he showed remarkably little paternal interest and to whom he remained all but a virtual stranger. Furthermore, Kitty had proven no companion; they shared no common topic of conversation, no mutual interests (apart from the children). He was no more interested in the romantic novels she was reading than she was in his military treaties. And she was incapable of providing the foyer needed to attract him. Thus Wellington permanently fled wife and family ties, with the exception of Kitty's soldier brother, Edward Pakenham, whom he brought out to Portugal with him.

After completing a stint as Chief Secretary to the Lord Lieutenant of Ireland, and participating in the Copenhagen campaign, Wellesley was promoted to the rank of Lieutenant General in April 1808 and given the temporary command of British forces in Portugal against the French. Upon returning briefly to England again, he was then appointed Commander in Chief of the British Army and made Marshal-General of the Portuguese Army. The total force put at his disposal ranged from between fifty and eighty thousand men over the next few years, though the British entirely volunteer force rarely numbered much more than thirty thousand men, about whose quality Viscount Wellington (as he was named on 4 September 1809 following the Battle of Talavera) was constantly complaining.

And yet what manner of man was this Wellington, "this curiosity of curiosities," as John Cam Hobhouse called him, who, although famous in Britain, remained unknown to Europeans and even to most French general officers? In 1812, when he began the final stage of the long hard campaign to oust the French from Portugal and Spain, because of his slender, muscular figure, the forty-three-year-old Wellington appeared taller than his average height would indicate, his brown hair set off by blue eyes against a well-bronzed complexion, and of course by his astonishingly large and ugly proboscis, which detracted from an already less than handsome face. Abstemious of food and drink, Wellington retained his youthful figure, aided by his equestrian feats. And though an excellent horseman, he was very hard indeed on his stable, going through fifteen mounts in just two years of campaigning in Portugal. From his days at Eton he had always been somewhat unsociable and remote, as his fellow officers perennially attested. He would brook no insubordination and did not take kindly to threats, whether from politicians and officers, or in his limited social life. For example, years later, when London's best-paid upper-middle-class whore, Harriet Wilson, threatened to expose in her forthcoming autobiography the fact that a younger Arthur Wellesley had prior to his marriage paid her for her favors, unless he sent her a very large sum of money forthwith (a tactic she tried successfully on other well-known public figures), the Duke of Wellington, as he then was, outraged by this attempt at blackmail, sent her a four-word reply: "Publish and be damned!" and she did.[15]

He was a surprisingly intense and private officer, filling his trunks with all manner of historical, political and even grammatical works, with little time for hail-fellow-well-met officers. Indeed, even as a young man he "was emerging as one who did not suffer superiors gladly," as his biographer, Elizabeth Longford, so marvelously put it.[16] Even less so in the Peninsular Campaign did he suffer the presence of incompetent or outrageous inferior officers. His taciturnity was legion, verbal emissions rarely spanning more than the briefest of replies to questions, a half-dozen words sufficing nicely as he saw it. His troops and officers tended to find him grim to the point of being unapproachable if they lacked a very good reason to see him. Ensign Gronow's view was typical, finding him "very stern and grave-looking . . . in deep meditation."[17] And yet he was not pompous, and never had more than two sentries posted at his office or tent, where French officers of equivalent rank would have had a platoon or more. Indeed, he had as little time for smug, self-important men as he did for empty conversation. On the other hand he did have a good sense of humor. For instance, on one occasion after Waterloo, when, as he arrived at a crowded London function with Lady Shelley on his arm, the high personages about them drew back, making a path for him, the Duke quipped with a rare twinkle in his eye—"It's a fine thing to be a great man, is it not?"[18]

When it came to serious affairs, however, no man could have been less ostentatious, more down to earth and dependable. At the same time, even at the risk of being misunderstood, and with the same blunt "publish-and-be-damned" attitude he took toward Harriet Wilson, Wellington never underestimated his own importance vis-à-vis his troops on the battlefield. "When I come myself, the soldiers think what they have to do the most important since I am there . . . and they will do for me what perhaps no one else can make them do."[19] He said this in pride, not as a boast. And this was confirmed time and again over the years, as Captain John Kincaid confirmed—"We would rather see his long nose in the fight than a reinforcement of ten thousand men any day"—that from an officer whose life depended on Wellington's supreme ability. And yet the Duke had no illusions about his own greatness and invincibility, and freely acknowledged the fact when he faced a supreme opponent, such as the French Emperor. But for all his solemnity of demeanor and serious approach to his profession, he could smile occasionally and even laugh, although the latter sounded more like a deep resounding "whoop" than anything mirthful.

His opinion concerning most of his officers was generally denigrating, as when he complained to his brother William that there was "nothing so stupid as a gallant officer" in battle, who rushes out, sword in hand, without thinking. The cavalry in particular were his bête noire, whom he never ceased to berate. They "never . . . think of manoeuvering," they just "gallop at every thing, and then gallop back. One would think they cannot manoeuvre, excepting on Wimbledon Common."[20] And having personally led one famous cavalry charge in India, and having also commanded all cavalry units in his army since then, he was better qualified than most to make this judgment. He then pointed out what he expected to find in a good leader. "That quality which I wish to see the officers possess . . . is a cool, discriminating judgement in action."[21] That really summed up Wellington himself. But as matters stood, most of the time he had to hold their hands, he complained. "If I detach one of them, he is not satisfied unless I go to him, or send the whole Army; and I am obliged to superintend every operation of the troops."[22] In the same breath, however, he acknowledged, "There is nothing I dislike so much as these extended operations which I cannot direct myself."[23] He simply did not like to delegate authority, which in part can explain his thoroughly analyzed battle plans, as for example the twenty-seven paragraphs of detailed instructions he issued before the siege of Badajoz.[24] But unlike Napoleon's battle plans, which gave few if any tactical instructions, Wellington's did—too many.

Nor was Wellington particularly pleased with Colonel Torrens, the Military Secretary at the Horse Guards, ultimately responsible for assigning his senior officers to the Peninsula. "Really, when I reflect upon the characters and attainment of some of the General officers of this army . . . on whom . . . I am to rely . . . I tremble."[25] But after further batches of hopeless officers, Wellington finally gave up, imploring the Prime Minister, Lord Liverpool—"I only beg you not to send me any violent [political] party men. We must keep the spirit of party out of the army, or we shall be in a bad way indeed."[26] One especially disagreeable officer was Foreign Minister Lord Castlereagh's half-brother, the egregious Charles Stewart, who was poisoning the government against Wellington. In this particular case Wellington was fortunate, as Stewart made his retreat homeward, while selling his wild steed, Copenhagen, to his commander, who would soon render him famous. More frequently officers were simply cronies of the Duke of York and incompetent, or general officers with offensive habits, such as Sir William Erskin, who not only was a wretched military commander but as Wellington put it, always "blind [drunk] as a beetle."[27] The case of General Sir Thomas Picton was a bit different, however. This eccentric officer was sometimes seen leading his troops into battle wearing a red nightcap and black cape, or a blue coat and broad-brimmed top hat, beating his horse with an umbrella. But it was neither the general's umbrella nor his nightcap that upset Wellington, so much as his personal habits, he describing Picton as "a rough foul-mouthed devil as ever lived."[28] Picton had one compensating factor on his side, however—he was a hellion in battle and a good, reliable soldier—and thus Wellington kept him on.

Wellington's politics were as straightforward as the man himself. A staunch Tory, he supported the prosecution of the war against the French, in opposition to the pacifist Whigs and Radicals, including his own brother, Richard, now Earl of Wellesley, who served briefly as Foreign Secretary under the Perceval administration. Although Wellington himself was a member of parliament for several years, he rarely attended the sessions of the House of Commons, and when he did, was dismayed by what he saw as the chaos, inefficiency and sheer lack of organization of the entire parliamentary system. Nor was he a strong supporter of his own party. "I never felt any inclination to dive deeply in party Politics," he told Sir John Moore. "I may be wrong but the conviction in my mind is that all the misfortunes of the present [Hanoverian] reign, the loss of America, the success of the French revolution, etc., etc., are to be attributed in a great degree to the Spirit of Party in England; & the feelings I have for a decided party politician are rather that of contempt than any other. I am very certain that his wishes & efforts for his party very frequently prevent him from doing that which is best for the Country;

& induce him to take up the cause of foreign powers against Britain, because the cause of Britain is managed by his party opponents."[29] And when asked by his brother William what his politics really boiled down to, Wellington replied: "I serve the public & not any administration"—it was as simple as that. The public weal, the good of the nation, was always his first and only aim. And years later, when he put this directness of purpose and philosophy into action at the Congress of Vienna, even the corrupt and cynical Talleyrand praised him. "He [Wellington] never indulged in that parade of mystification that is generally employed by Ambassadors. Watchfulness, prudence and experience of human nature, were the only means he used: and it is not surprising that . . . he acquired great influence as a result."[30] He applied the same directness to his own military career, never once asking for honors or titles for himself.

Wellington's campaign in Portugal began in earnest in 1810 with the approach of a French army under the one commander, after Napoleon himself, whom he respected. Marshal Ney was a good corps commander, to be sure. He "is brave and nothing more," Napoleon said of him. He was "good for leading 10,000 men in battle, but other than that, he was a real blockhead."[31] As for Soult, "He is much better at saying where any army should go, than in actually knowing what to do with it once it was there."[32] On the other hand André Masséna was "decisive, courageous, bold . . . a very superior man" whom the Emperor ranked with Davout as his two best commanders among all the generals and marshals of the Empire.[33] Wellington was in complete accord. "The ablest [general] after Napoleon was, I think Masséna," he told Earl Stanhope. When he "was opposed to me in the field, I never slept comfortably," and that was the only time he ever acknowledged that.[34]

And in the autumn of 1810 Wellington did indeed face Masséna, and despite his initial victory over that marshal at Bussaco on 27 September 1810, Wellington had only 51,000 men (half of them British) against superior advancing forces, and thus he continued to fall back toward Lisbon and the coast. What Masséna did not know, however, was that Wellington was preparing a most extraordinary surprise that would have utterly bewildered Napoleon himself. To begin with, neither Napoleon nor Masséna had made any attempt to know anything about Wellington the man, or his military tactics, and that was to prove their undoing.

Upon accepting his appointment to command the armies in Portugal, Wellington had commented: "My die is cast, they may overwhelm me, but I don't think they will outmanoeuvre me. First, because I am not afraid of them, as everybody else seems to be; and secondly, because if what I hear of their system of manoeuvre is true, I think it a false one as against steady troops. I suspect all the continental armies were more than half beaten before the battle was begun—I, at least, will not be frightened beforehand."[35] Just as no one had ever challenged Napoleon's courage and utter fearlessness, so too, no one, certainly not Masséna or Napoleon, had ever challenged Wellington's, though perhaps they would have found his utter calm and complete self-confidence regarding them somewhat dismaying.

Wellington was outnumbered at nearly every battle in the Peninsula, and even at the greatest one later at Vitoria, he never had more than 78,000 troops under his command, two-thirds of whom were Spanish or Portuguese, while at times the French had more than 300,000 men in Spain alone. But in the autumn of 1810, being pressed by superior forces once again, Wellington slowly fell back, not in desperation, but methodically, gradually leading Masséna, "the old fox," into one of the most elaborate traps in the annals of military history.

Far ahead, between the sea and the Tagus River, employing over 10,000 Portuguese laborers, Wellington had prepared three formidable lines of fortresses. The longest one, twenty-nine miles long, linked mountain tops, ridges and hills with 152 forts and hundreds of cannon, Wellington having forced tens of thousands of Portuguese peasants to move from the valley and slopes below where he burned their crops, mills and entire villages, cutting down their orange groves, olive trees and every living thing. The result of his three such fortified lines left a desert of more than fifty miles of scorched earth before the unsuspecting French. And although Napoleon claimed Masséna was "stubborn . . . and never discouraged,"[36] when in mid-November the marshal made the final approach to Lisbon and the Lines of Torres Vedras, as Wellington's extraordinary fortifications and desolate valleys were called, Masséna halted in his tracks and looked about him in utter disbelief at the blackened land and hilltops bristling with fortresses. He had never seen anything like it. When reconnaissance patrols then confirmed what lay before them, the enormity of what Wellington had done was brought home to him, even entire hills and ridges having been artificially leveled for gun emplacements. For the first time in his brilliant military career, the able André Masséna, Prince of Essling, who was "never discouraged," found himself morally defeated, and refusing further combat, on 14 November 1810, gave the order to retreat to Santarém.[37] Wellington, long frustrated by Napoleon's continuous, unchallenged conquests, had inflicted a major victory, without a major battle, completely out-maneuvering the French, resulting in their evacuation of the country . . . when only thirty miles from their goal of Lisbon.

And yet, at what a price, with villages laid waste, the precious orange and olive trees—which would take many years to replace—destroyed, thousands of Portuguese homeless, indeed destitute, and ultimately fifty thousand of them subsequently dying of famine as a result of Wellington's brilliant, meticulous but deadly defenses. On the other hand, had Masséna's rapacious forces pillaged and destroyed Lisbon—as they had already done so frequently to Spanish cities—and thus remained in Portugal for years to come, would it have been any better? At times the decision between the right and wrong solution is unanswerable.[38]

Nevertheless, the real fight, the final putsch to end the French domination of the Iberian Peninsula did not begin until 1812, when Wellington attacked and seized Ciudad Rodrigo, Badajoz and Salamanca, all falling to the English general's victorious armies between January and July of that year. A thunderstruck Général Maxime Foy, himself wounded by British forces at Bussaco, praised Wellington, comparing him to "our great Turenne." "Hitherto we had been aware of his prudence, his eye for choosing a position, and his skill in utilizing it. At Salamanca he has shown himself a great and able master of maneuver."[39] Wellington's own comments after the battle of Salamanca were, however, a little more prosaic. "I was never so fagged. My gallant officers will kill me. . . ."[40] Fagged or not, his victory brought conquest as his armies swept into Madrid—King Joseph, Marshal Soult and the French armies hurriedly fleeing northward from the Spanish capital, which Wellington duly entered on 12 August 1812.

Despite some setbacks the following year Wellington led another successful army in a forced march of 400 miles in a mere forty days to Vitoria, where in June 1813 he defeated an astonished Marshal Jourdan. This staggering defeat for the French—Jourdan even lost his baton—was followed a month later by Wellington's defeat of Soult at the battle of Pamplona, followed in turn by the related battles of the Pyrénées at the end of July, where as usual Wellington commanded in his famous gray frock coat and trousers. Although in various battles horses were shot beneath him and favorite officers and ADCs killed, thus far Wellington himself went unscathed. "I begin to believe that the finger of God is upon me," he commented afterward, relating events to his brother William. "I agree with you that the finger of God is upon you, but I shudder at the risks you run," the exasperated clergyman replied.[41]

And finally on 7 October 1813 the glorious day came for which Wellington and the Government had been awaiting for decades: the British army entered France. It was there on 12 April 1814, after driving Soult from Toulouse and successfully surviving the full brunt of a bullet that had smashed into the hilt of his sword, driving it deeply into his thigh and putting him in bed for a week, that Wellington learned of Napoleon's abdication six days earlier.[42]

For "El liberador de España," and now one of *"les libérateurs de la France,"* the war was over, or so it would seem. The British volunteer army, which Wellington had at times cursed, had truly proven its worth, he later praising it as "the most complete machine for its numbers now existing in Europe . . . I could have done anything with it," and indeed had.[43] But, alas, the British Government in all its wisdom now ordered it to be partially demobilized, and the rest sent to fight the Americans in the War of 1812, a decision which almost proved fatal to Wellington fifteen months later. In the course of the grueling Iberian campaign, Wellington had successfully fought and defeated Marshals Jourdan, Kellermann, Marmont, Masséna, Mortier, Ney, Soult and Victor, not to mention an even larger number of renowned generals, including Drouet d'Erlon, Foy, Gazan, Junot, Laborde, Marchand, Reille and Reynier. But to an arrogant Napoleon Bonaparte, who had never personally fought against this British opponent who had defeated every marshal and general he could muster, even when they had an overwhelming superiority of troops, Wellington remained "a mere Sepoy General."*

Meanwhile the British Government, being more practical than Napoleon, preferring verified results when estimating a man's merits as opposed to empty rhetoric, duly rewarded Wellington with the title of Duke and hundreds of thousands of pounds in cash and property, as the conquering hero returned briefly to England and a tumultuous welcome. He afterwards returned to Paris in August 1814 in the guise of Britain's first ambassador to the newly restored Court of the Tuileries. But even for the Duke, things soon became too hot, after bullets whizzed past his head, and death threats multiplied, as humiliated Bonapartists and "patriots" cowardly attempted to assassinate the celebrated general. Having failed to kill him face to face on the field of battle, they now attempted to do so from dark alleys when the unarmed ambassador's back was turned. Wellington, though as brave a man as any was not a fool, however, and on the insistence of the British Government, in January 1815 was dispatched to the Congress of Vienna, to replace Foreign Secretary Lord Castlereagh, and where on 7 March he learned of Napoleon's escape from Elba. Following the signing of the Treaty of Chaumont on 25 March 1815 against the deposed Emperor, Wellington set out for his new headquarters at Bruxelles to take up again the sword he thought he had sheathed once

Sepoy—Indian soldier.

and for all at Toulouse the year before. The confrontation that had escaped the two foes for so long was to take place after all.

On 7 June Napoleon informed the nation and the world that he would be reopening hostilities against the Allies and would "soon be leading the children of the nation into battle, *pour la patrie*—for the sake of the fatherland. We—the Army and I—shall do our duty . . . and you must be prepared to die rather than survive and see France degraded and dishonored."[44] For those who had carefully followed Napoleon's long and destructive career, it was the usual clear signal to expect an all-out French attack, while behind the scenes for the past four days a flurry of secret communications had been passing between the Tuileries and the War Ministry, as orders were issued appointing the last batch of army commanders, including Lieutenant-General Jérôme Bonaparte, "Prince Jérôme," as a divisional commander in General Reille's IInd Corps.[45] The "legitimate war," as Napoleon so nobly described it at the Tuileries on 11 June,[46] was about to break out.

Setting out from the darkened capital at 3 A.M. on the twelfth, Napoleon and his staff quickly proceeded northward via Soissons, Laon and Avesnes. Upon reaching Beaumont on the fourteenth he ordered General Drouet d'Erlon's Ist Corps to advance between Avesnes, Maubeuge and Solre-sur-Sambre, Reille's IInd Corps to station itself between Solre-sur-Sambre and Leers and General Vandamme's IIIrd Corps along with Lobau's VIth Corps to take up positions around Beaumont. As for Gérard's IVth Corps, they were to occupy a position between Philippeville and Florenne, while Grouchy's Corps of Reserve Cavalry remained at Valcourt, Bossus and Gayolle. The Imperial Guard under the command of Marshal Mortier were, of course, to remain around Napoleon's temporary general headquarters at Beaumont.[47]

The Emperor gave his usual prebattle pep talk to his army at Beaumont on the fourteenth, reminding French soldiers on this anniversary of their great past victories at Marengo and Friedland, that they now had "some marching to do, some battles to fight" in order to protect themselves against "the most unjust of aggressions" by the Allies. "The time has come," he repeated, "to conquer or perish."[48]

Summoning Marshal Soult, Napoleon then dictated his marching orders: twelve regiments of Grouchy's cavalry would be sent in advance to screen a three-pronged attack against Charleroi just across the Belgian frontier. General Dominique Vandamme's IIIrd Army Corps would launch the offensive at 2:30 A.M. on the fifteenth, leading a powerful central column northward, including the Comte de Lobau's VIth Corps, which would follow, at four o'clock, the Imperial Guard's "Young Guard" as well as the remainder of Marshal Grouchy's Reserve Cavalry. Meanwhile a left column would set out for Charleroi at 3 A.M., along the west bank of the River Sambre, involving General H. C. M. J. Reille's IInd Corps, which was to secure Marchienne en route, as General Drouet d'Erlon's Ist Corps marched on Thuin. At the same hour General Maurice-Etienne Gérard's IVth Army Corps (there was no Vth Corps) would form a right column, advancing from Philippeville on Charleroi. Thus, between 2:30 A.M. and 8 A.M. on 15 June Napoleon would launch a powerful army some 122,652 strong, including 21,652 cavalry and 358 pieces of ordnance[49] in a very concentrated area to the northeast with the purpose of securing the Sambre and the direct road from Charleroi to Bruxelles. Although a small army when compared to those of 1812 or 1814, it was composed of well-seasoned commanders and troops, most of them veterans of at least a dozen major campaigns, and morale was superb. Napoleon for his part was confident of a quick, decisive victory.

But one must always contend with the unexpected. In Napoleon's case the unexpected struck with bewildering rapidity. First Marshal Adolphe Mortier, the commander of the elite Imperial Guard, and an excellent as well as reliable soldier, suddenly came down with a crippling case of sciatica, which left him bedridden at Beaumont, requiring his second-in-command and Chief-of-Staff, General Comte Antoine Drouot, to assume full command, in addition to his other duties. The next unexpected incident occurred with Soult. With very little experience as Chief-of-Staff, Soult sent only one set of orders to each of the corps commanders, instead of taking the precaution of entrusting copies to several different officers, as Berthier had always done. For reasons that were never fully explained, the orders did not reach Vandamme's bivouac until 5 A.M. on the fifteenth, a delay that nearly derailed the entire campaign, for the orders had instructed his IIIrd Corps to have set out at 2:30 A.M. and spearhead the entire campaign! In fact, when Soult's officer finally did arrive with the orders, Vandamme could not be found anywhere near his headquarters. One of Vandamme's ADCs was sent posthaste to find him. At some distance from camp, however, the officer's horse stumbled and fell on him, breaking the officer's leg, leaving him half-conscious and immobile in an isolated area. Still without word or instructions when he later returned to his headquarters, Vandamme was informed that Comte de Lobau's VIth Corps was marching up the road behind him, and thus it was he discovered that he should have left hours earlier. The result was that Vandamme forced Lobau's entire corps, nearly 11,000 men, to halt while his, Vandamme's, 18,000 troops struck out on the double.

Napoleon had deliberately allowed for ninety minutes between the departure of each corps in order to permit an unencumbered route, but which instead now developed into a state of utter confusion, not to mention extraordinary delays for everyone, including the Imperial Guard and the remainder of Grouchy's calvary. In brief, a traffic jam several kilometers long involving the entire central column of nearly 60,000 men, thousands of horses and hundreds of caissons, limbers and carts congesting the road all the way to Charleroi. This in turn disrupted General Gérard's corps, of over 15,400 men, also advancing to Charleroi in the right column, forcing them to alter direction veering away to another bridgehead on the Sambre to the east of Charleroi at Châtelet. And although the left column, under Generals Reille and d'Erlon, left on time and reached their objectives, they, too, were slightly delayed by unexpectedly heavy Prussian resistance.

Thus when Napoleon himself reached Charleroi before noon on the fifteenth,[50] he was not greeted as he had expected by Vandamme in a secured city. Indeed, Vandamme did not arrive there until about three o'clock, some five hours late. But that was not the only reason for Napoleon's foul mood as he descended in Charleroi. While en route he was alerted by Gérard that one of his best divisional commanders, General Bourmont, along with two of his officers, had defected at five o'clock that very morning. The reason for his treachery, explained Bourmont in a note he left behind, was that he did not "want to help establish a bloody despotism in France that would lead to the downfall of the country." But, he closed, Gérard need have no fear—"You will not see me joining the Allies. I shall not give them any information capable of harming the French Army, which I dearly love, and to which I shall always feel deeply attached."[51] But of course upon crossing the Sambre and enemy lines, he had freely surrendered to an astonished Prussian Colonel von Schutter, immediately disclosing details about Napoleon's battle plans for that very afternoon, all of which were in turn passed on to General von Ziethen, commanding the Ist Corps round Charleroi. Fortunately for Napoleon the arrogant Ziethen put little store in the word of a turncoat French general who had deserted his own army even as hostilities were breaking out. Nor did he bother to forward this information to Commander in Chief Blücher's headquarters until 1:30 that afternoon, by which time Napoleon and the French Army were securely in control of the Sambre, Charleroi and the road to Bruxelles. Later in the day when Bourmont was brought to Sombreffe to meet Blücher, the honorable old Prussian found the haughty Comte de Bourmont so contemptible as to refuse to exchange more than a few curt words with him.[52]

What had been so meticulously prepared by Napoleon was a shambles, and his invasion schedule thrown into full disarray, thanks to Soult, Vandamme and Bourmont. The only good news, it seemed, was the sudden arrival of Marshal Ney at Charleroi at 3:30 that afternoon,[53] who upon stepping out of the crowd of troops, was greeted by Napoleon. "Hello, Ney. I am happy to see you," but then without further ado informed him: "You are going to take command of the Ist and IInd Army Corps. I am also giving you my Guard's light cavalry, but do not use them [without my authorization]. Tomorrow you will be joined by Kellermann's cuirassiers. Go now and push the enemy up the road towards Bruxelles and take up your position at Quatre-Chemins [sic, Quatre-Bras]."[54] Ney was to head the drive to the capital, Napoleon told him, while Grouchy's IIIrd and IVth Corps were to move up to Fleurus and Sombreffe to confront the Prussians.[55] As for Napoleon's decision to put Ney of all persons in a position of great trust at the head of two army corps, after the episode with Bourmont, and Ney's earlier threat to bring the Emperor back to Paris in an iron cage, one cannot help recalling Napoleon's own remark to Caulaincourt back in April 1814: "He [Ney] is on our side for the moment, but I have no assurances what he will be doing in an hour from now. . . ." Clearly Ney's nonappearance at Beaumont had worried the Emperor, now aggravated by the loss of Mortier. During the Russian campaign he had had ten marshals in the field . . . he was now down to three, counting Soult as Chief of Staff.

After handing over command of the left column to Ney, Napoleon then removed Grouchy from the Cavalry Corps and promoted him to command the right wing of the army. This turned out to be an appalling decision for which the Emperor was later to pay dearly. In fact, Grouchy, though an excellent cavalry officer, had never before commanded two infantry corps, a position far more suited to the veteran Davout. Compounding the situation now, Grouchy's two new subordinate commanders, Vandamme and Gérard, shocked by this unexpected appointment—of a man whom they considered an incompetent upstart—at first chafed at the news and loudly protested, deriding it. On the other hand, had Ney swapped commands with Grouchy, it would perhaps have proven better for everyone. (But this was not to be Napoleon's last error of judgment during this campaign.) And then to exacerbate the situation, both Vandamme and Gérard were barely on speaking terms with Soult, who reciprocated their animosity. But even Vandamme's dislike of Soult was nothing as to Ney's personal hatred of this man, dating back nearly two decades and, if anything, intensified during the Spanish campaign when Ney had openly refused to cooperate with, or provide troops for, Marshal Soult.[56] Nor for that matter was Soult trusted or liked by the other principal officers of the Armée du Nord today. Having always been an extremely cold and remote commander, with very few friends in the entire officer corps, his position now was if anything worse—considered as he was a turncoat for having served as King Louis's War Minister until just before Napoleon's return to Paris in March.

At the very outset of a massive offensive, Napoleon thus found his schedule thrown completely out of kilter, the element of surprise lost, his battle plans in Prussian hands and his army high command rent with jealousy and discord. A lesser commander might have given up and turned back, or lost hope, not so Napoleon Bonaparte.

The Emperor's immediate aim now was simple and direct. As in previous battles over the past decade, he wanted to break the hinge connecting the two opposing armies before him, thereby greatly reducing their strength and cutting communications between them. He could push forward to break first one, and then the other, or so he hoped. But in fact he had already encountered stronger resistance than he had expected from von Ziethen's Ist Corps along the Sambre. The French forces only repulsed them thanks to the intervention of a powerful detachment of the Imperial Guard.

As for Prussian strategy, all had been carefully considered in the first week of May, when Wellington and Blücher had met at Tirlemont. It had been agreed that in event of just such an attack, Ziethen's corps would hold the French as long as possible and then fall back—two of its three divisions toward Fleurus, the remainder toward Gosselies—while the IInd, IIIrd and IVth Corps hastening from Blücher's former GHQ at Namur and to the north, were to concentrate round Sombreffe, in an attempt to close ranks with Wellington's force, thereby strengthening the Allied hinge.[57] "You will await the development of the enemy's maneuvers at Fleurus, and *you will give the Duke of Wellington and me all the news as quickly as possible*,"* Blücher had personally instructed von Ziethen.[58] Now he expected to see those very precise orders executed.

*Author's italics.

Chapter XI

Eve of Battle

"Bruxelles has ceased to be a provincial city since the arrival of Wellington here. His general headquarters has become a veritable capital in itself."

> Ambassador Comte Pozzo di Borgo to
> Foreign Minister Count Nesselrode,
> Bruxelles, 4 June 1815

A Napoleonic battle on this occasion was considered very much a social event, with distinguished diplomats and army officers transferring from Vienna, London and Saint Petersburg to Bruxelles, bringing with them mistresses, hangers on, family and, occasionally, even wives. They were, in turn, supplemented by a swelling number of aristocratic families from England, all keen on the dazzling prewar festivities and the prospects of seeing gallant officers riding off to battle. Indeed, the Belgian capital was crowded with the British upper classes, vying with one another for suitable temporary residences, and who, once established, launched a variety of receptions, dinners and balls. British, Belgian, Dutch, German and French nationalities mixed in a frantic confluence of gatherings and glitter.

Despite a very full professional schedule, the center of all this attention, the Duke of Wellington himself somehow also found time to attend some of these social events between April and June, including several hours languidly spent on the afternoon of 13 June at a leisurely cricket match in the Belgian capital in the company of a lovely young woman, where champagne flowed amid tête-à-têtes more preoccupied with social chatter and army appointments than with the excellence of the bowling or the number of wickets. But Comte Pozzo di Borgo, the Russian Ambassador—and Napoleon's old bête noire—temporarily attached to Wellington's headquarters, was not taken in by the ambling social gait of the Duke as he related in considerable detail to Russian Foreign Minister Count de Nesselrode, praising Wellington's "ceaseless efforts to organize the armies of the various countries."[1]

Although King Louis at his transposed court at Ghent had given his blessing to the decision by the Allies to oust Napoleon from the Tuileries and destroy his power once and for all, with neither army nor money at his disposal to offer the Allies in their preparations against Napoleon, any contribution made by him proved as illusory as the crown he wore. Indeed, how could it have been otherwise with the French government in exile "in a state of complete ministerial anarchy," as Pozzo ruefully described it, Wellington scathingly dismissing it as a congregation of "ministers without a ministry."[2]

Indeed, throughout the campaign, the Allies, in one form or other, proved almost as much of a trial for Wellington as the Napoleonic forces. Not the least of which stemmed from King William, the ruler of the newly created Netherlands, who insisted on having his twenty-two-year-old son, the Prince of Orange, command the assembling Belgo-Dutch army— though he was without divisional experience in the field—against the most brilliant army commander in European history, Napoleon Bonaparte! The House of Orange, keen on quickly building its own followers, scoured the field for court and army officers, high ranking and ancient titles predominating, and those preferably French. Nor was there any shortage of young men volunteering for quick fame and fortune at what promised to be the battle of the century. The Prince of Orange was of course as ignorant and useless as most of them, arrogantly insisting upon preposterous military privileges to which he had not the remotest claim. But excellence and loyalty in officers, men well prepared for the anticipated campaign, did not therefore unduly concern the House of Orange. Indeed, Wellington complained about their deliberate "removal of almost all the German officers from the Belgian regiments, men on whom most reliance could have been placed." Instead, they had been replaced "by officers who had risen under Buonaparte, and . . . admirers of his system and government,"[3] in other words, a veritable fifth column undermining the integrity of the entire army. Nor was the Prince of Orange's personal staff much better, apart from his excellent Chief of Staff, Major General J. V. de Constant Rebecque, which was reflected in the lack of discipline and training of his army. And what the Prince of Orange did not undermine, King William's new War Minister, General Janssens, did. Having fought the British in South Africa and Java, Janssens displayed open hostility to Wellington and anything British and deliberately appointed high officers throughout his ministry who had personally sympathized with or served in Bonaparte's army. The situation was simply intolerable and Wellington, who had seen a great deal of crass political and military stupidity and incompetence in India, England and the Peninsula, hardly found the present situation encouraging. How could the Allies possibly hope to cope with Napoleon's crack army under such circumstances? It seemed madness.

But at last, after considerable pressure by the Allies, King William of the Netherlands had recognized that nothing effective could be done without appointing Wellington Field Marshal and Commander in Chief of the entire Anglo-Dutch-Belgian force—thereby superseding the Prince of Orange. It was a beginning, a most critical beginning. But the good news stopped there, for the one thing King William would not do was remove the Prince of Orange—or "the Little Frog," as his detractors referred to him—from the scene, and instead he was giving him command of one of the three corps Wellington was now forming. Fortunately, the appointment of the younger son, the eighteen-year-old Prince Frederick, to the head of his own "corps" was not to affect the outcome of Waterloo, where he did not participate. But clearly the tide of battles could hang on such egregious appointments, and nearly did. Yet as the pragmatic Wellington acknowledged, Napoleon had to be stopped, regardless of the political compromises one had to swallow. If he, Wellington, remained on the field, at least he would have a good chance of controlling events. If he simply gave up in despair and returned to Britain in this hour of need, disaster would surely strike the coalition, for there was no other Allied commander of his ability even remotely capable of coping with the situation. Wellington was the last and only hope.

Even the faithful Blücher, now in his seventies, was hardly fit to command the entire operation, nor would he have been acceptable to either Kings Louis or William. To put it mildly, Wellington now found himself in an excruciatingly disagreeable position. But although he was never a wild optimist, he was, for all that, an Englishman—a stubborn, dour Anglo-Saxon determined to see the thing through, regardless of the forbidding plethora of discouraging signs and events thus far. He would use the Dutch and Belgian forces, however unreliable they were, and he would integrate the English King's German Legion and Hanoverian troops, for without *all of them*, he simply had no army.

After carefully assessing the situation and less than a week after his arrival in Bruxelles, on 11 April, Wellington organized the entire military force put at his disposition. Although requesting a minimum British force of 55,000 men—including 40,000 infantry and 15,000 cavalry[4]—he knew that many of his 47,000 Peninsular Army veterans had been disbanded or were crossing the Atlantic or were in Canada, and that London traditionally balked at sending British troops to the Continent. Indeed, in this instance the Government even refused to activate the militia (on grounds that war had not been declared officially). It would prove an onerous tug-of-war with London over obtaining British troops—he had found only 14,000 upon his arrival[5]—and he was not sanguine.[6] Nonetheless, he knew that Prime Minister Lord Liverpool was sincere in his personal pledge of support and was fully behind him—despite fierce Whig opposition to the war. Yes, it was going to be difficult. Wellington could only do his best with "the instruments" that were provided, as he put it.

Setting about his task, the Duke decided to strengthen unreliable units by intermingling British and Allied brigades in every division (excepting the first). Beginning with the Prince of Orange's 1st Corps, he added General Cooke's entirely British Division (including Maitland's and Byng's Brigades), and General Alten's division (including the KGL, or King's German Legion, an Hanoverian brigade, and Sir Colin Halkett's 5th British Brigade). While Lord Hill's IInd Corps included Adam's 3rd British Brigade, Clinton's division and Colville's 4th and 6th brigades. Wellington's own Reserve Corps assigned two British brigades (Kempt's and Pack's) to Picton's division, and General Lambert's brigade to Cole's division, supported by Nassau and Hanoverian troops. But what a choice as commander for the Cavalry Corps—none other than John Paget, the second Earl of Uxbridge, who, a few years before, had run off with the wife of Wellington's ailing younger brother, Henry Wellesley. Curiously enough, however, it did not appear to interfere in any way with their professional relationship, and in any event Wellington needed Uxbridge, considered to be the finest cavalry officer in the British Army. Lord Uxbridge's Corps included English, Scottish and Irish regiments—the Life Guards, the Horse Guards, Scots Greys and Inniskillings Dragoons— and also several German Legion units.[7] It was a well-tried means of strengthening divisions of untrained or unreliable troops, and of course Napoleon had done the same over the years.

But in addition Wellington had also organized the administration for the distribution of supplies, uniforms, food, arms, artillery and ammunition. To be cooperative and efficient an army had to be well looked after. Naturally, the Duke also saw to the basic fortifications he would need at his back when the fighting began, as he ordered improvements at Nieuport, Ostend and Antwerp, as well as in more forward positions at Ypres, Menin, Tournai, Courtrai, Mons, Oudenaarde, Ghent and of course at Bruxelles.

If Wellington finally succeeded in part, it was, however, only after an acrimonious and even harrowing correspondence between his Bruxelles headquarters and London. Wellington had powerful Whig opponents in England, not to mention most of the Royal family, and in particular, the Commander in Chief of the entire British Army, Frederick, Duke of York, who apparently resented both Wellington's lack of sycophancy and his singularly successful military career (the like of which had eluded the Royal Duke). Indeed, the Duke of York made no effort to conceal his resentment against this man who had once served as a battalion commander under him in Flanders over twenty years earlier. Then when Wellington bypassed the usual chain-of-command, appealing directly to York to promote and return his veteran Peninsular troops and field commanders, the Duke of York snapped: "The power of appointing to commissions is not invested in you; you will be pleased to recommend to me such officers as may appear to you most deserving. . . ."[8] Sir John Moore, at the Horse Guards, would continue to make the appointments, including that of the bumptious and incompetent Sir Hudson Lowe, as his chief staff officer, whom Wellington ultimately succeeded in replacing, however, with a trusted Peninsular veteran, Quartermaster General Sir William de Lancey. "They [the Duke of York and the Horse Guards] never showed me any . . . favour or confidence . . . from the first day I had a command to this hour," Wellington bitterly remembered long after. To be sure, a large number of officers were sent out to him, but generally not the senior Peninsular veterans he wanted. Indeed, "I am overloaded with people I have never seen before, and it appears to be purposely intended to keep those out of my way whom I wish to have," Wellington complained to the Secretary of War, telling him frankly that in his opinion "the [Anglo-Belgian-Dutch] Army is not a very good one."[9] It was strong talk but exactly what one expected of him.

Fortunately for Wellington, though the Duke of York and Sir John Moore could control the officers sent to Belgium, not so army field operations, which were directed by the government. War Secretary Lord (Earl) Bathurst did his best to meet his requests and needs as did Lord Mulgrave, Master General of Ordnance, who not only sent all the artillery, weapons and munitions ordered, but even anticipated many of his desires.

And yet by the second week of May Wellington was far from pleased with the overall results. "I have got an infamous army, very weak and ill-equipped, and a very weak staff," he told Lord Stewart. "In my opinion they are doing nothing in England. They have not raised a man." Although this was an exaggeration in some respects—as commanders inevitably must to obtain their basic requirements, which are invariably whittled down by the politicians at home—nevertheless, there was much in it. For instance, even by the eve of battle in mid-June, London had sent Wellington only just under 14,000 troops, in addition to those he had found upon his arrival, for a total British force of 27,985—*less than half he had requested.* And yet, ironically, in the final analysis it was upon that small nucleus of British troops that the difference between victory and defeat would depend . . . and that was no exaggeration.

Although the Allies anticipated fielding a combined armed force of some 600,000 men, the Austrians under Prinz Schwarzenberg were not expected until July or so. Meanwhile Czar Alexander was still understandably furious about the revelation by his ambassador to France, Comte Pozzo di Borgo, of the secret, albeit unexecuted, treaty of 3 January 1815 between Britain, France and Austria, *against* Prussia and Russia.* Thus, although as intent as ever on seeing an end to Napoleon Bonaparte and any further French aggression, nevertheless, much to Pozzo's discomfort in Bruxelles, he dragged his feet in mobilizing an army under the command of Barclay de Tolly. The Czar was simply holding out for a much higher English subsidy. "The fact of the matter is," Russian Foreign Minister Count Nesselrode wrote Comte Pozzo on 1 May, "that Lord Castlereagh owes us these reparations as just compensation for his fine treaty of 3 January, for which he was largely responsible." In any event "another two million pounds sterling will not kill them [England]."[10] Some 40,000 cavalry, considerable infantry and 680 cannon could be dispatched the moment London agreed to the Russian terms, Nesselrode added.[11]

Thus it was to be only the Allies actually *sur place,* upon whom Wellington could reasonably count, chiefly the Prussians, and they proved to be a mixed blessing. In fact, the strongly anglophobic sentiments expressed by some influential officers, including General von Ziethen, General Grolman and Graf von Gneisenau had, if anything, been intensified by the disclosure about the secret Anglo-French-Austrian pact against Prussia and Russia. But fortunately the Prussian commander in chief, the rough, half-literate, warm-hearted and loyal Field Marshal Prinz

*Because of extravagant territorial claims in Poland and Saxony.

Blücher von Wahlstadt,* with his thin gray hair, short trimmed brown mustache, squat figure and good sense of humor—whom Wellington had first met socially in London the previous year—supported the British 100 percent. No courtier he, bluff and direct, a man after the Duke's own heart.

After much work and considerable anxiety, by June 1815 the Duke of Wellington found himself at the head of a field army of 92,309 men, including 68,829 infantry and 14,474 cavalry,[12] divided into four corps: Ist Corps under the Prince of Orange, 25,233 infantry, the IInd Corps, 24,033 strong under the command of Lieutenant General Lord Hill, Wellington's own Reserve Corps of 20,563 infantry and 912 cavalry, and Lieutenant General Earl of Uxbridge's predominantly British Cavalry Corps of 10,155 men, but also including a few brigades of German, Belgian and Dutch cavalry as well.[13]

To the Anglo-Allied force was to be added Prinz Blücher's Prussian army of 130,246 men,[14] including his Ist Corps of 32,692 commanded by Lieutenant General von Ziethen, Major General von Pirch's IInd Corps of 32,704 men, Lieutenant General von Thielemann's IIIrd Army Corps 24,456 strong, and General Graf Bülow von Dennewitz's IVth Corps of 31,102 infantry and cavalry.[15]

It sounded impressive, a total allied force of 222,555 men versus a French army of 122,652. Although the majority of the Prussian army comprised seasoned reliable troops, nevertheless a large number were not, including unwilling conscripts from Saxony and the former French Rhineland States, thousands of whom were to desert in and after battle.

But Wellington's own immediate command was much more sensitive, weaker and badly trained. Of the 92,309 men put at his disposal, just under 28,000 were British and completely trustworthy and even then green volunteers outnumbered veterans. Unlike Wellington, who had appealed largely in vain to the Horse Guards and Duke of York for the transfer to Belgium of his veteran senior officers and seasoned troops from the Peninsular Army—"the most complete machine . . . in Europe"—Napoleon's army was comprised mostly of veterans of numerous campaigns, which put an entirely different slant on things. And of course Napoleon would never have dreamt of placing the callow, untried Prince of Orange or Prince Frederick in command of a corps or division. What is more, Prussian officers were in a position to translate their Anglophobia in the field, as for example when Ziethen refused to inform Wellington of the large French encampment at Beaumont on 13 and 14 June, or to

*Gebhard Leberecht, Prinz Blücher von Wahlstadt, 1742–1819.

send him a message posthaste regarding the initial French attack early on the fifteenth, in total disregard of Blücher's written instructions to Ziethen issued back in May to do so.

The Royal Prussian Army, which under Frederick the Great had reached an excellence praised by all, thereafter declined rapidly in quality. Then, following enormous defeats at Jena-Auerstädt in October 1806, the Prussian King, Wilhelm III ordered the rebuilding of the entire military structure, a task carried out by such able reformers as Gneisenau, Grolman, Clausewitz and Scharnhorst. Thus by 1815 the Prussian King had a partially reconstructed, more modern, better-trained and equipped force that on 18 March he duly mobilized as "The Royal Prussian Army of the Lower Rhine." But regular standing armies were of necessity rather small, and full mobilization had required the recruitment of tens of thousands of men to fill the ranks. Often they came from a variety of newly acquired regions and territories, producing Brandenburg Cuirassiers, Neumärk Dragoons, Lithuanian Regiments, Elbe National Cavalry, Lieb Hussars, Silesian Cavalry, Pomeranian Hussars, Lützow Cavalry, Berg and Saxon Hussars, West Prussian Uhlans, and so on.[16] Needless to say, not all were of the same quality. Indeed, just how unsteady the otherwise seemingly magnificent new Prussian military machine was became manifest on the night of 2 May, when two entire Saxon brigades recently arrived at Liège threatened to mutiny. Blücher immediately took the drastic action required of the moment, ordering that entire Saxon division to disarm and disband, its regimental flags burned and seven of its officers executed. Blücher had not forgotten that some 6,000 Saxon troops had deserted in mid-battle at Leipzig in 1813, defecting to the Allies. He had no intention of entering the forthcoming campaign with a division of armed potential enemies at his back. And just how right he was, would be proven in mid-June, following the Battle of Ligny, when another 10,000 Rhinelanders—more loyal to the Napoleonic Confederation of the Rhine than to a Prussian king—deserted the army as well.[17] This then was the army of which Blücher took command on 12 March after having first attempted unsuccessfully to decline that appointment. No genius, Blücher, with little tactical or strategic ability, nevertheless he was an experienced and fully reliable commander, and in 1815 supported by an excellent, skilled, professional staff. His Chief of Staff for the Army, Lieutenant General von Gneisenau and Chief of the General Staff, Major General von Grolman[18] were responsible for plotting maneuvers and issuing the orders concerning the army's movements. And if Fredrick William had brought Prussia to the verge of bankruptcy financing his new military miracle, it still was not all that he had hoped for. Indeed, only 57 percent of its combat strength, or 74,080 men, were trained members of the regular army, the remaining Landwehr units having been hastily assembled.[19] Nonetheless, the total of 136 infantry battalions, 126 cavalry squadrons and 38 batteries of artillery (304 pieces of ordnance) looked very formidable indeed, especially when compared with Wellington's hodgepodge army, with its small British nucleus.[20] Hence, Napoleon entered the field of battle on 15 March grossly underrating his Prussian foes and completely unaware of the sweeping changes in the officer corps structure and tactical ability of this force, combined with Blücher's unflinching resolve to cooperate with his British ally. Not for nought was Blücher nicknamed by his troops Alte Vorwärts—"Old Marshal Forward March."

It was agreed in May 1815 that once all the armies were in place Wellington and Blücher would carry out an early combined attack on France: Wellington would advance southward via Mons and Cambrai; Blücher would lead his forces through Charleroi and Maubeuge; 150,000 Russian troops would cross the frontier east of the Moselle, east of Thionville and Metz, driving for Nancy; 200,000 Austrians, parallel and east of the Russians, would march in the same direction between the Russians and the Rhine, with other forces invading from Switzerland and through the Côte d'Azur.

In the event that Napoleon attacked first, however, Wellington anticipated the French thrust to come in one of three places: Tournai, Mons or Charleroi, their immediate objectives including the destruction of the Allied armies and the seizure of Bruxelles. The most likely route, thought Wellington, would be via Mons, which was on the main highway from Paris to Bruxelles, offering not only the easiest access all the way to the Belgian capital, but the shorter by ten miles as compared to the Charleroi route. On the other hand Mons was well fortified, whereas Napoleon was renowned for his preference for rapid advances and avoidance of sieges. Tournai was a second choice, as Wellington saw it, due to the excellent roads and flat terrain so ideal for maneuvers. The final possibility, and least likely, involved a French attack through Charleroi, with its road leading the last thirty-two miles directly to Bruxelles. But as Napoleon had already torn up the French roads on the other side of the frontier leading to Beaumont, Philippeville and Charleroi, this seemed an important negative consideration. Thus it was that by the beginning of June, Wellington's armies faced south and west towards Mons and Tournai while Blücher's troops occupied Charleroi and the eastern sector.

But what strategy and tactics would Napoleon employ in the eventuality of such an attack? Wellington, who had made only a patchy study of the Emperor's past campaigns, was convinced that rather than hitting the Allied forces head on, he would try to envelop them by swinging far to the west of their army, thereby cutting all British communications with the Channel ports and possible reinforcements or means of escape. As for the reports of large French concentrations between Maubeuge and Beaumont, those Wellington thought to be mere feints, to divert his attention from the real attack, and he for one was not about to be taken in by that old, obvious ruse. Meanwhile, he had also deliberately deployed his troops in scattered positions, to act as a general net in which to catch the French, rather than to concentrate them in one area. And although he considered it far too early to expect an attack, if one came he could always assemble all troops together in less than twenty-four hours. Accordingly, he positioned Hill's IInd Army Corps between Tournai and halfway to Mons, with units at Ath, Grammont, Renai, Oudenaarde and Alost. The Prince of Orange's Ist Corps was now located between Uxbridge's Cavalry around Ninove and the Dender River to the west, as far as Hill's Corps, with units dispersed behind Mons, Soignies, Braine-le-Comte, Enghien and Nivelles. Wellington's own Anglo-Dutch Reserve Corps extended around Bruxelles, from Vilvorde to Hal.

The Prussians were to protect the crossing of the Sambre, General von Ziethen's Ist Corps extending from Charleroi over to Châtelet and Fosses, while further to the east von Thielemann's IIIrd Corps would be deployed between Dinant and Ciney. Von Pirch's IInd Corps would be stationed between Gembloux just off the Roman Road, and Namur. The IVth and final corps, Bülow's, would be situated to the northeast, between the Roman Road and Liège, thereby protecting Prussian communications with the Rhine and Cologne.

In the event of a French attack, both Wellington's army and Blücher's were to draw together, taking up predetermined positions. That is precisely what the Prussians were now doing in an orderly and expeditious manner—Von Ziethen's divisions going to Fleurus and Gosselies, while Blücher with the rest of the Prussian army was redeploying round Sombreffe, thereby strengthening the Allied hinge with Wellington. And yet the nagging question persists: why? Why were both Wellington and Blücher taken totally unaware by Napoleon?

"Surprise" was one of the critical elements required in executing a successful military campaign, as Blücher's brilliant but still relatively unknown forty-five-year-old staff officer, Colonel Karl von Clausewitz, was shortly to make famous in his classical study, *Vom Kriege (On War)*. And despite the blunders and accidents plaguing the first day of the French offensive, a major tactical surprise had been achieved, if not fully exploited. Again one must ask why the Allied commanders were taken completely unawares. Both Blücher and Wellington were in good health, and alert to the gravity of the situation facing them by this redoutable Napoleon Bonaparte and his splendid French army, which had been successfully ravaging the whole of Europe almost incessantly for the better part of the past two decades.

Even if Ziethen was certainly responsible for a very slow response in notifying Wellington of the French incursion on 15 June, though informing Blücher promptly, in fact, both Wellington and Blücher had been receiving a series of reports from as early as 9 June. At that time General Sir William Dörnberg at Mons, British Intelligence Chief, Lieutenant-Colonel Colquhoun Grant—"in and near France"—and General von Ziethen at Charleroi had filed sightings of large French forces moving up. On 12 June Dörnberg had personally written to Wellington informing him of a spectacular French troop concentration of at least 100,000 men taking place between Avesnes and Philippeville—information that was then immediately passed on to Blücher. By the thirteenth and fourteenth both Dörnberg at Mons and von Pirch at Marchienne reported to their respective headquarters similar predictions of an imminent attack. Given this background it seems inconceivable that neither Wellington nor Blücher was prepared for what followed.

Nevertheless, it was Wellington alone who had been responsible for overall disposition and strategy of British, Dutch and Belgian forces, incorrectly applied as it turned out, because he had failed to put himself in his opponent's shoes. Although Wellington was a methodical commander when it came to traditional logistics—seeing to it that his troops were provided with sufficient supplies of food, clothing, arms and munitions—not so when it involved studying complicated documents involving the history of an enemy's successes in the field. Wellington, though facing perhaps the greatest military genius in modern European history, could not be bothered to study carefully Napoleon's battles and the reasons for his extraordinary success year after year. He preferred instead the common-sense approach, as he called it. To be sure, he would occasionally study or discuss briefly one of his battles, such as Marengo, or Austerlitz or Wagram or the Russian campaign, acknowledging "how very skillful in his manoeuvres" Napoleon always was, but he failed to do so methodically, ploy by ploy, battle by battle. Wellington himself had no variety of strategy he rigorously applied according to a set of specific circumstances. More accustomed as he was to a defensive rather than an offensive role, it simply did not occur to him—as a result of this failure to study thoroughly his most formidable opponent—that Napoleon himself might follow just such a logical system. Wellington knew that in a great number of battles Napoleon had created feints along the main front while sweeping round the opposing enemy's flanks to envelop it, and simply thought he would do the same again now. However, a closer examination would have revealed that that particular strategy had been used to meet very precise conditions. Alas for Wellington, the circumstances were now very different indeed, and hence his frightful miscalculations and subsequent defensive strategy. On the other hand, to be perfectly fair to the British commander, Napoleon himself had made the same error, having dismissed Wellington as "a mere Sepoy general," one not worth studying, despite the steady series of defeats he had inflicted on the French army in the Peninsular. In the long run one of Napoleon's greatest errors was to underestimate and fail to understand his English opponent.

As for the French Emperor's approach to battle, several factors had to be considered. He liked speed and efficiency of attack, and of course appreciated the importance of tactical surprise. He did not want to lose more men and equipment than necessary, not because he valued human life, but because his numbers were limited to begin with. Hence he invariably avoided costly, plodding, massive frontal attacks and sieges whenever possible, opting instead for his favorite strategy, "*le manoeuvre sur les derrières*" or "*attaque tournante*," or "*la bataille napoléonienne*," as it was popularly called.[21] This maneuver permitted him to skirt around a single army that had extended itself too far from its allies, supporting forces or lines of communication, as he enveloped and struck suddenly at the rear. This he successfully used some thirty times and was the Emperor's favorite strategy when his own forces *were superior in number* to those of the enemy. Clearly, it was this one which Wellington now had been expecting. But Napoleon had another maneuver, involving "an attack on the central position,"[22] he referred to it, which allowed him to attack *when he was outnumbered*. This strategy was applied successfully only twice in Napoleon's career, however, at Rivoli in 1797 and at Leipzig in 1813.[23] It was a strategy superb in its simplicity and devastating in effect, involving the driving of a shaft—literally comprising an entire French army—into and thus separating, superior enemy forces. But, of course, this could only be used when it was believed that the French Army would not be swallowed up and destroyed by the very armies it was attacking. Hence at best it was a risky venture. But needless to say, attempting weaker attacks against superior concentrations would have afforded much less chance of success, and as Napoleon said time and again, "battles should not be fought without having a 70 percent chance of success."[24]

Napoleon himself best explained his thinking on this strategy. "There are systems one applies on the battlefield," he began, "just as when laying siege to a fortress, and in this case it means concentrating all one's firepower on a single point [the hinge where the two opposing armies meet]. Once the breach is made, the enemy loses its balance and whatever he does thereafter is to little avail, for the place or force is taken. In such an operation one must never scatter one's attacks, but instead concentrate them," he stressed.[25] One must strike as hard as possible in one place with the maximum number of troops, cavalry and artillery, first to act as a wedge opening the breach, then widening it by pushing back both sides. The beauty of using the "central position" approach was, as General Camon points out, that "it was not necessary to attack and defeat an entire front. To the contrary, the surest and least costly means of gaining a victory was by executing a vigorous blow, resulting in a local disintegration but one extensive enough as to lead to the subsequent crumbling and disorganization of the enemy's entire front."[26]

It was this risky strategy of driving through a central position that Napoleon had now applied at Charleroi, as he stood poised between Wellington's force to the west and Blücher's to the east. He was indeed facing superior forces, their combined strength of 222,555 men against his 122,652.[27] But problems had already arisen. To begin with, surprise and speed were essential, and although initially catching the Allies and Prussians off guard when seizing Charleroi, nevertheless, many valuable hours had been lost during that operation and immediately thereafter. What is more, Wellington's army could not be attacked now as Napoleon had planned because the British commander quite unwittingly had left it dispersed in several different areas. Napoleon's army simply had no single, massed Anglo-Dutch-Belgian target to smash through. But one large force did remain there, of course—the Prussians, which he could attack and destroy while driving on to Bruxelles. The hope was that the British forces would then crumble and disintegrate psychologically as a result.

Fear, too, could win battles. Time and speed were the critical elements now, but first Blücher's force—which admittedly had proven much more of an obstacle at Charleroi and along the Sambre than Napoleon had expected—had to be dealt with. Clearly, this was no longer the Prussian Army he had defeated so deftly at Jena-Auerstädt back in 1806.

All was normal, indeed almost lifeless, in Bruxelles on 15 June, until just after three o'clock in the afternoon, when the peace was suddenly disturbed by the clatter of hoofs as three dispatch riders, approaching from three different directions, reined in sharply before Wellington's general headquarters, insisting upon seeing the great man himself. The first report was from Blücher at Namur, informing him of the French attack at Charleroi and that he was moving Prussian field headquarters to Sombreffe. The next dispatch came from the Prince of Orange reporting from his headquarters at Braine-le-Comte, that although none of his units was under fire, guns could be heard in the direction of Charleroi, while also noting that one of his scouting parties had encountered a French advance unit along the Roman Road at Binche (just a few miles to the west of Charleroi). The final report came from Ziethen repeating the information Blücher had sent, Ziethen's arriving *eleven hours* after the event. Although there was the fullest cooperation between Wellington and Blücher, and their liaison officers were most expeditious, Baron von Müffling representing Blücher at Bruxelles, and Lieutenant-Colonel Sir Henry Hardinge serving Wellington at Prussian headquarters, a man like Ziethen could foil the best-laid plans. And yet none of the three reports before him gave Wellington the essential details he required. What was the strength of the French attack, how far on either side of Charleroi did it extend and in what direction was the major thrust heading? Without such elementary information a competent commander could not commit major forces, and yet Wellington did have to act.

It was indeed both humiliating and irritating, of course, for both he and the Prussians had been caught completely off guard. Where had Prussian reconnaissance units and pickets been, that they utterly failed to observe the movement of 122,652 men and tens of thousands of horses, caissons and wagons? Clearly Ziethen had not executed the most basic precautions required of an advance army corps. But now it was too late, and meanwhile Wellington's thirty-three-man staff watched him intently, awaiting orders. The moment they had all awaited had come.

For Wellington, however, there were still a few elementary questions to be resolved. Was the attack at Charleroi the main thrust of the French Imperial Army, after all, or was it merely a diversion, or was it perhaps just one of several attacks at various different places? What Wellington needed was time in order to await further dispatches from all along the allied line, from Tournai on the Scheldt to the west, all the way across to the Prussian IIIrd Corps near Ciney to the east, a front over eighty miles wide. Having received no further news by five o'clock, all he could do was to order his troops to concentrate at their prearranged divisional assembly points.

Meanwhile, the arrival of the couriers had naturally caused rumor and speculation to sweep the Belgian capital, and perhaps in part to allay any possible panic, Wellington agreed to attend the ball given that evening for the British Army's upper echelons by his old friend and aide-de-camp, General Lennox, the Duke of Richmond. In fact, most of Wellington's senior officers would be attending this long-awaited social event and it proved an ideal place to meet his commanders. But at about ten o'clock that evening, just before leaving for the Richmonds', Wellington issued more orders to his field commanders, which included the dispatching of a cavalry screen to the west between Oudenaarde and Ghent—where there was no hint whatsoever of a major French presence. Lord Hill's IInd Corps was to stay near the River Dendre (west of Bruxelles), Orange's Ist Corps were ordered to Nivelles, Enghien and Soignies, and finally Uxbridge's cavalry corps were to hold themselves in readiness at Ninove, also well to the west, while Wellington's own Reserve Corps remained round Bruxelles. With Prussians on the south side of the Roman Road now, this left the entire length of the Charleroi–Bruxelles road *entirely undefended.*

There was in fact no allied hinge to smash through—one simply did not exist. The full impact of Napoleon's actions still had not sunk in. As matters stood now, on the fifteenth, even if Wellington were to summon all his army, "at least half his force would be beyond effective supporting distance at Quatre Bras on the morrow," David Chandler points out, with the closest troops being Cooke's 1st Division at Braine-le-Comte, Colville's 4th Division at Enghien and Alten's 3rd Division at Nivelles.

Indeed, it was only later that night at the Richmonds' supper that other British and Prussian reports finally confirmed for Wellington how very wrong he had been and that Napoleon's full army was indeed at Charleroi. He now learned that at two o'clock that afternoon (the fifteenth) the Prince of Orange's Chief of Staff, Baron de Constant Rebecque, extremely anxious about this enormous gap existing between Nivelles and Sombreffe—in the absence of the Prince, who was at the Richmonds'—had ordered General

Perponcher to move Prinz Bernhard von Saxe-Weimar's brigade from Nivelles to occupy Quatre Bras.[28] It was they who subsequently first confronted Ney's troops around Frasnes. Indeed, with news of this first clash at 8 P.M. that same evening, Constant Rebecque then promptly ordered Van Bijlandt's 1st Brigade there to support Saxe-Weimar, further disregarding Wellington's orders to remain at Nivelles. Constant Rebecque's intelligent disobedience was responsible for the Allies gaining control of the critical crossroads at Quatre Bras, thereby being in place to repel Lefebvre-Desnoëtte's initial advance later. At the same time it saved the line of communications with Blücher, and as David Chandler succinctly added, "This act of insubordination also saved Wellington's reputation."[29] Indeed it changed the course of the entire campaign.

"Napoleon has humbugged me, by God!" Wellington exclaimed to the Duke of Richmond upon receiving this catastrophic news. "I have ordered the army to concentrate at Quatre Bras."[30]

After taking three and a half hours' sleep, Wellington was at work again by 5:30 A.M. on the sixteenth, and at seven o'clock heading south along the Bruxelles–Charleroi road on his favorite horse, Copenhagen, having redirected his own Reserve Corps to await his orders at Mont-Saint-Jean. Upon reaching Quatre Bras at ten o'clock, Wellington studied the situation closely, where two of the Prince of Orange's divisions were now deployed in an arch around the crossroads. Satisfied with the present disposition of troops, Wellington, with Dörnberg, his ADCs and the Prussian liaison officer von Müffling, turned east on the eight-mile road to Sombreffe for a war council with *"Alte Vorwärts"* Blücher at the village of Brye.[31]

Meanwhile, although the French had secured Charleroi, it seemed that neither Ney nor Grouchy had been following Napoleon's orders to the letter. Grouchy and his column, instead of advancing quickly on the chief Prussian concentration in the act of assembling round Sombreffe, apparently lost his ardor as the full impact of the new commander's responsibilities sank in. Indeed, so slowly did he advance that early in the evening of the fifteenth Napoleon himself had to personally urge Grouchy to greater effort. And yet nightfall also found a large portion of Gérard's IVth Corps still camping along the southern bank of the Sambre, with the remainder of Grouchy's right wing encamped along the road between Châtelet and Fleurus, and behind them the Imperial Guard between Charleroi and Gilly.

Instead of moving up smartly to Quatre Bras as ordered, Ney, too, seemed moribund. It was maddening. General Lefebvre-Desnouëttes's advance cavalry upon reaching Frasnes at 5:30 did, in fact, successfully repulse the occupying Nassau battalions there, who fell back to Bossut Wood. But when Lefebvre-Desnouëttes then requested infantry support in taking those woods, Ney refused. Instead of securing Bossut Wood and setting up his headquarters that night at Quatre Bras as ordered— just two kilometers away—Marshal Ney inexplicably withdrew to Frasnes. As a result, dusk found Ney's left wing camped in a line extending from Marchienne to Gosselies, and thence up to the forward observation posts at Frasnes.[32] Ney himself passed the night at Gosselies, just a few miles north of Napoleon's headquarters at Charleroi.

What had happened to the Ney of old? There is no single answer. But clearly the forty-six-year-old Marshal was tired, unconvinced, indeed a reluctant supporter of Napoleon, whom, back in March he had promised to bring back to King Louis in an iron cage. The fire, the enthusiasm of the Ney of 1805 was in 1815, dead it would seem. To be sure, von Ziethen's force (under Steinmetz) had been forced out of Gosselies, but that was all. The first Allied troops (four battalions of Saxe-Weimar's Nassauers) *only occupied Quatre Bras at seven P.M.* on the fifteenth. Why had Ney not permitted Lefebvre-Desnouëttes's light cavalry to seize Bossut Wood? What indeed had happened to Michel Ney?

Thus both Ney and Grouchy had further delayed the Emperor's scheduled advance. Nevertheless, both left and right wings were now in a position to continue quickly the next day against the Anglo-Allied forces at Quatre Bras and the Prussians at Sombreffe. And when Napoleon returned to his headquarters at Charleroi at eight o'clock that evening after nearly fifteen hours in the saddle, at least he could assume that all was ready for the morrow, when the Allied hinge would finally be pierced and severed.

Early on the morning of the sixteenth Napoleon therefore drew up the orders for the next phase of those operations: "I am moving Marshal Grouchy's 3rd and 4th Infantry Corps up against Sombreffe," he informed Ney, and "I am taking my [Imperial] Guard to Fleurus where I shall arrive before noon . . . and I shall clear the road [of the Prussians] as far as Gembloux." "My *principe général* for today's campaign is to divide my army into two wings, with one reserve force. Your [left] wing will be comprised of the Ist Corps' four divisions, the IInd Corps' four divisions, two divisions of light cavalry and the Comte de Valmy's [Kellermann's] two divisions, for a total force of between 45,000 and 50,000 men." Grouchy's right wing was to comprise Vandamme's IIIrd Corps, Gérard's

IVth Corps and the cavalry corps of Pajol, Milhaud and Exelmans, which he estimated at about the same total strength as Ney's.[33]

Before advancing north today, however, Ney was to *reinforce* his hold of Quatre Bras, posting his first division six miles before that crossroads, six infantry divisions actually around that crossroads and still another to the east at Marbais, "in the event I need it later," as Napoleon put it. Next, he was instructed to replace General Lefebvre-Desnoëttes's division of Young Guard light cavalry with Kellermann's corps of 3,000 cuirassiers or heavy cavalry. Then, if all went according to plan, he told Ney, "You will start marching for Bruxelles this evening [the sixteenth] arriving there at seven o'clock tomorrow morning. I shall support you with the Guard . . . and should like to arrive there myself tomorrow [the seventeenth] just after you."[34]

While Ney was doing this Napoleon would be moving up to Fleurus on the sixteenth, bringing up his IVth Corps from Châtelet to a position near Ligny. "If the enemy is at Sombreffe, I want to attack him. Indeed, I want to attack him, even if he is beyond it at Gembloux, securing that position as well. And after having done that I want to leave tonight [the sixteenth] and order my left wing to advance on and attack the English. Therefore *do not lose a moment*, because the faster our objectives are achieved the better that will be for the rest of the operation," he told Grouchy. "Keep the road open for me" to Fleurus, where he expected to arrive by 11 A.M. at the latest. As for the enemy force they would be encountering . . . "The Prussians cannot muster more than 40,000 men," the Emperor assured Grouchy.[35] Soult, of course, would be confirming all this with more detailed orders shortly.

Napoleon's intentions could not have been clearer, with Ney continuing from Quatre Bras on to Bruxelles, driving the scattered Anglo-Allied forces—there was no line there—while Grouchy was to destroy the Prussians at Sombreffe. As for the Imperial Guard serving as a reserve corps, "I shall deploy it in conjunction with one wing or the other, as the situation requires, but I'll only use it at Sombreffe if absolutely necessary."[36] As Napoleon Bonaparte saw it, there would be some fighting at Sombreffe on the sixteenth, but certainly no major battle.

What the French leader did not know, however, and what in consequence was going to have dire results for him, was that Ney had not advanced to and secured Quatre Bras on the fifteenth as ordered, preliminary to a triumphal march on Bruxelles, but had instead camped with his main force around Gosselies at eight o'clock that evening. And yet his powerful left wing, some 45,000 strong was clearly in a position to brush aside the Nassauer's 4,000 men holding Quatre Bras and to drive on to the capital. Meanwhile, of course, at the same hour that Ney was ordering his troops to stack arms for the night (at eight o'clock), eight miles to the west of Quatre Bras, at Nivelles, Chief of Staff Constant Rebecque was issuing orders to reinforce Prinz Bernhard at Quatre Bras with General Bijlandt's brigade.

Nor was Napoleon himself helping matters now, for instead of drawing up his battle plans for the following day as was his wont and dispatching them to his field commanders during the night, those instructions did not leave his headquarters at Charleroi until eight o'clock the next morning. But what was happening to the French Army? Why were Napoleon and Ney behind schedule? Indeed, why had Ney not informed his commander in chief that he had not reached his objective of Quatre Bras? Evidently something was very much amiss, thus allowing Wellington valuable time in which to extricate himself from his own nearly fatal earlier assessment and inaction. Rather than driving a strong wedge between the two Allied armies, Ney's unaccountable delay had in fact permitted them *to close some of the gap between them.* And yet it was still not too late, for even early on the sixteenth the French Marshal could have driven forward and seized the critical crossroads of Quatre Bras with his greatly superior numbers. But instead of marching briskly before the crack of dawn that day, the Ney of yore was to be found, not in his saddle at the head of his column, but in bed, and like Napoleon at Charleroi, at the same time dithering away whole hours, waiting, he said, for written instructions confirming what he had already been told personally by the Emperor himself the day before . . . this even as strong Allied reinforcements were mobilizing to reinforce Quatre Bras from the north and west.

Although Ney failed to send an accurate report on the situation at Quatre Bras, on the morning of the sixteenth Napoleon was informed of a continuing unexpected Prussian buildup around Sombreffe, as Blücher's forces arrived from Namur. Finally roused, the Emperor broke camp and headed northeast to Fleurus, reaching the front at Saint-Amand at 11 A.M. as previously planned. A major battle was about to begin after all, and he had not even bothered to inspect the terrain properly nor study the dispositions of the enemy until the last minute.

Grouchy's right wing was taking up positions, however, his IIIrd Corps' 17,000 men under Vandamme already facing von Ziethen's Ist Corps of 32,000 men,[37] although neither Gérard's IVth Corps of more than 15,000, nor the accompanying Imperial Guard was yet in place.

Therefore, Napoleon, though finally set on attacking and destroying the exposed Prussian position in the level, slightly elevated open fields stretching from the northeast of the village of Saint-Amand to the village of Ligny and beyond to Sombreffe, would have to await the arrival of the rest of his troops. Meanwhile, Comte de Lobau's VIth Corps, a force of 10,000 men, was to remain at Charleroi, uncommitted until Napoleon ordered it forward to support Ney or Grouchy. Finally, by the end of the morning, an impatient Napoleon Bonaparte saw his right wing deployed before him including 58,000 infantry and the 12,500 troopers of Pajol's Ist and Exelman's IInd Cavalry Corps, supported in turn by 210 pieces of artillery.

The Prussians, too, had been preparing, Graf von Ziethen's Ist Corps joined by General von Pirch's IInd, of nearly thirty-three thousand men, just after noon. After two o'clock they in turn were reinforced by Lieutenant General von Thielemann's nearly thirty thousand men, until Napoleon found himself facing—not 40,000 as he had predicted—but 76,000 Prussian infantry, 8,000 cavalry and 224 guns! In fact, Blücher had taken up a position along a seven-mile-long front, including ten hamlets and villages, extending from the Roman Road and the village of Wagnelé, before Saint-Amand, La Haye, past Ligny along the main road to Sombreffe, as far as Boignée and Balâtre to the southeast. But as Napoleon quickly realized, the Prussian forces—even allowing for the unexpected arrival of Bülow's IVth Corps of thirty-one thousand men— were both far too greatly dispersed and exposed. In his defensive position Blücher could rely on the four bridgeheads and stout village houses and on the marshy Ligne brook, which meandered to the southwest past Potriaux and Ligne village, but on little else.

It was just behind the Prussian lines at the hamlet of Brye and at Bussy Windmill that Wellington met with Blücher after one o'clock,[38] explaining the dispositions of his own army, while pointing out what Napoleon himself had seen: that the Prussian position was overly exposed and extended. The French, Wellington said in his wonted forthright manner, "had it in their power to cannonade them and shatter them to pieces" while the Prussians could not easily advance and attack the French, because of the extensive marshy area separating them. "I said that if I were in Blücher's place with English troops, I should withdraw all the columns I saw scattered about the front, and get more of the troops under shelter of the rising ground. However, they seemed to think they knew best, so I came away very shortly," a testy Wellington concluded.[39] Before he left, around two o'clock, however, the Prussians asked him to bring his army over to support them at Sombreffe, the Duke replying as he swung into the saddle, "Well, I will come, provided I am not attacked myself."[40]

In the realization now that he would apparently be facing the whole of Blücher's force—a factor he had not even considered earlier—at two o'clock Napoleon dictated orders to Chief of Staff Soult for Marshal Ney's Ist and IInd Corps to march from Quatre Bras (which he still thought to be in their hands):[41]

It is His Majesty's intention that you attack whatever force is now before you [at Quatre Bras], and after vigorously driving it back, you will turn in our direction, so as to bring about the envelopment of those enemy troops [Blüchers's] . . . If on the other hand the latter are overthrown first, then His Majesty will maneuvre in your direction so as to assist you in your operations there.[42]

Coming up the Namur Road, he was to attack and crush Blücher's totally exposed right rear. If Ney's entire force could arrive by 6 P.M. that evening, Napoleon could at the same time throw in the Imperial Guard against the Prussian front positions, wrapping up the victory and probably destroying two-thirds of the mighty Prussian army within a single afternoon. But in the final analysis, as Napoleon now well realized, the key to a decisive victory would be the use of Ney's left wing with which to envelop the right rear, entrapping the Prussians—the very maneuver Wellington had been expecting round Mons.

If all went well, the battle of Ligny would indeed be over by sunset, a mere mopping-up operation left so far as Wellington's dispersed army was concerned, followed by the seizure of Bruxelles and the expulsion of the Allies from the entire left bank of the Rhine. It was really quite simple, if Ney carried out his orders. But in fact Napoleon had already made three grievous errors: He had assumed that Ney had already seized Quatre Bras; that Wellington had a motley army still spread all over Belgium; and that the Prussians were a pushover.

Chapter XII

Waterloo

"Everyone . . . is agreed that the destruction of Bonaparte's power is the primary, irrevocable objective of the war."

> *Foreign Minister Nesselrode to*
> *Ambassador Pozzo di Borgo, 5 June 1815*

"Pray keep the English [in Bruxelles] quiet, if you can. Let them all prepare to move, but neither in a hurry nor a fright, as all will yet turn out well."

> *Wellington to Sir Charles Stuart*
> *Waterloo, 3 A.M., 18 June 1815*

"Mon plan de campagne, c'est une bataille."

> *Napoleon*

"My only plan is to stand my ground here to the last man."

> *Wellington*

The Battle of Ligny, as it was subsequently to be called, began in earnest between two-thirty and three o'clock under leaden skies, along a seven-mile-long front as some 140 French cannon opened fire against General von Ziethen's Ist Corps's defensive positions in and around the villages of Saint-Amand and Ligny, and Pirch's IInd Corps behind them. One hundred Prussian cannon at Saint-Amand and another sixty at Ligny returned the fire with an intensity that took Napoleon by surprise,[1] as 84,000 Prussians firmly rebuffed the first of many determined onslaughts by some 70,500 French troops.[2] The principal Prussian position continued from its most forward point at the village of Saint-Amand[3] all the way back to Sombreffe; its right flank extended from Saint-Amand, Saint-Amand La Haie and Wagnelé straddling the Roman Road, thence forming a rough triangle back to Blücher's headquarters on the heights of Sombreffe. Thielemann's IIIrd Corps were still in the midst of manning the Prussian left flank along the heights and hills from Sombreffe to Mont Potriaux, Tongrenelles, Boignée and Balâtre.

Vandamme's IIIrd French Corps, assisted by one of Reille's divisions, attacked the Prussians at their strongest point, at the center and right center situated principally at Saint-Amand, while Gérard's IVth Corps launched the first of a series of fierce attacks against Ligny, as Pajol's and Exelman's cavalry struck Thielemann's IIIrd Corps along the Prussian left flank. Discovering that he would not be outnumbering and outgunning the Prussians as he had anticipated and with all Vandamme's and Gérard's troops already deployed against the key Prussian positions at Saint-Amand and Ligny, at 2 P.M. Napoleon dispatched a hurried order to Ney "at Quatre Bras" to join him forthwith: "Do not lose a moment . . . This [Prussian] Army is lost if you act quickly. The fate of France is in your hands."[4] If Ney's troops could arrive by six o'clock at the latest, sweeping down the road from Quatre Bras to fall upon Blücher's by then drained and thinned ranks, victory, total victory was his. "The outcome of the war can be decided in three hours' time," Napoleon assured Gérard. "If Ney executes his orders thoroughly, the Prussian Army will be taken completely by surprise, not a cannon will escape."[5]

But as Napoleon himself had often repeated throughout his career, nothing is certain in a battle, not even with the best of troops and clearest of orders, and Ney's and General Drouet d'Erlon's actions on the sixteenth proved the validity of this axiom once again. For although one of Napoleon's staff officers then intervened personally, ordering d'Erlon's Ist Corps of nearly 19,000 men to come to the aid of the Emperor, while en route to Sombreffe, d'Erlon was later intercepted by a second imperial officer whom d'Erlon misunderstood to have ordered him to march on

Saint-Amand instead. When d'Erlon's column then did appear over the horizon from the wrong direction at 5:30 behind his own beleaguered troops, a startled General Vandamme alerted an equally astonished Napoleon, who like Vandamme thought that d'Erlon's corps was possibly an enemy force! At that very moment, in the midst of preparing to launch his principal attack of the day, a puzzled Napoleon delayed all orders for the next hour until he could ascertain the identity of this mystery corps. Finally, at about 6:30, upon establishing that it was indeed the Ist French Corps, the Emperor dispatched a third officer to inform d'Erlon that he was in the wrong area, and was instead to maneuver back and around the Prussian right rear as originally directed. Meanwhile, a by now bewildered Comte d'Erlon became utterly confused as a *fourth* courier, this time from Marshal Ney, ordered him to march quickly back to support Ney's left wing, and hence *to disregard the Emperor's instructions*. As d'Erlon afterward explained, "I felt that for the Marshal to recall me in spite of Napoleon's wishes, he must have been in a most perilous position."[6] In any event Drouet d'Erlon, who by now had marched within two kilometers of Vandamme's troops, turned about and countermarched back to Ney—leaving only General Durutte's division with Napoleon— thereby effectively keeping his fresh troops out of all fighting on the sixteenth of June.[7]

Back at Sombreffe, Field Marshal Blücher on the other hand was perfectly confident of victory, despite Wellington's earlier warning at Bussy Windmill that the Prussians were both too extended and too exposed and would be "damnably mauled" by French fire power. Blücher was basically happy with his defensive positions, manned and supported by 84,000 troops and 224 guns, although admittedly his ability to attack was greatly restricted because of the marshy banks of the meandering Ligne brook. Not only was Thielemann's IIIrd Corps secure in their hilltop positions along the left flank by the time hostilities began, but Blücher also expected Graf Bülow's IVth Corps, 31,000 strong, including his thirty-seven squadrons of cavalry and eleven batteries of guns (totaling eighty-eight pieces).[8] And then if Wellington did in fact arrive with at least 40,000 Allied troops, surely a great victory was to be his, thought Blücher.

But of course Wellington, already aware of the growing force before him at Quatre Bras, had only promised to come there if he had not a full-fledged attack of his own with which to contend. Furthermore, unknown to Blücher, General Bülow, who should have been moving his troops up smartly as ordered on the 15th, was like Ney caught dawdling, in his case back at Liège instead of advancing from Hannut, only five miles from Sombreffe. And although Bülow later claimed his IVth Corps had not received his orders until 11 A.M. on the fifteenth, Thielemann's IIIrd Corps, in a similar position, had managed to arrive on time to support his commander in chief.[9] If Blücher could not positively count on Wellington, he certainly could have expected a seasoned veteran like Bülow to march ten miles in twenty-four hours to reach Sombreffe. A pattern of lassitude of frightening proportions was beginning to emerge in both French and Prussian armies: Soult, Vandamme, Grouchy and Ney hamstringing Napoleon's well-prepared plans, and a nonchalant Graf Bülow deliberately keeping his entire army corps far from the field of battle.

Meanwhile, the two principal battles, at Ligny and Saint-Amand, continued to rage unabated as tens of thousands of brave troops hurled themselves at one another's guns and bayonets. Vandamme finally, if temporarily, ejected Ziethen from Saint-Amand at four o'clock,[10] which was followed by a powerful Prussian counterattack, including Pirch at Brye. At this point the valiant Prince Blücher, on seeing the Imperial Guard maneuvering and thinking the French Army about to retreat, personally led a spectacular cavalry charge at the head of forty-seven squadrons and the Tippelskirsch Division against Saint-Amand and Saint-Amand la Haie.[11] Although the Field Marshal was successful in retaking and holding Saint-Amand for the next few hours, it had been at great cost. This, of course, is precisely what Napoleon had hoped he would do: expend both his forces and munitions, and quickly deplete his reserves before the French had even launched their major attack of the day.

Unlike Saint-Amand, the fighting at Ligny—held by the 3rd and 4th Prussian Brigades and some sixty cannon of General Jagow and reinforced by other units—was even more stubborn and deadly, and into whose vortex of human destruction were thrown large contingents of cavalry from both sides. By four o'clock Gérard's attack had become so fierce and remorseless that Blücher ordered in a brigade of reserve cavalry, as well as another infantry brigade from the IIIrd Corps behind Ligny. This gave the Prussians a total force of 14,000 men [by eight o'clock], against Gérard's 16,000 or so men,[12] but Bülow's phantom corps still was not in sight.

The French had thrown attack after attack at Saint-Amand and Ligny, and although the Prussians still held their line between Wagnelé and Saint-Amand,[13] Napoleon estimated that Blücher's reserves had now been more or less committed. By 7:30 P.M., with no more hope of any help from d'Erlon's elusive and fast-fading corps, Napoleon gave the order for the long-delayed and final major attack against Ligny, where the Prussians had been holding on with extraordinary ferocity for some five hours, while Grouchy's cavalry struck hard against Thielemann's positions between Tongrenelles and Boignée.[14]

Thus by eight o'clock, in the midst of a heavy rainstorm, the Imperial Guard, forming two powerful, separate columns of infantry supported by heavy cavalry, fell upon Ligny from the east and west. Horrific hand-to-hand fighting and savage cavalry attacks ensued as the Prussians were finally swept from the narrow streets of the village. *"Alte Vorwärts"* Blücher, at the head of another counterattack, this time of thirty-two squadrons of von Röder's magnificent Ist Cavalry Corps,* riposted with a horrendous clash of flesh and steel. But at this moment a bullet felled Blücher's galloping mount, throwing down the Field Marshal, who was left unconscious and trampled in the quagmire as two more French cuirassiers charges passed over him.

If Ligny itself held out desperately until about nine o'clock, it was at a terrible price to both sides, as one surviving French infantry captain starkly summed up the toll. "In a moment, Major Hervieux, commanding the regiment, and two battalion commanders . . . had been killed: another battalion commander . . . was slightly wounded and had his horse killed under him; five captains were killed and three wounded, two adjutants and nine lieutenants and sub-lieutenants were killed, seven wounded, and close to seven hundred rank-and-file killed and wounded."[15] His regiment had been annihilated.

As night fell the Prussians were in full retreat while the French began the fearful task of collecting and identifying their dead and wounded, and the ambulances were brought up through the mud as close as possible to heaps of corpses of men and horses. Although Blücher himself was carried off the battlefield by a faithful ADC, he left behind twenty-one cannon in French hands and 18,772 Prussian casualties. With a mere 13,721 French casualties and remaining in control of the battlefield, Napoleon had won another victory, but not a total one. The much-mauled Prussians made an orderly retreat in the night,[16] and it was not until the morning of the seventeenth that Napoleon ordered Grouchy to begin their pursuit. By then it was nearly too late.

---

*Lieutenant General von Röder had twenty-seven squadrons, and five attached.

Blücher had made errors and paid for them. He had gone into battle without a well-defined plan, and in the course of it had expended men and munitions without an eye to the future. By the time he needed fresh reserves to support his counterattacks and meet the French main thrust, there were none. He left the battlefield not only with his ranks greatly depleted by casualties, but also suffered an additional nine thousand or so deserters.

Napoleon had been much slower to act on the sixteenth than Blücher, however, dispatching battle instructions to his commanders hours late and not even reaching the front himself until 11 A.M., only to find that half his men still were not there, preventing him from launching his first full attack for another four hours. He had already wasted the better part of the day, and a stormy sky threatened to unleash its own ingredients of confusion. Had he arrived earlier that morning, he could have caught Ziethen's single still-isolated corps and defeated it before Blücher arrived with the rest of the army. Nevertheless, Napoleon's basic plan was a good one and probably would have worked well, despite previous mistakes, if d'Erlon's corps had not only arrived late and gone to the wrong position, but then turned about, and marched off the battlefield and back to Ney. And yet Napoleon still had another ten thousand fresh troops of the VIth Corps he had brought up from Charleroi to Fleurus, which he had then completely forgotten about. Had things been managed better, the Prussian Army would perhaps have been destroyed by now, Wellington's dismembered, and the subsequent events and suffering made unnecessary.

Ney's puzzling inactivity on the morning of 16 June was to prove disastrous for the French in the battle for Quatre Bras. When Chief of Staff Soult's letter of instructions confirming Napoleon's orders of the previous day reached Marshal Michel Ney at Gosselies at 6:30 A.M. that day, he still had not moved an inch in the past thirteen hours. Instead of ordering his troops forward, after a good breakfast, the marshal left the village at seven o'clock to inspect the situation at the forward outpost at Frasnes. "Ney's conduct on the morning of the 16th," admits Napoleonic expert General Camon, "is absolutely incomprehensible."[17] Fleury de Chaboulon, however, attributed the deadly laxity of Ney, Soult, Grouchy and others to something more understandable. "These men were simply sick and tired of war," he reflected.[18] In Ney's case there was of course the added element of his long-festering feud with Soult, especially since the Peninsular campaign. There also remained the simple fact that these commanders, *all of them*, were equally sick and tired of Napoleon Bonaparte and his madcap schemes.

Indeed, today Ney only broke camp *at noon*, after receiving another testy note brought at 11 A.M. by Napoleon's ADC, General Flahaut, ordering him to do so, and reiterating the *"ordre du mouvement du jour."*[19] He was reminded to hold Quatre Bras with seven divisions while stationing another at Marbais (for Napoleon's use at Sombreffe in the event he needed it later). At the same time General F. E. Kellermann's eight regiments of cuirassiers—some nearly four thousand troops that had replaced General Lefebvre-Desnouëttes's Imperial Guard division, now on their way back to Napoleon—were also to be held in reserve for the Emperor's later use.[20] "It is my express desire that you be ready to march [from Quatre Bras] on Bruxelles," he concluded.[21] Thus in the light of Napoleon's clearly stated objectives and orders, issued on the fifteenth and repeated on the sixteenth. Ney's *"funeste erreur"* [horrendous mistake][22]—as Fleury called it—his subsequent inaction and failure to seize Quatre Bras remains as baffling to this day, as Napoleon's equal failure to issue the day's campaign plans to his field commanders until late on the very morning of the sixteenth and thereby greatly delaying that engagement. Both Napoleon and Ney had begun the day with inexplicable blunders that ultimately were to cost them dearly.

The result was that the first part of Reille's IInd Corps at Gosselies only reached Frasnes at 1:30 P.M.[23] But when Ney then ordered Reille's 24,336 men[24] to attack the meager Allied force at Bossut Wood— Perponcher at this time holding Bossut Wood and the Quatre Bras junction with only one division of 7,806 men—General Reille refused to march! He needed reinforcements, another brigade, and Foy's division as well, he pleaded. And thus at 2 P.M. Ney once again ordered the attack.

Advancing from Frasnes, the French force now divided into three principal columns and some separate cavalry marching north to seize the crossroads of Quatre Bras that controlled direct access to Bruxelles from Charleroi, Namur and the east. General Bachelu's 5th Infantry Division (4,294 men),[25] forming the right column, was to advance to the east of the Bruxelles road, securing Piraumont Farm and continuing to Quatre Bras, while Foy's 9th Infantry Division (5,493 men) formed a central column straddling the Bruxelles road itself. Meanwhile, Jérôme Bonaparte's 6th Infantry Division (8,019 men) was to secure Pierrepont Farm and Bossut Wood, converging on the critical road junction from the left.

Thus, under a protective barrage of shot, shell and canister from Reille's fifty guns and howitzers, the three columns advanced to capture

Quatre Bras.[26] Shortly before 3 P.M., as the French IInd Corps was closing steadily, Wellington, who had just returned from the Bussy Mill meeting with Blücher, was welcoming the arrival of the first units of his Reserve Army from Mont-Saint-Jean, including Picton's elite 5th Infantry division of 6,745 men and twelve guns, with a brigade of cavalry attached.[27] Ney was quickly beginning to see for himself the results of his unwonted nocturnal and matinal procrastination.

Although the Prince of Orange's initial cavalry charge at 3:30 to hurl back Reille's force was easily rebuffed by very accurate French fire; nevertheless, Wellington's forces continued to grow, the arrival of the Duke of Brunswick's contingent of nearly 7,000 giving the Allies some 23,000 men against Reille's 24,000.[28] The odds were nearly even by 4 P.M. when an officer arrived in Ney's camp, handing him a dispatch from Staff Headquarters with Napoleon's two o'clock order to come to Wagnelé and Sombreffe to execute the enveloping operation so critical for the day's success.[29] Meanwhile, Comte d'Erlon's Ist Corps, which had been eagerly awaited at Quatre Bras, was, unknown to Ney, intercepted in its northerly march from Gosselies by Colonel Forbin-Janson from imperial headquarters, ordering d'Erlon to redirect his Corps to Wagnelé![30] An astonished General Drouet d'Erlon halted his column, immediately sending his personal chief of staff, General Delcambre, to Ney to explain that he had changed directions on Napoleon's orders and had gone instead to fight another battle![31]

Upon receipt of this report from Delcambre, an even more astonished Marshal Ney, turning purple with rage, all but rebuked the young officer who had just brought Napoleon's order for him to bring his wing to attack Sombreffe—"Tell the Emperor what you have seen here!" he said, his arm sweeping the horizon indicating the thousands of fresh troops swelling Wellington's army. "I will hold on where I am," Ney literally shouted at the unfortunate officer at his side, "but nothing more," he stressed, if d'Erlon did not come to his rescue soon. He would *not* be coming to Sombreffe! Thereupon turning on the wretched General Delcambre, Ney ordered him to return to d'Erlon with instruction *to disregard Napoleon's orders* and to proceed to Quatre Bras posthaste![32]

Translating his pent-up anger against Napoleon, Ney, who had until this point been unenthusiastic at best, now threw himself with a frenzy at the head of his lancers. As devastating as was Ney's mighty charge against General Picton's freshly arrived 5th Division at Quatre Bras, now deployed in squares of bayonets, it was nonetheless forcefully repulsed by them and in particular by Lieutenant General Kempt's crack 8th British Brigade and Major General Pack's 9th British Brigade.

Undaunted by these losses, at 5 P.M. Marshal Ney ordered the Comte de Valmy's—General Kellermann's—IIIrd Cavalry Corps's 11th and 12th Divisions to accomplish what the lancers had failed to do: to take the crossroads. It was madness verging on professional incompetence ordering up these elite troopers whom Napoleon had kept in reserve to be released only at the crisis in battle, simply to use them to smash through a wavering Allied line. Kellermann, reputedly the best cavalry commander in the French Army, balked at such a suicidal order. But Ney insisted, joining them himself, as nearly 4,000 cuirassiers advanced up both sides of the Bruxelles road, and Kellermann, at the head of a column of twenty-five of the finest squadrons in the entire army, duly gave the order: *"Pour charger . . . au galop! En avant . . . Marche!"* With trumpets echoing the charge, the troopers in their heavy helmets and shining breastplate, with sabers drawn and roaring *"Vive l'Empereur!"* thundered forward in a mighty mass of steel and horseflesh at Picton's Division,[33] all deployed in a line of large bristling infantry squares. Barely reaching the safety of the 92nd Regiment's square, Wellington personally directed the first volley against the clamoring cuirassiers when only thirty yards from their lines, bringing down hundreds of horses and riders.[34] A bewildered French cavalry suddenly found themselves halted in their tracks by a formidable wall of smoke, flame and canister fired at point-blank range by five batteries of field artillery positioned between the mighty British squares, which in turn were emitting lethal rolling half-company volleys of impenetrable musketry all along the Allied line.

But though Wellington's troops finally stopped Kellermann's extraordinary charge—"the finest fellows I ever saw," Colonel Frazer called them[35]—it was at a high price. With bravery, steady fire and cold steel, but insufficient artillery and little cavalry (some Dutch and Belgian squadrons were soon fleeing the field), they had beaten back the French attack . . . if just narrowly. Weaving through a field littered with downed horses and writhing, sometimes dismembered soldiers, the French IIIrd Cavalry Corps beat a bloody retreat. Indeed, Kellermann himself barely made it back, as his horse was shot from under him, he escaping at the last minute by grabbing hold of two passing horses.[36] But with men exhausted by the effort and ammunition supplies dangerously low—bayonets replacing empty cartridge pouches—it seemed unlikely that the Allies could withstand another such attack.

Meanwhile, much to his surprise, an exhausted Marshal Ney, upon returning from this charge, in which he had had a second mount shot from beneath him, now received yet another, even more urgent message from Napoleon:

Regardless of the situation Marshal Ney now finds himself in, it is absolutely imperative that Comte d'Erlon's orders [to come to Sombreffe] be executed. *It is of very little consequence what happens over there* [at Quatre Bras].[37]*

Covered in mud and sweat, his uniform torn, Ney read it, cursed a blue streak at the staff officer impudent enough to have brought him such a contemptuous order, and leapt upon his third mount of the afternoon.[38] Mustering a hodgepodge combination of all the cavalry he could find— cuirassiers, lancers and hussars—Ney hurled them again at the hard-pressed Allied lines.[39]

It was at this very low point in the battle that Wellington finally saw fresh reinforcements arrive from Mont Saint-Jean and Nivelles, beginning with two brigades of Alten's 3rd Division.[40] Picton, though himself seriously wounded, immediately formed one of these—Sir Colin Halkett's brigade—into four regimental squares on either side of the Bruxelles road, extending all the way to Bossut Wood in support of the Brunswickers. Unknown to Picton, however, the Prince of Orange then countermanded those orders, redeploying Halkett's pristine British brigade into a thin line, over Halkett's most vehement protests.

No sooner had this been accomplished than Ney's cavalry reached them, savagely cutting through Halkett's four exposed regiments (all but annihilating the 69th Regiment in the process) before falling upon Picton's brigades once again. Wellington as usual was everywhere, and after bolstering the left flank and rallying the remnants of Halkett's regiments into squares again, he succeeded in driving the French back. It had been a very closely run thing.

More allied reinforcements continued to arrive, including two more Brunswick battalions and General Cooke's all-British Guards Division, and an additional five batteries of artillery as well as caissons of fresh musket and rifle ammunition, permitting Wellington to prepare a little surprise of his own.

Finally at 6:30 P.M., with 36,000 men and 70 guns, the Duke launched a successful, if bloody, British counterattack all across the line, throwing Reille's IInd Corps back from Bossut Wood, Gémioncourt Farm and Piraumont Farm. By nine o'clock that evening the Allies had regained all the ground they had lost earlier, thereby ending the battle of Quatre Bras, but at the high price of 5,200 casualties as opposed to Ney's 4,100.[41] As for d'Erlon's corps, it was still marching, having not fired a

*Author's italics.

single shot all afternoon, as a result of the astonishing tug-of-war of orders and counter-orders between Ney and the French Emperor.

"I attacked the English position at Quatre Bras with all I had," Ney afterward told Napoleon, "but an error on the part of the Comte d'Erlon deprived me of a fine victory. . . . Everyone today did his duty except the Ist Corps [d'Erlon's]."[42] Indeed, the error was to cost him more than a mere victory. Though his judgment was partly true, it was not fair on d'Erlon, who had been genuinely torn between two conflicting loyalties and seemingly unchallengeable authorities. Napoleon, however, naturally found fault in another direction. "If Marshal Ney had attacked the English with all his troops, he would have crushed them, and at the same time given the Prussians their coup de grâce. And if after having committed that first error he had not made his second blunder, by preventing the Comte d'Erlon from joining me . . . Blücher's entire army would have been captured or destroyed."[43] Ney then shifted the blame again— "How did the Emperor conceive it possible to fight two battles on the same day?" he asked.[44] But of course the marshal had also failed to point out that if he had advanced on the afternoon of the fifteenth as ordered, he could have occupied Quatre Bras practically unopposed. And even if he had arrived after Perponcher's 7,800 men had seized the crossroads, with a single corps of 24,000 he could have dislodged them with veritable ease.

Confusion reigned in French and Prussian camps the night of 16 June following the battles of Ligny and Quatre Bras. Napoleon's victory over Blücher's superior forces, leaving the Prussian Field Marshal himself a temporary victim on the battlefield threatened the already-uncertain Allied unity. Complaining that Wellington had betrayed the Prussians, in the absence of Blücher, Chief of Staff Gneisenau (who personally liked the British no better than did Napoleon himself) ordered the army to advance to the north and toward Liège and the ultimate safety of the German frontier. Indeed, it was only because of Blücher's most unexpected reappearance in the early hours of the morning of the seventeenth—battered, weak and reeking of gin and garlic as he was—that von Gneisenau's plan was rescinded. The army would instead march due north as far as Wavre in order to regroup and help Wellington. There would be no retreat to the Rhine.[45] Both the Alliance and Prussian honor required it, for Blücher had given his word, and in any event the indestructible old Prussian warhorse liked and respected the British commander in chief, and on such things the fate of armies and history hinge.

Meanwhile, after successfully defeating Ney, the Allies remained in full control of Quatre Bras. Passing the night at the nearby village of Genappe, Wellington returned to GHQ at Quatre Bras early on the morning of the seventeenth, where at 7:30 A.M. he received a full report as to what had transpired at Ligny. "Old Blücher has had a damned good licking and gone back to Wavre,"[46] a disconcerted Wellington gloomily acknowledged to Captain Bowles of the Coldstream Guards, as the full impact of the Prussian débâcle began to sink in. With the French victorious there, if he remained at Quatre Bras now, Wellington would be isolated, greatly outnumbered and more than likely defeated once Napoleon joined Ney. On the other hand, if he fell back the same distance as the Prussians, perhaps he could finally close the hinge and coordinate another, more successful attack with them.

When at 9 A.M. a Prussian officer duly arrived from Blücher confirming the retreat to Wavre, Wellington replied that his Allied Army would proceed north on the Bruxelles road to Mont Saint-Jean, about three miles from Waterloo. There they would prepare to meet the French Army again, but on the sole condition that Blücher send at least one corps to bolster his numbers and to replace the thousands of Dutch and Belgians who had deserted him in mid-battle on the sixteenth. Wavre was less than ten miles from the village of Mont Saint-Jean and Wellington's plan seemed feasible and realistic, and thus toward noon the Allied forces gradually began an orderly withdrawal from Quatre Bras. "I suppose in England they will say we have been licked. I can't help it; as they [the Prussians] have gone back, we must go too,"[47] Wellington said as he flung himself into the saddle once again.

As for the French Emperor, his actions continued to remain uncharacteristic and unpredictable. Usually one to sum up a military situation quickly and accurately and to act on it with decision and alacrity, Napoleon had, during this campaign, been ill during the night, late in rising in the morning, and equally lax in making decisions, and as Davout had already remarked in Paris, later still in putting them into effect. Many hours had been lost on the fifteenth, on the morning of the sixteenth, and yet again during the night of the sixteenth and the morning of the seventeenth.

Upon retiring late on the sixteenth, Napoleon had confidently but erroneously assumed that Wellington, hard-pressed by Ney, would be falling back in disarray, and fleeing at the prospect of having to face him. (These two commanders, Napoleon and Wellington, never would understand one another.) Meanwhile, not only had Bonaparte permitted Blücher's army to escape intact on the sixteenth, but was slow in dispatching Grouchy's cavalry to pursue and destroy them once and for all the following day. Nor could Napoleon even be bothered to send out patrols to establish the route or general direction taken by the hasty Prussian retreat. For just as he felt that Wellington would literally be running away, so, too, he had assumed that Blücher's army was fleeing in panic eastward toward Liège and the Rhine. It was only after eleven o'clock on the morning of the seventeenth, with a report in hand from General Pajol indicating that Blücher was indeed in full retreat on the Namur Road to Liège, that Napoleon authorized Generals Pajol and Exelmans to "clear the way to Namur and Maastricht in pursuit of the enemy."[48] Nevertheless, he took the precaution of asking for confirmation of the enemy's plans. It was "important to learn what precisely Blücher and Wellington mean to do," Napoleon insisted, "in the event that they do intend to join forces . . . and fight."[49]

Napoleon only began to realize how greatly he had miscalculated when at 7 A.M. on the seventeenth his ADC, General Flahaut, returned from a reconnaissance patrol to report that the Duke of Wellington's entire army was still at Quatre Bras. Napoleon was genuinely taken aback. An hour later he finally issued Ney's orders "to take up your position at Quatre Bras." Should the Allied Army prove too powerful, the Emperor himself would march there directly with Lobau's VIth Corps and Drouot's Imperial Guard Division from Marbais.[50]

What Napoleon still did not know, however, was that the few thousand Prussians whom Pajol had come across heading panic-stricken for Namur were largely deserting Rhinelanders and convoys of ambulances, and that at this very moment the entire Prussian Army was retiring quickly, not east, but northward, beyond Tilly, Mellery, Gentine and Mont Saint-Guibert.[51] This was to prove a most costly error for the French. Instead of resting on the seventeenth "to conclude this operation and bring up fresh supplies and rally scattered army units,"[52] as he ordered, Napoleon could have simultaneously advanced quickly with a sufficient force to destroy Blücher's retreating army in a final decisive engagement. That in turn would have left Wellington with no alternative but to withdraw, or else fight Napoleon's entire force alone in an all-out battle that would have probably resulted in a resounding defeat for the British. It was almost too late when Napoleon finally realized this on the seventeenth, at last detaching Grouchy's entire right wing of two corps to pursue Blücher's rear guard, while assembling the rest of his army, 69,000 strong, with which to attack Wellington at Quatre Bras.[53]

Nonetheless, neither Wellington nor Napoleon had plans of renewing battle immediately on the seventeenth. Wellington's forces had of course suffered a high number of casualties—5,200 exclusive of desertions—the day before, while both sides required fresh supplies and reorganization.

Napoleon for his part was apparently content with maintaining the same senior officers in their present posts, despite Soult's nearly disastrous work as chief of staff, resulting in critically long delays in dispatching orders and communications. But it was Michel Ney in particular who was singled out for Imperial disapprobation. "It was with great dissatisfaction that the Emperor saw that you did not succeed [at Quatre Bras] yesterday," Ney's old enemy Soult wrote on 17 June, either in crushing the British or in following orders by sending d'Erlon to him, thereby depriving the Emperor of an opportunity of "totally destroying" the Prussian Army and taking "perhaps some 30,000 Prussian prisoners."[54]

Smarting under these orders from the insufferable Soult, the humiliating castigation from Napoleon, and with the knowledge of his own many failures on the sixteenth, it was hardly surprising that the actions and attitude of an embittered Marshal Ney continued to baffle logic and a wary French Emperor.[55] Napoleon's most recent message on the seventeenth had ordered Ney "to attack the enemy at Quatre Bras" and destroy his entire army. Yet upon reaching that crossroads himself sometime after two o'clock that afternoon, 17 June, Napoleon found not a shot being fired, not a French soldier in sight![56] Moving south several kilometers, Napoleon instead found Ney and his men sitting around fires enjoying a leisurely lunch, thereby permitting Wellington's unimpeded, orderly and peaceful withdrawal to the north. Not only had Ney "displayed an inexcusable inertia"—as Camon put it[57]—and failed to launch a full-scale attack against Wellington, he had not even made an attempt to halt or hinder his withdrawal. Outraged, Napoleon upbraided a mortified Ney before his staff, ordering him to march immediately. Although it was the troops that Napoleon had personally brought there now who first attacked the withdrawing Allied force, d'Erlon's corps and cavalry were soon in pursuit as well in the direction of Genappe, followed by Reille's and Lobau's corps, Napoleon himself leading the Imperial Guard with Drouot at a full gallop.[58]

Once again everything that could have gone wrong for the French was continuing to do so, aided and abetted, it would seem, by nature itself. For just as the French cavalry was closing hard on Lord Uxbridge's rearguard cavalry and artillery, a terrific thunderstorm unleashed torrents of rain, quickly rendering fields still wet from previous storms nearly impassable, and the road a mire of mud. As a result, after Genappe the

French pursuit slowed considerably. "The tracks were so deep in mud after the rain that we found it impossible to maintain any order in our columns," one French soldier complained.[59] Neither cavalry nor infantry could advance rapidly, the heavy weight of the 3,440 lbs 12-pounders and 2,070 lbs 6-pounders*[60] driving wheels deeper and deeper, rendering them and their teams of horses—twelve, ten and eight per limber—all but immobile. Thus by 6:30 that evening Wellington was safely in position with his troops and artillery in the vicinity of Mont Saint-Jean and his general headquarters beyond at the village of Waterloo.

When the French finally began to arrive, they set up camp for the night in the rain along the Bruxelles road, in the neighboring fields south of the intersection of the secondary road connecting Braine l'Alleud and Ohain, and around the Belle Alliance Inn on the Nivelles-Mont Saint-Jean Road. Despite the continuing downpour, Napoleon spent the next several hours in the saddle inspecting troop positions, conferring with field and battery commanders, and drawing up plans for the morrow's battle.

After getting a couple of hours' sleep at his GHQ at Gros Caillou Farm, he awakened at three A.M. on the 18th to find a message from Marshal Grouchy [61] informing him that Blücher was heading in his general direction, for Wavre—and not for Liège after all—and assuring the Emperor that he would "follow them and prevent them from reaching Bruxelles or Wellington."[62] Dispatched by Grouchy from Gembloux at ten P.M. on the seventeenth, the marshal had taken an entire day just to discover in which direction the Prussians were going! But it did not occur to Napoleon now to order Grouchy to maneuver to the west, between Mont Saint-Jean and Wavre, thereby shielding his army from a possible Prussian attack. Indeed, the Emperor sent no reply whatsoever. And thus the hapless marshal was only to resume his prodigiously slow pursuit to the north the next day at 8 A.M. (18 June), when Vandamme's Corps finally set out—after a healthy eleven-hour rest. It seemed that even the fate of the French Empire could not instill in Grouchy a sense of urgency.

In the meantime Napoleon's sole anxiety appears to have been that Wellington's army might escape during the night, little realizing that his English opponent was as determined as he to meet in a decisive battle, and in his case to destroy Napoleon Bonaparte and the French Army once and for all. As for Wellington, he was pleased with the battlefield he had chosen along the Braine l'Alleud–Ohain road, with its protecting ridge and access to supply roads behind him, so necessary for the transport of men and munitions. And although von Clausewitz fully concurred,

*Including limbers.

describing this as a "very advantageous position,"[63] not so Napoleon, who thought Wellington "trapped" between his army and the Soignes Forest to their backs. "If he were defeated, all retreat would be impossible," he boasted. "Now I've got them, those English," he smiled before retiring for the night.[64]

As this time Napoleon had along the Bruxelles road 254 pieces of ordnance and some 74,500 men,[65] comprising the Imperial Guard, Comte d'Erlon's Ist Army Corps, Comte Reille's IInd Corps, Lobau's VIth Corps, as well as the IInd and IVth Reserve Cavalry Corps, for a total of 104 battalions of infantry and 113½ squadrons, or 15,830 troopers.[66] Far to the east, at Gembloux, Marshal Grouchy had nearly another 30,000 men, including Vandamme's IIIrd and Gérard's IVth Corps.[67]

Mostly unseen by the French but now facing them behind Mont Saint-Jean, Wellington had assembled a combined Anglo-Allied force of approximately 74,300 men including Orange's Ist Army Corps, Lord Hill's IInd, the Army Reserve and Lord Uxbridge's Cavalry Corps, for a total of 84½ battalions of infantry, 93 squadrons of cavalry (14,457) and 157 guns, the largest being the British 9-pounders.[68] Well to the west of Waterloo, Prince Frederick had another 17,000 men in reserve near Hal, although it was a contingent of Blücher's force—at least another 40,000 men—upon which Wellington was really depending, and which Napoleon of course was expecting Grouchy to neutralize.[69]

But, since the Prussians had suffered enormous initial losses—nearly 31,000 since Charleroi, including killed, wounded and desertions[70]—not to mention their exhausting flight northward from Ligny throughout the seventeenth, Napoleon for one thought it most unlikely that Blücher would be in a position to demand of his men another forced march to come to Wellington's aid many miles to the west.

Numerically the two opposing armies were almost perfectly equal, but in reality, as already seen, Napoleon's was far superior, with an extremely high percentage of veterans at every level, while French cavalry was superior both in numbers, officer training and heavy equipment, Wellington having no equivalent cuirassiers. Finally, in ordnance the French greatly out-gunned the Anglo-Allied army at Mont Saint-Jean by nearly one hundred guns, including a large number of powerful 1802-3-model 12-pounders (which the British 9-pounders could not match in range). And unlike the Duke, Napoleon was an artillery officer who knew how to use his batteries with devastating effectiveness. Wellington not only had inferior artillery and cavalry (only one half being British, and the combined total some 1,373 less than the French),[71] but a mostly untrained army as well. And even the better part of the 28,000 British troops were in raw, inexperienced units, supported of course by Peninsular veterans,[72] while the rest included Nassauers, Hanoverians and a large number of unreliable Dutch and Belgian infantry and cavalry, thousands of whom had already fled under fire at Quatre Bras on the sixteenth. What is more, Napoleon could count on many experienced corps or divisional commanders—e.g., Drouot, d'Erlon, Reille, Lobau, Kellermann, Milhaud, Foy, Bachelu, Domon, Donzelot, Durutte, Jacquinot, Jeanin, Marcognet, Piré and Subervie—all well-tried veterans, opposed to Wellington's smaller number of reliable commanders—Hill, Uxbridge, Picton, Clinton, Cook, Colville and Alten (the Duke of Brunswick having been killed at Quatre Bras).

On the other hand, Wellington had the distinct advantage of having selected his own site for the battle this time, one he had first reconnoitered the year before and then again just recently. As for Napoleon's more powerful and dependable army, it was still too small for an attacking force against a defended position and there existed serious problems of jealousy and lack of cooperation among the senior officer corps. Clearly, this would be a tough fight, with many unknowns in the balance, including the fact that this would be the first direct confrontation between Wellington and Napoleon . . . a battle worthy to record for history.

"Battles should not be fought if one cannot calculate at least a 70 percent chance of success. And yet [at times] one should fight even where there appears to be no chance of winning, since by its very nature, the outcome of a battle is never predictable. But once it has been decided to fight, one should do so to the very end, to conquer or perish."

Napoleon to Marshal Jourdan, 28 July 1809

"I cannot discover the policy of not hitting one's enemy as hard as one can, and in the most vulnerable place."

Wellington

"Napoleon never had so fine an army as at Waterloo."

Wellington

It was only with the first light on the morning of 18 June that the dispositions of the two opposing forces could finally be seen. Chassé's 3rd
Dutch-Belgian Division was holding Wellington's extreme right flank
round the village of Braine l'Alleud, joined next by Clinton's Division
behind the Braine l'Alleud road, along with Cooke's and finally Alten's
division reaching the junction with the Bruxelles road. There Wellington's
own Reserve Corps held the center of the Anglo-Allied front along the
Ohain road, straddling the intersection with the Bruxelles–Charleroi road
facing La Haie Sainte farm, Picton's division continuing from there along
the Ohain road as far as Papelotte and La Haie* where Saxe-Weimar's
brigade secured the left flank, supported to the rear by Uxbridge's cavalry. It was a very dense battlefield.

Napoleon had drawn up his army in a line parallel to Wellington's
and roughly perpendicular to the Bruxelles–Charleroi road, which it also
straddled. His left flank, beginning at the Mont Saint-Jean–Nivelles road
and continuing to the Bruxelles road, then extended to the French
extreme-right position opposite La Haie. Napoleon's extreme left, west of
the Bruxelles road, was manned by Piré's cavalry and Reille's Corps—
the divisions of Prince Jérôme, Foy and Bachelu—the cavalry of
Kellermann and Guyot behind them. The right, or east, of the Bruxelles
road and French front line was held by Comte d'Erlon's Ist Corps, including the divisions of Quiot du Passage (Allix's), Donzelot, Marcognet and
Durutte with Jacquinot's cavalry at the extreme-right flank, while they
were supported to the rear by Milhaud and Lefebvre-Desnouëttes. Just
before and to the right of the Belle Alliance Inn, Napoleon had thrown
up an enormous battery of ten divisions of artillery of 84 guns, while in
central reserve along the high road were Lobau's VIth Corps and the
Imperial Guard.[73]

The French Emperor's battle plan was rather primitive. He intended
to smash and seize Wellington's positions at La Haie Sainte and the
crossroads directly behind that farm and drive on to and occupy Mont
Saint-Jean Farm, thereby "cutting the Bruxelles road and the entire right
flank of the English Army where their principal forces are situated,"

---

*Not to be confused with La Haie Sainte.

while d'Erlon's corps would be "turning the enemy's left."[74] In the unlikely event of a Prussian attack from the east, d'Erlon's Ist Corps was to carry the brunt of the burden, supported later by the Guard and "a detachment of troops from Marshal Grouchy, whom the Emperor was awaiting momentarily."[75] Ney was to direct all the above operations, using massed concentrations of artillery, cavalry and infantry.

Nine o'clock found Napoleon at breakfast at the small Caillou farmhouse with his brother Jérôme, General Reille and a few other officers, instead of on the battlefield ordering the guns to begin the opening barrage as originally planned for that hour.[76] The rain that had continued throughout the night had rendered the area one vast morass. "Messieurs," he addressed his officers, "if my orders are properly executed, we will sleep in Bruxelles this evening."[77] Because of the soggy ground, however, troops were not even fully deployed until 10:30, and Napoleon postponed his main offensive until eleven o'clock that morning and yet again till 1 P.M.[78]

The initial diversionary bombardment and attack finally began at 11:50 A.M., from the extreme French left flank against Hougoumont Farm, a general sporadic firing developing all along the French front by noon.[79] Today, as on the sixteenth, Napoleon's poor choice of commanders, including Ney, Grouchy and his own brother, Prince Jérôme, was again to have dire results for him.

Heading the diversion, Jérôme's orders were to draw as much of Wellington's powerful center to the extreme left as possible, preparatory to the major offensive planned for one o'clock. Encountering very stiff resistance from the Nassauers and Hanoverians around Hougoumont Farm[80] and the British guards within that farm, however, Jérôme fell into his own trap, recklessly throwing in all four of his regiments, only to be repulsed each time. Then in desperation he finally forced Foy to part with as much as half his own division to satisfy Jérôme's ego in taking what was denied him. Foy protested vigorously but to no avail. After all, Jérôme was the Emperor's brother. Meanwhile, Hougoumont was reinforced lightly by the Coldstream Guards and the Scots Guards, who continued to repulse everything thrown at them, despite a heavier commitment by Reille. In fact, Reille should have ordered the reckless young Bonaparte back, instead of jeopardizing Napoleon's entire operations, but apparently he was too afraid of the Emperor to chance that. Indeed, any good commander would have attacked Hougoumont with howitzers first before committing troops as mere cannon fodder, as Bonaparte was doing. Prince Jérôme, however, obstinately hammered against the stone and brick walls of Hougoumont with human flesh and of course the casualties mounted and mounted.

In the meantime, just before one o'clock, as Napoleon was about to give the order for his super battery at La Belle Alliance to blaze away preparatory to launching his main attack, an unexpected movement of what appeared to be a large troop concentration was spotted emerging some eight miles away to the northeast in the direction of Wavre, at the village of Chapelle-Saint-Lambert. Once again, just as at Ligny, Napoleon was forced to suspend operations until he could establish the identity of this mysterious force. With both Blücher and Grouchy reportedly now in that direction, it could have been either one. This time he did not have to wait long, however, as Colonel Marbot reported a half-hour later that, alas, it was General Graf Bülow von Dennewitz with the first units of the Prussian IVth Army Corps heading directly for the exposed French right flank.

Having already come up against unexpected British tenacity at Hougoumont, and in the certain knowledge that he would shortly be outnumbered, Napoleon could now act in one of two ways: he could continue with his full-scale attack as planned and hope that Grouchy would yet join him in time to defeat the Allies, or else make a strategic withdrawal to the south. "Even now we have a sixty percent chance of winning,"[81] he concluded, and remembering Grouchy's still unanswered letter of the night before, he hurriedly dictated a brief note informing him of the arrival of the Prussians. "Therefore do not lose a moment in closing in this direction to join us in crushing Bülow, whom you will certainly take by complete surprise."[82] A fast courier could reach Grouchy at Walhain, within an hour's time, he estimated . . . incorrectly, as it turned out (it would take four hours). He could win yet, and it was simple enough to hold his own for just a short while before Grouchy's reinforcements arrived, when he could spring his surprise and make his kill.[83] The more cautious Clausewitz, however, thought otherwise. Fully aware that the Prussians would soon be arriving in force, "a more careful man would have broken off the engagement and retreated," he thought. But instead, the Prussian colonel continued, Napoleon persisted "with a foolhardy stubbornness and audacity."[84]

Throwing caution to the wind, Napoleon quickly calculated the measures necessary to meet this fresh, unexpected threat and then acted. Calling up Comte Lobau, he ordered his VIth Corps's 20,330 men and 32 guns to maneuver in an easterly direction across the Bruxelles road to a position between the village of Plancenoit and the dirt road skirting the Bois de Paris, where he would be supported by Domon's 3rd and Subverie's 5th Cavalry divisions. This would provide temporary protection along the secondary front anticipated along his right, exposed eastern flank—similarly to what he had done at Ligny—but of course at the expense of weakening units reserved for the main push against Wellington's center.

At 1:30 P.M. Napoleon finally unleashed the sledgehammer fury of his 84 guns from the Belle Alliance Inn in a deafening barrage, and for the next thirty minutes the ground rolled beneath the armies' feet as immense clouds of smoke rose and hung low in the damp air. The batteries of 12-pounders, sending cannon balls hurtling 1,800 meters over the road and ridge and out of sight, fell some three hundred meters beyond Wellington's front lines, raining fear, havoc and death on the Allies. But the massacre Napoleon envisaged did not take place, in part because his gunners could not see most of the Allied troops on the other side of the ridge, and because instead of ricocheting at high speed as cannon balls generally did, they just splashed furiously, sinking into the mud along the forward edge of the ridge.

At two o'clock three of Comte d'Erlon's Ist Corps divisions advanced according to plan, but to Napoleon's dismay, committed a foolish, even deadly, blunder as they did so. For instead of deploying in smaller units, by battalion (*colonne de division par bataillon*), two of the divisions proceeded in two separate, monstrous columns (*colonnes de bataillon par division*) two hundred men abreast, General Durutte's division alone correctly marching by battalion. And thus continuing forward, unprotected even by the usual advance cavalry—with only General Travers's single brigade of cuirassiers accompanying them—they marched toward their slaughter.[85] Nor did Ney or even Napoleon intervene to correct d'Erlon's maneuver, which at the same time made it impossible for the immense columns to form easily into battalion squares in the event of an Allied cavalry attack.

Thus as d'Erlon's three columns advanced with parade-ground perfection right up the deadly slope to the crest of the ridge, behind which Wellington was concealing most of his troops, one of Quiot du Passage's* brigades assaulted the stoutly held La Haie Sainte Farm on the Bruxelles road, while another attacked the gravel pit just beyond it.[86] Meanwhile, Quiot's main force and the divisions led by Generals Donzelot and Marcognet continued to march in their splendid columns through a hail of musketry and artillery under which they "appeared to wave like high-standing corn blown by sudden gusts of wind . . . their caps and muskets . . . flying in the air."[87] But nonetheless they succeeded in

---

*Général de Division Comte Allix de Vaux, not present at Waterloo now, was replaced as commander by Général de Brigade, Baron Quiot de Passage.

routing Van Bijlandt's exposed 1st Dutch-Belgian Brigade in Wellington's left center, earlier hard hit by the crashing fire of Napoleon's 24 *"belles filles,"* as he lovingly referred to his 12-pounders.[88] However, although Travers's veteran cuirassiers also destroyed one of Ompteda's battalions, the rest of the Allied line managed to hold. The incomparable Picton led one infantry attack after another, repelling d'Erlon's divisions with dreadful losses,[89] as Ponsonby's and Somerset's cavalry charges sabered the fleeing troops, while taking some three thousand prisoners as well. And although to the far right General Durutte was momentarily successful in expelling Saxe-Weimar's Nassauers from both Frischermont and Papelotte,[90] nevertheless the gamble on an initial overwhelming infantry attack against the Allied center had failed.

Not only had d'Erlon forgotten to deploy his infantry correctly, but he had made the error of doing so against part of Wellington's finest troops (including Picton's crack 5th Infantry Division, comprising Kempt's 8th British Brigade, Pack's 9th British Brigade and the 5th Hanoverian Brigade, totaling some 6,745 men).[91] The redoutable Sir Thomas Picton, already badly wounded at Quatre Bras on the sixteenth, had held the ridge against vastly superior forces, but paid heavily for it. And even Anglophobe eyewitness Fleury de Chaboulon praised the English, *"insensible au danger* [reckless boldness], and for withstanding the charges of our infantry and cavalry with such great firmness."[92] For not only did Thomas Picton die at the head of his division, but of the total of his fifteen brigade and regimental commanders, thirteen were either killed or wounded before the day was out, with Picton's troops suffering equally grievous casualties, reflecting as nothing else could their remarkable determination to stop the French. Pack's brigade had repulsed General de Marcognet's division from Ohain Road, while the Nassauers finally dislodged Durutte from Papelotte Farm, as Lord Uxbridge's corps swept back two-thirds of d'Erlon's powerful corps. British cavalry, like Picton's infantry, were to pay a very high price for their bravery, however, and in this case far extended themselves against the French; before the day was out, Uxbridge's first two brigades alone reported some one thousand casualties, or 40 percent of his entire corps. His commanders took even proportionately higher dead and wounded, Uxbridge and seven of his nine officers commanding units included on the casualty list, and Sir William Ponsonby dying the most valiant and perhaps most agonizing death of all, brought down by seven French lancers.[93] If by 3 P.M. Wellington still held his line—and this was but the first attack—he was no doubt wondering just how long he could continue to do so.

To everyone's relief the end of this phase of the battle was marked by a sudden lull in the fighting, except for Reille's corps to the west, around Hougoumont. Wellington used this respite to bring up reinforcements for La Haie Sainte and the reoccupation of the gravel pit. General Kempt, though himself wounded, now replaced Picton at the head of the 5th as their commander's remains were carried from the battlefield. And on the far left of the British line, Prince Bernhard von Saxe-Weimar's 2nd Nassau Brigade of his 2nd Dutch-Belgian Infantry Division reoccupied the village of Papelotte.[94]

It was at this time that another message arrived from Grouchy (dispatched from Walhain at 11:30 A.M.) who, having not yet received Napoleon's 1:30 P.M. instructions, requested authorization to advance to the north.[95] Still nine miles from Wavre, he nevertheless heard the distinct thunder of the battle round Mont Saint-Jean shortly thereafter, but deliberately chose to ignore it over the loud urging of an insubordinate General Gérard to alter course and come to the aid of Napoleon. The plodding Grouchy was intent on only one thing, resuming his pursuit of *his* Prussians, although unknown to him half of them had already set out at dawn for Waterloo while Grouchy was still in bed.

Back at Mont Saint-Jean, scarcely had the men returned to their own positions when at 3:30 P.M. Napoleon again ordered Marshal Ney to try to take the farm at La Haie Sainte on the critical Bruxelles–Charleroi Road, which its sturdy walls and buildings abutted, while moving the Imperial Guard right up that road, replacing Lobau's VIth Corps (now forming a defensive perimeter along the French right flank against the Prussian threat).[96] Once again Napoleon's "belles filles," his 12-pounders, erupted in full voice, a prelude to a second attack, as Ney personally led the first two brigades of d'Erlon's Ist Corps in a dazzling assault against La Haie Sainte Farm, only to be repulsed again by a battalion of the superb King's German Legion.[97] But now the hot-headed and impulsive Ney once again misjudged the situation, thereby introducing a fearful chain of events.

It began as he himself was withdrawing. Noticing the road behind the British line filled with a long stream of wounded men and ambulances, as well as some frontline troops pulled back out of range of the French artillery, mixed with large numbers of empty caissons and hundreds of deserting Dutch-Belgian cavalry, Ney incorrectly jumped to the conclusion that Wellington's entire army was fleeing. Without informing Napoleon, he immediately called up General Milhaud's crack IVth Cavalry Corps, including General Delort's 14th Cuirassier Cavalry, followed by Desnoëttes's ten squadrons of the Guard's light cavalry. The result was that at four o'clock Ney, *"emporté par sa bouillante ardeur"* ("carried away in the heat of battle"),[98] made a mad, uncoordinated—if magnificent—cavalry charge—5,000 strong—right up the slope of the center Allied position on the west side of the Bruxelles Road–Braine l'Alleud Road crossroads.[99] But the bewildered French artillery commanders, whose principal battery had been pounding this very sector—as amazed as Napoleon himself by the spectacle—had to cease fire suddenly to avoid killing their own commanding officer and the accompanying cavalry.[100] Ney had done it again! It was a staggering tactical blunder, involving an unplanned attack on a large scale by the army's precious, but fast-dwindling cavalry.

Lacking any artillery cover, not to mention infantry support, thousands of brave cavaliers flung themselves up a soggy and by now well-trampled slope, their horses soon exhausted in the effort, as they found themselves before a formidable line of British regiments drawn up in tightly packed red squares.[99-101] "Prepare to receive cavalry!" came the command, and even French steel breastplate proved no protection against the rolling volleys from Brown Bess muskets and Baker rifles and fearsome double-shot spewn forth from accompanying British artillery.[102] Indeed, so intense was British artillery fire that the muzzles of some guns were soon "bent down by the excessive heat . . . [and] many touch-holes melted away," Sergeant-Major Edward Cotton recalled.[103] And yet Ney's hapless warriors in a terrible moving mass plunged forward still farther, approaching the cannons' mouth at point-blank range in their "fatal charge," as Napoleon called it from his observation post. "Never did cavalry behave so nobly or was received by infantry so firmly," Colonel Sir Augustus Frazer attested.[104] The first salvoes and volleys, bringing down a large number of horses, "created indescribable confusion," Ensign Gronow reported. "The horses of the first rank of cuirassiers, in spite of all the efforts of their riders came to a stand-still, shaking and covered with foam, at about twenty yards' distance from our squares: and . . . resisted all attempts [by their officers] to force them to charge the line of serried steel. . . . [Thus] unable to renew the charge, but unwilling to retreat, they brandished their swords with loud cries of *'Vive l'Empereur!'* and allowed themselves to be mowed down by the hundreds rather than yield."[105]

The British, too, paid a horrific price: Gronow described his regimental square as "an perfect Hospital . . . It was impossible to move a yard without treading on a wounded comrade, or upon the bodies of the dead."[106] It was worse for the exposed French cavalry, who paid a very lethal price indeed for their "awful grandeur" and Ney's bloody miscalculation. After a final shattering volley braced with more double-shot and canister, they finally retreated from what Chandler calls "the corpse-strewn crest,"[107] assisted by Uxbridge's cavalry.[108]

And yet incredibly, despite atrocious losses, Ney's cavalry regrouped at the bottom of the slope, battered and blown as they and their horses were, and mounted another attack—this time at a painful walk amid the tangle of hundreds of their own dead and wounded and slaughtered horses. Again the British squares, "suffocated by the smoke and smell of burned cartridges,"[109] turned back the elite, but by now shattered, remnants of Ney's cavalry charge. Napoleon, with his eye to his telescope, watched "in despair"[110] as this folly unfolded before him, and when upon his return Ney demanded reinforcements, snapped: "Where the devil do you expect me to find them!"[111]

Then at five o'clock, without waiting for Napoleon's orders or approval, an impatient General François Kellermann and his IIIrd Cavalry Corps (3,858 men)[112] and Baron Guyot's division of cuirassiers (2,068 men)[113] threw in their forces behind Ney now "ivre d'intrépidité" ("drunk with excitement").[114] Emerging from the little valley separating Hougoumont from La Haie Sainte, a mass of 9,000 French troopers[115] drove pell-mell along a five-hundred-yard-wide front straight at the British. "The whole space between La Haie Sainte and Hougoumont appeared one moving, glittering mass," eyewitness Captain Siborne recalled, "and as it approached the Anglo-Allied position, undulating with the conformation of the ground, it resembled a sea in agitation. . . . Like waves following in quick succession, the whole mass now appeared to roll over the ridge . . . and the devoted [British] squares seemed lost in the tumultuous onset." "Hard pounding this," a more prosaic Wellington called it. "Let us see who will pound the longest."[116] "Never, no never, did the French strike their adversaries with such murderous force," exclaimed Fleury de Chaboulon from the French lines.[117]

And yet, however spectacular it was, this "tempestuous and hazardous" attack was repulsed by a hail of musketry and a rush of British cavalry, "thundering murderous work," according to one English soldier.[118] The superb French cavaliers, undaunted and seemingly impervious to threats of imminent death and dismemberment regrouped yet again. With Milhaud's IVth Cavalry reforming behind Kellermann and Guyot, they hurled themselves up the hill against the equally tough, but by now greatly weakened, squares, as both Generals Friand and Michel fell wounded* and Ney had his fourth and last horse shot from beneath him.[119] But well after six o'clock and "the most frightful carnage I have

*Michel subsequently died.

ever witnessed," as Ney later admitted, even *"le brave des braves"* had had enough as he made his way on foot back to the French lines, unnoticed even by his own admittedly severely mauled warriors.[120]

Never before had he come up against such magnificent infantry, (though he neglected to bring up any of his own, and indeed with only one battery of horse artillery). Nevertheless, Reille's and d'Erlon's infantry were just a few hundred yards away, waiting for his orders to advance. It was simply gross professional incompetence, something one might expect of a green company commander panicking under fire the first time, but not of a *Maréchal de l'Empire.* And as Wellington had quietly boasted many months prior to this battle, no French cavalry—"not even the Imperial Guard"—could stand up against the best British squares, which had indeed proven their worth. But the toll had been heavy on both sides, leaving the Allies with very little cavalry left intact.

Nevertheless, Napoleon, who had earlier predicted to Soult that today would be "a picnic," was incredulous at this unheard-of resistance by an opponent in the field, particularly by Wellington and the British, whom he had always denigrated and dismissed with an arrogant wave of the hand. He quickly reassessed the situation. Smarting under the rebuff and humiliation dealt him at the hands of "that Sepoy general," and regardless of Ney's tragic blunders, Napoleon ordered *another attack* against La Haie Sainte. This time Ney was more successful as part of Donzelot's 2nd Infantry Division, some cavalry and a few guns finally ousted the King's German Legion—now out of ammunition—from the farm. Immediately bringing up their artillery to the farm, the French trained a fresh, devastating cannonade on Wellington's already badly shaken center, which included Baron Ompteda's 2nd King's German Legion Brigade and Graf Kielmansegge's 1st Hanoverian Brigade, both in the words of David Chandler, "virtually annihilated." Ompteda himself a fatality.[121] Wellington's center was now on the verge of collapse. Never in his career had the Duke faced such brutal firepower and murderous cavalry.

The indomitable Ney, his spirits revived because of this success, and once again feeling that victory was within his grasp, apprised Napoleon of the situation, pleading for fresh reserves to be brought up from the Imperial Guard. Indeed, this was probably all that was needed to break decisively through what remained of Wellington's center position. But having already heard and answered that same plea at the cost of large numbers of excellent units and irreplaceable commanders with no results to show for it, Napoleon declined to part with his precious reserves. What is more, he had just discovered that the Young Guard had been routed from Plancenoit, and clearly he felt he would badly need the remaining fourteen battalions in reserve.

Meanwhile, much earlier that afternoon, by one o'clock, Field Marshal Prince Blücher had joined Bülow von Dennwitz's IVth Corps at Chapelle-Saint-Lambert, to the northeast of the battlefield. Despite the pain and exhaustion resulting from Ligny, he personally reconnoitered the approaches to the French right flank. But he could not move quickly, nor were his decisions fast in coming, and it was not until 4 P.M. that Bülow's first two brigades were seen debouching from the Bois de Paris. [122] At a point close to the farm of Frischermont they started heading in the direction of Plancenoit, some three kilometers away, along the southern end of the hastily extended French right. Napoleon for his part watched impotently as the Prussians easily scattered the wounded General Domon's 3rd Cavalry Division of less than a thousand men at five o'clock. But three brigades of Comte Lobau's VIth Corps, supported by thirty pieces of artillery, promptly challenged Bülow's equal ordnance and swelling infantry, successfully pushing them back for the moment. However tired the Prussians may have been from their forced march from Wavre today, nonetheless, with the rest of Bülow's corps now arriving, they had a crushing numerical superiority with their 31,000 against Lobau's 7,000, and by six o'clock the French had again abandoned Plancenoit.

Coming under Prussian cannon fire himself for the first time, Napoleon dispatched General Duhesme's Division of eight battalions of Young Guard infantry, totaling over 4,000 men, along with twenty-four pieces of ordnance. Duhesme retook Plancenoit, so critical for maintaining the French right flank, while Durutte attacked Papelotte. [123] This was no time for half measures. But capturing Plancenoit from the mortally wounded Duhesme, Bülow once again threatened Napoleon and French control of the Bruxelles Road itself. Meeting this challenge, the Emperor then deployed eleven of his remaining Guards battalions in as many separate squares, from La Belle Alliance along the Bruxelles highway down to Rossommée Farm. Now facing east toward a wall of massing Prussians, he ordered another attack on Plancenoit, led by two battalions of Morand's Old Guard chasseurs. By 7 P.M. not only was that village of 500 souls again back in French hands, but Papelotte and La Haie secured by Durutte's 4th Infantry Division as well. Experience had won the day. Lobau had regained all the land he had earlier lost. [124]

By 7 P.M. Prince Jérôme was still vainly laying siege to the redoubtable Hougoumont Farm along the Allied right, while Donzelot's, Quiot's and Marcognet's divisions were in control as far as Papelotte and La Haie to the Allied left, Blücher temporarily thrown back. Although the sun broke through at long last, promising light for another two hours, Napoleon's situation was still desperate as further Prussian reinforcements continued to come up. In fact, once again he found himself faced with two options: a rapid strategic withdrawal in an attempt to salvage his army and regroup, or . . . he could attack and pray that Grouchy arrived in time.

But if he withdrew, he was left only with the option of regrouping round Philippeville in an uncertain attempt at defending the French northern frontier from the inevitable second Allied invasion, while Rapp, Lecourbe and Davout brought up reinforcements. If all failed, however, Napoleon had to face the alternate probability of returning to Paris defeated, as he had done so abjectly in 1812 following the appalling catastrophe of the Russian campaign. There was no future for Napoleon, it seemed . . . unless he surprised Wellington, launching a final, supreme attack, throwing in everything he had, using the last of his reserves, his much-vaunted Old Guard. And as he was wont to say, "by its very nature, the outcome of a battle is never predictable."[125]

Thus it was, facing probable political annihilation and the last hope of shoring up his wobbly empire if he failed, Napoleon decided on an overwhelming attack against Wellington's center before La Haie Sainte. And once again, as so many times in the past, "the brave presence of the Guard and a dramatic talk by Napoleon inflamed the troops," Fleury duly noted.[126] "Never had Bonaparte committed a greater error," commented von Clausewitz from the Prussian lines. "There has always been an immense difference between leading an invincible army in an orderly withdrawal from a battlefield in the face of an overwhelmingly superior force, and returning like a veritable fugitive, guilty of having lost and abandoned an entire army."[127]

Regardless, a desperate Napoleon facing just such a superior force—Wellington and his Prussian reinforcements—now deployed two Guard battalions between Hougoumont and La Haie Sainte, handing over the remaining seven Guard battalions to Ney with which to spearhead the drive across the Ohain road, while ordering a heavy artillery barrage against the much-pounded Allied center. Both Reille's and d'Erlon's corps, along with the remaining cavalry, were to support the Imperial Guard's thrust forward, while Napoleon reluctantly remained behind with the last four Old Guard battalions.

Then after 7 P.M., just as he was about to give the signal for the attack, Napoleon suddenly heard a loud cannonade exploding along his right flank to the northeast, which General Dejean shortly after identified as the arrival of von Ziethen's Ist Corps. It was too late after all. To advance now was suicide. But the French Emperor—a man with no future—deliberately lied to Ney, stating that it was Grouchy's troops arriving, coming to the rescue, and not the Prussians. With cheers of *"Vive l'Empereur! Vive Napoléon!"* bellowing forth from thousands of throats, Ney gave the order to charge.[128]

As the column of seven Guard battalions in a "dark waving forest of bear-skin caps,"[129] seventy-five men abreast, supported by two batteries of horse artillery, advanced, they divided—apparently by accident—into two separate columns. While General Friant's grenadiers in the front part of the column continued forward, the chasseurs under General Morand peeled off to the left. They immediately came under heavy fire by Allied guns and Chassé's 3rd Division of Dutch-Belgian infantry, as the main body continued forward where most of Wellington's troops still lay concealed once again behind the banks of the Ohain road, just ahead of them. Meanwhile, to their left the chasseurs unexpectedly found themselves facing General Adams's light brigade, as it emerged abruptly from the cornfield before them, while Colonel Colborne's 52nd fell upon their left flank with a stinging fire, startling and momentarily halting the entire French advance. Taking advantage of the moment to rise from the concealed embankment, Wellington in his blue coat, white buckskin breeches and gold Spanish sash, waved his hat, signaling the Allies all along the front to counterattack.

Less than sixty yards away, some 40,000 Allied troops appeared as if out of nowhere, firing a steady stream of lethal volleys into the exposed front ranks of the astonished Imperial Guard, and then shouting, charged with bayonets as the remaining two brigades of Allied cavalry under the command of Generals Vivian and Vandeleur swept across the road. Despite Ney's repeated orders to advance and the Guard's drummers rolling out the *"pas de charge,"*[130] the marshal's troops and frontline Imperial Guard broke and fled for their lives.

A desperate Napoleon hurriedly formed his last three Guard battalions into squares in the very path of his fleeing troops, but even he could not stop the massive flight, and all gave way as this immense wall of humanity poured forth, their cries of *"Vive l'Empereur,"* now replaced by *"Sauve qui peut!"* [Everyone for himself.] At the same time on the other side of the Bruxelles–Charleroi highway, the Young Guard managed valiantly to hold on to Plancenoit under a heavy Prussian barrage for another couple of hours, thereby covering the escape route to Charleroi for the precipitous retreat of the Armée du Nord.

With the Old Guard's withdrawal completed by 8 P.M., a dazed and gloomy Napoleon Bonaparte himself turned away from the battlefield of Waterloo and his extraordinary defeat, and "entirely disappeared," as Ney put it, without having notified him or the other field commanders of his plans.[131] The crush of the troops in their southerly retreat became overwhelming as the imperial coaches and Napoleon's famous dark blue and gilt berline were seen fleeing the scene. "A complete panic at once spread throughout the whole field of battle," reported one official version of the battle, as the greatest army in the world broke and fled in "great disorder"[132] before the *"issue funeste de la bataille"* ["fatal outcome of the battle"].[133]

"In an instant the whole army was nothing but a mass of confusion . . . and it was utterly impossible to rally a single unit,"[134] Ney admitted. Napoleon had abandoned his army in Egypt and in Russia and now again at Waterloo. "All was lost by a moment of terrifying panic. Even the cavalry squadrons accompanying the Emperor were overthrown and disorganized by these tumultuous waves,"[135] said the official Army report. And Ney, much bruised from his last fall and limping painfully, covered in mud and exhausted—with not even one of his staff officers willing to help or offer him a mount—now followed on foot swallowed up in the mob. "I owe my life to a corporal who supported me on the road, and did not abandon me during the retreat," that marshal acknowledged.[136]

Meanwhile, with some British and Prussian cavalry units already hard on their heels,[137] it took Napoleon and his staff an entire hour just to clear the bottleneck over Genappe's narrow stone bridge spanning the Dyle, where artillery limbers, caissons, carts and horses were locked together holding back the entire French army. Indeed, with the sudden blare of Prussian cavalry trumpets and the rush of Gneisenau's dragoons, Uhlans and Pomeranians around the imperial cortège, Napoleon himself barely escaped capture, as he leapt from his berline onto his waiting horse. Leaving behind a fortune in gold, bank notes and diamonds, including his sister Caroline's 300,000-franc necklace, personal papers and hat, he galloped off down the Charleroi road followed by Drouot, Bertrand and his staff.

But upon reaching Quatre Bras, instead of finding Girard's reserve division (ordered earlier from Ligny)* waiting for him, he came upon over three thousand French soldiers, long dead, in immense rows, completely stripped of their clothing and possessions by scavenging French and British soldiers and local Belgian inhabitants, their white bodies bruised, mutilated and streaked in dry blood, rigid and refulgent in the June

---

*Girard, of course, had been killed.

moonlight.[138] With no organized French units left around him, nor word of Grouchy, and Gneisenau's troopers again fast approaching, a tearful Napoleon mounted his horse and continued to lead the French retreat from Waterloo.[139]

Earlier at 9:30 P.M. (on the eighteenth), a weary Wellington and "Old Blücher"—as the Duke affably referred to "my neighbor and fellow labourer"[140]—had finally met at the appropriately named Belle Alliance Inn. The Prussian Army band struck up a vigorous "God Save the King" as they congratulated each other warmly over their narrowly won but most spectacular victory. If Wellington had not realized before just how shattered Prinz Blücher had been as a result of his traumatic battlefield experience at Ligny, he now did as he appraised the black-and-blue Prussian wheezing before him. After ascertaining that the British had only a little light cavalry left in fresh enough condition with which to pursue the French, following the fiercest and most savage cavalry attacks in modern history, it was agreed that Prussian cavalry led by Gneisenau would be dispatched immediately, augmented on the morrow by the Ist and IVth Corps.[141]

There were in fact three matters the two field marshals differed on, however, as they toasted their grand victory: the name of the battle, the destruction of Parisian monuments, and the fate of Napoleon. Although Blücher suggested the "Belle Alliance" as an ideal name for this historic event, Wellington preferred "Waterloo," and with the largest army present, he won the day. On a more serious note, Blücher was most keen on destroying all Parisian war memorials commemorating previous Prussian defeats, and dramatically insisted on his right to blow up the Pont d'Iéna in particular. Nevertheless, Wellington managed to convince him that there were more pressing matters at present and that they could consider that at a later date. And then there was the thornier question of what to do with Napoleon. "Blücher wants to kill him," Wellington told Sir Charles Stuart, but "I advised him to have nothing to do with so foul a transaction. . . . if the sovereigns wished to put him to death, they should appoint an executioner, which should not be me. . . ."[142]

Finally, as for his professional views on that day's fighting, the Duke drily observed: "Napoleon did not manoeuvre at all; he just moved forward in the old style in columns, and was driven off in the old style."[143] And while admitting that Bonaparte "never had so fine an army as at Waterloo," he equally declared that he himself "never saw the British infantry behave so well,"[144] firmly believing that they had "given Napoleon his death blow," as he put it.[145] "Our battle . . . was one of giants: and our success was most complete" he afterward reported to Prinz Schwarzenberg; "God grant I may never see another!"[146]

The frenzy and confusion Napoleon had found earlier at Genappe was now repeated at Charleroi, where he arrived at five o'clock in the morning of the nineteenth, as bands of fleeing soldiers mixing with the stream of the first convoys of the wounded and the twenty-one pieces of captured Prussian artillery blocked the sole bridge crossing the River Sambre there, some bursting its wooden parapets and plunging into the rain-swollen waters below. Food, clothing, weapons, ammunition, overturned carriages and carts lay before them. And then with the tocsin sounding again to alert them to a possible Prussian approach, the soldiers turned, not to protect the column, but to plunder the Army's treasury wagon as they hacked with swords and bayonets to grasp the heavy sacks containing 20,000 gold francs each. In the words of historian Houssaye, *"Tout fut pillé."*[147] ("Everything was pillaged.")

But as tired as he was, the dismal sight was too much for Napoleon, who, setting out an hour later, reached Philippeville at 9 A.M. (the nineteenth). Here at least he hoped to find some semblance of order and see his army units regrouping. Instead he found unabated confusion and only 2,600 men from a dozen different regiments.[148] But at least his staff and commanders began to drift in, and he soon had with him Bertrand, Drouot, Dejean, Flahaut, Bussy, Bassano, Fleury, Reille and Soult. For the first time since the end of the battle Napoleon was able to dispatch orders to commanders he had abandoned, as well as to nearby garrisons, where he hoped to assemble his cavalry, artillery and infantry. In addition he now dictated two letters to Fleury for Joseph Bonaparte, acting as Regent in his absence: one for his ministers, the other personal. Explaining briefly what had transpired at Waterloo, he said—"I believe the Deputies will be made to understand that it is their duty to join me in saving France . . . All is not lost by a long chalk. . . . I shall call up one hundred thousand conscripts. The fédérés and the National Guard will provide another one hundred thousand men. . . . I can call up a levée en masse in Dauphiné, at Lyons, in Burgundy, Lorraine and Champagne. . . . I shall soon have three hundred thousand soldiers under arms with which to face the enemy! . . . Then I'll simply crush them once and for all!"[149] Still in this defiantly optimistic mood he appointed the lukewarm Soult to take over command of the Army concentrating at Philippeville, and commandeering three of that marshal's carriages, Napoleon and his staff set out for Laon.

Meanwhile, Grouchy's right wing, down to 25,000 men, which had been fighting General von Thielemann's 17,000 Prussians at Wavre and

Limale, on learning of the defeat the next day (the nineteenth), ordered a swift and brilliant withdrawal for his army via Namur and Givet. Having defeated the pursuing Prussians in two sharp if minor battles, Marshal Grouchy's forces reached Philippeville on the twentieth, and were then taken over by Soult, giving him a grand total of just 55,000 troops—as opposed to Blücher's approaching 66,000 and Wellington's 52,000 men.[150] But "Old Nick" Soult (as his officers and men facetiously referred to him), as cold, uncommunicative and solitary as ever, personally felt the situation following the débâcle of Waterloo was utterly hopeless. He only wanted to escape while he still could, and giving orders to evacuate Philippeville, he continued with the French Army on its retreat for Soissons where, a few days later, pleading "ill health," he in turn would hand over supreme command to Grouchy and in the best Napoleonic tradition abandon them all.[151]

By the time Napoleon himself reached Laon, after six o'clock on the evening of the twentieth, he had changed his mind again. He would not stay to rebuild the Army after all, he would go to Paris. He had to go to Paris to save the nation . . . and his throne. After traveling throughout the night from Laon, the dust-covered Emperor emerged from the calèche in the courtyard of the Elysée at 5:30 A.M. on 21 June, where he was greeted by a grim Foreign Minister Caulaincourt. "If I return to Paris," Napoleon had told General Bertrand at Philippeville, "and I have to get my hands bloody, then I'll shove them in right up to the elbow!"[152] Was that his solution, after having left 64,600 French casualties—25,000 dead and seriously wounded just at Waterloo and tens of thousands of horses and 220 cannon behind him in the fields of Belgium[153]—was he now bent on bringing down the apocalypse on France as well?

Chapter XIII

End of the Napoléonade

"You must have heard what I have done; and I hope you are satisfied. I never saw such a battle . . . and never before did I gain such a victory. I trust it is all over with Napoleon Bonaparte. We are in hot pursuit of him."

   Wellington to General Dumouriez, 20 June 1815

"Europe's great expectations have been fulfilled. You have now achieved the ultimate glory. Your complete victory over Buonaparte proclaims you the greatest captain of your century. . . ."

   King William of the Netherlands to Wellington, 20 June 1815

"We have taken Napoleon's hat. It is to be hoped that we will now end in capturing the man himself."

   Metternich to his daughter, 22 July 1815

"This creature at once greater than life and so unfathomable, this phenomenon the like of whom shall never be seen again. . . ."

   Pozzo di Borgo on Napoleon

The late June afternoon found Napoleon sitting at his desk in the groundfloor library of la Malmaison, contemplating the large leather tomes of Alexander von Humboldt's study of the American wilderness, *Voyages aux Contrés Equinoxiales du Nouveau Continent.*[1] His imagination was stirred by what was hinted at and what was left unsaid: the vast unknown, the marvelous opportunities. And he now discussed these in conjunction with his own proposed journey to the United States with the sixty-nine-year-old savant, mathematician, and founder of the Ecole Polytechnique, Gaspard Monge. Joseph, Lucien and Jérôme, along with several officers and officials, had agreed to accompany him there, but Napoleon alone was already planning vast explorations "from Canada to the tip of Cape Horn"[2] to take up where Humboldt had left off. Napoleon was no explorer, however, despite his professions of great scientific curiosity. For him, "exploration" no doubt meant discovering a new, unclaimed region for a new realm, a new kingdom, fresh conquest. He put it differently, however. "Henceforth without an army and empire, only the sciences remain strong enough to attract me . . . I want to start a new career, leaving behind some works truly worthy of me!"[3] Behind Monge stood the walls of books, the long row of mahogany bookcases still rich and red in the warm light. He would miss this house, this room full of memories of the faithless but wonderful Josephine. But he could not remain here, his days were numbered, the very hours ticking quietly by. At the end of the long room Fleury de Chaboulon and Baron Fain were sitting at a table beneath the vaulted multicolored ceiling, writing orders and letters that Napoleon had continued to dictate since his return to la Malmaison on 25 June.

Hortense had greeted him at the tented entrance of the Cour d'Honneur earlier, as they walked across the drawbridge into the deep shade of the immediate *"petit jardin"* of this 726-hectare estate. Napoleon had in fact been deeply touched by the kindness of his stepdaughter ever since his arrival in Paris on 20 March. There had been considerable coldness and tension before that, because of Napoleon's divorce of her mother, Josephine, in December 1809, and more recently because of Hortense's struggle in the public courts in 1814 to obtain legal custody of her children (including Louis Napoleon, the future Napoleon III). The attempt to wrest legal control of them from her deranged husband, Louis Bonaparte, the former king of Holland, had simply brought the wrath of the entire Bonaparte clan down upon her.

But since the Emperor's return, Hortense's simplicity and warmth, which had so won over Czar Alexander the year before, had likewise finally conquered a still-embittered Napoleon. And now, in Josephine's house, the final reconciliation was taking place. Nor was Hortense insensible to Napoleon's mute respect for the Josephine he had so adored, *malgré tout*, and who had died under this very roof on 29 May 1814. Her spirit haunted the rooms, now once again filled with the flowers she had so loved, and when Hortense and Napoleon walked arm in arm through the large English garden, past the roses, past the winding lake and regal swans, down the allée of tulip trees, under ancient oaks and beeches, he was often speechless and moved to tears, frequently breathing with some difficulty. "That poor Josephine," he said. "I cannot get used to living here without her. I always expect to see her emerging from a path gathering one of those flowers, which she so loved. . . . She was the most graceful woman I have ever known. . . . Make another portrait of her for me, this time for a locket."[4] The confusion of sentiments and the rapidity of events occurring since his return to Paris early on 21 June had left Napoleon in a singularly reflective mood as they passed the cypress Josephine herself had planted in celebration of the battle and victory of Marengo. And the Napoleon who had paced his suite of apartments in the Louvre and then the Elysée, and who generally avoided the beauties of nature, now spent hours wandering slowly along the forested paths of the 70-hectare park. He was a prisoner of the past, trying furiously to unscramble the significance of the immediate events that had brought him here, now literally a prisoner of the French government, in the house where it had all begun back in 1799. He wanted to forget, it was a mass of chaos in his mind, and yet it was imperative that he remember, analyze and understand all that had transpired.

"I am sorry to see you at Paris, Sire," Caulaincourt, the Duc de Vicence, had told him upon his return to the Elysée on Wednesday, the 21st (of June). "It would have been preferable not to have left your army, for it is that which ensures your power, your safety,"[5] to which Joseph had fully concurred. They had been both right and wrong. Napoleon had always owed everything to his army, but now there was no army. Nevertheless, despite his wheezing lungs, aggravated by tension, exhaustion and the emotion of the moment, Napoleon did want to go on, as he told his brothers Joseph, Lucien and Jérôme, and his ministers at the Elysée later that same morning of the twenty-first.

"Our misfortunes are great," he acknowledged. "I have come back to repair them, to build a great and noble movement for the nation and the army. If the nation rises to the call, the enemy will be crushed. But, if to the contrary, extraordinary measures are not taken, and instead they simply argue, all is lost. The enemy is now in France. I need to save the fatherland, and must be invested with enormous power, by means of a temporary dictatorship. . . . In the interests of *la patrie*" this had to be done immediately.[6] If Carnot and Davout were ready to rally to the old call, "*la patrie en danger*," ready to call up the fédérés, the national guard, the conscripts, and place Paris under "a state of siege," it certainly was not too late. Caulaincourt and Fouché had opposed this, however,[7] preferring instead to appeal to the Chamber of Representatives and the Chamber of Peers for help and support. Nevertheless, Napoleon's faithful old counselor, Comte Regnault de Saint-Jean d'Angély, was not sanguine. As a member of the Chambers he understood their mood, and that mood, he advised, was adamantly against Napoleon. Victory invites friends; disaster, enemies. And when on the very morning of his return Bonaparte than asked Regnault point blank: "Tell me frankly. It's my abdication they want, isn't it?" The Comte replied, "I believe, Sire, that however painful it is for me now, it is my duty to enlighten Your Majesty on the realities of the moment. Given the current situation, I believe it preferable if Your Majesty were not to oppose it, and instead to offer his abdication of his own accord, before the Chambers demand it."[8] There were few men Napoleon would listen to with respect and Comte Regnault, sitting there thoughtfully, was one. But then Lucien had strongly protested. "The well-being of the *patrie* must always be the first rule of the land," he insisted, "and since the Chambers do not appear at all disposed to join the Emperor, to work with him to save France, then he must save it by himself. He must assume dictatorial powers, put France under martial law, and call upon all patriots and good Frenchmen to come to its defense."[9] Carnot warmly endorsed this. Once again Napoleon was stirred: "The nation's patriotism, its hatred of the Bourbons, its attachment to my person—all offer us immense resources, we are not yet lost!"[10]

At that moment they were interrupted by an urgent message from the Chamber of Representatives, however, Napoleon turning livid as he read the document:

"The Chamber of Representatives declares that the independence of the nation is threatened.

"The Chamber declares itself in permanent session. Any attempt to dissolve it is a crime of high treason. Whosoever becomes guilty of such an attempt will be considered a traitor of the country and adjudged forthwith as such."[11]

"I knew I should have dismissed those people over there before I left Paris [on the twelfth]. Now it's finished," he said, asking who had dared propose this egregious declaration.[12] "Lieutenant-General de La Fayette," Napoleon's old enemy, he was told. Denouncing that general, his thoughts no doubt returned to all the difficulties he had had throughout his career with this La Fayette, whom he had tried so unsuccessfully to win over, and then buy off with honors. This had included the offer of a seat in the Senate with its handsome lifetime income (but turned down by La Fayette on at least four separate occasions) and the Grand Cordon of the Legion of Honor (which La Fayette had dismissed, publicly declaring the Legion itself to be "ridiculous" and "contrary to all my principles").[13] But then La Fayette had never been one of Napoleon's sycophants. When years earlier he had criticized La Fayette for opposing his regime, La Fayette had told him to his face: "What do you want of me, then? I live secluded in the countryside. I have retired from all political life. I avoid all occasions to speak in public. But when someone asks me if your regime conforms to my ideas of freedom, I reply, of course not. . . .[14]," It was hardly the sort of thing Bonaparte liked to hear. "Everyone in France has accepted the Empire," Napoleon had complained to the Conseil d'Etat back in 1808, "but there is one man who has not, that is La Fayette. He has never conceded an inch,"[15] and, in fact, Napoleon had secretly admired him for his integrity, for not having given in when everyone else had been easily bought off or intimidated. Nevertheless, this did not stop him from denouncing La Fayette or destroying his son's military career; although such acts of vengeance did nothing to alter the situation.

"A republican in Provence, a partial-republican by the time he reached Lyons, an absolute Emperor upon entering Paris, Napoleon has since discovered that he had no future if he did not accept constitutional approval," La Fayette had commented when Napoleon had then proclaimed his Additional Act to the Constitutions. But the result was hardly a resounding success, La Fayette pointed out, describing the combination of previous imperial constitutions and the Additional Act as "a strange hodgepodge of imperial, liberal and terrorist measures."[16] And after speaking to Sir Charles Stewart (half-brother of Lord Castlereagh, not to be confused with Sir Charles Stuart), who had told him that "peace with the Powers is not possible unless you hand over Bonaparte,"[17] La Fayette met privately with Joseph Bonaparte at the Palais Royal, echoing these sentiments. "I hope it [Napoleon's reign] comes to an end quickly,"[18] he had told him. This was blunt speaking, to be sure, but language the Bonapartes understood.

Then on 21 June, after hearing the results of the motion by La Fayette, which the combined Chambers had just pronounced, declaring themselves in permanent session and warning him against silencing them, Napoleon snapped, "I am going to dissolve the rebellious Assembly! I have the right to do so.[19] . . . I want to declare in my turn my right to sit in permanent session with my ministers and the Conseil d'Etat at the Tuileries, and to summon around me the six thousand men of my Imperial Guard."[20] But force was not the answer, he realized. "I shall not consider doing this, for it would be more effective, politically speaking, that dictatorial powers were granted me by the Chambers. . . .[21] Instead, however, the representatives are going to canvass the provinces and turn the country against me. . . . No, I am no wretched party hack. I shall not be the one to cause a civil war . . . I do not want to be the king of a jacquerie [mob]."[22] And then becoming gloomier and more resigned, he said, "If France no longer needs me, I shall indeed abdicate."[23]

Though they realized the battle was not over, extending Napoleon's already sweeping powers was hardly acceptable to the Chamber. Nevertheless, Lucien, for one, returned to the Chamber of Representatives that same Wednesday the twenty-first to make one last plea on behalf of Napoleon, calling upon them to unite with his brother to rid France of the common danger threatening them. "I beg of you, citizens, in the sacred name of the country, rally, all of you rally round the leader whom the nation has just solemnly again placed at its head. Remember that our well-being depends on our union, and that you cannot separate yourselves from the Emperor and abandon him to his enemies, without losing the country itself, without violating your oaths of office, without sullying our national honor forever."[24] This was greeted with hoots, shouts and boos, and again it was Gilbert de La Fayette who rose to answer him, this time with vehement, unwonted indignation. "By what right does he [Lucien] have the effrontery to accuse France of letting down the Emperor? The nation has followed him loyally across the sands of Egypt and the wastes of Russia, across fifty battlefields, sharing his reverses along with his successes. And indeed it is for thus having followed him so faithfully that today we must count the cost in the blood shed by three million Frenchmen!"[25]

"The truth has been revealed at last. . . . You know as well as we do, that it is against Napoleon alone that Europe has declared war," Henry Lacoste's voice echoed across the Chamber. "As for me, I declare that I can see only one man standing between us and peace. Let him leave and the country will be saved."[26]

By now the Chamber was in an uproar and had turned irrevocably against the Emperor once and for all. Before the day was out, both Chambers had elected five members each to form a joint committee to deal with the national crisis—La Fayette serving on the Chamber of Representative's Committee, while the five members selected by the Chamber of Peers were Bonapartists to a man: Cambacérès, Thibaudeau, General Drouot, General Andréossy and General Dejean.

Convening at 11 P.M. that same evening, La Fayette addressed the ten-man Committee, calling for Napoleon's abdication and the creation of a special commission "to negotiate directly with the Allied Coalition."[27] A majority vote carried both motions.[28] And "in order to maintain the honor of the head of State," they agreed to grant Napoleon *"une heure de grâce"* in which to respond to their ultimatum. It had been La Fayette's initial act declaring the Chambers to be in permanent session and denouncing any tyrannical act to suppress them, the Duc de Castries pointed out, and it was really that "revolutionary motion, in the best style of the Constituent Assembly of 1789, which marked the inevitable downfall of Napoleon. . . ."[29]

General Solignac, heading a small delegation, brought the abdication ultimatum to the Elysée on Thursday 22 June, and an outraged Napoleon grandly said, "I shall never abdicate. The Chamber is composed of jacobins and hot-heads."[30] But Regnault, calming him, explained the reality of the moment. "Sire . . . time is running out, enemy troops are advancing on us. Do not leave the Chamber, the nation, the right to accuse you of having been the sole obstacle to peace. In 1814 you sacrificed yourself for the good of everyone. Repeat that grand and generous sacrifice today."[31] It had happened much more quickly than Napoleon had expected, but by now he had already had enough, more than enough, and summoning Lucien, he dictated his second abdication, in his "Declaration to the French People" that same day:

> "In beginning the war to maintain our national independence, I was counting on the union of all our efforts, but since then the circumstances appear to me to have changed, and I offer to sacrifice myself to the hatred of the enemies of France. . . . My political life is over and I proclaim my son, under the title of Napoleon II, *Empereur des Français*."[32]

And thus three days later, on Sunday 25 June, the ex-Emperor moved from the Elysée Palace to Rueil and La Malmaison, where he now looked back upon the swirl of events. But as Regnault had pointed out, time was indeed slipping past them; though here at La Malmaison, in the eye of the hurricane which was ravaging France, the unearthly stillness was deluding. There was no fighting, no hustle and bustle of couriers, no marching troops . . . just a sylvan solitude. To be sure, the house was not empty—Generals Bertrand, Gourgaud, Montholon and the two brothers Generals Lallemand were present daily, along with his chamberlain, the Comte de Las Cases, and his equerry, Baron de Montaran[33]—in addition to four young ordnance officers, some pages and ADCs. When not discussing the most recent war bulletins and their plans for leaving the country, everyone's major preoccupation was with a reported royalist plot involving some five hundred troopers to kidnap Napoleon, just as he had the Duc d'Enghien.

Hortense, for one, found the tension unbearable—"We were continuously on the alert," she acknowledged.[34] But then everyone was anxious, except Napoleon, it seemed, who appeared totally indifferent to everything, including his own safety. Thirty dragoons of the Imperial Guard were picketed around the grounds of the house, though several of them were still suffering from wounds at Waterloo and most were inadequately armed. In addition, as many as three hundred more Imperial Guards, grenadiers and chasseurs remained in barracks in nearby Rueil, while outside dozens of gendarmes circulated round the walls of the estate.[35]

Nor had tension within the mansion diminished with the arrival of General Beker late on 25 June with orders from War Minister Davout to "exercise the most active surveillance in order that His Majesty does not leave la Malmaison, and to prevent any attempt against his person. You will guard all avenues on all sides leading to la Malmaison,"[36] reminding him that "the interests of the country require that the evil-doers [i.e. Bonapartists] be prevented from using his name to cause uprisings in the country."[37] These were of course the very reasons why Fouché had wanted Napoleon to quit the capital in the first place. It was evident to one and all that he was no longer a free man. "Who would have ever thought that I would see the Emperor of the French held prisoner at Malmaison!" Hortense exclaimed in dismay.[38]

In fact, from the outset the one thing Fouché, who had skillfully jockeyed himself into the position as president of the provisional executive commission of five* ruling France, wanted desperately was to be rid of Napoleon Bonaparte altogether. Indeed, no sooner had the Emperor arrived at Malmaison than Fouché bluntly asked him to leave, and proceed instead to the Channel and sail from France. Davout for his part, in what can only be described as a rage, went so far as to threaten to

*The members included Fouché, Carnot, Caulaincourt, Grenier and Quinette.

arrest Napoleon personally if he did not leave forthwith.[39] He had lost the war; he had abdicated; he had made his decision. Normal life in France could not resume until he had left the country, permanently. Jackals snapping at his heels did not unduly dismay Napoleon, however, who wrote on the twenty-fifth and then again the following day when he received no reply, that he would not leave la Malmaison just to become a prisoner elsewhere, probably in some Channel fortress while awaiting the necessary British safe-conduct passes and appropriate passports to materialize.

Although various refuges had been considered for Napoleon by his friends—including England, Russia and Austria—all had been finally rejected in favor of America, though this ultimate choice was hardly to Fleury's liking. "What will you do there?" he asked. Napoleon, apparently having forgotten his plans of exploration, replied: "They will give me some land, or I shall buy some, and we will cultivate it. . . . I shall live on the products of my fields and flocks." "That is all very well and good, Sire, but do you really believe that the English will let you cultivate your fields in peace?" Fleury persisted. If that did not work out, Napoleon said, there were other havens available. "I will go to Mexico . . . I will go to Buenos Aires, or to California, or if worse comes to worst, I will travel from sea to sea until I find a sanctuary against the evil and persecution of man."[40] He had not even left Malmaison and he already had the haunted mentality of the fugitive. But first things first, and before he could even leave the house, he had to have the American passports as well as the safe-conduct passes from the Duke of Wellington.[41] In addition he demanded that two French warships be put at his disposal, for as he put it, he had no intention of finding himself a "prisoner in the Tower of London."[42]

Naval Minister Denis Decrès quickly acceded to his request, ordering two frigates near Rochefort, *La Saale* and *La Méduse*, to prepare provisions and accommodations for the Emperor's journey to the "Nouveau Continent." But awaiting the British safe-conduct passes to permit him to sail was another story. When asked, Wellington informed Fouché that he had no authority to issue them. A variety of other approaches were then made, though apparently his friends were unaware of the extent of British hostility. ("We wish that the King of France would hang or shoot Bonaparte, as the best termination of the business," Prime Minister Lord Liverpool was even now confiding to Lord Castlereagh.[43]) One such approach included Lucien Bonaparte's offer to go to London personally to obtain the necessary documents from Lord Liverpool's government, to which Napoleon gave his approval. But the Lucien of 1815 had not changed one whit from the Lucien of 1799, and on reaching Boulogne, instead of crossing to England, he sailed for Italy, where he was promptly imprisoned. As for Jérôme, who had also pledged to go into exile in America with Napoleon, he instead bolted to Germany and the protection of his wife's family in Württemberg. The bounding Bonapartes were back in form; only the faithful Joseph remained by Napoleon's side. Meanwhile, Fouché applied more pressure, ordering his two secretaries, Fleury de Chaboulon and Baron Fain, away from Napoleon, thereby reducing his entourage to Bassano (Maret), LaValette, Flahaut, Gourgaud, Montholon, Las Cases and Bertrand.[44]

But there were other matters to be seen to now that Napoleon knew he would be shortly leaving France. Before departing from the Elysée, he had contacted his old banker, Jacques Laffitte, to arrange for supplementary funds to cover his immediate travel expenses, as well as for the investment of nearly six million francs.[45] There were also personal effects to be seen to: Fouché personally authorized Napoleon to take two traveling carriages from the Tuileries, as well as sheets, towels, clothes, silver service for a dozen persons, his *"Quartiers Généraux"* china, and an additional 100,000 francs for travel expenses to America, while Barbier, his librarian, was to select four hundred volumes from the Rambouillet library and remove all the books from the Trianon. Nor did his valet, Marchand, forget such items as the marble bust of Napoleon's son and several small paintings by Isabey of his son and Marie-Louise, as well as a small bronze bust of Napoleon.[46] While packing the necessary papers and maps he needed, Napoleon also included a small flacon of red fluid he had Marchand attach to his lower left braces, the poison he would take if events required it.

Given his house arrest, Napoleon's leave-taking of his troops had to be done in the form of a proclamation in which he assured them that he "will follow your steps, even in my absence, and I carry with me the happy certainty that it [the Army] will prove itself by providing the eminent services the country expects of it." And although "you and I have been calumniated by men unworthy of appreciating our accomplishments" because of the "mark of attachment you have shown for me. . . . [Nevertheless] Soldiers! A little more work yet and the [Allied] Coalition will be broken by you. Save the Honor and independence of the French people. Remain to the very end the soldiers I have known for twenty years and you will be invincible."[47] And he did indeed follow their footsteps closely as a dozen colored pins were daily moved on the map in his study, indicating the approach of British, Prussian and Austrian troops.[48]

Although life at la Malmaison seemed deceptively quiet, the long queue of carriages parked just outside the green and gold wrought-iron gates of the estate belied that. In fact Napoleon's brothers, Joseph in particular, LaValette, Bassano, Flahaut, La Bédoyère, General Caffarelli, Monsieur Pogg and the Duc de Rovigo were all in regular attendance in the south wing of the house Hortense had put at his disposal.

False but crude rumours circulating in the Faubourgs St. Honoré and St. Germain about Hortense, regarding her role in plotting for Napoleon's return from Elba, not to mention her personal relations with her step-father, had led to her ostracism and isolation from most society. Nevertheless, the Duchesse de Saint-Leu, as ex-Queen Hortense now called herself, had several visits by loyal friends, in particular by the Comtesses Bertrand, de Montholon and Caffarelli, as well as by the Comtesse Regnault and the Duchesses de Rovigo and de Bassano. In addition three of her ladies-in-waiting also shared her north wing of the house, where friends were received in the the long "petite galérie" (or music room).

Since Napoleon's divorce the brothers Bonaparte—Joseph, Lucien and Jérôme—and Madame Mère, who now also visited la Malmaison, maintained little more than formal relations with Hortense, that is, when they simply did not cold-shoulder her altogether. She had sought legal custody of her two sons from her husband Louis, and on 10th June (1815) Napoleon had finally authorized that legal separation,[49] which did nothing to enhance her already frigid relations with the Bonaparte clan. Nevertheless they all met formally at dinner in the neo-classical dining room as a phalanx of marble statues looked down upon them, after which Napoleon generally retired next door to his conference room or to his study with Bassano, LaValette or Joseph, leaving the ladies and other officers to a more convivial time with music, cards and conversation chez Hortense at the other end of the house.

Joseph Fouché pushed through the Decree of 26 June, Article Five of which forbade French warships to sail with Napoleon without the British safe-conduct passes mentioned earlier, and Admiral Decrès tried on more than one occasion to have it rescinded to permit Napoleon to leave France as quickly as possible. Finally, late on the twenty-eighth, with news of the Prussian armies encircling Paris, Fouché finally consented.[50] Fouché clearly felt that Napoleon's continued presence was a threat to him and his ruling clique, as well as an obstacle to concluding an armistice. Napoleon had overthrown the legal government of France on two previous occasions[51] and was certainly capable of doing so again aided by thousands of discontented Bonapartists swelling the capital.[52]

And then everything changed as the clatter of horses and the crunch of carriage wheels on the gravel drive, attended by the sharp challenge of sentries, suddenly broke the stillness outside la Malmaison just after three o'clock in the morning of the twenty-ninth. Moments later, Napoleon was awakened by his valet with news that the Duc Decrès and Comte Boulay de la Meurthe were downstairs with an urgent message for him. Descending the small staircase leading to the ground floor and his study, he was informed by Decrès that the Prussian army was approaching Rueil and that it was imperative that Napoleon leave now to avoid capture.[53] And although Napoleon then gave instructions for everyone to prepare to leave later in the day, he personally was in no hurry to do so himself, to the consternation of a much-agitated Hortense. More than once thereafter he was reminded of the urgency of the hour, and although sending some of his young officers down to the Seine to survey the situation vis-à-vis the Prussians, he continued to postpone his departure. He simply did not like being pushed by anyone, whether it was Fouché and his five-man commission, or the enemy. But of course he also dreaded leaving France, knowing there was little chance of his ever returning.

Later that morning, when French infantry regiments passing along the highway adjacent to la Malmaison cheered him with a noisy *"Vive l'Empereur!"*, Napoleon impetuously asked General Beker to go to Paris to obtain the Commission's permission for him to rejoin the army and repulse the enemy. "Explain to them that I have no intention of seizing power, that I simply want to fight the enemy, crush them and by gaining a victory, force them to negotiate with us on more favorable terms. After that, I shall continue on my way. Go now, General, I am counting on you,"[54] and handed him a note to present to Fouché:

> In abdicating public power, I have not renounced the most noble right of the citizen, the right to defend my country.
>
> The approach of our enemies to the capital leaves no more doubt as to their intentions and bad faith.
>
> Under these grave circumstances, I offer my services as a general, still considering myself the *premier soldat de la patrie.*[55]

Carnot was one member of the Executive Commission ready to endorse Napoleon's offer, believing him to be the only man in France capable of repulsing the Allies. Fouché, on the other hand, did not appreciate Bonaparte's noble gesture—"Is he making fun of us? . . . [56] That man is out of his mind no doubt. Does he want to drag us all down with him?"[57] Napoleon, he said, was acting "as if a sense of his own fatal position had now made him willing to plunge the country into the abyss with him."[58] Having no intention of encouraging or joining him, Fouché reminded his colleagues that it was an armistice they sought, not battle, and ordered a reproved and chastened General Beker immediately back to la Malmaison, where he found Napoleon awaiting him in his green Grenadiers uniform, eager to rejoin the French Army. But one look at Beker's expression disabused him of such action.

Once again descending from his small bedroom, a resigned Napoleon reappeared shortly thereafter in bourgeois attire and a gray dress coat,[59] ready once again to depart for the coast, as Hortense quietly handed him a 200,000-franc diamond necklace he had given her previously as a gift.[60] He would need it, she said, as three carriages appeared on the opposite side of the house of the Cour d'Honneur, where Napoleon's faithful Imperial Guardsmen, officers and friends were waiting to bid him adieu and God's speed, but whom the ex-Emperor had not the courage to face. He would go to America, he told Hortense, where "those who bore his name could join him," including his illegitimate nine-year-old son by Eléonore Dennuelle de la Plagine,[61] who had visited him here the day before. Now he looked up one last time. "How beautiful Malmaison is, isn't it, Hortense? It would be wonderful to be able to stay here," he had told her earlier,[62] but now it was too late as he entered the unmarked calèche with his brother Joseph and General Beker; Messrs. Gourgaud, de Montholon and de Las Cases mounting a second carriage; his staff and younger officers settling in the third one. A second group of carriages with Madame de Montholon, the Comtesse de Las Cases and her son and others took a different route. As the bridge over the river at Châtou had already been blown up by French troops anticipating a Prussian attack and the main Neuilly bridge to the capital barricaded by government troops, Napoleon's cortège instead headed for Saint-Cloud and Rambouillet, thence on to Tours, Poitiers and Niort,[63] where Joseph, who had left them earlier, en route, rejoined them on 2 July.[64]

On reaching the Channel port of Rochefort on the third, Napoleon sent the Duc de Rovigo to exchange 100,000 francs in notes for gold, which Marchand then sewed into a dozen buckskin belts. Here he learned that Fouché had reneged on his promise to let him have the books from the Rambouillet library.[65] It was a small but telling sign as to what to expect from him.

Although delegations of Rochefort townsmen and troops begged Napoleon not to abandon them, he dismissed them impatiently, explaining that they and their representatives had rejected his offer of help in the Chambers. Meanwhile the news from Paris was bad, where on 7 July Prussian troops entered the capital, confirmed the same day by the special naval telegraph link between Rochefort and the capital. Nor was the situation much better here where the British ship-of-the-line, the 74-gun *Bellerophon*, under the command of Captain Maitland, was at anchor nearby, keeping London informed of every step Napoleon was taking.

On 8 July the imperial party, told that the two frigates were ready for them, proceeded to Fouras opposite the Ile d'Aix and at 10 P.M. were rowed out to the frigate *La Saale*, where Captain Philibert gave Napoleon "a correct" if cool reception.[66]

In fact, both Philibert and Captain Poncé of the sister ship, *La Méduse*, had received long, precise and "Very Secret" instructions from Naval Minister Decrès several days earlier[67] informing them that "the two frigates are to carry him who was formerly our Emperor to the United States of America. . . . Napoleon is traveling incognito" Decrès continued, and "the greatest secrecy must be maintained. . . . Once [he is aboard] the frigates must put to sea within twenty-four hours at the latest, the winds permitting and if not prevented from doing so by enemy cruisers." They were to sail "as quickly as possible . . . landing Napoleon and his suite, either at Philadelphia or at Boston, or at such other port of the United States as would be most promptly and easily reached." If en route they were involved in hostile action, "the frigate not carrying Napoleon, will sacrifice itself by holding off the enemy, in order to give the other one with him on board the opportunity of escaping. . . . I remind the captains of their duties as well as their discretion regarding anything else that might not have been foreseen by the present orders. . . . The commanders of the frigates, the officers and their crews, are commended to treat his person with all the courtesy and respect due his position and the crown that he wore. Aboard ship the fullest honors will be accorded him. . . . He will use the interior of the frigates for his lodgings, as he deems fit. . . . His dinner table and his domestic arrangements will be executed according to his orders." And finally Decrès reminded them "that the person of Napoleon has been placed under the safekeeping and the loyalty of the French people, his immediate safety specially entrusted to the captains of the *Saale* and the *Méduse*. . . ." Decrès, a tough naval officer, was only too aware of all he personally owed this Napoleon Bonaparte, who had raised him in his youth from an obscure rear-admiral to the Naval Ministry and War Cabinet, the title of Duke and great wealth. Unlike Davout, who had now already written off Napoleon completely—indeed, ready to imprison him if necessary—Decrès was bent on protecting him in his hour of distress.

But the *Saale* did not sail within the prescribed twenty-four hours and Napoleon found her captain less than forthcoming. The *Bellerophon* blocked the way, Philibert contended, and thus the ninth passed, and the tenth and the eleventh with the frigate still at anchor. Rovigo and Las Cases were sent several times to fetch the necessary passes ensuring them a safe passage to the United States, one unmolested by the British, but returned empty-handed. Meanwhile the Emperor's horses, carriages, and large items from Paris began arriving, but finding insufficient transport laid on, Napoleon ordered some items—including his horses—to be sold then and there. After angry words with the captain of the *Saale*, who refused to quit his anchorage, Napoleon finally left the vessel in a huff on the twelfth of July and installed himself on the Ile d'Aix.

The next day Joseph suggested that he, posing as the Emperor, give himself up to the English, thereby permitting Napoleon time in which to escape, but Napoleon rejected his scheme. Some young naval officers suggested that the Emperor escape with them on board a small coastal freighter, but again the proposal was declined, and finally in despair, an American brig, the *Commerce*, was chartered and boarded by Napoleon, Bertrand, Rovigo and the others. And while all was being made ready to put to sea, Las Cases and General Lallemand were again sent to the *Bellerophon* to confer—unsuccessfully as it turned out—with Captain Frederick Maitland about safe-conduct passes.[68] Nevertheless, Maitland, acting in a friendly manner, indicated that the Admiralty and Lord Liverpool's government had authorized him to receive Napoleon and his party on board his warship and bring them to England, if they so wished. Upon returning to Napoleon a *conseil de guerre* was held to consider the situation. The Comte de Las Cases, the Duc de Rovigo and General Bertrand all urged Napoleon to accept the British offer, despite the lack of safe-conduct passes, while Generals Lallemand, Montholon and Gourgaud feared a trap.

But after a fortnight of travel, tension and uncertainty a weary Napoleon had had enough, and trusting Maitland as "an English gentleman" told his Grand Marshal of his decision. "Bertrand, it is not without some danger, in putting myself in the enemy's hands, but it is better to risk confiding oneself to their honor than to be handed over to them as de jure prisoners."[69] He then addressed a formal letter to the Prince Regent informing him of his decision:

> Royal Highness, exposed to the factions which divide my country and to the enmity of most of the great European powers,

I have concluded my political career. Like Themistocles [before the Persians] I come to take my place before the hearth of the British people. I place myself under the protection of their laws, which I now claim of Your Royal Highness, as that of the most powerful, most consistent and most generous of my enemies.[70]

At six o'clock the following morning, Saturday, 15 July, Napoleon prepared to board the *Bellerophon*, no doubt ignorant of this warship's brilliant role in the great French defeat at Trafalgar on 21 October 1805, when its captain, John Cooke, was killed, along with one hundred fifty of its officers and crew.[71] Before transferring from the French brig, *l'Epervier*, General Beker asked if he would be allowed to accompany him to the *Bellerophon*, to which Napoleon replied: "Do nothing of the kind. It would soon be said that you handed me over to the English." The general, deeply moved, with tears in his eyes, kissed the Emperor's hand as he took his final leave—*"Sire, soyez plus heureux que nous."*[72] ("Sire, I hope you will be happier than us.")

Within a few hours, under a full press of sail, the *Bellerophon* was far out to sea, Napoleon watching—for the last time—as the shores of France slipped forever from his sight and his life.

That same fifteenth of July, before having received the Admiralty dispatch regarding the events on the *Bellerophon*, writing from his London residence at Fife House, Prime Minister Lord Liverpool was instructing Foreign Secretary Viscount Castlereagh:

I am desirous of apprising you of our sentiments respecting Bonaparte. If you should succeed in getting possession of his person, and the King of France does not feel sufficiently strong to bring him to justice as a rebel, we are ready to take upon ourselves the custody of his person, on the part of the Allied Powers; and, indeed, we should think it better that he should be assigned to us than to any other member of the Confederacy . . . [and] that the discretion [of his punishment] should be vested entirely in ourselves, and that we should be at liberty to fix the place of his confinement.

Although Malta, Gibraltar and Great Britain were considered for his ultimate incarceration, the Prime Minister concluded that "the best place of custody would be at a distance from Europe, and that the Cape of Good Hope or Saint-Helena would be the most proper stations for that purpose."[73]

Four days later a small item appeared on page three of the Parisian newspaper *La Quotidienne*, reporting to the capital:

> The last remaining subject of disquiet for Europe has just disappeared: Buonaparte is held prisoner. The man who banished peace and tranquility from the world for so many years has finally been condemned to perpetual rest. That same energy which upset and ravaged the universe is now *enchainée à jamais*.[74]

Unlike the campaign of 1814, the five-man Executive Commission representing the French government and headed by Joseph Fouché, announced that it wanted to cease fighting immediately and sign an armistice. On Friday, 23 June, its first set of *"Instructions pour Messieurs les Plénipotentiaires de la Commission du gouvernement auprès des Puissances alliées"* stated that their primary objective was "to save the country" and this involved "two basic questions, national independence and maintaining the integrity of our national frontiers."[75] The abdication of Napoleon, Fouché's instructions argued, "automatically returns the nation to a position of peace with the other Powers, since their only aim had been to remove him." On the other hand, this initial French negotiating team—including La Fayette, D'Argenson, General Sébastiani, Comte de Pontécoulant, Comte de La Foret and Benjamin Constant[76]—informed the Allies that they for their part must "renounce without reservation any plans to again place the French Government under the Bourbon family," whom Fouché referred to as "strangers to our national values (*moeurs*)." Instead, Napoleon having abdicated, "his rights and claims devolve upon his son. The Powers cannot tamper with this principle of heredity established by our constitutions, without overthrowing our very independence." Not only must the national independence of France be respected and its boundaries be left intact, but "there remains another sacred duty which France must observe—that is to stipulate the safety and inviolability of the Emperor Napoleon once he has left his territory." What is more, "the choice of place to which the Emperor will retire shall be subject to discussion, and the place fixed for his residence be found acceptable to the Emperor himself."[77]

The document and its demands were as arrogant as they were unrealistic and were quickly rejected at the first meeting with the Prussians on Monday, 26 June. When on the twenty-seventh the next set of instructions were drawn up by Fouché's committee, the tone and aims were already much more amenable, no longer insisting on the rights of Napoleon II or his place in a future government. "As regards the question of form of government to be taken by France, provisionally, our negotiators will limit themselves to discussing only those matters proposed to them."[78] Louis XVIII and the Bourbons would not be welcomed back to France, however. "It is perfectly clear, therefore, that it is not the re-establishment of that family that the French nation desires" and they were confident that "the noble character of the Duke of Wellington" would not "want to force France to submit to a government which is hostile to the wishes of the great majority of the people," said Caulain-court's replacement at the Foreign Ministry, Bignon, and fully supported by the Executive Commission.[79] As Fouché reminded the Allies, "force can be used to place him [Louis XVIII] back on the throne, but will be unable to maintain him there very long."[80] Nevertheless, Fouché later confessed that this whole ploy of claiming to support the Bonaparte family and strongly opposing the Bourbons was a lie. "The necessity of the moment required that I pretend [je feignis] to plead the cause of Napoleon II . . . in order to deceive the vigilance of the parties involved." In reality, he claimed, "I already regarded the question as having been irrevocably settled in favor of the Bourbons"[81]—whereas in fact he was supporting neither the cause of Napoleon II nor of Louis XVIII at this time, but rather, that of the Duc d'Orléans.

Meanwhile, even as Napoleon was leaving Malmaison on Thursday, 29 June, the military situation was deteriorating quickly as the Allies' 110,000 troops were surrounding Paris.[82] The Prussian Ist Corps was already at Aulnay, their IVth Corps at Bourguet and IIIrd Corps at Dammartin and marching southwesterly towards Saint-Germain, while Wellington's main force at Saint-Martin and Lagneux was moving on Louvres,[83] even as Grouchy's army was reaching the safety of Paris. In the east and south several powerful Austrian armies were also closing in on them, their forces pouring through Germany, the Swiss Alps and Italy. While General Wreda's corps and Archduke Ferdinand were closing in on Nancy, General Rapp at Strasbourg was caught in a pincer movement as he was attacked by Prince von Württemberg from the south and Prince von Hohenzollern from the north. At the same time General Colloredo was advancing on Lecourbe's corps at Belfort. Two more Austrian corps, under Field Marshal von Frimont and General Bubna, were entering Savoy against Marshal Suchet's forces, Frimont attacking Mâcon via

Geneva, and Bubna crossing Mont-Cenis heading for Grenoble and Lyons, while another Austrian force approached Nice and the Var.[84] In the distance, Barclay's great Russian Army was slowly heading for the Rhine. With the collapse of Grenoble on 30 June, the extent of the disaster about to befall the French was becoming apparent to almost everyone, even to the hitherto resolute Davout, though Carnot was as determined as ever to hold on, even if it meant a full-scale siege of Paris.[85]

But by Sunday the second of July, the military situation had deteriorated further, Marshal Suchet having already surrendered in the east to von Frimont, while Paris, almost completely encircled, was about to come under Allied guns, with Wellington's force now at Gonesse, and Blücher's Ist Corps at Meudon, his IVth at Versailles and the IIIrd at Plessis-Piquet.[86]

Despite his many clashes with Napoleon, Davout knew that France still had a fighting chance with him free and at the head of France's armies, but with his abdication, and on the same 29 June as his departure for the coast, Davout, who along with Carnot had always resisted surrender—"must one lost battle decide the fate of a great nation?"[87]—finally wrote to Fouché in his capacity as President of the Executive Commission acknowledging that "there now remains no other means of saving the country, except by concluding an armistice and immediately recognizing Louis XVIII."[88] Three days later, on Saturday the first of July, a full Conseil de Guerre was duly convened at Villette. Although it was agreed that "Paris could hold out for at least twenty days,"[89] it was also acknowledged nevertheless that that feat in itself would lead to no positive results. In fact, under the present circumstances the defense of the capital would be disastrous for the country, Davout felt. Indeed, "dismemberment of France, the pillage and devastation of the capital would perhaps be the fruit of the rash defense which you [Carnot] now propose. . . ."[90] They had no choice but to sue for peace, and Soult, making one of his last public appearances before fleeing to the south, concurred.

When the War Council broke up in the early hours of the second, Fouché hurriedly convened the Executive Commission at the Tuileries. "The discussion was pretty grim, and given the unanimous negative answer by the War Council, the Commission decreed that Paris would not be defended and instead would be handed over to the Allies."[91] It was all over, and the next day, Monday, 3 July, the eighteen articles comprising the armistice, the Convention of Paris, as it was called, were quickly drafted and signed.[92] At six o'clock the following morning, meeting on the Neuilly bridge, the Convention was approved and ratified by all parties, Davout signing for France. On Wednesday the fifth, still in his capacity as President of the temporary Commission, Fouché informed the country:

"Frenchmen," peace was necessary to restore the country: "stand united and put behind us all our ills. The peace of Europe is inseparable from your own. Europe wants your tranquillity and happiness."[93]

If neither eloquent nor moving it was typical of Fouché, and the way had been prepared for the formal peace treaty, the second Treaty of Paris signed on 20 November 1815.[94] This saw France reduced to her boundaries of 1789, ordered to pay war indemnities totaling 700,000,000 francs and made to suffer a large army of occupation.

The reestablishment of peace did not mean the return to national order, however, as the pent-up fury of the hitherto suppressed royalists wreaked revenge, unleashing the "white terror" on Bonapartists and republicans throughout the country: riots, attacks, accusations, murders in Lyons, Uzès, Montpellier, Nîmes, Bordeaux, Toulouse, Marseille and Toulon ensued. And even as Bonapartist commanders and troops attempted to withdraw, the news came of the assassination of Marshal Brune at Avignon on the second of August and of General Ramel a few days later at Toulouse, followed by the great witch-hunt by King Louis's new administration, as hundreds of army officers and government officials were charged with having aided and abetted Napoleon in betraying their lawful ruler. Louis XVIII not only endorsed this unplanned terror but encouraged it. Examples had to be made to discourage any further such attempts in the future.

At nine A.M. on Thursday the seventh of December 1815, Marshal Ney descended the steps of the Luxembourg Palace into the gray wintry light of the vast garden, surrounded by a company of veterans, including troops of the late royalist leader, de La Rochejaquelein. Upon entering the waiting carriage lent by Monsieur Le Grand, with Abbé de Pierre, curé of Saint-Sulpice Church, Ney was surprised to find them driving silently through the palace gardens and not into the street. King Louis, who had returned to Paris on 8 July, had insisted upon the greatest secrecy for this execution, and beyond the barren trees ringing the palace grounds, five thousand National Guardsmen remained ready to spring into action if Bonapartist conspirators attempted to intervene, as rumored, to save the condemned man.

Preceded and followed by two platoons of cavalry, even at this slow pace the procession reached the extreme southern gates within a few minutes. Passing through the immense gates just opposite the Observatory, Ney was ordered down and directed to a position fifty paces to the left, his back turned to a new, partly constructed stone wall. He was by now weary of everything, of the mad happenings since 13 March when he had announced his intention of joining Napoleon on his march to Paris. He was weary of the civil war and acrimony, of the débâcle of the Waterloo campaign, where he had seemed to want so badly to die by leading his cavalry in those astonishing charges against Wellington's army. Nor had it been better or less bitter since his arrest at the Château de Bessonies on 3 August, where he had been betrayed by a disloyal officer, it was said.

He had been then brought to the Conciergerie for a courtmartial, where Marshal Jourdan presided over Ney's seven colleagues-in-arms: Generals Gazan, Claparède and Villalete, and Marshals Augereau, Masséna and Mortier (Moncey having adamantly refused to partake in this abhorrent charade).[95] But they had found a way of escaping their duty on 9 November as Jourdan declared the military court incompetent to try a Peer of France. Ney was instead to appear before the Chamber of Peers.

The trial had finally opened on 21 November, in the austere neoclassical hemicycle where the peers sat, their backs to the wall and inner courtyard of the Luxembourg Palace, facing the accused against a backdrop of statues, columns and of course Napoleon's empty golden throne. There were dozens of soldiers and a couple of sailors among the members present throughout the fortnight of hearings to follow, including four fellow marshals: Kellermann, Pérignon, Sérurier and Victor. It was humiliating for him, an ordeal far worse than the bloody slopes of Mont Saint-Jean, as the charges were read out against "Michel Ney, born at Sarrelouis, in 1769, Marshal, Peer of France, Duc d'Elchingen, Prince of Moskowa, Chevalier de Saint-Louis, Grand-Aigle of the Legion of Honor, Commander of the Ordre du Christ," accusing him of "high treason and an attack against the *sûreté de l'Etat*."[96]

Back on 24 July, King Louis had promulgated his ordinance on this subject, dealing primarily with those who "have betrayed the King before 23 March or who have attacked France and the Government by main force," and followed it shortly thereafter by an initial list of fifty-seven military and political figures to be accused and tried, including nineteen marshals and generals.[97] Marshal Davout for one was outraged, and even more so when he discovered that the top people in Napoleon's Government, including Fouché, Decrès, Caulaincourt and himself, had not even been named. Those army officers now accused "have merely obeyed the orders I gave them in my capacity as War Minister," Davout protested to the King. "Therefore you must replace all their names with mine alone. . . . That is a favor I ask in the best interests of the King and country."[98] But the King was determined to see many heads roll, with the full blessing of Lord Liverpool and the British Government, Lord Liverpool stressing that "a severe example" had to be made "of the conspirators who brought back Bonaparte."[99] Thus Davout's request was denied out of hand. Summoning his highest officers on the first of August, Marshal Davout warned "that those who have had the misfortune to be named on the fatal ordinances should think about their safety. They have not a moment to lose."[100] Later that same day the first warrants were issued as dozens of the highest army officers of the land fled the country or went into hiding, including the unfortunate Ney.

General Lefebvre-Desnoëttes, after cutting off his famous cavalry officer's mustache, was seen disappearing in the guise of a traveling salesman, which General Amiel quickly and successfully imitated. LaValette was last seen escaping from the Conciergerie disguised in his wife's dress. Of all the general officers in the army, General Drouot, the former commander of the Imperial Guard, alone went to Paris to give himself up, while General Vandamme was the sole officer to remain at his post, from which he was dismissed by Davout's successor, Marshal Macdonald.[101] Nor were the majority of the accused to be saved by the traditional French amnesty, as the nineteen marshals and generals were accused of high treason and ordered to stand trial. But of that number only five had the misfortune to be captured, tried and executed, including the twenty-nine-year-old General La Bédoyère (apprehended when visiting his wife before sailing for America), Generals Faucher (brothers), Mouton-Duvernet, and Chartran. Fourteen other generals and politicians were condemned to death in their absence, including Generals Bertrand, Brayer, Clausel, Debelle, d'Erlon, the Lallemand brothers, LaValette, Rovigo (Savary) and Travot. Others, either tried and found guilty or simply accused but not tried, were dismissed from office or banished, including Bassano, Boulay de la Meurthe, Cambacérès, Carnot, Defermont, Fouché, Masséna, Merlin de Douay, Quinette, Regnault de Saint-Jean d'Angély, Soult and Thibaudeau. Ironically, General Cambronne, who had been in on the plot from the beginning to overthrow the King, was acquitted, and Grouchy was declared incompetent to stand trial, though as "guilty" as Ney.[102]

It was for Ney that the great show-trial had been reserved; he was to serve as "the severe example" for the nation as he faced his 150 fellow peers now present. And why was it that Ney was brought to trial, but not his three superior officers? Soult and Davout were not even tried, and Soult, as Louis XVIII's former War Minister, had certainly been one of the greatest traitors in the land. He, however, appeared to have strong political allies. As for the great culprit, Napoleon Bonaparte, the man responsible for ousting and replacing King Louis after bringing down his government in an armed coup, and dragging France—finally at peace with all Europe—into a deadly war that he alone wanted, resulting in civil war throughout France and over 64,000 French casualties on the battlefields of Belgium, he was not even brought to trial.

Thus it was the hapless Ney, one of the most unpopular senior officers in the French army, who had been singled out as Napoleon's surrogate and the nation's scapegoat. Victor de Broglie was one of the few to defend him against the charges brought against him during the trial at the Luxembourg, protesting, "There can be no crime without criminal intent. . . . I can find in the accusations brought against Marshal Ney neither premeditation, nor plan to commit treason," he argued. What then was he guilty of? He had in fact simply been "carried away by his emotions at the last moment, caught up in the whirl of events. There are some events in life which are simply beyond the scope of human justice," de Broglie concluded.[103] But the Chamber of Peers was set on revenge, not justice, as Comte Lynch leaped to his feet like a madman calling for "La guillotine!" seconded by Ney's fellow colleague-in-arms, Marshal Marmont, insisting that "No man could be found guilty with greater justice."[104] It all bode ill for the vote to follow.

Thus, a little before five o'clock in the afternoon on Wednesday, the sixth of December, the votes having been tallied, Ney was found to be

> guilty of having maintained intelligence with Buonaparte in order to second the progress of his arms against French territory on the night of 13–14 March; of having aided him with troops and men; by speeches in public places, broadsheets, posters and printed material, of having directly incited the citizens to fight one another; of having encouraged soldiers to pass over to the enemy [Napoleon]; finally, of having committed treason against the King and State, and of having participated in plots and attacks, whose purpose was to destroy the government, and change the order of succession of the throne.
>
> All crimes foreseen by articles 77, 87, 88, 89, 92, 93, 96, and 102 of the Penal Code, and by the military law of Brumaire V.

> In consequence, in application of the aforesaid articles we do hereby condemn Michel Ney . . . to the penalty [of death] prescribed by these diverse dispositions.

When asked by the President of the Court whether he had anything to say "about the application of the penalty," Ney replied: "Nothing at all, My Lord."[105]

The results had been a foregone conclusion. Of the 150 peers, 5 had abstained from voting, demanding instead an appeal for clemency to the King. Seventeen had called for Ney's deportation to a penal colony, while 122 had demanded the death penalty, including his 4 fellow marshals, Pérignon, Kellermann, Sérurier and Victor; one admiral, Ganteaume; and a bevy of generals, among them Beurnonville, Compans, Dessolles, La Tour-Maubourg, Lauriston, Maison, Monnieur, and Soulès.

Led back to the third-story room in the west wing of the Luxembourg serving as his prison, Ney ate well, and then slept soundly until four o'clock in the morning of Thursday, 7 December, when his wife and two sons and his sister, Madame Gamot, were brought to him. His wife, Aglaé-Louise, fainted on the stone floor and his sister fell to her knees sobbing, when he informed them that he was to be executed by a firing squad a few hours hence. His two sons alone—the eldest eleven years old—stood bewildered, somber and silent. And though his wife then went to the Louvre at 9 A.M. to plead before King Louis for her husband's life, she was informed that he had just sat down to breakfast and could not be disturbed. She waited.

At 9:19 A.M., Comte de Rochechouart, Military Governor of Paris, faced Marshal Ney as he stood in the street before a firing squad of twelve men. Having refused to kneel and be blindfolded, Ney remained smartly at attention in his marshal's uniform. "A man such as I does not get down on his knees," he said loudly and firmly, as a group of curious pedestrians stopped across the street to watch the spectacle. Then covering his chest with his right hand he addressed the firing squad. "Soldiers, straight at the heart!" Ney commanded as the order was given: "*Apprêtez armes!*" and Ney continued, "Frenchmen, I protest against my judgment. My honor . . ." but was interrupted—"*Joue! Feu!*" and he fell to the ground as the traditional drums rolled and the members of the firing squad cried out, "*Vive le roi!*"[106] Of the twelve shots fired, three had shattered the Marshal's face.

In conformity with military regulations, the body remained exposed where it fell on the place of execution for a quarter of an hour.

"Thus came to an end a warrior justly famed for his valor, but who dishonored a heroic life by an act of treason without equal in history," declared the editor of the *Journal des Débats*. "Failing to recognize the King's authority, cowardly putting his life under the orders of the foreigner [Napoleon], are actions so unworthy of a Frenchman, that they silence any commiseration which we might have otherwise felt for him . . . *Voilà donc une grande justice accomplie.*"

And thus concluded what Ney himself had so aptly predicted, "the final act of the Napoléonade."[107]

EPILOGUE

The arrival of H.M.S. *Northumberland* with Napoleon Bonaparte at the tropical island of Saint Helena on 15 October 1815, while thereby ending his long rapacious career, at the same time seemed suddenly to intensify the mystery of the man himself. The questions were then asked: *Who was he? What was he?* But of the hundreds of contemporaries who attempted an explanation, two alone seemed best to understand the complexity of their task. Comte Pozzo di Borgo, who had known him since his childhood in Corsica, described Napoleon as "this creature at once greater than life and so unfathomable, this phenomenon the like of whom shall never be seen again, who was a moral and political universe unto himself. . . . Even yet not understood . . . he is destined to remain obfuscated in a sublime, gigantic shadow. He is a great enigma and almost impossible to explain. Until now his panegyrists have shown themselves inferior to their subject, while his detractors have descended even lower than his worst deeds."[1]

Nevertheless Chateaubriand probably came closer to understanding the many conflicting qualities of Bonaparte than anyone else, when writing after the events of Waterloo.

"The bloody dráma of Europe is concluded, and the great tragedian, who for twenty years has made the earth his theatre, and set the world in tears, has left the stage forever! He lifted the curtain with his sword, and filled the scenes with slaughter. . . . His part was invented by himself, and was terribly unique. Never was there so ambitious, so restless, a spirit; never so daring, so fortunate, a soldier. His aim was universal dominion, and he gazed at it steadfastly with the eye of an eagle and appetite of a vulture.

"He combined within himself all the elements of terror, nerve, malice and intellect: a heart that never trembled, a mind that never wavered from its purpose. The greatness of his plans defied speculation, and the rapidity of their execution outstripped prophecy. Civilized nations were the victims of his arts, and savages could not withstand his warfare. Scepters crumbled in his grasp, and liberty withered in his presence. The Almighty appeared to have entrusted to him the destinies of the globe, and he used them to destroy. He shrouded the sun itself with the clouds of battle, and unveiled the night with his fires. His march reversed the course of nature: the flowers of the spring perished, the fruits of autumn fell; for his path was cold, and cheerless, and desolate, like the political changes which he produced, he was still the same. Ever ambitious, ever inexorable; no compassion assuaged, no remorse deterred, no dangers alarmed him. . . . He proved himself the Attila of the West. . . . He made war before he declared it; and peace was with him a signal for hostilities. His friends were the first whom he assailed, and his allies he selected to plunder. . . . He would have enslaved the land to make the ocean free, and he lacked only the power to enslave both. . . . This bloodstained soldier adorned his throne with the trophies of art, and made Paris the seat of taste as well as power. . . . The weight of the chains which he imposed on France was forgotten in their splendor; it was glorious to follow him, even as a conscript. . . .

"Let us reflect on his enormous abuse of power, on his violated faith, and shameless disregard of all law and justice. . . . Great he unquestionably was, great in the resources of a misguided mind, great in the conception and execution of evil, great in mischief, like the pestilence; great in desolation, like the whirlwind. . . . Awful indeed will be the sentence of history [on his reign]; but when will posterity finally be a disinterested tribunal? When will the time arrive that Europe will have put off mourning his crimes?"[2]

APPENDICES

APPENDIX I

CHRONOLOGY OF EVENTS

1813:

1 December   Declaration of Frankfurt.

1814:

January   Allies invade France.

February–March   Congress of Châtillon. Initial peace negotiations fail.

1 March   Treaty of Chaumont (actually signed on ninth). Twenty-year pact. Great Britain, Russia, Prussia and Austria agree to prosecute war against France with vigor.

25 March   Allied manifesto ordering France to depose Napoleon.

29 March   Empress Marie-Louise and King of Rome flee Paris.

31 March   Napoleon, Ney, Macdonald and Berthier reach Fontainebleau.

Paris capitulates to Allies: Czar Alexander and King Frederick William of Prussia enter French capital.

1 April   French Senate appoints provisional government, headed by Prince Talleyrand.

3 April   Corps Législatif deposes Napoleon.

6 April   Corps Législatif offers crown to Louis XVIII.

6 April	Napoleon signs unconditional abdication of crown.
11 April	Treaty of Fontainebleau concluding abdication of Napoleon: signed by Russia, Prussia, Austria and France.
12 April	Duc d'Angoulême enters Paris.
12–13 April	Napoleon attempts suicide.
19 April	Talleyrand signs Armistice with Allies.
24 April	Louis XVIII lands at Boulogne.
3 May	Louis XVIII enters Paris.
4 May	Napoleon lands at Elba.
30 May	Treaty of Paris signed, bringing peace to Europe.
September	Congress of Vienna convenes.

1815:

26 February	Napoleon escapes from Elba.
1 March	Napoleon lands at Golfe Juan.
13 March	Allied Declaration outlawing Napoleon.
20 March	Napoleon enters Paris.
25 March	Allies confirm coalition to prosecute war against Napoleon.
April	Napoleon announces Additional Act.
1 June	Champ de Mai ceremony.
12 June	Napoleon leaves Paris to join Armée du Nord.
16 June	Battles of Ligny and Quatre Bras.
18 June	Battle of Waterloo.
21 June	Napoleon returns to Paris.
22 June	Combined Chambers demand Napoleon's abdication. Napoleon abdicates in favor of Napoleon II.
25 June	Napoleon moves from Elysée to Malmaison.
29 June	Napoleon leaves Malmaison for Rochefort.
8 July	Louis XVIII reenters Paris.
15 July	Napoleon boards H.M.S. *Bellerophon* and sails for Plymouth.
24 July	Louis XVIII promulgates ordinances against traitors.
15 October	H.M.S. *Northumberland* lands Napoleon on Saint Helena.
November	Second Treaty of Paris, war concluded.
21 November–6 December	Trial of Marshal Ney.
7 December	Execution of Marshal Ney.

APPENDIX II

THE THIRTY-TWO MILITARY DIVISIONS OF METROPOLITAN FRANCE AND CONQUERED TERRITORIES

1st   division: Paris
2nd division: Mézières
3rd   division: Metz
4th   division: Nancy
5th   division: Strasbourg
6th   division: Besançon
7th   division: Grenoble
8th   division: Toulon
9th   division: Montpellier
10th division: Toulouse
11th division: Bordeaux
12th division: Nantes
13th division: Rennes
14th division: Caen
15th division: Rouen
16th division: Lille
17th division: Amsterdam
18th division: Dijon
19th division: Lyons
20th division: Périgueux
21st division: Bourges
22nd division: Tours
23rd division: Bastia
24th division: Bruxelles
25th division: Wesel
26th division: Mayence
27th division: Turin
28th division: Genoa
29th division: Florence
30th division: Rome
31st division: Groningue
32nd division: Hambourg

APPENDIX III

NAPOLEON'S ABDICATION DECLARATION, 22 JUNE 1815
"DECLARATION AU PEUPLE FRANCAIS"

"En commençant la guerre, pour soutenir l'indépendance nationale, je comptais sur la réunion de tous les efforts, de toutes les volontés, et le concours de toutes les autorités nationales. J'étais fondé à en espérer le succès, et j'avais bravé toutes les déclarations des puissances contre moi.

"Les circonstances me paraissent changées; je m'offre en sacrifice à la haine des ennemis de la France: puissent-ils être sincères dans leurs déclarations, et n'en avoir voulu réellement qu'à ma personne. Ma vie politique est terminée; et je proclame mon fils sous le titre de Napoléon II, Empereur des Français.

"Les ministres actuels formeront provisoirement le conseil de gouvernment. L'intérêt que je porte à mon fils m'engage à inviter les Chambres à organiser, sans délai, la régence par une loi.

"Unissez-vous tous, pour le salut public, et pour rester une nation indépendante.

NAPOLÉON."

"Au palais de l'Elysée,
ce 22 juin 1815."

APPENDIX IV

COMMAND STRUCTURE OF FRENCH AND ALLIED ARMIES AT WATERLOO

A. FRENCH IMPERIAL COMMAND
EMPEROR NAPOLÉON.

AIDES-DE-CAMP TO NAPOLEON:

1. Général de Division Lebrun, Duc de Plaisance
2. Général de Division Comte Drouot
3. Général de Division Comte Flahaut de la Billarderie
4. Général de Division Comte Dejean
5. Général de Brigade Baron Bernard
6. Général de Brigade Comte de La Bédoyère
7. Général de Brigade Baron Bussy
8. Général de Brigade Baron Letort (killed at Waterloo)

SENIOR FIELD COMMANDERS:

Marshal Michel Ney, Prince of Moskowa
Marshal Emmanuel de Grouchy

CHIEF OF STAFF FOR THE ARMY:

Marshal, Duc de Dalmatie, Jean de Dieu Soult

CHIEF OF THE GENERAL STAFF:

Général de Division Comte Bailly de Monthion (wounded at Waterloo)

DEPUTY CHIEFS OF THE GENERAL STAFF:

1. Général de Brigade Baron Gressot
2. Général de Brigade Baron Couture
3. Général de Brigade Lebel

SENIOR STAFF OFFICERS:

1. Adjudant-commandant Baron Michel
2. Adjudant-commandant Baron Stoffel
3. Adjudant-commandant Babut
4. Adjudant-commandant d'Hincourt
5. Adjudant-commandant Petiet

COMMANDER IN CHIEF OF ARTILLERY FOR THE ARMY:

Général de Division Comte Ruty.

COMMANDER IN CHIEF OF ENGINEERS FOR THE ARMY:

Général de Division Baron Rogniat

GENERAL ADMINISTRATION:

Comte Daru, Intendant General

IMPERIAL WAR CABINET:

Hugues Maret, Duc de Bassano

PERSONAL SECRETARIES TO HIS MAJESTY:

Baron Fain
Fleury de Chaboulon

CHAMBERLAIN TO NAPOLEON:

Vicomte Turenne

CORPS COMMANDERS:

I Corps, Général de Division Drouet Comte d'Erlon
II Corps, Général de Division Comte Reille
III Corps, Général de Division Comte Vandamme
IV Corps, Général de Division Comte Gérard
IV Reserve Cavalry Corps, Général de Division Comte Milhaud
Imperial Guard, Général de Division Comte Drouot
      (replacing Marshal Mortier, Duc de Treviso)
VI Corps, Général de Division Mouton, Comte de Lobau

B. ANGLO-ALLIED ARMY

COMMANDER IN CHIEF:

Field Marshal Arthur, Duke of Wellington, K.G., G.C.B.

MILITARY SECRETARY TO THE FIELD MARSHAL:

Lt. Colonel Lord Fitzroy Somerset (wounded at Waterloo)

AIDES-DE-CAMP TO THE FIELD MARSHAL:

1. Lt. Colonel J. Fremantle
2. Lt. Colonel C. F. Canning (killed at Waterloo)
3. Hon. Sir Alexander Gordon, K. C. B. (killed at Waterloo)
4. Hereditary Prince of Nassau-Usingen
5. Major Hon. Henry Percy
6. Captain Lord Arthur Hill
7. Lieutenant Hon. George Cathcart

CHIEF OF STAFF FOR THE ARMY:

Colonel Sir William Howe de Lancey, K.C.B. (killed at Waterloo)

COMMANDER IN CHIEF OF THE ROYAL ARTILLERY:

Colonel Sir George Adam Wood

COMMANDER IN CHIEF OF ROYAL ENGINEERS:

Lt. Colonel James Carmichael Smyth

PRUSSIAN ATTACHÉ AT BRITISH HEADQUARTERS:

Major General von Müffling

ADJUTANT-GENERAL STAFF, QUARTERMASTER-GENERAL STAFF:

CORPS COMMANDERS:

I Army Corps, William, H.R.H., the Prince of Orange (wounded)
II Army Corps, Lieutenant General Lord Hill, G.C.B.
Army Reserve, under Wellington's direction
Cavalry Corps, Lieutenant-General, the Earl of Uxbridge, G.C.B.
N.B. Of Wellington's total general staff, 12 officers were killed, 46 wounded, and 3 missing.

C. PRUSSIAN ARMY

COMMANDER IN CHIEF:

Field Marshal Prince Blücher von Wahlstadt

QUARTERMASTER-GENERAL AND CHIEF OF STAFF FOR THE ARMY:

Lieutenant General Count von Gneisenau

AIDES-DE-CAMP TO THE FIELD MARSHAL:

1. Major Huser
2. Captain of Cavalry von Jasmund
3. Captain von Stosch
4. 1st Lieutenant Rothe

CHIEF OF THE GENERAL STAFF:

Major General K. von Grolmann

SENIOR STAFF OFFICERS:

1. Colonel von Pfuel
2. Colonel von Thile
3. Lt. Colonel von Witzleben
4. Major von Lützow
5. Captain von Vigny

COMMANDER IN CHIEF OF ARTILLERY:

General of Infantry Prince August of Prussia

CORPS COMMANDERS:

I Corps, Lieutenant General von Ziethen

II Corps, Major General von Pirch

III Corps, Lieutenant General von Thielemann (Colonel von Clausewitz serving as his Chief of Staff)

IV Corps, General of Infantry, Graf Bülow von Dennewitz

APPENDIX V

NAPOLEON'S MARCH ON PARIS, 1–20 MARCH 1815

 1 March, Lands at Golfe Juan, Cannes

 2 At Grasse

 3 Reaches Barrême

 4 Dines at Digne, sleeps at Malijai

 5 Passes night at Gap

 6 Passes night at Corps

 7 Laffrey, enters Grenoble, joined by de La Bédoyère

 8 Grenoble

 9 Passes night at Bourgoin

10–12 Lyons

13 Leaves Lyons, night at Mâcon

14 Night at Chalon

15 Spends night at Autun

16 At Avallon

17–18 Auxerre, joined by Ney

19 Passes night at Pont-sur-Yonne

20 Reaches Fontainebleau in morning, at Tuileries by 9 P.M.

BIBLIOGRAPHY

A. BOOKS

Alleaume, Charles, "Les Cent Jours dans le Var," Société d'Etudes Scientifiques et Archéologiques de Draguignan, *Mémoires*, vol. 49 (Draguignan: Oliver Joulian, 1938).

Arbuthnot, Harriet Fane, *The Journal of Mrs. Arbuthnot, 1820–1832* (London: Macmillan, 1950), vol. I.

Audiffret-Pasquier, Etienne Denis, Duc d', *Histoire de mon temps. Mémoires du Chancelier Pasquier, duc d'Audiffret-Pasquier* (Paris: Plon, 1894), six vols, see vol. III (1814–1815).

Bac, Ferdinand, *Le Secret de Talleyrand* (Paris: Hachette, 1933).

Bartel, Paul, *Napoléon à l'île d'Elbe* (Paris: Perrin, 1950).

Bartlett, C.J., *Castlereagh* (London: Goldsmith College, 1967).

Beauharnais, Eugène de, *Mémoires et correspondance politique et militaire du prince Eugène* (Paris: Lévy, 1858–60), 10 vols.

Beauharnais, Hortense de, *Mémoires de la Reine Hortense* (Paris: Plon, 1927), vol. II.

Beker-Martha, *Le Général Beker* (Paris: Didier, 1876), which includes, "Relation de la mission du Lieutenant-Général Beker auprès de l'Empereur."

Bertier de Sauvigny, G., *La Restauration* (Paris: Flammarion, 1955).

Bertrand, Henri Gatien, *Cahiers de Sainte-Hélène* (Paris: Albin Michel, 1949–50), 3 vols.

Boigne, Eléonore Adèle, Comtesse de, *Mémoires de la Comtesse de Boigne* (Paris: Mercure de France, 1987), 2 vols.

Bonaparte, Jérôme, *Mémoires et correspondance du roi Jérôme et de la reine Catherine* (Paris: Dentu, 1861–66), 7 vols.

Bonaparte, Joseph, *Mémoires et correspondance politique et militaire du roi Joseph* (Paris: Perrotin, 1853–54), 10 vols.

Bonaparte, Lucien, *Mémoires secrètes sur la vie privée, politique et littéraire de Lucien Bonaparte, prince de Canino* (Paris: Delaunay, 1818).

Bonaparte, Napoléon, *Correspondance de Napoléon* (Paris: Imprimérie Impériale, 1869), vols. XXVIII, XXXI (out of 32 total).

Bourrienne, Louis Antoine Fauvelet de, *Mémoires sur Napoléon, le Directoire, le Consulat, Empire et la Restauration* (Paris: Ladvocat, 1829–30), 10 vols.

Bowden, Scott, *Armies at Waterloo. A Detailed Analysis of the Armies that Fought History's Greatest Battle* (Arlington, Texas: Empire Games Press, 1983).

Brett-James, Antony, *Wellington at War, 1794–1815. A Selection of His Wartime Letters* (London: Macmillan, 1964).

————. *The Hundred Days, Napoleon's Last Campaign from Eye-Witness Accounts* (London: Macmillan, 1964).

Camon, Hubert, *La Guerre Napoléonienne: Batailles* (Paris: Chapelot, 1910).

Campbell, Neil, *Chronique des événements de 1814 et 1815* (Paris: Pichot, 1873).

Campbell, Neil, *Napoleon at Fontainebleau and Elba* (London: J. Murray, 1869).

Canuel, Simon, *Mémoires sur la guerre de Vendée en 1815* (Paris: Dentu, 1817).

Carnot, Lazare-Nicolas, *Mémoires historiques et militaires* (Paris: Baudouin, 1824).

————. *Révolution et Mathématique* (Paris: L'Herne, 1984).

Castlereagh, Robert Stewart, Viscount, *Correspondence, Despatches, and other Papers of Viscount Castlereagh* (London: Murray, 1853), vol. 10.

Castries, René de la Croix, duc de, *La Fayette* (Paris: Tallandier, 1981).

Caulaincourt, Armand de, *Mémoires: La campagne de Russie, l'agonie de Fontainebleau* (Paris: Perrin, 1986).

Chamans de LaValette, Antoine Marie, *Mémoires et souvenirs* (Paris: Fournier, 1831), vol. II.

Chandler, David G., *Campaigns of Napoleon* (New York: Macmillan, 1966).

————. *Waterloo—The One Hundred Days* (London: Osprey, 1988).

Chardigny, Louis, *Les maréchaux de Napoléon* (Paris: Tallandier, 1977).

Chastenay, Victorine de, *Mémoires, 1771–1855* (Paris: Perrin, 1987).

Chateaubriand, François René de, *De Buonaparte et des Bourbons* (Pamphlet, published March, 1814).

————. *Mémoires d'Outre-Tombe* (Paris: Flammarion, 1948), 4 vols.

Clausewitz, Karl von, *Campagne de 1815 en France* (Paris: Chapelot 1900).

Cobban, Alfred, *A History of Modern France* (Baltimore: Penguin, 1961), vol. 2: 1799–1945.

Connelly, Owen, *Napoleon's Satellite Kingdoms* (New York: Free Press, 1965).

Constant de Rebecque, Benjamin, *Journal intime* (Paris: Ollendorff, 1895).

Cotton, Edward, *A Voice from Waterloo. A History of the Battle Fought on the 18th June 1815* (Brussels: Hotel du Musée, 1913).

Creevey, Thomas, *The Creevey Papers* (London: Murray, 1903), 2 vols.

Croker, John Wilson, *The Croker Papers, 1808–1857* (London: J. Murray, 1900), vol. I.

D'Arblay, Frances Burney, *The Diary and Letters of Madame D'Arblay* (London: H. Colburn, 1846), vol. 7.

Davout, Louis Nicolas, *Correspondance du Maréchal Davout, Prince d'Eckmühl, ses Commandements, son Ministère, 1801–1815* (Paris: Plon, 1885), vol. IV.

De Lancey, Magdalene, *A Week at Waterloo in 1815, Lady de Lancey's Narrative* (London: Murray, 1906).

Desmarest, Pierre Marie, *Témoignages historiques, ou, Quinze ans de Haute Police sous le Consulat et l'Empire* (Paris: Levasseur, 1833).

Dhumez, Hubert, "Cannes et les Cent-Jours," *Mélange inédits Relatifs au passé du pays cannois. Collections: Documents, textes inconnus pour servir à l'Histoire du pays de Cannes et de sa région*, vol. 6 (Cannes: Aegitna, 1961).

Dumoulin, Evariste, *Histoire complète du procès du maréchal Ney* (Paris: De Launay, 1815) 2 vols.

Fain, Agathon Jean François, *Mémoires du Baron Fain, premier secrétaire du cabinet de l'Empereur* (Paris: Plon, 1908).

Fleury de Chaboulon, Edouard, *Les Cent-Jours. Mémoires pour servir à l'histoire de la vie privée, du retour et du règne de Napoléon en 1815* (Paris: Rouveyre, 1952), see vol I (of two).

Florange, Charles, *Le vol de l'aigle (1815. Napoléon, la marche sur Paris* (Paris: Clavreuil, 1932).

Fortescue, John, *Wellington* (New York: Dodd, Mead, 1925).

Fouché, Joseph, *Les Mémoires de Fouché* (Paris: Flammarion, 1945).

François, Charles, *Journal du capitaine François, 1792-1830* (Paris: Carrington 1903–1904) Vol. II.

Frazer, Augustus, *Letters of Colonel Sir Augustus Frazer* (London: Murray, 1859).

Gaudin, Michel Martin Charles, Duc de Gaëte, *Mémoires, souvenirs, opinions et écrits du Duc de Gaëte* (Paris: Colin, 1926), vol I.

Girod de l'Ain, Gabriel, *Joseph Bonaparte, Le Roi Malgré Lui* (Paris: Perrin, 1970).

Gotteri, Nicole, *Soult, Maréchal d'Empire, et homme d' Etat* (Besançon: Editions La Manufactures, 1991).

Gourgaud, Gaspard, *Mémoires pour servir à l'histoire de France sous Napoléon* (Paris: Didot, 1823), two vols.

Gouvion Saint-Cyr, Laurent de, *Mémoires pour servir à l'histoire militaire sous le Directoire, le Consulat et l'Empire* (Paris: Anselin, 1831), four vols.

Gronow, Rees Howell, *Captain Gronow, His Reminiscences of Regency and Victorian Life, 1810–60*. Edited by Christopher Hibbert (London: Kyle Cathie, 1991).

Grouchy, Emmanuel de, *Mémoires du maréchal Grouchy* (Paris: Dentu, 1873–74), 5 vols.

Guizot, François, *Mémoires pour servir à l'histoire de mon temps* (Paris: Michel Lévy, 1858–1867), see vol. I (of 8 vols).

Harris, James, Earl of Malmesbury, *Letters of the First Earl of Malmesbury, 1745–1820* (London: Bentley, 1870).

Haswell, Jock, *The First Respectable Spy: The Life and Times of Colquhoun Grant* (London: Hamilton, 1969).

Hayman, Peter, *Soult, Napoleon's Maligned Marshal* (London: Arms & Armour, 1990).

Hobhouse, John Cam, *Lettres écrites de Paris pendant le dernier règne de l'Empereur Napoléon* (Gand: Houdin, 1847).

Hortense, Reine, *Mémoires de la Reine Hortense* (Paris: Plon & Nourrit, 1927), 3 vols.

Houssaye, Henri, *1814* (Paris: Bartillat, 1986).

———. *1815. Vol. I: La Première Restauration—Le Retour de l'Ile d'Elbe—Les Cent Jours* (Paris: Perrin, 1896).

———. *1815. Vol. II: Waterloo* (Paris: Bartillat, 1987).

———. *1815. Vol. III: La Seconde Abdication—La Terreur Blanche* (Paris: Perrin, 1914).

Jouquin, Jacques, *Dictionnaire analytique, statistique et comparés des vingt-six maréchaux du premier empire* (Numéro spécial, 146) of the *Revue de l'Institut Napoléon* (Paris: Tallandier, 1986).

Lacour-Gayet, Georges, *Talleyrand, 1754–1838* (Paris: Payot, 1930), vols II and III.

La Fayette, Gilbert de, *Mémoires, Correspondance et manuscrits du général de La Fayette* (Paris: Fournier Aîné, 1837–38), six vols, see vol. V.

Lamarque, Jean Maximilien, *Mémoires et souvenirs du général Maximilien Lamarque* (Paris: Fournier jeune, 1835–36), 3 vols.

Lamothe-Langon, Etienne Léon Caron de, *Les après-dîners de S.A.S. Cambacérès* (Paris: Fournier-Valdès, 1946).

Larpent, Francis Seymour, *The Private Journal of F. Seymour Larpent, Judge-Advocate General during the Peninsula War, from 1812 to its close* (London: R. Bentley, 1853), vol. I.

Las Cases, Marie-Joseph, Emmanuel Dieudonné, comte de, *Mémorial de Sainte-Hélène* (Paris: Flammarion, 1951), two vols.

La Tour du Pin, Henriette-Lucy (Dillon), Marquise de, *Mémoires de la Marquise de La Tour du Pin, Journal d'Une Femme de Cinquante Ans (1778–1815)* (Paris: Mercure de France, 1989).

Lefebvre, Georges, *Napoleon* (London: Routledge & Kegan Paul, 1969), vol. II: *From Tilsit to Waterloo*.

Lennox, Sarah, *Life and Letters of Lady Sarah Lennox* (London: Murray, 1901), two vols.

Lennox, Lord William, *Three Years with the Duke, or Wellington's Private Life* (London: Murray, 1853).

Longford, Elizabeth, *Wellington* (London: Weidenfeld and Nicolson, 1969), vol. I: *The Years of the Sword*.

Louis-Philippe d'Orléans, *Mon journal, événements de 1815* (Paris: Michel Lévy, 1849), two vols.

Madelin, Louis, *Le Consulat* (Paris: Hachette, 1945).

———, *Fouché, 1759–1820* (Paris: Plon, 1903), 3 vols.

———, *Talleyrand* (Paris: Flammarion, 1944).

Manceron, Claude, *Napoléon reprend Paris (20 mars 1815)* (Paris: Laffont, 1965).

Marchand, Louis, *Mémoires de Marchand, Premier Valet de Chambre et Exécuteur testamentaire de l'Empereur* (Paris: Plon, 1952–1955), vol. I: *L'Ile d'Elbe—Les Cent-Jours*.

Marmont, Auguste Frédéric Louis Viesse de, *Mémoires du duc de Raguse* (Paris: Perrotin, 1857), in nine vols, see vol. VII.

Masséna, André, *Mémoires de M. le Maréchal Masséna, Duc de Rivoli, Prince d'Essling, sur les événements qui ont eu lieu en Provence, pendant les mois de mars et d'avril 1815* (Paris: Delaunay, 1816).

Masson, Frédéric, *Napoléon et sa famille* (Paris: Ollendorff, 1914), vols. I, II, III, IV, VIII, IX, X and XI.

Maxwell, Sir Herbert, *The Life of Wellington* (London: S. Low, Marston & Co., 1899), vol. II.

Molé, Louis Mathieu, *Le Comte Molé, sa vie et ses mémoires* (Paris: Champion, 1922–30), six vols, see vol. I.

Mollien, Francis Nicolas, comte, *Mémoires d'un ancien ministre du Trésor . . . 1800 à 1814* (Paris: Fournier, 1837), four vols.

Montholon, Charles Tristan, *Mémoires pour servir à l'histoire de France sous Napoléon, écrits sous sa dictée* (Paris: Ladvocat 1822–25), eight vols.

Mowat, R. B., The *Diplomacy of Napoleon* (London: Edward Arnold, 1925).

Müffling, Karl Friedrich Ferdinand von, *Passages from My Life* (London: Murray, 1853).

Napier, William F. P., *A History of the War in the Peninsula and the South of France, 1807–1814* (London: Murray, 1886), six vols.

Ney, Michel, *Mémoires du maréchal Ney* (Paris: Fournier, 1833), 2 vols.

Orieux, Jean, *Talleyrand, ou le sphinx incompris* (Paris: Flammarion, 1970).

Ouvrard, Gabriel Julien, *Mémoires de G-J Ouvrard, sur sa vie et ses divers opérations financières* (Paris: Moutardier, 1826), three vols.

Paget, Henry William, Marquess of Anglesey, *One-Leg, The Life and Letters of Henry William Paget, 1st Marquess of Anglesey* (London: Jonathan Cape, 1961).

Picton, Thomas, *Mémoires of Sir Thomas Picton* (London: Murray, 1836).

Pietromarchi, Antonello, *Lucien Bonaparte, Prince Romain* (Paris: Perrin, 1980).

Pons de L'Herault, André, *Souvenirs et ancecdotes de l'Ile d'Elbe* (Paris: Plon, 1897).

Pozzo di Borgo, Charles-André, *Correspondance diplomatique du comte Pozzo di Borgo, ambassadeur de Russie en France, et du comte de Nesselrode, 1814–1818* (Paris: Calmann-Lévy, 1890), vol. I.

Rapp, Jean, *Mémoires du général Rapp, aide de camp de Napoléon* (Paris: Lacroix, 1895).

Reinhard, Marcel, *Le Grand Carnot* (Paris: Hachette, 1952), see vol. II: *L'organisateur de la victoire, 1792–1832*.

Rémusat, Charles de, *Mémoires de ma vie* (Paris: Plon, 1941), vol. I: Enfance et Jeunesse—La Restauration Libérale (1797–1820).

Salvandy, A. N. de, *Observation critique sur le champ de mai*. (Pamphlet).

Savary, Anne Jean Marie René, duc de Rovigo, *Mémoires pour servir à l'histoire de l'Empereur Napoléon* (Paris: Bossange, 1828), eight vols.

Schama, Simon, *Citizens, A Chronicle of the French Revolution* (London: Viking, 1989).

Shelley, Frances, *The Diary of Frances Lady Shelley, 1787–1817* (London: J. Murray, 1912), vol. I.

Siborne, Herbert Taylor, *Waterloo Letters* (London: Cassell, 1891).

Soult, Jean de Dieu, *Mémoires du maréchal général Soult* (Paris: Amyot, 1854), three vols.

Staël-Holstein, Anne Louise Germainede, *Mémoires, Dix ans d'exile* (Paris: Plon, 1904).

Stanhope, Philip Henry, *Notes of Conversations with the Duke of Wellington, 1813–1851* (London: Murray, 1888).

Stewart, Robert, Viscount Castlereagh, *Correspondence, Despatches, and other Papers of Viscount Castlereagh*, 3rd Series: Military and Diplomatic (London: John Murray, 1853), see vol. 10.

Suchet, Louis Gabriel, duc d'Albufera, *Mémoires du Maréchal Suchet, duc d'Albufera sur ces campagnes en Espagne depuis 1818 jusqu'en 1814* (Paris: Bossange, 1828), two vols.

Talleyrand-Périgord, Charles Maurice de, *Mémoires du Prince de Talleyrand* (Paris: Calmann-Lévy, 1891–92), five vols, see vols. II and III.

Thibaudeau, Antoine Clair, *Mémoires de A. C. Thibaudeau, 1799–1815* (Paris: Plon, 1913).

Thiébault, Dieudonné Charles Henri, *Mémoires du général baron Thiébault* (Paris: Hachette, 1962).

Thiry, Jean, *Les Cent-Jours* (Paris: Berger-Levrault, 1943).

Timbs, John, *Wellingtonia: Anecdotes, Maxims and Characteristics of the Duke of Wellington* (London: Ingram, Cooke, 1852).

Troyat, Henri, *Alexandre Ier, le sphinx du nord* (Paris: Flammarion, 1985), Tulard, Jean, *Bibliographie critique des mémoires sur le Consulat et l'Empire* (Paris, Genève: Droz, 1971).

———. *Murat, ou l'Eveil des Nations* (Paris: Hachette, 1983).

———. *Napoleon, The Myth of the Saviour* (London: Methuen, 1985).

Vigée Lebrun, Marie Elisabeth Louise, *Souvenirs* (Paris: Fournier, 1853–1857), 3 vols.

Vigier, Comte, *Davout, Maréchal d'Empire, duc d'Auerstaedt, prince d'Eckmühl (1770–1823)* (Paris: Ollendorff, 1898), see vol. I.

Vitrolles, Baron de (Eugène d'Arnauld), *Mémoires* (Paris: Gallimard, 1950), see vol. II.

Wagener, Françoise, *Madame Récamier, 1777–1849* (Paris: Lattès, 1986).

Watson, J. Steven, *The Reign of George III, 1760–1815* (Oxford: Clarendon Press, 1985).

Webster, Charles, *Congress of Vienna, 1814–1815* (London: G. Bell, 1950).

Weller, Jac, *Wellington at Waterloo* (London: Longmans, 1967).

Wellington, Arthur, Duke of, *The Dispatches of Field Marshal the Duke of Wellington, during his various Campaigns* (London: John Murray, 1834–38), vol. XII.

———. *Supplementary Despatches, Correspondence, and Memoranda of Field Marshal Arthur, Duke of Wellington, K.G.* (London: John Murray, 1858–64), vols. IX, X, XI.

Wilson, Harriette, *Harriette Wilson's Memories of Herself and Others* (London: P. Davies, 1929).

Woodward, Llewellyn, *The Age of Reform, 1815–1870* (Oxford: Oxford University Press, 1962).

Zieseniss, Jérôme, *Berthier, Frère d'Armes de Napoléon* (Paris: Belfond, 1985).

B. **PERIODICALS CONSULTED**

The Morning Chronicle   *Gazette de France*
Morning Post   *Gazette Officielle*
Observer   *Journal des Débats*
The Times   *Journal de l'Empire*
                           Journal de Paris
                           Moniteur Universel
                           La Quotidienne

NOTES

CHAPTER I

"ILE DU REPOS"

1. Henry Houssaye, *1815: La Première Restauration—Le Retour de l'Ile d'Elbe, Les Cent Jours* (Paris: Perrin, 1896), p. 173. (Hereafter this work will be referred to as Houssaye, *1815: Cent Jours*.) See also Louis Marchand, *Mémoires de Marchand, Premier Valet de Chambre et Exécuteur Testamentaire de l'Empereur* (Paris: Plon, 1952), vol. I: *L'Ile d'Elbe—Les Cent-Jours*, for a general coverage of this event.
2. Declaration of Frankfurt, December 1, 1813. R. B. Mowat, *The Diplomacy of Napoleon* (London: Edward Arnold, 1925), p. 285.
3. Castlereagh to Liverpool, 29 January 1815. Mowat, p. 286.
4. Caulaincourt to Napoleon, 14 February 1815. Quoted by Mowat, p. 293.
5. See Jérôme Zieseniss, *Berthier, Frère d'Armes de Napoléon* (Paris: Belfond, 1985), pp. 260–61.
6. Mowat, p. 295. Henri Troyat, *Alexandre Ier, Le Sphinx du Nord* (Paris: Flammarion, 1980), pp. 258 ff. The Treaty of Fontainebleau was signed by Metternich (Austria), Nesselrode (Russia) Hardenberg (Prussia), and by Caulaincourt, Ney and Macdonald. Castlereagh refused to sign it. Mowat, p. 295: Henri Houssaye, *1814* (Paris: Christian de Bartillat, 1986), pp. 634 ff.
7. Professor Alfred Cobban gives a figure of 860,000 French alone (between ages of twenty-three and forty-four). See Alfred Cobban, *A History of Modern France* (Baltimore: Penguin Books, 1961), vol. 2: 1799–1945, p. 65.

8. Napoleon to Général de Brigade, Jean-Baptiste Dalesme (1763–1832) 4 mai 1815. See Marchand, *Mémoires*, I, p. 32.

9. Guillaume-Joseph Roux, Baron Peyrusse, 1776–1860. Trésorier-Général de la Couronne during the "100 Days." Antoine Drouot, 1774–1847, artillery officer, War Minister at Elba, Deputy Commander of the Imperial Guard during the "100 Days."

10. Houssaye, *1815: Cent Jours*, p. 146.

11. Houssaye, *1815: Cent Jours*, pp. 153–54.

12. Houssaye, *1815: Cent Jours*, p. 150.

13. Houssaye, *1815: Cent Jours* pp. 153–54.

14. Marchand, *Mémoires*, I, p. 68.

15. Marie-Louise to Emperor Franz, 31 août 1814.

16. Quoted by Neil Campbell, *Napoleon at Fontainebleau and Elba* (London: Murray, 1869), pp. 327–28, 331.

17. Houssaye, *1815: Cent Jours*, p. 167.

18. Houssaye, *1815: Cent Jours*, pp. 167–68, discusses the details of the clauses of the Treaty of Fontainebleau.

19. Houssaye, *1815: Cent Jours*, p. 168.

20. Houssaye, *1815: Cent Jours*, p. 166.

21. Campbell, *Napoleon at Elba*, pp. 343, 345.

22. Houssaye, *1815: Cent Jours*, p. 168.

23. Houssaye, *1815: Cent Jours*, p. 176.

24. Comtesse de Boigne, *Mémoires de la Comtesse de Boigne* (Paris: Mercure de France, 1986), vol. II, pp. 304–7. She reports plans relating to Napoleon's escape, delivered by Dr. Marshall upon his return from Elba in January 1815.

25. Houssaye, *1815: Cent Jours*, p. 169.

26. Marchand, *Mémoires*, I, p. 69: Campbell to Castlereagh, 28 September 1815, *Napoleon at Elba*, p. 297.

27. Mariotti to Talleyrand, 28 septembre 1815, quoted by Houssaye, *1815: Cent Jours*.

28. Houssaye, *1815: Cent Jours*, p. 171.

29. Napoleon to Campbell. Neil Campbell, *Chronique des événements du 1814 et 1815* (Paris: Pichot, 1873), p. 78.

CHAPTER II

THE SOVEREIGN OF THE ISLAND OF ELBA

1. Henry Houssaye, *1815* vol. I: *La Première Restauration—Le Retour de l'Ile d'Elbe, Les Cent Jours* (Paris: Perrin, 1896), p. 181 ff.

2. For details see Charles Alleaume, "Les Cents Jours dans le Var," Société d'Etudes Scientifiques et Archéologiques de Draguignan, *Mémoires*, vol. 49 (Draguignan: Oliver Joulian, 1938), p. 15. See also Fleury de Chaboulon, *Mémoires pour servir l'histoire* (Paris: Cornet, 1901), vol. I, p. 93. There are contradictory dates regarding the arrival of Fleury on Elba, 9 January and also 12 or 13 February 1815. On 24 or 25 February 1815, Napoleon dispatched Chevalier Colonna to apprise Murat of events. Napoleon, *"L'Ile d'Elbe et les Cents Jours. Correspondence*, vol. XXXI, p. 24. For another view of this, see *Jean Orieux, Talleyrand, ou le Sphinx Incompris* (Paris: Flammarion, 1970), pp. 617 ff.

3. Alleaume, *Cent Jours*, p. 15, and Charles Florange, *Le vol de l'aigle (1815): Napoléon, La marche sur Paris* (Paris: Clavreuil, 1932), pp. 11–13. Houssaye, *1815: Cent Jours*, I, p. 191.

4. Henri Gracien Bertrand, *Lettres à Fanny, 1800–1815* (Paris: Albin Michel, 1979), p. 403.

5. Alleaume, *Cent Jours*, p. 15.

6. Ibid.

7. Florange, *Vol de l'Aigle*, p. 9.

8. Florange, *Vol de l'Aigle*, p. 11.

9. Comtesse de Boigne, *Mémoires de la Comtesse de Boigne* (Paris: Mercure de France, 1986), vol. I, p. 307.

10. Florange, *Vol de l'Aigle*, p. 15.

11. Florange, *Vol de l'Aigle*, pp. 16–17

12. Alleaume, *Cent Jours*, p. 7.

13. Florange, *Vol de l'Aigle*, pp. 18–19.

14. Florange, *Vol de l'Aigle*, p. 22.

15. Florange, *Vol de l'Aigle*, p. 21.

16. See Hubert Dhumez's excellent article, "Cannes et le Cents-Jours," *Mélange inédits relatifs au passé du pays cannois. Collection: Documents, textes, inconnus pour servir à l'Histoire du pays de Cannes et de sa région*. vol. 6 (Cannes: Aegitna, 1961), p. 117. A scholarly piece of work by Dhumez.

17. Dhumez, "Cannes," pp. 118–19.

18. Archives Nationales, Fte III. Var 12 (liasse 1813).

19. Dhumez, "Cannes," p. 123.

20. Dhumez, "Cannes," p. 127.

21. Dhumez, "Cannes," p. 127. In a later report by Poulle.

22. Valentinois to Marshal Soult, le 3 mars 1815. Arch. Nat., Fte III. Var 12 (liasse 1813).

23. "La nuit de Malijay." Published in *Illustration*, 21 septembre 1931.

24. Paul Canestrier, "Rapport d'un envoyé secret de Napoléon," p. 1. Report dated 2 June 1815, Antibes, by Officier d'Ordonnance Rey, in 8-page pamphlet, "Sur les bords du Var, pendant les Cents Jours."

25. Florange, *Vol de l'Aigle*, pp. 28–32.

26. Canestrier, "Rapport," pp. 1–3.

27. Dhumez, "Cannes," p. 130.
28. Dhumez, "Cannes," p. 129.
29. Arch. Nat., Fte III. Var 12 (liasse 1813).
30. Ibid.
31. Alleaume, p. 22. (Quotes Bonaparte to Cambronne.)
32. Alleaume, *Cent Jours*, pp. 23–24.
33. Alleaume, *Cent Jours*, p. 23.
34. Alleaume, *Cent Jours*, p. 25.
35. Ibid.
36. Jean-Charles-Marc-Antoine Raymond de Lacépède. Arch. Nat., Fte III. Var 12 (liasse 1813). See also Dhumez, "Cannes," p. 122 ff.
37. Arch. Nat., Fte III. Var 12 (liasse 1813).
38. Ibid.
39. Bouthillier, arrêté, dated 2 mars 1815—Archives du Var. Arrêtés du Préfet. Registre 29., no. 680.
40. Ibid.
41. Dhumez, "Cannes," p. 135.
42. Bouthillier to Interior Minister Montesquiou, Arch. Nat., Fte III. Var 12 (liasse 1813).
43. Ibid.
44. Arch. Nat., Fte III. Var 12, (liasse 1813).
45. Dhumez, "Cannes," p. 137.
46. Alleaume, *Cent Jours*, p. 41. In fact, Pons, though given a passport, this time was arrested by Bouthillier even before reaching Masséna.
47. Préfet Bouthillier to Interior Minister, le 3 mars 1815. Arch. Nat., Fte III, Var. 12, (liasse 1813).
48. André Masséna, *Mémoires de M. le Maréchal Masséna, Duc de Rivoli, Prince d'Essling, sur les événements qui ont eu lieu e Provence, pendant les mois de mars et d'avril 1815* (Paris: Delaunay, 1816), p. 4. This 89-page pamphlet was prepared as a defense and apologia for his actions at this time.
49. Masséna, *Mémoires*, p. 6.
50. Masséna, *Mémoires*, p. 4.
51. Alleaume, *Cent Jours*, p. 41.
52. *Moniteur Universelle*, address, 9 mars 1815.
53. Alleaume, *Cent Jours*, pp. 31–35.
54. Alleaume, *Cent Jours*, p. 35.
55. Alleaume, *Cent Jours*, p. 31.
56. Houssaye, *1815: Cent Jours*, p. 242.
57. Ibid.
58. Quoted by Florange, *Vol de l'Aigle*, plate XIX.
59. Houssaye, *1815: Cent Jours*, pp. 246–56.
60. Florange, Vol de l'Aigle, p. 74.
61. Florange, *Vol de l'Aigle*, p. 73.

62. Florange, *Vol de l'Aigle*, pp. 90–91, reprints "Décret Impériale, donné à Grenoble, le neuf mars 1815."

63. Florange, *Vol de l'Aigle*, p. 76.

64. G. Bertier de Sauvigny, *La Restauration* (Paris: Flammarion, 1955), pp. 97–98. Houssaye, *1815: Cent Jours*, p. 269.

65. Bertier, *Restauration*, pp. 97–98; Houssaye, *1815: Cent Jours*, pp. 260–61.

66. Bertier, *Restauration*, p. 98; Houssaye, *1815*, p. 264.

67. Florange, *Vol de l'Aigle*, p. 81.

68. Florange, *Vol de l'Aigle*, p. 82.

69. Florange, *Vol de l'Aigle*, pp. 82, 83.

70. Florange, *Vol de l'Aigle*, p. 85.

71. Houssaye, *1815: Cent Jours*, pp. 226–27, and 290–91. Angoulême was to command a southern army of the 9th, 10th, and 11th military districts.

72. "Proclamation donnée au Château des Tuileries, le 12 mars 1815," reprinted by Claude Manceron, *Napoléon Reprend Paris (20 mars 1815)* (Paris: Laffont, 1965), p. 22.

73. Houssaye, *1815: Cent Jours*, p. 301. See footnote, and p. 305.

74. Manceron, *Napoléon Reprend*, p. 119.

75. Ibid.

76. Manceron, *Napoléon Reprend*, p. 103.

77. Manceron, *Napoléon Reprend*, p. 120.

78. Manceron, *Napoléon Reprend*, p. 118

79. Manceron, *Napoléon Reprend*, pp. 144–45.

80. Manceron, *Napoléon Reprend*, pp. 147–48.

81. Ney to Sous-Prefect de Bourcia and Prefect Cappelle. Manceron, *Napoléon Reprend*, p. 25.

82. Bertier, *Restauration*, p. 99.

83. Manceron, *Napoléon Reprend*, p. 53.

84. Houssaye, *1815: Cent Jours*, pp. 313–14.

85. Houssaye, *1815: Cent Jours*, p. 313.

86. Manceron, *Napoléon Reprend*, p. 84.

87. Houssaye, *1815: Cent Jours*, pp. 317–18.

88. Total of 10 infantry regiments, 3 cavalry regiments, 4 engineers regiments, 2 artillery (30 cannon). See Houssaye, *1815: Cent Jours*, p. 301.

    A. *From Grenoble* (7th Military District):
       5th, 7th, and 11th Infantry regiments
       4th Hussards
       3rd Génie
       4th Artillery regiment
    B. *From Lyons*:
       20th and 24th Infantry regiments
       13th Regiment of Dragoons
    C. *Additional troops*:

23rd, 36th, 39th, 72nd and 76th Infantry regiments
3rd Hussards
4th Field Artillery
Troops from Elba
1 battalion of retired officers

CHAPTER III

"THE DISTURBER OF THE PEACE OF THE WORLD"

1. Henry Houssaye, *1815*, vol. I. *La Première Restauration—Le Retour de l'Ile d'Elbe, Les Cent Jours* (Paris: Perrin, 1896), p. 22; G. Bertier de Sauvigny, *La Restauration* (Paris: Flammarion, 1955). For general information, see pp. 14–15 and 95.

2. Bertier, *Restauration*, pp. 10, 14–15. Salt was reintroduced in 1806 and tobacco in 1810.

3. Bertier, *Restauration*, p. 10.

4. See Louis Chardigny, *Les maréchaux de Napoléon* (Paris: Tallandier, 1977).

5. Bertier, *Restauration*, p. 11.

6. Ibid. Professor Lefebvre provides other examples of the sharp decline in the commercial life of the Nation, e.g., by 1811 Marseilles had only nine ocean-going merchant ships left (as opposed to 330 in 1807), and that city's manufactures fell from 50 million in 1789 to just 12 million by 1813, while her population dropped by one-fifth. Georges Lefebvre, *Napoleon* (London: Routledge & Kegan Paul, 1969), vol. II, pp. 171 ff. See also Professor Jean Tulard's *Napoleon, The Myth of the Saviour* (London: Methuen, 1985), pp. 196–206, and 283 ff.

7. Tulard, *Napoleon, The Myth*, p. 319.

8. Claude Manceron, *Napoléon Reprend Paris (20 mars 1815)* (Paris: Laffont, 1965), p. 11.

9. Bertier, *Restauration*, p. 12.

10. Bertier, *Restauration*, p. 13.

11. Bertier, *Restauration*, pp. 13–14.

12. Bertier, *Restauration*, p. 15.

13. Bertier, *Restauration*, p. 21.

14. "Chevaliers de la Foi," Bertier, *Restauration*, p. 19.

15. Bertier, *Restauration*, pp. 69–71.

16. Bertier, *Restauration*, p. 76.

17. Bertier, *Restauration*, p. 80.

18. "Maître de la garde-robe"

19. Bertier, *Restauration,* p. 95.
20. Bertier, *Restauration,* pp. 16–97.
21. Masséna, *Mémoires,* pp. 3 ff.
22. Manceron, *Napoléon Reprend,* pp. 105, 106.
23. See Baron de Vitrolles (E.F.A. d'Arnaud), *Mémoires* (Paris: Gallimard, 1884), 3 vols., especially vol. II, 1810–1814, pp. 349 ff. Houssaye, *1815: Cent Jours,* p. 327.
24. See Vitrolles, *Mémoires,* II, p. 232.
25. *Journal des Débats,* 18 mars 1815.
26. Ibid.
27. *Journal des Débats,* 15 mars 1815.
28. *Journal des Débats,* 18 mars 1815.
29. *Journal des Débats,* 15 mars 1815.
30. Ibid.
31. Houssaye, *1815: Cent Jours.* pp. 321–22.
32. Ibid.
33. Berry reached Melun at noon, 17 March. Manceron, p. 140.
34. Houssaye, *1815: Cent Jours,* p. 343. The Treasury paid out the full sum of 400,000 francs at 4 P.M. that same day.
35. Manceron, *Napoléon Reprend,* p. 138.
36. Vitrolles, *Mémoires,* II, p. 921. Houssaye, *1815: Cent Jours,* pp. 340–41.
37. Vitrolles, *Mémoires,* II, p. 323, Houssaye, *1815: Cent Jours,* pp. 340–41.
38. Vitrolles, *Mémoires,* pp. 321–22: Auguste Frédéric Louis Viesse de Marmont, *Mémoires du duc de Raguse* (Paris: Perrotin, 1857), in 9 vols. Houssaye, *1815: Cent Jours,* p. 341.
39. Fleury de Chaboulon, *Mémoires pour servir à l'histoire* (Paris, Rauveyre, 1901), vol. I, p. 210.
40. Manceron, *Napoléon Reprend,* p. 49.
41. Fleury, *Mémoires,* op. cit.
42. "courir sus"
43. Reine Hortense, *Mémoires de la Reine Hortense,* vol. II (Paris: Plon, 1927), p. 4.
44. Fleury, *Mémoires,* vol. I, p. 248.
45. Ibid.
46. See Tulard, *Napoleon, The Myth,* pp. 283 ff. Manceron, *Napoléon Reprend,* p. 247. Niepperg became her lover in September 1815.
47. Houssaye, *1815: Cent Jours,* p. 344.
48. *Journal des Débats,* 18 mars 1815.
49. *Journal des Débats,* 19 mars 1815.
50. Bertier, *Restauration,* pp. 102–03.
51. Bertier, *Restauration,* p. 103. Houssaye, *1815: Cent Jours,* pp. 413–33. See Houssaye for a most detailed coverage of Angoulême's armies and march. In addition to Angoulême's own force of 5,500 men, General Rey, with another, much smaller force, quickly surrendered to Bonaparte's army, while

a third royalist army, under General Ernouf (5,000 men), was defeated at the Durance and fell back to Marseille. Angoulême won a battle at Loriol and pushed on toward Lyons. The Duc d'Angoulême subsequently surrendered with the last royal army at La Palaude on 8 April, from which he was sent to Sète, then deported to Spain.

52. *Journal de Paris*, 18 mars 1815. Houssaye, *1815: Cent Jours*, p. 335.

53. Though bearing no date, King Louis's proclamation was issued on 18 March 1815.

54. Manceron, *Napoléon Reprend*, p. 97.

55. Manceron gives this figure, *Napoléon Reprend*, p. 194.

56. Houssaye, *1815: Cent Jours*, op. cit.

57. Houssaye, *1815: Cent Jours*, pp. 351–52.

58. Blacas informed Vitrolles earlier that evening (19 March). Vitrolles, *Mémoires*, II, p. 354; Houssaye, *1815: Cent Jours*, pp. 351.

59. Vitrolles, *Mémoires*, II, op. cit.

60. Vitrolles, *Mémoires* Ibid; Houssaye, *1815: Cent Jours*, p. 353.

61. Houssaye, *1815: Cent Jours*, op. cit.

62. Houssaye, *1815: Cent Jours*, p. 326.

63. Houssaye, *1815: Cent Jours*, p. 356.

64. Chamans de LaValette, Antoine Marie, *Mémoires et souvenirs* (Paris: Fournier, 1831), II, p. 159. See also Houssaye, *1815: Cent Jours*, p. 354 ff, 360 ff.

65. Hortense, *Mémoires* II, pp. 329–33.

66. Hortense, *Mémoires* II, pp. 333; Houssaye, *1815: Cent Jours*, pp. 362–63.

CHAPTER IV

THE BROTHERS BONAPARTE

1. Pietromarchi, Antonello, *Lucien Bonaparte, Prince Romain* (Paris: Perrin, 1980), pp. 30–31.

2. Pietromarchi, *Lucien Bonaparte*, pp. 39–40.

3. Pietromarchi, *Lucien Bonaparte*, p. 43.

4. Pietromarchi, *Lucien Bonaparte*, p. 51.

5. In theory, the appointment as Minister was made by the three Consuls: Napoleon, Cambacérès and Lebrun. See Frédéric Masson, *Napoléon et sa famille* (Paris: Ollendorf, 1920), vol. I (1769–1802), p. 302.

6. Pietromarchi, *Lucien Bonaparte*, pp. 90–92.

7. Jean Tulard, *Napoleon, the Myth of the Saviour* (London: Methuen, 1984), pop. 85–86.

8. Pietromarchi, *Lucien Bonaparte*, pp. 75–76. Pietromarchi suggests that

some five million votes were cast. See also Alfred Cobban, *A History of Modern France* (Harmondsworth, Middlesex: Penguin, 1967), vol. 2, p. 13.

9. Pietromarchi, *Lucien Bonaparte*, p. 79.
10. Pietromarchi, *Lucien Bonaparte*, p. 81–95.
11. Pietromarchi, *Lucien Bonaparte*, pp. 127–129.
12. Masson, *Napoléon*, II, pp. 15–17, and 21.
13. Pietromarchi, *Lucien Bonaparte*, pp. 140–41.
14. Pietromarchi, *Lucien Bonaparte*, p. 140.
15. One of the three government bodies of the Consulate, the other two being the Corps Législatif and the Senate. It was the Senate (men hand-picked by Napoleon) who elected the members of the Tribunate.
16. Louis Madelin, *Le Consulat* (Paris, Hachette, 1945), p. 241.
17. Pietromarchi, *Lucien Bonaparte*, pp. 155–61.
18. Pietromarchi, *Lucien Bonaparte*, p. 159.
19. Marie-Elisabeth Louise Vigée-Lebrun, *Souvenirs* (Paris: Fournier, 1853) I, p. 202.
20. Pietromarchi, *Lucien Bonaparte*, pp. 155–61.
21. Pietromarchi, *Lucien Bonaparte*, p. 159.
22. Pietromarchi, *Lucien Bonaparte*, p. 203.
23. Pietromarchi, *Lucien Bonaparte*, p. 207.
24. Pietromarchi, *Lucien Bonaparte*, p. 213.
25. Pietromarchi, *Lucien Bonaparte*, pp. 215–25.
26. Pietromarchi, *Lucien Bonaparte*, pp. 227–29.
27. Lucien Bonaparte, *Mémoires secrètes sur la vie privée, politique et littéraire de Lucien Bonaparte, prince de Canino* (Paris: Delauney, 1818).
28. Pietromarchi, *Lucien Bonaparte*, p. 237.
29. Pietromarchi, *Lucien Bonaparte*, pp. 236, 239.
30. Pietromarchi, *Lucien Bonaparte*, p. 239.
31. Pietromarchi, *Lucien Bonaparte*, p. 244.
32. Masson, *Napoléon*, I, pp. 36, 37, 39.
33. Masson, *Napoléon*, I, pp. 94, 95.
34. Masson, *Napoléon*, I, p. 118.
35. Masson, *Napoléon*, I, p. 126.
36. Masson, *Napoléon*, I, p. 127.
37. Masson, *Napoléon*, I, p. 132.
38. The sole exception being Jérôme Bonaparte, who was a close school friend of Eugène de Beauharnais. Masson, *Napoléon*, I, p. 135.
39. Letter from Foreign Minister Charles Delacroix to Joseph Bonaparte, 6 May 1796. Masson, *Napoléon*, I, pp. 192–93.
40. Masson, *Napoléon*, I, pp. 212, 214.
41. Masson, *Napoléon*, I, pp. 212–18.
42. Ibid.
43. Masson, *Napoléon*, I, pp. 248–49.
44. Masson, *Napoléon*, I, p. 282.

45. Masson, *Napoléon*, I, p. 341.
46. Masson, *Napoléon*, I, pp. 405 ff.
47. Masson, *Napoléon*, I, p. 409.
48. Masson, *Napoléon*, I, p. 410.
49. Masson, *Napoléon*, II, p. 342.
50. Masson, *Napoléon*, II, p. 344.
51. Masson, *Napoléon*, II, pp. 346, 347.
52. Masson, *Napoléon*, II, p. 372.
53. See Senatus-Consulte of 24 floréal an XII (18 May 1804), and Masson, *Napoléon*, II, pp. 381–82.
54. See Masson, *Napoléon*, II, pp. 383, 384.
    As Prince Imperial he received 1 million francs per annum and another 333,333 francs as Grand Elector. On 4 August 1804 he received 300,000 francs and another 50,000 on 14 September 1804.
55. Masson, *Napoléon*, II, p. 449.
56. Masson, *Napoléon*, II, p. 452.
57. Masson, *Napoléon*, II, p. 457.
58. Masson, *Napoléon*, III, p. 127.
59. Masson, *Napoléon*, III, pp. 16–17, regarding Lombardy.
60. Masson, *Napoléon*, III, pp. 190–92, 315.
61. Masson, *Napoléon*, III, p. 240.
62. Masson, *Napoléon*, IV, p. 75.
63. Masson, *Napoléon*, IV, p. 244, on 10 May 1808.
64. Masson, *Napoléon*, IV, p. 245.
65. Masson, *Napoléon*, IV, p. 357.
66. Masson, *Napoléon*, IV, p. 371.
67. Masson, *Napoléon*, IX, pp. 131 ff. He returned to France and Mortefontaine in June 1812.
68. Masson, *Napoléon*, IX, p. 349.
69. Masson, *Napoléon*, IX, pp. 294–95.
70. Masson, *Napoléon*, IX, p. 409.
71. Masson, *Napoléon*, IX, p. 427.
72. Masson, *Napoléon*, I, p. 130.
73. Masson, *Napoléon*, II, p. 54.
74. Masson, *Napoléon*, II, pp. 56, 57.
75. Masson, *Napoléon*, II, p. 57.
76. Masson, *Napoléon*, II, pp. 58, 59.
77. Masson, *Napoléon*, II, pp. 59–60.
78. Masson, *Napoléon*, II, p. 61.
79. Masson, *Napoléon*, II, p. 295.
80. Masson, *Napoléon*, II, pp. 299–300.
81. She was born on 6 February 1785. Jérôme was born on 9 November 1784.
82. Masson, *Napoléon*, II, pp. 301 ff., p. 314.
83. Masson, *Napoléon*, III, pp. 89, 93.

84. Masson, *Napoléon*, III, p. 89.

85. Masson, *Napoléon*, III, pp. 90–91.

86. Masson, *Napoléon*, III, p. 93.

87. Bonaparte to Pius VII, 24 May 1085, Masson, III, p. 155.

88. Masson, *Napoléon*, III, p. 93.

89. Masson, *Napoléon*, III, p. 95.

90. Masson, *Napoléon*, III, pp. 95–96, 97. Napoléon to Letizia, 23 avril 1805.

91. Masson, *Napoléon*, III, p. 98.

92. Masson, *Napoléon*, III, pp. 155, 157.

93. Masson, *Napoléon*, III, p. 103.

94. Masson, *Napoléon*, III, p. 106.

95. Masson, *Napoléon*, III, p. 107.

96. Masson, *Napoléon*, III, p. 101.

97. Masson, *Napoléon*, III, p. 158.

98. Masson, *Napoléon*, III, pp. 160–61. In 1806, while serving at sea Jérôme received 750,000 francs, yet incurring even greater debts.

99. Masson, *Napoléon*, III, p. 161.

100. Masson, *Napoléon*, III, p. 371.

101. Masson, *Napoléon*, III, p. 297.

102. Granted this rank by Napoleon, 14 March 1807.

103. Masson, *Napoléon*, III, pp. 409–11, 418.

104. The Bonapartes were divorced by a special act of the State Assembly of Maryland on 2 January 1813. Following Jérôme's "marriage" to Catherine, Elizabeth Bonaparte tried to remarry on at least two occasions, which Napoleon personally quashed through direct intervention. See Masson, *Napoléon*, III, p. 441. She never married again.

105. Masson, *Napoléon*, IV, p. 326.

106. Masson, *Napoléon*, IV, p. 195.

107. Masson, *Napoléon*, IV, p. 321.

108. Masson, *Napoléon*, IV, p. 390 ff.

CHAPTER V

A DEADLY ENEMY

1. Marquise de La Tour du Pin, Henriette-Lucy Dillon, *Mémoires de la Marquise de La Tour du Pin, Journal d'une femme de cinquante Ans (1778–1815)* (Paris: Mercure de France, 1989). See pages 196 ff. for life on the farm, Talleyrand, clothing, etc.

2. Jean Orieux, *Talleyrand, ou le sphinx incompris* (Paris: Flammarion, 1970), pp. 218–19.

3. La Tour du Pin, *Mémoires*, p. 340.
4. Orieux, *Talleyrand*, p. 454, quotes Hortense.
5. La Tour du Pin, *Mémoires*, p. 340.
6. Victorine de Chastenay, *Mémoires*, *1771–1815* (Paris: Perrin, 1987), p. 560.
7. Comte de Molé, *Mémoires*, vol. I, p. 272. See also G. Lacour-Gayet, *Talleyrand*, *1754–1838* (Paris: Payot, 1930), vol. III, 1815–1838, pp. 49–50.
8. Chastenay, *Mémoires*, p. 560.
9. La Tour du Pin, *Mémoires*, pp. 340–41.
10. Orieux, *Talleyrand*, pp. 454–55.
11. La Tour du Pin, *Mémoires*, pp. 340–41.
12. Orieux, *Talleyrand*, p. 431.
13. Molé, *Mémoires*, I, p. 272, also Lacour-Gayet, *Talleyrand*, III, pp. 49–50; and Orieux, *Talleyrand*, p. 450.
14. Chastenay, *Mémoires*, p. 598.
15. Chastenay, *Mémoires*, p. 566.
16. Molé *Mémoires*, I, p. 272; and Lacour-Gayet, *Talleyrand*, III, p. 50.
17. Ibid.
18. Molé, *Mémoires*, I, p. 272.
19. Chastenay, *Mémoires*, p. 560.
20. Lacour-Gayet, *Talleyrand*, II, p. 44.
21. Ibid.
22. Lacour-Gayet, *Talleyrand*, II, p. 43.
23. Lacour-Gayet, *Talleyrand*, II, p. 46.
24. Lacour-Gayet, *Talleyrand*, II, p. 47.
25. Lacour-Gayet, *Talleyrand*, II, p. 46.
26. Lacour-Gayet, *Talleyrand*, II, p. 47.
27. Lacour-Gayet, *Talleyrand*, II, p. 48.
28. Lacour-Gayet, *Talleyrand*, II, p. 322.
29. Le Marquis de Noailles, *Le Comte de Molé sa vie et ses mémoires* (Paris: Champion, 1922–30) (six volumes), I, p. 193.
30. Noailles, *Comte de Molé*, I, p. 193, and Lacour-Gayet, II, pp. 322–23.
31. Orieux, *Talleyrand*, p. 418.
32. Orieux, *Talleyrand*, pp. 420–24.
33. Orieux, *Talleyrand*, p. 422.
34. Ibid.
35. Ibid.
36. Orieux, *Talleyrand*, p. 605; Lacour-Gayet, II, p. 439.
37. Orieux, *Talleyrand*, pp. 393–96.
38. Orieux, *Talleyrand*, p. 448.
39. Orieux, *Talleyrand*, p. 397.
40. Orieux, *Talleyrand*, p. 433.
41. Ibid.

42. Orieux, *Talleyrand*, p. 442.
43. Orieux, *Talleyrand*, p. 443: announced on 5 June 1806.
44. Created, signed at Berlin, 21 November 1806.
45. Orieux, *Talleyrand*, p. 451.
46. Ibid.
47. Orieux, *Talleyrand*, pp. 449–53.
48. Orieux, *Talleyrand*, p. 455.
49. Orieux, *Talleyrand*, p. 462.
50. Orieux, *Talleyrand*, p. 466.
51. Ibid.
52. *Mémoires du Prince de Talleyrand*; Orieux, p. 574.
53. Orieux, *Talleyrand*, p. 466.
54. Orieux, *Talleyrand*, p. 467.
55. Orieux, *Talleyrand*, p. 468.
56. Orieux, *Talleyrand*, p. 470.
57. Talleyrand to Metternich. Orieux, *Talleyrand*, p. 471.
58. Orieux, *Talleyrand*, p. 472.
59. Orieux, *Talleyrand*, p. 486.
60. Orieux, *Talleyrand*, p. 570. See also Louis Madelin, *Talleyrand*. (Paris: Flammarion, 1944).
61. Orieux, *Talleyrand*, p. 585.
62. Orieux, *Talleyrand*, pp. 477–78.
63. Orieux, *Talleyrand*, p. 473.
64. Orieux, *Talleyrand*, p. 511.
65. Lacour-Gayet, *Talleyrand*, II, p. 272.
66. Lacour-Gayet, *Talleyrand*, II, p. 273.
67. Napoleon to Caulaincourt. Armand de Caulaincourt, *Mémoires: La campagne de Russie, L'agonie de Fontainebleau* (Paris: Perrin, 1986), p. 200.
68. Orieux, *Talleyrand*, p. 536.
69. Orieux, *Talleyrand*, p. 574.
70. Ibid.
71. Orieux, *Talleyrand*, p. 575.
72. Orieux, *Talleyrand*, pp. 576–77.
73. Caulaincourt, *Mémoires*, p. 548; Lacour-Gayet, II, p. 193.
74. Frédéric Masson, *Napoléon et sa famille* (Paris: Albin Michel, 1926), vol. VIII, p. 271.
75. Orieux, *Talleyrand*, p. 577.
76. See Orieux, *Talleyrand* pp. 573, 713–16, on the Maubreuil affair.
77. Napoleon to Joseph Bonaparte, 8 February 1814. Lacour-Gayet, *Talleyrand*, II, p. 336.
78. Orieux, *Talleyrand*, p. 583.
79. Orieux, *Talleyrand*, p. 589.
80. Orieux, *Talleyrand*, p. 598.
81. Wellington to Castlereagh, Paris, 25 December 1814. Viscount Castlereagh

(Robert Stewart, 2nd Marquess of Londonderry), *Correspondence, Despatches, and Other Papers of Viscount Castlereagh* (London: Murray, 1853), vol. 10. pp. 226–27.

82. Lacour-Gayet, *Talleyrand*, II, p. 431.

83. Pozzo di Borgo, Charles-André, *Correspondence Diplomatique du Comte Pozzo di Borgo, ambassadeur de Russie en France, et du Comte de Nesselrode, 1814–1818* (Paris: Calmann Lévy, 1890), vol. I, pp. xii–xiii.

84. Castlereagh to Wellington, Vienna, 25 October 1814. Castlereagh, *Correspondence*, vol. 10, p. 173.

85. Wellington to Castlereagh, Paris, 5 November, 1813. Castlereagh, *Correspondence*, vol. 10, p. 183.

86. Castlereagh to Wellington, October 25, 1814. Castlereagh, *Correspondence*, vol. 10, p. 173.

87. Castlereagh to Wellington, Oct. 25, 1814, Castlereagh, *Correspondence*, vol. 10, pp. 173–74

88. Castlereagh to Wellington, Oct. 25, 1814, Castlereagh, *Correspondence*, vol. 10, p. 174.

89. Castlereagh to Wellington, Oct. 25, 1814, Castlereagh, *Correspondence*, vol. 10, p. 175.

90. Ibid.

91. Wellington to Castlereagh, November 5, 1814, Castlereagh, *Correspondence*, vol. 10, p. 183.

92. R. B. Mowat, *The Diplomacy of Napoleon* (London: Arnold, 1924), p. 299; Charles Maurice de Talleyrand, *Mémoires du Prince de Talleyrand* (Paris: Calmann-Lévy, 1891–92), II, 561–65.

93. Mowat, *Diplomacy of Napoleon*, p. 299.

94. Mowat, *Diplomacy of Napoleon*, p. 299; Talleyrand, *Mémoires*, II, 561–65.

95. Liverpool to Castlereagh, Bath, January 12, 1815. Castlereagh, *Correspondence*, vol. 10, pp. 239–40.

96. Liverpool to Wellington, Bath, January 11, 1815, Castlereagh *Correspondence*, vol. 10, p. 243.

97. J. Steven Watson, *The Reign of George III, 1760–1815* (Oxford: Clarendon Press, 1985), p. 565.

98. Lacour-Gayet, *Talleyrand*, II, p. 432.

99. Orieux, *Talleyrand*, p. 618.

100. Lacour-Gayet, *Talleyrand*, II, p. 333.

101. Orieux, *Talleyrand*, p. 618.

102. Orieux, Talleyrand, pp. 618–19. See also Ferdinand Bac, *Le Secret de Talleyrand* (Paris: Hachette, 1933); and Paul Bartel, *Napoléon à l'île d'Elbe* (Paris: Perrin, 1950).

103. Lord Clancarty to Castlereagh, Vienna, 11 March 1815, Castlereagh, *Correspondence*, vol. 10, pp. 263–69.

104. Clancarty to Castlereagh, Vienna, 18 March 1815, Castlereagh, *Correspondence*, vol. 10, p. 276.

105. Quoted in *Le Moniteur universel*, 13 April 1815, and discussed by Mowat, *Diplomacy of Napoleon*, p. 300.

106. Article 3 quoted by Talleyrand, *Mémoires*, III, 136–39, and discussed by Mowat, p. 300.

107. Castlereagh to Wellington, London, 26 March 1815, Castlereagh *Correspondence*, vol. 10, pp. 285–86.

108. Castlereagh to Wellington, Downing Street, 3 April 1815, Castlereagh, *Correspondence*, vol. 10, 297.

109. Nesselrode to Castlereagh, Vienna, 2 April 1815, Castlereagh, *Correspondence*, vol. 10, p. 297.

110. Lord Clancarty to Stratford Canning, Vienna, 29 March 1815, Castlereagh, *Correspondence*, vol. 10 p. 288.

CHAPTER VI

"THE MOST WRETCHED OF ALL PROFESSIONS"

1. See Henry Houssaye, *1815: La Première Restauration, Le Retour de l'Ile d'Elbe, Les Cents Jours* (Paris: Perrin, 1896), p. 371. Molé refused to compromise his name by associating himself with Napoleon now, and finally decided against joining the ministry when Carnot was named, though Napoleon needed his "name" and forced him to accept Ponts et Chaussées. Etienne Pasquier, *Mémoires du Chancelier Pasquier* (Paris: Plon, 1894), III, 1814–1815, pp. 165–66, 177.

2. Antoine-Marie Chamans de LaValette, *Mémoires*, II, p. 164.

3. Lazare-Nicolas Carnot, *Exposé de ma conduite politique*, p. 22.

4. LaValette, Pasquier's old friend, resented Fouché's reappearance in the government. Napoleon had also offered Foreign Affairs to LaValette. Pasquier, *Mémoires*, III, p. 167.

5. Louis Madelin, *Fouché, 1759–1820* (Paris: Plon, 1903), vol. I, p. 136.

6. Madelin, *Fouché*, III, p. 438.

7. *Moniteur*, le 13 octobre 1793. Madelin, *Fouché*, I, p. 122.

8. Madelin, *Fouché*, I, p. 126.

9. Madelin, *Fouché*, I, p. 135.

10. Simon Schama, *Citizens: A Chronicle of the French Revolution* (London: Viking, 1989), p. 780.

11. Les représéntants à la Convention, 7 nivôse an II, Aulard IX, 713. Madelin, *Fouché*, I, p. 139.

12. Madelin, *Fouché*, I, p. 138.

13. 30 frimaire an II, Arch. Nat., F7 4435. Madelin, *Fouché*, I, p. 138.

14. Schama, *Citizens*, p. 783.

15. To the Comité du Salut Public, 16 frimaire an II, Aulard, IX, p. 363 (Madelin, *Fouché*, I, p. 137).

16. Victorine de Chastenay, *Mémoires, 1771–1815* (Paris: Perrin, 1987) p. 363.

17. Chastenay, *Mémoires*, pp. 364, 366.

18. Chastenay, *Mémoires*, pp. 363, 329.

19. Chastenay, *Mémoires*, p. 368.

20. Ibid.

21. Chastenay, *Mémoires*, pp. 339, 374

22. Chastenay, *Mémoires*, p. 364.

23. Madelin, *Fouché*, pp. 387–88 (letter to Mme de Custine, 9 September 1815).

24. Chastenay, *Mémoires*, p. 364.

25. Madelin, *Fouché*, I, p. 388.

26. Madelin, *Fouché*, I, p. 386.

27. Chastenay, *Mémoires*, p. 371; Madelin, *Fouché*, II, p. 438.

28. Chateaubriand, François-René, *La Monarchie suivant la charte*, p. 111; Madelin, *Fouché*, II, p. 435.

29. Madelin, *Fouché*, II, p. 400.

30. Madelin, *Fouché*, II, p. 393.

31. Madelin, *Fouché*, II, p. 385.

32. Pierre Marie Desmarest, *Témoignages Historiques* (Paris: Lavasseur, 1833), p. 219. See also Madelin, *Fouché*, I, p. 419.

33. Madelin, *Fouché*, I, p. 411.

34. Madelin, *Fouché*, I, p. 416.

35. François Guizot, *Mémoires pour servir à l'histoire de mons temps* (Paris: Michel Lévy, 1858–1867), I, p. 73.

36. Madelin, *Fouché*, I, p. 397.

37. Fouché to Gaillard, 25 mars 1818, Madelin, *Fouché*, I, p. 397.

38. Madelin, *Fouché*, I, p. 397.

39. Madelin, *Fouché*, I, p. 460.

40. Madelin, *Fouché*, I, p. 462.

41. Madelin, *Fouché*, I, p. 404.

42. Madelin, *Fouché*, I, p. 402.

43. Madelin, *Fouché*, I, p. 441.

44. Guizot, *Mémoires*, I, p. 73.

45. Madelin, *Fouché*, I, p. 405.

46. Madelin, *Fouché*, I, p. 384.

47. Madelin, *Fouché*, I, p. 384.

48. Madelin, *Fouché*, I, p. 384.

49. Madelin, *Fouché*, I, p. 383.

50. Chastenay, *Mémoires*, p. 611.

51. See Madelin, *Fouché*, I, pp. 353–56.

This election was fradulent, of course, as already pointed out in Chapter IV, re Lucien's role as Interior Minister.

52. See Alfred Cobban: *A History of Modern France* (Baltimore: Penguin, 1961), vol. III, 1799–1945, pp. 16–17.

53. Talleyrand to Etienne Pasquier, *Mémoires*, III, p. 331. See also, Madelin, *Fouché*, II, p. 437.

54. Le Bailli de Crussot to Beugnot, Madelin, *Fouché*, II, p. 438.

55. Madelin, *Fouché*, II p. 322.

56. Madelin, *Fouché*, II, p. 313. 10 Mars 1794 at Nantes *vs* royalist émigrés.

57. Madelin, *Fouché*, II, p. 317.

58. Madelin, *Fouché*, II, p. 319.

59. Madelin, *Fouché*, II, p. 321.

60. Madelin, *Fouché*, II, p. 329 ff.

61. Madelin, *Fouché*, II, p. 328.

62. Madelin, *Fouché*, II, pp. 330–31.

63. Chastenay, *Mémoires*, p. 611.

64. Fouché, *Mémoires*, II, pp. 309–10.

65. Madelin, *Fouché*, II, p. 334.

66. Ibid.

67. Madelin, *Fouché*, II, p. 342.

68. Madelin, *Fouché*, II, p. 339 ff.

69. Madelin, *Fouché*, II, pp. 349–59.
France was divided into four police districts.

70. Madelin, *Fouché*, II, p. 348.

71. Pasquier, *Mémoires*, vol. III, p. 17.

72. Madelin, *Fouché*, II, p. 353.

73. Madelin, *Fouché*, II, p. 353; Duc d'Otrante aux Préfets, le 31 mars 1815, *Moniteur universel*, le 4 août 1815.

74. Madelin, *Fouché*, II, p. 353.

75. Madelin, *Fouché*, II, p. 354.

CHAPTER VII

A LAND IN TURMOIL

1. Henry Houssaye, *1815: La Première Restauration—Le Retour d'Elbe, Les Cent Jours* (Paris: Perrin, 1896), p. 483.

2. Houssaye, *1815: Cent Jours*, pp. 440–42.

3. Benjamin Constant de Rebecque, *Mémoires sur les Cents Jours* (Paris: Bechet, 1822) II, pp. 47 ff; Houssaye, *1815: Cent Jours*, p. 545.

4. Houssaye, *1815: Cent Jours*, p. 498. I.e., those who had previously worked

for him but now betrayed him, and who had instead allied themselves directly with Louis XVIII.

5. Houssaye, *1815: Cent Jours*, pp. 486 ff.
6. Houssaye, *1815: Cent Jours*, pp. 486 note 1, among his brothers.
7. Ibid.
8. Ibid.
9. "Mémoires de Molé," *Revue de la Révolution*, XI, p. 39; Houssaye, *1815: Cent Jours*, pp. 483, 389.
10. Benjamin Constant de Rebecque, *Journal Intime* (Paris: Olendorff, 1895), p. 100; Houssaye, *1815: Cent Jours*, p. 494.
11. Houssaye, *1815: Cent Jours*, p. 494.
12. Marie-Joseph de Las Cases, *Mémoriale de Sainte-Hélène* (Paris: Flammarion, 1951), VI, pp. 93–95.
13. Announced 29 March 1815.
14. *Bulletin de Lois*, 24 mars 1815, announced its abolition; Houssaye, *1815: Cent Jours*, p. 528.
15. Re article in the *Nain Jaune* of 10 mai 1815; Houssaye, *1815: Cent Jours*, p. 529.
16. Houssaye, *1815: Cent Jours*, p. 530.
17. Houssaye discusses them in *1815: Cent Jours*, p. 533.
18. Houssaye, *1815: Cent Jours*, p. 534.
19. Houssaye, *1815: Cent Jours*, p. 536.
20. "Fragment des Mémoires de Molé," *Revue de la Révolution*, XI, p. 90; Houssaye, *1815: Cent Jours*, p. 536.
21. *Journal de Paris*, 19 mars 1815, Françoise Wagener, *Madame Récamier, 1777–1849*, p. 270 (Paris: Lattès, 1986).
22. Wagener, *Récamier*, p. 270.
23. Houssaye, *1815: Cent Jours*, p. 540.
24. Constant to Récamier, 19 mars 1815, Constant, *Mémoires*, II, p. 122.
25. Quoted by Wagener, *Récamier*, p. 270.
26. Houssaye, *1815: Cent Jours*, p. 547.
27. Houssaye, *1815: Cent Jours*, pp. 542–43.
28. Houssaye, *1815: Cent Jours*, p. 545.
29. Pasquier, *Mémoires*, III, p. 170.
30. Ibid.
31. Houssaye, *1815: Cent Jours*, p. 545.
32. Caulaincourt to Pasquier, Pasquier, *Mémoires*, III, p. 178.
33. LaValette to Pasquier, Pasquier, *Mémoires*, III, p. 218.
34. Houssaye, *1815: Cent Jours*, p. 550; A. N. de Salvandy , *Observation critique sur le champs de mai* (pamphlet).
35. Constant, *Mémoires*, II, p. 72.
36. Constant, *Mémoires*, II, p. 72; Houssaye, *1815: Cent Jours*, p. 553.
37. Houssaye, *1815: Cent Jours*, p. 554.
38. Houssaye, *1815: Cent Jours*, pp. 555–56. For election results, p. 556.

39. Pasquier, *Mémoires*, III, p. 174.
40. Pasquier, *Mémoires*, III, pp. 177–79.
41. Ibid.
42. Pasquier, *Mémoires*, III, pp. 177–79.
43. Fouché to Pasquier, March, 1815, Pasquier, *Mémoires*, III, p. 171.
44. Houssaye, *1815: Cent Jours*, p. 493.
45. Houssaye, *1815: Cent Jours*, p. 485.
46. Lazare Carnot, *Révolution et Mathématique* (Paris: L'Herne, 1984), pp. 92–95.
47. Carnot, *Révolution et Mathématique*, pp. 36–101.
48. Carnot, *Révolution et Mathématique*, pp. 95, 101.
49. Carnot, *Révolution et Mathématique*, p. 272.
50. Carnot left the Comité du Salut Public on 5 March 1794. In May 1794 he was elected President of the Convention.
51. Elected to the Corps Législatif on 4 November 1795.
52. Carnot, *Révolution et Mathématique*, pp. 120–24.
53. Inspecteur Général de Revues, 7 February 1800; War Minister, 2 April 1800.
54. Carnot, "On revolution," essay by Carnot, published in *Révolution et Mathématique*, pp. 126, 358.
55. *Révolution et Mathématique*, p. 272.
56. Carnot, *Révolution et Mathématique*, pp. 356–57.
57. Carnot, *Révolution et Mathématique*, pp. 1–186.
58. Marcel Reinhard, *Le Grand Carnot* (Paris: Hachette, 1952); volume II: *L'organisateur de la Victoire, 1792–1832*, pp. 132, 269–71.
59. Reinhard, *Carnot*, II, pp. 27–28.
60. Reinhard, *Carnot*, II, p. 28.
61. Reinhard, *Carnot*, II, p. 29.
62. Ibid.
63. Reinhard, *Carnot*, II, pp. 134–35.
64. Reinhard, *Carnot*, II, p. 31.
65. Reinhard, *Carnot*, II, p. 32; and Napoleon to Metternich, Klemens von Metternich's *Mémoires*, I, p. 179.
66. Las Cases, *Mémorial*, le 9 juin 1818; and Reinhard, *Carnot*, II, p. 33.
67. Reinhard, *Carnot*, II, p. 39.
68. Reinhard, *Carnot*, II, p. 18.
69. Reinhard, *Carnot*, II, p. 304.
70. Reinhard, *Carnot*, II, p. 22.
71. Ibid.
72. Reinhard, *Carnot*, II, p. 311.
73. Houssaye, *1815: Cent Jours*, p. 500.
74. Houssaye, *1815: Cent Jours*, p. 503.
75. War Minister Davout to Interior Minister Carnot, 13 April 1815. Maréchal Davout, *Correspondance du Maréchal Davout, ses Commandements, son*

Ministère, 1801–1815, notes by Ch. de Mazade (Paris: Plon, 1885), vol. IV, pp. 438–39. Davout provides two examples—at Rouen and Abbeville—where, though the Prefects were perfectly loyal to Napoleon, everyone else, particularly the mayors and city officials, were openly hostile to the Empire.

76. Houssaye, *1815: Cent Jours*, p. 521.
77. Houssaye, *1815: Cent Jours*, pp. 521–24.
78. Houssaye, *1815: Cent Jours*, pp. 500–05.
79. Houssaye, *1815: Cent Jours*, p. 496; Constant, *Mémoires*, II, pp. 90–91.
80. Houssaye, *1815: Cent Jours*, pp. 504–05.
81. Regnault to Pasquier, Pasquier, *Mémoires*, III, p. 174.
82. Houssaye, *1815: Cent Jours*, p. 457.
83. Houssaye, *1815: Cent Jours*, pp. 504–05.
84. Brune was murdered at Avignon following Waterloo.
85. Houssaye, *1815: Cent Jours*, pp. 514–16. For Davout's complaints about rebellious state at Marseille, now placed under martial law, see Davout to Marshal Suchet Duc d'Albuféra, 17 mai 1815, Davout, *Correspondance*, IV, p. 540.
86. Houssaye, *1815: Cent Jours*, p. 512.
87. Houssaye, *1815: Cent Jours*, pp. 510–15.
88. Houssaye, *1815: Cent Jours*, p. 503.
89. Houssaye, *1815: Cent Jours*, pp. 506–08.
90. Alfred Cobban, *A History of Modern France*, vol. II, p. 65. Cobban estimates that nearly 900,000 were killed, excluding young conscripts, ages 18–22.
91. Sent out on 4 April 1815. Reinhard, *Carnot*, II, p. 315. Went to military divisions on 20 April.
92. Houssaye, *1815: Cent Jours*, p. 510.
93. Reinhard, *Carnot*, II, p. 318.
Bigot de Préameneu's "Exposé de la Situation de l'Empire" discusses clerical animosity. See also Reinhard, *Carnot*, II, p. 317. The Protestants of the Cevennes reacted sharply to anti-Protestant acts by the nation's Catholics, and thus supported Napoleon.
94. Reinhard, *Carnot*, II, pp. 317–18.
95. Reinhard, *Carnot*, II, pp. 318–19.
96. Houssaye, *1815: Cent Jours*, p. 561.
97. Houssaye, *1815: Cent Jours*, pp. 562–63.
98. Houssaye, *1815: Cent Jours*, pp. 563–64.
99. Houssaye, *1815: Cent Jours*, p. 568.
100. Houssaye, *1815: Cent Jours*, p. 565.
101. Houssaye, *1815: Cent Jours*, p. 566.
102. Houssaye, *1815: Cent Jours*, p. 567.
103. Ibid.
104. Ibid.

105. Houssaye, *1815: Cent Jours*, p. 568.
106. Carnot to Napoleon. Carnot, *Révolution et Mathématique*, p. 358.
107. Davout, *Correspondance*, IV, note 1, p. 552, to send 15th, 26th, 27th, 43rd and 65th regiments.
108. Houssaye, *1815: Cent Jours*, p. 570.
109. Ibid.
110. Ibid.
111. Houssaye, *1815: Cent Jours*, pp. 571–73.
112. Houssaye, *1815: Cent Jours*, p. 573.
113. Houssaye, *1815: Cent Jours*, pp. 574–75.
114. Houssaye, *1815: Cent Jours*, p. 576. He quoted all the above rebel corre-spondence, found in General Canuet's *Mémoire sur la guerre de Vendée*, pp. 346–49.
115. Houssaye, *1815: Cent Jours*, p. 577.
116. Pasquier, *Mémoires*, III, p. 195.
117. Pasquier, *Mémoires*, III, p. 171.
118. Houssaye, *1815: Cent Jours*, p. 581.
119. Pozzo di Borgo, to Nesselrode, Bruxelles, 11–23 mai 1815, in Charles-André Pozzo di Borgo, *Correspondance diplomatique du comte Pozzo di Borgo, ambassadeur de Russie en France, et du comte de Nesselrode, 1814–1818* (Paris: Calmann Lévy, 1890), p. 122, and Pozzo to Nesselrode, Bruxelles, 4 mai 1815, p. 112.
120. Pasquier, *Mémoires*, pp. 194–95.
121. Pasquier, *Mémoires*, III, p. 195.
122. Houssaye, *1815: Cent Jours*, pp. 586–89, and Fleury de Chaboulon, *Mémoires de Fleury de Chaboulon* (Paris: Rouveyre, 1901), II, pp. 27–42. Ottenfels used the alias Henri Werner.
123. Houssaye, *1815: Cent Jours*, p. 590; see also Fleury's account (above). This also involved Talleyrand's intercepting a secret message sent by Fouché (by M. de Saint Léon) to Metternich, calling for the replacement of Napoleon with the Duc d'Orléans. See Pasquier, *Mémoires*, III, p. 199.
124. Houssaye, *1815: Cent Jours*, p. 590.
125. Caulaincourt to Pasquier, Pasquier, *Mémoires*, III, p. 178.
126. Houssaye, *1815: Cent Jours*, p. 581 and Pasquier, *Mémoires*, III, p. 195; See also Pozzo di Borgo to Nesselrode on this, Pozzo, *Correspondance*, vol. I, p. 130 ff.
127. Houssaye, *1815: Cent Jours*, pp. 620–21.
128. Houssaye, *1815: Cent Jours*, p. 622.
129. Houssaye, *1815: Cent Jours*, pp. 622–23.
130. See also Pasquier, *Mémoires*, III, p. 199.
131. Houssaye, *1815: Cent Jours*, pp. 623–26. *Correspondance* de Napoléon, 21906, and Constant, *Journal de l'Empire*, 15 and 16 mai 1815.
132. Houssaye, *1815: Cent Jours*, pp. 623–26.
133. Houssaye, *1815: Cent Jours*, p. 624; Napoléon *Correspondance*, 21908.

720 men per battalion. Arch. Nat. AF IV, 1936, 1940, Davout to Napoleon, 7 juin 1815.

134. Houssaye, *1815: Cent Jours*, p. 625.

135. Houssaye, *1815: Cent Jours*, pp. 625–26.

136. Reinhard, *Carnot*, II, p. 324.

137. Ibid.

138. Ibid.

139. Reinhard, *Carnot*, II, p. 324. Carnot was named Grand Officier on 15 May 1815, and Comte de l'Empire on 2 June 1815.

CHAPTER VIII

"NEITHER PEACE NOR TRUCE"

1. Marshal Davout, *La Correspondance du Maréchal Davout, Prince d'Eckmühl. Ses commandements, son Ministère, 1801–1815* (Paris: Plon, 1885), vol. IV, p. 352.

2. Comte Vigier, *Davout, maréchal d'Empire, Duc d'Auerstaedt, Prince d'Eckmühl (1770–1823).* (Paris: Ollendorff, 1898), vol. I, p. 7.

3. Vigier, *Davout*, I, p. 4.

4. Vigier, *Davout*, I, p. 66.

5. Vigier, *Davout*, I, p. vii.

6. Vigier, *Davout*, I, p. vii.

7. Vigier, *Davout*, I, p. viii.

8. Ibid.

9. Vigier, *Davout*, I, p. vii.

10. Vigier, *Davout*, I, p. x.

11. Vigier, *Davout*, I, pp. 18–19.

12. Vigier, *Davout*, I, p. 102.

13. Vigier, *Davout*, I, p. 89.

14. Louis Chardigny, *Les maréchaux de Napoléon* (Paris: Tallandier, 1977), p. 193.

15. Vigier, *Davout*, I, p. 110.

16. Vigier, *Davout*, I, p. 213.

17. See David G. Chandler, *The Campaigns of Napoleon* (New York: Macmillan, 1966), pp. 495–97.

18. Vigier, *Davout*, I, p. 213; Chardigny, *Maréchaux de Napoléon* p. 144.

19. Jérôme Zieseniss, *Berthier, Frère d'armes de Napoléon* (Paris: Belfond, 1985), pp. 197 ff; Chardigny, p. 144.

20. Chardigny, *Maréchaux de Napoléon*, p. 92.

21. Zieseniss, *Berthier*, pp. 252–53.
22. Chardigny, *Maréchaux de Napoléon*, p. 147.
23. Napoleon to Davout, 10 avril 1815, *Correspondance de Napoléon*, 21790.
24. Davout had sold the Hôtel de Monaco (or, de Sagan), at 57 rue Saint-Dominique in 1812, and now lived at 39 rue Saint-Dominique; Kellermann not far away on the same street; Masséna, at the Hôtel Bentheim, 92 rue Saint-Dominique; Soult, Hôtel de Périgord, 57 rue Saint-Dominique and Suchet, at 55 rue Saint-Dominique. See Jacques Jouquin's *Dictionnaire analytique statistique et comparés des vingt-six maréchaux du premier empire*, numéro spécial, 146, of the *Revue de l'Institut Napoléon* [Paris: Tallandier, 1986], pp. 124–29.
25. Napoleon to General Caulcaincourt, 3 avril 1815 (21759).
26. Napoleon's "Lettre circulaire aux souverains," Paris, 3 avril 1815 (21769).
27. Napoleon to Davout, 21 mars 1815 (21692).
28. Davout to Gouvion Saint-Cyr, 23 mars 1815, Davout, *Correspondance*, IV, p. 365.
29. Davout to Masséna, 24 mars 1815. Davout, *Correspondance*, IV, pp. 369–370.
30. Davout to Masséna, 25 mars 1815. Davout, *Correspondance*, IV, p. 369.
31. Napoleon to Davout, 13 avril 1815, *Correspondance de Napoléon*, 21798.
32. Davout to General Pajol, 26 mars 1815, Davout, *Correspondance*, IV, p. 371.
33. Davout to General Souham, 29 mars 1815. Davout, *Correspondance*, IV, pp. 378–80; Davout to General Clausel, 5 avril 1815, Davout, *Correspondance*, IV, pp. 403–05.
34. Napoleon to Davout, 26 mars 1815 (21723); and Napoleon to Davout, 30 mars 1815 (21747) re the creation of eight Corps d'Observation.
35. Napoleon, "Decree," 28 mars 1815 (21737); and Davout, *Correspondance*, IV, p. 409.
36. Napoleon to Davout, 10 avril 1815 (21785); Napoleon to General Andréossy, 3 avril 1815 (21767).
37. Napoleon to Caulaincourt, 3 avril 1815 (21759); Napoleon to Davout, 2 avril 1814 (21756); Napoleon to Davout, 15 mai 1815 (21910).
38. Fouché to Pasquier. See *Mémoires du Chancelier Pasquier* (Paris: Plon, 1891), vol. III, p. 170.
39. Of Napoleon's initial army of 655,000 men, only 85,000 or so returned to France (including Germans, Poles, Italians, etc.). In addition, some 200,000 trained army horses (cavalry, artillery, etc.) were also killed or had died. He also lost his entire artillery. See Chandler, *Campaigns*, pp. 756 and 853.
40. Napoleon to Gaudin, 2 avril 1815. Napoleon, *Correspondance* (21761).
41. See Gaëte, *Mémoires, Souvenirs, Opinions et Ecrits du Duc de Gaëte* (Paris: Colin, 1926), vol. I, pp. 304–09.

42. Ibid.
43. Davout's projected Ministerial budget for July was put at 72 million. Henry Houssaye, *1815: Waterloo* (Paris: Bartillat, 1987), p. 30.
44. Houssaye, *Waterloo*, pp. 28, 31. The loan of 150 million francs was included in the budget presented to the Chambers on 19 June 1815.
45. On Ouvrard, see Houssaye, *Waterloo*, pp. 28–29.
46. On the National Guard, see Carnot's "Exposé de la situation de l'Empire," of 14 June (in *Moniteur*, 15 June 1815). Exact amount: 29,920,120 francs. Houssaye, *Waterloo*, p. 29.
47. Napoleon to Mollien, 14 avril 1815 (21803).
48. Napoleon to Mollien, 14 avril 1815 (21803).
49. Houssaye, *Waterloo*, p. 30. Treasury balance, ca. 670,000 francs.
50. Napoleon to Decrès, 22 avril 1815. Napoleon, *Correspondance* (21836): reduced to 50 million.
51. Napoleon to Decrès, 14 avril 1815. Napoleon, *Correspondance* (21808).
52. Napoleon to Decrès, 22 avril 1815. Napoleon, *Correspondance* (21836).
53. Napoleon to Decrès, 22 avril 1815. Napoleon, *Correspondance* (21836). 60,000 to 80,000 men for coastal artillery and defenses were assigned from the navy and conscripted locally. Decrès was responsible for coastal defenses.
54. See Alan Schom's *Trafalgar, Countdown to Battle, 1803–1805* (New York: Atheneum, 1990), p. 83.
55. Henry Houssaye made a study of these contributions in *1815: La Première Restauration—Le Retour de l'Ile d'Elbe, Les Cent Jours* (Paris: Perrin, 1896), p. 630.
56. Houssaye, *1815: Les Cent Jours*, pp. 630–31.
57. Houssaye, *1815: Les Cent Jours*, p. 631.
58. Davout to Soult, 10 avril 1815, Davout, *Correspondance*, IV, pp. 423–24.
59. Napoleon to Cambacérès, 18 avril 1815. Napoleon, *Correspondance* (21820).
60. Napoleon to Davout, 10 avril 1815 (marshals) (21790), and Napoleon to Davout, 7 juin 1815 (22025).
    Generals Briche, Curto, D'Aultanne, Dessoles, Dupont, Leclerc, Loverdo, Maison, Monnier, Edmond Périgord, Souham.
61. Napoleon to Davout, 26 mars 1815 (21723).
62. Décret, Napoleon (21855), 20 avril 1815, and Napoleon, 26 mars 1815 (21723).
63. 59,600 of a total of 90,000 on duty. Houssaye, *Waterloo*, p. 35.
64. Napoleon to Davout, 17 avril 1815 (21819).
65. Ibid.
66. E.g., Napoleon created the "Section de la Guerre," of the Comité de Défense of the Conseil d'Etat on 20 avril 1815 (21828). For Conseil des Finances, see no. 21853.
67. See Houssaye, *Waterloo*, p. 37. Army recruits, Napoleon to Davout, 3 mai

1815 (21874). 3 mai 1815 Napoleon to Davout (21874).

52,446 deserters rejoined by mid-June. Houssaye, *Waterloo*, p. 37.

46,419 recruits joined by 11 June. Houssaye, *Waterloo*, p. 16.

68. See e.g., Toulouse, Marseille: 22 avril 1815, Décret, Napoleon (21831)—created 3 volunteer regiments, or Corps Francs.

69. Napoleon to Andréossy, 3 avril 1815 (21767), Napoleon calls up 120,000 National Guards and Imperial Guards; he was short 240,000 muskets for Army. Davout to Napoleon, 12 avril 1815—workers to build muskets in houses; 15 avril (21811), Napoleon to Davout; 3 mai 1815, Napoleon to Davout (21874). Napoleon calls for up to 120,000 recruits for 1815, and 100,000 *"anciens soldats."*

100,000	National Guards
20,000	imperial guards
120,000	recruits
100,000	*anciens soldats*
340,000	total.

70. Napoleon to Davout, 3 mai 1815 Napoleon, *Correspondance* (21872).

71. Napoleon to Davout, 27 avril 1815 (21845).

72. Napoleon to Davout, 3 mai 1815 (21872).

73. Napoleon to Conseil des Finances (Conseil d'Etat), 29 avril 1815 (21853).

74. See Houssaye's study of this problem, *Waterloo*, p. 26. See also Rapport du 16 mai 1815, by Ordonnateur Daure, and Davout's letters 1587, 1595, 1656, 1670, 1785 and 1693, and Napoleon's *Correspondance*, 21872 and 21915.

75. Davout, *Waterloo*, p. 27.

76. Napoleon to Gaudin, 16 avril 1815 (21816).

77. Napoleon to Davout, 3 mai 1815 (21873).

78. Napoleon to Davout, 13 avril 1815 (21798).

79. Napoleon to Davout, 11 avril 1815 (21795), and of 13 avril 1815 (21798).

80. Napoleon to Davout, 13 avril 1815 (21798).

81. Napoleon to Davout, 11 avril 1815 (21795).

82. Napoleon to Davout, 15 avril 1815 (21811).

83. Ibid.

84. Ibid.

85. Napoleon to Davout, 2 mai 1815 (21950).

86. Napoleon to Davout, 15 avril 1815 (21811).

87. Napoleon to Carnot, 22 mai 1815 (21958).

88. Napoleon to Davout, 13 avril 1815 (21798).

89. Ibid.

90. Napoleon to Davout, 10 mai (21887).

91. Houssaye, *Waterloo*, p. 18.

92. Napoleon to Davout, 15 avril 1815 (21811).

93. Napoleon to Davout, 15 avril 1815 (21811). This is very reminiscent of

his demands on the Navy for the emergency ship construction during the invasion preparations for Britain, 1803–1805, when he gave Admiral Decrès just a few months in which to construct some two thousand transport vessels.

94. Houssaye, *Waterloo*, p. 20.
95. Davout to Daru, 15 avril 1815, Davout, *Correspondance*, IV, p. 441.
96. Napoleon to Davout, 9 mai 1815 (21885).
97. Napoleon to Davout, 3 mai 1815 (21874); Napoleon to Mollien, 9 mai 1815 (21886).
98. Napoleon to Davout, 9 mai 1815 (21879).
99. Davout to Mollien, 17 avril 1815, Davout, *Correspondance*, IV, p. 451.
100. Houssaye, *Waterloo*, pp. 17, 19. Vincennes was producing 6 million cartridges per month (by May).
101. Napoleon to Davout, 26 mars 1815 (21723).

CHAPTER IX

MOBILIZATION

1. Napoleon, *Correspondance de Napoléon* (Paris: Imprimérie Impériale, 1869), Tome XXVIII: Napoleon to Davout, 30 mars 1815 (no. 21747); Napoleon's Decree of 30 avril 1815 (21855); first army formation, 12 mai 1815, Napoleon to Davout (21895).
2. Napoleon's Decree of 30 avril 1815 (21895).
3. Ibid.
4. See Henry Houssaye, *1815: Waterloo* (Paris: Bartillat, 1987), p. 12; Davout's report to Napoleon, 25–26 mars 1815.
5. See Houssaye, *Waterloo*, pp. 36–37; Napoleon to Davout 3 mai 1815 (21874) re recruits; 12 mai 1815 (21896) Napoleon to Davout re pressgangs.
6. Napoleon to Davout, 3 mai 1815, Napoléon, *Correspondance* (21874).
   1. "Armée de Réserve de Lyon" (for 7th, 8th, 19th Military Districts covering the Dauphiné and Provence)
   2. Armée de Réserve de Bordeaux (11th and 20th Military Districts)
   3. Armée de Réserve de Toulouse (9th and 10th Military Districts)
   4. Armée de Réserve de Paris (1st, 2nd, 3rd, 4th, 5th, 6th, 12th, 13th, 14th, 15th, and 16th Military Districts)
7. Napoleon to Davout, 12 mai 1815, Napoleon, *Correspondance* (21896).
8. Louis Madelin, *Fouché, 1759–1820* (Paris: Plon, 1945), II, p. 277.
9. Napoleon's "Allocûtion à l'Armée," 9 avril 1815, *Correspondance de Napoléon* (21779).

10. Napoleon to Davout, 17 avril 1815 (21819); Napoleon to Davout, 12 mai 1815 (21895).

11. Napoleon to Davout, 12 mai 1815 (21895); Napoleon to Davout, 22 mai 1815 (21952).

12. Napoleon to Davout, 23 mai 1815 (21960).

13. Napoleon to Davout, 22 mai 1815 (21952).

14. Napoleon to Davout, 23 mai 1815 (21960).

15. Ibid.

16. Ibid.

17. Napoleon to Davout, 23 mai 1815 (21963).

18. Napoleon to Davout, 22 mai 1815 (21950).

19. Napoleon to Davout, 20 mai 1815 (21930).

20. Napoleon to Davout, 18 avril 1815 (21823); Napoleon to Davout, 9 mai 1815 (21881).

21. Napoleon to Davout, 7 mai 1815 (21877).

22. Napoleon to Davout, 23 mai 1815 (21961), re horses, Versailles.

23. Napoleon to Davout, 3 mai 1815 (21873).

24. Napoleon to Davout, 9 mai 1815 (21879).

25. Napoleon to Davout, 9 mai 1815 (21879).

26. Napoleon to Davout, 12 mai 1815 (21892).

27. Napoleon to Davout, 13 mai 1815 (21900).

28. Napoleon to Davout, 22 mai 1815 (21930).

29. Napoleon to Davout, 22 mai 1815 (21952); 19 mai (21926).

30. Napoleon to Davout, 20 mai 1815 (21930).

31. Napoleon to Davout, 23 mai 1815 (21961).

32. Napoleon to Davout, 24 mai 1815 (21963).

33. Napoleon to Davout, 25 mai 1815 (21968).

34. Napoleon to Davout, 24 mai 1815 (21966).

35. Etienne-Denis Pasquier, *Histoire de mon temps, Mémoires du Chancelier Pasquier, duc d'Audiffret-Pasquier* (Paris: Plon, 1894), III, p. 110.

36. Napoleon to Davout, 25 mai (21979).

37. Napoleon to Davout, 29 mai 1815 (21987).

38. Soult was ordered to prepare the marching plans for the Armée du Nord, 3 juin 1815 (22005). Napoleon to Soult; Davout to Soult, 22 mai 1815 (Davout's threatened resignation).

39. Davout to Carnot, 15 avril 1815; Davout to Daru, 15 avril 1815, re uniforms, low morale. *Correspondance du Maréchal Davout, Prince d'Eckmühl, ses Commandements, son Ministère, 1801–1805* (Paris: Plon, Nourrit, 1885), vol. 4, pp. 441–43.

40. Napoleon to Davout, 1 mai 1815 (21861).

41. Napoleon to Davout, 1 mai 1815 (21861)—294 battalions; and Napoleon to Davout, 1 mai 1815 (21860). The 284 National Guard battalions were to be divided as follows:
    I. 105 battalions assigned to the Armée du Nord.

II. 42 battalions assigned to Armée de la Moselle.

III. 35 National Guard battalions attached to Armée du Rhin.

IV. 46 battalions assigned to Corps d'Observations du Jura.

V. 56 Guard battalions assigned to Armée des Alpes.

42. E.g., Davout to General Gérard, 9 mai 1815. Davout, *Correspondance*, IV, pp. 509–12; Napoleon to Carnot, 12 mai 1815 (21898).

43. Davout to Gérard, 9 mai 1815 Davout, *Correspondance*, IV, pp. 509–12. Napoleon to Carnot, 12 mai 1815 (21898).

44. Napoleon to Davout, 12 mai 1815 (21894); Napoleon to Davout, 1 mai 1815 (21860); Napoleon to Davout, 15 mai 1815 (21909); Napoleon to Carnot, 12 mai 1815 (21898); Houssaye, *Waterloo*, p. 8; Napoleon to Davout, 1 mai 1815 (21861), National Guard strength to start at 500 men, build up to 750—quote, note p. 99; Houssaye, *Waterloo*, p. 37. The 90,000 included guardsmen to defend cities as well. Carnot's report to Chambre des Pairs, 13 juin 1815 (*Moniteur*, 15 juin 1815); Houssaye, *Waterloo*, p. 91 (called up by Napoleon's Decree of 10 avril 1815). Houssaye, *Waterloo*, pp. 11, 37; 45,903 mobile National Guards in reserve, 90,000 in northern forts, depots, interior cities.

45. Houssaye, *Waterloo*, p. 35.

46. 94,000 former soliders who had completed military service; 85,000 1814 deserters; 32,800 men on temporary or extended leave. Houssaye estimates that less than half of the 94,000 retired soldiers were capable of serving—Houssaye, *Waterloo*, pp. 13, 14; some 25,000 now coming forth to provide an additional 56 battalions. Houssaye, *Waterloo*, p. 5.

47. Houssaye, *Waterloo*, p. 5 E.g., 7,553 troops from Napoleon's Imperial Guard were detached for duty elsewhere in the country, leaving 20,755, added to the 158,174 men along the front. Houssaye, *Waterloo*, p. 37.

48. Houssaye, *Waterloo*, p. 32, note 4; and "Rapport," by Davout, 21 mars 1815. Imperial Guard ultimately comprised twelve infantry regiments (Chasseurs, Grenadiers and Jeune Garde), and six cavalry regiments (Lanciers Rouges, Chasseurs and Grenadiers). See Napoleon to Comte Drouot, Aide-Major de la Garde Impériale, 30 mai 1815 (21994). 1,000 men per regiment (e.g., 4,000 men in the four Young Guard regiments).

49. Grouchy to Davout, 6 avril 1815. Davout, *Correspondance*, IV, p. 408.

50. Davout to Napoleon, 8 juin 1815, Houssaye, *Waterloo*, p. 38, note re National Guard.

51. Davout to Carnot, 13 avril 1815, Davout to Carnot 15 avril 1815; Davout to Napoleon, 15 avril 1815, Davout, *Correspondance*, IV, pp. 432–36, 442–43.

52. Davout to Suchet, 13 avril 1815, Davout, *Correspondance*, IV, p. 432.

53. Davout to Napoleon, 15 avril 1815, re Le Havre, Cherbourg, Davout, *Correspondance*, IV, pp. 393–94.

54. Davout to General Morand, 3 avril 1815, Davout, *Correspondance*, IV, pp. 393–394.

55. Napoleon to Davout, 16 avril 1815 (21813).
56. Napoleon to Carnot, 20 avril 1815 (21813).
57. Napoleon to Carnot, 10 mai 1815 (21889).
58. Napoleon to General Caffarelli, 11 mai 1815 (21891).
59. Napoleon's response to the Electoral College of Seine-et-Oise, 14 mai 1815 (21905).
60. Electoral College of Seine-et-Oise, response to Napoleon, 14 mai 1815 (21905).
61. Napoleon to Fouché, 13 mai 1815 (21902).
62. Napoleon to Comte Drouot, 17 mai 1815 (21920).
63. Napoleon to Fouché, 18 mai 1815, (21923).
64. Napoleon to Carnot, 19 mai 1815 (21925).
65. Napoleon to Conseil des Ministres, 21 mai 1815 (21945).
66. Napoleon to Davout, 22 mai 1815 (21948), creates Armée de la Loire. Napoleon to Général Corbineau (ADC), 21 mai 1815 (21944).
67. Napoleon to Conseil des Ministres, 21 mai 1815 (21945).
68. Napoleon to Davout, 22 mai 1815 (21949).
69. Napoleon to Davout, 22 mai 1815 (21949).
70. Napoleon to Davout, 22 mai 1815 (21952).
71. Napoleon to Davout, 3 juin 1815 (22000).
72. Napoleon to Carnot, 17 mai 1815 (21921), placing Marseille under *"état de siège;"* Napoleon to Fouché, 18 mai 1815 (21923); 31 mai 1815, Napoleon to Davout—Nantes, Poitiers; 13 mai 1815, Davout to Napoleon, re state of siege to be declared at Le Havre.
73. Houssaye, *Waterloo*, p. 37.
74. Napoleon to Davout, 15 mai 1815 (21910).
75. Napoleon to Davout, 16 mai 1815 (21915). Napoleon to Davout, 22 avril 1815 (21835).
76. Houssaye, *Waterloo*, p. 17; Napoleon to Decrès, 22 avril (21836).
77. Napoleon to Davout, 27 avril 1815 (21845).
78. Napoleon to Davout, 2 mai 1815 (21863, 21864, 21865) and Napoleon to Davout, 12 mai 1815 (21893).
79. Napoleon to Davout, 5 juin 1815 (22009); Napoleon to Davout, 12 mai 1815 (21892); Napoleon to Davout (21865).
80. Napoleon to Davout, 5 juin 1815 (22009), Napoleon to Davout, 12 mai 1815 (21892).
81. Napoleon to Davout, 2 mai 1815 (21865). He ordered redoubts, etc., to be begun by 5 May, though one month later little had been accomplished.
82. Napoleon to Davout, 1 mai 1815 (21862); and 2 mai 1815, Napoleon to General Comte Dejean, premier inspecteur général de génie (21869).
83. Napoleon to Davout, 2 mai 1815 (21867).
84. Napoleon to Davout, 27 mai 1815 (21973).
85. Napoleon to Davout, 27 mai 1815 (21973).
86. Napoleon to Davout, 27 mai 1815 (21973).

87. Napoleon to Davout, 27 mai 1815 (21973).
88. Napoleon to Davout, 27 mai 1815 (21973).
89. Napoleon to Davout, 10 mai 1815 (21888).
90. Napoleon to Davout, 6 juin 1815.
91. Napoleon, "Note pour la défense de Paris," 30 mai 1815 (21995).
92. Drafting students from Saint-Cyr Academy and Ecole Polytechnique.
93. Alfred Cobban, *A History of Modern France*, vol. II, 1799–1945, pp. 13, 17. 3,011,007 *vs*. 1,562 for the Consulship, and 3,572,329 *vs*. 2,579 for the Empire.
94. Napoleon to Cambacérès, quoted by Etienne-Léon Caron de Lamothe-Langon, *Les après-diners* de S.A.S. Cambacérès (Paris: Fournier-Valdès, 1962), p. 325.
95. Fleury de Chaboulon, *Mémoires de Fleury de Chaboulon* (Paris: Rouveyre, 1952), I, p. 151.
96. Recorded by Fleury, *Mémoires*, II, p. 87.
97. Fleury, *Mémoires*, II, p. 81. Votes:

Civilian:	1,288,357—yes	4,207—no
Army:	222,000—yes	320—no
Navy:	22,000—yes	275—no
		4,802

98. Fleury, *Mémoires*, II, p. 81.
99. Marchand, *Mémoires*, I, p. 156.
100. Louis Marchand, *Mémoires de Marchand* (Paris: Plon, 1952); *L'Ile d'Elbe—Les Cent Jours*, p. 151.
101. Owen Connelly, *Napoleon's Satellite Kingdoms* (New York: Free Press, 1965), pp. 323–26.
102. Marchand, *Mémoires*, I, pp. 149–50. Napoleon moved into Elysée Palace 21 May 1815.
103. Marchand, *Mémoires*, I, pp. 157–58.
104. For background see Houssaye, *1815*, I, p. 549 ff; the *Moniteur, Journal de l'Empire, Journal de Paris* of 1, 2, 3, and 4 June 1815.
105. Marchand, *Mémoires*, I, p. 141.
106. Houssaye, *1815: Les Cent Jours*, p. 595.
107. Houssaye, *1815: Les Cent Jours*, p. 598.
108. Houssaye, *1815: Les Cent Jours*, p. 598.
109. Marchand, *Mémoires*, I, p. 145.
110. See Jérôme Zieseniss, *Berthier, Frère d'armes de Napoléon* (Paris: Belfond, 1985), p. 212.
111. Housaye, *1815: Les Cent Jours*, p. 595.
112. Fleury de Chaboulon discussed the ceremony in his *Mémoires* II, pp. 77 ff; Houssaye, *1815: Les Cent Jours*, p. 599.
113. Napoleon, *Correspondance*, Discours, 1 juin 1815 (21997). This speech by Electoral College Delegates quoted in Fleury's *Mémoires* II, pp. 66–81.

114. Houssaye, *1815: Les Cent Jours*, p. 599.
115. What is more, this national plebiscite, like the previous ones held under the Empire and Consulate before it, were not decided by ballot. Instead, each eligible voter (perhaps a quarter of the population) "voted" by writing his vote in a bound register in his city or village, before the gathered municipal officials and soldiers to witness. Needless to say, one was often not free to vote as one wished, if one desired to live peacefully thereafter in that community. But as entire municipal administrations were openly against Napoleon, those mayors encouraged strong opposition, hundreds of thousands of votes were registered opposing the Acte Additionnel in Toulon, Marseille, Montpellier, Perpignan, Toulouse, Bordeaux, etc.; votes, it might be added, which were suppressed entirely by Interior Minister Carnot, or his officials.

    For Napoleon's first of June speech, see his *Correspondance*, XXVIII, 1 juin 1815 (21997).
116. Napoleon's speech, 1 juin 1815 (21997).
117. For general background, see John Cam Hobhouse, *Lettres écrites de Paris, pendant le dernier règne de l'Empereur Napoléon* (Gand: Houdin, 1817), II, pp. 389–92. *Moniteur*, 2 juin 1815, and Napoleon's speech, 1 juin 1815 in his *Correspondance* (21997).
118. Hobhouse, French version, *Lettres*, II, pp. 329–92.
119. Fleury du Chaboulon, *Mémoires*, II, p. 84.
120. *Mémoires et souvenirs du Comte LaVallette* (Paris: Société Parisienne d'Edition, 1905), p. 365.
121. Fleury, *Mémoires*, II, p. 85.
122. Chambre des Pairs, to Napoleon, Tuileries, Napoleon, *Correspondance*, 11 juin 1815 (22038).
123. Chambre des Représentants, to Napoleon, 11 juin 1815 (22038).
124. Napoleon's response to Chambre des Représentants (22039).
125. Napoleon to Davout, 11 juin 1815 (22043).
126. Napoleon to Davout, 11 juin 1815 (22042).
127. Napoleon, "Ordre Général de Service, Pendant l'Absence de l'Empereur," 11 juin 1815 (22044).
128. See Fleury, *Mémoires* I, pp. 106 ff.
129. Napoleon's Decree, 11 juin 1815 (22045).

CHAPTER X

"POUR LA PATRIE"

1. Elizabeth Longford, *Wellington*, vol. I: *The Years of the Sword* (London: Weidenfeld and Nicolson, 1969), p. 10, footnote.
2. Longford, *Wellington*, I, pp. 19, 21.

3. Longford, *Wellington*, I, p. 77.
4. Longford, *Wellington*, I, pp. 83 ff.
5. Longford, *Wellington*, I, p. 81.
6. Longford, *Wellington*, I, pp. 82, 83. Corruption practices also by Lieutenant Dodd.
7. Longford, *Wellington*, I, pp. 62–67.
8. Ibid.
9. Longford, *Wellington*, I, pp. 85–95.
10. Longford, *Wellington*, I, p. 92.
11. Stanhope, Philip Henry, *Notes of Conversations with the Duke of Wellington, 1813–1851* (London: J. Murray, 1888), p. 182.
12. Longford, *Wellington*, I, p. 94.
13. Harriet Arbuthnot, (Fane), *The Journal of Mrs. Arbuthnot 1820–1832* (London: Macmillan 1950), vol. I, p. 169.
14. Ibid.
15. Longford, *Wellington*, I, p. 166.
16. Longford, *Wellington*, I, p. 77.
17. Rees Howell Gronow, *The Reminiscences and Recollections of Captain Gronow* (London: Bodley Head, 1964), p. 28.
18. Lady Shelley, *The Diary of Frances Lady Shelley, 1787–1817* (London: J. Murray, 1912), vol. I, p. 7.
19. Francis Seymour Larpent, *The Private Journal of F. Seymore Larpent. Judge-Advocate General during the Peninsular War, from 1812 to Its Close* (London: R. Bentley, 1853), I, p. 285 (9 August 1813).
20. Longford, *Wellington*, I, p. 275.
21. Wellington to General Alexander Campbell (1811). Arthur, Duke of Wellington, *The Dispatches of Field Marshal, the Duke of Wellington, during his various Campaigns* (London: John Murray, 1834–1838), vol. VII, p. 546.
22. Longford, *Wellington*, I, p. 282.
23. Longford, *Wellington*, I, p. 328.
24. Longford, *Wellington*, I, p. 269.
25. Wellington to Colonel Torrense, 29 August 1810. Wellington, *Supplementary Despatches, Correspondence, and Memoranda of Field Marshal Arthur, Duke of Wellington, K.G.* (London: John Murray, 1858–1864), vol. VI, p. 582.
26. Wellington, *Despatches*, V, p. 392, 2 January 1810 to Lord Liverpool.
27. Longford, *Wellington*, I, pp. 217, 313.
28. Longford, *Wellington*, I, p. 207.
29. Longford, *Wellington*, I, p. 332.
30. Gronow, *Reminiscences* (1964), p. 374.
31. Jacques Jourquin, *Dictionnaire analytique, statistique et comparé des vingt-six maréchaux du premier empire*, numéro spécial no. 146, of the *Revue de l'Institution Napoléon* (Paris: Tallandier, 1986), p. 161.
32. Jourquin, *Dictionnaire*, p. 164.
33. Jourquin, *Dictionnaire*, p. 156.

34. Longford, *Wellington*, I, p. 230.
35. John Wilson Croker, *The Croker Papers (1808–1857)* (London: John Murray, 1900), I, pp. 12, 13.
36. Jourquin, *Dictionnaire*, p. 156.
37. The Lines of Torres Vedras and Wellington, see Longford, *Wellington*, I, p. 233 ff.
38. Longford, *Wellington*, I, p. 242. She gives a figure of 50,000 famine victims.
39. Charles Oman, *A History of the Peninsular War* (Oxford: Oxford University Press, 1902–1930), vol. V, p. 473.
40. Longford, *Wellington*, I, p. 282.
41. Quoted by Longford, *Wellington*, I, p. 330.
42. Longford, *Wellington*, I, p. 282.
43. Longford, *Wellington*, I, p. 323.
44. Napoleon before the opening of the Chambers, at the Palais des Représentants, 7 June 1815.
45. E.g., Napoleon's correspondence with Davout, Soult and Drouot. Napoleon, *Correspondance de Napoléon* (Paris: Imprimerie Impériale, 1869), vol. XXVIII (nos, 22002, 22003, 22004, 22005, 22006, 22016, 22017, 22023, 22025, 22049).
46. Napoleon before the Chambre des Représentants, 11 June 1815, *Correspondance*, no. 22089.
47. Henry Houssaye, *1815: Waterloo* (Paris: Bartillat, 1987), pp. 101–04.
48. Houssaye, *Waterloo*, pp. 101–04.
49. The actual strength of the French Army varies slightly according to the source. Scott Bowden in *Armies at Waterloo* gives a figure of 122,652 men and 358 guns (p. 42); Houssaye's *Waterloo*, pp. 101–4 lists approximately 124,000 men and 370 guns, while David G. Chandler in *The Campaigns of Napoleon* (New York: Macmillan, 1966) gives a figure of 122,721 troops, including 89,000 infantry, 221,000 cavalry and 366 guns, page 117. According to Général Chaix, the Ecole Royale Belge (Military Academy) gives Napoleon 128,088 men and 344 cannon; Wellington, 93,643 men and 186 cannon; the Prussians, 117,697 men and 312 cannon. Letter to author of 2 June 1991.
50. General H. Camon, *La Guerre Napoléonienne: Les Batailles* (Paris: Chapelot, 1910), p. 18.
51. Boumont to General Gérard, 15 juin 1815, quoted by Houssaye, *Waterloo*, pp. 111–12.
52. Von Ziethen's report prepared at Gilly, at 1:30 P.M., Houssaye, *Waterloo*, pp. 112–13.
53. Chandler, *Campaigns*, p. 1029.
54. Ordre du Jour, le 15 juin 1815. Napoleon, *Correspondance*, XXVIII (22056). Houssaye, *Waterloo*, pp. 120.
55. Chandler, *Campaigns*, p. 1029.
56. Camon, *Guerres Napoléoniennes, Batailles*, pp. 448, 452. See Sir Peter

Hayman, *Soult, Napoleon's Maligned Marshal* (London: Arms and Armour, 1990), pp. 92–95.

57. Lt. Col. Colquhoun Grant, not to be confused with General Colquhoun Grant, also serving in this army.

58. Blücher to Ziethen, Liège, le 5 mai 1815, Houssaye, *Waterloo*, p. 115. Chandler, *Campaigns*, p. 1027.

CHAPTER XI

EVE OF BATTLE

1. Pozzo di Borgo to Nesselrode, Bruxelles, le 28 avril 1815, *Correspondance diplomatique du comte Pozzo di Borgo, ambassadeur de Russie en France, et du comte de Nesselrode, 1814–1818* (Paris: Calmann Lévy, 1890), vol. I, p. 113.

2. Pozzo to Lieven, Bruxelles, 4–16 mai 1815, Pozzo di Borgo, *Correspondance Diplomatique*, I, p. 115.

3. Jac Weller, *Wellington at Waterloo* (London: Longmans, 1967), p. 31. Wellington, *Supplementary Despatches*, X, p. 182. *The Dispatches of Field Marshal, the Duke of Wellington, during his various Campaigns* (London: John Murray, 1834–38), 12 volumes. Wellington, *Supplementary Despatches, Correspondence, and Memoranda of Field Marshal Arthur, Duke of Wellington, K.G.* (London: John Murray, 1858–1864), 11 volumes.

4. Longford, *Wellington*, I, p. 401.

5. Wellington, *Supplementary Despatches*, X, pp. 215, 182.

6. Weller, *Wellington at Waterloo*, p. 33.

7. Weller, *Wellington at Waterloo*, p. 34; Houssaye, *Waterloo*, pp. 105–6.

8. Wellington, *Supplementary Despatches*, X, p. i, Duke of York to Wellington, 28 March 1815.

9. Wellington to Bathurst, 4 May 1815, *Supplementary Despatches*, X, p. 216.

10. Nesselrode to Pozzo di Borgo, 1–13 mai 1815. Pozzo, *Correspondance*, I, p. 143.

11. Ibid.

12. See Weller, *Wellington at Waterloo*, pp. 242–43, and then pp. 237 ff for the rest of the figures for the Anglo-Allied Army mentioned here.

13. See Appendix I of this book for breakdown of each corps.

14. Bowden, *Armies at Waterloo*, pp. 199, 201; Karl von Clausewitz, *Campagne de 1815 en France* (Paris: Chapelot, 1900), p. 26, gives 115,000.

15. See Appendix II of this book for Prussian Army Command.

16. Bowden, *Armies at Waterloo*, p. 142.

17. Bowden, *Armies at Waterloo*, pp. 146, 147.

18. Bowden, *Armies at Waterloo*, p. 158. Lists Blücher's staff in detail. Gneisenau (1760–1831).
19. Bowden, *Armies at Waterloo*, p. 149.
20. Bowden, *Armies at Waterloo*, pp. 199, 201, 272.
21. General H. Camon, *La Guerre Napoléonienne, Les Batailles* (Paris: Chapelot, 1910), pp. 17 ff; and Chandler, *Campaigns*, pp. 162 ff.
22. Camon, *Batailles*, p. 35.
23. Camon, *Batailles*, pp. 35, 36.
24. Napoleon to Jourdan, 28 juillet 1809, Camon, *Batailles*, p. 542.
25. Camon, *Batailles*, p. 17.
26. Camon, *Batailles*, p. 19.
27. For army figures, Clausewitz, *Campagne de 1815*, p. 20; Houssaye, *Waterloo*, p. 106.
28. David G. Chandler, *The Campaigns of Napoleon* (New York: Macmillan, 1966), pp. 1031–32.
29. Chandler, *Campaigns of Napoleon*, p. 1032.
30. Chandler, *Campaigns of Napoleon*, pp. 1032, 1033. See also Baron von Müffling, *Passages from My Life* (London: Murray, 1853), p. 230, and Wellington's *Dispatches*, XII, pp. 472 ff.
31. Weller, *Wellington at Waterloo*, p. 51.
32. Bulletin de l'Armée, Charleroi, le 15 juin 1815, au soir, Napoleon, *Correspondance* (22056).
33. Napoleon to Ney, 16 juin 1815, *Correspondance* (22058).
34. Ibid.
35. Napoleon to Grouchy, 16 juin 1815, *Correspondance* (22059).
36. Napoleon to Ney, 16 juin 1815, *Correspondance* (22058).
37. Von Clausewitz gives Ziethen only 27,000. Clausewitz, *Campagne de 1815 en France*, Paris edition, p. 209.
38. Clausewitz, *Campagne*, p. 71.
39. Sir Herbert Maxwell, *The Life of Wellington* (London: S. Low Marston & Co., 1899), II, pp. 19–20.
40. Chandler, *Campaigns*, p. 1040; Clausewitz, *Campagne*, p. 71, for a different version.
41. Clausewitz, *Campagne*, Paris edition, p. 78; Clausewitz quotes the four orders issued by Soult/Napoleon to Ney on 16 June 1815, pp. 77–79.
42. Camon, *Batailles*, p. 454. Clausewitz, *Campagne*, p. 75.

CHAPTER XII

WATERLOO

1. Karl von Clausewitz, *La Campagne de 1815 en France* (Paris: Chapelot, 1900), pp. 85–87, gives a figure of 76 cannon at Saint-Amand and about 60 at Ligny. Prussians had 100 guns at Saint-Amand firing from 1,000-meter-long area, and had another 60 guns at Ligny. Prussians fired very frequently, using up their ammunition much faster than the French. Prussians had 224 guns at the battle of Ligny, the French a total of 210.
2. David G. Chandler, *The Campaigns of Napoleon* (New York, Macmillan, 1966), pp. 1038, 1044. See also Chandler's excellent *Waterloo: The Hundred Days* (London: Osprey, 1990) for a more detailed coverage of the campaign. Clausewitz's troop figures give the Prussians 78,000 men and the French about 75,000, p. 97 of *Campagne de 1815*. I give 84,000 Prussians, 70,500 French.
3. Saint-Amand, population 200 persons; Ligny, population 443.
4. General Camon, *La Guerre Napoléonienne, Les Batailles* (Paris: Chapelot, 1910), pp. 450 ff.
5. Clausewitz, *Campagne de 1815*, p. 75.
6. Camon, *Batailles*, p. 475.
7. Camon, *Batailles*, pp. 454–60, and Chandler, *Campaigns*, p. 1043. Professor David Chandler attributes d'Erlon's wrong position to his possible confusion of Wagnée and Wagnelé on his map. Chandler's letter of 1 August 1991 to author.
8. Scott Bowden, *Armies at Waterloo* (Arlington, Texas: Empire Games Press, 1983), p. 197. Clausewitz gives a slightly lower strength to Prussian units.
9. Clausewitz, *Campagne*, pp. 49–50.
10. Clausewitz, *Campagne*, pp. 83 ff.
11. Camon, *Batailles*, p. 459.
12. Clausewitz, *Campagne*, p. 88.
13. Clausewitz, *Campagne*, p. 91.
14. Clausewitz, *Campagne*, p. 89.
15. Charles François, *Journal du capitaine François (1792–1830)*, (Paris: Carrington, 1903–1904), vol. II, pp. 879–81.
16. Casualties at Ligny, see Bowden, *Armies at Waterloo*, p. 372.
17. Camon, *Batailles*, p. 468.
18. Fleury de Chaboulon, *Mémoires de Fleury de Chaboulon* (Paris: Rouveyre, 1901), vol. II, p. 120.
19. Napoléon to Ney, 16 juin 1815, *Correspondance de Napoléon* (Paris: Imprimérie Impériale, 1869) Tome XXVII (22058).
20. Napoléon, Ordre, 16 juin 1815, Charleroi, *Correspondance* (22058).
21. Napoleon, *Correspondance*, 16 juin 1815 (22058).

22. Fleury, *Mémoires*, II, p. 139.
23. Camon, *Batailles*, p. 470.
24. Reille's IInd Corps had a full strength of 20,478 men, plus Kellermann's attached IIIrd Reserve Cavalry Corps of 3,858, for 24,336.
25. Bowden, *Armies at Waterloo*, p. 106.
26. Ibid. 6/12-lb. guns, 22/6-lb. guns, 2/6-inch howitzers, 8/5½-inch howitzers, to which must be added Kellermann's twelve guns. Bowden, 124.
27. Bowden, *Armies at Waterloo*, pp. 252, 258. (Two batteries, six guns per battery).
28. Bowden, *Armies at Waterloo*, p. 258: 6,893 men, 16 guns.
29. Clausewitz quotes it, *Campagne*, p. 57. Duc de Dalmatie, Major-Général, Maréchal d'Empire, devant Fleurus, le 16 juin 1815, à 2 heures. Soult to Ney.
30. Camon, *Batailles*, p. 472. D'Erlon first received Ney's order to advance to Quatre Bras at 12:15 P.M.. 16 June. Henry Houssaye, *1815: Waterloo* (Paris: Bartillat, 1987), pp. 200–01.
31. Ibid.
32. Camon, *Batailles*, p. 475.
33. Houssaye, *Waterloo*, pp. 208–09.
34. Jac Weller, *Wellington at Waterloo* (London: Longmans, 1967), p. 60.
35. Chandler, *Campaigns*, p. 1053; Camon, *Batailles*, p. 474. Sir Augustus Frazer, *Letters of Colonel Sir Augustus Frazer* (London: John Murray, 1859), p. 98.
36. Weller, *Wellington at Waterloo*, pp. 61–64.
37. Camon, *Batailles*, p. 473.
38. Weller, op. cit.
39. Weller, *Wellington at Waterloo*, p. 63.
40. Weller, *Wellington at Waterloo*, p. 64.
41. Chandler, *Campaigns*, p. 1053; Camon, *Batailles*, p. 474.
42. Camon, *Batailles*, p. 474, note 2.
43. Napoleon, conversation, to Fleury. Fleury, *Mémoires*, II. p. 134. Fleury and Baron Fain served as Napoleon's personal secretaries at this time. Fleury was apparently at Napoleon's side throughout the campaign.
44. Ney to Fouché and provisional government, 26 June 1815.
45. Chandler, *Campaigns*, p. 1057–58.
46. Chandler, *Campaigns*, p. 1060.
47. Ibid.
48. Camon, *Batailles*, p. 477, and Napoleon to Emmanuel de Grouchy, Mémoires du Maréchal de Grouchy (Paris: Dentu, 1874), V, pp. 35 ff.
49. Camon, *Batailles*, p. 477.
50. Camon, *Batailles*, pp. 476, 486. Duplicated by Soult to Ney, noon 17 juin 1815 (Camon, p. 483).
51. Camon, *Batailles*, p. 478.
52. Napoleon to Ney, Camon, *Batailles*, p. 476.

53. Chandler's analysis, *Campaigns*, p. 1059.
54. Soult to Ney, midi, le 17 juin 1815, Camon, *Batailles*, p. 483.
55. Sir Peter Hayman offers no insight into the situation now. See his otherwise interesting biography, *Soult, Napoleon's Maligned Marshal* (London: Arms and Armour, 1990). See also Nicole Gotteri, *Soult, Maréchal d'Empire et homme d'Etat* (Besançon La Manufacture, 1991), pp. 476–477.
56. Camon, *Batailles*, p. 484.
57. Camon, *Batailles*, p. 486.
58. Camon, *Batailles*, p. 486; Chandler, *Campaigns*, p. 1061.
59. Chandler, *Campaigns*, p. 1062; Camon, *Batailles*, p. 486.
60. French artillery: the 12-pounder gun, Model 1802–3, weighed 1,950 pounds and its limber 1,490 pounds. The French 6-pounder weighed 880 pounds and its limber 1,130, while the 6.54 howitzer (Gribeauval) weighed 700 pounds and its limber 1,365. The British 9-pounder weighed 1,510 pounds and its limber 1,760 pounds; the British 6-pounder weighed 576 pounds and its limber 1,065 pounds, and the British 5.5-inch howitzer, 448 pounds and its limber, 1,125 pounds. It took twelve horses to pull a French 12-pounder, ten to pull the 6.54-inch howitzer and the 8-pounder and eight horses to haul the 6- and 4-pounders. The British, on the other hand, used only six horses per team for their largest artillery piece there, the 9-pounder. See Weller's excellent chart, *Wellington at Waterloo*, p. 177.
61. Louis Marchand, *Mémoires de Marchand, Premier Valet de Chambre et Exécuteur Testamentaire de l'Empereur* (Paris: Plon, 1952), vol. I, pp. 162–63.
62. Camon, *Batailles*, p. 489.
63. Clausewitz, *Campagne*, p. 169.
64. Napoléon, "Campagne de 1815," *Correspondance*, XXXI; and Camon, *Batailles*, p. 488.
65. Bowden, *Armies at Waterloo*, pp. 327, 131, 272. 122,652 French Armée du Nord on 15 June. 18,421 casualties (600 at Gilly, 13,721 at Ligny, 4,100 at Quatre Bras), leaves 104,231 men. Of these Grouchy had 29,731 at Wavre. Adjusted total at Waterloo, 74,500 (see Bowden's figures, above pages). Chandler gives French Army 71,947 and 246 guns now. Chandler, p. 1065. (This includes 15,765 French cavalry). Camon gives Napoleon 78,000 men at Waterloo, *Batailles*, p. 98.
66. Bowden, *Armies at Waterloo*, p. 131. After deducting 18,421 casualties from 122,652, giving Grouchy 29,731. Napoleon gives a figure of 34,000 men. Napoleon, "Campagne de 1815," *Correspondance*, XXXI, p. 179. Camon gives Grouchy 33,000.
67. Ibid.
68. Bowden, *Armies at Waterloo*, p. 271. Bowden gives adjusted figure of 74,326. All above ordnance figures exclude rockets. Chandler (*Campaigns*) gives Wellington a force of only 67,661, including a cavalry of 12,408

and 156 guns. (Napoleon incorrectly claimed that Wellington had 90,000 men and 255 guns. Napoleon, "Campagne de 1815," *Correspondance*, vol. XXXI, p. 156. British guns—9-pounders, 6-pounders, 5.5-inch howitzers.) See also Weller, *Wellington at Waterloo*, p. 177.

69. Bowden, *Armies at Waterloo*, pp. 261–68.
70. The Prussian force, originally 130,246 (including officers) and 15,857 cavalry, 7,123 artillery, 103,343 infantry. Bowden, pp. 199, 201. On 18 June, reduced to 99,374, after deducting 30,772 casualties (Bowden, *Armies at Waterloo*, p. 327).
71. Bowden, *Armies at Waterloo*, pp. 261–68.
72. Bowden, *Armies at Waterloo*, p. 272.
73. Napoleon, "Campagne de 1815," *Correspondance*, XXXI, p. 183. Chandler gives 84 guns, Camon, p. 492.
74. Napoleon, "Campagne de 1815," *Correspondance*, XXXI, p. 1832.
75. Napoleon, "Campagne de 1815," XXXI, p. 183.
76. Marchand, *Mémoires*, I, p. 163.
77. Marchand, *Mémoires*, I, p. 163.
78. Camon, p. 494.
79. Camon, pp. 497 (and 494).
80. Chandler, pp. 1072–73.
81. Chandler, p. 1076.
82. Clausewitz reproduces this entire order, pp. 150–51 (see also p. 149). Camon, p. 500. Soult to Grouchy, ca. 1.15 p.m., 18 juin 1815 (quoted by Camon, p. 500).
83. Clausewitz, p. 157. In fact the 1:30 letter did not reach Grouchy until 7 P.M. according to Clausewitz, it having been sent the long way around via Quatre Bras and Gembloux.
84. Clausewitz, pp. 157, 166.
85. Chandler, p. 1076. 12–pounders carried a maximum range of 1,800 meters, while 8–pounders carried only 1,500 meters.
86. Camon, pp. 503–04.
87. Edward Cotton, *A Voice from Waterloo. A History of the Battle Fought on the 18th June, 1815*. (Brussels: Hotel du Musée, 1913), p. 126.
88. Camon, p. 504. Chandler, pp. 1073, 1077. "Belles filles"—name given by Napoléon to the Imperial Guard's 12-pounders.
89. Chandler, p. 1078.
90. Chandler, pp. 1077 and 1078.
91. Bowden, *Armies at Waterloo*, p. 252. General Sir James Kempt, 8th British Brigade; Brigadier General Sir Denis Pack, 9th British Brigade.
92. Fleury de Chaboulon, *Mémoires*, II, pp. 140–41.
93. For all statistics on Lord Uxbridge's Cavalry Corps, see Bowden, *Armies at Waterloo*, pp. 268–71. On battle events, see also Chandler, pp. 1078–79, and of course Camon's excellent work. (Lieutenant General, the Earl of Uxbridge. Major General Lord Edward Somerset (1776–1842) had com-

manded the 4th Light Dragoons during the Peninsular War. At Waterloo he commanded the Brigade of Household Cavalry. He was the fourth son of Henry, 5th Duke of Beaufort. Major General Sir William Ponsonby, killed at Waterloo.)

94. Chandler, p. 1079.
95. Camon, p. 506.
96. Chandler, p. 1079.
97. Ibid.
98. Fleury, *Mémoires*, II, p. 142.
99. Chandler, p. 1080.
100. Chandler, p. 1079.
101. Ibid.
102. Chandler, p. 1080.
103. Cotton, *Voice from Waterloo*, p. 116.
104. Chandler, p. 1081.
105. Rees Howell Gronow, *Captain Gronow, His Reminiscences of Regency and Victorian Life 1810–60*, edited by Christopher Hibbert (London: Kyle Cathie, 1991), p. 137.
106. Gronow, *Reminiscences*, p. 137.
107. Chandler, p. 1084.
108. Camon, p. 508.
109. Gronow, *Reminiscences*, p. 114; Chandler, p. 1081.
110. Fleury de Chaboulon, *Mémoires*, II, p. 145.
111. Houssaye, *Waterloo*, pp. 389 ff.
112. Bowden, *Armies at Waterloo*, pp. 83 and 124; Chandler, p. 1084; Camon, p. 509.
113. Bowden, *Armies at Waterloo*, p. 83. Camon states that Napoleon ordered Guyot to march, pp. 501–10.
114. Fleury de Chaboulon, *Mémoires*, II, p. 145.
115. Chandler, p. 1084; Bowden, pp. 83, 124.
116. Quoted by Cotton, *Voice from Waterloo*, p. 311.
117. Fleury de Chaboulon, *Mémoires*, II, p. 148.
118. "This is thundering murderous work," one of Halket's soldiers commented. Cotton, *Voice from Waterloo*, p. 117.
119. Ney to Fouché, le 26 juin 1815.
120. Ibid.
121. Chandler, p. 1086.
122. The Prussians used the term *brigade* instead of the rough British or French equivalent, *division*. The average Prussian brigade was almost 6,000 men (e.g., Hake's 6,642; von Funcke's 6,853; Losthen's 5,902; and Hiller's 5,774). See Bowden, *Armies at Waterloo*, p. 197.
123. Camon, pp. 510–11.
124. Camon, p. 512.
125. Napoleon to Jourdan, 28 July 1809.

126. Fleury de Chaboulon, *Mémoires*, II, p. 141.

127. Clausewitz, p. 167.

128. Camon, pp. 513–14.

129. Cotton, *Voice from Waterloo*, p. 125.

130. Chandler, pp. 1087, 1088.

131. Ney complained of Napoleon's desertion of his army in a letter to Joseph Fouché in his capacity as head of the provisional government, 26 June 1815.

132. Official French report, "Bataille de Mont Saint-Jean."

133. Fleury, *Mémoires*, II, p. 150.

134. Official French report, "Bataille de Mont Saint-Jean."

135. "Bataille de Mont Saint-Jean."

136. Ney to Fouché, 26 June 1815.

137. Clausewitz, pp. 188 ff. for the Prussian pursuit.

138. Houssaye, *Waterloo*, pp. 422–26; Fleury, *Mémoires*, II, pp. 150–52; and Marchand, *Mémoires*, I, pp. 164–66.

139. Houssaye, *Waterloo*, p. 428, quotes Colonel Baudus re Napoleon's tears, corroborated by Marchand and Fleury.

140. Wellington to Prinz Schwarzenberg, 26 June 1815, in Wellington, *The Dispatches of Field Marshal, the Duke of Wellington during his various Campaigns* (London: John Murray, 1858–65), II, p. 510.

141. Clausewitz, pp. 189, 191, 193.

142. Wellington to Sir Charles Stuart, 28 June 1815, Wellington, *The Dispatches*, XII, p. 242.

143. Wellington to Lord Beresford, 2 July 1815, Wellington, *The Dispatches*, XII, p. 529.

144. Wellington to Prinz Schwarzenberg, Joncourt, 26 June 1815, *The Dispatches*, XII, p. 510.

145. Wellington to Lord Uxbridge, Le Cateau, 23 June 1815, *The Dispatches*, XII, pp. 499–500.

146. Wellington to Schwarzenberg, Joncourt, 26 June 1815, *The Dispatches*, XII, p. 510.

147. Houssaye, *Waterloo*, pp. 429–31.

148. Houssaye, *Waterloo*, pp. 432, 440.

149. Fleury, *Mémoires*, II, pp. 155, 156. On Joseph Bonaparte, see Gabriel Girod de l'Ain, *Joseph Bonaparte, Le Roi Malgré Lui* (Paris: Perrin, 1970), pp. 317 ff.

150. Clausewitz, pp. 202, 215, gives Blücher 60,000 men and Wellington 50,000; see Chandler, p. 1094 for slightly different figures.

151. Chandler, p. 1091; Napoleon, *Correspondance*, XXVIII, Napoleon to Joseph Bonaparte, Philippeville, 19 juin 1815; Chandler, p. 1090. See Hayman, *Soult*, p. 231.

152. Marchand, *Mémoires*, I, p. 167.

153. Bowden, *Armies at Waterloo*, p. 327. Total Coalition dead, wounded, de-

serters, prisoners at Waterloo, 24,143: 6,998 Prussians, and *17,145* Allies (Dutch, Belgian, British, Germans). Separate British losses at Waterloo were 8,458. During the entire campaign in Belgium, France lost 64,602 men as casualties, including 43,656 at Waterloo and during the retreat. The Allies suffered total casualties of 62,818, including Prussian figures of 40,237, and Allies of 22,581. Of the British losses of 8,458, 460 included officers, thereby giving the British the highest percentage of casualties among the Allies, i.e. approximately 30%. The French of course had approximately 51% "casualties" when including in that figure prisoners, deserters, etc. All the above figures are based on Bowden's calculation, Armies at Waterloo, pp. 324–27. Thus, according to him, the entire campaign in Belgium resulted in 127,420 casualties.

On captured guns, Chandler gives a figure of 220 French guns taken at Waterloo by the Allies (and Prussians), p. 1098, though Clausewitz gives a figure of 260.

CHAPTER XIII

END OF THE NAPOLÉONADE

1. Von Humboldt coauthored this thirty-volume work with Aimé Bonpland and K. S. Kunth, later completed by Humboldt's *Géographie du Nouveau Continent*.
2. Henri Houssaye, *1815*, vol. III: *La Seconde Abdication—La Terreur Blanche* (Paris: Perrin, 1914), p. 215.
3. Houssaye, *1815: La Seconde Abdication*, p. 215.
4. Queen Hortense, *Mémoires de la Reine Hortense* (Paris: Plon, 1927), III, p. 27.
5. Fleury de Chaboulon, *Mémoires de Fleury de Chaboulon* (Paris: Rouveyre, 1901), II, p. 166.
6. Fleury, *Mémoires*, II, p. 167.
7. Fleury, *Mémoires*, II, p. 168.
8. Fleury, *Mémoires*, II, 169. Regnault to Napoleon.
9. Fleury, *Mémoires*, II, p. 169.
10. Fleury, *Mémoires*, II, p. 170.
11. Duc de Castries, *La Fayette* (Paris: Tallandier, 1981), p. 355.
12. Fleury, *Mémoires*, II, p. 171.
13. Castries, *La Fayette*, p. 314.
14. La Fayette to Napoléon, Castries, *La Fayette*, p. 306.
15. Castries, *La Fayette*, pp. 339–40.

16. Castries, *La Fayette*, p. 352. 21 juin 1815.
17. Castries, *La Fayette*, p. 366.
18. Castries, *La Fayette*, p. 350. 21 avril 1815. La Fayette to Joseph Bonaparte, at Palais Royal.
19. Castries, *La Fayette*, p. 357.
20. Castries, *La Fayette*, p. 358.
21. Fleury de Chaboulon, *Mémoires*, II, p. 167.
22. Castries, *La Fayette*, p. 359.
23. Castries, *La Fayette*, p. 358.
24. Fleury, *Mémoires*, II, p. 175. Lucien's speech.
25. Gilbert de La Fayette, *Mémoires, Correspondances et manuscrits du général de La Fayette* (Paris: Fournier Aîné, 1837–1838), vol. V, p. 453.
26. Fleury, *Mémoires*, II, pp. 174–75.
27. Fleury, *Mémoires*, II, p. 178.
28. 21 juin 1815, La Fayette calls for Napoleon's abdication before the Committee's joint meeting. Castries, *La Fayette*, p. 361.
29. Castries, *La Fayette*, p. 357.
30. Napoleon to Regnault, Fleury, *Mémoires*, II, p. 180.
31. Regnault to Napoleon, 22 juin 1815. Fleury, *Mémoires*, II, p. 180.
32. Napoleon's abdication "Déclaration au peuple Français," 22 juin 1815: See *Journal des Débats*, 23 juin 1815; Fleury, *Mémoires*, II, p. 182.
33. Louis Marchand, *Mémoires de Marchand, Premier Valet de Chambre et Exécuteur Testamentair de l'Empereur* (Paris: Plon, 1952), vol. I: *L'Ile d'Elbe—Les Cent Jours*, pp. 177, 181.
34. Hortense, *Mémoires*, III, pp. 26, 28, 30.
35. Hortense, *Mémoires*, III, p. 30.
36. Davout to Beker, Paris, le 27 juin 1815, Houssaye, *1815: La Seconde Abdication*, p. 210, and Fleury, *Mémoires*, II, p. 211. See also General Beker, *Relation de la Mission du Lieutenant-Général Comte Beker auprès de l'Empereur* (Paris: Didier, 1876).
37. Davout to Beker, le 25 juin 1815, 4 P.M., quoted by Marchand, *Mémoires*, I, pp. 182–83.
38. Hortense, *Mémoires*, III, p. 31.
39. Hortense, *Mémoires*, III, pp. 31, 32. Fleury, *Mémoires*, II, p. 216.
40. Fleury, *Mémoires*, I, pp. 222–23.
41. Fleury, *Mémoires*, II, p. 210. Hortense, *Mémoires*, III, pp. 22–23.
42. Hortense, *Mémoires*, III, pp. 31 ff.
43. Liverpool to Castlereagh, Wellington, *Supplementary Despatches, Correspondence, and Memoranda of Field Marshal Arthur, Duke of Wellington, K.G.* (London: John Murray, 1863), vol. 11, p. 47.
44. Fleury, *Mémoires*, II, p. 212.
45. Marchand, *Mémoires*, II, p. 380, mentions this and then quotes Napoleon's letter to Laffitte, dated, "longwood, Ile de Sainte-Hélène, ce 2 avril 1821," See also Marchand, *Mémoires*, I, p. 182.

46. Marchand, *Mémoires*, I, p. 178.
47. Quoted in entirety, Marchand, *Mémoires*, I, p. 175.
48. Hortense, *Mémoires*, III, p. 34. Fleury, *Mémoires*, II, pp. 212 ff.
49. Napoléon, Paris, le 10 juin 1815, to La Princesse Hortense, quoted by Hortense, *Mémoires*, II, p. 385.
50. Hortense, *Mémoires*, III, p. 35, footnote.
51. 18 Brumaire 1799, and 20 March 1815.
52. Upon returning to her mansion in the rue Cerutti, Hortense was contacted by a group of Bonapartist officers. Hortense, *Mémoires*, III, pp. 56 ff.
53. Fleury, *Mémoires*, II, p. 229.
    On 29 June the Commission informed both Chambers that "l'approche de l'ennemi, et la crainte d'un mouvement à l'intérieur (bonapartiste), lui avaient imposé le devoir sacré de faire partir Napoléon." Fleury, *Mémoires*, II, p. 234.
54. Fleury, *Mémoires*, II, p. 214.
55. Quoted by Fleury, *Mémoires*, II, p. 214.
56. Fleury, *Mémoires*, II, pp. 214–16.
57. Joseph Fouché, *Les Mémoires de Fouché* (Paris: Flammarion, 1945), p. 502.
58. Fouché, *Mémoires*, p. 502.
59. Hortense says grey, Marchand says brown.
60. Hortense, *Mémoires*, III, p. 36–37.
61. Hortense, *Mémoires*, III, p. 33, note 1, and p. 37.
62. Hortense, *Mémoires*, III, p. 39.
63. See note 3, p. 45, of Hortense *Mémoires* III. Marchand states that Joseph did not rejoin Napoleon until the fifth, at Rochefort, Marchand, *Mémoires*, I, p. 200.
64. Ibid.
65. Marchand discusses the gold and librarian Barbier's problems. Marchand, *Mémoires*, I, p. 200.
66. Marchand, *Mémoires*, I, p. 201.
67. Fleury, *Mémoires*, II, pp. 231–34, where these complete instructions are to be found.
68. Marchand, *Mémoires*, I, p. 203.
69. Marchand, *Mémoires*, I, pp. 203–04.
70. Quoted by Marchand, *Mémoires*, I, p. 205.
71. Alan Schom, *Trafalgar, Countdown to Battle, 1803–1805* (New York: Atheneum, 1990), p. 346.
72. Marchand, *Mémoires*, I, p. 206.
73. Viscount Castlereagh (2nd Marquess of Londonderry), *Correspondence Despatches, and other Papers of Viscount Castlereagh*. 3rd Series: Military and Diplomatic (London: Murray, 1853), vol. 10, p. 430.
74. *La Quotidienne, ou La Feuille du Jour*, mercredi, le 19 juillet 1815.
75. "Instructions pour Messieurs les Plénipotentiaires de la Commission du

Gouvernement auprès des Puissances alliées," 23 juin 1815, quoted by Fleury, *Mémoires*, II, 238–48.

76. Fleury, *Mémoires*, II, p. 251.

77. Instructions of 23 June 1815.

78. "Instructions Pour Messieurs les Commissaires Chargées de Traiter d'un Armistice, Paris, le 27 juin 1815," quoted by Fleury, *Mémoires*, II, pp. 253–57; Houssaye, *1815: La Seconde Abdication*, pp. 168 ff.

79. 1 July 1815, Bignon to his commissioners—Andréossy, Comte Boissy d'Anglas, Flaugergues, Valence, Labenardière. Fleury, *Mémoires*, II, pp. 270–72.

80. Fleury, *Mémoires*, II, pp. 275–76.

81. Fouché, *Mémoires*, p. 503.

82. Von Clausewitz gives Wellington 50,000 (with another 10,000 behind the lines in garrisons, etc.) and Blücher 60,000 (with another 10,000 behind the lines) exclusive of the IInd Prussian Corps not present during this part of the campaign against Paris. Karl von Clausewitz, *La campagne de 1815 en France* (Paris: Chapelot, 1900), p. 215.

83. Clausewitz, *Campagne*, pp. 200–01.

84. For a survey of this phase of operations, see Clausewitz, *Campagne de 1815*, p. 220.

85. Davout quotation, Fleury, *Mémoires*, II, p. 289.

86. Clausewitz, *Campagne*, p. 202.

87. Davout quoted, Fleury, *Mémoires*, II, p. 289.

88. Davout to Fouché, 29 juin 1815, Fleury, *Mémoires*, II, p. 261.

89. Fleury, *Mémoires*, II, pp. 287–88.

90. Davout before Conseil de Guerre, at Villette, ½ juillet 1815, presided over by Davout, Fleury, *Mémoires*, II, pp. 287–88.

91. Fouché, *Mémoires*, p. 507.

92. Fleury, *Mémoires*, II, pp. 295–99.

93. Houssaye, *1815: La Seconde Abdication*, pp. 296 ff.

94. Houssaye, *1815: La Seconde Abdication*, pp. 560 ff.

95. Houssaye, *1815: La Seconde Abdication*, pp. 568–69.

96. *Journal des Débats*, mercredi, le 22 novembre 1815.

97. Ordnance du 24 juillet 1815, published in *Gazette Officielle* of 23 July and *Moniteur* of 26 July. See also Houssaye for text, *1815: La Seconde Abdication*, p. 429.

98. Davout quoted in Houssaye, *1815: La Seconde Abdication*, III, p. 434.

99. Liverpool to Castlereagh, Fife House, 15 July 1815, Castlereagh, *Correspondence, Despatches*, vol. 10, p. 431.

100. Davout to commanding officers, 1 August 1815. Houssaye, *1815: La Seconde Abdication*, pp. 426 ff.

101. See Houssaye, *1815: La Seconde Abdication*, p. 436.

102. For full list, see Fleury, *Mémoires*, II, pp. 327–29 and Houssaye, *1815: La Seconde Abdication*, pp. 427–33.

103. Quoted by Evariste Dumoulin, *Histoire complète du procès du maréchal Ney* (Paris: Delaunay, 1815), II, pp. 330–32; and Houssaye, *1815: La Seconde Abdication*, p. 578.
104. Houssaye, *1815: La Seconde Abdication*, p. 578.
105. See *Journal des Débats*, jeudi, le 7 décembre 1815, pp. 1, 2, 3, 4, for the trial. The entire proceedings were immediately published in two cahiers.
106. Record of his execution taken from *Journal des Débats*, 8 décembre 1815, and from Houssaye, *1815: La Seconde Abdication*, pp. 583–85.
107. *Journal des Débats*, vendredi, 8 décembre 1815.

EPILOGUE

1. Pozzo di Borgo, *Correspondance Diplomatique*, I, p. viii.
2. François René de Chateaubriand, *De Buonaparte et des Bourbons* (pamphlet, published March 1814).

INDEX

Additional Act, 132–34, 207–9, 299
  plebiscite on, 208–9, 216
Alexander I, Czar of Russia, 9, 96, 99–
  101, 160, 177, 296
  and Allied declaration of war against Na-
    poleon, 106
  Congress of Vienna and, 101, 103–4
  Fouché and, 121
  and invasion of France, 3
  and kidnapping and execution of En-
    ghien, 93
  and Napoleon's abdication, 99
  and Napoleon's exile on Elba, 104
  and Napoleon's public renunciation of
    war, 173
  and preparations for war against Napo-
    leon, 246
  Talleyrand and, 88, 97, 100
  and Treaty of Paris, 5
Alten, Karl August von, 271, 279
Amiens, Treaty of, 4, 38, 71
Andréossy, General, 91, 187, 194, 301
Angoulême, Louis-Antoine, Duc d', 41, 51,
  53, 212
  royalist uprisings and, 170, 174
Antibes, Napoleon's attempt to neutralize
  garrison at, 15–16, 19
Armée du Nord, French:
  creation of, 185–86
  mobilization of, 194
  Napoleon's joining with, 219–20
  in retreat, 290

Artois, Charles-Philippe, Comte d', 5
  Fouché and, 121–23
  and Napoleon's invasion of France, 27,
    42–44, 46, 122
Assaye, battle of, 225–27
Austria:
  Congress of Vienna and, 101–3, 105–6
  in invasion of France, 312
  in preparing for war against Napoleon,
    246, 249
Autichamp, Comte d', 150–51, 153–54
Auxerre, Napoleon's arrival in, 29–31

Bachelu, General, 268, 279
Badajoz:
  peace of, 62
  siege of, 230
Barras, Paul, 67, 141
Bassano, Duc de, see Maret, Hugues, Duc
  de Bassano
Beauharnais, Hortense de, 160, 305–7
  divorce of, 305
  Napoleon's house arrest and, 302, 305
  Napoleon's reconciliation with, 296–97
  on Talleyrand, 87
Beauharnais, Josephine de, 63–64, 296–97
  Davout and, 164–65
  death of, 297
  and kidnapping and execution of En-
    ghien, 93
  Napoleon's divorce from, 172, 296
  Napoleon's insulting of, 72

Index

Beauharnais, Josephine de, *(cont.)*
Napoleon's marriage to, 67–68
and Napoleon's relationship with Talleyrand, 95
in plotting against Napoleon, 120
Beker, General, 302
and Napoleon's surrender to British, 310
and Prussian encirclement of Paris, 306–7
Bellerophon, H.M.S., Napoleon's boarding of, 308–10
Bernadotte, Jean, 70, 166
Berry, Charles-Ferdinand, Duc de, 33
and Napoleon's invasion of France, 41–44
and Napoleon's march on Paris, 47, 51–52
Berthier, Alexandre, Prince de Neuchâtel et Valengin, 36, 53
comparisons between Davout and, 193–94
conflicts between Davout and, 166
Napoleon abandoned by, 4–5
and Napoleon's march on Paris, 54
suicide of, 214
and Westphalian trade with Britain, 83
Bertrand, Henri, 309
in exile with Napoleon, 6, 8
in invasion of France, 14, 16–18, 25, 30–31, 33
and Napoleon's march on Paris, 55–56
in retreat, 291, 293–94
Bijlandt, General Van, 256, 259, 283
Blacas d'Aulps, Comte de, 33, 40–41, 52–53
Fouché and, 121
and Louis's flight from France, 53
and Napoleon's invasion of France, 41, 43–44
and Napoleon's march on Paris, 47–48
Blücher von Wahlstadt, Prinz Gebhard Leberecht, von, 238–40
aides of, 248
and Allied control of Quatre Bras, 256
and battle of Ligny, 259–61, 263–67, 272–73
and battle of Quatre Bras, 269, 272
and battle of Saint-Amand, 265–66
and battle of Waterloo, 277, 281, 288–89, 292
Bourmont's meeting with, 238–39
and French army in retreat, 294
and French attack on Charleroi, 254
in invasion of France, 3, 313
and Napoleon's war preparations, 174
in preparing for war against Napoleon, 240, 243, 247–51, 253
in retreat, 273–74, 276

tactical errors of, 267
Bonaparte, Alexandrine Jouberthon, 63–64
Bonaparte, Caroline, 209–10
Bonaparte, Christine, 59–60
Bonaparte, Elizabeth Patterson, 77–82
Bonaparte, Jérôme, 58, 74–84, 119, 296–97
and battle of Quatre Bras, 268
and battle of Waterloo, 279–80, 289
Champ de mai ceremonies and, 213
education of, 76
finances of, 77–78, 80–81
in line of succession, 72, 78
marriages of, 77–82
military command of, 236
Napoleon's Continental System defied by, 83
and Napoleon's planned trip to United States, 304
Napoleon's relationship with, 76–84, 210
naval career of, 76–78, 80–81
plots against, 100
self-promotions of, 80
Westphalian crown assumed by, 74–75, 81–84
womanizing of, 80, 83
Bonaparte, Joseph, 57–58, 63, 65–75, 84, 296–97
Additional Act and, 134
as ambassador to Rome, 68–69
and battle of Waterloo, 293
Champ de mai ceremonies and, 213
Constant and, 131
country estates acquired by, 69
creative writing of, 69–70
crown of Naples and Sicily assumed by, 73–74
crown of Spain assumed by, 74–75
on desire for peace, 38
education of, 66
finances of, 66–67, 71–73
in flight from Madrid, 234
Fouché's relationship with, 118
and French occupation of Rome, 69
French politics and, 67–68, 71
Jérôme Bonaparte and, 81
in line of succession, 72–73
military command of, 73–74
Napoleon rejoined by, 209–10
Napoleon's abdication and, 299
and Napoleon's defeat, 297
Napoleon's defeat, 297
Napoleon's house arrest and, 305
and Napoleon's joining with Armée du Nord, 220

and Napoleon's planned trip to United
States, 304, 307, 309
Napoleon's relationship with, 66–67, 70–
75
piracy of, 59
power hunger of, 70–73
Talleyrand and, 100
Bonaparte, Josephine, *see* Beauharnais,
Josephine de
Bonaparte, Julie Clary, 66–67
Bonaparte, Letizia, 59, 64
and Jérôme Bonaparte's marriage, 78–79
Bonaparte, Louis, 58, 72–75, 84, 296
Batavian crown assumed by, 74–75
divorce of, 305
in line of succession, 72
military command, 73
Bonaparte, Lucien, 58–66, 72, 84, 296–97
Additional Act and, 134
as ambassador to Spain, 61–62
ambitions of, 62
background of, 58
Champ de mai ceremonies and, 213
Fouché's relationship with, 61, 118–19
under house arrest in Britain, 65
jealousy of, 63
life in Rome of, 64–65
marriage of, 63–64
Napoleon rejoined by, 210
Napoleon's abdication and, 298, 300
Napoleon's Consulate and, 60–61
and Napoleon's escape from Elba, 65
and Napoleon's joining with Armée du
Nord, 220
and Napoleon's planned trip to United
States, 303–4
Napoleon's reconciliation with, 65–66
offensive manner of, 61
piracy of, 59, 61
political career of, 59–64
power hunger of, 70
private life of, 61
wealth of, 59–60, 62, 64–65
Bonaparte family, 57–58
Fouché's investigations of, 119, 126
Napoleon rejoined by, 209–10
Borghese, Pauline, 7–8, 14
Boudin, General, 29–30
Bourmont, Louis-Auguste, Comte de, 32,
238–39
Bourrienne, Louis de, 123, 142
Bouthillier de Chavigny, Comte de, 17–18
and Napoleon's invasion of France, 21–25
Brayer, General:
Champ de mai ceremonies and, 213

and Napoleon's march on Paris, 27–29,
55
Brune, Guillaume-Marie, 146
assassination of, 314
mobilization and, 195–96, 200
royalist uprisings and, 203
Bruxelles, 236–42
Napoleon's planned drive into, 236–40,
253–59, 268
prewar festivities in, 241–42
Wellington in, 241–42, 244
Bubna von Littitz, Ferdinand von, 312–13
Bülow von Dennewitz, Graf, 247
and battle of Ligny, 260, 264–65
and battle of Waterloo, 281, 288
in preparing for war against Napoleon,
250

Cadoudal, Georges, 93, 120
Cambacérès, Jean-Jacques de, 108, 185,
215, 301
Cambronne, Pierre-Jacques, 316
and attack on Antibes, 15, 19
Cannes captured by, 17–18
in capture of Grasse, 20
in exile with Napoleon, 6, 8
in invasion of France, 14–15, 17–20, 25
Camon, Hubert, 253, 267, 275
Campbell, Sir Neil:
Napoleon's exile and, 1, 7–10, 13
and Napoleon's invasion of France, 14–15
and violation of Treaty of Fontainebleau, 9
Cannes, Napoleon's capture of, 17–22
Carnot, Lazare-Nicolas-Marguerite, xii, 109,
136–49, 175–76
Additional Act and, 208
and Allied encirclement of Paris, 306,
313
and Allied invasion of France, 298
Champ de mai ceremonies and, 217
commerce and industry influenced by,
149
in communicating government ideas and
programs to peasantry, 148–49
comparisons between Davout and, 163
critics of, 141
Davout's conflicts with, 199
energy of, 140–43
on fédérés, 158
loyalty and honor of, 141
mobilization and, 158–59, 175, 182–83,
188, 195, 199–203
on monarchy, 136
in Napoleon's new government, 129–30
Napoleon's relationship with, 137, 139,
141–42

Carnot, Lazare-Nicolas-Marguerite, *(cont.)*
  physical appearance of, 140–41
  prefects replaced by, 145–47
  private life of, 140
  in propaganda effort, 203
  on public opposition to Napoleon, 176
  and public opposition to war, 148
  in recruiting soldiers, 195
  and restoration of law and order, 143–49
  retirement of, 139–40
  during Revolution, 138–39, 142–43
  royalist uprisings and, 151–52, 201–2
Castlereagh, Robert Stewart, Lord, 1, 9–10, 221
  and Allied declaration of war against Napoleon, 106
  and Allied invasion of France, 3
  Congress of Vienna and, 101–2, 104–6
  and Napoleon's abdication, 99
  and Napoleon's escape from Elba, 105
  and Napoleon's exile on Elba, 10, 104–5
  and Napoleon's surrender, 310
  and preparations for war against Napoleon, 246
  Talleyrand's relationship with, 101–3
Caulaincourt, Armand de, Duc de Vicence, 2–5, 97, 106, 137, 171–72, 297–98
  Additional Act and, 133
  and Allied declaration of war against Napoleon, 108, 128
  and Allied invasion of France, 298
  Champ de mai ceremonies and, 219
  mobilization and, 192
  Napoleon's attempted suicide and, 2, 5, 7
  and Napoleon's defeat, 297
  on Napoleon's incongruous acts, 156
  and Napoleon's mistrust of Ney, 239
  and Napoleon's public renunciation of war, 172, 174
  Talleyrand's relationship with, 91
  war with Allies predicted by, 135
Chamber of Representatives, French, Napoleon's abdication demanded by, 298–301
Champ de mai ceremonies, 210–19
  Additional Act and, 133
  celebrities at, 212–13, 217
  Dubois d'Anger's speech at, 215–16
  electoral delegates at, 214–16, 218–19
  foreign ambassadors absent from, 213–14
  Napoleon's speech at, 216–17
  purpose of, 214, 218–19
Chandler, David G.:
  on battle of Waterloo, 286–87
  on French attack on Charleroi, 255–56
Charleroi, 253–56

Napoleon's attack at, 254–56
  Napoleon's retreat to, 290, 293
  Napoleon's strategy at, 253–54
Chastenay, Victorine de:
  Fouché and, 107, 113, 118, 122
  on Talleyrand, 85, 88
Chateaubriand, François-Auguste-René de, xiii, 97, 126
  on Constant's political conversion, 132
  on Fouché, 114
  on Napoleon, 320–21
Clarke, Henri-Jacques, Duc de Feltre, 43
  and Louis's flight from France, 53
  Napoleon abandoned by, 198
  and Napoleon's march on Paris, 50
Clary, Désirée, 66, 68, 70
Clausel, Bertrand, 174, 199–200
Clausewitz, Karl von, 251
  and battle of Waterloo, 276–77, 281, 289
Congress of Vienna, 9–10, 100–106, 171
  aims of, 100–101
  and Allied declaration of war against Napoleon, 106, 108
  and Napoleon's escape from Elba, 105–6
  and Napoleon's exile on Elba, 104–5
Constant, Benjamin, 51, 71
  Additional Act authored by, 132–34
  on Napoleon's rule, 129, 131–32
  political conversion of, 132
Constant Rebecque, Baron J. V. de, 243
  and Allied control of Quatre Bras, 256, 259
  and French attack on Charleroi, 255–56
Consulate, Napoleon's creation of, 60–62, 70, 75–76, 165, 168
Continental System, 36, 83, 95, 99
Cooke, General, 271, 279
Corps d'Observation du Var, creation of, 186, 195–96
Custine, Madame de, Fouché and, 113, 122

Daru, Comte, 188, 191, 199
Davout, Louis, Duc d'Auerstaedt and Prince d'Eckmühl, xii, 108, 161–71, 173–76, 273
  administrative skills lacked by, 168, 198
  and Allied encirclement of Paris, 313
  aristocratic background of, 162
  in calling for Napoleon's departure from France, 302–3
  campaign plans and strategy drafted by, 187
  Champ de mai ceremonies and, 212–13, 217
  comparisons between Berthier and, 193–94

critics of, 165–66
in Eygptian Expedition, 1662–63, 165
energy of, 170
on fédérés, 158
impatience of, 196–97
logistical concerns of, 187–90. 193, 197–99
loyalty of, 165–68, 183–84
military career of, 162–67
military training of, 161–62
mobilization and, 158–59, 170, 173–75, 179, 182–83, 186–91, 193–201, 203, 205
and musket production, 189–90
and Napoleon's invasion of France, 12–13
Napoleon's relationship with, 161–69, 171, 183–84, 190, 195–99, 232, 308–9
Ney's trial and, 315–17
officers criticized by, 199
in organizing War Ministry, 168–71
and planning for defense of Lyons, 198, 205
private life of, 164–66
on public opposition to Napoleon, 176
and public opposition to war, 148
in recruiting soldiers, 195, 199
reputation of, 164, 166, 169
and restoration of law and order, 143, 147, 150
during Revolution, 162
royalist uprisings and, 151–52, 174, 201, 203–4
in Russian Campaign, 166–67
in selecting field commanders, 185, 197
uniform procurement program and, 191
War Minister appointment of, 161, 167, 171
wealth of, 165
Decrès, Denis, 37, 41, 108
Champ de mai ceremonies and, 217
comparisons between Davout and, 167
comparisons between Fouché and, 114
Jérôme Bonaparte and, 78, 80
and Napoleon's allegations against Talleyrand, 98
and Napoleon's planned trip to United States, 303, 308
Napoleon's relationship with, 308–9
naval budgets and, 180–81, 188
and planning for defense of Paris, 206–7
and Prussian encirclement of Paris, 306
Dejean, Comte Jean-François, 205, 290, 301
Dessolles, General, 43–44, 47, 51
Digne, Napoleon's march on, 22–25
Donzelot, General, 282, 287, 289

Dörnberg, Sir William, 251, 256
Drouet, Jean-Baptiste, Comte d'Erlon, 42
and battle of Ligny, 263–67
and battle of Quatre Bras, 269, 271–72
and battle of Waterloo, 277, 279–80, 282–84, 287, 289
marching orders of, 236–38
in pursuit of Allies in retreat, 275
Drouot, Antoine, 202, 237, 274–75
and battle of Quatre Bras, 274
in exile with Napoleon, 6, 8
in invasion of France, 14, 25
Napoleon's abdication and, 301
and Napoleon's march on Paris, 55–56
in pursuit of Allies in retreat, 275
in retreat, 291, 293
Dubois d'Angers (representative of electors), 215–16
Durutte, General, 264, 282–83, 288

Egyptian Expedition, 162–63, 165
Elba:
entertainment on, 7–8, 10
Napoleon's cabinet on, 6, 8
Napoleon's escape from, xi, 9–14, 65, 105–6, 235
Napoleon's exile on, 1, 3–4, 6–13, 65, 104–5
Enghien, Duc d', kidnapping and execution of, 93, 98–99, 172
Erlon, Comte d', see Drouet, Jean-Baptiste, Comte d'Erlon

Fleury de Chaboulon, Edouard, 296, 303–4
Additional Act and, 208
and battle of Quatre Bras, 267–68
and battle of Waterloo, 283, 286, 289, 293
and Fouché's plot against Napoleon, 155
on Napoleon's Champ de mai speech, 217
and Napoleon's escape from Elba, 105
and Napoleon's invasion of France, xi, 12–13, 23, 31
and Napoleon's march on Paris, 49
and Napoleon's planned trip to United States, 303
on public dissatisfaction with Napoleon, 218
Fontainebleau, Treaty of, xi, 5–6, 8–10, 100, 105
Fouché, Joseph, Duc d'Otrante, xii, 36, 86, 107, 109–26, 137, 175–76, 311–14
Additional Act and, 133
and Allied encirclement of Paris, 306–7, 313
and Allied invasion of France, 298

Index

Fouché, Joseph, Duc d'Otrante, *(cont.)*
  and armistice with Allies, 311–13
  bribes accepted by, 114, 118
  in calling for Napoleon's departure from
    France, 302, 304–5
  calmness of, 115
  Champ de mai ceremonies and, 212
  Church opposed by, 109–11
  comparisons between Carnot and, 138,
    141, 146
  comparisons between Napoleon and, 112–
    13
  comparisons between Talleyrand and, 88–
    90, 92, 113–15, 119
  demeanor of, 112–20
  disabling qualities of, 119–20
  energy of, 112, 115–16, 126
  fédéré movement and, 156, 158
  on foreign policy, 118–19, 122, 124
  and French surrender to Allies, 314
  independence of, 115
  Jérôme Bonaparte and, 80
  and kidnapping and execution of En-
    ghien, 93
  liberal police policies of, 125–26, 146
  Lucien Bonaparte's relationship with, 61,
    118–19
  Lyons anti-Christianization campaign of,
    110–12, 114, 117
  Napoleon's despotism and, 175
  Napoleon's doom predicted by, 154
  and Napoleon's invasion of France, 122–
    23
  and Napoleon's planned trip to United
    States, 304
  Napoleon's relationship with, 92, 99,
    115–20, 122–26, 128–30, 154–55
  physical appearance of, 112
  in plotting against Napoleon, 98, 119–20,
    154–56, 196
  press censorship and, 125–26, 149
  private life of, 113–14
  on public opposition to Napoleon, 176
  on reinstating regency, 39, 121–22
  and restoration of law and order, 143–45
  during Revolution, 109–12
  royalists arrested by, 202–3
  royalist uprisings and, 151–56
  sadism of, 111–12
  social and ideological barriers tran-
    scended by, 116–17, 124
  Talleyrand's relationship with, 89, 122,
    124
  war with allies predicted by, 135
  wealth accumulated by, 117–18
Foy, Maximilien-Sébastien, 234

  and battle of Quatre Bras, 268
  and battle of Waterloo, 279–80
France:
  Allied invasions of, 3–4, 234–35, 298,
    312–13
  Allied occupation of, 39
  armistice between Allies and, 311–13
  budget estimates of, 177–81
  calls for Napoleon's departure from, 302–
    6
  Congress of Vienna and, 101–3
  corrosion of administration structure of,
    143
  creation of new Empire of, 208
  demobilization of army of, 40–41
  desire for peace in, 37–38
  economic decline of, 36–38, 40, 180
  fédéré movement in, 156–58
  Louis's flight from, 52–53, 55, 170
  malaise of uncertainty in, 134–35
  martial law in, xii
  military intervention in Rome by, 69
  mobilization of, 158–59, 170, 173–220
  Napoleon's invasion of, xi–xii, 11–35,
    41–51, 122–23
  Napoleon's reorganizing and consolidating
    hold on, 128–35, 137, 144, 146
  opposition to war in, 148
  Papal States seized by, 64
  peasantry of, 50, 148–49
  press censorship in, 125–26, 130–32,
    149
  reinstating regency in, 39–41
  royalist uprisings in, 51, 146–56, 170,
    174, 176, 186, 201–4
  Spain occupied by, 75
  in surrendering to Allies, 313–14
  trade relations between Britain and, 36,
    83, 95
  war casualties of, 176
  Westphalia occupied by, 82
  in withdrawing from Portugal, 233–34
  in withdrawing from Spain, 234–35
Francis II, Emperor of Austria, 8, 95, 171
Frazer, Sir Augustus, 270, 285
Frederick William III, King of Prussia,
  248–49
  and Allied declaration of war against Na-
    poleon, 106
  Saxon claims of, 101, 103–4
French Revolution:
  Carnot during, 138–39, 142–43
  Davout during, 162
  Fouché during, 109–12
  Talleyrand's flight to United States dur-
    ing, 86

Index

Ganteaume, Honoré, 16, 76–77
Gaudin, Martin-Michel-Charles, Duc de
 Gaëte, 108, 170
 and Napoleon's war preparations, 175,
 177–78, 183, 188–89
Gérard, Maurice-Etienne:
 and battle of Ligny, 259, 263, 265
 and battle of Waterloo, 284
 marching orders of, 236–39
 and Napoleon's planned drive into Bruxelles, 257–58
Gneisenau, August Wilhelm von, Graf, 246,
 248, 272
 and Napoleon's retreat from Waterloo,
 291–92
Golfe Juan, Napoleon's landing at, 15–16,
 18, 21, 23, 34–35
Gosselies, Ney's advance to, 257–59
Grasse, Napoleon's capture of, 20, 22
Great Britain:
 Congress of Vienna and, 101–3
 in declaring war against Napoleon, 124–
 25
 Fouché's negotiations with, 120, 124
 France invaded by, 234–35
 industrial dominance of, 149
 Lucien Bonaparte's house arrest in, 65
 and Napoleon's Continental System, 36,
 83, 95
 and Napoleon's planned trip to United
 States, 303, 309
 and Napoleon's public renunciation of
 war, 173
 Napoleon's surrender to, 309–11
 and preparations for war against Napoleon, 244–46
 and royalist uprisings in France, 151,
 153–54, 203
Grenoble, 25–27
 alleged royalist retaking of, 51
 Napoleon's arrival in, 26–27
 Napoleon's march on, 22–23, 25–26, 45
Grouchy, Emmanuel de, xiii, 312, 316
 in advance to Sombreffe, 256–58
 and battle at Wavre, 293–94
 and battle of Ligny, 260, 266
 and battle of Quatre Bras, 267
 and battle of Waterloo, 277, 280–81,
 284, 289–90
 Champ de mai ceremonies and, 212
 field command of, 184, 187
 inexperience of, 239
 marching orders of, 236–39
 mobilization and, 204
 and Napoleon's planned drive into
 Bruxelles, 239, 257–58

and Napoleon's retreat from Waterloo,
 292
 and pursuing Allies in retreat, 274, 276
 royalist uprisings and, 174, 201

Hardenberg, Count Karl August von, 5
 Congress of Vienna and, 101, 104
Hill, Lord Rowland:
 and battle of Waterloo, 277
 and French attack on Charleroi, 255
 and preparations for war against Napoleon, 244, 247, 250
Hobhouse, John Cam, 218, 228
Holland, Louis Bonaparte's assumption of
 crown of, 74–75
Hortense, Queen of Holland, see Beauharnais, Hortense de
Houssaye, Henri, 9, 127, 213, 293

India, Wellington's posting in, 223–27
Italy:
 Davout's command in, 165
 Napoleon's assumption of crown of, 74

Joachim I, King of Naples, see Murat,
 Joachim
Jourdan, Jean-Baptiste:
 Champ de mai ceremonies and, 212
 Ney's trial and, 315
 Wellington's defeat of, 234–35

Kellermann, François-Etienne, Comte de
 Valmy, 257
 and battle of Quatre Bras, 268, 270
 and battle of Waterloo, 286
Kempt, General, 269, 284

La Bédoyère, Charles de, 23, 26, 213
Lacépèdes, Raymond de, 21–22
La Fayette, Gilbert de, 219, 299–301
Lamarque, Jean-Maximilien, 152
 mobilization and, 199–200, 203
 royalist uprisings and, 186, 203
La Rochejacquelein, Auguste de, 150–51
La Rochejacquelein, Louis de, royalist upris-
 ing and, 150–51, 153–54, 156, 203
La Tour du Pin de Gouvernet, Henriette-
 Lucy, Marquise de, 86–88
LaValette, Antoine Chamans de, 109
 Additional Act and, 133
 Champ de mai ceremonies and, 219
 in escaping from France, 316
 and Napoleon's war preparations, 182
Lefebvre-Desnoëtte, Comte Charles, 42, 268
 in advance to Quatre Bras, 256–57
 in escaping from France, 316

Index

Ligny, battle of, 258–61, 263–67, 272–73
Liverpool, Robert Bank Jenkinson, Lord, 1
  and Allied invasion of France, 3
  Congress of Vienna and, 103
  and Napoleon's planned trip to United
    States, 303, 309
  and Napoleon's surrender, 310–11
  and preparations for war against Napo-
    leon, 244
  and royalist uprisings in France, 153–54
  Wellington's complaints to, 231
Lobau, Comte de:
  and battle of Ligny, 260
  and battle of Quatre Bras, 274
  and battle of Waterloo, 277, 279, 281,
    284, 288
  Champ de mai ceremonies and, 212
  marching orders of, 236–38
Longford, Elizabeth, 222, 229
Lons-le-Saunier, Ney at, 31–32
Louis XIV, King of France, 36, 98
Louis XVI, King of France, 41
  execution of, 115, 157
  Napoleon compared with, 157–58
Louis XVIII, King of France, xi, xiii, 9–11,
  198
  and Allies' preparations for war against
    Napoleon, 242–43
  apathy of military toward, 42
  and armistice between France and Allies,
    312–13
  budget estimates of, 177–79
  Congress of Vienna and, 102–3
  crown offered to, 4
  flight from France of, 52–53, 55, 170
  Fouché and, 120–23, 125, 154–55
  government in exile of, 107–8, 126, 130,
    169
  leadership abilities lacked by, 41, 52
  logistical arrangements of, 188
  Marmont's planned coup against, 48
  Napoleon compared with, 137
  Napoleon replaced by, 39
  and Napoleon's advance on Paris, 28–29,
    31–33, 47, 51–54
  Napoleon's coup against, 11, 13, 130
  Napoleon's finances and, 9–10
  and Napoleon's invasion of France, 16,
    20–22, 22–24, 27–33, 41–47, 122
  Ney's execution and, 314, 318–19
  Ney's trial and, 315, 318
  powers assumed by, 40–41
  public support for, 39–41, 176–77
  religious intolerance under, 40
  and royalist uprisings in France, 150–51,
    153

  Soult's loyalty to, 185
  Talleyrand's relationship with, 100
  white terror on Bonapartists and republi-
    cans encouraged by, 314–17
Lyons:
  alleged royalist retaking of, 51
  fortification plans for defense of, 198,
    205–6
  Fouché's anti-Christianization of, 110–12,
    114, 117
  Napoleon's arrival in, 27–28
  Napoleon's march on, 45–46
  as obstacle to Napoleon, 25

Macdonald, Jacques, Duc de Tarente, 4–5,
  52–53, 316
  and Louis's flight from France, 53
  and Napoleon's invasion of France, 27,
    42, 46
  and Napoleon's march on Paris, 52, 55
Madelin, Louis, 62, 114, 116–17
Madrid, Wellington's entrance into, 234
Mahratta Confederacy, Wellington's battle
  with chiefs of, 225–27
Maitland, Frederick, 308–9
Malartic, Comte de, 152–53
Malmaison, Napoleon's house arrest in,
  301–7
Marchand, Jean-Gabriel, 25–26, 51
Marcognet, General, 282–83, 289
Maret, Hugues, Duc de Bassano, 55, 108,
  181
  and Napoleon's invasion of France, 12–
    13, 23
Marie-Antoinette, Queen of France, 41, 157
Marie-Louise, Empress of France, 8, 171
  Napoleon abandoned by, 49–50
  and Napoleon's invasion of France, 28
  and Napoleon's march on Paris, 50
Marmont, Auguste-Frédéric de, Duc de Ra-
  guse, 4, 37, 41, 317
  and Louis's flight from France, 53
  palace coup planned by, 48
Marseille, royalist opposition in, 146–47,
  201, 203–4
Masséna, André, Prince d'Essling:
  French mobilization and, 173–74
  and Napoleon's invasion of France, 16,
    18, 20–24, 42, 51
  Napoleon's invitation to fight to, 220
  Napoleon's opinion of, 232
  in Peninsular Campaign, 232–34
Metternich, Klemens von:
  and battle of Waterloo, 295
  Carnot and, 142
  Congress of Vienna and, 101, 103

Fouché and, 124, 155
and signing of Treaty of Fontainebleau, 5
on Talleyrand's relationship with Louis, 100
Michel, General, 286–87
Milhaud, General, 284, 286
Molé, Mathieu-Louis, Comte de, 108
mobilization and, 192
Napoleon's complaints about Talleyrand to, 92
and Napoleon's electoral college plan, 131
revolutionary Left feared by, 129
on Talleyrand, 87–88
Mollien, François-Nicolas, 108, 170
and Napoleon's war preparations, 175, 177–80, 182–83, 191
Montesquiou, Interior Minister, 22–23
Fouché and, 121
and Napoleon's march on Paris, 47–48
Moore, Sir John, 231, 245
Morand, General, 288, 290
Morangiès, Baron de, 21–22, 24
Mortier, Edouard-Adolphe, 185, 236–37
Müffling, Baron Karl Friedrich Ferdinand von, 254, 256
Murat, Joachim, 16, 74
bribes offered to Talleyrand by, 94
conflicts between Davout and, 166
Congress of Vienna and, 101, 103
Fouché and, 122
and kidnapping and execution of Enghien, 93
Napoleon rejoined by, 209–10
in plot to overthrow Napoleon, 98

Naples and Sicily, Kingdom of, Joseph Bonaparte's assumption of crown of, 73–74
Napoleon I, Emperor of France:
abdications of, xiii, 3–6, 65, 75, 99–100, 235, 298–303, 306, 311, 313
Additional Act and, 132–34, 208–9, 299
Allied declaration of war against, 106, 108, 124–25, 128
and Allied encirclement of Paris, 306–8, 313
and Allied invasion of France, 298
Allies' preparation for war against, 240, 242–53
appeals for support made by, 202
Armée du Nord joined by, 219–20
attempted suicide of, 2–3, 5, 7
in Auxerre, 29–31
and battle of Ligny, 260–61, 263–67, 272
and battle of Quatre Bras, 267–75
and battle of Saint-Amand, 265–66

and battle of Waterloo, 276–95
Bellerophon boarded by, 308–10
Bonaparte family reunited with, 209–10
boredom of, 11
bravery of, 226
break between Lucien Bonaparte and, 63–64
British surrender of, 309–11
Bruxelles drive planned by, 236–40, 253–59, 268
campaign plans and strategy drafted by, 187, 253–54
Carnot's relationship with, 137, 139, 141–42
Champ de mai ceremonies and, 213–19
charisma of, 135, 218
commercial community alienated by, 202
comparisons between Davout and, 163–64, 169
comparisons between Louis and, 137
comparisons between Wellington and, 226, 230, 277–78
conscription under, 37–38
Consulate created by, 60–62, 70, 75–76, 165, 168
Continental System of, 36, 83, 95, 99
coronation of, 73, 78–79, 213
coup d'état of 18 Brumaire of, 61, 70
Davout's relationship with, 161–69, 171, 183–84, 190, 195–99, 232, 308–9
decline in health of, 143–44, 155–56, 273
Decrès's relationship with, 308–9
despotism of, 175
determination of, 25
eagles distributed to troops by, 218
egoism of, 38, 74, 105
in Egyptian Expedition, 162–63, 165
electoral colleges and, 131, 134, 160, 175, 202, 216
energy of, 3, 7, 31, 112, 196
in escaping from Elba, xi, 9–14, 65, 105–6, 235
evil deeds and words of, xi
in exile on Elba, 1, 3–4, 6–13, 65, 104–5
in exile on Saint Helena, 142, 320
favorite military strategies of, 252–53
fédérés and, 156–58
field armies created by, 185–86
finances of, 9–10, 28, 67, 69
first marriage of, 67–68
Fouché's relationship with, 92, 99, 115–20, 122–26, 128–30, 154–55
France invaded by, xi–xii, 11–35, 41–51, 122–23

Napoleon I, Emperor of France: (cont.)
   Grand Empire plan of, 74
   history's judgment of, xiii
   Hortense's reconciliation with, 296–97
   hostility against Allies reopened by, 236
   house arrest of, 301–7
   indecisiveness of, 196
   international news manipulated by, 78
   Jérôme Bonaparte's relationship with, 76–
      84, 210
   Joseph Bonaparte's relationship with, 66–
      67, 70–75
   and kidnapping and execution of En-
      ghien, 93
   and kidnapping of Spanish royal family,
      98
   logistical concerns of, 187–91, 197–98
   Louis overthrown by, 11, 13, 130
   Louis's replacing of, 39
   Lucien Bonaparte's reconciliation with,
      65–66
   lust for power of, 74
   in march on Paris, 21–22, 25, 27–29,
      31–33, 45, 47–56
   members of new regime of, 108–9, 116,
      123–24, 129–30
   military career success of, 67
   military commanders selected by, xii–xiii,
      183–85, 187, 197, 280
   mobilization and, 158–59, 173–206, 219
   on musket production, 189–90, 197
   named Consul for life, 120, 139, 207
   on naval budget cuts, 180–81
   new peerage created by, 26
   optimism of, 3
   parliamentary government scorned by,
      207–8
   Peninsular campaign and, 232–33
   and planning for defense of Lyons, 198,
      205–6
   and planning for defense of Paris, 205,
      207
   plots against, xi, 10–11, 93, 96–100,
      104–5, 115, 119–20, 154–56, 196,
      302
   on power, 57
   as practical, 33
   press censorship under, 125, 130, 132
   private life of, 67–68, 72, 171–72, 296
   public opposition to, xii, 146–48, 151–
      52, 154, 156, 176–77, 192, 201–3,
      218
   public support for, 49–50, 144–45
   public works projects proposed by, 144
   and pursuing Allies in retreat, 273–75
   in recruiting soldiers, 195, 199, 204

   in reorganizing and consolidating hold on
      France, 128–35, 137, 144, 146
   republicanism supported by, 28
   in retreat from Waterloo, 290–94
   revolutionary Left feared by, 129–30, 137
   romances of, 66, 68
   sadism of, 78
   stubbornness of, 38
   in surrendering to British, 309–11
   Talleyrand's relationship with, 87, 89–93,
      95–99
   United States trip planned by, 296, 303–
      4, 307–9
   war publicly renounced by, 172–74
   Wellington underestimated by, 252, 287
   wife and son separated from, 8
   womanizing of, 209
   world conquest as ambition of, 90, 96
Napoleon II, King of Rome, 8, 171–72, 312
National Guard, French, 204–7
   in defense of Lyons, 205
   in defense of Paris, 206–7
   mobilization of, 200, 205–7
   new offensive role of, 186
   royalist uprisings and, 204
Navy, French Imperial:
   budgets of, 180–81, 188
   mobilization and, 204, 206–7
Neipperg, Adam Adalbert, Graf von, 8, 50,
      171
Nesselrode, Graf Karl Robert von, 5, 241–
      42, 262
   and Allied declaration of war against Na-
      poleon, 106
   Congress of Vienna and, 101, 104
   and preparations for war against Napo-
      leon, 246
Ney, Aglaé-Louise, 34, 318
Ney, Michel, xiii, 4–5, 185
   and Allied control of Quatre Bras, 256
   and Allied invasion of France, 4
   background of, 31
   and battle of Ligny, 260–61, 263–64,
      267
   and battle of Quatre Bras, 267–72, 274–
      75
   and battle of Waterloo, 280, 282, 284–
      87, 289–91
   Champ de mai ceremonies and, 212
   execution of, 314–15, 318–19
   in failing to advance to Quatre Bras,
      257–59, 261
   and Napoleon's advance on Paris, 28,
      31–32
   and Napoleon's invasion of France, 12,
      24, 28–32, 43, 45, 47

Napoleon's invitation to fight to, 220
Napoleon's opinion of, 232, 275
and Napoleon's planned drive into
    Bruxelles, 239, 257–59
Napoleon's relationship with, 32–33
and Napoleon's retreat from Waterloo,
    291
Napoleon supported by, 32–33, 47, 50
in Peninsular Campaign, 232
and pursuing Allies in retreat, 273–76
scapegoating of, 317
and signing Treaty of Fontainebleau, 5
Soult's feud with, 239–40, 267–68
tactical blunders of, 257–59, 261, 285–
    87
trial of, 315–18

Ompteda, Baron, 283, 287
Orange, William, Prince of:
    and Allied control of Quatre Bras, 256
    and battle of Quatre Bras, 269, 271
    and battle of Waterloo, 277
    and French attack on Charleroi, 254–56
    and preparations for war against Napo-
        leon, 243–44, 247, 250
    Wellington's complaints about, 242–43
Orléans, Louis-Philippe, Duc d', 312
    Fouché and, 155
    and Napoleon's invasion of France, 43–44
Ouvrard, Gabriel-Julien, 179, 188

Pack, General:
    and battle of Quatre Bras, 269
    and battle of Waterloo, 283
Pajol, Claude-Pierre:
    and battle of Ligny, 260, 263
    and pursuing Allies in retreat, 274
    royalist uprisings and, 174
Papal States, French seizure of, 64
Paris:
    Allied encirclement of, 305–8, 312–13
    Allied occupation of, 99
    Champ de mai ceremonies in, 210–19
    flight of upper bourgeoisie and aristocracy
        from, 51–52
    fortification plans for defense of, 205–8
    march of fédérés in, 157
    Napoleon's entrance into, 55–56
    Napoleon's march on, 21–22, 25, 27–29,
        31–33, 45, 47–56
    Napoleon's popularity in, 144–45
    Napoleon's retreat to, 294
    reaction to Additional Act in, 207–8
    second Treaty of Paris, 314
    in surrendering to Allies, 313
    Treaty of, 5, 100

Pasquier, Etienne-Denis de, 98, 108–9,
    135, 146
    Additional Act and, 133
    Fouché and, 116, 121, 124, 154–55
    mobilization and, 192, 198
    and Napoleon's despotism, 175
Peninsular Campaign, Wellington in, 228–
    30, 232–35
Perponcher, General, 256
    and battle of Quatre Bras, 268, 272
Peyrusse, Guillaume-Joseph, Baron, 6, 9,
    55
Philibert, Captain, 308–9
Philippeville, French retreat to, 293–94
Picton, Sir Thomas, 231
    and battle of Quatre Bras, 269–71
    and battle of Waterloo, 279, 283–84
Pirch, General von:
    and battle of Ligny, 263
    and battle of Saint-Amand, 265
    in preparing for war against Napoleon,
        247, 250–51
Pius VII, Pope, 64, 68, 79
Pons de l'Hérault, André, 6
    and Napoleon's invasion of France, 14,
        16–17, 23
Portugal:
    campaign to oust French from, 228–30,
        232–35
    French withdrawal from, 233–34
Poulle, François, 17–21, 23
Pozzo di Borgo, Count Charles André, 102,
    262
    and Allies' preparations for war against
        Napoleon, 242, 246
    and battle of Waterloo, 295
    on Fouché, 128, 154–55
    on Napoleon, 295, 320
    Wellington and, 241–42
Prussia:
    army rebuilt by, 248–49
    and battle of Ligny, 260, 263–67, 272–
        73
    and battle of Saint-Amand, 263, 265
    Congress of Vienna and, 101–6
    and French attack on Charleroi, 254–55
    and Napoleon's planned drive into
        Bruxelles, 238–40, 253–54
    Paris encircled by army of, 305–8, 312
    in preparing for war against Napoleon,
        240, 246–50, 253
    Sombreffe buildup of, 259

Quatre Bras:
    Allied control of, 256–57, 259
    Allied withdrawal from, 273

Quatre Bras: *(cont.)*
  battle of, 267–75
  Ney's failure to advance to, 257–59, 261
Quiot du Passage, Baron, 282, 289

Récamier, Juliette, 131–32
Regnault de Saint-Jean d'Angély, Michel-
    Louis, Comte, 135, 146
  Napoleon's abdication and, 298, 301
Reille, H. C. M. J.:
  and battle of Ligny, 263
  and battle of Quatre Bras, 268–69, 271
  and battle of Waterloo, 277, 279–80,
    284, 287, 289
  marching orders of, 236–38
  in pursuit of Allies in retreat, 275
Richmond, Charles Gordon-Lennox, Duke
    of, 255–56
Robespierre, Maximilien-François de, 58,
    66, 142
Rome:
  French military intervention in, 69
  Joseph Bonaparte as ambassador to, 68–
    69
  Lucien Bonaparte's life in, 64–65
Roux-Laborie (Talleyrand's secretary), 99–
    100
Rovigo, René Savary, Duc de, 76, 109,
    124, 212, 309
Russia:
  Congress of Vienna and, 101–6
  Napoleon's campaign in, 166–67, 176
  in preparing for war against Napoleon,
    249

Saint-Amand, battle of, 263, 265–66
Saint Helena, Napoleon's exile on, 142, 320
Saint-Leu, Duchesse de, *see* Beauharnais,
    Hortense de
Savary, René, *see* Rovigo, René Savary,
    Duc de
Saxe-Weimar, Prinz Bernhard von:
  and battle of Waterloo, 279, 283–84
  Quatre Bras occupied by, 256, 259
Saxon, Lieutenant Colonel, 223–24
Schwarzenberg, Prinz Karl Philipp zu, 3
  and battle of Waterloo, 292
  and Napoleon's abdication, 99
  and preparations for war against Napo-
    leon, 246
Sombreffe, 256–59
  Grouchy's advance to, 256–58
  Prussian buildup around, 259
Soult, Jean de Dieu, xiii, 184–85, 317
  and Allied encirclement of Paris, 313
  and battle of Ligny, 261

and battle of Quatre Bras, 267–68, 275
and battle of Waterloo, 287
Blacas's charges against, 43
Champ de mai ceremonies and, 212
Davout's conflicts with, 199
and French army in retreat, 294
Joseph Bonaparte's conflict with, 73
marching orders of, 236–37, 239
Napoleon abandoned by, 185
and Napoleon's invasion of France, 12,
    20, 31, 41–43
and Napoleon's joining Armée du Nord,
    219
Napoleon's opinion of, 232
and Napoleon's position near Ligny, 258
Ney's feud with, 239–40, 267–68
Wellington's defeat of, 234–35
Spain:
  campaign to oust French from, 228–30,
    232–35
  French occupation of, 75
  French retreat from, 234–35
  Joseph Napoleon's assumption of crown
    of, 74–75
  kidnapping of royal family of, 98
  Lucien Bonaparte as ambassador to, 61–
    62
  on Napoleon's Continental System, 95
Staël, Germaine de, 63, 104, 116
  Napoleon's fear of, 129–30
Stanhope, Philip Henry, Earl, 226, 232
Stewart, Sir Charles, 231, 299
Stuart, Sir Charles, 262, 292
Suchet, Louis-Gabriel, 43, 174, 312–13
Suzannet, Monsieur de, 150–51, 153–54

Talleyrand-Périgord, Charles-Maurice de,
    Prince de Bénévent, 9–10, 85–108,
    121
  administrative philosophy of, 90–91
  and Allied declaration of war against Na-
    poleon, 106
  arrogance and independence of, 92
  bribes demanded and received by, 94–95,
    96n
  charm of, 87–88
  comparisons between Fouché and, 88–90,
    92, 113–15, 119
  Congress of Vienna and, 100–104
  diplomatic philosophy of, 91–93
  as emigré in United States, 86–89
  foreign policy goals of, 90, 96–97, 99
  Fouché's relationship with, 89, 122, 124
  heritage of, 87
  and kidnapping and execution of En-
    ghien, 93, 98–99

and kidnapping of Spanish royal family, 98

Louis's relationship with, 100

and Lucien Bonaparte's Spanish mission, 61–62

motto of, 91

and Napoleon's abdication, 99

and Napoleon's Continental System, 95

and Napoleon's exile on Elba, 10, 104–5

and Napoleon's invasion of France, 34

Napoleon's relationship with, 87, 89–93, 95–99

physical appearance of, 88

in plotting against Napoleon, 96–100, 120

on reinstating regency, 39

seizure of Church property proposed by, 89

social life of, 88–89

vices of, 87

warmth lacked by, 88

wealth of, 36

womanizing of, 88–89

Thielemann, Johann Adolf von, 247

in battle of Wavre, 293–94

and battle of Ligny, 260, 264–66

in preparing for war against Napoleon, 250

Tipu Sultan, 224

Torrens, Sir Robert, 230–31

Trafalgar, battle at, 94–95, 310

Travers, General, 282–83

Travot, General, 152–53

United States:

Napoleon's planned trip to, 296, 303–4, 307–9

Talleyrand as emigré in, 86–89

Uxbridge, John Paget, Earl of:

and battle of Waterloo, 277, 279, 283, 286

and French attack on Charleroi, 255

and preparations for war against Napoleon, 244, 247, 250

in retreat, 275

Valentinois, Duc de, 18–20

Vandamme, General:

Allied retreat and, 276

and battle of Ligny, 259, 263–64

and battle of Saint-Amand, 265

and battle of Waterloo, 277

marching orders of, 236–39

and Napoleon's planned drive into Bruxelles, 257–58

surrender of, 316

Var, Napoleon's march across, 21–22

Vaudémont, Madame de, Fouché and, 122–23

Vitoria, battle at, 233–34

Vitrolles, Baron de, 44, 52–53

and Louis's flight from France, 53

and Napoleon's march on Paris, 48

Vom Kriege (Clausewitz), 251

War Ministry, French:

budgets of, 170, 179

Davout's appointment to, 161, 167, 171

Davout's organization of, 168–71

mobilization and, 195–96, 198, 204

Waterloo, battle of, xii–xiii, 276–95

comparative strengths of armies in, 277–78

Napoleon's choice of commanders in, 280

Napoleon's last attack in, 289–90

Napoleon's retreat from, 290–94

Napoleon's strategy in, 279–82

Ney's blunders in, 285–87

site of, 276–78

sudden lulls in, 284

Wavre:

battle at, 293–94

Blücher's retreat to, 273, 276

Wellesley, Catherine "Kitty" Pakenham, 227–28

Wellesley, Richard, Earl of, 222–25, 231

Wellington, Arthur Wellesley, Duke of, 221–36, 240–56, 262

and Allied control of Quatre Bras, 256

and Allied declaration of war against Napoleon, 106

Anglo-Dutch-Belgian force commanded by, 243–45, 247, 251

appointed Commander in Chief of British Army, 228

and armistice between France and Allies, 312

attempts on life of, 235

in battle against Tipu Sultan, 224

in battle of Assaye, 225–27

and battle of Ligny, 260, 264–65, 267, 272–73

and battle of Quatre Bras, 269–71, 273–75

and battle of Waterloo, 276–80, 282–84, 286–87, 289–90, 292, 295

bravery of, 226

in Bruxelles, 241–42, 244

Champ de mai ceremonies and, 212

command techniques of, 225–26, 230, 232

Index

Wellington, Arthur Wellesley, Duke of,
    (cont.)
  comparisons between Napoleon and, 226,
    230, 277–78
  Congress of Vienna and, 101–3, 106
  early military career of, 222–27
  education of, 222–23
  Fouché's secret negotiations with, 156
  and French army in retreat, 294
  and French attack on Charleroi, 254–55
  French mobilization and, 204
  heritage of, 221–22
  in India, 223–27
  in invasion of France, 3, 312–13
  logistical concerns of, 244–45
  medals and honors of, 226–27, 235
  Napoleon's abdication and, 235
  and Napoleon's planned trip to United
    States, 303
  Napoleon's underestimation of, 252, 287
  and Napoleon's war preparations, 174–75
  Napoleon underestimated by, 251–52
  in occupation of France, 39
  officers criticized by, 230–32, 242–43,
    245
  in Peninsular Campaign, 228–30, 232–35
  physical appearance of, 228–29
  politics of, 231–32
  in preparing for war against Napoleon,
    240, 242–53
  private life of, 227–29
  reputation of, 224–25
  in retreat, 273–76
  sense of humor of, 229–30
  troops inspired by, 230
Westphalia, Kingdom of:
  British trade with, 83
  French military occupation of, 82
  Jérôme Bonaparte's assumption of crown
    of, 74–75, 81–84
  Jérôme Bonaparte's departure from, 84
William I, King of the Netherlands, 101,
    242–43, 295
Wilson, Harriet, 229–30

Ziethen, General von, 238, 240, 246–48
  and battle of Ligny, 259–60, 263
  and battle of Saint-Amand, 265
  and battle of Waterloo, 290
  and French attack on Charleroi, 254
  in preparing for war against Napoleon,
    250–51
Zweig, Stefan, 120, 126